ENTREPRENEURIAL FINANCE
The Art and Science of Growing Ventures

Academics and practitioners from a range of institutions across Europe provide a cutting-edge, practical, and comprehensive review on the financing of entrepreneurial ventures. From sourcing and obtaining funds, to financial tools for growing and managing the financial challenges and opportunities of the startup, *Entrepreneurial Finance: The Art and Science of Growing Ventures* is an engaging text that equips entrepreneurs, students and early-stage investors to make sound financial decisions at every stage of a business' life. Largely reflecting European businesses and with a European perspective, the text is grounded in sound theoretical foundations. Case studies and success stories as well as perspectives from the media and from experts provide real-world applications, while a wealth of activities give students abundant opportunities to apply what they have learned. A must-have text for both graduate and undergraduate students in entrepreneurship, finance and management programs, as well as aspiring entrepreneurs in any field.

Luisa Alemany is an associate professor in entrepreneurial finance at ESADE Business School and holds an M.B.A. from Stanford University, California, and a PhD from the Universidad Complutense, Madrid. Her research focuses on business angels, venture capital, impact investing, and entrepreneurship education for children. From 2009 to 2017, Dr Alemany was the director of the ESADE Entrepreneurship Institute. She is currently the academic sponsor of ESADE Business Angels Network (BAN) and is active at the European level, where she has been a director of the board of the European Business Angels Network (EBAN). She also holds seats in different investment committees, both in venture capital and impact investing. She is part of the first European women-only business angels network, Rising Tide I and II. Dr Alemany has held positions at Procter & Gamble, McKinsey & Co., and Goldman Sachs. She also has experience in venture capital and private equity, having worked for the funds Europ@Web and The Carlyle Group.

Job J. Andreoli is a senior lecturer and PhD candidate at the Center for Finance of the Nyenrode Business Universiteit and the Nyenrode New Business School in the Netherlands. In addition, he leads the Nyenrode Incubator in Amsterdam and is on the advisory board of a venture capital firm. Prior to joining Nyenrode, Mr Andreoli has worked as a strategy consultant for Ernst & Young (EY) and Capgemini and was responsible for setting up the Strategy and Innovation practice of Atos Consulting. He has also been involved in startups and working with small and medium-sized enterprises that tend towards financial distress. Mr Andreoli holds an M.Sc. degree in Strategic Management from Rotterdam School of Management, Ersamus University and an M.Sc. in Education from VU Amsterdam.

ENTREPRENEURIAL FINANCE

The Art and Science of Growing Ventures

LUISA ALEMANY
ESADE Business School

JOB J. ANDREOLI
Nyenrode Business University

CAMBRIDGE
UNIVERSITY PRESS

CAMBRIDGE
UNIVERSITY PRESS

University Printing House, Cambridge CB2 8BS, United Kingdom

One Liberty Plaza, 20th Floor, New York, NY 10006, USA

477 Williamstown Road, Port Melbourne, VIC 3207, Australia

314–321, 3rd Floor, Plot 3, Splendor Forum, Jasola District Centre, New Delhi – 110025, India

79 Anson Road, #06–04/06, Singapore 079906

Cambridge University Press is part of the University of Cambridge.

It furthers the University's mission by disseminating knowledge in the pursuit of education, learning, and research at the highest international levels of excellence.

www.cambridge.org
Information on this title: www.cambridge.org/9781108421355
DOI: 10.1017/9781108368070

First published 2018

Printed and bound in Great Britain by Clays Ltd, Elcograf S.p.A.

A catalogue record for this publication is available from the British Library.

Library of Congress Cataloging-in-Publication Data
Names: Alemany, Luisa, editor. | Andreoli, Job, editor.
Title: Entrepreneurial finance : the art and science of growing ventures / edited by Luisa Alemany, ESADE Business School, Job Andreoli, Nyenrode Business University/New Business School.
Description: New York : University of Cambridge, [2018] | Includes bibliographical references and index.
Identifiers: LCCN 2017061576| ISBN 9781108421355 (hbk. : alk. paper) | ISBN 9781108431859 (paperback : alk. paper)
Subjects: LCSH: New business enterprises – Finance. | Small business – Finance. | Venture capital. | Entrepreneurship.
Classification: LCC HG4027.6 .E58 2018 | DDC 658.15/92–dc23
LC record available at https://lccn.loc.gov/2017061576

ISBN 978-1-108-42135-5 Hardback
ISBN 978-1-108-43185-9 Paperback

CONTENTS

FIGURES

TABLES

CONTRIBUTORS

Luisa Alemany is an associate professor in entrepreneurial finance at ESADE Business School and holds an M.B.A. from Stanford University, California, and a PhD from the Universidad Complutense, Madrid. Her research focuses on business angels, venture capital, impact investing, and entrepreneurship education for children. From 2009 to 2017, Dr Alemany was the director of the ESADE Entrepreneurship Institute. She is currently the academic sponsor of ESADE Business Angels Network (BAN) and is active at the European level, where she has been a director of the board of the European Business Angels Network (EBAN). She also holds seats in different investment committees, both in venture capital and impact investing. She is part of the first European women-only business angels network, Rising Tide I and II. Dr Alemany has held positions at Procter & Gamble, McKinsey & Co., and Goldman Sachs. She also has experience in venture capital and private equity, having worked for the funds Europ@Web and The Carlyle Group.

Job Andreoli is a senior lecturer and PhD candidate at the Center for Finance of the Nyenrode Business Universiteit and the Nyenrode New Business School in the Netherlands. In addition, he leads the Nyenrode Incubator in Amsterdam and is on the advisory board of a venture capital firm. Prior to joining Nyenrode, Mr Andreoli has worked as a strategy consultant for Ernst & Young (EY) and Capgemini and was responsible for setting up the Strategy and Innovation practice of Atos Consulting. He has also been involved in startups and working with small and medium-sized enterprises that tend towards financial distress. Mr Andreoli holds an M.Sc. degree in Strategic Management from Rotterdam School of Management, Ersamus University and an M.Sc. in Education from VU Amsterdam.

Torben Antretter Research Associate and PhD Candidate at the Chair for Entrepreneurship of the University of St. Gallen (HSG). His research is mainly focused on entrepreneurial finance with special emphasis on venture capital. At the HSG, he further leads an interdisciplinary project that aims to build algorithmic models to support data-driven investment decisions. Before joining the Chair for Entrepreneurship, Torben worked in management consulting, focusing on financial transformation. Besides his research at the university, he is active as an entrepreneur in the field of LegalTech. With his venture he currently raised € +25 million in venture capital and private equity financing. He holds a MSc degree from the University of Muenster, where he was awarded the National Scholarship of the Haniel Foundation.

Tiago Botelho joined Norwich Business School (NBS) as a Lecturer in Business Strategy in August 2015. Prior to joining NBS he held teaching positions (lecturer, teaching assistant, and tutor) at the University of Glasgow, University of Strathclyde, Universidade Nova de Lisboa and Piaget Institute.

From 2011 to 2013, Tiago was part of a research team lead by Colin Mason and Richard Harrison in an ESRC project on business angel exits. His research interests are in entrepreneurial finance and methodological applications. The first stream of his research has been on business angels' decision-making criteria. The second has questioned the comparability of different methodologies to address this issue. Tiago has published in several academic journals.

Tiago holds a BA degree in Economics from the Universidade Autónoma de Lisboa and a Masters degree in Finance and Business Economics from Fundação Getúlio Vargas, Escola de Pós-Graduação em Economia, Rio de Janeiro, Brazil. He completed a PhD in Management at the University of Glasgow on the topic of business angel investing criteria.

Timothy Bovard is Adjunct Professor of Entrepreneurship at INSEAD and Adjunct Professor at Columbia Business School where he teaches Entrepreneurship Through Acquisition. He also teaches in the MBA program, guest lectures at Chicago Booth School of Business, and is a regular speaker at conferences on search funds and entrepreneurship through acquisition.

Timothy is the Founder and CEO of Search Fund Accelerator (SFA), the first-ever accelerator accompanying highly motivated entrepreneurs seeking to acquire businesses to run as CEOs. Created in 2015, SFA provides unparalleled mentoring and support to searchers throughout the search, acquisition and post-acquisition phases, providing all needed equity from its fund of committed capital.

As Founder and former President of CPI S.A., Timothy created Europe's leading book manufacturer. Through a series of twenty acquisitions over twelve years, he built CPI into a group with over €500 million in sales and 4000 employees in fifteen plants across Europe. Timothy is President of the Association Petits Princes, a leading French charitable organization that realizes the dreams of severely ill children.

Timothy holds a BS in Management from Rensselaer Polytechnic Institute, an MA in Political Science from the University of North Carolina at Chapel Hill and an MBA with Distinction from INSEAD.

Jan Brinckmann is Associate Professor of Entrepreneurship and Strategy at ESADE Business School. He is Director of the Entrepreneurship Lab of the ESADE MBA Program, Director of the ESADE Entrepreneurship Research Group and is Academic Director of EWorks ESADE's entrepreneurship support activities. Before coming to ESADE, he taught at Loyola University Chicago and Cornell University and was a visiting scholar at Stanford University and Case Western Reserve University. He published extensively in leading academic entrepreneurship journals and is editorial review board member of the *Journal of Business Venturing and Entrepreneurship: Theory and Practice.*

He founded and leads Karma Ventures. He is member of the board of Aklamio, Kviar Groupe, Red Points and Value Desk. He made over eleven seed and follow-on investments in companies including Aklamio, First Stop Health, Juniqe, Red Points, Magin Software, ValueDesk and Savedo. He was investor and advisor to Icebergs, acquired by Pinterest. In addition he leads ESADE support for the KIC InnoEnergy incubator. He also created and teaches at the Founders Academy for the Bertelsmann Foundation and the Corporate Academy for the Pioneers Club.

Jan holds a PhD in entrepreneurship from the Technical University of Berlin and a Master of Economics and Business Administration from University of Hanover.

Stefano Caselli is Full Professor of Banking and Finance and the Vice Rector for International Affairs at Bocconi University. He is a member of the board of directors of SDA Bocconi School of Management. He conducted numerous research, training and consulting projects both with the most important financial institutions at European level and corporations for valuation and corporate governance issues. His research activities focus on the relationship between banking and industrial systems, facing issues of banking strategy and corporate governance, investment banking and private equity and venture capital.

He is the author of numerous books and articles on the subject. His works have been published in Journal of Financial Intermediation, Journal of Banking and Finance, European Financial Management, Journal of Financial Services Research, Journal of Applied Corporate Finance, among others. He is also the founder and the director of the 'Start-up Day' platform for Bocconi, devoted to facilitate the start-up process for Bocconi students and alumni.

He has extensive experience as independent director in several boards as well as advisor of investment committees. Among them: Generali Real Estate SGR S. p.A., Santander Consumer Bank S.p.A., SIAS S.p.A.

He holds a MSc in Business Administration from the University of Genoa and a PhD in Financial Markets and Institutions from the University of Siena.

Josep Duran is an Investment Manager at the European Investment Fund (EIF), a cornerstone investor in Private Equity and Venture Capital funds across Europe. He joined EIF in 2015 at its Innovation and Technology Investments division in Luxembourg, where he has led investments and participated in the board of several VC funds, and has closed co-investment deals with some of the most relevant Business Angels in Europe. He is an active member of the investment ecosystem and is also a regular speaker in some of the main events in the continent.

Before joining EIF, He was investment associate at Caixa Capital Risc, the venture capital division of CaixaBank where he invested in tech startups in their early stages. He was also Entrepreneurship Program Manager at La Salle University of Barcelona, where he also led the Business Angels Network.

He holds a degree in Telecommunications Engineering from the Universitat Ramon Llull and an MBA from the same university. He has also received executive education from the European Venture Capital Association and Cambridge University.

EUROPEAN
INVESTMENT
FUND

Oscar Farres is Head of Unit in the Innovation and Technology Investments team at the European Investment Fund (EIF) in Luxembourg, a European institution that provides risk finance to benefit small and medium-sized enterprises (SME) across Europe. At EIF, he has invested in VC funds across Europe with a focus on the ICT sector and sits on their Advisory Boards. He is a seasoned speaker in VC industry events and contributor to publications in the field of venture capital.

Prior to joining the EIF, Oscar developed his professional career at two Spanish VC funds, Caixa Capital Risc and Debaeque Venture Capital, where he invested in internet and software startups. During this period, he invested and sat on the Boards of companies such as Groupalia, BuyVIP, ApeSoft, Icinetic, and HelpMyCash among others. In 2003, he co-founded Kineto Project, a technology startup in the fitness space.

EUROPEAN
INVESTMENT
FUND

He holds an Electronics Engineering degree from the Universitat Ramon Llull and an MBA degree from IESE Business School with an exchange at MIT.

Dietmar Grichnik is Chair Professor of Entrepreneurship and Director of the Institute of Technology Management at the University of St. Gallen (HSG). He is the Initiator and Co-Director of the Center for Entrepreneurship and the Global Center for Entrepreneurship and Innovation. In addition, he is the Dean of the School of Management and Board Member of the Institute of Media and Communications Management and the Institute of Business Education and Educational Management at HSG.

Before joining HSG, Dietmar served on the faculties of WHU – Otto Beisheim School of Management and Witten/Herdecke University in Germany. Moreover, he held a visiting professorship at University of Melbourne, was guest professor

University of St.Gallen

at Harvard Business School and lecturer at the Swiss Federal Institute of Technology (ETH) Zurich.

The main focus of his work is on entrepreneurial cognition and emotions, entrepreneurial finance and entrepreneurial decision-making. He has published seven books and several articles in leading journals such as *Journal of Business Venturing, Research Policy, Entrepreneurship Theory & Practice* and *Journal of Economic Behavior and Organization*. He served as an associate editor for *R&D Management Journal* and reviews currently on the editorial board of *Journal of Small Business Management* among others.

He holds a Diploma in Business Administration and in Business Education, as well as a PhD in Business Administration from University of Cologne, Germany.

Lisa Hehenberger is a Lecturer in Strategy and General Management at ESADE business school. Her research focus is on applying organizational theory to study the evolution of venture philanthropy and social impact investment. She teaches courses in social entrepreneurship, impact investing and strategy.

She is a member of the European Commission's Expert Group on Social Business (GECES) and the OECD's Expert Group on Social Impact Investment, and has been a member of the French National Advisory Board and the Impact Measurement Working Group of the Social Impact Investment Task Force established by the G8.

Until recently, she was the Research and Policy Director of the European Venture Philanthropy Association (EVPA). She set up and ran EVPA's Knowledge Centre, conducting and publishing research, and collecting and disseminating data and knowledge. She also coordinated EVPA's policy initiatives, facilitating the dual transfer of knowledge between policy makers and practitioners. Previously she worked in investment banking at UBS and GB Investment Banking in London, Madrid and Barcelona.

She has a PhD in Management from IESE Business School and a Master's degree in Business and Economics from Stockholm School of Economics and HEC (CEMS).

Peter Hiscocks built the entrepreneurship resources within the University of Cambridge, from the original Cambridge Entrepreneurship Centre to Cambridge Enterprise and achieved a considerable increase in the level of commercialization. He is a Senior Lecturer in Entrepreneurship and Innovation Management at the Judge Business School and is managing several research projects on the success factors for new hi tech business ventures. For the last four years he has been Head of Executive Education but has just stepped down from this role.

He is a scientist who worked in business; initially large companies, then consultancy and finally starting his own companies. He worked in consulting for fifteen years and was one of the founding members of two consulting businesses that grew to have several hundred professional staff. Overall he has

ESADE
Business School

UNIVERSITY OF
CAMBRIDGE
Judge Business School

founded ten companies; is Chairman of three growth companies and is on the board of three others: he has achieved the successful sale of five companies. He is the co-founder of a £30 million seed-fund in the North East of England and is on the advisory board of a VC firm.

He is a graduate from the University of Cambridge.

Isidro Laso is Head of Startups and Scaleups sector of the European Commission, known as Startup Europe (www.startupeuropeclub.eu). Since 2013 He is continuing policy fellow at the Cambridge University's CSaP where he works on the intersection of research and policy with other academics. In 2015 he was selected as thought leader at United Nations ITU. Isidro is also member/observer of several advisory boards to international networks of start-ups. He is visiting lecturer to CEPADE (business school of the Universidad Politecnica de Madrid) as well.

Since becoming an European Commission official in 2001 he has managed research projects and drafted research and innovation strategy objectives. From 2010 he has been focused on creating a new endeavour within the EU institutions related to startups: the Startup Europe initiative. Isidro has written many books and papers, some of which have been translated into many languages.

He had his first taste of entrepreneurship at university, where he created a junior enterprise. After graduating he set up his own software business in the agritech domain. He then moved to the research and innovation department of an IT international company. This gave him the opportunity to create a new department within his company offering change management projects to customers, to complement traditional ICT projects.

He holds an engineering degree from the Universidad Politecnica de Madrid.

Benoît Leleux is the Stephan Schmidheiny Professor of Entrepreneurship and Finance at IMD in Lausanne (Switzerland), where he was also Director of the MBA program (2006–2008) and Director of Research and Development (2004–2008). He is currently the co-Director of Foundations for Business Leadership (FBL).

He was previously Visiting Professor of Entrepreneurship at INSEAD and Director of the 3i VentureLab and Associate Professor and Zubillaga Chair in Finance and Entrepreneurship at Babson College.

He is the author of *Investing Private Capital in Emerging and Frontier Market SMEs* (2009), *Nurturing Science-Based Ventures: An International Case Perspective* (2008), *From Microfinance to Small Business Finance* (2007), and *A European Casebook on Entrepreneurship and New Ventures* (1996). His latest book *Private Equity 4.0: Reinventing Value Creation* was published in March 2015 by Wiley. His teaching cases have earned more than nineteen European case writing awards. Prior to his academic career, he was the head of corporate venturing for a leading agribusiness conglomerate in South East Asia.

He earned an MSc in Agricultural Engineering and an MEd in Natural Sciences from the Catholic University of Louvain, an MBA from Virginia Tech and his PhD at INSEAD, specializing in Corporate Finance and Venture Capital.

Johanna Mair is Professor of Organization, Strategy and Leadership at the Hertie School of Governance in Berlin. She is the PACS Distinguished Fellow at Stanford University and the academic co-director of the Social Innovation and Change Initiative at the Harvard Kennedy School. From 2001 to 2011 she served on the faculty at IESE Business School and has held a visiting position at the Harvard Business School and INSEAD.

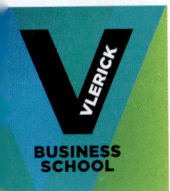

Dr Mair's research focuses on how novel organizational forms and institutional arrangements create economic value and social impact and the role of innovation in this process. Her works has been published in leading academic journals including the *Academy of Management Journal, Academy of Management Perspective, Journal of Management, Journal of Management Studies, Organization Studies* among others. Her book with Christian Seelos on *Innovation and Scaling: How effective Social Entrepreneurs create Impact* makes this research accessible to a broader audience.

She earned her PhD in Management from INSEAD.

Sophie Manigart is Full Professor at the Department of Accounting and Corporate Finance at Ghent University and partner of the Vlerick Business School. Her research interests are entrepreneurial finance, including the supply side (venture capital, business angels, crowdfunding, bootstrapping) and the demand side (entrepreneurs and entrepreneurial companies).

She was guest professor at London Business School and IE Business School, and research fellow at the Wharton School, University of Pennsylvania. Her research has been published in international journals like *Journal of Business Venturing, Journal of Management Science, European Financial Management, Entrepreneurship Theory and Practice*, or *Small Business Economics*, and in numerous book chapters.

She was founder and director of the first Belgian business angels network, Vlerick BAN, and director of BAN Vlaanderen. She is involved in the investment committee of Baekeland-fund, the risk capital fund for spin-offs of Ghent University and Qbic II Venture Fund, among others. She is an independent board member of Gimv (quoted private equity firm), of AXA Belgium (insurance company) and Ovinto (a high tech growth company). She has consulted on entrepreneurial finance for policy makers at the regional, national and European level.

She holds a degree in Civil Engineering, and an MBA and a PhD from Ghent University.

Colin Mason is Professor of Entrepreneurship in the Adam Smith Business School, University of Glasgow. His research and teaching are in the area of entrepreneurship and regional development. His specific research interests are in entrepreneurial finance and entrepreneurial ecosystems.

He has written extensively on business angel investing and has been closely involved with government and private sector initiatives to promote business angel investment, both in the UK and elsewhere. He was joint winner of the ESRC's 2015 Outstanding Impact in Business Award for his research with Professor Richard Harrison on business angels. His other research interests include high-growth firms, home-based businesses, entrepreneurship education and more generally in the concept of 'entrepreneurial campuses'. His research is often featured in the media and he is a contributor to both newspapers and business magazines.

Professor Mason has served on a number of European Commission Expert Groups. He is the founding editor of the journal *Venture Capital: An International Journal of Entrepreneurial Finance* (published by Taylor and Francis Ltd.).

He has a Master of Arts degree from the University of Edinburgh and a PhD from the University of Manchester.

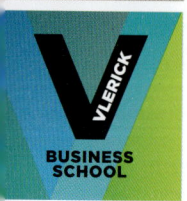

Miguel Meuleman is Associate Professor in Entrepreneurship at Vlerick Business School and visiting professor at Imperial College Business School. His research focuses on management buyouts and buy-ins, venture capital and private equity, new venture creation and entrepreneurial finance more generally.

He has published several articles in journals such as *Journal of Business Venturing, Journal of Management Studies, Entrepreneurship Theory & Practice, Strategic Entrepreneurship Journal* and *Research Policy*. He has also co-authored a book on entrepreneurial finance and has written a number of teaching cases. He has initiated the Entrepreneurial Buyout Academy at Vlerick Business School to promote entrepreneurship through acquisition. Additionally, he has been involved in many initiatives to make entrepreneurship education more effective including BRIDEE (Bridging Entrepreneurship Education & Design) and the EFER European Entrepreneurship Colloquium. He also received the Excellence in Teaching Award at Imperial College Business School in 2017.

Professor Meuleman is a member of the investment committee of the Ark Angel Fund, a business angel fund that provides seed capital investments to start-up companies in Belgium. He has been involved in numerous consulting projects on new business development in established companies and start-up firms in multiple industries.

He holds a PhD in Applied Economic Sciences at Ghent University.

Peter Roosenboom is Professor of Entrepreneurial Finance and Private Equity at the Rotterdam School of Management, Erasmus University. He has been an invited speaker at influential conferences and seminars in the private equity industry and has advised the Dutch government on private equity and the financing of small and medium-sized enterprises (SMEs).

His research has been published in finance and accounting journals such as the *Review of Financial Studies, Journal of Financial and Quantitative Analysis, Review of Finance and Contemporary Accounting Research*. He is a member of the Editorial Boards of the *Journal of Banking & Finance* and *Multinational Finance Journal*. His research has been widely covered in newspapers and magazines.

He holds a PhD degree in finance from Tilburg University.

Sara Seganti is EVPA's Training Manager. She joined EVPA's Knowledge Centre in March 2017 after more than ten years working as training and project manager in the venture philanthropy and social investment sectors.

Before, she also provided secretariat support to the Italian Advisory Board to the Social Impact Investment Taskforce established under the UK's Presidency of the G7.

She holds a Master's Degree in Social Enterprises Management from SDA Bocconi School of Management.

Alexander Stoeckel is a Partner and Board Member at venture capital firm btov. He joined the firm in 2007. He has studied international business administration at the European Business School (EBS) in Oestrich-Winkel and Paris, and at the International School of Management (ISM) in Dortmund and San Diego.

Prior to btov, he has worked as fund-of-fund manager for Hauck & Aufhäuser Private Bankers, and as Assistant Executive Manager for KPMG. From May 2015 to May 2017, he was a Board Member for the Seed Money & Venture Capital Chapter of the Swiss Private Equity & Corporate Finance Association (SECA).

He holds an MBA from the University of Oxford.

Hans Vanoorbeek is Adjunct Professor at Vlerick Business School. He supports the school in its activities around entrepreneurship through acquisition. Together with Professor Miguel Meuleman he co-founded the Platform for Entrepreneurial Buyouts ('PEBO'), where he contributes with his experience as a practitioner. He is also Adjunct Professor at INSEAD where he teaches the Leveraged Buy Out elective.

He is managing partner and co-founder of BV Capital Partners since mid 2003, a private equity holding which invests the money of its two partners in small- and medium sized enterprises in the Benelux. He is also a Director at Aquasourca SA in Luxembourg, the private equity investment vehicle of the family Defforey (founding family of French food retail chain Carrefour), where he is responsible for their international investments. He is a senior advisor of Chequer's Capital, a French private equity firm, for the Benelux. He is currently a shareholder and board member of several companies.

Before this he was active in London in private equity between 1996 and 2004. He was a partner at BC Partners and an Associate Director at IK Investment Partners. In that capacity, he served in several boards.

He holds an MBA from Harvard University, a master's degree in Applied Economics from University College London, a master's degree in Law and a bachelor's degree in philosophy from KU Leuven.

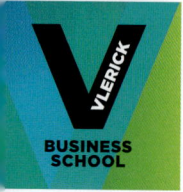

Peter Witt is Full Professor of Technology and Innovation Management at the University of Wuppertal and a director of the Jackstädt Center of Entrepreneurship and Innovation Research. His research interests are innovation management, entrepreneurship and corporate governance. He has published in refereed academic journals like Entrepreneurship & Regional Development, Journal of Business Economics, Management International Review, and R&D Management.

He is department editor for entrepreneurship and SME at the Journal of Business Economics. From 2008 to 2015, he was the president of the German entrepreneurship association (FGF e.V.).

Before joining University of Wuppertal, Peter was a full professor of innovation management and entrepreneurship at the University of Dortmund as well as a full professor of entrepreneurship at WHU, Otto Beisheim School of Management in Vallendar.

He holds a Diploma in Economics from the University of Bonn and a PhD in Management from WHU.

PREFACE

THE ART AND SCIENCE OF 'AN ENTREPRENEURIAL (FINANCE) BOOK'

It was the end of July of 2016, and a group of more than fifty professors from technical universities and business schools from around Europe were gathered at Harvard University. They were all there because of their passion for entrepreneurship, in all its different specialities and forms. Many of them were teaching courses on 'Entrepreneurship', 'Entrepreneurial Marketing' or 'Social Entrepreneurship'. There was also a group focusing on 'Innovation and Design Thinking'. However, the group we were part of was the most appealing one (of course): the faculty of 'Entrepreneurial Finance'

Luisa was teaching a workshop on the way she had designed her course at ESADE in Barcelona. Around twenty-five professors joined the discussion. It was interesting to share knowledge in a new field and to be able to ask questions to colleagues who were facing the same challenges as they introduced their students in Europe to the ever-evolving field of financing for new ventures. Then, somebody asked a basic question: '*So, which book are you using for your classes?*' '*Well, actually, there is no such a book for the European context. Of course, there are some good textbooks when it comes to explaining the financing path of an entrepreneur in the USA. The ways of doing business, Silicon Valley, alternative financing, legal issues, etc. Some of them offer global coverage, but their focus on Silicon Valley and IPOs makes some students think that there is no alternative to raising funds if you are not based there. I use chapters from many different books . . .*' replied Luisa.

Suddenly the room fell silent. '*Then, why don't we write a book. We need to have a textbook, and if it is not available we have to create one,*' Job added. After the summer break (always well-deserved), Job contacted Luisa and they committed to start working together on a proposal in the autumn.

The story of this book is all about entrepreneurship. Just as entrepreneurs do, we identified a need and decided to do something about it. We put together a short proposal, including the proposed table of contents, *the executive summary* and the 'dream team'; a list of professors, the leading experts in particular topics, who could each contribute a chapter to the textbook. We thought that in an entrepreneurial book co-creation was a good idea.

Once the short proposal was ready, we needed to find our 'investor'. In fact, as our entrepreneurial endeavour was a textbook, we needed to find the best publishing house to make our dream come true. After reviewing in some depth the publishers of books covering the topic, or aspects of it, we identified our favourite publisher. And as entrepreneurs do, Job contacted the editor in charge of Management books at Cambridge University Press (CUP). It was our lucky day! The editor, Valerie Appleby, replied promptly with a positive response, acknowledging that she also had identified a need in the market, and shared with us the good news that she would be interested in hearing more about the book. We were really excited! Imagine an entrepreneur receiving an email back from a venture capitalist saying that he wants to know more about the startup and is happy to meet. Well, the rest is history.

We really hope that you enjoy the book, and we look forward hearing from you: Alemany_Andreoli_EF@outlook.com and @EntrFinance

Luisa	&	Job
Twitter: @LuAlemany		LinkedIn.com/in/JJAndreoli

THANK YOU

Entrepreneurial finance has grown steadily over the past few decades, adding both width and depth to the options available to entrepreneurs and investors for financing ventures. We have carefully selected the experts on the different areas from leading European institutions, creating a difference in 'tone of voice' but, at the same time, assuring that the provided content is best of breed. We feel proud and privileged to have worked with so many leading professors, practitioners, investors and entrepreneurs, the collaboration has been a pleasure and the outcome is worthwhile. Thank you all!

To Paula Parish for her patience while doing all the editorial work and Valerie Appleby for being super entrepreneurial and helpful along the way, supporting us in all our 'crazy' ideas . . .

A special gratitude to Bert Twaalfhoven who enabled the EFER European Entrepreneurship Colloquium at Harvard University, where Luisa & Job met.

We would also like to thank our institutions, ESADE and Nyenrode, for the support and encouragement to pursue our dream, and of course, our families, for the long hours spent in front of the laptop during family vacations and weekends. Yes, we made it!

Finally, to Amsterdam for the inspiration, the city where it all started . . .

STRUCTURE OF THE BOOK

This book is organized in five parts. Each of the parts has a distinct topic:

- **Part I: Funding Sources** This part of the book reviews all the alternative sources of financing available to entrepreneurs. Chapter 2 looks in depth at incubators, accelerators and crowdfunding. Chapter 3 considers business angels, from who they are, to how they select, invest and exit their investments. Chapter 4 covers venture capital, private equity and corporate venture capital. Finally, Chapter 5 reviews the public sources of financing available to entrepreneurs.

- **Part II: Funding Process** This part is devoted to the process of obtaining financing for a new venture. Chapter 6 explains how investors source their deals and how they screen them. This is particularly important for first-time entrepreneurs who are trying to raise funding. Chapter 7 examines in some depth the process of preparing a good business plan that will allow the entrepreneurs to understand how much money is needed, its timing and other relevant metrics such as cash burn rate or break-even point. Chapter 8 discusses the valuation of new ventures using the venture capital method. Finally, Chapter 9 looks at the fascinating topic of negotiating the key terms of the deal with investors. In doing so, we move from finance to law, but, in fact, we will see that terms almost always have a financial impact.

- **Part III: Growing the Venture** Once the entrepreneur has raised funds from equity investors, the focus moves to growth and control. In Chapter 10, we review the tools used by venture capitalists and business angels to monitor the evolution of the business plan. We include key metrics for some of the most common business models. Then, in Chapter 11, the focus turns to corporate governance, including key issues such as the board of directors or employee stock option plans. Chapter 12 concludes with considering the concept and practicalities of intellectual property.

- **Part IV: Alternative Routes to Entrepreneurship** This part moves from starting a new venture to becoming an entrepreneur by acquisition, and concludes by looking in depth at social entrepreneurship. Chapter 13 covers management buy-ins and buyouts. In these circumstances, the acquired company is used as a platform for becoming an entrepreneur. The process of acquiring a company requires a completely different approach than starting from scratch, and the chapter covers the process step-by-step. Chapter 14 reviews search funds and the search process involved in acquiring a company. Chapter 15 explores the special situation of acquiring a failing company and turning it around. Finally, in Chapter 16, we look at social entrepreneurship and venture philanthropy, the latter being a very interesting source of financing in the social sector.

- **Part V: Harvesting and the Future of Entrepreneurial Finance** Chapter 17 takes a detailed look at the final stage of the entrepreneurial finance process for investors, that is, exiting the venture. The chapter explores the different exit options available to successful entrepreneurs, considering in depth the topics of acquisitions (trade sales) and initial public offerings (IPOs). Finally, Chapter 18 concludes with some of the trends and future evolution of this exciting topic of entrepreneurial finance.

PART I

FUNDING SOURCES

CHAPTER

1

INTRODUCTION TO ENTREPRENEURIAL FINANCE

LUISA ALEMANY

ESADE Business School

JOB J. ANDREOLI

Nyenrode Business University

This chapter has been designed to act as your guide as you begin your journey in entrepreneurial finance. It will serve as a road map, allowing you to choose between reading the book from start to finish or, if you are looking for very specific advice, to jump directly to the relevant chapter or topic. We will look at the differences and similarities between entrepreneurial finance and more traditional fields of finance, such as corporate finance. Finally, we will discuss the different stages that a new venture may go through as it grows, and some of the financial challenges that both the founders and investors in the business might meet along the way.

VIEW FROM THE MEDIA

FINANCIAL TIMES   FT

Investors hail future of German flying taxi start-up

Lilium funding tops $100m as electric aircraft company aims for 2019 lift-off

SEPTEMBER 5, 2017 BY PEGGY HOLLINGER, INDUSTRY EDITOR

The race is on to bring an end to traffic jams after a German start-up founded two years ago by four university students secured $90m in funding from tech entrepreneurs to develop a flying taxi. Munich-based Lilium secured the funding from Chinese social media giant Tencent, Skype founder Niklas Zennström's Atomico, Twitter co-founder

Ev Williams' Obvious Ventures, and LGT, the private bank owned by Lichtenstein's royal family. The fundraising follows an earlier funding round which raised $10m, bringing the total so far to more than $100m. Daniel Wiegand, the chief executive who with three others founded Lilium while at the Technical University of Munich, said the investment made Lilium 'one of the best funded electric aircraft projects in the world'. It would enable the company to accelerate the commercial development of a five-seat electric aircraft. Lilium in April completed a successful test flight of a full-scale two seat version of the aircraft – which takes off and lands vertically but transitions to forward propelling flight once in the air. ... Lilium is hoping to make its first manned flight by 2019 and to have an on-demand service by 2025. Mr Gerber said the aircraft would be capable of travelling 300 kilometres or more in a single charge, with a cost per kilometre that would be competitive against ground travel.

www.ft.com/content/e1f443c8-91a2-11e7-bdfa-eda243196c2c

LEARNING OBJECTIVES

After reading this chapter you will be able to:

* Understand what we mean when we talk about entrepreneurial finance.
* Become familiar with the definitions of 'entrepreneurship' and 'finance' and the fit of entrepreneurial finance with both fields.
* Appreciate the similarities and differences between entrepreneurial finance and corporate finance.
* Differentiate between the stages of new venture development and the sources of financing available.

Where Are We Going Next?

This chapter begins with a short story about an entrepreneur to illustrate the concept of entrepreneurial finance. It will then answer the question 'what is entrepreneurial finance?' by exploring exactly what we mean by entrepreneurship and finance. We will then clarify the differences, and similarities, between corporate finance and entrepreneurial finance. The chapter continues with an analysis of the different stages of a new venture from a financial perspective, and by looking at the sources of financing available for each stage. We hope that you enjoy the ride!

1.1   An Entrepreneurial Finance Story

We are often asked the question: 'so what exactly *is* entrepreneurial finance?' And it is sometimes difficult for us to explain. One answer might simply be 'well, it is finance for entrepreneurs'. And that's correct. However, the next question that we are asked is 'and how is finance for entrepreneurs different from finance for anybody else?' This is where the explanation becomes more detailed and, sometimes, more confusing.

Let us start by telling you a story. It happened on a typical day of teaching. Luisa was teaching an intensive course in finance to a group of Master of Science students from RENE. RENE is a very interesting programme on Renewable Energy that is offered by four European universities:[1] *KTH-Royal Institute of Technology* in Stockholm, *Instituto Superior Tecnico* in Lisbon, *Ecole Polytechnique*, Paris and *Università Politécnica de Catalunya*, Barcelona. As part of their Master's degree, some of the students have an intensive week on entrepreneurship at ESADE Business School, in Barcelona.

It was a very intensive day, at the end of a very intensive week, for the RENE students. It meant eight hours of basic accounting and finance for some very smart students, who were highly motivated to find a brilliant idea that could help to reduce pollution, to provide cleaner energy or to make our world more sustainable. The topics that we covered in class that Friday were the balance sheet and the profit and loss account. This is part of basic accounting. Many of them (actually, nearly all of them) understood for the very first time the difference between an 'investment' and an 'expense' – a very important concept when you are thinking about starting your own business. Also, we looked at how assets and liabilities balance out and, that if you owe more money than you have, then you are in big trouble and it might be 'game over'. I could see, as the class progressed, how all these definitions were engaging them. The fact that accounting and finance use numbers was something that engineers love. Better than marketing and strategy, right?

Later, we reviewed the concept of cash flow and how selling does not always translate into cash. This happens quite frequently, for example, if your customer is another company that is planning to pay you in 60 days. Well, that's if you are lucky. So, you might have sold, let's say, €10,000 of services, but the money has not yet been paid into your bank account. You are expecting to be paid in 60 days, so you will have a balance of €10,000 in your 'Accounts receivable'.

Finally, in the second part of the afternoon, the students worked in groups on a case study to build the financial plan for a new company, a wind farm. It was challenging for them; it was their first contact with accounting and finance. But smart teams perform well when confronted with challenges. It was a very long day. But they survived!

As I was packing my laptop and class material, one of the students, Niklas, approached me. He was very excited because he was already working on a plan for a new company, and he felt that today's class had been very useful. Of course,

1 This programme counts with the support of KIC-InnoEnergy and is accredited by the European Institute of Innovation and Technology. To learn more visit: www.innoenergy .com and https://eit.europe.eu

I was very happy to hear that. Professors are always happy when a student tells them that the class was worthwhile. But in this case, I was very interested as the student asked me if he could show me the presentation he had prepared about his business idea.

It was Friday, 6:30 PM, but I was really keen to hear about it, especially when Niklas mentioned the name of the venture[2]. He went through the slides, which were very well laid out, I have to admit (I'm used to seeing a lot of presentations in class), so I congratulated him. He mentioned that one of his co-founders, Eva, had experience in design. Anyway, the opportunity that he and his team had identified was to produce vegetables, such as tomatoes, broccoli, onions or even lettuce in the Nordic countries. They were planning to use new technology that they were developing in their home university as part of their Master's degree that would allow the production of 'Mediterranean' vegetables, which need a lot of sun and warm weather, in labs close to the final customer. With this idea, they were solving two key problems. First, they could ensure stable prices for Nordic consumers, as they would not be dependent on the weather conditions in southern Europe or the effect of supply and demand in the market[3]. Second, they were significantly reducing transportation costs, as their plan was to produce locally, close to the customer, in areas surrounding the cities, using electric vehicles or even bicycles to distribute the vegetables to the customer's home or office. In addition, they could ensure attractive and competitive prices, as they were cutting out many of the intermediaries. Finally, they thought that their competitive advantage, and the reason why customers would buy from their startup, was that Nordic people were tired of not having continuous access to fresh vegetables, limiting their options for a healthy and varied diet.

The last-but-one slide was full of numbers. I have to admit that I do love numbers and financial plans, but this wasn't the most appealing slide in the deck. Niklas asked me to review it. I quickly went through the numbers of his financial plan.

The following is an excerpt from the conversation we had:

Luisa: Well, Niklas, you've done a good job of putting all the numbers together. I see that you have prepared a profit and loss account here, right?

Niklas: Yes, that is what I was trying to do. Adding in the money coming from the revenue, which will be subscriptions, and then subtracting all the expenses that we think we are going to have, such as employees, rent or marketing.

Luisa: I see, so these are your assumptions.

Niklas: Yes. And we have also estimated that we will need €460,000 for the land where we are growing the vegetables, around 5,000 square metres, in six different locations, to start with.

2 For reasons of confidentiality, we do not use the actual name and have changed some of the details of his plan.
3 In January 2017, there was a steep increase in the price of basic vegetables across Europe, and worldwide, due to the bad weather, including floods, that reduced production in southern Europe, affecting the price of basic products.

Luisa: Very good, and you have already checked that this is the appropriate size for the production that you are forecasting?

Niklas: Yes, we have talked to an agricultural expert who has confirmed that this is the right size. So, we basically need €460,000 to start this company. And we think that we can get this money from a grant, or maybe from crowdfunding.

Luisa: Niklas, let me ask you a question: do you need all the money upfront? Or can this investment be staged?

Niklas: Umm, well, I don't know. I just know that this is the money we need.

Luisa: Ok. Now, going back to your numbers, I see that in year 1 you are already selling your entire production, exactly the same amount as in year 2.

Niklas: Well, yes, we are being very conservative here, as we are charging 15% less than supermarkets and we are assuming only 1,500 subscriptions paying a fixed fee of €60 per month.

Luisa: Hahaha, entrepreneurs always say their figures are conservative . . .

Niklas: But they actually are!

Luisa: Maybe you are right, but let me go back to my point. If you are starting in year 1, then you will need to find the land. You mentioned six locations. Then you need to build your 'labs'. That will probably not happen overnight. Once the labs are ready, you will most likely have to do some testing of the quality of the crop, which, by the way, takes some weeks to grow. I'm not an expert, but a tomato will not be ready in a week for sure . . .

Niklas: Oh, yes, well, true.

Luisa: But that is not all. Once the crop has been tested and the quality is high enough, you can start advertising your company and your service. Again, even if you think 1,500 people is not many, you will have to reach them somehow, and then convince them to buy from you.

Niklas: Yes, but we are counting on our friends from University and also our families to be our customers.

Luisa: Of course, they will be your first customers, but the point I'm trying to make here is that most likely, your first year will be a full year of expenses and that the revenues will not come in in January. Maybe in June. Maybe in October. You need to take all the steps into account – one after the other. Some of them might work in parallel. Therefore, you are going to need more money than just the one needed for the big investment, as you will not have income on the very first day.

Niklas: I see.

At this point, I could see that Niklas was looking sad. He was kind of disappointed with himself because he hadn't realized all of this. But of course, how can you know before somebody explains it to you. So Luisa tried to encourage him.

Luisa: Yes, sorry, I don't mean to give you bad news here. As we saw in class today, the profit and loss account is one thing, especially once the business is up and running at full speed, and the cash flow is another. But don't worry, it is normal; you've never heard of this before. Believe me, putting down some numbers, as you have already done, is the first step, and a very important one, and you are certainly on the right path.

Niklas: Thanks, we were just trying to build a financial plan, without really knowing exactly what that was. We looked on the internet. But I feel that now, having gone through this afternoon's exercise of building a financial plan, I will be able to go back and re-work the numbers for my startup.

Luisa: Of course you can! And you can count on me to review them. Now, my quick calculation, from looking at your numbers, and taking into account everything that we just talked about, is that you are going to need between €1 and €1.2 million. So, what do you say to that?

Niklas: That much? Uff, I hope you are not right! We have heard about accelerators, business angels and venture capital, and if we need that amount of funding it sounds like we will need to go down that road rather than follow our initial idea of getting a grant or raising some money from crowdfunding. I don't think the banks will give us a loan. This is very complicated!

Luisa: Niklas, don't worry, it is not complicated, it is just a question of learning about the different options. What you do in your Master's in Renewable Energy is complicated. You are looking for new ways of creating energy! This thing about business angels and venture capital sounds complex because you have heard about it but you don't know how it works. Look, congratulations on your project, I truly believe you have something very interesting here! It is Friday evening. You are in Barcelona. Now, enjoy the weekend and try to re-do your numbers next week. After that, contact me again, and let's see how can we move things forward.

Niklas: Thanks a lot! And yes, it is Friday. I was so tied up with what we saw today that I almost forgot! Have a great weekend as well. I'll send you an email next week from the North!

Niklas' story illustrates some of the first questions faced by entrepreneurs once they have come up with an amazing idea and they start to put their plans into action. At some point in time, you will need to estimate the resources needed to make your dream a reality. Resources such as talent, assets or contacts will be part of the equation, and money, whilst not necessarily your first priority, will be needed to make it work.

1.2   What Is Entrepreneurial Finance?

Entrepreneurial finance is a recently emerged field of finance that sits at the crossroads of entrepreneurship and finance.[4] Before getting to the definition of

---

4 First research in the entrepreneurial finance field started in the late 1990s. One of the first papers on the topic of entrepreneurial finance is Gorman and Sahlman (1989).

'entrepreneurial finance', it is interesting to think about the meaning of its components.

As regards '**entrepreneurship**', there are several definitions that have evolved over time. Some of them are included in Table 1.1.

Table 1.1 Definitions of 'Entrepreneurship'		
Year	Author	Definition
1755	R. Cantillon	The entrepreneur is an 'adventurer', who invests in the purchase of goods and materials, combines them to obtain new products with the incentive of selling these in the future at uncertain prices. The entrepreneur takes risks and identifies and realizes fruitful business opportunities.
1934	J. Schumpeter	The entrepreneur is an individual who exploits market opportunity through technical and/or organizational innovation and through new combinations taking place in: • Introduction of new products. • Introduction of new production methods. • New markets. • New forms of organization. • Reorganization of an exiting organization.
1973	I. Kirzner	The entrepreneur is a person who discovers previously unnoticed profit opportunities. The entrepreneur's discovery initiates a process in which these newly discovered profit opportunities are then acted on in the marketplace until market competition eliminates the profit opportunity.
1990	H. Stevenson and J. C. Jarillo	Entrepreneurship is a process by which individuals – either on their own or inside organizations – pursue opportunities without regard to the resources they currently control
2000	S. Shane and S. Venkataraman	Entrepreneurship is an activity that involves the discovery, evaluation, and exploitation of opportunities to introduce new goods and services, ways of organizing, markets, process, and raw materials through organizing efforts that previously had not existed. Entrepreneurship includes the study of the sources of those opportunities and the forms they take, the processes of opportunity discovery and evaluation, the acquisition of resources for the exploitation of these opportunities and the individuals that discover, evaluate, gather resources and exploit them.

As we can see from the different definitions,[5] entrepreneurship relates to the discovery of an opportunity and the steps that need to be taken to make it a reality. It is not just applied to the creation of new businesses, but they are, in most cases, its main focus.

In order to start an entrepreneurial endeavour, entrepreneurs need resources. Resource acquisition is, in fact, one of the main lines of research in entrepreneurship. And one of the key resources that the entrepreneur will need is money, as we saw in the previous section. This is where finance comes into play.

There is a multitude of definitions of '**finance**' but its origin seems to be as a French word that was later adopted by English speakers in the eighteenth century. Its original meaning relates to 'the management of money'. From there, finance has spread into many different fields, and with many different definitions, depending on the user group.

In general, finance relates to obtaining money, to investing money and to understanding the cost and the best use of money. It is sometimes referred to in the context of governments and countries, sometimes of markets and companies and often to ourselves, as in 'personal finance'. In this book, we are interested in the type of finance that relates to businesses, and that is known as 'corporate finance'.

In corporate finance, there are two major topics that relate to corporations. The first one is investing. This looks at how owners or managers in companies decide where to invest their budgets. They may choose to invest in a new machine, a new factory, entering new markets, launching new products or relaunching existing ones, or in many other projects that may affect the existing business. The second topic is financing. Where do you get the money needed to invest in or to run your business? How do you finance your investment plan? How much will that cost you? In fact, we are back to the basics of accounting; the company's balance sheet. The first topic (investing) refers to the assets of the company and the second one (financing) to its liabilities and equity.[6]

So in this context, let's go back to the initial question, 'what exactly *is* entrepreneurial finance?' If we combine the two fields we get:

'The art and science of investing and financing entrepreneurial ventures'[7]

Typically, entrepreneurial finance involves mainly private funding, as opposed to public funding, when we are talking about corporate finance. It is true that a very successful entrepreneurial venture might end up reaching the stock market, as a way of harvesting and giving liquidity to its investors, and at this point we are talking public funding.

This definition is not limited to startups, as a new entrepreneurial venture may also take place within a corporation or family business, as in the case of corporate venturing or intrapreneurship. It can also take place when an entrepreneur

---

5 The references to the original papers can be found at the end of this chapter.
6 To go deeper into the topic of corporate finance, see Brealey (2016).   7 Own definition.

acquires an existing business. We will cover that in Part IV of this book, Chapters 13 to 15. Although we are talking finance here, we have not yet mentioned the word 'profit'. Not because we don't like profits. We do. A lot. But because entrepreneurial finance also involves social businesses, where the main goal is the social return. However, financial sustainability is a must. Chapter 16 will introduce you to the specific characteristics of financing social businesses.

1.3 Differences and Similarities between Corporate Finance and Entrepreneurial Finance

Corporate finance focuses on existing businesses and the challenges they face to grow in order to deliver a healthy return to their investors. We could say that corporate finance's underlying goal or mantra is to increase shareholder value. So this assumes that there is already value in the business, and the key question is how to increase this value.

In contrast, entrepreneurial finance relates to an entrepreneur's first challenge to acquire the funding to be able to test whether there is an actual opportunity that can be made into a business – a real one, that has the potential to become financially sustainable. The challenge starts way before the generation of value. It actually begins during the opportunity phase, as aspiring entrepreneurs start to develop their ideas, or become more serious about them when creating a first prototype, or when they try to get a first feel that a market for this product or market exists, with customers that are willing to pay. In Section 1.4 we will discuss the different stages of venture financing.

One of the key differences between entrepreneurial finance and corporate finance is that in the latter you have historical information that will help you to forecast the future. However, this is not a guarantee of accurate forecasting, believe me. But at least the financial information is there. In the case of a startup, there is no previous history, or not a lot, and the future is unknown. In most cases, the founders will be working on a very innovative solution that will solve an existing need. In other cases, they will be generating the need, as they plan to enter a totally new market.

Another major difference between the two fields is that in corporate finance we assume that projects or investments will have a positive net present value (NPV) – if not, they will not be implemented by senior management.[8] In entrepreneurial finance, losses are part of the game, since in the early years most of the money is ploughed into investments and expenses that, hopefully, at some point in the future, will translate into positive cash flows. You might be wondering who would be likely to be interested in investing in or starting a company that will almost certainly lose money. Well, it's a very reasonable question. As we will see, while in corporate finance most of the returns will come from the

8 Sometimes top management might approve negative net present value investments because they consider them to be 'strategic'.

existing company, in entrepreneurial finance investors will make a profit when they divest from the venture. And at that point it might be generating a profit or it might not. It is the increase in the value of the shares in the company that matters.

Corporate finance theories are based on an important assumption, that investors are rational.[9] This means that they will estimate the risk of each investment opportunity and either choose the option with the lower risk given the same expected return or the one with the higher return given the same level of risk. When investing in new startups, investors are confronted with two issues. First, the level of risk and the expected return that the investor requires for each specific new venture is very difficult to estimate. Unfortunately, we cannot rely on established theories such as the capital asset pricing model (CAPM) which allow us to estimate the expected return while understanding the level of risk.[10] Second, investors in new ventures may not have the profile of a 'typical' investor. Perhaps they are not as 'rational' as established corporate finance theory assumes? For example, imagine that an investor is offered two options. Option 1 is €100 in hand. Nice. Option 2 is a lottery ticket, or one stock in a new venture. This lottery ticket (or one stock) has a 50 per cent chance of returning €200 and a 50 per cent chance of getting nothing. Let's imagine that both options will pay out at the same time. Now, which would a 'rational' investor pick? What would you do?

Let's do the calculations. The expected return of option 1 is €100. What about the expected return of option 2? 50 per cent of €200, plus 50 per cent of zero. That's exactly €100. Therefore, the two options provide the same expected return. Now, let's examine their risk profile. Well, without doing any calculations you can see that there is no risk involved in option 1. You are guaranteed to receive €100. However, in option 2, although your expected return is €100 euros, you might end up with nothing.

Maybe investors in entrepreneurial ventures are not 'rational', as defined in traditional finance, as they are picking the lottery ticket (or the stock), instead of the less risky option. In fact, an investor might come up with different answers to the two-option challenge if we changed the characteristics of the options. For example, what if, rather than €100, you were offered either €10,000 or a lottery ticket that might yield €20,000 or nothing at all? Would you choose the lottery ticket? What if you had to pay some money up front to play the game? What if the money that you pay upfront goes to something that you really like, something that is socially beneficial or that is related to one of your hobbies? In fact, rationality is mixed with passion, a bit of fun and a lot of uncertainty in

---

9 The first models that related risk to return assuming that investors are rational where defined by nobel prize winners professors H.M. Markowitz (1952) and by W. F. Sharpe (1964). Currently, there is a new branch of corporate finance, known as 'behavioral finance', that study investors' irrationality.

10 If you are interested in learning more about CAPM, see Sharpe (1964).

entrepreneurial finance. In Chapters 2 to 4, we will review the profile and motivations of the different types of investors.

A UK company without clients raises $50 million and is bought in three years for $500 million

DeepMind Technologies, headquartered in London, is a British artificial intelligence company that was founded in 2010 by Demis Hassabis, Shane Legg and Mustafa Suleyman. DeepMind made headlines in 2016 when its AlphaGo program beat a human professional Go player for the first time.

Hassabis and Legg met at University College London's Gatsby Computational Neuroscience Unit. From 2010 to 2014, without a product or client, the company raised $50 million in funding from venture capitalists such as Horizons Ventures, Founders Fund and entrepreneurs such as Scott Banister (IronPort and Paypal) and Elon Musk (Tesla). On January 2014, still without revenues, Google announced the acquisition of DeepMind for $500 million.

The main aspects of corporate finance and entrepreneurial finance are summarized in Table 1.2.

As we can see in Table 1.2, although both forms of finance have a number of characteristics in common, the focus is different, as the needs of an established corporation are different from the needs of a newly-created company.

Table 1.2 Key characteristics of entrepreneurial finance versus corporate finance

Topic	Entrepreneurial Finance	Corporate Finance
Funding sources	• Friends and Family • Crowdfunding • Incubators/accelerators • Business angels • Venture Capital • Private Equity	• Banks • Capital markets
Funding process	• Deal sourcing and Screening • Financial plan • Valuation • Term sheet	• Standard due diligence • Financial plan • Collateral to back loan
Growth	• Monitoring & key metrics • Corporate Governance • Protecting knowledge • Private Equity	• Capital budgeting • Mergers & acquisitions • Private Equity • Initial public offering (IPO)
Harvesting	• Exiting (selling) Initial public offering (IPO)	• Dividends

1.4   Stages of Venture Development and Sources of Financing

Entrepreneurial finance is not only relevant at the starting point of a new company. It covers the different stages that the venture will go through if it is successful in its endeavours. There are different classifications of the life of a venture. In this book, we divide the life of a company into four main stages.[11] Figure 1.1 details the four stages and their main characteristics.

1.4.1   Seed Stage

The seed stage begins with the idea for developing a new product or service. In most cases, a company will not yet have been established, but its founders will have identified an opportunity and be willing to devote time to it. They will try to validate their idea, produce a first prototype and reach the market. Reaching the market and getting the first customer, who will ideally pay for the product or service,[12] might be achieved within a short or a very long period of time. For example, if the startup provides a consulting business, the seed stage might be very short; as short as a month, or even a week. However, if the business is in the biotechnology field, getting access to the first customer will take many years, as

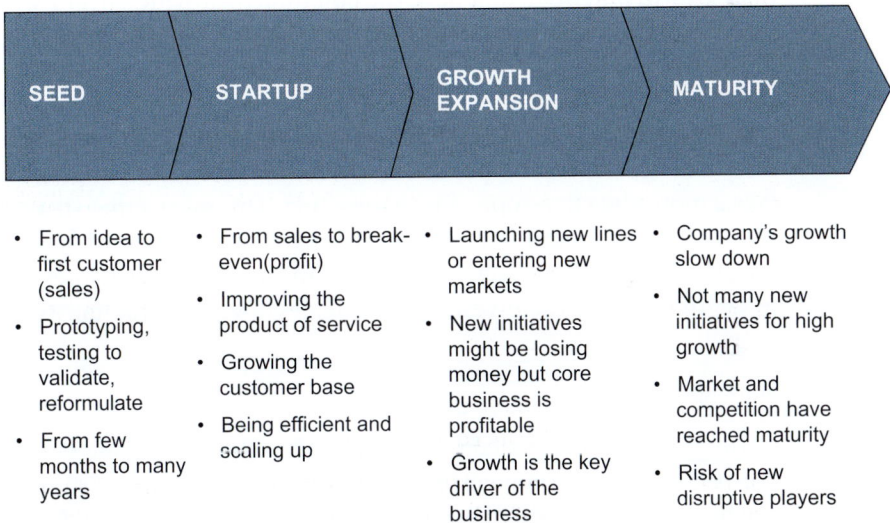

SEED	STARTUP	GROWTH EXPANSION	MATURITY
• From idea to first customer (sales)	• From sales to break-even(profit)	• Launching new lines or entering new markets	• Company's growth slow down
• Prototyping, testing to validate, reformulate	• Improving the product of service	• New initiatives might be losing money but core business is profitable	• Not many new initiatives for high growth
• From few months to many years	• Growing the customer base	• Growth is the key driver of the business	• Market and competition have reached maturity
	• Being efficient and scaling up		• Risk of new disruptive players

Figure 1.1 Stages of venture development.

11 There are other classifications of the stages of a venture development depending on different perspectives. In this book we are interested in its financial perspective.
12 In general, a seed stage finishes when revenues start to come in. However, we need to acknowledge the different nature of many internet or technology ventures. Some companies have many users or customers, but they do not pay to use their service, like in the case on Wallapop or Whatsapp.

the process of testing and approval is very lengthy. Therefore, it cannot be said that seed stage covers the first year, or a fixed period of time. It varies according to the activity of the business and its specific characteristics.

Depending on the type of business, the founders will need funding (until they start selling) to finance this period of time. Examples of the use of funding are paying salaries, investments in tangible or intangible assets and other expenses. At the very beginning, the first financing source will be the founders' own savings, known as 'bootstrapping', with perhaps some support from friends and family, also known as the '3Fs' (friends, family and fools). The support from the 3Fs is very important, as they are the people who know the founding team best, and it is a positive indication for other investors. Having some 'skin in the game' will signal to the seed investors that the owner and those around her believe in the venture (and, more specifically, believe in the founder). Also, if the business meets certain criteria, or has an important research base or innovation component, there may be research grants and public funding available. Chapter 5 reviews public funding for entrepreneurs.

If the entrepreneurs still need financing, they can launch a crowdfunding campaign, approach an incubator or an accelerator. Chapter 2 covers these funding sources in detail. Next in line is the business angel. However, business angels are not interested in all types of business. Only those businesses with high-growth potential, that have the potential to provide a healthy return in the long term, will be able to raise capital from angels. Chapter 3 explores the topic of angel investors.

Although venture capitalists generally invest during the start-up stage (see the following section), there are some venture funds that focus on seed investing. They look for the same types of companies as the business angels, but they will take a more objective approach to investing. This means that they will ask for a great deal more information, undertaking a deeper level of analysis and due diligence before becoming shareholders in the venture. Chapter 4 presents an in-depth review of the investment strategies of venture capitalists.

1.4.2   Start-up Stage

By this point in time, the company is already selling its products or services or, at the very least, has some customers. It will remain in the startup stage until it reaches break-even, which is the stage at which the startup is able to cover all its costs. The company will then no longer need additional external financing, and will be sustainable.

Having its first customers is a very important milestone for the venture, as this is a proof that there is initial demand for the product or service. However, the first customers are often friends of or people who are close to the entrepreneur, so there is still much to learn about the potential customer base. Understanding the cost of acquiring a customer is a key metric (known as CAC, customer acquisition cost), as it is very important that the value of a customer to the business (known as LTV, or lifetime value) is higher than the cost of acquiring it. There are other costs in the business, and they need to be covered too. But if the LTV is higher than the CAC, the business could potentially reach profitability if it keeps on growing. Chapter 10 takes an in-depth approach to the topic of key metrics and the ways in which investors monitor the evolution of the venture.

At this stage in the company's life cycle, it is still consuming cash, as its income is not yet sufficient to cover its expenses. Depending on the financial needs of the company, the most suitable source of financing will be business angels or venture capitalists. As a rule of thumb, if the business requires less than €1 million, a syndicate of business angels might be willing to provide the financing. If a larger sum is required, then venture capital will be the most likely route, with the investor investing in the venture in what is called 'Series A'. Depending on the cash consumption of the venture and its rate of growth, there might be successive rounds of venture funding. They will be called 'Series B', 'Series C' and so on. We explain how to estimate the venture's financial needs and the best timing for this in Chapter 7. In a few cases, perhaps in one out of ten venture-backed startups, or even fewer, they will achieve stock exchange listing for an initial public offering (IPO). All you need to know about IPOs is explained in Chapter 17.

1.4.3   Growth Stage

The growth stage starts once the company has reached break-even and is becoming profitable. It may not be generating a lot of profit yet, but the important point is that it is no longer losing money. Most of the cash generated will go to finance growth. Additional financing can be raised, but now banks may come into play, as the company will, most likely, meet the credit control requirements of traditional financial institutions.

1.4.4   Maturity Stage

The maturity stage begins once the growth of the market or the company stabilizes at normal rates. The company will not make large investments at this stage, will be carrying out 'business as usual' and will try to maintain its current market share. Everything you need to know about finance for mature companies can be found in any good corporate finance book. However, if you are interested in acquiring a mature company and becoming an entrepreneur by acquisition, Chapters 13 to 15 of this book will give you more information. In the case of entrepreneurship by acquisition, private equity can be an ideal source of financing.

In summary, there are different types of financing available according to the size and timing of the new venture's financial needs, as well as the milestones

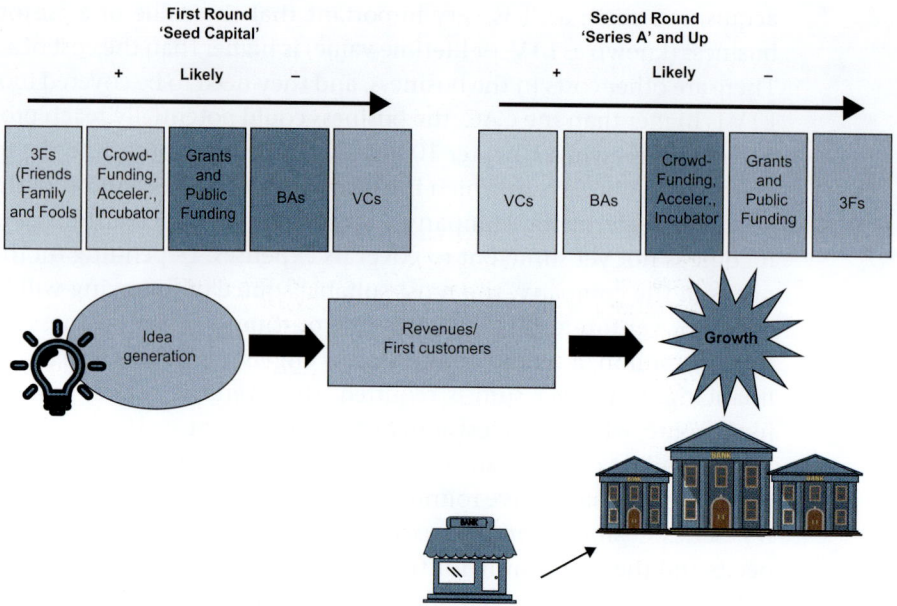

Figure 1.2 Early stages of a new venture and sources of financing.

achieved. Understanding which type of investor is suitable for your company is important. Figure 1.2 summarizes the different alternative sources of financing for the seed round and the first start-up round. Each source of financing comes with positives and negatives, and considerations to be borne in mind for the present as well as for the future. Learning as much as you can about entrepreneurial finance is crucial for people like Niklas, as it was for the many other entrepreneurs that you will encounter as you work your way through this book. Some are well known, some are not famous at all, but they all had the drive and the courage to follow their dreams. And for this endeavour, they counted on the support of the investors that believed in them.

So funding options come available dependent upon the venture development phase. The remainder of this section will assess the funding options in more detail see figure 1.3.

The sources relied upon in the very early phase (merely idea and initial qualification) of a venture are the entrepreneurs themselves and the people closest to them. First to invest anything is typically the entrepreneur. They see an opportunity and feel the urge to pursue it. The funding comes from their own savings account or they approach their family and close relations in the hope of obtaining funding from them. Although the funds are typically limited, the benefit of obtaining the funds through these means is that the entrepreneur is not yet required to issue equity. A support in these very early stages with restricted access is a business incubator. Although not directly providing capital, this source enables the entrepreneur to speed-up the development

Seed	Startup	Growth	Maturity
» Entrepreneur	» Entrepreneur	» Crowdfunding	» Venture Capital
» Family and Friends	» Family and Friends	» Business Angel	» Commercial Bank Loan
» Incubator	» Incubator	» Government Programme	» Private Equity
» Accelerator	» Accelerator	» Corporate Strategic Partnership	» Mezzanine Capital
» Crowdfunding	» Crowdfunding	» Venture Capital	» High Yield Bonds
» Business Angel	» Business Angel	» Corporate Venture Capital	» Public Debt
» Government Programme	» Government Programme	» Venture Debt	» IPO
» Corporate Strategic Partnership	» Corporate Strategic Partnership	» Asset-Based Loan	
» Venture Capital	» Venture Capital	» Trade Credit	
	» Corporate Venture Capital	» Commercial Bank Loan	
	» Venture Debt	» Private Equity	
	» Asset-Based Loan	» Mezzanine Capital	
	» Trade Credit	» High Yield Bonds	

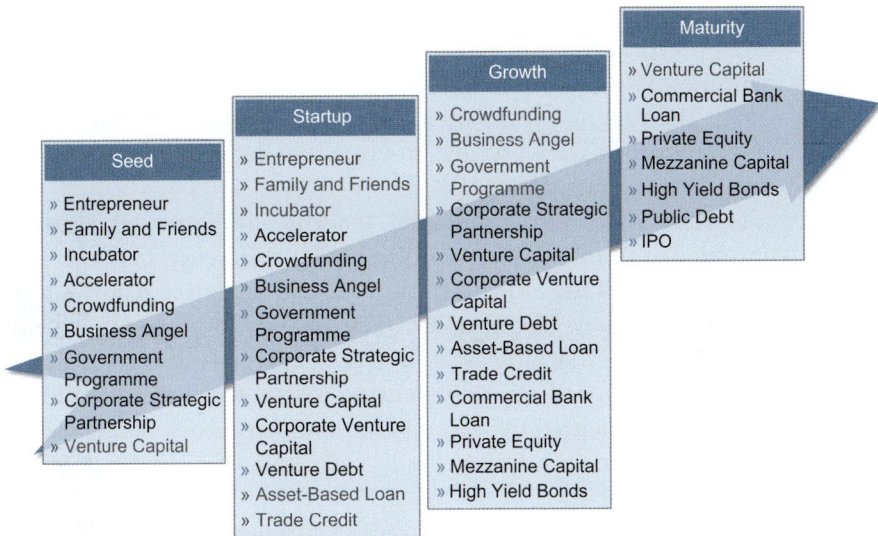

Figure 1.3 Sources of funding by venture development phase.

process through peer entrepreneur contact and obtaining valuable external contacts.

Sources of funding extending into the start-up phase are accelerator, crowd-funding, angel investors and government programmes. These sources require the venture to be slightly more developed from the start and extend their support into the phase where the venture is revenue generating. An accelerator is again largely support as opposed to merely capital. Business angels or angel investors are typically former successful entrepreneurs that have money, time and experience and enjoy actively supporting new ventures with all of these. Both accelerators and angel investors require the venture to give out part of its equity as compensation. Governments programmes refer to grants, subsidies, tax benefits or loans that governments provide to support and stimulate entrepreneurship as well as to incentivize initiatives aimed at particular societal needs.

The corporate strategic partner seems to have the broadest application area when related to the venture development. From the entrepreneur's point of view, seeking support from and partnering with established companies helps to build credibility and get access to a corporate network that might be relevant while further developing the venture. From the corporate's point of view, bonding with young innovative ventures is a means to build understanding of new trends and have a first-row seat to seeing the venture grow, appreciating their impact and developing a new supplier or buyer relation. This relation may have the form of funding support or merely providing credibility, distribution support or PR and branding benefits.

Venture Capital (VC) refers to professionals that invest large amounts of capital (typically up to Euro 10 million) in high-risk–high-return early-stage ventures. The venture reimburses the VC by giving it a significant minority stake. The role of VCs in their portfolio companies remains largely financial and imposes a rigid reporting structure that details the status quo and planned investments going forward.

Venture debt and asset-based lending are forms of loans available to entrepreneurs in the start-up phase. The difference between the two is the availability of assets in the venture, while the latter requires assets as security for the loan, the former is especially developed for venture capital backed ventures lacking assets and a steady cash flow for a more traditional form of debt financing. Debt venture is structured as a loan for a number of years complemented by warrants for company stock. Ventures in the growth phase and able to prove a steady cash flow can opt for a traditional commercial bank loan.

In the growth stage, more funding forms become available. Trade credit provides a form of spontaneous funding by allowing the entrepreneur to pay later for the goods that he already obtained. Trade credit is a vendor loan, typically without interest but coming at the expense of foregoing a discount that would be obtained when paying earlier. Factoring works the other way around, selling accounts receivable to a factoring company for a discount on the face-value of the money that should be received in due time. So, a venture sells its accounts receivable (of say Euro 100,000) to a factoring company for Euro 80,000. The venture has the benefit of receiving its money directly and without debtor risk but this comes at the expense of selling it at a discount. The discount is dependent upon a number of variables, amongst which is the credit worthiness of the debtors. The factoring company now works on gathering the full (Euro 100,000) from the acquired debtors.

Mezzanine capital is a hybrid form of debt and equity funding used by ventures that have built an established reputation and track record of positive cash flows. The reason for attracting additional capital is often to fund an expansion plan. This form of debt funding for high-risk ventures provides a relatively high interest rate and allows the capital providers to convert their loan into an equity stake in the venture.

The maturity and harvesting stage of venture development reveal three more key forms of funding. Private equity provides very large amounts of capital (potentially over a Euro 100 million) into ventures in return for a controlling stake and involves itself actively in the operations and streamlining of the venture. Public debt refers to ventures attracting debt from public markets by issuing bonds. The Initial Public Offering (IPO) refers to the first time that a (formerly private) stock is offered to the public. At the time of the IPO lots of capital is raised for the company and after the IPO the equity of the company is freely tradeable. This is the point in time that private companies become public companies.

KEY TAKEAWAYS

- Entrepreneurial finance is a field at the crossroads of entrepreneurship and finance.
- Corporate finance and entrepreneurial finance have some similarities and some differences. Corporate finance has a focus on existing businesses while entrepreneurial finance focuses on new ventures or in acquisition of existing business as a way of becoming an entrepreneur.
- A new venture will go through different stages: seed, startup, growth and maturity. Depending on the stage and the financial need there are different sources of financing available.
- Understanding the positives and negatives of each financing source is key to avoid surprises in the future.
- Entrepreneurship by acquisition and the financing of social enterprises is also part of entrepreneurial finance.

END OF CHAPTER QUESTIONS

1. What are the key questions that a first-time entrepreneur might have when thinking about finding financial resources for its venture?
2. Which would be the next steps that you would recommend Niklas to take? What other advice do you have for him?
3. When do we say that a company is in its seed stage?
4. When does a company move from startup to growth?
5. How do we know that a company has reached maturity?
6. What are the sources of financing that are covered in this book?
7. What are the main steps in the process of financing a new venture?

FURTHER READING

Bartlett, J. W. and Economy, P. (2002). *Raising Capital for Dummies*. Wiley Publishing.

Draper, W. and Schmidt, E. (2011). *The Startup Game: Inside the Partnership between Venture Capitalists and Entrepreneurs*. Palgrave Macmillan.

Gompers, P. and Lerner, J. (2001). *The Money of Invention*. HBS Press.

Lutoff-Carroll, C., Pirnes, A. and Withers LLP (2009). *From Innovation to Cash Flows*. Wiley.

Manigart, S. and Meuleman, M. (2004). *Financing Entrepreneurial Companies*. Larcier.

Osterwalder, A. and Pigneur, Y. (2010). *Business Model Generation*. Yves Pigneur.

Ries, E. (2011). *The Lean Startup*. Crown Publishing Group.

Sahlman, W., Stevenson, H, Roberts, M. and Bhidé, A. (1999). *The Entrepreneurial Venture*. 2nd edition. Harvard Business School Press.

Timmons, J., Spinelli, S. and Zacharakis, A. (2004). *How to Raise Capital: Techniques and Strategies for Financing and Valuing Your Small Business*. McGraw Hill.

REFERENCES

Brealey, R., Myers, S. and Allen, F. (2016). *Principles of Corporate Finance*. 12th edition. McGraw-Hill.

Cantillon, R. (1755). *Essai sur la nature du commerce en général*. History of Economic Thought Books.

Gorman, M. and Sahlman, W. A. (1989). What do venture capitalists do? *Journal of Business Venturing*, 4(4), 231–248.

Kirzner, I. (1973). *Competition and Entrepreneurship*. The University of Chicago Press.

Markowitz, H. M. (1952). Portfolio selection. *Journal of Finance*, 7, 77–91.

Schumpeter, J. A. (1934). *The Theory of Economic Development*. Harvard University Press.

Shane, S. and Venkataraman, S. (2000). The promise of entrepreneurship as a field of research. *Academy of Management Review*, 25(1), 217–226.

Sharpe, W. F. (1964). Capital asset prices: A theory of market equilibrium under conditions of risk. *Journal of Finance*, 19, 425–442.

Stevenson, H. and Jarillo, C. (1990). A paradigm of entrepreneurship as a field of research. *Academy of Management Review*, 3, 45–57.

End of Chapter Case Study

WUAKI.TV[13]

On his way back from London, Jacinto Roca couldn't stop thinking about the decision he'd have to take in a few hours' time. He'd just had his third meeting with Hiroshi Mikitani, Rakuten CEO and founder, and the offer was on the table. He wasn't really sure that selling the company to Japan's 'Amazon' was the best idea, particularly because less than a year ago €2m had been raised from two venture capital funds, so cash flow was not, for the time being, an obstacle to potential growth.

To make matters worse, Spain's economic climate continued to go downhill, unemployment was 20% and the risk premium had been breaking records since early 2012. At that time, in late May, the possibility of Spain having to suddenly exit the Euro was being discussed. The spotlight had been on Greece, then Portugal, and now Spain.

---

13 This case was written by Professor Luisa Alemany, with help from Jacinto Roca, founder of Wuaki.TV and is intended to be used as the basis for class discussion rather than to illustrate either effective or ineffective handling of a management situation. The case was made based on primary data with the financial support of the ESADE Entrepreneurship Institute (2013).

Wuaki.TV

The idea of Wuaki.TV began in late 2008. Jacinto and his partner Josep had a theory that internet TV would be the next great revolution. In mid 2009 they got to work and started up the company. The founder team invested its own money plus some from family and friends and after rounding up about €250,000, work began on product engineering and contacting foremost international producers about quality content.

Six months later, now with something to show potential investors, they managed to raise €1m from business angels including several ESADE BAN (Business Angels Network) members. The year was 2010, the credit squeeze had a stronghold on the Spanish economy and obtaining a loan was almost like finding the Holy Grail. The investors obviously believed in Jacinto and the Wuaki team's potential.

Right from the start, the Wuaki project was shown to investors with an exit strategy. This is quite usual amongst startups, particularly if the management team are business school graduates. Jacinto was a former ESADE student and well aware of how important a well signposted exit is for investors. The big difference, however, was to not just design an exit strategy but to apply it from day one onwards.

Their market survey pinpointed two types of potential buyers. Firstly, international players, such as Amazon, Google and Netflix, interested in geographic expansion. Secondly, nationwide players in the television industry, such as Canal+, Antena3 and Tele5, interested in taking advantage of Wuaki's technological developments. So Jacinto and his partner Josep along with the first investors in Wuaki, Manel and Marc, agreed to stay in contact with these companies.

In mid 2011, already with a substantial number of subscribers, €2m of funding was raised from two venture capital companies.

Rakuten

The Japanese company Rakuten, aka the Japanese 'Amazon', was founded in 1997 by Hiroshi Mikitani, a Harvard Business School graduate, and floated on the JASDAQ in 2004.

Although Rakuten was originally an e-business it soon expanded into other realms, starting an aggressive globalization strategy in 2010 based mainly on buyouts. Its most famous buyouts include Buy.com in USA and PriceMinister in France. Rakuten is reckoned to have invested more than $1,000m in all. In 2011 the company had some 10,000 employees and was pushing ahead with its plans for global growth.

Rakuten and Their Interest in Wuaki.TV

In the last quarter of 2011, Hiroshi contacted Jacinto and suggested a meeting in Barcelona. The meeting went well and was followed by another work session to get to know each other better, in Tokyo this time. Hiroshi's personality, values and corporate philosophy tallied well with Jacinto's. They seemed to hit it off. Jacinto believed in Hiroshi's idea of a team of entrepreneurs around the globe helping Rakuten go global.

The cost of penetrating the internet TV industry and the European market was high for Rakuten. It would be possible but Wuaki had a head start of three years' work with a subscriber base of 250,000 and more than thrity employees.

The last meeting with Rakuten took place in London. The offer was on the table. Wuaki's board had the information and finance-wise, the proposition was very attractive. It was true that Wuaki did not need the money just then and by investing in its business growth, it would increase in value. Returns for investors could be higher with a little patience. But there were obviously risks. On the one hand, the Spanish economic climate, and on the other, the impending arrival of tough competitors and new projects in the industry. The same old story: the higher the returns, the greater the risk.

The Decision

Time was running out and after negotiating for so long, Jacinto wasn't sure he was thinking clearly. It wasn't just a matter of finance, there was a personal side to the deal. He and his partner had created Wuaki. It was their "baby" and they were entrepreneurs. Rakuten's buyout put a different slant on everything. The plane had just landed at Barcelona and he suddenly remembered his usual tactic when assailed by doubts: he switched his mobile on and called his father.

Questions for Discussion

1. What would you do if you were Jacinto? How do you feel about selling to Rakuten?
2. If you were one of the early business angel investors in the business sitting on the board of directors, what would you vote to do?
3. What is your reaction to Rakuten's proposal if you are the venture capital fund that invested in Wuaki.TV a year before?

EARLY SOURCES OF FUNDING (1): INCUBATORS, ACCELERATORS AND CROWDFUNDING

JOB J. ANDREOLI

Nyenrode Business University

This chapter considers three sources of early funding and support for new ventures. As will become apparent, these sources of early funding have only become available since the early 2000s, and they have resonated well judging from their adoption, especially in the European context.

Entrepreneurs tend to recognize market opportunities on a fairly regular basis and are optimistic about the market potential thereof. If they are serious about pursuing a perceived opportunity, capital is needed to transform the opportunity into a proposition that can be brought to the market. The challenge is to generate proof of the added value of an opportunity early on, to support the process of obtaining funding. That is where the sources addressed in this chapter come in.

In the early 2000s, three new sources of early funding were introduced, helping entrepreneurs to develop credible propositions and providing investors with more reliable indicators of success at an early stage. These three sources are incubators, accelerators and crowdfunding. Each of these funding sources treats validation, proof of concept and possibly first testing differently. This chapter will discuss these aspects in more depth and review the added value that these new sources offer compared to the more traditional means of raising capital.

As will become apparent, these forms of funding have complemented the 'art' of obtaining funding with 'science'. They do so by helping entrepreneurs, through a pre-defined and structured approach, to effectively convey their message to investors and at the same time address the key challenges for growth of the venture.

VIEW FROM THE MEDIA

FINANCIAL TIMES   FT

How trial by crowdfunding sorts winners from losers

Fundraising on online platforms is gaining ground among inventors

APRIL 5, 2017 BY BRIAN GROOM

Joe Lemay, a former software engineer and sales executive, was fed up with scribbling notes in meetings and losing them, so he came up with an imaginative solution: a notebook that can be microwaved. After jotting down ideas in the book, users scan and save their notes to the cloud via an app. They then microwave the book with a mug of water to erase the writing, making it clear and ready to be reused. The Rocketbook Wave raised $1.3m on crowdfunding platform Indiegogo in 2015, dwarfing the original $20,000 goal. Further campaigns followed: Rocketbook Innovations, the company Mr Lemay co-founded, has so far raised $4.2m for notebook products on Indiegogo and Kickstarter, another platform. Mr Lemay is typical of a growing number of company owners who are using crowdfunding not just to launch businesses, but to test the market's response to new products and seek customers' help in developing them.

'The funds are needed for the first build of products and it's ideal to validate that anyone cares about the product before spending time and money on it,' he says. 'Throughout the process, we engage our backers. They weigh in on design options, give us ideas for useful features and even vote on which product we do next,' adds Mr Lemay. ... Product validation applies mainly to rewards-based crowdfunding – a market dominated by Kickstarter and Indiegogo – in which backers contribute small sums in exchange for a reward that is often the item produced, such as a watch, album or film. Rewards-based platforms accounted for just under 10 per cent of the $34bn raised globally through crowdfunding in 2015, according to consultancy Massolution. So far the technique is a route that has appealed mainly to smaller entrepreneurs, though larger companies such as General Electric, toymaker Hasbro and brewer Anheuser-Busch have also worked with Indiegogo to aid their product development. ... Crowdfunding is not an easy route, however. It requires time and effort. Two-thirds or more of projects fail to achieve their funding target. Mr Lemay failed with his first crowdfunding project, a whiteboard system. Failures, though, can be useful in identifying quickly whether products are likely to flop, before spending years and millions developing them. ...

www.ft.com/content/f35f46f0-f92a-11e6-bd4e-68d53499ed71

LEARNING OBJECTIVES

After reading this chapter, you will be able to:

- Define incubator, accelerator and crowdfunding.
- Review the key drivers for their origination and development.
- Assess when each of these early sources of funding is appropriate for a growing venture.
- Understand the value and pitfalls of each method from both an entrepreneur's and investor's perspective.
- Establish the market proof of these early sources of funding in the success of ventures.

Where Are We Going Next?

This chapter defines incubators, accelerators and crowdfunding and reviews their respective roles in the early stages of a venture. Insight into the added value and limitations of each funding option is also provided. While these elements are primarily examined from the entrepreneur's perspective, attention is also given to that of the investor. Both perspectives prove to be important, as new ventures will seldom be in a position to qualify for debt, and the entrepreneur will therefore be particularly keen to gain the investor's confidence. Although all forms of funding considered in this chapter are relatively new, the final section will discuss early proof of their contribution to venture growth and the business ecosystem.

2.1   Definition and Origination of the Early Funding Sources

The three sources of early funding discussed in this chapter all originated in the early 2000s. As a consequence, their definitions – in particular, of incubators and accelerators – have not yet been established and vary in the literature. Moreover, the terms are sometimes even used interchangeably, although the forms have distinct differences.

Although the three forms of early funding will be explored in detail later in the chapter, this section is included to reveal the distinctive traits of the different funding sources. As will become apparent, there is a key difference between the three funding sources in their primary orientation and in the venture development phases to which they are applicable. Clarifying these differences may prevent entrepreneurs from wasting unnecessary time while seeking capital.

2.1.1   Pre-market Funding

Before investigating early sources of funding, an entrepreneur may tap into another funding source that is not provided in the market. This 'pre-market' source of funding is referred to as 'bootstrapping'.

Bootstrapping describes the activity of obtaining capital from one's own savings, personal loans and from close relatives. This form of capital is provided to the entrepreneur without giving away ownership in the company. As a rule, bootstrapping generates only small amounts of money. It is often referred to as 'the triple F', being family, friends and fools! The distinctive trait of this form is that obtaining the capital is rarely, if at all, related to the business concept but is provided because of the entrepreneur's personal means and relationship with the funder. As such, it is not a qualification of the business concept or market potential, as opposed to all other forms of funding.

Besides the necessity for the entrepreneur to resort to this kind of funding early on, the main advantage of bootstrapping is that it allows the entrepreneur to retain complete control of the venture. This means that the entrepreneur is free to determine the development of the venture and to reap all future financial benefits from it. It also allows the entrepreneur to focus on the customer instead of having the burden of searching for and being accountable to outside investors. The business may remain self-funded during later stages as well, e.g. through extending supplier trade credit terms. Many experienced entrepreneurs endorse this form of funding, e.g. 'Stay self-funded as long as possible' (Garrett Camp, co-founder of Uber).

Bootstrapping is usually undertaken at the stage when the entrepreneur has perceived an opportunity and is still developing the business concept. The early funding sources addressed in this chapter are the first external (or market) sources, rather than this type of FFF-funding.

2.1.2   Definition of the Early Market Sources

The definition of crowdfunding is quite widely agreed upon. However, the exact legal implications of crowdfunding differ at a country level throughout Europe and these continue to evolve. The challenge lies in differentiating between incubators and accelerators, as definitions of the terms vary in the literature, and in practice each form reveals a number of variations. For this reason, this section includes both a definition and an illustration of the key differences between incubators and accelerators.

The following definitions of the three sources of early funding are in common usage:[1]

- **Incubator**: an organization that provides startups with a shared operation space and also provides young businesses with networking opportunities, mentoring resources and access to shared equipment.
- **Accelerator**: an organization that offers startups support services and funding opportunities, in intense programmes lasting several months that include

---

1 Incubator and accelerator in line with 'What is a business accelerator and how does it differ from an incubator' by Startup Europe (11 August 2016), crowdfunding in line with definition of European Commission (ec.europa.eu, retrieved April 2017).

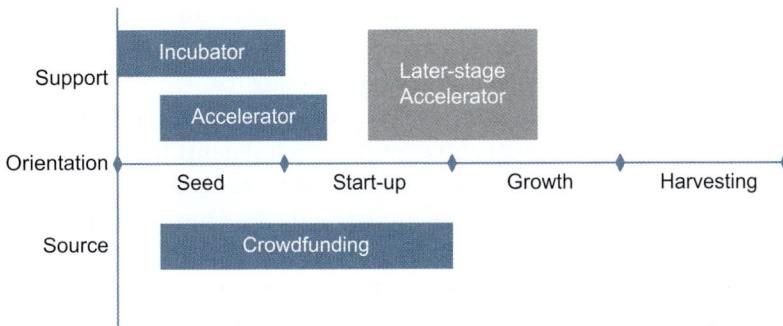

Figure 2.1 Early sources of funding by orientation and venture development phase.

mentorship, office space and access to capital and investment in return for startup equity.
• **Crowdfunding**: an emerging alternative form of financing that connects those who can give, lend or invest money directly with those who need financing for a specific project.

By reviewing the academic literature on these sources of early funding, common characteristics and traits emerge. Figure 2.1 visualizes three key elements: primary orientation, venture development phase and the existence of another form of accelerator that may support later-stage ventures. By applying these distinctions, possibly even in combination, entrepreneurs can select the funding source that provides them with the required support.

The horizontal axis reflects the four venture development phases as defined in Chapter 1. For external funding purposes, these phases range from seed (left) to harvesting (right). The vertical axis does not have a scale but indicates the orientation of the funding source, being either support or source. The positioning and length of the bars reveal the primary orientation of the early sources of funding in relation to the venture development phases for which they are typically applied.

The orientation indicates a source to be either 'support' or 'source', but it actually refers to more than just that. Incubators and (later-stage) accelerators have a support orientation and are primarily focused internally. Their primary orientation is on the development of the venture itself and they support that development with various tools, templates and networks. By optimizing the processes internally, investors are attracted and market success attained. Crowdfunding, on the other hand, has a source orientation and is primarily directed towards the (external) user/buyer and is used to generate market proof for the venture. All forms ultimately consider both internal and external elements for venture success however their initial focus may differ.

Of the three sources of early funding, incubators are the only one that supports the search for funding as of the start of the seed phase. Although incubators come in different forms and have varying origins, they typically provide support while the entrepreneur is developing the initial opportunity or concept. Accelerators and crowdfunding support in the development of a venture require a more developed concept to generate funding.

Finally, as indicated, another type of accelerator exists. This accelerator may be used in a later stage of the venture development. It applies in the case of a revenue-generating company that, for whatever reason, is not attaining the levels of growth that had been envisioned. The later-stage accelerator assesses the main cause(s) for underperformance and addresses that in a time-bound programme. This form is mentioned in this chapter on early sources as it is often, in news reports and the literature, placed in a category that includes (early-stage) accelerators, although it has distinct differences. Later-stage accelerators are discussed in more detail in section 2.4.

2.1.3   Distinct Differences

The reason that the terms incubator and accelerator are used interchangeably is that these forms have a number of similarities. Both forms provide support to ventures for growth in their earlier stages and go on to deliver startups. Moreover, in order to intensify learning and speed up the path to growth, both also provide access to a network of peer entrepreneurs and mentors.

Table 2.1 sets out some key differences between incubators and accelerators:

The distinctions shown in Table 2.1 relate to incubators and accelerators in their core form. In practice, combinations of both can be found, mixing the core traits of each form.

Incubators are mainly located in colleges or universities, to stimulate entrepreneurship within the student body. They can also be found within corporates, to nurture their internal innovation potential. In the latter case, the specialization may be more focused rather than purely horizontal. Incubators

Table 2.1 Differences between an incubator and accelerator

	Incubator	Accelerator
Specialization	Horizontal	Vertical(s) / Theme(s)
Target	Individuals	Teams
Entrance	Restricted	Open
Support	Organic growth	Boost growth
Programme	None	Generic
Duration	Months – Years – No limit	3–6 months
Financial contribution	None – Small amount	Larger amount (€10,000 – up)
Compensation	None – Small fee (e.g. rent)	Equity stake (5–10%)

are discussed in more detail in Section 2.2. Accelerators specialize in one or more vertical(s) or theme(s), and boost growth through an intensive programme aimed at 'Demo Day'. More information on accelerators is provided in Section 2.3.

In crowdfunding, different forms have also emerged over the years, all referencing the potential reward for the providers of capital (called 'funders' for financial rewards or 'backers' for non-financial rewards). Of the many variations, four key forms are elaborated on in Section 2.5, where further information is provided as to when each form is appropriate and on their potential benefits for entrepreneurs.

2.1.4   Key Drivers in Development

Before diving into each source of early funding in turn, the background to the origination and initial development of the three sources is considered. As will become clear, all three forms are quite recent developments and have gained ground rapidly in the market.[2]

Entrepreneurship is recognized as a key determinant to ensure economic growth, innovation and job creation.[3] Policymakers therefore promote entrepreneurship and actively facilitate it.[4] As a result of improvements in technology, as well as the growing interest of investors in this sector, technological startups have shown particularly strong growth. Most countries revealed signs of recovery in startup rates in 2016, although the startup rates in many countries are still below the levels that existed before the financial crisis of 2008–9 (see Figure 2.2). This is particularly important for Europe, as it has a greater reliance on small and medium-sized enterprises than the United States.[5]

The concept of providing a shared office space for the development of companies began in 1959 in the Batavia Industrial Center in New York. It became the world's first business incubator, providing a shared office and support to a number of companies. Incubators have developed more widely since the 1980s, being typically attached to universities, providing an infrastructure that acts as a 'playground' for aspiring entrepreneurs. The first accelerator was Y Combinator in Boston (2005) and Seedcamp in London (2007) was the first accelerator to be set up in Europe.[6] The first crowdfunding platforms to be established were ArtistShare in the United States (2003), followed by Sellaband in the Netherlands (2006).

Accelerators have helped to reshape the tech industry and proved to be a successful breeding ground for developing new business models and turning ideas into

---

2 Derived from Brunet *et al.* (2017a), Massolution (2016) and Zhang *et al.* (2016).
3 European Commission (ec.europa.eu/growth/smes_en).   4 European Commission (2012).
5 OECD (2016).
6 Note 'Nowadays, both Y Combinator and Seedcamp have expanded and changed their program offerings, and now consider themselves to be seed funds, a distinct group from accelerators' (European Accelerator Report 2015 by S. Brunet, M. Grof & D. Izquierdo, 2016).

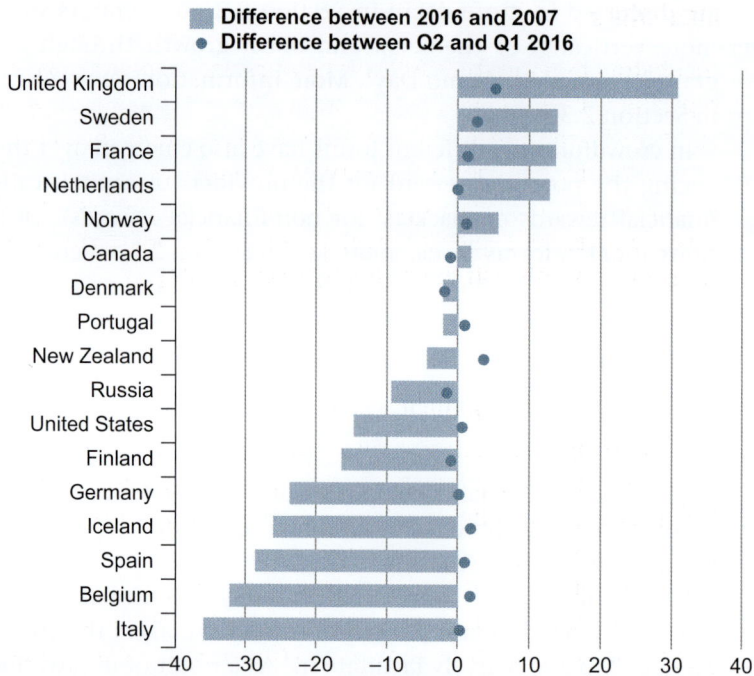

Figure 2.2 Global difference in enterprise creation.
Source: OECD (2016)

viable businesses. The accelerator industry has shown a strong growth rate world-wide. In the period from 2011 to 2016, the year-on-year growth rate (CAGR) in the number of accelerators in Europe was 47 per cent and in North America 39 per cent.[7] This growth can also be explained by the interest of investors. The qualification of startups for accelerators can aid as pre-selection and as such can help investors in funnelling and selecting the initiatives that they would likely invest in.

Europe only surpassed North America in the number of accelerators in 2015. However, there are still large differences in the levels of investment committed by these accelerators to their startups. Table 2.2 illustrates this:

Table 2.2 Accelerator programmes around the world in 2016[8]				
	Europe	North America	Rest of World	Total
Accelerators (#)	193	178	208	579
Startups (#)	3,701	3,269	4,335	11,305
Investment (MM)	US$ 50	US$ 107	US$ 49	US$ 206

7 Approximation for accelerator industry growth, based on Brunet *et al.* (2016) and Brunet *et al.* (2017b).
8 Derived from Brunet *et al.* (2017b).

2.2   Incubators

Incubators provide the earliest type of formal support that entrepreneurs can typically access. Their differentiating trait is that they support ventures very early on in the process of developing their (often merely) business idea. So entrepreneurs may be in the very early stages of developing an idea, or may already have a 'clickable demo' or minimal viable product (MVP), but are in any case pre-revenue. Typically, incubators are attached to either non-profit institutions such as universities or directly to corporates.

2.2.1   Forms

Incubators guide the entrepreneur through the early development phases, e.g. assessing the opportunity, researching the potential and building the business plan. The purpose of incubators is to support the entrepreneur in this process, from the creative aspects of the startup to the more analytical planning stage and assessment of the market approach. To facilitate this, the most basic incubator consists of a physical location that provides a general infrastructure and network for its participants. In this case, the incubator is little more than a meeting point for (aspiring) entrepreneurs. The benefit for the entrepreneurs is that it enables them to network, obtain feedback and learn from each other's experiences. Variations exist according to specialization, type of programme and duration. Some incubators have a specialization, tied in with their origin.

A noteworthy example is SETsquared (UK, linked to Universities of Bath, Bristol, Exeter, Southampton and Surrey), which is ranked first in the Global Top 25 University Business Incubator ranking of UBI Global. It provides space and support for early-stage high growth-potential ventures. Over the past 10 years, it has helped to raise over US$1.5 billion in investment and funding.[9] For universities, an incubator is a means of encouraging its students to engage in entrepreneurship. It stimulates them to apply their learning by developing a product or service and gaining experience in commercializing it. Incubators attached to corporates focus on initiatives that produce innovative offerings and expand the corporate's existing business. It is a means by which these companies generate new business, retain employees with entrepreneurial aspirations and signal to the market their engagement with innovation. The programme may be extended by including employee training and by linking with the local network.

9 UBI Global (2016).

2.2.2   Process

Most incubators have restricted membership, requiring the entrepreneur to be part of a certain institute or company. Access to the incubator is limited upfront by this affiliation: as such, the initial selection for most incubators is predetermined, given that they only allow applications from individuals who are directly associated with the founding institute. When making a selection from within this subset, attention is mainly given to the qualities of the individuals, as a key determinant of their potential success. In some cases, applicants will pitch their idea. From this subset, a number of applicants are chosen to form the next cohort of the incubator.

The incubator is the location (unless virtual) for infrastructure and support, and is dedicated to networking and to limiting distractions for the entrepreneurs. Key activities might include generic training, but they often do not. A mentor will be appointed to the entrepreneurs, to support their development and to bridge any questions or challenges that they may experience. The selection of a mentor is key in the success of the entrepreneur and the incubator, as these mentors will maintain ongoing personal contact with the entrepreneurs and coach them as they develop their venture. The mentors are therefore not only appointed according to their knowledge and experience, but also for their personal traits and experience as an entrepreneur.

The incubator's network and invited experts are another factor driving the success of the incubator. Typically, well-known entrepreneurs or business leaders from the incubator's network (co-sponsors or alumni) will be invited to give presentations that inspire the participants as well as advice that helps them to avoid the common pitfalls early on in developing a venture.

2.2.3   Benefits and Concerns

The success of an incubator in nurturing new ventures is determined for a large part by the quality of its mentors. The mentors will be in regular contact with the participants of the incubator and steer and advise them on how to proceed. In addition, a strong network of peer participants, alumni, partners and experts is an important factor in the success of the incubator, as well as the extent to which the incubator actively maintains contact with the local network.

The primary role of the mentor is to build a relationship with the entrepreneur(s) and to challenge them, while maintaining momentum. As well as the experience the mentor brings, he or she will need to find an approach that will stimulate performance while allowing the entrepreneur to make their own decisions. Mentoring has similarities with coaching, whereby telling the entrepreneur what to do is not the mentor's purpose; rather, it involves providing them with guidelines and allowing them to develop their own approach.

The key benefit of an incubator for aspiring entrepreneurs is the process of learning about entrepreneurship in a confined environment. However, both young and experienced entrepreneurs can aim to join an incubator. The latter group likely does so because of the access it provides to the network, while the former group is more likely to do so because of the generic process support it provides for the skills the young entrepreneurs still need to master. By building on the experience of their predecessors and the incubator's (corporate) partners, the participants become more effective in their approach to building a venture. The managed and protective office space allows the entrepreneurs to focus on their venture and feel supported at the same time. The peer network proves to be useful for feedback and support, meaning that ideas are challenged and validated early on, allowing for higher success rates.

The concerns raised about incubators relate to the offering. An incubator needs to be more than just a meeting point; having no fixed programme raises questions about the likely progress and dedication of the entrepreneurs.[10] The second concern relates to mentors, who are typically required to provide their services unpaid. Mentors are willing to do so because they wish to support entrepreneurs, but they also see it as a means for them to get involved in new and promising ventures. Their involvement, therefore, is not always entirely without self-interest. The third concern regards the attitude of the entrepreneurs. Once admitted to the incubator, the urgency of proving their venture may be lessened, having reached their first true milestone. This achievement might come too early for them to retain a focus on the value proposition and client.

Two final remarks on incubators. An incubator can be expected to have an impact on the local ecosystem. The incubator fosters entrepreneurship with spillover effects in terms of job creation and economic development. Also, just as academic rankings matter to universities, the ranking of an incubator is also a means by which the host (university or corporate) can differentiate itself. UBI Global assesses the performance of university incubators bi-yearly, as represented in Table 2.3.

These assessments take a broad perspective, looking at variables such as the value for the ecosystem, economy enhancement, talent retention, value to clients and post-incubation performance. For their 2017/2018 report, an

10 Mitra (2013).

Table 2.3 University business incubator: Europe Top 10[11]

#	Incubator	University	Country
1	SETsquared	University of Bath; University of Bristol; University of Exeter; University of Southampton; University of Surrey	United Kingdom
2	PoliHub Startup District & Incubator	Polytechnic University of Milan	Italy
3	INiTS Universitäres Gründerservice Wien	Vienna University of Technology; University of Vienna	Austria
4	YES!Delft	Delft University of Technology	Netherlands
5	Uppsala Innovation Centre	Uppsala University; Swedish University of Agricultural Sciences	Sweden
6	UtrechtInc	Utrecht University; University Medical Center Utrecht; University of Applied Sciences Utrecht	Netherlands
7	Business-Incubator of National Research University Higher School of Economics	National Research University, Higher School of Economics	Russia
8	ITU SEED (ITU CEKIRDEK)	Istanbul Technical University	Turkey
9	BLC3 Incubadora	University of Coimbra; University of Minho; School of Technology and Management of Oliveira do Hospital; University of Beira Interior; University Nova Lisbon; Catholic University of Portugal	Portugal
10	Parque Tecnológico de la Salud de Granada (PTS Granada)	University of Granada	Spain

Source: UBI Global (2016)

incubator programme's relative performance is assessed across 21 dimensions, with the aim to identify strengths and weaknesses, generate actionable metrics, and provide recommendations on how they can further improve their performance.[12]

11 'Global Benchmark 15/16 report – Top University Business Incubators' by UBI Global (2016).
12 'KPI Directory' by UBI Global (2017).

Let's Practise: Case Study

INCUBATOR – YES!Delft Case[13]

This case is based on the true story of how three TU Delft students started their own business. It describes the difficulties they experienced in trying to get their ideas to work and deciding on which market to enter. The technology itself was developed at TU Delft and has exciting potential benefits for many other market applications and product ideas, many of which are currently being explored by Spring-Solutions.

Jan stuffed his hands deep inside his pockets as he walked across the market square in Delft. The autumn air was cool. The summer was fading, and as he looked up at the tall church spire of the Nieuwe Kerk at the east side of the square he remembered those long summer days spent as an undergraduate here in Delft. Life was so much easier then, he mused to himself. A smile grew on his face as he thought about those untroubled days sharing a six bedroom house on Raamstraat, behind the railway station.

He stopped at the ABN-Amro cash machine to withdraw €50. Money was tight. Although Jan was no longer a student he was not yet earning the large salary that all graduates hoped would be theirs once they completed their studies. Instead of opting for employment Jan had decided on having a go at starting his own business with two friends André and Dirk. This is where he was heading now to see his two business partners to make a decision: which market to select for their technology. The outcome of which would become their business.

As Jan stood in line waiting to use the cash machine he thought back to a year ago when he and his friends decided to have a go at starting and running their own business. They had all completed their Master's degrees in Mechanical Engineering. It was during their time studying at the 3mE faculty that they met a young professor called Ryan Timmer. He had recently completed his PhD on statically balanced mechanisms and had been successful, with the help of TU Delft, in gaining a number of patents for his technology. Professor Timmer, however, while extremely passionate about the technology was less interested in forming a business to exploit the technology. His personal interest and passion was in further exploring and understanding the technology rather than in exploring its applications. Jan and Dirk had attended a presentation by Professor Timmer at TU Delft and had been very impressed with the technology. Indeed, they had been so impressed that they had wanted to develop the technology further and start their own business. Meetings followed with Professor Timmer and people from the incubator at YES!Delft.

The key advantage with this technology is that unlike conventional static spring balanced systems this technology enables the weight to be varied. The technology can be applied to develop balanced mechanisms for ergonomic

13 Case by Paul Trott (2016) from TU Delft and University of Portsmouth (abbreviated).

consumer products. For example, it is possible to have a vertically moveable overhead cupboard that functions without motors/actuators. The cupboard feels weightless, independent of its weight or content.

Jan collected his cash from the ABN-Amro machine and eased off towards De Kurk. He was not looking forward to the meeting with André and Dirk. For almost a year, while they completed their studies they had been exploring possible market applications. They had explored some wacky and crazy ideas such as: bicycle racks that can be raised off the ground, electrical appliances in the home that could be raised off the ground to create extra space and even beds that can be raised to create space. Although they now had to select a market application on which to focus, the truth was that they were still exploring new applications that might benefit from their technology. There were currently three main options: moving cabinets, moving monitors/television screens and moving tables/desktops. Six months ago each of them was supporting different options. Since then their market analysis and their own personal preferences had coalesced around two of the three options: moving kitchen cabinets and moving tables. They had obviously done their analysis, but the decision they were about to take is partly based on fact, partly based on previous experiences from other sources and guesswork. So which market should they select?

Adjustable kitchen cabinets – Storage space is always in short supply, especially in kitchens. One of the most common solutions is to stack up high. High cupboards, closets up to the ceiling and high shelves are common in every house. Lifting above your head is heavy and many users, young and old, are not able to reach the upper shelves or have a poor view of them. As a result the storage space used is often inefficient. The solution is moving wall cabinets that can be moved up and down the wall as required.

Adjustable table tops/desks/work stations – This is potentially a very lucrative market due to increasing health and safety regulations. This means people at work require work stations that adjust to the person's seating position height. The number of people spending time working at their computers also seems to be increasing every year.

There are so many questions that need to be addressed. A large potential market seems like a compelling reason to enter a market, but success in a smaller market would be better than failure in a large market. If the new product is a discontinuous one there may be a level of market education required. Some new products take a long time to succeed. One only has to consider PCs, CD players and MP3 players. The rate of diffusion and level of consumer adoption can have a significant impact on the level of profitability for firms. The table attempts to bring together some of the factors that need to be considered before deciding which market application is most likely to be successful for Spring-Solutions.

Factors to consider for selecting a market application of their technology:

	Potential size of European Market	Market attractiveness (M Porter)	New product classification	Adoption and diffusion issues	Potential Profit for Spring- Solutions versus likelihood of success
Moving Kitchen Cabinets	16 million kitchens each year	Barriers to entry?	Extent of newness?	Technology unknown?	Potential profit high but high entry barriers
Moving television screens	100 million televisions sold each year	Power of suppliers?	Improvement?	Who to approach in the supply chain	Extensive competition margins low
Moving table/ desk tops at workplace	unknown	Power of buyers?	New to the company?	People purchasing not the same as end consumer who benefits	Too many unknown factors
Others	?	?	?	?	?

Questions for Discussion

1. Analyse the three main market applications being considered by Dirk, Jan and André. Explain: which one would you choose? Use the market analysis models and frameworks suggested in the table (or others you are familiar with) to help you with your analysis.
2. Dirk, André and Jan also considered many other applications for their technology. Use your own creativity and come up with one further market application that could benefit from this technology.
3. What do you consider to be the key added value of the incubator YES!Delft in the entrepreneurial aspirations of students?

YES!Delft helps entrepreneurs to build leading technology companies. It is the incubator of the Delft University of Technology. Although founded by and fully linked to the university, it is also funded by the city of Delft and the province of Zuid-Holland as it clearly provides benefits for the local economy/community. Over the years YES!Delft adopted a number of accelerator traits, such as the requirement to have a business plan at the start and focus on the team. It does not request an equity stake, but does include a moral obligation to give back once a venture becomes successful (defined as having a value of over €1 million). To help the ventures attain success, YES!Delft is more than just a location and actively supports the growth of ventures by means of mentors and programme. Noteworthy ventures that resulted from this incubator are Ampelmann, Senz, Epyon, NightBalance, and Eternal Sun. In the Global Benchmark report 2015/16, YES!Delft ranks 4th in Europe and 9th worldwide.[14]

14 UBI Global (2016).

2.3   Accelerators

While incubators 'incubate' ventures, fostering innovation in preparation for a market launch, accelerators 'accelerate' ventures, speeding up innovation and their market potential. Both are early sources of support for funding, as they focus on supporting the creation of startups. However, there are a number of noticeable differences, as provided in Table 2.1. This section will look at the specific characteristics of an accelerator and its applicability for entrepreneurs.

It is important to note that this form of funding is often referred to using slightly different terms. These terms include 'seed accelerator', 'startup accelerator', 'pre accelerator' or 'venture accelerator'.

2.3.1   Forms

Typically, accelerators have a physical location where the founders of the venture work on building their venture. An accelerator is rarely just virtual. The application process is open and targeted at teams. This means that it does not have upfront restrictions as to whom can apply, as long as their interests fit in with the vertical(s) or theme(s) of the accelerator. Teams are admitted in cohorts for a programme of typically three to six months. So the selected teams start at the same time and work towards 'Demo Day'. This is a carefully orchestrated day when the entrepreneurs pitch their venture to invited investors.

Different forms of accelerators exist depending on the specialization, the type of programme, the intensity and quality of the mentorship and the strength of the external network.

As shown in Figure 2.1, accelerators come into play in seed phase and extend into the startup phase. Acceptance into an accelerator is very competitive, e.g. in the United States there was a 1.5 per cent acceptance rate for Y Combinator in 2014 (compared to 5.1 per cent and 5.9 per cent for Stanford and Harvard respectively of student acceptance in that same year).[15] In Europe, the Startup Sauna accelerator (Finland) mentions a 'mere 2%' acceptance rate, and the Startupbootcamp an average of 2–3 per cent.[16] As a result of the intensified level of competition and decreasing admission rates, teams that apply for accelerators increasingly tend to differentiate themselves more and apply with more developed concepts, such as 'clickable demos' or MVPs.

---

15 Rao (2015).
16 Startupsauna '700 applications, a mere 2% acceptance rate – meet our spring '16 batch' (20 April 2016, www.startupsauna.com); Startupbootcamp (SBC) indicates averages of: 300–500 applicants, 50 per cent are selected for an interview (possibly through Skype), 20 teams are invited for the final selection days, of which half are admitted to the accelerator programme (based on interview with Marc Wesselink (Managing Director SBC Amsterdam) on 17 May 2017).

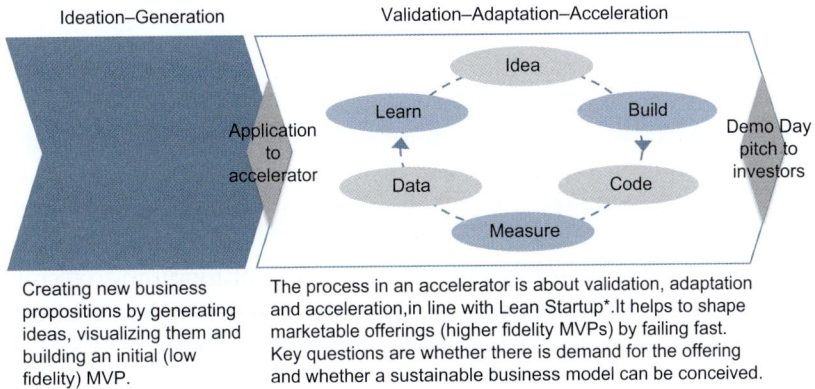

Figure 2.3 Overview of the accelerator process.[17]

2.3.2   Process

As admission to an accelerator is made in cohorts, the start of the programme and the finishing point (at 'Demo Day') are the same for all participants. By organizing it 'batch-wise', training can be more efficiently delivered and the progress of the teams aligned, fostering joint learning and networking.

The training provided in the programme is typically generic. This training helps with the development of concepts, creating the vision and mission of ventures, assessing the market size, reviewing different business models, profiling and team building, working out the preliminary financials and preparing a compelling proposition for future investors.

These activities are very focused, and it is an intense experience for the entrepreneurs, given the limited duration that any venture is allowed in the accelerator. The purpose is, as mentioned, to boost growth by providing process support in building the pitches for the startup, aimed at obtaining capital commitments on 'Demo Day'.

A mentor is appointed to support each team and maintain the momentum. This mentor has regular contact with the team to measure progress and help out with any specific questions. These questions may involve the application of the generic training to a particular venture. All activities in an accelerator are about validation, adaptation and acceleration, in line with the lean startup methodology (see Figure 2.3).

Accelerators are typically sponsored by corporates. For those sponsors, being associated with an accelerator programme is a means of showcasing their involvement with innovation and of staying in touch with the development of new initiatives.

17 Lean Startup(*), methodology derived from *The Lean Startup* by E. Ries (2011).

2.3.3   Benefits and Concerns

Good accelerators are highly skilled in screening applicants, only allowing ventures in that really have a chance of becoming successful in the market.

As with incubators, the quality of an accelerator is largely determined by the quality of its mentors. Their ability to link a mentor to a startup is a key differentiating factor, setting the good accelerators apart from the less successful ones.

The benefits for the entrepreneur of working with an accelerator are abundant, relating to the process, network and external effects of the programme. The network fosters new networks, particularly amongst the various entrepreneurs who participate in the accelerator and ask each other for feedback. It also allows the entrepreneurs to build partnerships with corporates. The external effects for the venture include the signalling effect and PR exposure that being selected for an accelerator brings. This selection raises the odds of gaining access to capital.

Another benefit for the entrepreneurs is the steep learning curve and vast amount of hands-on experience that involvement with an accelerator brings. It is often referred to as a new approach to learning, compared with going to a business school. In other words, to *be* the business case instead of reading about one.

A notable benefit for the local community is that an accelerator has a spillover effect. Accelerators can have a positive impact on the regional entrepreneurial mindset, activities and funding opportunities. Therefore, having thriving accelerators in the locale will improve business in that region.[18]

Being involved in an accelerator also has its pitfalls. In particular, the entrepreneurs need to participate actively from the outset, rather than wasting too much time celebrating the achievement of being accepted onto the programme. The entrepreneurs need to avoid being overwhelmed by the process, which can be distracting because of the many and various meetings that are scheduled. It can also be confusing, as the people they meet may give conflicting advice. Finally, the strong focus on obtaining funding during 'Demo Day' may distract the entrepreneurs from focusing on the client and the value proposition itself.

A concern that has been raised about accelerators is the variable quality of funding sources, referring to the actual intention of investors to invest. Demo Day typically sees an abundant number of investors in attendance, but their actual willingness to invest seems to sometimes be in doubt.

Another concern relates to the fact that many accelerators are also commercial organizations. To compensate for their support in the development of a venture, they typically ask for a stake in the venture. This equity stake in the venture is the key revenue model for the accelerator. The delicate part is that this stake, however small it may seem, is non-dilutable up to a fixed, minimal future value of the venture. This means that the share owned by the accelerator does

---

18 Hathaway (2016).

not dilute with subsequent investments until the specified value is exceeded. Entrepreneurs often tend to underestimate the impact of the non-dilution disclosure on their holdings. As the following example will reveal, this trait requires serious consideration.

Suppose that startup ABC is invited to join accelerator XYZ and receives a €25,000 stipend. Before being formally admitted, the founders of ABC will be required to sign a contract including some basic etiquette, the support they can expect and a financial paragraph. This latter paragraph details the investment that XYZ is making including their equity stake in the venture. Some services (such as housing, infrastructure, training) might be charged for, but only at a cost-price level. The actual benefit for accelerator XYZ is the small, non-dilutable stake (of typically 5–10 per cent) in ABC.

Let's suppose the equity stake is 6 per cent with an upper limit of €4 million and assess the consequence for the stake of the founders of having a number of investments in the venture:

i.   An initial investment by the accelerator of €25,000 for a 6% non-dilutable equity stake in the venture
ii.   The venture develops further and arrives a point that it needs more money. It pitches for €200,000, and is successful in doing so with an investor for a 12.5% stake
iii. In a subsequent round, an investor is found for €400,000, requiring a 16% stake
iv.   Finally, an investor for €1,000,000 for a 20% stake becomes involved.

Before looking at the calculations below, calculate the impact of each investment on the valuation of the venture. Assess the effect of each investment on the valuation of the venture, calculate the stakes held by each shareholder and the effect on the holdings of the founding team of venture ABC. Conclude with an assessment of the value of the accelerator's equity share and compare it to a scenario where there was no non-dilutable disclosure in the contract.

The calculation is as follows (let's assume steady growth of the venture):

i.   Venture ABC is currently valued at €416,667. The valuation is calculated as €25,000/6%. This results in a 94% shareholding for ABC and 6% for XYZ
ii.   Venture ABC is now valued at €1,600,000 (calculated as €200,000/12.5%). This results in a 12.5% shareholding for the new investor and cumulative 87.5% shareholding for ABC and XYZ. Without special arrangements this would result in an 82.25% (calculated as 94%*87.5%) share for ABC and 5.25% (calculated as 6%*87.5%) for XYZ. However, since XYZ's share does not dilute, XYZ retains 6% and ABC's shares decrease even further to 81.5% (100% - 12.5% - 6%)
iii. Venture ABC is now valued at €2,500,000 (calculated as €400,000/16%). This results in a 16% shareholding for the new investor and cumulative

84% shareholding for ABC, XYZ and the former investor. Again, without special arrangements this would result in a 69.1% (being 82.25%*84%) share for ABC, 4.45% for XYZ (being 5.25%*84%) and 10.5% (being 84% *12.5%) for the former investor. As XYZ does not dilute (retains 6%), the shareholdings of ABC are further reduced to 67.5% (the result of 100% - 6% - 10.5% - 16% or 69.1% - (6% - 4.4%)).

iv. Venture ABC is now valued at €5,000,000 (calculated as €1,000,000/20%). The investment results in a 20% shareholding for the last investor and 80% cumulative for all prior investors/founders. Without special arrangements, this would result in a 54% share for ABC, 4.8% for XYZ and 8.4% for the former investor and 12.8% for the subsequent investor. As the value of the venture surpassed the upper limit, XYZ now holds an interest of 4.8% in ABC worth €240,000.

Concluding, the worth of the shareholding of accelerator XYZ after the last investment is €240,000 (4.8% of €5,000,000). Without the non-dilutable disclosure, their shareholdings would have been 3.5% worth €175,000. The founders of ABC, decreasing their stake in the venture by 1.3% as result, absorb the difference in shareholdings themselves.

Note that ABC absorbed more of XYZ before the venture reached the upper limit valuation of €4,000,000. That is, before the final round, ABC absorbed 1.6% (as XYZ's shareholdings would have been 4.4% after the subsequent investor).

Pan-European examples of this form include Startupbootcamp and Wayra. See Figure 2.4 for an overview of the Top 10 accelerators in Europe by capital invested in the startups that joined their programme. As well as revealing the scope of their operations, the visual also shows how the accelerators are funded and the number of startups they accelerated in 2016.

All of these accelerators have built up impressive portfolios of ventures. To mention a few from their large and ever-growing portfolio, Wayra ventures include playgiga.com, hubbub.net and stocardapp.com while those of Startupbootcamp include relayr.io (see end-of-chapter case), sendcloud.com and startmonday.com.

2.4   Later-stage Accelerators

Later-stage accelerators speed up the market success of businesses that are already an established company. The purpose is to build these companies into 'scale-ups'. In terms of the venture development phases discussed in Chapter 1, these accelerators support the process from the startup to the growth phase.

The companies that apply for this form of support will already have a revenue-generating business, but feel that its growth is too limited and its potential is not being fully realized. So while an incubator and accelerator are designed to

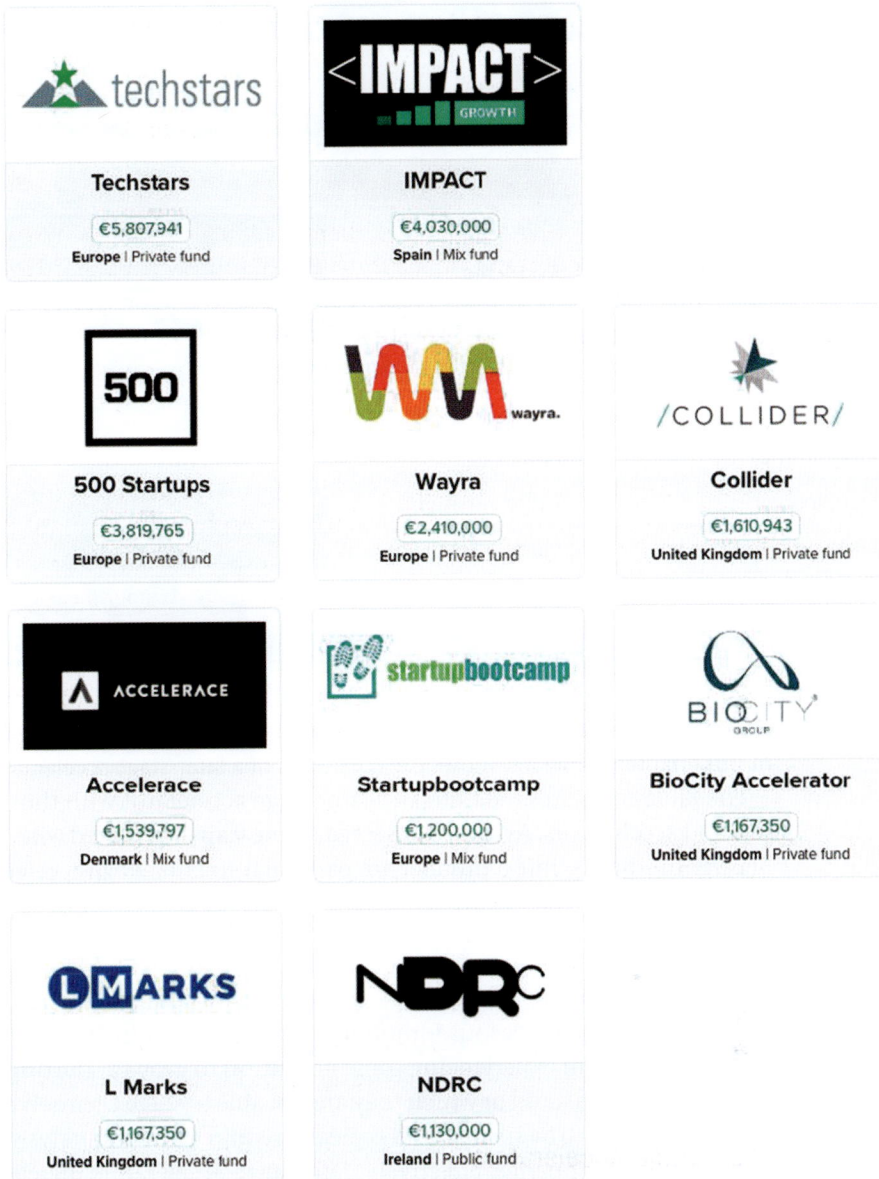

Figure 2.4 Top 10 accelerators by capital investment: Europe (2017).
Source: Brunet et al. *(2017)*

develop concepts into a startup, this form of support is aimed at identifying the factor(s) limiting growth and address them using a tailored approach.

As shown in Figure 2.1, later-stage accelerators do not occur in the earlier stages of funding, as this form of support only becomes an option later in the startup phase.

Table 2.4 Comparing three support sources of funding

	Incubator	Accelerator	Later-stage Accelerator
Specialization	Horizontal	Vertical(s) / Theme(s)	
Purpose	Build startups		Build scale-ups
Target	Individuals	Teams	
Entrance	Restricted	Open	
Dev. stage – Entrance	Seed		Startup
Acceptance	Batches / Cohorts		Ongoing
Support	Organic growth	Boost growth	
Programme	None	Generic	Tailored
Duration	Large variation	3–6 months	
Financial contribution	None – Small amount	Larger amount (€10,000 +)	
Compensation	None – Small fee	Equity stake (5–10%)	
Dev. stage – Graduation	Startup		Growth

However, given their relationship to accelerators in particular, the topic is included in this chapter. Table 2.4 shows the core traits of a later-stage accelerator.

The table compares the traits of a later-stage accelerator with those of incubators and accelerators. As can be observed, some traits are shared with those forms of early funding, while a number are particular to later-stage accelerators.

2.4.1   Forms

To be considered by a later-stage accelerator, a company is required to be revenue-generating. Reasons for joining the accelerator include the company's management team experiencing some limitation to growth, the origin of which they do not understand or which they are not able to solve themselves. Thus, the issue is expected to be specific and typically requires further analysis. In order to support these companies effectively, later-stage accelerators increasingly focus on one or a few verticals (industries) or themes.

Application to a later-stage accelerator is open yet competitive, and companies are accepted on a continuous basis. In line with incubators and accelerators, the later-stage accelerator has a physical location where the management teams will meet during the programme.

Typically, the programme will be tailored to the needs of the company, yet still compressed into a three to six month time span. The programme typically consists of a number of days spread throughout the duration, as opposed to the full-time involvement that is expected by accelerators and incubators.

The purpose of the programme is two-fold: first of all, to assess the factors limiting the growth of the company and, secondly, to address them, enabling the desired growth. As well as the mentors that support the process, the later-stage accelerator has an extensive network of corporate partners to accelerate market traction where possible.

2.4.2 Process

The first challenge for the later-stage accelerator is to assess the specific limiting factor(s) for the growth of the company. So while an accelerator provides generic, conceptual support, later-stage accelerators focus on assisting a company with a specific challenge.

The mentors in this form of accelerator support the company through the entire process of finding the core cause for diminished growth, and coach their management teams towards solving it. For this reason, the mentors are highly skilled and experienced. Furthermore, the accelerator will rely on an extensive network of partners and investors who can become involved when appropriate.

These are some of the typical challenges that companies entering an accelerator face:

- Lack of a growth plan for the next stage – growing the business further requires a different skill set and structure than building it did.
- Lack of brand identity – a very skilled salesman generates all the revenue but the company has not developed its brand and message, as a result of which the company is loosely knit and lacks coherence.
- Lack of funding – the entrepreneurs have already allocated capital, but now need more capital to fund growth. However, the bank will not commit and the entrepreneurs lack other means of attracting capital.

2.4.3 Benefits and Concerns

The key challenge for the later-stage accelerator is the effective assessment of the company, identifying the factor(s) that limit its growth and potential so that these can be appropriately addressed. This focus on limitations is important because the approach chosen during the accelerator programme will be tailored to the company's key challenge(s).

The benefit for the company is primarily related to being relieved of its key obstacles to growth once the programme has been completed. On top of that, involvement with the accelerator provides a valuable network of peer entrepreneurs and corporate partners to further accelerate growth. Another benefit for the company's management team is that the later-stage accelerator provides an environment that allows for thorough reflection, supported by knowledgeable mentors. This forces the management team to focus on those things that are of prime importance for the success of the business and which will set the company apart from others in the market. This is achieved by them being actively coached by a mentor who helps the company to focus and to develop metrics to make progress measurable.

Accelerators can find it difficult to attract the right kind of talent to support their offering. The small pool of mentors meeting the skill level required to coach these companies limits their opportunities for growth.

This form of later-stage accelerator is offered by freelance coaches and companies. Examples include the global Gazelles International network (founded by Verne Harnish) and companies such as GoFastForward (The Netherlands) and Prelude Group (UK).

GoFastForward – Snappcar growth acceleration[19]

Snappcar (2011) was amongst the early ventures to develop a peer-to-peer carsharing community. After 1½ years of operation, the founder of Snappcar (Victor van Tol) experienced diminished growth. In consultation with GoFastForward, the assessment of 'spreading too thin' was made, requiring the company to make a strategic choice: either proceed with offering carsharing both B2B and Peer2Peer (P2P) and accept the growth rates or focus on a segment, refine the offering and develop that specific market as steppingstone for international expansion. Victor chose to focus by devoting the company's resources on the P2P market in The Netherlands and further develop the Snappcar-offering in this particular market. Supported by a crowdfunding campaign that generated more than €2 million, this focus was rewarded with accelerated growth rates in The Netherlands and it allowed Snappcar to acquire its peers in Sweden and Denmark.

2.5   Crowdfunding

The final early source of funding covered in this chapter is crowdfunding. This source of early funding has rapidly gained interest and is frequently required by investors when considering ventures in order to get an initial indication of the market response. This level of interest in crowdfunding has been fuelled by its broad applicability, including the number of venture development phases involved, the types of initiatives and the seemingly low-cost threshold of usage.

Figure 2.1 revealed the primary orientation and venture development phases for the sources of funding covered in this chapter. In this visual, crowdfunding is characterized by both an external orientation and a broad spectrum of development phases during which it can be used. Moreover, as detailed below, this source of funding exists in different forms. This variation allows crowdfunding to be applied across a wide range of initiatives of for-profit and also not-for-profit

---

19 Example of a later-stage accelerator application, based on interview with Rutger Prent (CEO GoFastForward), reviewed by Victor van Tol (CEO Snappcar), 28 April 2017.

businesses (see inserts for two highly successful applications: Brewdog is a for-profit example, The Ocean CleanUp case is a not-for-profit).

Brewdog: Early investors in craft beer attain almost 2,800% return[20]

BrewDog was founded in 2007 by James Watt and Martin Dickie, who started operations in Dickie's mother's garage. The brewer funded its expansion in 2009, by raising money directly from its fans; eight years and four rounds of crowdfunding later, the brewer nowhas a total of 55,000 investors. The long-shot bet on craft beer is paying off massively for the first 1,300 investors. The Scottish craft brewer announced on 10 April 2017 that investors who supported its initial equity crowdfunding effort back in 2010 have secured a return of nearly 2,800%. TSG Consumer Partners has acquired approximately 23% of the company, in a GBP 213million transaction involving GBP 100million to fund BrewDog's continued global expansion, and the balance of proceeds to provide for early shareholder liquidity. At the current GPB 1bn valuation, shares purchased in the crowdfunding campaign Equity for Punks I, which closed in February 2010, are now worth 2,765% of their original value. Even craft beer fans that invested in Equity for Punks IV, which closed in April 2016, have seen the value of their shareholding increase by 177% in just one year.

2.5.1   Forms

As the name suggests, crowdfunding relies on a crowd to obtain funding. It does so by generating small amounts of capital from a large pool of individuals and companies, typically using the Internet. In essence, crowdfunding exposes an initiative to the public, making clear how much money is needed to launch a project or business. Crowdfunding could also be carried out using traditional media, but it is greatly facilitated by the Internet.

This form of funding is in its infancy; the earliest reference made to the term was in 2006.[21] Ever since, it has shown strong growth worldwide. Although the usage and volumes differ considerably by country,[22] over the period 2012 to 2015, a year-on-year global growth rate in fundraising volume of 134 per cent was estimated.[23]

Because it is so new, crowdfunding lacks a clear taxonomy and provides limited transparency.[24] Definitions of the various forms differ from country to country, making international comparisons difficult. From a legal perspective,

20 Based on press-release of BrewDog 'BrewDog announces £100m investment from TSG Consumer Partners' (www.brewdog.com) and CNN (money.cnn.com) on 10 April 2017, reviewed by Sarah Warman (BrewDog Global Head of Marketing, on 10 October 2017).
21 According to Word Spy (www.wordspy.com).
22 For country-level detail, see 'Current State of Crowdfunding in Europe' (2016) by CrowdfundingHub (www.crowdfundinghub.eu).
23 Based on crowdfunding fundraising volume from Massolution (2016).
24 Zhang *et al.* (2016).

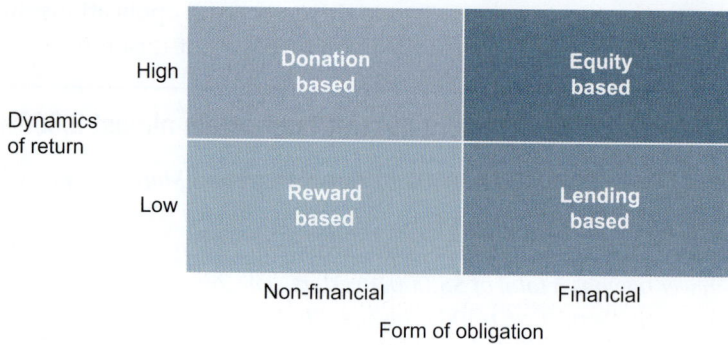

Figure 2.5 Main forms of crowdfunding.

many governments are still working on the enactment of laws and legal frameworks.[25] There is clearly a need to do so, as the impact of crowdfunding is increasing and it is not governed under the traditional financial system. Crowdfunding is considered to be part of the so-called 'alternative finance' industry. Alternative finance refers to financial channels and instruments that emerge outside of the traditional financial system, which includes regulated banks and capital markets.[26]

Crowdfunding comes in different forms, and entrepreneurs can choose the most appropriate form, according to the purpose of their initiative. Four main forms can be identified: donation-based, reward-based, lending-based and equity-based crowdfunding. Figure 2.5 structures these categories according to two variables: the form of the obligation and the dynamics of the return.

The form of obligation refers to the responsibility of the initiator to the provider of capital, which may be either financial or non-financial returns. The dynamics of the return indicates whether the return for the investor is pre-defined (low) or dependent upon the performance of the venture (high). Combining the possible outcomes for these two variables provides the four main forms of crowdfunding.

As mentioned, the applicability of the form is dependent upon the initiative and intentions of the entrepreneur. Each form is described in short below:[27]

- **Donation-based**: investment in the initiative does not generate a tangible reward; the return on investment for the investors is merely 'a good feeling'.
- **Reward-based**: investment in the initiative is rewarded by a product or service produced by the venture; the return takes the form of payment-in-kind.

---

25 Derived from CrowdfundingHub (2016a).
26 Cambridge Judge Business School: Cambridge Centre for Alternative Finance (www.jbs.cam.ac.uk).
27 Derived from the four forms given in CrowdfundingHub (2016b).

- **Lending-based**:[28] the investment takes the form of a loan made to the entrepreneur to develop the initiative in return for interest payments and principal after a certain time.
- **Equity-based**: the investment provides the investors with equity in the initiative, entitling them to a share of the future profit and typically voting rights on key matters.

Involving the public in funding an initiative provides entrepreneurs with many benefits, which are not only financial in nature but which also relate to assessment of the traction and viability of the initiative. As such, crowdfunding is much more than just another funding source: it is also a valuable marketing tool and reveals the initial market response to the initiative.

2.5.2   Process

There are three parties involved in a crowdfunding campaign: the initiator, the public and the mediating organization. The initiator is to the entrepreneur in search of funding, the public is the group of individuals and companies being targeted and the mediating organization is the platform that makes the initiative visible and connects the initiator to the public.

By providing exposure to the entire market, crowdfunding actually reverses the normal process of market selection. In a traditional funding search, entrepreneurs identify the most appropriate investors to whom to pitch their initiative. This approach requires entrepreneurs to make an upfront selection of potential investors and then target them with their investment proposal. For this approach to be successful, a judicious selection of potential investors needs to be made and the investment proposal needs to fit their respective portfolios. Despite making all the necessary preparations, for various reasons, the selected investors might not be interested, making a new search necessary. Crowdfunding turns this selection process around. By getting involved in crowdfunding, entrepreneurs open themselves up to being selected by investors. The proposition is made visible to all potential investors who, subject to the initiative and the choices made by the entrepreneur, may be rewarded in different ways.

The initiative for launching a crowdfunding campaign lies with the entrepreneur. Instead of looking for specific investors who meet their investment requirements, they will now involve themselves in assessing what kind of message needs to be conveyed to which audience. Defining the audience helps to determine which platform is the most appropriate. Many hundreds of crowdfunding platforms have emerged as result of the popularity of crowdfunding as means of searching for funding. Basically, these platforms represent a gateway for entrepreneurs in making their initiatives known to the public.

Following the rapid emergence of crowdfunding, many platforms were set up as mediating organizations. To differentiate themselves, these platforms

---

28 Also known as 'debt-based', 'peer-to-peer' (P2P) or 'marketplace lending'.

originally specialized in certain sectors. However, many have since withdrawn their services due to the high level of competition. The remaining platforms now have broader offerings.

The means to differentiate their platform is to stand out in performance. The number and exposure level of crowdfunding campaigns that meet their target funding measures this performance. For this reason, crowdfunding organizations are selective in the initiatives they allow on their platforms. Another reason is that they are compensated with a percentage of the revenue generated. To improve the chances of reaching the targeted amount, they offer additional services to help the entrepreneurs shape their message.

VOICE OF THE EXPERT: Pim Betist (the Netherlands)[29]

Pim is an entrepreneur and pioneered crowdfunding as founder of Sellaband in 2006 in Amsterdam. Sellaband was the world's first crowdfunding platform with a reward based model. Under the slogan 'You are the Record Company' it raised more than 3m dollars in less than 1.5 years from over 50,000 music fans, enabling unsigned artists from 27 countries to record professional albums. Pim now leads Ripplestarters, an

organisation that enables the growth of innovative startups and scale-ups and recently co-founded Voordegroei, a crowdlending platform for scale-ups.

How did you come to think of the crowdfunding approach?
My friends were all artists looking for funding to realize their music projects. I saw the amount of fans they had on MySpace and simply said: why not ask them for ten bucks each? Surely you'll raise enough money to hit the studio and record an album for them. The concept worked and was a big inspiration to platforms like Kickstarter and Indiegogo which launched a few years after we did.

What advice would you give to (aspiring) entrepreneurs with regard to crowdfunding?
Get expert advice before you even consider starting a campaign. It's not rocket science, but there are a lot of pitfalls. You need to choose the right form, the right platform, understand the implications of getting funded by a large group of people and most of all understand that raising money from the crowd can be a lot of fun, but also means hard work, before, during and after the campaign.

2.5.3   Benefits and Concerns

The current spotlight on the legal aspects of crowdfunding and the varying treatment of crowdfunding in different European countries is of concern to

29 Interview with Pim Betist (Amsterdam, 10 May 2017).

entrepreneurs, and may influence the future growth of this source of funding. As discussed earlier, the pace of technological developments has enabled the rapid diffusion of crowdfunding worldwide.[30] This, in turn, has given impetus to the discussion of its harmonization across Europe. At the present time, individual countries in Europe have developed their own rules and regulations, which means that the European market is not a level playing field.[31] The European Banking Authority recognizes the divergence of crowdfunding lending practices and that convergence of these practices across the European Union is desirable.[32] Likewise, the European Securities and Market Authority indicated that supervision of crowdfunding platforms should be intensified to protect equity investors and allow further growth.[33] The lack of an unequivocal taxonomy also limits the transparency of comparisons of crowdfunding across countries.

Crowdfunding provides many benefits for entrepreneurs. For one, it lowers the transaction costs involved in finding investors. It also expands their reach and thereby the potential set of investors. This increases the chances and speed of obtaining funding.

There are other benefits for entrepreneurs. Spreading the word about the initiative through a crowdfunding campaign also acts as a marketing tool, rapidly revealing the initial market response and building investor credibility. It is a means for entrepreneurs to 'sense and respond', to engage the audience and adjust the initiative to best meet the market needs.

For investors, the key benefit is that it reduces search and transaction costs. Crowdfunding exposes them to new and unthought-of propositions, while also producing feedback from the target market. This explains the take-up of crowdfunding by institutional investors and why they are rapidly increasing their adoption of it.[34]

Crowdfunding also has some drawbacks for both entrepreneurs and investors. For the entrepreneur, there is the reputational risk, meaning that the level of visibility may prove harmful if the crowdfunding goal is not met. Also, by sharing the initiative early on, the risk of being copied by a rival firm or entrepreneur is increased. A particular concern is the use of lending-based crowdfunding. The entrepreneur will be personally liable for repayment of the loan, irrespective of success and the legal form of the venture. For investors, while they increasingly trust crowdfunding platforms,[35] the main concern about such campaigns is that the options for doing a proper due diligence are diminished when compared to the traditional approach of presentations and business plan reviews.

Examples of well-known financial crowdfunding platforms in Europe include Crowdcube (UK, equity), SmartAngels (France, lending), FundedByMe (Swedish,

---

30 Cusmano (2015).
31 Cusmano (2015) and CrowdfundingHub (2016a); for more information, visit
    www.crowdfundinghub.eu or www.eurocrowd.org
32 Opinion given by the EBA (26 February 2015); for more information, visit eba.europa.eu
33 Advice given by the ESMA (18 December 2014); for more information, visit esma.europa.eu
34 'Professional investors join the crowdfunding party' in Financial Times (16 March 2017).
35 CrowdfundingHub (2016c).

combining equity and debt) and non-financial platforms such as Verkami (Spain, reward), Betterplace.org (Germany, donation), Produzioni dal Basso (Italy, donation and reward). Occasionally, financial and non-financial returns are combined in one platform, such as Angel.me (Belgium, equity and reward).[36]

Let's Practise: Case Study

CROWDFUNDING: The Ocean Cleanup case.[37]

It all started when then 16-year-old Boyan Slat was scuba diving in Greece and was surprised to see more plastic than fish. What surprised him even more, after digging deeper into the plastic pollution problem, was no one had made serious attempts to combat this issue. The question 'Why don't we just clean it up?' lingered in his mind, and led him to devote his high school science project to understanding the problem, as well as researching why a cleanup was considered impossible. It quickly became clear that a cleanup using vessels and nets would take thousands of years, cost tens of billions of dollars and be harmful to sea life and lead to large amounts of carbon emissions.

There are five major plastic accumulation zones in the world where ocean currents converge. These accumulation zones are commonly called "garbage patches". The vast majority of ocean plastic will not go away by itself but instead slowly break down into micro plastics. After a year of experimenting with ideas and simple tests, Boyan came up with the idea to develop a passive concentration system. He envisioned using the ocean currents to his advantage, and letting them be the driving force behind catching and concentrating the plastic. Instead of going after the plastic, you could let the plastic come to you.

Initially, his idea did not gain traction. Boyan had just started studying Aerospace Engineering at TU Delft but continued working out his concept in parallel. After six months, he decided to quit his studies and founded The Ocean Cleanup, with just €300 of savings as a starting capital. Then one night in March 2013, things changed. The TEDx video was picked up by several news sites, from which it spread to hundreds of thousands of people. The idea went viral. In a matter of days, it allowed The Ocean Cleanup to recruit an initial team, as well as raise the first US$ 90,000 using crowdfunding. And so, The Ocean Cleanup project took off.

While the idea to use passive systems to rid the world's oceans of plastic was first floated in 2012, it was still just that – an idea. That is also the reason for him to hold back from the many interview requests (over 450) he receives from media worldwide. In order to investigate whether the cleanup technology is indeed an effective method to remediate the Great Pacific Garbage Patch, The Ocean Cleanup started off by performing a broad-scoped feasibility study, covering areas including engineering, oceanography and recycling. A voluntary team

---

36 For a more comprehensive overview, please see 'Current State of Crowdfunding in Europe' by CrowdfundingHub (2016).
37 Based on interview with Joost Niepoth (23 May 2017), additions by Joost Dubois and Boyan Slat.

of close to 100 scientists and engineers spent a year on completing the 528-page study, which was published on 3 June 2014. Although a lot of the work is now outdated, the feasibility study provides insight into the early stages of The Ocean Cleanup, and some of its indicative conclusions remain relevant today.

The next step was to secure the money for the next phase, so together with releasing the scientific study, a large-scale crowd funding campaign kick-started. With the support of over 38,000 funders from 160 countries, over US$ 2 million was raised in 100 days. This success brought The Ocean Cleanup one step further in its quest of ridding the oceans of plastics. The money raised helped The Ocean Cleanup initiate the engineering process as well as a series of expeditions. The collected oceanographic data is used by their engineers when designing the cleanup system. A total of US$ 2,154,282 was raised, making it 'the most successful non-profit crowdfunding campaign in history' at the time, according to crowdfunding platform ABN Amro's SEEDS, who facilitated the campaign.

Questions for Discussion

1. Do you see another means for Boyan (at the time) to gather the funding for his research?
2. Choosing a crowdfunding campaign is a start but does not in itself ensure the gathering of US$ 2 million (especially not in donations!). What traits would you highlight in your crowdfunding message?
3. So the campaign generated US$ 2 million. What other benefits do you see from using this approach (instead of e.g. finding a philanthropist)?

This success kick-started The Ocean Cleanup in its quest of cleaning the oceans of plastics, 'We created this mess, so don't tell me that we cannot clean this up together!' (Boyan, 2012). Boyan keeps on building insights and growing his organization.[38] The Ocean Cleanup is organized as a project, for which it defined the milestones that lead up to the ultimate goal of cleaning the ocean. It works from milestone to milestone, as stepping-stones, gathering the resources and funding to attain the next development stage. The next step, which comprises the construction and testing of large-scale operational pilots could thus be initiated. It was followed up by a number of investments. More recently (November 2016 – May 2017) these initial successes were complemented by US$ 21.7 million in donations. The latest funding round brings The Ocean Cleanup's total funding since 2013 to US$ 31.5 million. This new contribution allowed The Ocean Cleanup to initiate large-scale trials of its cleanup technology in the Pacific Ocean in late 2017. This significant funding round is led by San Francisco-based philanthropists Marc and Lynne Benioff and an anonymous donor. Other supporters include the Julius Baer Foundation, Royal DSM, and Silicon Valley entrepreneur/investor Peter Thiel.

---

38 Boyan Slat is awarded the United Nation's Champions of the Earth (17 November 2014), thereby being the youngest winner of this award, for his inspiring efforts to cleanup the ocean.

2.6   Market Proof of these Early Sources of Funding in the Success of Ventures

Starting up a venture has become easier and cheaper, facilitated by technology and connectivity. The three sources discussed in this chapter provide a means to support funding of the venture in its early stages. All of these sources are rather new. The question now is whether these sources of funding have contributed to the success of ventures.

2.6.1   Challenges of Measuring Contribution

One way of assessing the contribution of the early sources of funding could be to compare the success rate of ventures that used these sources to those that did not. The literature shows that nine out of ten startups die within three years.[39] The question now is whether ventures emerging from incubators, accelerators or supported by crowdfunding have a lower failure rate than those that did not use these sources. The question is also whether simply measuring the failure rate is enough of an indicator to prove the value of these early sources of funding.

Measures for assessing success are numerous, but no agreement on the most accurate metric has been reached. The suggested measures include total follow-up funding, years in operation after the funding, the valuation of ventures and the number of exits.[40]

For now, however, the results are still patchy. Accelerators have only been around since the early 2010s. As such, the ventures they have supported are in their early years and still have to prove their value over the years to come. The same goes for crowdfunding. An exit from an equity crowdfunding campaign typically takes five to ten years, while this form of funding only came into existence in 2006.

The measurement challenge is further complicated by the selection process for incubators and accelerators. The entrepreneurs who wish to join these programmes must apply and be selected. Comparing their successes to the entire population of aspiring entrepreneurs makes the assessment of the added value of an individual programme biased.

Furthermore, the use of incubators, accelerators or crowdfunding does not ensure success in the market. For these initiatives to flourish, the broader ecosystem in which they operate needs to be conducive as well.

2.6.2   Arguments in Favour of Early Sources of Funding

Notwithstanding the challenges mentioned above, there are reasonable arguments in favour of the positive contribution of these early sources of funding. These arguments include the much-improved learning curve of entrepreneurs, the lowered transaction costs for investors, the growth of the industries involved and spillover effect for regional economies.

---

39 Riggins (2016).
40 Shieber (2014).

Certainly, the chances of obtaining funding and attaining market success are improved for participating entrepreneurs. The months they spend in an incubator or accelerator allow them to step up their learning curve through sharing experiences, networking and participating in the programme.

For investors, the effective selection of ventures in which to invest is improved. Arguably, the funnel of potential initiatives for them to invest in improves as a result of the selection and support process inherent in the programmes. Similarly, once a crowdfunding campaign has been launched, the market can select out those initiatives that appeal. An investor can use this initial market assessment for making investments.

Over the past decade, the number of incubators and accelerators has grown rapidly. This growth can be perceived as indicator of their expected contribution. Again, the same argument goes for crowdfunding, which has shown strong growth since its origination.

Another argument in their favour is the entrepreneurial energy that results from incubators and accelerators. The local community typically flourishes when such a programme exists, thereby supporting the existence of a spillover effect on the wider regional ecosystem.

Finally, research from the Judge Business School at Cambridge University found that 'company survivorship' was raised by 10 to 15 per cent in the fifth year following the exit from accelerator programmes.[41] Similarly, Hochberg's research (MIT Sloan) concluded that the average valuation of ventures two years after having participated in accelerators was significantly higher than the average overall.[42] Although this finding is still biased, as previously remarked, these findings help to support the arguments for the positive contribution of these early funding sources.

Startup Europe's Accelerator Assembly is the network for startup accelerator programmes in Europe.[43]

Born out of the European Commission's leadership towards supporting tech entrepreneurs, Accelerator Assembly is a key part of the EU initiative called Startup Europe.

The Accelerator Assembly is an industry-led network, delivered by Bisite Accelerator, with the support of Nesta, How to Web, Techstars London, UPGlobal, Betahaus and Wayra UK.

The European Commission's Startup Europe initiative was created to connect tech entrepreneurs across Europe, providing networks, resources and information to help them start up their business and grow, creating new jobs and transforming the economy and society.

---

41 Birdsall *et al.* (2013).
42 Shieber (2014).
43 For more information see www.acceleratorassembly.eu/

KEY TAKEAWAYS

- Incubators, accelerators and crowdfunding are recently developed sources of early funding, which have rapidly built up their market impact in Europe.
- These sources of early funding are applicable at distinct phases in venture development.
- Both entrepreneurs and investors benefit from their availability, as it lowers transaction costs as well as improves exposure.
- There is no standard definition of incubators and accelerators, given their recent introduction and ongoing development.
- There are different legal arrangements applied to crowdfunding internationally, which can be a limiting factor for its growth.

END OF CHAPTER QUESTIONS

1. What are the pre-market sources of funding available to an entrepreneur? What is their common denominator and makes it attractive for the entrepreneur?
2. What are the key considerations for an entrepreneur when looking for funding in the market?
3. How does an incubator support the venture development process, and what motivates the incubator to do so?
4. Mention the typical process support that can be expected in an accelerator. What is the key difference of this support compared to the one that can be expected in an incubator?
5. Entering an accelerator proves to be challenging. Moreover, the challenge does not end then. How can an entrepreneur improve upon their chances for getting most out of the time they spend in an accelerator?
6. How does a later-stage accelerator differ from an accelerator? How does this difference become apparent from the support that a later-stage accelerator offers?
7. In return for €20.000 funding in a venture, the accelerator obtained an 8% non-dilutable equity stake with upper limit of €5 million. At Demo Day, the entrepreneurs are negotiating with an investor for additional capital. Up to how much more funding can they obtain if they do not wish to compensate for more than 1% of the non-dilution clause of the accelerator?
8. Besides making financial means available, what are other benefits to an entrepreneur for launching a crowdfunding campaign?
9. Why is a crowdfunding campaign of a venture often required by a potential subsequent investor? How does this investor benefit from the crowdfunding campaign?
10. Assessing the added value of incubators, accelerators and crowdfunding proves to be cumbersome. What are the challenges in qualifying this contribution? How would you address this and what measures do you think are appropriate?

FURTHER READING

Cambridge Centre for Alternative Finance (jbs.cam.ac.uk).

CrowdfundingHub (www.crowdfundinghub.eu).

European Accelerator reports (www.gust.com).

Global Accelerator Network (www.gan.co).

Global Entrepreneurship Monitors (www.gemconsortium.org).

Moe, M. (2017): *The Global Silicon Valley Handbook*. 1st edition. Grand Central Publishing.

Ries, E. (2011): *The Lean Startup*. Crown Publishing Group.

Schwienbacher, A. and Larralde, B. (2012): *Crowdfunding of entrepreneurial ventures*, in *The Oxford Handbook of Entrepreneurial Finance*. Oxford University Press.

Startup Europe (www.startupeuropeclub.eu).

UBI Global bi-yearly incubator rankings (www.ubi-global.com).

REFERENCES

Birdsall, M., Jones, C., Lee, C., Somerset, C. and Takaki, S. (2013). *Business Accelerators: The Evolution of a Rapidly Growing Industry*. Judge Business School, University of Cambridge.

Brunet, S., Grof, M. and Izquierdo, D. (2016). *Global Accelerator Report 2015*. Gust and Fundacity.

S. Brunet, M. Grof & D. Izquierdo (2017a). *European Accelerator Report 2016*. Gust and Fundacity.

Brunet, S., Grof M. and Izquierdo, D. (2017b). *Global Accelerator report 2016*, by Gust and Fundacity.

CrowdfundingHub (2016a). *Crowdfunding Crossing Borders*. CrowdfundingHub.

CrowdfundingHub (2016b). *Current State of Crowdfunding in Europe*. CrowdfundingHub.

CrowdfundingHub (2016c). *Equity Crowdfunding*. CrowdfundingHub.

Cusmano, L. (2015). *New Approaches to SME and Entrepreneurship Financing: Broadening the Range of Instruments*. OECD Centre for Entrepreneurship.

European Commission (2012). *The Entrepreneurship 2020 Action Plan*.

Hathaway, I. (2016). What startup accelerators really do. *Harvard Business Review*, 1 March 2016.

Massolution (2016). *Crowdfunding Industry 2015 Report* on crowdexpert.com

Mitra, S. (2013). The problems with incubators, and how to solve them. *Harvard Business Review*, 26 August 2013.

OECD (2016). *Entrepreneurship at a Glance 2016*. OECD Publishing.

Rao, L. (2015). Meet Y Combinator's new COO. *Forbes*, 26 August 2015.

Ries, E. (2011). *The Lean Startup*. Crown Publishing Group.

Riggins, N. (2016). What is a business accelerator and how does it differ from an incubator. startupeuropeclub.eu, 11 August 2016.

Shieber, J. (2014). [Updated] These are the 15 best accelerators in the U.S., 10 March, 2014.

UBI Global (2016). *Global Benchmark 15/16 report – Top University Business Incubators*. UBI Global.

UBI Global (2017). *KPI Directory*, April 2017. UBI Global.

Williams, A. (2017). Professional investors join the crowdfunding party. *Financial Times*, 16 March 2017.

Zhang, B., Wardrop, R., Ziegler, T., Lui, A., Burton, J., James, A. and Garvey, K. (2016). *Sustaining Momentum*. Cambridge Centre for Alternative Finance

Let's Practise: Case Study

ACCELERATOR: Startupbootcamp case.[44]

In August 2013 Marc Wesselink (managing director Benelux of Startupbootcamp (SBC)) received an application to the NFC & Contactless Accelerator programme regarding a new business proposition. It was Jackson Bond (47, American, co-founder of what would later become Relayr) saying that they would like to do 'something in the cloud' followed by 'a management platform for IoT (internet of things) in the cloud'. While this message was still rather vague and the application purpose was still lacking, Marc did understand that Jackson was part of a team with two former Cisco-executives and decided to set up a Skype interview. This interview triggered Marc and they were invited for a four day collaboration in September at the SBC hub in Amsterdam with nineteen other ventures. During the four days, Jackson and his team (also consisting of Paul Hopton, 42, English and Harold Zapp, 56, German) talked to over seventy mentors. From the feedback of these mentors, the team chemistry became apparent and the SBC decided to invite them to join the three months SBC accelerator program.

During the programme the Relayr-team had a hard time validating their proposition with customers and was made aware of the need to (re-)define their proposition. The overall comment was 'Nice thought of having such platform, but we need to see something more tangible'. That is when the 'wunderbar' was conceived, a bar with a number of sensors that operates as a gateway. These sensors are connected to the gateway via Z-Wave (protocol for wireless and IP communications) that can be placed in and around any building to measure key variables (e.g. temperature, CO_2-density). Any time these sensors measure a dissonant value, it communicates that via the gateway to the online platform. For example, when the temperature in the fridge is above 5 degrees Celsius the sensor gives a signal through the platform to any device, which in turn informs the owner so he/she knows not to keep food in there too long. The MVP (minimal viable product) built for Demo Day attracted Conrad Electronics (one of Europe's largest electrical distributors and retailers) and led to the payment and pre-order of 5,000 wunderbars. Having secured this order, Relayr was now able to finalize the development and produce the wunderbars. Conrad as initial customer spurred the interest of other large companies (e.g. Bosch, Siemens, Samsung), that have built their own sensors in their electronics but

44 Based on interview with Marc Wesselink (17 May 2017).

use the cloud platform of Relayr to communicate the data to the consumers. Besides, a business angel invested and brought the proposition to the United States, leading to new clientele and a larger investment by Kleiner Perkins Caufield & Byers (a Silicon Valley based venture capital firm) and another from Munch Re (one of the world's leading reinsurers based in Germany).

Questions for Discussion

1. Being the entrepreneurs, what market would you focus on to launch your product? Would you start by offering it B2B or B2C?
2. What do you consider to be the true added value for Relayr from joining the accelerator?
3. From the accelerator's point of view, given the large amount of applicants they receive every year, what is their take-away from this particular case?

SBC was founded in 2010. The first programme was officially launched by Alex Farcet in Copenhagen in 2010. In 2012, its co-founders Carsten Kolbeck, Patrick de Zeeuw and Ruud Hendriks expanded SBC to Amsterdam, Berlin, Madrid and Dublin. Over the years till 2017 it developed into a global family of industry-focused accelerators, having nineteen programmes on five continents in fourteen cities (of which six are in Europe). SBC supports early-stage tech founders to rapidly scale their companies by providing direct access to an international network of mentors, partners, and investors in their industry. It is affiliated with the Global Accelerator Network (GAN) and ranks seventh in Europe by capital investment (€1,200,000 (2.5% of total)) and eighth by number of startups accelerated (80 (2.2% of total)) in 2016.[45]

Relayr is now (mid 2017) a company employing over 200 employees from 20 nationalities, based in 7 offices across Europe and USA.[46] As the company states 'Relayr is a rapidly-growing IoT company providing enterprise middleware and IoT solutions for the digital transformation of industries. As a thought leader in enterprise IoT, Relayr enables interoperability through industrial-grade platforms. Their software enables comprehensive data analytics and management, empowering businesses to create new solutions and revenue streams with data collected from any device, through any connectivity, throughout any IT ecosystem.' To provide this offering Relayr raised US$23 million on 20 October 2016, making a total of US$37 million in funds raised since their inception in 2013.[47]

---

45 Based on Brunet *et al.* (2017).
46 Retrieved from relayr.io (24 May 2017).
47 Retrieved from pitchbook.com (24 May 2017).

EARLY SOURCES OF FUNDING (2): BUSINESS ANGELS

COLIN MASON

Adam Smith Business School, University of Glasgow

TIAGO BOTELHO

Norwich Business School, University of East Anglia

Business angels are private individuals – predominantly cashed-out entrepreneurs – who invest their own money in new and early-stage businesses and, having invested, then draw upon their own business experience to support these ventures in a variety of ways. As such, they are often referred to as informal investors, or informal venture capitalists. Whereas the attention of scholars and the media is largely focused on institutional venture capital, business angels actually finance substantially more businesses, although their investments are much smaller, hence the overall amount they invest is smaller.

This chapter will examine the role that business angels play in the financing of entrepreneurial ventures. It starts with a consideration of definitional issues – who are business angels? The shift in the nature of angel investing from being a largely invisible and individual activity to one that is increasingly organized into visible groups is then discussed. This is followed by a review of the types of investments that business angels make. The remainder of the chapter examines how business angels make their investment decisions and the key criteria that they take into account in their investment decisions. This discussion is structured around the stages in the investment decision – deal origination, initial screening of opportunities, detailed evaluation, negotiation and contracting, the post-investment relationship with the entrepreneur and the exit.

VIEW FROM THE MEDIA

FINANCIAL TIMES   FT

With a little help from our friends, family ...

OCTOBER 4, 2016 BY ANDREW BOUNDS

You have a good idea, but how do you go about raising cash to turn it into a business?

Red's True Barbecue, founded: 2012, amount raised: £4.5 m, sources: Founders, angels

James Douglas was fortunate when he and Scott Munro teamed up to open a barbecue restaurant in Leeds. He had £150,000 from selling his first business, an estate agency, and the local RBS bank manager loved the food, which has a strong emphasis on grilled meat. Started with a £300,000 bank loan and around £265,000 of their own money, the American-style smokehouse restaurant was soon looking to expand. Mr Douglas and Mr Munro were introduced to Ian Neill, former chairman of Wagamama, who put together a consortium of eight investors in the restaurant sector. Dubbed the 'Super Eight', they put in a combined £2m using the UK's Enterprise Investment Scheme, which offers tax breaks. Over beef brisket served with their trademark sauces, which are now available in supermarkets, Mr Douglas says they turned down several offers from venture capital funds: 'We didn't want dumb money and we didn't want pressure money, with people on our case every week. We wanted people that could help us with expansion.'

After three funding rounds, the chain has eight restaurants from London to Manchester, with a Newcastle branch opening soon.

www.ft.com/content/685fc05a-63db-11e6-8310-ecf0bddad227

LEARNING OBJECTIVES

After reading this chapter you will be able to:

- Understand where business angels fit into the financing structure of entrepreneurial ventures.
- Recognize the profile of business angels.
- Appreciate the way in which the operation of the angel market is changing and understand the implications for entrepreneurs.
- Understand their investment process and specifically their investment criteria and how they make their investments.
- Assess the evidence on investment returns.

Where Are We Going Next?

The chapter opens by considering where business angels fit into the financing structure of an emerging entrepreneurial business. We then present a profile of business angels. This is followed by a discussion of the evolution of angel investing from one that was undertaken largely by individuals operating informally and below the radar to the current situation in which angels are organizing themselves into managed investment groups. We consider the implications of this change for entrepreneurs. We then consider the entire investment process, from deal sourcing, through investment decision, deal structure, post-investment relationship and finally the exit. This section also draws a distinction between how angels operate in the real world and the way in which they are portrayed in some TV shows such as the famous *Dragon's Den*.

3.1   Business Angels and their Market Positioning

New entrepreneurial businesses are likely to need to raise external finance in order to grow. Typically they will raise equity finance because they will initially go through a period in which their costs exceed their revenues as they undertake product development and invest in staff, systems and infrastructure to achieve sales. This stage – which may extend over several years in the case of technology-intensive firms and those growing rapidly – is referred to as the 'valley of death'. Businesses at this stage will not be able to raise debt finance because they lack the trading history, positive cash-flow and assets that a bank requires for security on a loan.

As we saw in Chapter 1, seed money (sometimes divided into pre-seed and seed) is the first capital raised by a start-up company. This provides the funds for the initial development of the company. This funding is used to create a prototype of the product, hire key members of the management team, rent space, find initial customers and launch initial marketing. As the business starts to gain market traction (moving from seed to startup stage), indicating proof-of-concept, it requires finance for market development, it will need to raise early-stage or 'Series A' finance to cover its financing needs for the next 12 to 24 months. Subsequent rounds of financing are termed 'Series B' and 'Series C'. These financing rounds – which are substantially larger – are raised by companies seeking a significant scaling-up of their activity.

Business angels focus on financing the seed and Series A stages. Pre-seed funding is likely to be dominated by the '3Fs' – the founder's own financial resources (including credit cards) and investment from family and friends, along with bootstrapping. Grants may also be available. Once these sources have been exhausted, firms will turn to external investors, notably business angels. The emergence of crowdfunding platforms and accelerators, as seen in Chapter 2, now offers a further source of finance. Businesses that are scaling up their activities and hence require much larger amounts of finance will seek venture capital – professional managers who raise finance from third parties (pension funds, banks, family trusts, etc.) to invest in businesses with high-growth potential (see Chapter 4 for more detail). Fast-growing businesses may raise several rounds of venture capital, with later rounds syndicated between several funds.

Because of the anonymity of most business angels, the statistical evidence that is available on their investment activity is only an estimate. However, there is consensus that business angels make significantly more investments than venture capital funds, or, to put this another way, firms that have raised finance from business angels are much more numerous than those raising money from venture capital funds. The European Business Angel Network (EBAN)[1] estimates that business angels made more than ten times as many investments as venture capital funds across Europe in 2015. Angels make smaller investments than venture capital funds, so the difference is smaller when the amount invested is considered. EBAN estimates that business angels invested €6.1 billion compared with €2.1bn by early-stage venture capital funds in 2015. This role in the financing of new businesses explains why governments have been willing to support angel investing with tax incentives, co-investment funds, support for networks and groups, angel training and investment readiness programmes.[2]

As equity investors, both business angels and venture capital funds will require a harvest event to realize their investment (harvesting is covered in detail in Chapter 17). One possible harvest event is an Initial Public Offering (IPO) in which the firm's shares are traded on a stock market. However, it is much more common for angel and venture capital investors to seek a 'harvest event' at an earlier stage in the development of their investee businesses by means of a sale to a larger, often international, company in what is termed a 'trade sale'. Strategic sales have the added benefit of providing the acquired business with access to a range of various non-financial resources of the acquiring company, notably distribution channels and professional management, to enable its further expansion.

3.2   Business Angels: Definition and Profile

Business angels are conventionally defined as *high net worth individuals who invest their own money, along with their time and expertise, directly in unquoted companies in which they have no family connection, in the hope of financial gain.* Although they invest in all sorts of situations, including management buyouts and buy-ins and rescue/turnaround situations, their typical investment is in a new and recently started business. The key point here is that business angels want to be active investors in the companies in which they invest, helping them to grow through funding as well as advice and access to networks. And while initially concentrated in developed economies, business angel investing is now a global phenomenon, albeit with variations in practice between regions.

---

1 For more information see www.eban.org
2 OECD (2011).

Having discretionary wealth that they can afford to put at risk is an obvious prerequisite for becoming a business angel. Business angels invest upwards of €10,000 per deal (sometimes, in excess of €100,000) and typically have a portfolio of two to five investments (but some angels have more). However, the available evidence suggests that most are 'comfortably off' rather than 'super-rich'. Most are successful, often cashed-out entrepreneurs, while the remainder either have senior management experience in large businesses (board member, partner) or have specialist business expertise (e.g. accountant). In other words, they are first-generation wealth (in contrast to 'old money').

There are two further important distinguishing features of business angels. First, they make their own investment decisions as opposed to investing in some form of pooled investment vehicle in which the investment decisions are made by fund managers. Second, business angels are investing their own money, which differentiates them from venture capital funds which are investing other people's money – their investment funds come from such sources as pension funds, banks and foundations and, as a result, they have a legal duty of care for how they invest such funds (this will be explained in detail in Chapter 4). Several implications arise from these features. Business angels do not have to invest if they do not find appropriate investments, whereas venture capital funds have a fixed life, typically of eight to ten years, and are looking to make the most of their investments in the first three years of the fund's life, after which they will be engaged in supporting their portfolio companies, making follow-on investments and seeking exits. Business angels can also make quicker investment decisions as they do not need to justify the decision to anybody. In addition, angels have less need for specialist financial and legal due diligence (as they invest earlier and there is not much to find out), so the costs for the investee business are lower. Finally, business angels can adopt idiosyncratic investment criteria, whereas venture capital funds have raised their investment funds to invest in specific types of businesses and so must follow these investment criteria when investing.

A key feature of the investment approach of business angels involves the support they provide to their investee businesses through a variety of hands-on roles. Four distinct roles have been identified:[3] (1) sounding board/strategic role; (2) supervision and monitoring; (3) role acquisition, and (4) mentoring role. In performing these roles, angels are leveraging the learning, skills, social capital and intuition that they have accumulated through their prior entrepreneurial and business experience. The opportunity to be involved with a business startup is a significant motive for business angels. Involvement also reduces information asymmetries and moral hazard and so is a means of risk reduction.[4] However, it should be acknowledged that the competence levels amongst business angels and

3 See Politis (2008).
4 Information assymetrics and moral hazard is discussed in detail in Chapter 6.

their consequent ability to add value is variable, and a career as a successful entrepreneur, or in a senior position in a large company, does not necessarily provide an individual with all of the skills required to be a successful business angel. Indeed, their initial investments typically involve a steep learning curve.

Business angels invest for a mixture of economic, hedonistic and altruistic motives. For some, investing is all about achieving a financial return, typically in the form of a capital gain that is accomplished through some form of harvest event, normally the acquisition of their investee company. However, many angels are also motivated in part by non-monetary considerations from which they derive psychic income. Studies are consistent in identifying that the fun and enjoyment arising from such investments, particularly through their hands-on involvement, is an important subsidiary reason for becoming a business angel. Some angels also express altruistic motives. Indeed, there is evidence that indicates that most business angels would be willing to forego *some* financial return to invest in businesses that were seen as socially beneficial.[5]

The characteristics of business angels exhibit a high level of consistency across developed countries. The majority – upwards of 80 per cent – are male. However, the proportion of women in the angel population is steadily increasing, reaching 12 per cent in a recent UK survey,[6] although this is still below the latest (2016) US figure of 26 per cent.[7] Most are in the 45–65 years age group – typically some 20 years older than the entrepreneurs that they finance. This reflects the length of time required to build significant personal net worth, the greater amount of discretionary wealth of this age group as their children cease to become financially dependent on them, and the age at which people with a successful business career might choose, or be forced to, disengage. Becoming a business angel is often a way for such individuals to remain economically active and stimulated. For example, cashed-out entrepreneurs in their 40s or 50s often report that they became business angels because they quickly became bored by a life of leisure. As one angel noted, 'the attractions of playing golf seven days a week quickly palls'. However, there is evidence that business angels are becoming younger. This may be linked to the younger age at which technology entrepreneurs in particular are starting – and cashing out – from their businesses.

Most business angels have had experience of business startups and growth. In many cases they are serial entrepreneurs. This implies that many angels have acquired the range of experience that it takes to start, manage and harvest a successful entrepreneurial venture – skills which have prepared them to conduct the due diligence necessary to evaluate the merits and risks of prospective investments and to add value of their know-how to the ventures that they invest in. The remainder are typically either people who have held senior positions in large companies or who have specialist commercial skills and are involved in

5 Some research on this topic has been done by Sullivan (1994).
6 Mason and Botelho (2014).
7 Sohl (2017).

working with entrepreneurial companies (e.g. accountants, consultants, lawyers) and whose wealth is derived from high income. In contrast, non-business professionals (e.g. doctors, dentists) and public sector employees are conspicuous by their absence from the ranks of business angels. Some studies suggest that becoming a business angel represents the third phase of an individual's career.[8] The first phase is the corporate career – where they develop managerial competence, build networks and develop a reputation. The second phase is entrepreneurial learning, often as consultants, in which they developed new competences by learning the 'logic' of entrepreneurial processes. The third phase is an integrated investment career phase in which they make use of their managerial and entrepreneurial learning in the firms in which they invest. The transition between the second and third phases often overlaps.

This profile masks considerable heterogeneity in the business angel population, not so much in terms of their demographics but rather in their investment activity, motivation and approach to investment. The most basic distinction is between *active angels* – those individuals with experience of investing and who are continuing to look for investments, *latent angels* – inactive investors who have made investments in the past, and *virgin angels* – individuals who are looking to invest but have yet to make their first investment. There are several typologies of active investors: (1) on the basis of their investment experience (i.e. the number of investments made); (2) on the basis of their competence (education, business and entrepreneurship background); (3) by type of contribution to their investee companies; and (4) by time spent on the investment process. These studies underline the differentiated nature of the supply of angel investment. Clearly, 'not everybody's money is green'. The implication for entrepreneurs is that they must ensure that the type of business angel who is offering to invest is both willing and capable of contributing the value-added that they require.

Various studies have focused on specific types of business angels. One category is the most active investors who account for a disproportionate amount of investment activity. Such angels are more financially driven and formalized in their approach, which reflects their experience of living through unforeseen problems and obstacles. Another category is 'takeover and turnaround artists' – business angels who specialize in investing in distressed companies with the aim of turning them around to start on a growth path again (see Chapter 15 for more information on the topic of restructuring and turnarounds).[9] These investors are 'performing the same function as . . . other types of business angels . . . – breathing new life into a business – but at the other end of the business spectrum – when the business is about to die.' (Visser and Williams 2001: 2). A further category is 'founder

---

8 Politis and Landström (2002).
9 Visser and Williams (2001) emphasize that T&T artists are distinguished from 'company doctors', who may be called in to turn a business round, but do not necessarily invest their own money, and from 'corporate raiders' who may, or may not, invest their own money but whose aim is to sell off valuable components of the business as soon as possible.

angels'.[10] Their differentiating feature is that they invest at an earlier stage than conventional angels and venture capital funds. They commit resources – financial, human and social capital and time – alongside the founder(s) of new firms seeking to commercialize technologies, in exchange for shares (as opposed to consultancy fees), making them indistinguishable from the founder. A final category is 'super angels'. These are highly successful – and hence extremely wealthy – entrepreneurs who, as a consequence, have the capacity to invest large amounts, in excess of several hundred thousand euros per year, year-on-year, with individual investments often exceeding €1 m. Because of their reputation, they attract a high-quality deal flow. Some super angels have established micro venture capital funds by pooling their capital with that of friends and close business colleagues.[11]

VOICE OF THE EXPERT: Candace Johnson (France)

Candace Johnson is a co-founder of SES, the world's pre-eminent satellite group and the architect of SES Global (Luxembourg). She is also the founder of Loral Cyberstar-Teleport Europe, Europe's first independent private trans-border satellite communications network, and Europe Online, the world's first Internet-based online service. President of EBAN (European Business Angels Network), Candance is a very active business angel and is also the President of three investment funds and the founder of the Global Telecom Women's Network (GTWN), Global Board Ready Women (GBRW) and the VATM, the German Association of Private Telecom Operators.

What is special about business angels?
Business Angels bring experience, expertise, networks, and oh, yes 'Smart Money'. This is what is special about them. They also invest their own money, so they can decide themselves when they want to exit.

What is the role of business angels in the entrepreneurial ecosystem in Europe?
For me, I consider Business Angels to be the most important part of the entrepreneurial ecosystem in Europe. Business Angels are there when the company has a product, first sales, and first clients. They help the entrepreneur 'scale-up' and they accompany the entrepreneur throughout all her or his various stages.

3.3   The Changing Structure of the Angel Market

Angel investing is undergoing a transformation from a largely invisible, atomistic market dominated by individual and small ad hoc groups of investors who strive to keep a low profile and rely on word-of-mouth for their investment

10 Festel and De Cleyn (2013).
11 Sudek *et al.* (2011).

opportunities, to a more organized and visible marketplace in which managed angel groups are becoming increasingly significant.[12] These groups are professional in their operation, with published routines for accessing deals, screening deals, undertaking due diligence, negotiating and investing. This process has gone the furthest in the United States, but is a global phenomenon. There is also evidence of the specialization of groups by industry sector (e.g. health care angel groups), type of investor (e.g. women-only angel groups) and affiliation (e.g. university-based groups). However, because the size of the invisible market cannot be measured it is unclear what proportion of angel investments are now channelled through angel groups.

Angel groups operate by aggregating the investment capacity of individual high net worth individuals (HNWIs). Some groups are member-managed while others are manager-led (this individual is often termed the 'gatekeeper').[13] They typically have a limited and selective membership of angels (typically 20–75 members, but some have over 100 members) who play an active role in the investment process. In the most common model – the 'dinner club' model – members will meet regularly to hear pitches by entrepreneurs. An alternative model consists of a tight inner circle of lead investors who provide the central decision-making function alongside the 'gatekeeper' and lead the group's investments, and a larger, outer ring of semi-passive investors who are given the opportunity to invest alongside the lead investors.

The emergence of angel groups reflects two sets of factors. First, individual angels are rarely involved in making follow-on investments. Typically, companies that have exhausted their angel investment will seek further finance from venture capital funds. However, angels and venture capitalists are poor bedfellows. Angels are vulnerable to dilution on account of the different investment instruments used by venture capital funds and because they are typically unable to make follow-on investments. As a consequence, they have increasingly sought to avoid investing with venture capitalists. Meanwhile, the ability of angels to pass on their investee businesses to venture capital funds to make follow-on investments has declined as venture capitalists have shifted their focus to larger investments. The implication is that angels have had to band together to create the 'deep pockets' needed to make follow-on investments. A second driver for the emergence of angel groups is that individual angels have found advantages in working together, notably in terms of better deal flow, superior evaluation and due diligence of investment opportunities, the ability to make more and bigger investments, the saving of time on the screening process, as well as social attractions.

Angel groups enhance the efficiency of the angel market. First, they reduce sources of inefficiency in the angel market. Because of the fragmented and invisible nature of angels, there was no mechanism for them to receive a steady flow of investment opportunities. Instead, they found their deals by chance. The entrepreneur's search for angel finance was equally a hit-or-miss affair. As a

12 Mason *et al*. (2016).
13 Paul and Whittam (2010).

consequence, investors and entrepreneurs both incurred high search costs. This encouraged many to drop out of the market as either suppliers or seekers of finance. Angel groups, in contrast, are generally visible and are therefore easier for entrepreneurs to approach. A further source of inefficiency was that each investment made by an investor has typically been a one-off that was screened, evaluated and negotiated separately. However, angel groups have been able to develop efficient routines for handling investment enquiries and screening opportunities, and have developed standardized investment documents.

Angel groups have also stimulated the supply-side of the market. They offer considerable attractions for HNWIs who want to invest in emerging companies, particularly those who lack the time, referral sources, investment skills or the ability to add value. Those angels who do have the networks and skills to be able to invest on their own are also attracted by the reduction in risk that arises from investing as part of a syndicate, notably the ability to spread their investments more widely and thereby achieve greater diversification, as well as access to group skills and knowledge to evaluate investment opportunities and provide more effective post-investment support. Other attractions of syndicates are that they enable individual angels to invest in particular opportunities that they could never have invested in as individuals, offer the opportunity to learn from more experienced investors and provide opportunities for camaraderie and schmoozing with like-minded individuals.

The ability of angel groups to add value to their investments is also much greater. The range of business expertise that is found amongst angel syndicate members means that in most circumstances they are able to contribute much greater value-added to investee businesses than an individual business angel, or even most early-stage venture capital funds. May and Simmons, leading angel syndicate practitioners in the United States, comment that 'when angels band together ... their smorgasbord of advice and strategic services frequently makes the difference between life and death for a start-up'.[14]

However, the emergence of angel groups may also reduce diversity in investing. The interaction between group members may influence individual behaviour. This can lead to 'herd behaviour', in which agents 'ignore their own information and imitate the behavior of other supposedly better informed agents'.[15] Alternatively, it can result in the emergence of 'communities of practice' which have a shared perspective on the world, resulting in a common way of thinking. In each case, the outcome is a reduction in the diversity in investment outcomes.

In summary, business angels are a subset of the informal investment market which is the main source of finance for the startup and early growth stage of businesses. This market comprises family and friends – the most numerous category, but the smallest in terms of investment size – and 'strangers' in the form of business angels, a diverse category of individual investors comprising

14 May and Simmons (2001).
15 Gale (1996: 681).

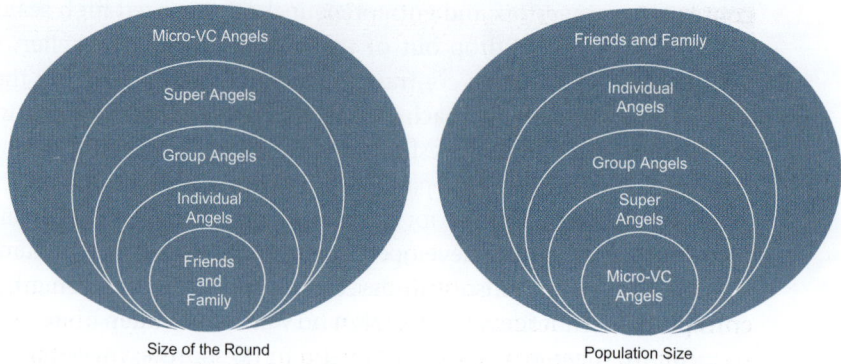

Figure 3.1 Sources of informal venture capital.
Source: Sudek et al. *(2011)*

solo angels investing on their own, those investing as part of a group and super angels (see Figure 3.1).

3.4   The Investment Process

From a theoretical point of view, agency theory is widely adopted as a framework to study the investment process.[16] An agency relationship is said to exist when one individual (the principal) engages another individual (the agent) to perform a service on their behalf. This involves the delegation of a measure of decision-making authority from the principal to the agent. Both are assumed to be economic-maximizing individuals. The central concern of agency theory is opportunism. The separation of ownership and control creates the risk that the agent will make decisions that are not in the best interests of the principal. This creates two types of risk for the principal (i.e. the investor). The first is adverse selection which arises as a result of informational asymmetries: the agent is better informed than the principal about their true level of ability. However, agents may deliberately misrepresent their abilities to the principal. The second risk is moral hazard. In situations where it is not possible for the principal to observe the behaviour of agents, the agent may shirk, engage in opportunistic behaviour that is not in the interests of the principal or pursue divergent interests that maximize their economic interests rather than those of the principal. Every investment decision also includes market risk – the risk that the business will perform less well than anticipated on account of competitive conditions (e.g. competition, demand, technological change).

However, the relevance of agency theory for business angels has been questioned. The conventional response to agency risk is to design contracts to provide protection. This is the approach of venture capital funds. However,

16 Agency theory is discussed in detail in Chapter 6.

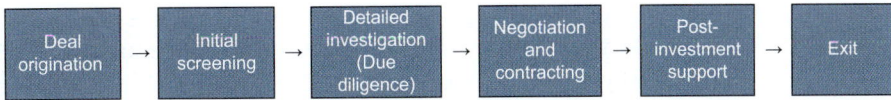

Figure 3.2 The stages in the business angel's investment process.

business angels are more likely to manage agency risk through active involvement with their investee businesses and by seeking common ground with the entrepreneurs. Indeed, Landström (1992) concludes that because of its assumptions agency theory is not valid in the business angel investment context. First, it assumes economic maximizing behaviour, but as discussed above, most angels are motivated by a mixture of motives. Second, the central assumption in agency theory is that the principal is likely to engage in opportunistic behaviour; however, the relationship between the angel and entrepreneur is more likely to be based on support and mutual trust. Third, the personal relationship between the angel and entrepreneur and the angel's involvement in their investee businesses reduces information asymmetries. Fiet (1995) suggests that angels focus on agency risk because they rely on the entrepreneur to manage market risk.

A number of discrete stages can be identified in the angel's investment process (see figure 3.2):

- Deal origination.
- Deal evaluation: this can, in turn, be sub-divided further:
  - pre-screen
  - initial screening
  - detailed investigation (often termed due diligence).
- Negotiation and contracting.
- Post-investment involvement.
- Harvesting.

This sequence is similar in most respects to the investment decision-making model of institutional venture capital funds (see Chapter 4). However, the approach of business angels is less exhaustive, less sophisticated and involves less time.

3.4.1   Deal Origination

In the so-called invisible market, business angels adopt a relatively ad hoc and unscientific approach to identifying investment opportunities. Informal personal contacts – business associates and friends – are the most significant sources of deal flow. Professional contacts are much less significant: of these, accountants are the most frequent sources, whereas few business angels receive deal flow from lawyers, bankers and stockbrokers. Those angels who are known in their communities also receive approaches from entrepreneurs. Some business angels also undertake their own searches for investment opportunities. In some cases – especially in the case of ad hoc investors – the entrepreneur is not a stranger but a business associate who is known to the angel (e.g. client, supplier). The most active investors have less reliance than occasional investors on 'public' sources (e.g. accountants, lawyers, etc.) for their deal flow and place more emphasis on their extensive and longstanding networks of 'private' relationships. However, these various sources of information differ in their effectiveness. The rejection rate at the initial screening stage for deals referred by business associates is lower than that for other referral sources. Of course, investing in businesses that are referred by trusted business associates and friends is an obvious way in which business angels can minimize adverse selection problems. As Riding *et al.* (1993) comment, 'even if the principals of the firm are unknown to the investors, if the investor knows and trusts the referral source risk is reduced'. Deal referrers are passing judgement on the merits of the opportunity and so are putting their own credibility and reputation on the line. In their case study of an Italian angel group, Croce *et al.* (2017) note that deals referred by venture capital funds were more likely to pass the initial screening stage. By contrast, non-personal sources such as accountants, lawyers and banks have a low likelihood of generating investments. The greater visibility of angel groups means that they can be approached directly by entrepreneurs, resulting in a high number of unsolicited approaches.

3.4.2   Deal Evaluation

The process of evaluating investment opportunities involves three distinct stages – pre-screen, initial screening and detailed investigation (or due diligence). The initial step taken by business angels is to assess investment opportunities for their 'fit' with their own personal investment criteria. The investment opportunity will also be considered in terms of its location (how close to home?), the nature of the business, the amount needed and any other personal investment criteria.[17] The business angel will also typically ask themselves two further critical questions: first, 'do I know anything about this industry, market or technology?' and, second, 'can I add any value to this business?' Clearly, the ability to add value is very often a function of whether the angel is familiar with the industry. If the answer to either question is negative, then the opportunity will be rejected at this point. In angel groups, the initial screening stage is typically undertaken by the gatekeeper where the 'fit' with the group's investment focus (e.g. sector, stage, size of investment, existing investment portfolio) is a key consideration.

Angels and gatekeepers then undertake a quick review of those opportunities that fall within their investment criteria to derive some initial impressions. Although most business angels expect a business plan, they are unlikely to

---

17 Mason and Rogers (1997).

read it in detail at this stage. Their aim at this point in the decision-making process is simply to assess whether the proposal has sufficient merit to justify the investment of time needed to undertake a detailed assessment. The market, financial considerations, the product or service and the entrepreneur are the key considerations at this stage.[18] Angels exhibit considerable scepticism about the value of financial information in the business plans of startups: as one investor in the Mason and Rogers (1997: 45) study commented, 'I take [financial projections] with a great pinch of salt, especially from accountants because they can tweak the assumptions and come up with any figure. So, it's the last thing I look at.' Nevertheless, investors want to see that there is the potential for significant financial return, that the principals are financially committed and what the money that is invested will be used for. Some angels will be flexible, willing to treat these criteria as compensatory (e.g. a strong management team would compensate for a distant location), whereas others will regard them as non-compensatory.[19] These stages (fit and initial screen) are typically undertaken very quickly – in the majority of cases, in less than 10 minutes and less than a minute if there is no fit.[20] The rejection decision is usually made on the basis of the accumulation of several perceived weaknesses or deficiencies – a 'three strikes and you're out approach'.[21] The Case Study below provides an example of a business angel undertaking the screening of an investment opportunity.

Let's Practise: Case Study

The Business Angel's Initial Screening Process

Background

We asked several business angels and angel group managers to review a real investment opportunity and 'think aloud' as they read it. This is the reaction of one experienced angel who has made in excess of forty investments in technology companies.

The business angel was given information about the following company which has £100,000 of equity already committed and is seeking a further £500,000 of equity from one or more investors.

The Investment Proposal

Overview

The company has developed a unique and new vision screening test for infants and toddlers – fast, accurate diagnostic, low cost, and de-skilled. The Intellectual

---

18 Mason and Rogers (1997).
19 Maxwell *et al.* (2011).   20 Mason and Rogers (1997) and Harrison *et al.* (2015).
21 Mason and Rogers (1997).

Property (IP) is proprietary. It will sell into the global ophthalmology and paediatric markets. The company is currently at the R&D – pre-revenue – stage.

Background

Between 2 and 4 per cent of children have strabismus (squint) – a chief cause of amblyopia ('lazy eye'). Amblyopia is responsible for visual loss in children and young adults – ten times more than all other causes combined. A squint has known psycho-social effects as well as medical implications, affecting early years' development as well as relationships and employment in later life. Efficiency of treatment reduces with age – after 7 or 8, loss of vision can be permanent. Hence early detection and treatment are imperative for successful treatment. However, the under-5 population of infants and toddlers typically do not undergo tests as they are a difficult age group to diagnose. A large proportion of squints are not noticeable to the unskilled eye. Therefore, many cases of squint and amblyopia go unnoticed until the early school years, by which time damage has already been done.

Currently, only manual tests are available to GPs, paediatricians and optometrists to detect and diagnose squints. These require skill and are diffi-cult to administer to the under 5s. The consequence is a combination of under-referrals, where small squints are missed due to the difficulty in diag-nosing, and over-referrals, whereby physicians are over-cautious and refer unnecessarily.

The Product

The team have developed the world's first commercially available automatic red eye removal technology to replace the 120-year-old manual test conducted by medical practitioners. The product is an ultra-simple, low-cost screening test conducted by taking a standard photo using a regular Smartphone camera. The picture is analyzed in real time and results are instantly and automatically interpreted, displayed and stored. The instant result displays 'Refer/ Don't Refer' options for the physician, with comments on the potential medical condition.

The core product is proprietary software which is currently designed to run on an Android Smartphone, but can run on any platform that has a processor and memory.

This means complete de-skilling of the screening procedure – it can be admi-nistered by a nurse or health visitor, as well as a GP's practice.

The technology has achieved proof-of-concept stage. It now needs further R&D in order to achieve reliable sensitivities and specificities. New and pro-prietary IP is being developed as part of the R&D; patent work is already underway with patent submission imminent. The proprietary elements of the IP are believed to be protectable and defensible. This approach to vision screening is new, innovative and, as far as we know, does not exist anywhere today.

Market Opportunity

Because of its simplicity, low-cost and ubiquitous characteristics this medical device can be used by GPs and paediatricians, optometrists and ophthalmologists, as well as by nurses and health visitors on a global basis. It is not restricted to any particular healthcare market, be it private or public, in a developed or emerging economy. The product addresses the two opposing problems: over-referrals and under-referrals. Both introduce great inefficiencies and costs into the healthcare system to the detriment of patients, doctors and funders of healthcare – insurance companies and public health services. This technology is very affordable (say, under $1,000 per unit) with massive distribution capabilities. It can easily become ubiquitous due to low costs, ease of use and the fact that it can run on handheld devices.

Although one of the key markets is the US private healthcare market, emerging markets such as Brazil, India and China are also important as they begin to develop good healthcare infrastructures. However, FDA clearance and a European CE mark will be required.

There are three distinct market segments to address:

- GPs and paediatricians (US – 190,000).
- Optometrists and ophthalmologists (US – 50,000).
- Screening programmes.

Competition and Competitive Issues

This new screening device primarily replaces a manual test conducted by medical practitioners at all levels which requires considerable skill and experience when dealing with the under-5 population, which, in turn, leads to the over-referrals and under-referrals. The 'competition' is therefore the 120-year-old manual Hirschberg test, and this is the twenty-first-century version of it. With the advent of camera-enabled Smartphones, with considerable processing power and memory, it is now possible to automate this manual test and to conduct it via a ubiquitous handheld device such as a Smartphone. Predictably, this automation introduces accuracy which is impossible to achieve with the naked eye.

Business Model and Strategy

The focus of the business is on licensing the technology and IP to one of the large players in the global ophthalmic devices market, some of whom we have existing relationships with and can access at the right level. These players have the market and distribution network in place and, importantly, already have a substantial footprint in the emerging and global market for ophthalmic devices. Our product fits well within their product strategy, either as a stand-alone device, or as an add-on to an existing product. This allows the company to continue to commercially supply customization, maintenance and upgrades/ enhancements services to licensees.

Management Team

The management team comprises experienced professionals combining technology industry expertise, a track record of building technology startups and exits, strong and proven R&D credentials and leading authorities in the field of optometry. They have considerable experience in licensing IP. Two of its members have successfully taken the original technology from idea to invention and all the way through to full commercialization, successfully licensing the technology to Nikon, Canon, Olympus and Konica in Japan.

Potential Exit

The intention is to achieve a very early trade sale to one of many large players in the ophthalmic devices market. These companies are very competitive and acquisitive, particularly seeking new technologies that may give them a competitive edge.

Future Funding Needs

This funding round will take the company well into Phase 2. A further £750,000 or so is likely to be required to get to profitability under the licensing model. But by that point in time, the expectation is that substantial parts of the proposition will have been de-risked, hence it is anticipated that the valuation will be much higher than currently. If the company is acquired beforehand, then less funding will be required.

The Business Angel's Reaction

OK, so it's a new technology, it's a vision screening test for infants and toddlers. So that's interesting. The IP is proprietary. I guess this must be protected? This first thing I would say is that health and technology is very difficult to sell in the UK. The UK's National Health Service (NHS) is not really innovative in buying health technology. So it's very difficult to sell innovation to the NHS. There are markets round the world that are more open to that, but obviously you are based here so getting into a US market or something means you have to have a sales office in the States, and so I suspect that half a million pounds is probably not enough to do that. It's at the R & D pre-revenue stage so you're taking a big chance. This is a risky proposition right now.

So now we've got the techy stuff about the problem you're tackling, squints and so forth. So the tests at the moment are not very good and this is a better way of doing it. The problem is that displacing existing practices is very tough. People might be happy to accept that current tests are not that great but they'll probably still rely on them because they've been doing them for years. So getting them to change and invest in a new piece of equipment to do it will be very difficult unless you can make that commercially very attractive and very easy for them.

One approach used by a previous company I invested in was they sold their technology not by machine but by the number of tests performed, so when the customer buys its machine, they don't actually buy it. They rent it on the basis of the number of operations they do. So basically the company gets so much for every procedure that's gone forward. That would be something I would suggest they might want to look at. However, the way that company sold their product did introduce a problem for them because it made them look a bit like a financing company because they were effectively leasing.

It sounds like it might be quite cheap. But if it's designed to run on an Android Smartphone it could also run on a small Android tablet or something like that. That's quite smart, I like that. I think that makes sense. Because it's a proprietary product, you could buy a standard Android tablet and put your own badging on it and stuff like that. I'd sell it as a combination. Work is under way. I think I would want to see that there's some serious patent searching going on and there isn't coverage in this area already. There probably is, so it's quite likely that you can't get a unique patent.

Selling to Brazil, India and China. But how do you get into them? They're all quite complicated. It's pretty difficult to do business unless you're willing to give envelopes stuffed full of money to people. China is really tough to do anything without good strong local partners. So you've got a real load of difficulty. Breaking into the US market frankly is a doddle compared to any of these, or indeed Europe.

The technology is affordable, under a thousand pounds a unit. In that case, you'll have to sell it. So you're effectively talking about a consumer product at a thousand pounds a unit. So you're talking about all the things that go along with a consumer product. You're talking about brand, advertising and the market presence and to have this kind of presence in the marketplace you need to have full page adverts in the medical practices, opticians, magazines and sponsor things at their conferences and all these sort of things because you're talking about selling huge quantities. You're never going to do that on half a million dollars.

The focus is on licensing the technology IP to win large players. Well, that might make sense. The trouble then is you become captive. I mean, if you license this technology to a big corporate, they're your marketing channel, they own your company and it is very difficult for you to do anything independently. Effectively, you're captive, almost a subsidiary.

The team is techy. It's not a marketing team. The CEO has run a software company to exit. That's good. He's been through a startup, an AIM listing and an exit. That's very positive. I would regard that as very important. Three years as a DC at an early-stage tech company, finance director and an MBE. Yes, he's very well qualified. The other guy is the doctor. And the CTO (Chief Technology Officer) knows all there is to know about the software.

You've got some trials, FDA clearance. Pre-revenue at phase one – that's where we are right now, ok. Then moving onto phase two, and that's where you're going to lose the million dollars.

There's several large global players. That's going to be tricky. Usually for something like this, a global player will want exclusivity and if they're going to put a lot of money into building a product on the back of your licence they will not want competition from one of their competitors selling the same technology. So that could be very, very tricky. But on the other hand, of course, exclusivity is a really dangerous thing because you effectively become captive of that company. It would be better if this was part of a wider product range and this was just one component of it. That might be easier for them to do, but if they're going to try and sell this as a stand-alone product they're going to want exclusivity.

The technical solution, it says, is non-trivial, but actually, once you've done it other people can look at what you're doing and can replicate it. So you'd have to be very careful about protection. Is it patentable? I think it is. Ok, and it will need more funding, right.

I wouldn't invest in this, it's too complex. It doesn't have a clear route to market at all. You're talking about developing a consumer device effectively with a thousand dollars. That's a real challenge to do, particularly as it's not a natural product for the UK market because health care in the UK doesn't tend to buy innovations. So you'd have to go internationally to do it or, as they say, license to a big international optical technology company. I would be very, very surprised if you could do that without having to give exclusivity to one company and at that point you would be a captive. You'd just be their development shop supplying them. They can negotiate your fees down and down and down. And then how are you going to exit?

Unless you've got other technology coming along later this doesn't really fit in my model of a company that can make a dent. Rather than go for the licensing thing, it might be better to go for a higher value, more specialist, purchaser that you could sell to. Why couldn't they go to the big global national optician chains – the Specsavers type operations – and try and do a deal with them. If they can produce the product and they can license it to, let's say the equivalent to Specsavers in the USA, one of these operations that's got several branches in every city. You go to them and you say, we'll exclusively license this to you, only for a year but you've got to promote it. That might be more interesting to them so they might say OK we might do that because that would give us a competitive advantage, we can put in our window that we're saving children's sight and so forth. That way, I think you could make a dent in that market.

If you're selling things at a thousand dollars, you cannot go from shop to shop selling it. That's just not going to work. You can't afford to send salesmen out for anything less than fifty grand, but you could go to a national chain and say we'll supply all your five hundred stores with our product. It's branded as our product but you have exclusivity over it for a year, eighteen months, something like that, so you can really promote it. You can say we've got this, nobody else has got it. Now if the company did that and did that with chains in Germany, France, America, Britain and so forth, it would then have a product that the big guys would want to get involved in. And I think that might be the way to go about it.

Questions for Discussion

1. Why did this business angel reject the opportunity? Was there a specific deal killer?
2. Is this business angel using a compensatory or non-compensatory approach to assessing this investment opportunity?
3. In the light of this business angel's critique, how would you advise the entrepreneur to re-work his proposal?

In situations in which the entrepreneur makes a pitch to an audience of potential investors, angels are influenced by the quality of the presentation. The level of interest amongst angels is significantly related to their evaluations of the quality and content of the entrepreneurs' presentations. There is a positive relationship between the perceived passion of the entrepreneur (enthusiasm and excitement) and evaluations of presentations.[22] At the other extreme, angels make negative inferences from a poor pitch about the entrepreneur's broader abilities. One angel commented as follows: 'if he can't sell to investors, how can he sell to customers?'.[23]

The process is rather different in angel groups, where the gatekeeper normally undertakes the initial screening on behalf of the individual angels who are members of the groups. First, gatekeepers are slower to say 'no'. They spend longer than solo angels on the screening. Second, their screening is less personalized. Personal – often idiosyncratic – issues are prominent in the screening by individual angels. In contrast, the gatekeepers place considerable emphasis on the group's investment criteria – these are typically few in number and dominated by industry sector, the amount of the investment and the likelihood of future funding rounds being required. Within these

---

22 Mitteness *et al.* (2012).
23 Mason and Harrison (2003).

constraints, they are open to considering a wide range of opportunities, not least because of the collective expertise of the group that they can draw upon. Third, gatekeepers give considerably greater emphasis to the financial aspects of the proposal, not just in terms of the frequency of comments but also in terms of the issues raised, notably valuation, the need for future funding rounds and returns. Those opportunities that pass the gatekeeper's screening might then be invited to pitch to the group.

The purpose of the initial screen is to filter out 'no hopers' in order to focus their time on those opportunities that appear to have potential. Indeed, angels reject the majority of the opportunities that they see. In their Canadian study, Riding et al. (1993) found that 72.6 per cent of opportunities were rejected at the initial impressions stage. Carpentier and Suret (2015) report that 70 per cent of the investment proposals submitted to a Canadian angel group were rejected at the pre-screen stage. This is similar to the 72 per cent rejection rate of an Italian angel group (Croce et al. 2017).

The minority of investment proposals that get through the initial screening stage are then subject to more detailed appraisal. The angel will read the business plan in detail, go over the financial information, do some personal research to gather additional information on market potential, competition and so on, and meet the principals. Indeed, getting to know the principals personally (by a series of formal and informal meetings) is the most vital part of the process. Most angels emphasize their intuition and gut feeling rather than performing formal analysis – although more experienced angels and angel groups adopt more sophisticated approaches.

The emphasis that angels give to particular investment criteria change as the opportunity passes from the initial screen to the detailed investigation stage.[24] Moreover, the rejection decision is likely to be made on the basis of identifying a single flaw. Detailed evaluation of tangible objective criteria ceases to be the drivers of angel decision-making and they start to consider less quantifiable intangibles. Getting to know the entrepreneur becomes decisive. Whereas the focus at the initial screening stage is on verifiable attributes such as skills, experience and track-record, it is intangibles such as leadership abilities, trustworthiness and enthusiasm that are the focus at the due diligence stage. Trust is particularly important. Business angels pay particular attention to key signals that indicate positive or negative displays of trust-based behaviours. Entrepreneurs displaying a comparatively large number of trust-building behaviours and comparatively few trust-damaging ones are more likely to receive offers of finance.[25] An early study found that business angels attach the greatest importance to the leadership capabilities of the principals, followed by the potential of the firm's market and products.[26] In other studies, the emphasis of investors is on management abilities, an understanding of what is required to be successful, a strong work ethic,

---

24 Riding et al. (2007); Maxwell et al. (2011); Mitteness et al. (2012).
25 Maxwell and Lévesque (2014).
26 Landström (1998).

integrity, honesty, openness and personal chemistry.[27] Rewards, the realism of the projections and potential also assume greater importance, while 'investor fit' becomes less of a consideration.

The primary deal killer is the perception of poor management. Feeney et al.'s (1999) approach was to ask business angels 'what are the most common shortcomings of business opportunities that you have reviewed recently?' This highlighted shortcomings in both the management (lack of management knowledge, lack of realistic expectations, personal qualities) and the business (poor management team, poor profit potential for the level of risk, poor fit, undercapitalized/lack of liquidity, insufficient information provided). People factors emerge as the dominant 'deal killer' in a study by Mason et al. (2017). Four themes dominate. First, by far the most frequently mentioned was the concern that the entrepreneur was not open and straightforward, believable, trustworthy and honest. Second, angels are looking to invest in entrepreneurs who appear knowledgeable and competent. Third, entrepreneurs have to exhibit realism, in particular about valuation and size of equity share. Finally, the angel has to feel that there is a personal rapport with the entrepreneur. This reflects the long and personal nature of the angel–entrepreneur relationship. This emphasis on the entrepreneur reflects the view of angels that agency risk is more of a threat than market risk: 'compared with venture capital investors, business angels place much more importance upon screening entrepreneurs than deals for market risk' (Fiet, 1995: 567). However, a positive decision to invest in an opportunity involves a consideration of management ability, alongside the growth and profit potential of the business. In other words, angels are looking to invest in businesses that show growth potential and have an entrepreneurial team with the capability to realize that potential.[28]

3.4.3   Negotiation and Contracting

Having decided, in principle, to invest, the business angel must negotiate terms and conditions of the investment that are acceptable both to themselves and to the entrepreneur. In agency theory, terms, deal structuring – mechanisms for allocating the rewards to the investor and entrepreneur – are an attempt to align the behaviour of the entrepreneur with that of the investor, while the terms and conditions attempt to control the behaviour of the entrepreneur. There are three main issues – valuation, structuring of the deal (share price, type of shares, size of shareholding, timing) and the terms and conditions of the investment, including the investor's role. It is not uncommon for opportunities that reach this stage not to proceed, with entrepreneurs' unrealistic view (in the opinion of the investors) of the valuation of

---

27 Haines et al. (2003); Mason and Stark (2004).
28 Feeney et al. (1999).

the business, and of the angel's contribution, being frequent reasons for not making an investment.[29]

Valuation is critical because it influences the return. However, there is no universally agreed method of valuing a small company. Market-based valuations are inappropriate because small businesses are not continually valued by the market, and appropriate comparator stocks are unlikely to be available. Asset-based valuations are more commonly used, although finance theory prefers earnings or cash-flow based valuations because they value the business in terms of the future stream of earnings that shareholders might expect from the business. However, these approaches are complex. Valuation of new and early-stage businesses adds further complications because they may only have intangible assets (e.g. intellectual property). It is therefore not surprising, especially since most angel investments are concentrated at startup and early stage, that methods of pricing and calculating the size of shareholdings are remarkably imprecise and subjective, based on rough rules of thumb or gut feeling. As investors, May and Simmons (2001: 129) note 'the truth about valuing a start-up is that it's often a guess'. For this reason, many angels prefer to use convertible preference shares which defer valuation until a later round of investment. But in practice, angels use a range of investment instruments from pure debt to pure equity.[30] You will find more information about new venture valuation in Chapter 8.

Angels draw up contracts as a matter of course to safeguard their investment from adverse selection and moral hazard, although their degree of sophistication varies. Contracts specify the rights and obligations of both parties and what will be done, by whom and over what time frame. Their objective is to align the incentives of the entrepreneur and the investor by means of performance incentives and direct control measures. Moreover, contracts are, of necessity, incomplete by their very nature. There are three reasons for this: it is costly to write complete contracts; it is impossible to foresee all contingencies; and because of asymmetric information. Key items on a term sheet are as follows: valuation, liquidation preferences, anti-dilution provisions, board representation, information rights, redemption rights, control rights, piggyback rights, registration rights and the investment instrument. Certain issues are non-negotiable: veto rights over acquisitions/divestments, prior approval for strategic plans and budgets, restrictions on the ability of management to issue share options, non-compete contracts required by entrepreneurs on the termination of their employment in the business, and restrictions on the ability to raise additional debt or equity finance.[31] These issues give investors a say in material decisions that could impact the nature of the business or the level of equity holding. However, there are also a number of contractual provisions to which angels attach low importance, and which might be considered to be negotiable.

29 Haines *et al.* (2003).
30 For example, in the UK the tax incentives available under the Enterprise Investment Scheme and Seed Enterprise Investment Scheme only apply to ordinary shares, hence most UK angels use this instrument to make their investments.
31 Kelly and Hay (2003).

These include forced exit provisions, investor approval for senior personnel hiring/firing decisions, the need for investors to countersign bank cheques, management equity ratchet provisions and the specification of a dispute resolution mechanism. Less experienced investors place relatively greater emphasis on the need to include a broad array of contractual safeguards to protect their interests, whereas experienced investors are more likely to include specific provisions that can impact the level of their equity stake (share options, ratchets) and the timing of exit (forced exit provisions). In other words, with experience business angels become more focused on those elements that can impact their financial return. We will look at term sheets in more depth in Chapter 9.

Investors recognize that the investment agreement must be fair to both sides. Contracts that favour the investor will be detrimental to the entrepreneur's motivation. In Mason and Harrison's (1996) study, two-thirds of investors and entrepreneurs considered that the investment agreement was equally favourable to both sides, and half of the investors reported that this was their objective. Indeed, a significant minority of investors believed that the agreement actually favoured the entrepreneur. Thus, the available evidence suggests that, in most cases, entrepreneurs are not exploited by investors when raising finance.

The inclusion of contractual safeguards does not give an indication of whether investors will be willing to invoke them to protect their interests. In practice, investors place a heavy reliance on their relationship with the entrepreneur to deal with any problems that arise.[32] Indeed, one of the purposes of establishing a contractual framework at the outset is to provide a basis for the development of a relationship between the parties. In other words, the contract is less a protection mechanism per se; rather, it is a means by which mutual behaviour expectations of all parties in the transaction can be clarified.[33]

Most angel investments involve input from professional advisors. For example, lawyers would normally review, and might draw up, the investment agreement, but would not be involved in the negotiations. Similarly, accountants may be consulted for advice but would rarely play a more prominent role. Thus, transactions costs are low.[34] One study reported that the entrepreneur's costs amounted to an average of 5.1 per cent of the funds raised (and 29 per cent reported no costs), while for the investor the average costs were 2.8 per cent of the amount invested (and 57 per cent reported no costs).[35]

The time taken by business angels to make investments is much quicker than that of venture capital funds. One study reported that the entire investment process rarely extended over more than three months, and often took less than a

---

32 Kelly and Hay (2003).
33 Landström *et al.* (1998).
34 Mason and Harrison (1996).
35 Lengyel and Gulliford (1997).

month. Most negotiations took less than a week to complete, whereas the evaluation could take up to three months or more. Thus, in nearly half of the investments less than a month elapsed between the entrepreneur's first meeting with the investor and the decision to invest; in 85 per cent of cases, the elapsed time was under three months.[36]

This process contrasts with what is portrayed in the *Dragon's Den* TV show (see next box).

Angel Investing As Entertainment: Does *Dragon's Den* Provide an Accurate Portrayal of Angel Investing?

Dragon's Den has turned business angel investing into popular entertainment for TV audiences in several countries. The dragons themselves – all successful entrepreneurs – have become celebrities. The programme was conceived and shown in Japan under title *Money Tiger* and first broadcast in the UK in 2005. It is now shown in several other countries. *Shark Tank* is the counterpart to *Dragon's Den* in the United States.

However, it is not an accurate representation of the process of raising money from business angels.

• The businesses are selected for their entertainment value rather than the worthiness of the investment. Tech businesses are under-represented.
• The dragons make their investment decision on the basis of the pitch rather than following detailed investigation of the business and entrepreneur. Moreover, their investment decision is very quick. The entrepreneurs may have pitched for only 30–60 minutes – although this is edited down to just a 5 or 10-minute clip on the programme. However, no angel would strike a deal within such a short time of meeting an entrepreneur. Not surprisingly, around half of the investments that are 'done' on TV do not proceed to a real investment, as subsequent due diligence reveals problems (see below).
• The deals that that the dragons seek to strike are very greedy in terms of the equity stake (often 30 to 40 per cent for a relatively small investment). This is very dilutive for the entrepreneur, and they would find themselves owning less than half of their business should they need to raise further finance in the future.
• Finally, the dragons are very aggressive, sarcastic and rude.

The most realistic aspect of the programme is the reasons that the dragons give for not investing in a business.

****

36 Mason and Harrison (1996).

Dragon Pulls Investment

A tech start-up firm which thought it had secured a £100,000 investment on the BBC's *Dragons' Den* TV show has had the funding pulled. Shortly after the show was aired, Peter Jones tweeted that his investment did not go through. The Glasgow-based firm had hoped to use the money to help fund the expansion of its Bluetooth tracker, Xupo, a coin-sized tracking sensor that helps people find misplaced personal items, by strengthening their position in the UK and to expand into Germany and France, followed by Italy and Spain. The tracker was launched by Strathclyde University graduates Raj Sark and Vincenz Klemt in 2014 after they raised nearly £27,500 in a crowdfunding campaign with Kickstarter. Xupo had forecasted £1 m in revenues in the next year.

During the show, Peter Jones had offered the investment for 30% equity of the business. However, just after the show Peter Jones tweeted: "My invest-ment with My Lupo (sic) didn't go through as some issues arose during due diligence. I still wish Raj all the best in the future."

www.bbc.co.uk/news/uk-scotland-scotland-business-38536108

Investment Funnel

The investment process has a very high attrition rate. Figure 3.3 shows the funding success rate of businesses approaching Canadian angel groups. In 2016, the thirty-five groups received over 5,000 approaches for funding. This is an increase of nearly 900 over the 2015 figure (19 per cent), which itself was 50 per cent higher than in 2014. Only 30 per cent of these businesses were selected

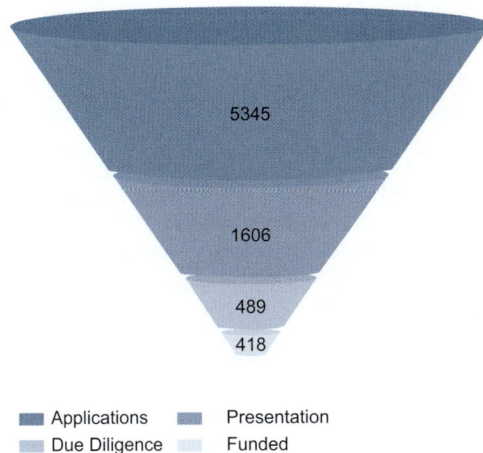

Applications   Presentation
Due Diligence   Funded

5345

1606

489

418

Figure 3.3 The funding funnel of Canadian angel groups.
Source: www.nacocanada.com/naco-academy/research/angel-activity-reports/

for presentation to investors. Among these businesses, just 30 per cent attracted sufficient interest for angels to perform due diligence (9 per cent of the original number that applied). Investors invested in the vast majority of the businesses that were subject to due diligence (85 per cent). The total number of businesses that successfully raised funding – 418 – is just 7.8 per cent of the total that applied for funding.[37] Case studies of angel groups report even lower funding rates – just over 2 per cent in the case of a Canadian group[38] and just 1 per cent in the case of an Italian group.[39]

3.4.4   Post-investment Involvement

From an agency perspective, monitoring is the main way in which principals attempt to mitigate the risk of opportunistic behaviour on the part of the agent going undetected (Chapter 11 is devoted to the topic of monitoring and control). It is this engagement, monitoring and involvement – which requires the need to meet the entrepreneur on a frequent basis – that explains why most angels invest locally.[40] In line with this expectation, most business angels play an active role in their investee businesses. There is a spectrum of involvement: at one extreme are passive investors who are content to receive occasional information to monitor the performance of their investment, while at the other extreme are investors who use their investment to buy themselves a job. However, most angels do not want day-to-day involvement, hence the typical involvement ranges from one day a week (or its equivalent) to less than one day a month.[41] Nevertheless, some angels are so involved, and involved so early, that they are indistinguishable from the entrepreneurs, and are seen by the entrepreneurs as being part of the entrepreneurial team.[42]

There are a number of roles that business angels play in their investee businesses: advice about the management of the business, contacts, hands-on assistance (e.g. legal advice, accountancy advice, provision of resources), providing business and marketing intelligence, serving on the Board of Directors or Advisory Board, preparing firms to raise venture capital and providing credibility and validation. One study emphasizes the role of business angels in helping their investee businesses to raise additional finance.[43] The nature and level of involvement is influenced by geography. The frequency of contact between angels and their investee companies is inversely related to the geographical distance that separates them. It will also be influenced by the performance of the

37 www.nacocanada.com/naco-academy/research/angel-activity-reports/
38 Carpentier and Suret (2015).
39 Croce et al. (2017).
40 Harrison et al. (2010).
41 Mason and Harrison (1996).
42 Festel and De Cleyn (2013).
43 Sørheim (2003).

business, with angels more involved at particular stages of business development and in crisis situations.

However, in contrast to agency theory, the involvement of angels in their investee businesses is not entirely motivated by monitoring considerations. First, as noted earlier, angels derive psychic income from their involvement in their investee businesses in the form of fun and satisfaction from being involved with new and growing businesses, and their belief that their experience, know-how and insights can 'make a difference'. May and Simmons (2001: 156) quote one investor as follows: 'I've never had as much fun in my life. It's a joy to see someone listen, take action and win.' Indeed, most business angels report that they have derived fun and enjoyment from their investments, often more than expected, in cases where the investment is still trading, although not when the business has failed. Psychic income returns are therefore related to business performance rather than compensating for financial loss. Second, angels see themselves as 'offering help' rather than 'checking up' on their investee businesses by acting as mentors, providing contacts, guidance and hands-on assistance.[44] Third, as Kelly and Hay (2003: 309) comment, 'from the outset, the relationship between the business angel and the entrepreneur appears to be more positive and trusting in character than the inherently adversarial one implied by agency theorists.'

A majority of entrepreneurs and angels regard their relationship as productive and consensual – although entrepreneurs have a more favourable view of its productiveness than angels.[45] One study reported that half of the entrepreneurs who had raised finance from business angels regarded their contributions as being helpful or very helpful.[46] Another study reported that entrepreneurs considered that the most valuable contribution of their business angel has been as a sounding board.[47] However, there has been no rigorous attempt to assess the impact of the value-added contributions that arise from this involvement of business angels on the performance of their investee businesses.

3.4.5   Harvesting

The nature of angel investing is based on achieving a financial return from a liquidity event rather than from an income stream, hence there is a need for an exit (Chapter 17 covers exits in detail). However, the evidence suggests that many business angels give very little thought to future exit routes and do not have clear exit plans at the time of investing.[48] There is no evidence

44 Mason and Harrison (1996).
45 Mason and Harrison (1996).
46 Mason and Harrison (1996).
47 Harrison and Mason (1992).
48 Harrison *et al.* (2016).

in studies of the post-investment involvement of angels in their investee business that preparing the business for an exit is one of their value-added contributions. This activity was not mentioned in any of the studies reviewed by Politis (2008) nor in a more recent study of the post-investment activities of angels.[49] Indeed, there is a common belief in the angel community that 'good investments will always find exits'. Angels are relaxed about the timing of the exit, with many willing to hold their investments for up to seven years or more.[50] Patience is regarded as an inherent requirement of being an angel investor.[51] Nevertheless, some angels do recognize that they need to adopt a more exit-centric approach to their investments. The following Case Study provides an example of this approach.

Let's Practise: Case Study

An angel investor – a lead angel in an angel group – talks about one of the group's exits.

The Investment

The company had used widely available technology to develop a very powerful, very user friendly software tool to allow mobile telecoms companies and others, on a desktop basis to call up and look at very detailed images of assets within their portfolio. They had also been doing some work in the energy sector, mainly around the nuclear industry and the renewable hydro-electric industry in the north of Scotland. Following the investment the company successfully penetrated the oil and gas market which transformed its performance.

The angel group made the investment because they considered that what the company was doing was smarter and faster than other companies, giving them a competitive advantage. The risk was that the company would not be able to capture sufficient new clients fast enough before the competition woke up to what they were doing.

The initial investment for £200,000 was made in February 2011 when the company had been trading for around ten years. A follow-on investment of £150,000 was made in March 2011 and a further £50,000 for working capital in the second half of 2012. The Scottish Co-investment Fund invested on a £1 for £1 basis in each of these rounds.

Preparing for the Exit

We began to think about the exit about two months before we invested. You can't invest in something before you've thought about how you're going to get out. You can't stick money into these companies without very specifically

---

49 Fili and Grünberg (2016)
50 Mason and Harrison (1994)
51 Harrison *et al.* (2016)

considering there will be an exit at some point in the future and that, ideally, you will make money.

The entrepreneurs were on-side with this. It was a husband and wife team that owned the majority of the shares in the business. They had decided that life was just too hard running the company, effectively, as a lifestyle business. What they wanted to do was to start to grow it properly and sell it.

We got one of our investors involved to help them get ready for an exit. This was prompted by two considerations. First, we had this concern that they ran the risk of being overtaken by competitors. Second, they had begun to receive inbound enquiries from their customers about whether they were for sale or not. So, it was definitely time to get our house in order. However, the entrepreneurs were also quite focused on the exit. But we were driving the process because they were busy running the business.

The Exit

They were bought by one of their customers. They approached the business but I think we flushed them out. We had a couple of expressions of interest and two executives from these companies had verbally asked to be kept informed. I think the ultimate buyer was one of the ones who'd asked verbally to be kept informed should anything look like happening.

One of the customers saw the value of what the company did as part of their own broader service offering. They recognized that they could take the company's capabilities and do it on a global basis. So, it was a bolt on in terms of the service lines that the company offers but, exploiting it on a global basis rather than on a fairly local basis.

The exit occurred in 2013, less than three years after the initial investment. The timing of the exit was influenced by our concern about competitive threats. There were early signs that our guys were not the only people capable of offering this service.

The process of exiting took about six months.

The deal was cash for the investors. The managers/founders were on a more conventional lock in structure involving a bit of cash up front, deferred consideration and that deferred consideration was partially dependent on hitting numbers for the next 18 months. The Scottish Coinvestment Fund had the same multiple and same internal rate of return (IRR) as the angels. We were quite happy with the exit. It was a decent IRR, it was done in about 2.5 years.

Reflections

It is possible that with a more competitive auction process we could have got a better price. But, at the end of the day, it was a small company with pretty limited management resources which limited their ability to continue to deliver the day-to-day business as well as handle a complex multi-party corporate finance transaction, even with help from us. So I think it would have run a very high risk by delaying the exit.

We started with three potential buyers and then we dropped to two. We tried, and failed, to get those two to come back at a higher headline price. We ended up with a lower risk to the headline price but we didn't achieve an actual increase. And, I think, if we'd been doing the process six, twelve months later, or if we had an under-bidder who was more enthusiastic and had put in a good full and final offer I would say we could have got an extra 20–40% on the headline offer price.

The two serious interested parties were seeing, primarily, the value of the oil and gas side of business. They attributed little, if no, value to the non-oil and gas side. A difference of six months might have demonstrated that there was value in the non-oil and gas side. Moreover, the oil and gas side was growing fast and so just substantiating those growth numbers by actual sales coming in, as was the case by the time we actually sold it, we had delivered on a large chunk of the forecast for the current year, pretty much bang on. That provided a great deal of comfort for the buyer who was, in effect, buying off the back of some projections which had been largely delivered by the time we actually completed.

So you can certainly construct a case that, in terms of headline offer price the increase in price would have been sufficient to compensate for the additional six months or so of time before the exit which might have improved the IRR. But, there were significant execution risks and in my experience you have to think very hard about turning down an offer that was acceptable in the hope that you will get a better one later because you don't always get it.

Questions for Discussion

1. Why did the angel group want an exit?
2. Why was the entrepreneur aligned with this objective?
3. How did the angel group drive the exit process?
4. What was the motive of the acquiring company to buy the business?
5. Why did the angel group consider this was not a perfect exit?

The evidence indicates that where exits occur, business angels typically exit and realize their capital gains within three to six years. The median time to exit in the UK is four years for high-performing investments and six years for moderately performing investments, possibly because of the limited opportunities to exit.[52] Often these investments are sold back to the management team, typically for a nominal price. Failures appear, on average, after two years.[53] In Finland, investments that had a positive outcome were five years old at harvest, whereas those which failed had an average holding time of 2.8 years. This would appear to confirm the investment cliché that 'lemons ripen before plums'.

Despite different time periods and geographical contexts, the small number of studies of returns to angel investing are remarkably consistent, indicating

52 Mason and Harrison (2002); Wiltbank (2009).
53 Mason and Harrison (2002).

that around half of all investments fail to generate a return while a minority of investments generate more than ten times cash return. For example, a UK study highlights the highly skewed distribution of outcomes, with 40 per cent of investments making a loss (34 per cent being a total loss), and another 13 per cent only achieving break-even or generating bank account-level returns. However, there was a significant subset of investments, some 23 per cent in total, which generated internal rates of return (IRRs) in excess of 50 per cent. In Wiltbank's (2009) study this small minority of successful investments (9 per cent each returned more than 10 times their investment) generated the majority (c. 80 per cent) of the cash generated by the entire sample of investments. A separate analysis of the returns distribution of technology and non-technology investments in the UK found no significant differences in the returns profile.[54] It is important to note that these studies only consider the capital gain on the original investment. However, many angels also attempt to draw back at least part of their investment in the form of a director's fee or interest on loans provided, either immediately or at some stage in the future when the business is financially stronger. Successful investments are positively related to the angel's experience, undertaking some due diligence, and involvement with the investee company.[55] The most common exit route for successful investments is a trade sale (i.e. sale of the company to another company), while an IPO only accounts for a small minority of the exits. Trade sales, along with sale to existing shareholders, were the most common exit routes for investments with little or no value. The preference of angels is to exit via a trade sale rather than an IPO.[56]

Comparison with the returns achieved by venture capital investors is problematic because the reporting unit is the fund, whereas angels invest on a deal-by-deal basis. However, Murray (1999) has reported deal-specific returns for one UK venture capital fund. Comparing the returns achieved by business angels with this information reveals a much higher loss rate by the venture capital fund (64 per cent) and a lower proportion of investments that generated a moderate return, but a very similar proportion of high-return investments (IRR in excess of 50 per cent). The interpretation of these differences is that because the venture capital fund is seeking to maximize the performance of the fund, it can be more ruthless with those investments that are performing moderately, in order to focus the time of its executives on supporting the best-performing investments whereas business angels invest on a deal-by-deal basis.[57]

A Finnish study sought to identify differences between the most, and least, successful investors. The most successful investors were more likely to be motivated by the fun and interest of making such investments, have a large deal flow and have a lower estimation of the value of their hands-on

54 Mason and Harrison (2004).
55 Wiltbank (2009).
56 Carpentier and Suret (2014).
57 Mason and Harrison (2002).

involvement. The least successful investors were more likely to be motivated by altruism, have a low deal flow and make few investments and rely to a greater extent on friends for deal flow. They were also more likely to make investments in friends' businesses and have a different pattern of hands-on involvement, over-emphasizing contributions that other research has suggested are least important in adding value.[58]

However, this focus on the exits that occur – both positive and negative – should not obscure the reality that most investments never achieve an exit. A survey of Scotland-based business angel groups found that these groups had collectively made 37 exits, representing just 4 per cent of their investments. The majority of groups – 12 of the 17 that provided data – had not made any exits. To some extent, this reflects the young age of many of the groups. Indeed, four of the five groups that have achieved exits were at least eight years old, with the three longest established groups accounting for 92 per cent of total exits. Nevertheless, the vast majority of groups that were between five and eight years old had not made any exits. Equally notable is the low number of failed investments, which account for 17 per cent of total investments. The three oldest groups account for 82 per cent of all losses. The implication is that these groups have a high proportion of 'living dead' investments – businesses that are generating sufficient revenue and profits to survive but are not performing sufficiently well to attract acquirers. Two-thirds of the groups reported that they had no formal strategy for dealing with the 'living dead' in their portfolios, creating the risk that these investments absorb unproductive time and further funding.[59]

KEY TAKEAWAYS

- Business angels play a critical role in the financing of entrepreneurial businesses at their seed, start-up and early growth stages, providing finance and expertise.
- Because of this, governments have introduced a range of initiatives to support the angel market.
- Business angels are typically successful entrepreneurs with disposable wealth. However, the angel population exhibits considerable heterogeneity.
- Angels are increasingly joining organized angel groups to make investments alongside other angels. This is having a significant impact on the nature of angel investing.
- The investment process comprises several stages. The pre-screen and screening stages are undertaken very quickly, with angels rejecting the majority of the opportunities they see. Typically angels invest in just 1 or 2 per cent of the opportunities that they consider.
- The investment criteria evolve as opportunities pass through the screening stage to due diligence. Concerns about the entrepreneur – their

58 Lumme *et al* (1998).
59 Mason *et al* (2015).

trustworthiness, competence, realism and ability to establish a rapport – are the key deal killers.

- Angel investing is high risk. Over half of their investments are unsuccessful. Returns are highly skewed: the small proportion of successful investments (between 1 in 5 and 1 in 10) generate the majority of the returns.
- The majority of investments never achieve an exit. Angel portfolios are dominated by 'living dead' investments – moderately profitable businesses that are not successful enough to achieve an exit.

END OF CHAPTER QUESTIONS

1. Why are business angels critical actors in the entrepreneurial ecosystem?
2. Angels are a heterogeneous population: in what ways might they be classified?
3. What are the implications of the emergence of angel groups on the nature of angel investing?
4. What are the pros and cons for an individual angel of joining an angel group?
5. What types of risks do angels face when investing?
6. In what ways does the investment evaluation differ at the pre-screen, screening and due diligence stages?
7. What are the main reasons why angels reject the investment opportunities that they consider?
8. Why do business angels engage with their investee businesses after making an investment?
9. Why do most angels not consider the exit when appraising investment opportunities?
10. What valuation techniques do angels use?
11. What might an exit-centric approach to investing look like?
12. Why do most of the businesses that angels invest in fail to produce any financial return?
13. What strategies should angels adopt towards their 'living dead' investments?
14. Why do angels prefer to exit via a trade sale rather than an IPO?
15. What advice would you give an entrepreneur who is planning to pitch to an angel or angel group?

FURTHER READING

Landström, H and Mason, C. (eds.) (2016). *Handbook of Research on Business Angels*. Edward Elgar.

Gregson, G. (2014). *Financing New Ventures: An Entrepreneur's Guide to Business Angel Investment*. Babson Expert Press LLC.

McKaskill, T. (2009). *An Introduction to Angel Investing*. Breakthrough Publications, www.drexit.net.

May, J. and Liu, M. M. (2015). *Angels Without Borders: Trends and Policies Shaping Angel Investment Worldwide*. World Scientific Publishing.

OECD (2011). *Financing High Growth Firms: The Role of Angel Investor*. OECD.

Peters, B. (2009). *Early Exits: Exit Strategies for Entrepreneurs and Angel Investors*. Meteorbytes Data Management Corporation.

White, B. and Dumay, J. (2017). Business angels: a research review and new agenda. *Venture Capital: An International Journal of Entrepreneurial Finance*, 17(3), 183–216.

REFERENCES

Carpentier, C. and Suret, J-M. (2014). Canadian business angel perspectives on exit: a research note, *International Small Business Journal*, 33(5), 582–593.

Carpentier, C. and Suret, J-M. (2015). Angel group members' decision process and rejection criteria: a longitudinal analysis, *Journal of Business Venturing*, 30(6), 808–821.

Croce, A., Tenca, F. and Ughetto, E. (2017). How business angel groups work: rejection criteria in investment evaluation, *International Small Business Journal*, 35(4), 405–426.

Feeney, L., Haines, G. H. and Riding. A. L. (1999). private investors' investment criteria: insights from qualitative data. *Venture Capital: An International Journal of Entrepreneurial Finance*, 1, 121–145.

Festel, G. W. and De Cleyn, S. H. (2013). Founding angels as an emerging sub-type of the angel investment model in high tech businesses, *Venture Capital: An International Journal of Entrepreneurial Finance*, 15(3), 261–282.

Fili, A. and Grünberg, A. (2016). Business angel post-investment activities: a multi-level review, *Journal of Management and Governance*, 20(1), 89–114.

Fiet, J. O. (1995). Risk avoidance strategies in venture capital markets. *Journal of Management Studies*, 32, 551–574.

Gale, D. (1996). What have we learned from social learning? *European Economic Review*, 40(3), 617–628.

Haines, G. H., jr., Madill, J. J. and Riding, A. L. (2003). Informal investment in Canada: financing small business growth. *Journal of Small Business and Entrepreneurship*, 16(3/4), 13–40.

Harrison, R. T. and Mason, C.M. (1992). International perspectives on the supply of informal venture capital. *Journal of Business Venturing*, 7, 459–475.

Harrison, R. T., Botelho, T. and Mason, C. M. (2016). Patient capital in entrepreneurial finance: a reassessment of the role of business angel investors, *Socio-Economic Review*, 14(4), 669–689.

Harrison, R. T., Mason, C. M. and Robson, P. (2010). Determinants of long-distance investing by business angels in the UK. *Entrepreneurship and Regional Development*, 22, 113–137

Harrison, R. T., Smith, D. and Mason, C. M. (2015). Heuristics, learning and the business angel investment decision making process, *Entrepreneurship and Regional Development*, 27(9–10), 527–554

Kelly, P. and Hay, M. (2003). Business angel contracts: the influence of context. *Venture Capital: An International Journal of Entrepreneurial Finance*, 5, 287–312.

Landström, H. (1992). The relationship between private investors and small firms: an agency theory approach. *Entrepreneurship and Regional Development*, 4, 199–223.

Landström, H. (1998). Informal investors as entrepreneurs. *Technovation*, 18, 321–333.

Lengyel, Z. and Gulliford, J. (1997). *The Informal Venture Capital Experience*. Local Investment Networking Company, London.

Lumme, A., Mason, C. and Suomi, M. (1998). *Informal Venture Capital: Investors, Investments and Policy Issues in Finland*. Kluwer Academic Publishers.

Mason, C. and Botelho, T. (2014). *The 2014 Survey of Business Angel Investing in the UK: A Changing Market Place*. Adam Smith Business School, University of Glasgow.

Mason, C., Botelho, T. and Harrison, R. (2016). The transformation of the business angel market: evidence and research implications. *Venture Capital: An International Journal of Entrepreneurial Finance*, 18(4), 321–344.

Mason, C. M. and Harrison, R. T. (1994). The informal venture capital market in the UK. In A. Hughes and D. J. Storey (eds.), *Financing Small Firms* (pp.64–111). Routledge.

Mason, C. M. and Harrison, R. T. (1996). Informal venture capital: a study of the investment process and post-investment experience. *Entrepreneurship and Regional Development*, 8, 105–126.

Mason, C. M. and Harrison, R. T. (2002). Is it worth it? The rates of return from informal venture capital investments. *Journal of Business Venturing*, 17, 211–236.

Mason, C. M. and Harrison, R. T. (2003). 'Auditioning for money': what do technology investors look for at the initial screening stage? *Journal of Private Equity*, 6(2), 29–42.

Mason, C. M. and Harrison, R. T. (2004). Does investing in technology-based firms involve higher risk? An exploratory study of the performance of technology and non-technology investments by business angels. *Venture Capital: An International Journal of Entrepreneurial Finance*, 6, 313–332.

Mason, C. and Rogers, A. (1997). The business angel's investment decision: An exploratory analysis. In D. Deakins, P. Jennings and C. Mason (eds.), *Entrepreneurship in the 1990s* (pp. 29–46). Paul Chapman Publishing.

Mason, C. and Stark, M. (2004). What do investors look for in a business plan? A comparison of the investment criteria of bankers, venture capitalists and business angels. *International Small Business Journal*, 22, 227–248.

Mason, C., Harrison, R. and Botelho, T. (2015). Business angel exits: strategies and processes. In J. G. Hussain and J. M. Scott (eds.), *Research Handbook on Entrepreneurial Finance* (pp. 102–124). Edward Elgar.

Mason, C., Botelho, T. and Zygmunt, J. (2017) 'Why business angels reject investment opportunities: Is it personal? *International Small Business Journal*. 35, 519–534.

Maxwell, A. L. and Lévesque, M. (2014). Trustworthiness: A critical ingredient for entrepreneurs seeking investors. *Entrepreneurship Theory and Practice*, 38(5),1057–1080.

Maxwell, A. L., Jeffrey, S. A. and Lévesque, M. (2011). Business angel early stage decision making. *Journal of Business Venturing*, 26, 212–225.

May, J. and Simmons, C. (2001). *Every Business Needs an Angel: Getting the Money You Need to Make Your Business Grow*. Crown Business.

Mitteness, C. R., Baucus, M. S. and Sudek, R. (2012). Horse vs. jockey? How stage of funding process and industry experience affect the evaluations of angel investors. *Venture Capital: An International Journal of Entrepreneurial Finance*, 14(4), 241–267.

Murray, G. (1999). Seed capital funds and the effect of scale economies. *Venture Capital: An International Journal of Entrepreneurial Finance*, 1, 351–384.

OECD (2011). *Financing High Growth Firms: The Role of Angel Investors*. OECD Publishing. http://dx.doi.org/10.1797/9789264118782-en

Paul, S. and Whittam, G. (2010). Business angel syndicates: an exploratory study of gatekeepers. *Venture Capital: An International Journal of Entrepreneurial Finance*, 12(4), 241–256.

Politis, D. (2008). Business angels and value added: what do we know and where do we go? *Venture Capital: An International Journal of Entrepreneurial Finance*, 10(2), 127–147.

Politis, D. and Landström, H. (2002). Informal investors as entrepreneurs: the development of an entrepreneurial career. *Venture Capital: An International Journal of Entrepreneurial Finance*, 4, 77–101.

Riding, A. L., Dalcin, P., Duxbury, L., Haines, G. and Safrata, R. (1993). Informal investors in Canada: the identification of salient charcteristics. Carleton University, Ottawa.

Riding, A. L., Madill, J. J. and Haines Jr, G. H. (2007). Investment decision making by business angels. In H. Landström (ed.), *Handbook of Research on Venture Capital* pp. (332–346). Edward Elgar Publishing.

Sohl, J. (2017). *A Cautious Restructuring of the Angel Market in 2016 With a Robust Appetite for Seed and Start-Up Investing*, Center for Venture Research, University of New Hampshire.

Sørheim, R. (2003). Business angels as facilitators for further finance: an exploratory study. *Journal of Small Business and Enterprise Development*, 12, 178–191.

Sudek, R., May, A. and Wilbank, R. (2011). *Angel Investing: Catalyst for Innovation*. Angel Resource Institute. www.angelassociation.co.nz/media/2014/04/Super-Angels-Report-ARI-10-18-11.pdf

Sullivan, M. K. (1994). Altruism and entrepreneurship. In *Frontiers of Entrepreneurship Research 1994 (pp. 373–380)*. Babson College.

Visser, R. and Williams, R. (2001). Prospecting for gold: how Dutch informal investors appraise small businesses in trouble. *Venture Capital: An International Journal of Entrepreneurial Finance*, 3, 1–24.

Wiltbank, R. E. (2009). *Siding With the Angels. Business angel investing: Promising Outcomes and Effective Strategies*. NESTA.

VENTURE CAPITAL, PRIVATE EQUITY AND CORPORATE VENTURE CAPITAL

JOSEP DURAN

European Investment Fund

OSCAR FARRES

European Investment Fund

In this chapter, you will be walked through the concepts of venture capital, private equity and corporate venture funds, helping you to understand how they operate, who invests in these funds and, most importantly, how they make money and why this is important for entrepreneurs.

Venture capital, private equity and corporate venture funds have emerged in the last decades as the ideal vehicles for channelling private and public money into the financing of innovation. Since the creation in Boston in 1946 by French immigrant George Doriot of the American Research and Development Corporation (ADRC)[1], considered to be the first venture capital firm, the industry has evolved to provide risk capital to innovative entrepreneurs in a model that has barely changed and is adapted to the particularities of the underlying asset: startup companies.

The venture capital industry is surrounded by a halo of secrecy, and not only the general public but also many entrepreneurs do not fully understand how venture capital funds work and what makes venture capitalists take the decisions they take. The goal of this chapter is to throw light on the functioning of the venture capital industry as it is today, in order to contribute to much more straightforward interaction between all the actors in the innovation process.

---

1 To learn more about George Doriot and the beginnings of venture capital you might like to read: Ante, S. (2008) *Creative Capital: George Doriot and the Birth of Venture Capital*, HBS Press.

VIEW FROM THE MEDIA

FINANCIAL TIMES   FT

Partech Ventures raises €400m fund for European and US start-ups

Two-thirds of investments to focus on emerging technologies such as virtual reality

JULY 10, 2017 BY ALIYA RAM

Partech Ventures, the France-based investment firm, has closed a €400m fund to invest in European and US technology start-ups, amid signs the funding freeze following the UK's vote to leave the EU is beginning to thaw. The fund is the seventh of its kind from Partech and is being backed by the European Investment Fund, a public-private partnership in the EU, and Bpifrance, France's sovereign wealth fund. ... Two-thirds of its investments will focus on European start-ups developing emerging technologies such as virtual reality, blockchain and drones, while the rest will go into companies in Silicon Valley, where Partech also has an office. ... European tech funding slowed sharply after the vote for Brexit in June 2016. Start-ups that already lag behind counterparts in the US and Asia in attracting early-stage investment saw venture capital investment drop by a third in the third quarter, according to Dow Jones VentureSource.

But this year a number of large venture capital groups have launched multimillion-dollar funds focused on the sector. Last month Brent Hoberman, co-founder of lastminute.com raised $60m to invest in technology start-ups across the region. In February, Atomico closed a $765m European tech fund to help new businesses expand. (...)

www.ft.com/content/78eb5444-640b-11e7-8526-7b38dcaef614

LEARNING OBJECTIVES

After reading this chapter, you will be able to:

- Understand the differences between venture capital, private equity and corporate venture funds.
- Recognize the key attributes of a fund.
- Appreciate the virtuous cycle of venture capital.
- Understand the economics of a venture capital fund and how fund investors and fund managers make money.
- Become familiar with the latest developments in European venture capital and wider industry trends.

Where Are We Going Next?

This chapter provides an understanding of how venture capital, private equity and corporate funds raise capital, invest in companies and make money. The basic characteristics of these three types of investment funds will be described, after which the chapter will focus on venture capital funds as the most dominant vehicle for financing innovation.

The full life cycle of a venture capital fund will be explained in detail so that the reader understands the dynamics of value creation that underpin this particular investment vehicle. The underlying economics of venture capital funds will be analysed, uncovering concepts like 'management fee' or 'carried interest', which still remain a mystery to most entrepreneurs. There is no better way to successfully raise money for your company than by understanding in depth how the money flows to venture capital funds, from there to portfolio companies, and, hopefully, after a successful exit, to the pockets of the entrepreneur, the venture capitalists and the investors in the fund.

Finally, we will take the opportunity to look at current trends in the European venture capital market, which has evolved significantly in recent years, and is competing on a global scale with some of the most developed ecosystems in the world. A clear understanding of where Europe stands in terms of venture capital investments is a key factor for success as an entrepreneur in a globalized economy.

4.1   Venture Capital, Private Equity and Corporate Venture Capital: Is It All the Same?

Terms like venture capital (VC) or private equity (PE) are often confused and may be used interchangeably, whereas actually both concepts, although sharing some similarities, have notable differences. In fact, we could consider venture capital as a subsector of the private equity industry. However, the growing relevance of the venture capitalist and the huge impact of the digital economy and life sciences in our current lives mean that venture capital deserves its own space in the finance industry.

Indeed, both venture capital and private equity funds are *temporary equity investors that provide capital, in exchange for equity (shares), to non-listed companies*. It is the stage, sector and level of risk that determines whether they are private equity firms or venture capital investors.

In this section, we will explain the differences between both types of investors, as summarized in Figure 4.1.

4.1.1   Venture Capital

Venture capital firms generally target emerging companies in their early stages of development. These companies are mainly technology or science-driven

	VENTURE CAPITAL	PRIVATE EQUITY
Stage	Seed / Start-up / Expansion	Growth / Replacement / Buyout / Turnaround
Activity sector	Technology, Telecom, Media, Biotech	Traditional business, consumer goods, industry
Market Growth	Two-digits	0% or GNP growth
Expected Return	50–60% annually	20–40% annually

Figure 4.1 Venture Capital versus Private Equity.

businesses, with an innovative or disruptive service or product. Yes, you are right, we are talking about what we all define as 'startups'. Here, the level of risk is much higher because the product or service that the founders are trying to push to the market is not yet proven, but of course the upside is almost unlimited if a venture firm is able to identify an extremely successful startup and sell it in a multi-billion euro transaction. How early the venture capitalist identifies and invests in the company also has important implications in the risk level and strategy of the fund. Investing a few hundreds of thousands of euros when Janus Friis and Niklas Zennström were designing the concept of Skype in a garage is a very different matter from investing several tens of millions in a pharma product in its later stages of development, before Big Pharma, say, acquires the company. Both are risky, but the expected returns and the skills of the fund managers are clearly different.

Venture capital funds can behave very differently, or may have different sizes or approaches, depending on the stage at which they are investing. We can classify venture capital funds into three groups according to the investment stage:

- *Seed*: typically small funds (some tens of millions), investing in very early-stage companies with a product or service under development. In the majority of cases, the company hasn't begun commercial operations. Ticket sizes range from a hundred thousand to a few hundreds of thousands.
- *Early stage/Startup*: medium-size funds (say, around €100m) targeting companies that already have a product or service in the market, with growing revenues and traction, but still trying to scale operations and fine tune the business model. The fund would invest from one to a few millions in the round.
- *Expansion*: the funds can have several hundreds of millions to invest in mature companies, with solid products or services and a consolidated business model. These companies might be looking to expand their activities and

tackle markets on a global scale. The ticket sizes in the rounds could amount to several tens of millions.

Whatever the stage, it should be noted that venture capital funds like to co-invest and syndicate when investing in startups. It's extremely common to see several investors participate in the same investment round in order to control the level of risk they're assuming. This means investing in just a portion of the round and also brings onboard different approaches and expertise from the partners that will take care of the portfolio company. And since in each investment round the company will need to talk with different investors, depending on the stage of the company, they might end up with a quite an eclectic list of shareholders.

VOICE OF THE EXPERT: Andreas Saari (Finland)

Andreas Saari is the Co-Founder and CEO of Wave Ventures, the first student-run venture capital fund in the Nordics. Wave Ventures aims to back the boldest founders and their ideas that arise from the university communities across the Nordics. Previously, Andreas led the startup and investor operations at the technology super event Slush, taking place in Helsinki every year in the Fall, and is now developing a new programme concept there. Andreas studies industrial engineering and management at Aalto University and loves downhill biking, other extreme sports and learning furiously about everything.

How does venture capital add value to the startups on top of the money provided?

As we are investing in the very earliest stages of the life-cycle of a company, sometimes even at the time of the founding, our help to the portfolio companies can take many forms and is often performed on-demand – below are three examples:

For first-time founders, some of the biggest value-adds might be our help in navigating the whole investment and VC landscape, funding possibilities and preventing the most common traps along the way.

Introductions are often a big (sometimes too big a) part of a VC's value-add. To shed some light on their type: right after or even at the time of raising the first round of outside capital, we spend time with the startup planning the next financing round (if one is needed) and go on to make the needed introductions in due course. Often times the very early-stage team also needs more talent pretty early on, so we put a lot of effort in identifying potential, uniquely good hires for that exact team.

In very practical terms, due to having a few of the best young lawyers in the region as part of our investment team, we have for example been able to help our portfolio companies with their legal paperwork and thus helping them save up to tens of thousands of euros in legal fees.

4.1.2   Private Equity

Private equity investors target mature companies in traditional sectors with proven business models that are trying to expand their business or consolidate their activity through a merger, acquisition, management transition or a number of other corporate transactions. Investing in the international expansion of a successful dental franchise, or buying significant stakes in an industrial company in order to merge it with another complementary portfolio company of the fund, would be typical private equity deals. These could range from a few million euros up to hundreds of millions, combining both equity and debt instruments. These companies are generally active in more traditional industries where the level of risk relies on the meeting of debt obligations, the effective management of the business or the evolution of the market, rather than on the product fit, technological or scientific innovation or the behavior of new consumers.

We could group private equity funds in the category of growth funds or leverage buyouts, although we could also include a large number of other approaches, like real estate funds, mezzanine funds, distressed funds, etc. They can be sector agnostic or specialized, and can target concrete geographies or take a global approach.

- *Growth funds*: target mature companies that are entering into new markets and are expanding their operations organically or though merger and acquisition (M&A) activities. They tend to be quite generalist in terms of industry scope and sometimes they overlap with late-stage or expansion VC funds. Some VC funds have their own growth divisions.
- *Leverage Buyout funds (LBOs):* target mature companies with stable cash flows. They seek to finance the transaction with a mix of equity and debt in order to obtain controlling stakes in the portfolio companies. The balance between equity and debt is very unique, because when they acquire a company they use a small amount of the fund as equity and they leverage a large percentage of the transaction with bank loans or subordinated debt. LBOs' investment teams can be closely involved when buying a company, by carrying out different restructuring techniques, cuts (HR, general costs, subsidiaries, etc), partnerships or M&A activities, in other words, doing everything they can to maximize the value of the asset before selling it again. Management buyouts (MBOs) and management buy-ins (MBIs), where the management acquires a company as a way of becoming owner and entrepreneur, are classic private equity deals and will be analysed in detail in Part IV of this book, covering Chapters 13, 14, and 15.

4.1.3   Corporate Venture Capital

A lot of large corporations, mainly involved in technology, have venture arms to invest in other young companies. In this field, there are almost as many approaches as there are companies. Corporate venture capital is a very well developed activity in the United States (Google Ventures, Intel Capital, Qualcomm Ventures, Walmart, etc.), and has become more and more significant in Europe in recent years (Bertelsmann, Telefónica, Orange, Allianz, Santander, Siemens, etc). They do it in many different ways, from sponsoring other independent venture firms, to having their in-house venture capital activities or creating acceleration programmes where they fund and mentor young companies, giving them access to their structural resources and knowledge. However, by this point you might already have guessed that they don't do it for charity. So, why do they spend their time, money and resources on investment activity when their core businesses are far removed from the buying and selling of shares from startups? Well, each large company will have their own explanation for this, but generally they are doing it for strategic reasons. Most of the venture arms of big companies are very closely linked to the company's business development, innovation[2] or strategy divisions[3]. Investing in startups is a fantastic way to be up to date on the latest trends and technologies to be found in the market. Also, investing in a young company with an innovative product or service could be a good strategy for acquiring the company at a later stage if the large company feels that adding the startup to its portfolio could be key for its future. In fact, there are some large corporations that base their growth and innovation on their M&A activity (e.g. Cisco, Qualcomm). This is very common in the USA, but unfortunately it is not that common in Europe, where relationships between startups and large corporations are very few and far between. Could this be a key point to tackle in the near future?

So, this sounds fantastic, doesn't it? I enroll my startup in one of these Telco acceleration programmes, I get some funding, they open all the doors that right now are closed to me and then they acquire my project and I become rich overnight. Well . . . yes and no. It is true that having a strategic investor in your company could be a determinant factor of success for your business. Who would not want to have access to the unlimited resources that are available to big companies? If they really support your activity, partnering with one of the giants in your field could be an enormous boost for your project. But, at the same time, there are a number of things you need to take into account. First of all, big companies take decisions either very quickly or very slowly, for better or for worse. You project may become 'non-strategic' overnight, and your access to their resources may be immediately withdrawn. Or even worse, the project might spend months and months in their gigantic decision process before they make any movement at all. And as you know, speed is something you cannot afford to neglect in your fragile and tiny business. In addition, some venture capital firms traditionally don't like to have strategic investors involved in the startups, at least in the early stages. The main reasons are that having a big

2 Chesbrough (2006);Chesbrough and Crowther (2006).
3 Vanhaverbeke *et al.* (2008).

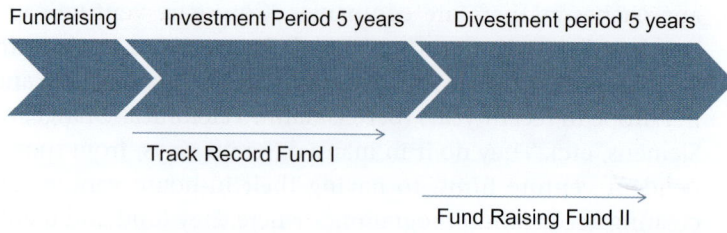

Figure 4.2 Life of a VC fund.

company as a shareholder could prevent competitors from approaching your company for an acquisition, or that strategic decisions could be blocked by the corporate investor if they are not benefiting from the overall strategy decided by a board of directors that you have never met. How can you avoid these drawbacks? Two key points: if you want a big company as an investor, hire good lawyers (do this for VC and PE investors too) and make sure that you have a strong 'champion', who pushes and fosters your project through the rambling corridors of the corporation.

4.2   The Virtuous Circle of Venture Capital

In the previous section, you will have discovered the basic descriptions of a venture capital and private equity fund. It is time to dive deeper and determine their role in the 'virtuous circle of venture capital' in which money from affluent investors, institutions, the financial sector and other asset managers flows into venture capital funds, is invested in startup companies that can innovate and grow, and then returned to the initial investors with a return commensurate to the risk that they are undertaking. The wise reader will draw parallels between a venture capital fund and a startup company, as both entities are confronted with similar challenges throughout their life cycles. It is not incorrect to say that a venture capitalist is an entrepreneur in a very particular industry.

The life of a venture capital fund will be explained below, but its first stage involves raising money from investors. Then, it is followed by an investment period that can be divided into two main stages: investing and then managing and controlling the portfolio of backed companies. Finally, the last stage is known as the divestment period, and this is when the venture capitalist exits from the startup by selling his stake. This life cycle is summarized in Figure 4.2.

4.2.1   Stage 1: Fundraising

The first step in the life of a venture capital fund is to find investors (also known as 'limited partners') willing to commit a certain amount of money to the fund (further detail about limited partners can be found in Section 4.3), following the legal set-up explained in Section 4.4 below. The commitment will last for the life of the fund, and the fund manager will call on the investors' money when it is needed for investments in the startups and to pay for management fees (more on management fees in Section 4.5 below). Therefore, not all the money committed by investors to a venture capital fund will be transferred to the fund on day one, but the consequences of not fulfilling a capital call from the fund manager are very punitive for the investor (they might lose all the money invested so far in the fund) as such a situation would damage the strategy of the fund.

A venture capital fund is a very particular investment vehicle in which:

- The investors' money will be locked in for 10 years, and in some cases even longer, as the fund life is extended in order to be able to sell all the portfolio companies. Investments in venture capital funds are rather illiquid.
- The investors do not know at the time of the initial investment the identities of the startup companies in which the fund will invest.
- Returns are heterogeneous across the asset class and vary considerably according to the year in which the fund is raised (the so-called 'vintage year'). In addition, the spread of returns between the best performing teams and the worst performing teams is huge.

Despite all this, billions of euros in new commitments flow into venture capital funds every year in Europe, so what is attracting all those investors to venture capital funds?

The main reasons are:

- Returns are not correlated with the stock markets due to the long-term nature of the venture capital investments, and this is great news for achieving diversification in your asset portfolio, as you will know from Modern Portfolio Theory.[4] In fact, venture capital funds raised during periods of financial crisis typically perform well as they invest in companies at the bottom of the cycle and hence pay lower prices. Due to its long holding period, the venture capital fund exits the companies once the crisis is over and can obtain juicy valuations in the sale process. The opposite might happen with funds raised at the peak of the economic cycle. Figure 4.3 shows net IRR performance for a large sample of private equity funds (including venture capital) as of end of June 2016.
- Top-performing VC funds generate double digit returns over a ten-year period. This is far above other traditional asset classes (e.g. stock markets, real estate, bonds). Cambridge Associates publishes a performance index for global VC/PE funds excluding the USA which, in its Q3 2016 edition,[5] shows that over a 10-year period (the standard term of a VC/PE fund) or longer, the asset class outperforms the stock markets:

4 See, for example, Elton et al. (2009).
5 Cambridge Associates (2017).

Table 4.1 VC/PE returns benchmarked against stock market indexes

	1 Yr	3 Yr	5 Yr	10 Yr	15 Yr	20 Yr	25 Yr
CA Global ex US Dev Mkts PE/VC (€)	12.4%	17.0%	14.5%	10.6%	12.4%	13.6%	13.5%
MSCI EAFE (€) mPME	5.9%	7.4%	12.0%	4.7%	5.6%	5.1%	5.2%
S&P 500 (US$) mPME	15.6%	11.8%	17.5%	8.7%	8.7%	8.2%	8.5%

Source: Cambridge Associates LLC, MSCI Inc., Standard & Poor's, and Thomson Reuters Datastream

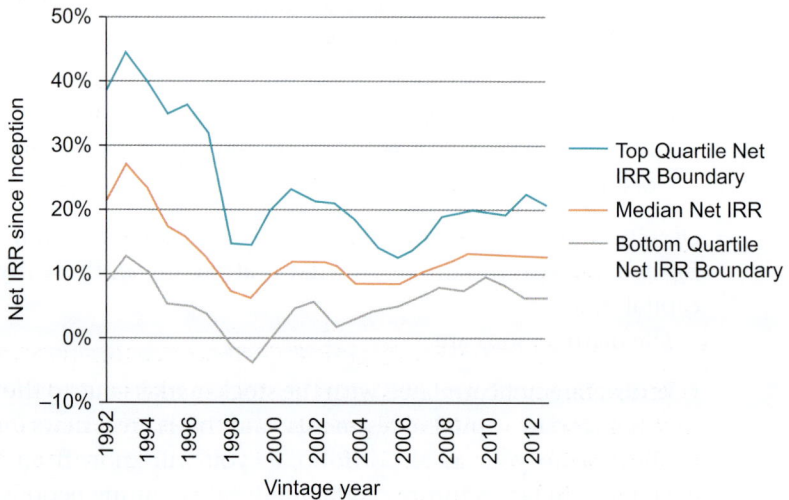

Figure 4.3 Net IRR by vintage year in PE funds as of 30 June 2016.
Source: Preqin Private Equity Online

- Additionally, venture capital funds provide a valuable insight into new industry trends and disruptive innovation which can be highly valuable, specifically for strategic investors such as big corporates.

Venture capital funds are hence a good addition to any investor's portfolio, as it diversifies risk while adding extra returns over long investment horizons. Despite the supporting data, the relatively short history of venture capital in Europe, and some stereotypes associated with recent boom-and-bust cycles (notably the 2000.com bubble[6]), has played against venture capital funds when it comes to incorporating alternative investment funds in the portfolio of institutional investors (for instance, pension funds or insurance companies that need to manage huge amounts of cash).

The main investors in European venture capital funds in 2015, according to Invest Europe[7], are shown in Figure 4.4.

6 For a narrated account of the dot com bubble period you can read Cassidy (2003).
7 Invest Europe (2016).

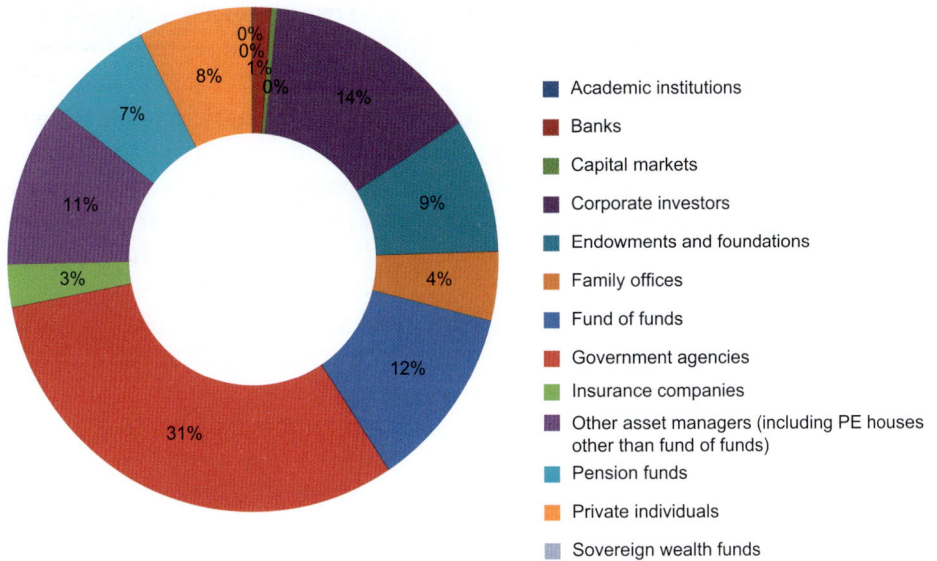

Figure 4.4 Investors in European venture capital in 2015.
Source: Invest Europe (2016)

From the data shown in Figure 4.4, we can see that public institutions are a cornerstone investor in European venture capital funds, followed by corporate investors and private fund of funds and other asset managers. This situation will be discussed in more detail in Section 4.6. Note that unclassified investors have been excluded from the above chart.

Different investors might have different criteria for investing in venture capital funds. For instance, public investors might value the policy impact of a particular investment strategy, or corporate investors might appreciate access to specific deal flow or industry knowledge. Despite the different motivations for investing in venture capital, in most cases financial return is one of the key criteria for all types of investors. In general, investors (LPs) in venture capital funds will look at the following dimensions in order to decide in which venture capital funds they will invest (disclaimer: this is not a comprehensive list of investment criteria, and criteria are not listed in order of importance):

- Track record. How did the team's investments perform in the past? Is the current investment strategy comparable to prior funds? Has there been any significant change in market conditions that will deem the previous track record irrelevant? Is the track record fully attributable to the current team members?
- Team. Is the team a long-standing one or is it a first-time team? Does the team have a combination of complementary profiles? How do the individual team members interact with each other? Have there been any team

departures? Is there any succession issue foreseen during the lifetime of the fund (10 years is a long time!)? How motivated are team members to commit to the fund?

- Fund strategy. Is the strategy of the fund in line with market developments? Is the capital deployment plan sensible and in accordance with the needs of the targeted sector and stage of development of the portfolio companies? Is the strategy supported by the deal flow that the team sees? Does the geographical diversification of the fund correspond to market dynamics and the team's footprint?
- Market opportunity. Is the fund tapping into an emerging market segment? What is the competitive positioning of the fund? Will the market opportunity last for the whole duration of the fund?
- Alignment of interests between the fund manager and the investors in the fund (also known as GP–LP alignment). What are the economic incentives for the team? Is the team incentivized by the carry or by the management fee (the economic incentives for venture capitalists will be discussed further in the next section)? What is the personal investment in the fund of the team members (i.e. 'skin in the game')?

4.2.2   Stage 2: Investing

Once a new venture capital fund is raised, it is time for the fund manager to deploy the money according to the envisaged strategy and build a portfolio of promising startups. The average venture capital fund has a fixed period of five years[8] to do the initial investments in startups and build the portfolio. This period is called the investment period, and after the end of the investment period the venture capital fund is not allowed to invest in new companies and can only provide follow-on capital to existing portfolio companies.

The construction of a portfolio has two key elements: the selection of individual companies and portfolio management.

Individual Company Selection

The selection of individual startups is a mix of science and art. The earlier the stage of development of the startup, the less quantitative data that will be available for analysis and the higher the risks associated with the development of the company. Even though the investment criteria might change slightly depending on the stage of development, sector and type of venture capital firm,

8 Five years is the standard in the legal documentation. Recently, some VC funds have built their portfolios earlier (in 3–4 years) but it remains to be seen if this trend translates into different terms in the legal documentation (shorter investment periods might be a consequence of the current boom cycle).

there is a set of core criteria most venture capitalists apply (and some advice for entrepreneurs):

- A clear and innovative value proposition. The startup needs to address one or several pain points for its target customers with a solution that is defendable vis-à-vis the competition. And no, an idea on its own is not enough. Execution is everything, so even seed-stage investors will request some kind of proof of product-market fit, and if the entrepreneur can show initial metrics it will be like music to the venture capitalist's ears. The good news, for ICT entrepreneurs at least, is that with decreasing infrastructure costs, launching a bootstrapped prototype in a short time frame has never been so easy.
- A highly scalable business model. And highly means highly. Venture capitalists target at least a 10× increase in the value of the startup in a short period of time (between five and ten years) in order to generate the portfolio-level returns expected by its limited partners. Scalability has two building blocks that are equally important: market size and business model. Market size will determine how far the entrepreneur can go in scaling the business. It is important not to fall into the 'top-down' analysis trap ('if 0.1% of the world population buys my product ... ') and instead do a proper bottom-up analysis ('if I invest this many resources in sales & marketing, I will reach that many people'). The business model of the startup will determine whether it is feasible for it to reach such a target, or whether the startup will explode in the process (scaling up a startup is similar to launching a rocket, a small defect in one screw might create massive havoc at high speed). Given that startups die typically because of a lack of cash to pay salaries at the end of the month, a business model that keeps working capital needs under control when growth rates skyrocket is a must. Alternatively, the entrepreneur needs a supportive venture capitalist who provides timely capital increases, but patience has its limit.
- The team of entrepreneurs is considered even more important than the product. In the end, the product will evolve and the business model might pivot, but the team should lead all these processes. The team is so important that it is the object of several clauses in the shareholders' agreement of the startup company. A key aspect is the complementarity of the team; investors dislike companies run by a single entrepreneur without a competent team.
- The exit plan. Selling the startup company before the end of the life of the fund is, as explained later in the chapter, the raison-d'être of a venture capital fund. Hence the exit strategy of a startup will be a key element of discussion between the venture capitalist and the entrepreneur, as it will determine the potential upside of the investment and will impact upon many strategic decisions (e.g. partnerships with large corporates, geographical expansion in foreign markets, profile of venture capital funds in follow-on rounds). It is important that the exit expectations of the entrepreneur and the venture capitalist are aligned, otherwise the topic will be a source of conflict sooner or later.

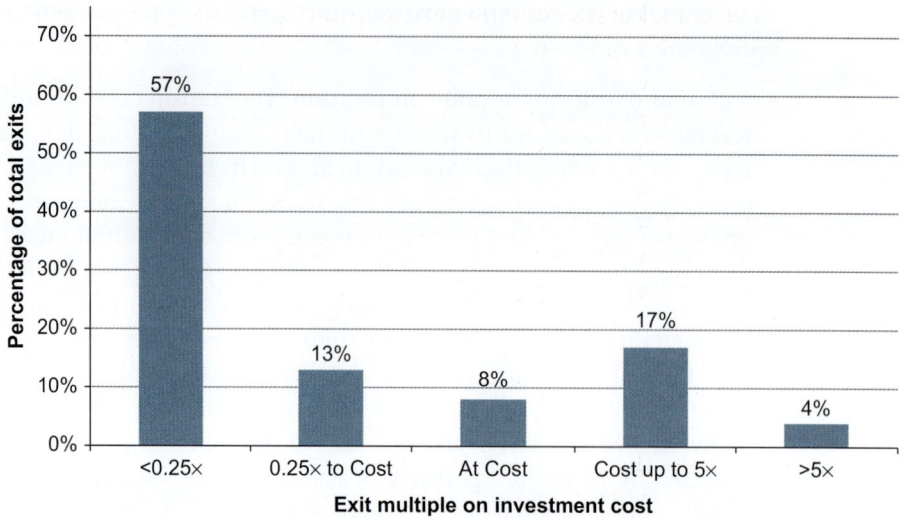

Figure 4.5 Distribution of exit multiples in European VC funds (1996–2016).
Source: European Investment Fund (2017)

In the end, venture capitalists select each individual portfolio company convinced that it will be a success story. The reality is, as discussed in the following section, that hugely successful startups are the exception in the portfolio of a venture capital fund.

Portfolio Management

The construction of a startup portfolio must take into account the particularities of the underlying asset, which carries a great deal of risk and unpredictability: startup companies by definition either launch new products in existing markets (taking product risk), or operate with tested products but in new markets (taking market risk), or take both risks. As the classic financial literature recommends, the best way to protect against uncertainty is to diversify your portfolio.[9] Hence diversification is a key element of any venture capital strategy. As a large percentage of startups will fail in the first few years of life, a venture capital portfolio should be ample enough to avoid a situation where a small number of write-offs ruin the overall results. Although data on the final outcomes of individual startups is hard to find, the European Investment Fund has conducted an analysis[10] on the exit multiples (value of the investment at exit over the cost of the investment) of more than 2,000 early-stage startup companies from its portfolio of venture capital funds in the 1996–2016 period. The results are shown in Figure 4.5.

9 The classic papers are: Markowitz (1991) and Sharpe (1964).
10 European Investment Fund (2017).

A first look at the data shows that up to 70 per cent of early-stage startups made insufficient returns to compensate for the invested capital, whereas only 21 per cent of early-stage startups returned proceeds that exceed the invested capital. Venture capitalists rely on the latter group to generate financial return at the fund level. It is worth noting that these figures are based on a sample of companies that have been invested in by professional venture capitalists, and hence have been selected following a comprehensive analysis that made the venture capitalists bullish about their potential returns.

The concept of capital allocation is equally as important as diversification. Intuitively, a venture capital manager would like to maximize the potential financial return at fund level by allocating as much capital as possible to the best performing companies in the portfolio, whilst at the same time minimizing its exposure to the failing companies that will unavoidably pop up. 'Backing the winners' is the Holy Grail of venture capital managers.[11] If most of the capital of a venture capital fund is allocated to the star company generating 10x returns, the fund will make a great return. The question is, how can winners be identified at the investment stage? Option theory will help us here. Winners do not need to be identified from the outset. Actually, if a manager invests in a company in the first place it should be because the company has all the necessary attributes to be a winner, but the high degree of product or market uncertainty will make it impossible to be completely sure at that point. Stage investing, i.e. dividing the financing round into several tranches that will be paid if certain milestones are met, and an adequate follow-on strategy in subsequent financing rounds, will help the venture capital manager to minimize its exposure to poorly-performing companies and allocate higher amounts of capital to companies that are performing well. Stage investing is covered in greater depth in Chapter 9.

4.2.3   Stage 3: Monitoring, Adding Value and Growing the Portfolio

Value creation in a venture capital fund has three main dimensions: company selection, portfolio management (as discussed in the previous section) and operational support to portfolio companies. The latter is a key element in the success of venture capital funds, especially in the seed and early stages due to the uncertainty surrounding startups. Entrepreneurs will be confronted with important decisions across functional domains (sales, operations, product development, finance, etc.) for which they seek advice from, among others, their investors. The background of the venture capital investor will play a key role in the type of support and value-add they can bring to the portfolio companies (whether it is operational or financial), as well as the network of contacts that the investor can access. Additionally, venture capital funds can employ specific people for value-add tasks: some venture capital funds work with venture

---

11 Some research has focused on whether venture capital funds are able to select the winners or whether they are actually creating them. See for example Baum and Silverman (2004).

partners, typically successful entrepreneurs or people with extensive operational experience in startups who will collaborate closely with a venture capital fund to provide specific support during short-term engagements with the portfolio companies, and are compensated according to the value created in the portfolio companies. Other venture capital funds have developed in-house value-add platforms consisting of full-time employees with an operational background who provide support to the portfolio companies, either directly or by organizing meetings with service providers (legal firms, Google for search engine marketing advice, Amazon for cloud storage hints, etc.). The operational support provided to portfolio companies is a key attribute for attracting the best startups to venture capital funds in competitive deals, where the entrepreneur has the luxury of choosing between several funding alternatives.

Interaction between the portfolio companies and its investors is formalized around Board of Directors meetings, where the main investors in the company take a seat and voting rights, and, informally, through weekly meetings to sort out the most urgent decisions for the startup. Board seats taken by investors also guarantee them a vote on important decisions concerning the management of the startup company and thus to protect their investment. For more information on corporate governance in startups, see Chapter 11.

4.2.4   Stage 4: Exiting (or Love Is Not Forever)

The ultimate goal of a venture capital fund is to provide adequate returns to its investors. Therefore, the moment of truth for any venture capitalist is the sale of its portfolio companies. The result of this exit process will determine whether the investors in the fund are satisfied, and hence will continue to support the venture capitalist in its subsequent fund or not. It is important to note the concept of temporary investors. Regardless of the stage at which these funds invest or the strategy they follow, a partnership with VC firms will always have a cut-off date. And this is very much related to their business model and the 'expiry date' of their funds. Because although love seems eternal in those early days, investors will already be thinking about the terms for divorce. And a very profitable divorce, too! Naturally, this will be backed up by a very controversial marriage agreement (the 'Term Sheet', discussed at length in Chapter 9), on a par with the most famous celebrity 'prenup'. Well, actually, they are not really that bad. It is probably the only way in which they can make money for themselves and their investors and, eventually, for you too.

The topic of exits is such an important one in venture capital that one of the key criteria for investing in a startup is whether, if the company is successful, there is a potential exit path, and what the size of such a deal might be (see Chapter 17 for all you need to know about exits). In order to ensure that the venture capital fund will be able to exit a portfolio company when the opportunity arises, the portfolio company's shareholders' agreement includes two specific clauses which will be familiar to any entrepreneur who has raised venture capital money: the 'drag-along' and the 'tag-along'. The drag-along clause ensures that if there is an interesting acquisition offer, the venture capital fund will be able to force the other investors in the company to sell its stake, as typically an acquirer will want to buy 100 per cent of the company. In other words, the venture capital fund will be able to drag other investors in the company into the sale process. The drag-along clause can be subject to certain conditions (valuation targets, time horizon, etc.). The purpose of the tag-along clause is to avoid an investor (and particularly the founder of the company) selling their stake to an acquirer, leaving the venture capital fund out of the deal. In other words, if any investor sells their stake in the company, the venture capital fund must have the right to tag along with the deal with its pro-rata of the company shares. Having said that, regardless of the legal clauses in the shareholders' agreement, a company sale will rarely occur without the agreement of both the entrepreneur and the investors, as the stability of the management team is a key element in the sale process. For more information on term sheets, see Chapter 9.

The main routes for a successful exit are briefly described below:

- **Initial Public Offering (IPO).** Listing in a stock market is considered one of the best possible outcomes for a startup company, as it tends to maximize the exit price. The IPO process requires the startup to be prepared for constant scrutiny from the markets and to present attractive financial statements in the years prior to the listing. In order to prepare for an IPO, many startups raise late-stage financing rounds that will help them to consolidate their financial position and adjust the organization to the challenges of stock markets. Venture capital funds are typically not allowed to sell their own shares in the company at the time of the IPO and hence have to wait until the end of a vesting period of between six and 12 months.
- **Trade sale.** Selling a portfolio company to a bigger company with a strategic interest in the technology, team or market share of the former is another way of maximizing value for a startup. Normally, trade sale processes are led by an independent M&A firm which prepares all the documentation and contacts potential acquirers in order to generate interest and spark an auction process. The valuation of the company will be determined by the strategic interest of the acquirer, the potential synergies, and the level of competition in the process. The chances of a successful trade sale are maximized if the startup has had previous contact or even commercial deals with the potential acquirers.
- **Secondary sale.** A secondary sale consists of selling the stake in the startup to another financial investor. The rationale for this exit process is to bring onboard financial investors with different risk–return objectives and different skill sets. For instance, seed-stage venture capital funds might be good at spotting emerging technologies and helping the entrepreneur to get the right product and team in place, whereas private equity funds might be

good at optimizing the cost structure of companies with a mature product offering. Both types of funds target companies at different stages and, therefore, as a portfolio company matures it might make sense for a venture capital fund to sell its stake to a private equity player that can maximize the valuation in the maturity stage of the company (e.g. Apax Partners buying the stake of financial investors in the Spanish real-estate portal Idealista). Another good reason for selling a company (or a stake in a company) to another financial investor is to generate liquidity in a venture capital fund when the term of the fund is reaching its end and the investors in the fund want to liquidate their portfolio positions. There are investment funds that specialize in secondary deals that provide liquidity to venture capital funds and startup founders. The characteristics of these funds are that they target lower multiples on the invested capital but, thanks to the shorter holding period, they can provide attractive IRR figures to their investors.

- **Share buy-back**. Share buy-back by the entrepreneur or the startup's management team is another exit scenario, which is more common in private equity than in venture capital, the reason being that generally the entrepreneur is not financially capable of buying the shares of the company at the market price (unless the company is not doing well and they are sold at a fire sale price) and hence needs to finance the purchase by borrowing money from a bank. Banks will only lend money to an entrepreneur or management team that has stable cash-flows that guarantee the repayment of the loan, a scenario that is more likely to happen in established companies in stable markets, rather than in young innovative companies in disruptive industries.

- **Write-off**. Losing all or most of the money in an investment is the most likely outcome of an investment in a startup company, as seen in Figure 4.5 above. There are many reasons that can lead to the failure of a startup that result in its liquidation and dissolution. During the liquidation period, some assets of the startup (patents, domain names, etc.) may be sold to third parties, or the whole startup may be sold at a nominal price to another company that is interested in keeping the team and the know-how.

4.3   Who Is Behind These Venture Capital and Private Equity Funds?

As you can see, managing one of these investment companies must be quite difficult. Fund managers are also entrepreneurs, who build their companies from scratch and must go to the market to raise capital with relatively limited experience. Does it sound familiar? As with startups, setting up an investment firm and raising a fund is much more difficult than it might seem at first sight. It's not entirely true that fund managers (i.e. venture capitalists or private equity investors)[12] raise funds without experience,

---

12 In this section, we will refer to 'venture capitalists' although it also applies to 'private equity investors', as both of them are creating and managing a fund.

because it is precisely the experience, or in the case of venture capitalists, the track record of investments that fund of funds investors are looking for. And obviously, the more limited their track record, the more difficult it is to raise the fund. On the other hand, the more successful they are at investing the money, the easier it is for them to raise a subsequent fund. We will see how it works in the following sections.

Typically, venture capitalists are experienced investors (and wealthy – they have to invest a percentage in the fund in order to align interests with the fund investors) with a relevant professional background in the sectors they are targeting for investment, a very extensive network of contacts (from which they receive the deal flow of projects they assess), and with both financial and operational experience. Because apart from managing large amounts of capital and investing and divesting, the partners of the funds like to have a seat on the board of the investees or act as advisors, at least. And they do this not just to control what the company is doing with their money (see Chapter 10 for more information on monitoring). They also get involved with the strategy to help the company to achieve the goals that will bring the business to the next level, e.g. another investment round, international expansion, recruiting talent or the exit. In both PE and VC firms, you will find a team around the partners who are able to add value to the portfolio companies in different ways. This approach varies from firm to firm, with the most hands-on investors being more intrusive whilst, at the same time, being the most helpful in the success of the portfolio. In VC funds, there may be successful entrepreneurs among the partners of the fund. Having the experience of having been through the process of starting up and exiting a company is priceless when it comes to investing in other similar initiatives. Entrepreneurs love to have other entrepreneurs investing in their companies, rather than former bankers or consultants, don't they? In private equity, the profiles are equally diverse, but you tend to find more senior consultants, investment bankers or executives from large companies who have decided to go and work in the equity industry.

4.4   What Does a Fund Look Like? Legal Structure

We can think of a VC fund or a PE fund as a regular business, but with a quite complex or sophisticated structure behind it. Since their activity is specialized and they are subject to a number of tough regulations, there are several essential components that funds need within their structure in order to run properly. Figure 4.6 shows a very simple structure, the GP–LP structure, which has been used widely across the globe for many years. Most funds use this concept, and it can be as simple as this one, or much more complex, depending on how many funds the firm has under management, the geographies in which they are active or the type of activities they are carrying out.

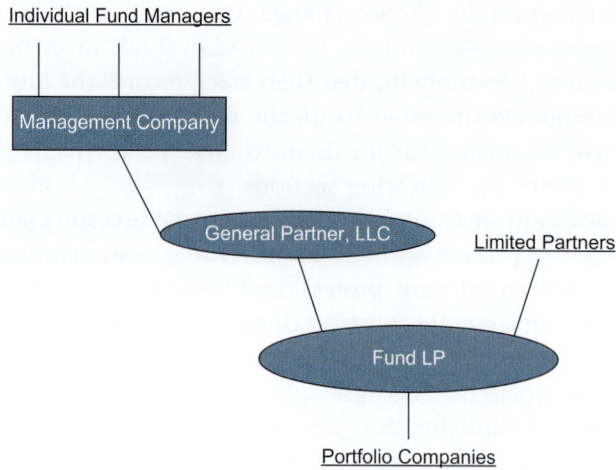

Figure 4.6 Structure chart of a VC fund.

The diagram has three main elements:

- *The Manager*: this is the management company, typically owned by the partners who founded the firm, and which is responsible for raising the funds. This is also the most visible part of the structure, commercially speaking, carrying the 'brand' of the fund. Balderton Capital, Sofinnova or EQT are well-known managers.
- *The General Partner LLC*: owned and controlled by the manager, it is usually set up as a limited partnership and is in charge of making the investment and divestment decisions of the fund.
- *The Fund LP*: is the limited partnership formed with the purpose of investing money. This is where the *Limited Partners* (the investors in the Fund) put their money to be managed by the fund's team.

In the majority of cases, we find only one manager, but there can be as many general partners as funds the manager has raised. Typically, the objective of the manager is to raise several funds to continue its activity, one after the other, or in parallel if they are allowed, ideally when the previous fund is coming to the end of the investment period. This will happen if the fund investors are happy with the performance of the first fund.

As previously mentioned, funds have a limited life-span. The most standard set-up is a ten-year period, with a five-year investment period (to build the portfolio) and another five years to manage the portfolio, make follow-on investments and exit the companies.

4.5   How Do Fund Managers and Fund Investors Make Money?

As in any other industry, understanding the business model and the economics behind all the players in the value chain is a key element for having the full picture and being able to make the right decisions. And this is no different in the case of venture capital funds.

It is true that venture capitalists are highly qualified professionals with pretty nice salaries. But in such a risky game as VC or PE, there must be a special motivation that keeps them engaged and makes them want to share the success of the performance of the fund they're managing. For example, it would hardly be fair if the fund investors in the VC funds that invested in King.com or Rocket Internet got huge returns whilst the partners managing the VC funds failed to benefit from their performance.

Generally speaking, there are two main sources of revenue from the point of view of venture capitalists (the actual 'venture capitalists'): the management fee and the carried interest.

The **management fee** is a periodic payment the manager receives from the fund investors to cover the salaries of the investment team that is working for the fund and other relevant costs, such as travel costs, rent or any other expenses related to the business activity. Typically, the management fee is calculated as a percentage of the total commitments to the fund during the investment period, and as a percentage of the net invested capital (cost of the active investments in the portfolio) after the investment period. The reason for this is that after the investment period the fund manager will have fewer portfolio companies to support, and therefore the resources devoted to fund management will be lower. Let's look at an example:

If a VC firm is managing a €100m fund and receives a 2% annual management fee during the investment period and 1.5% of the net invested capital during the divestment period (both on total commitments in order to simplify the calculations), what would the annual management fee be?

The management company will cash in €2m per year during the first five years (€100 m × 0.02) and €1.5m for the last five years.

That means that the investable amount is not €100m but €82.5m in case the investors do not allow the fund to reinvest the proceeds of the exits.

The management fee is subject to negotiation between the LPs and the fund managers (i.e. the venture capitalists) and is generally between 2.5 per cent and 1.5 per cent of total commitments during the investment period, decreasing during the divestment period when, in theory, the work and the costs associated with managing the portfolio should be lower because there will be fewer companies in the fund as exits materialize. The scale of the management fee depends on the sector, size and 'pedigree' of the fund. If the fund manager is able to raise a subsequent fund once the investment period of the previous fund is over, the management fees from the previous fund plus the management fees of the new one will be accumulated. I guess you can already see where part of the business lies.

Ok, so far so good. Fund managers have attractive salaries, money to pay the team, and perhaps even nice offices in the centre of the city. But given that raising a fund is quite difficult (fund investors are very selective) and fund managers are themselves investing a significant percentage in the fund they are raising (typically between 1–5%), there must be something else going on. Indeed, the carrot that keeps the investment team motivated throughout the life of the fund is the **carried interest**. This remuneration is defined as a percentage of the returns of the fund, which is used by the investors in the fund to incentivize the managers of the fund to maximize the returns. The typical split is the famous 80/20. That means that the fund manager is entitled to receive 20 per cent of the returns of the fund, and the LPs the remaining 80 per cent. But the beauty of it is that the fund manager will not have access to this carry until they are able to return the initial commitments to the fund investors plus a 'hurdle' (a minimum return the LPs expect from their investment) which could range from between 6 and 8 per cent per year. At this point, you can see that if the fund performs well, the managers and the investment team will earn much more than a nice salary. The only thing they need to do, apart from being sharp investors, is wait until they have returned all commitments plus the hurdle, which typically happens towards the end of the fund, some ten years later.

Let's Practise: Case Study

SPACE RETURNS (Part I)

Mery, John and Mikel are the founders and managing partners of the venture capital firm Space Returns. The three partners come from different backgrounds. Mery and John are both successful entrepreneurs who managed to sell their startups and make some business angel investments before setting up the fund. Mikel, on the other hand, was a top executive in one of the biggest technology companies in the USA, and has been a co-investor with Mery and John as a business angel in several companies. They got along well and decided to launch their own fund.

The firm was founded back in 2011, and in 2012 they raised their first fund, Space I, a €50m fund to invest in early-stage technology startups with a pan-European approach. After five years, they are drawing the investment period of the first fund to a close, having invested in twenty companies and already followed on in some of them. The limited partners are very happy, because the portfolio companies look promising and one of the companies has been already acquired with a good return. Over the next five years, they will focus on continuing to invest in the existing portfolio and exiting the companies. The initial plan was to invest one-third of the fund in initial tickets, with two-thirds reserved for follow-ons, and they are sticking to that plan. After five years, they have invested 65 per cent of the capital.

The economics of this first fund were quite standard, involving a 2.5 per cent annual management fee for the fund manager during the investment period, and 1.75 per cent flat fee for the rest of the life of the fund. Also, the fund managers will get 20 per cent carried interest once a hurdle of 6 per cent has been obtained if they are able to achieve positive returns.

Since the first fund is no longer investing in new companies, Space Returns is contacting a number of existing and new investors to raise its second fund, Space II. Space II will have a fund of €80m, with the same strategic and economic objectives as Space I, but with slightly increased ticket sizes to invest and more resources for follow-ons in order to back the winners all the way to the exit.

Questions for Discussion

1. What is the size of the management fee (in euros) that the team was able to cash in during the investment period of the first fund?
2. If the Space Return team is successful in raising its second fund right after the investment period of the first fund comes to a close, what would the accumulated management fee received by the management company be in 2020?
3. Suppose that in 2022 Space I is completely divested and total returns are €100m. Will the team receive any carry? If so, how much?

4.6   Trends in European Venture Capital

According to the data published by Invest Europe[13] (formerly known as European Venture Capital Association, EVCA), the European venture capital industry raised €5.3bn in new funds in 2015 (+8% YoY), invested €3.8bn in startup companies (+6% YoY), and received €2.1bn from divestments (+10% YoY). The relationship between the three metrics lies in the fact that funds raised in a specific year will typically be invested over the following five years (investment period of the fund), and divestments usually happen in the five years following the investment period.

4.6.1   Fundraising

By looking at the historical fundraising data in the 2007–15 period illustrated in Figure 4.7, we can see a clear correlation with the economic cycle. A severe correction took place from 2008 until 2010 following the global financial crisis, but fundraising activity in Europe has steadily picked up in recent years. Total funds raised in 2015 jumped 66 per cent above the record low in 2010, but were still 36 per cent lower than the 2007 figure.

A detailed analysis of the investors in venture capital funds in the 2007–15 period shown in Figure 4.8 reveals two related trends: on the one hand, the

13 Invest Europe (2016).

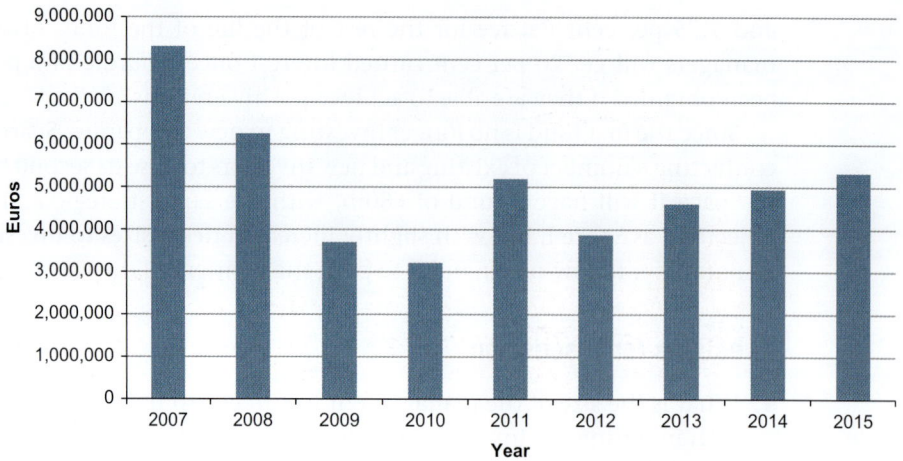

Figure 4.7 Fundraising volumes by European VC funds.
Source: Invest Europe (2016)

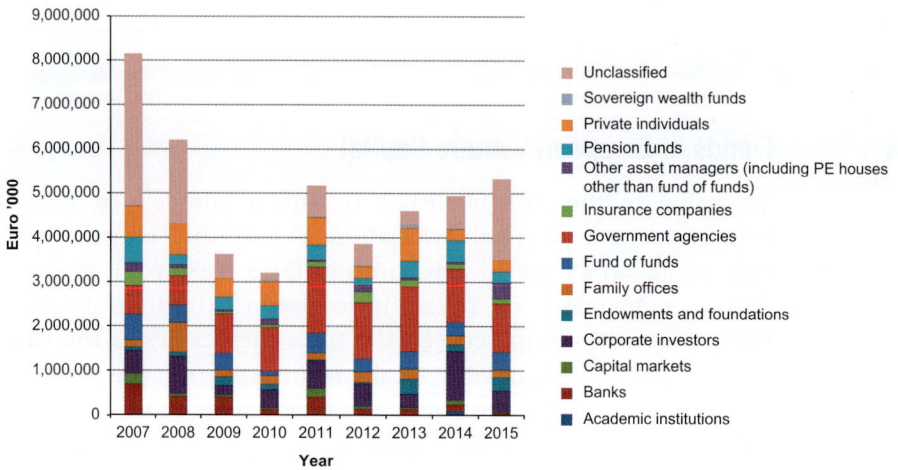

Figure 4.8 Investors in European VC funds.
Source: Invest Europe (2016)

amounts invested by private banks in venture capital funds has decreased dramatically following the global financial crisis. Private banks allocated €679m to venture capital funds in 2007, or 8.3 per cent of total funds raised, but only €43m in 2015, or a mere 0.8 per cent of total funds raised (although the three-year average is €101m or 2 per cent of total funds raised). On the other hand, the gap in venture capital fundraising has been, to a great degree, closed by government agencies: whereas such public institutions allocated €646m or 7.9 per cent of total funds raised in 2007, the figure jumped to €1.1bn or 20.7 per cent of total

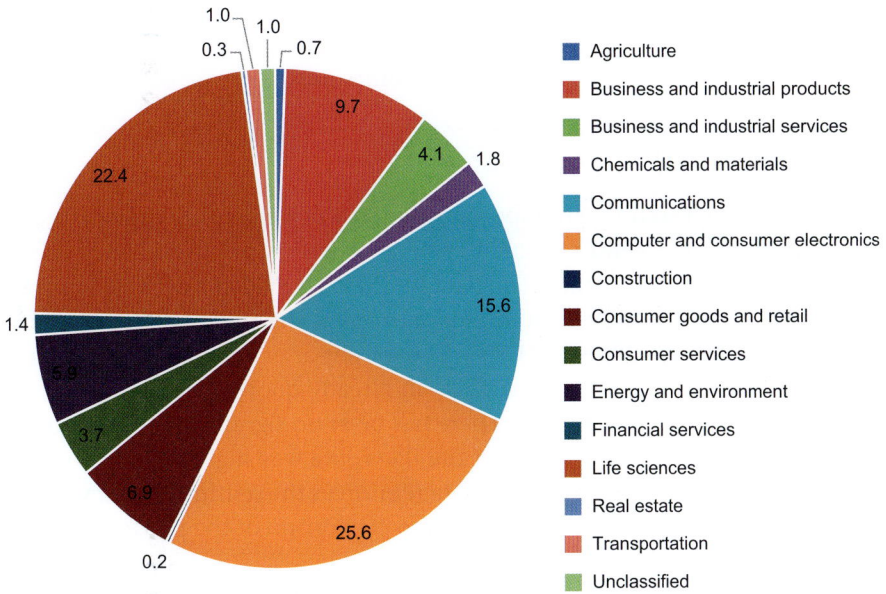

Figure 4.9 Venture capital investments by sector as percentage (2015).
Source: Invest Europe (2016)

funds raised in 2015 (the three-year average amounted to €1.3bn or 26 per cent of total funds raised). Public funding is hence a primary pillar in the venture capital industry. Institutions such as the European Investment Fund at a pan-European level, or local institutions in the European countries (e.g. British Business Bank in the UK or Instituto de Crédito Oficial in Spain) play a key role in the development of the venture capital industry and have become the largest single investors in the asset class.

4.6.2   Investments

The sectors preferred by venture capital investors are clearly shown in the data provided in Figure 4.9. In 2015, venture capital investments in European start-ups in the communications and computer and consumer electronics sectors (all subsectors of the ICT industry) represented 41.1 per cent of total investments, followed by the life sciences sector with 22.4 per cent of total investments. This is not radically different from the sector preferences back in 2007, when ICT investments represented 36.7 per cent of the total and life sciences 24.8 per cent. One interesting trend is the decline in the relative weight of energy and environment investments (or cleantech) from 10 per cent of total investments in 2007 to 5.9 per cent in 2015.

Venture capitalists select target sectors based on the ability of those sectors to provide the returns required by the venture capital model. Hence, sectors with large market size, exponential growth and scalable business models that optimize the use of capital are preferred by venture capitalists that target 10× returns in 5–10 years for their portfolio companies.

4.6.3   Divestment

The exit route is an important dimension for venture capitalists as it marks the end of the venture capital cycle and determines the financial returns of their portfolio companies. The data for 2015, provided by Invest Europe, shows that the most likely exit route for startups is the trade sale (22.4%), followed very closely by write-offs (21.9%). The sought-after IPO route (including sale of shares in the IPO or sale of shares of an already quoted company) barely represented 7 per cent of total exits. There has been no significant changes in these percentages since 2007, although the IPO route was slightly more popular in years of bullish stock markets. The data reinforces the sentiment that venture capital is a highly risky business, with a large proportion of the portfolio companies resulting in a write-off.

4.6.4   European Venture Capital Activity in the Global Context

A commonly accepted metric when comparing venture capital activity across countries or regions is to measure invested volumes in relation to gross domestic product (GDP), a measure of the size of a particular economy. In relation to European GDP, investment by European venture capital funds represented 0.025 per cent of total GDP according to the OECD,[14] with significant differences between countries as shown in Figure 4.10.

The European venture capital ecosystem still has a long way to go when compared to two of the most developed venture capital ecosystems: the USA and Israel. According to the OECD, the USA saw US$59.7bn invested in startups in 2015, or roughly 0.4 per cent of its GDP, more than ten times the European figures. Israel saw US$1.2bn invested in startups in the same year, a remarkable figure given the size of the country and almost 0.35 per cent of its GDP. Figure 4.11 shows the percentage of VC investment relative to GDP in selected countries.

4.6.5   Qualitative Trends. Signs for a Brighter Future

Despite lagging far behind the USA and Israel, and the hiccups of the macroeconomic environment in recent years, the European venture capital landscape has made great progress in recent years, alongside the development of the tech ecosystem. A few of the notable trends contributing to the consolidation of the venture capital landscape in Europe are:

14 OECD (2015).

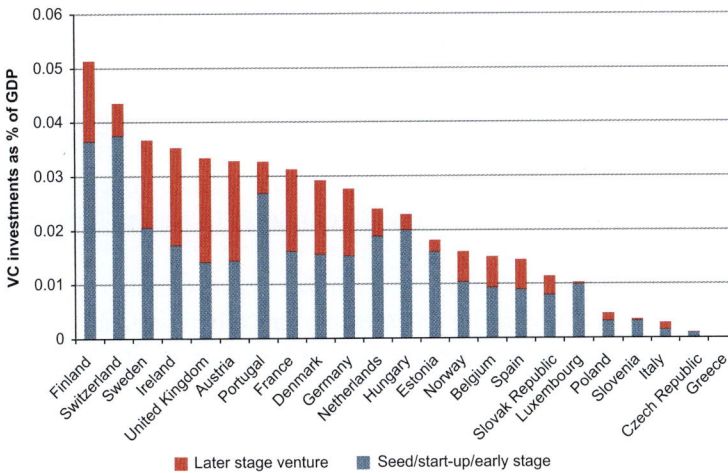

Figure 4.10 Venture capital investments as percentage of GDP in European countries.
Source: OECD (2015)

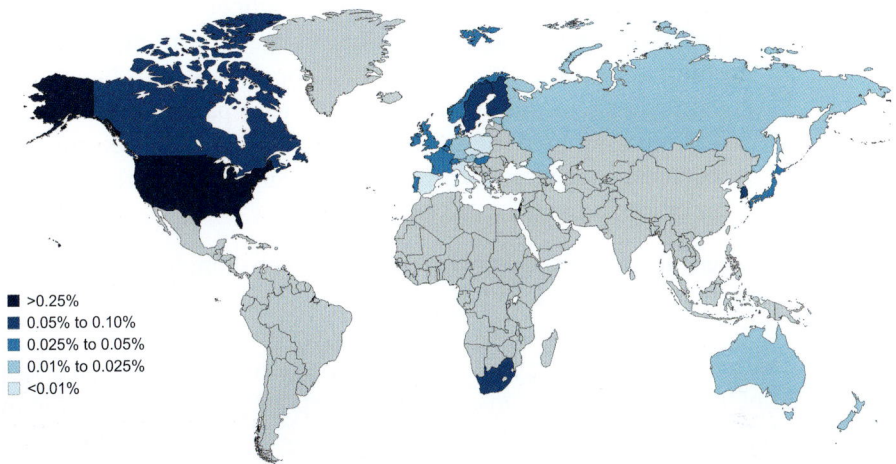

Figure 4.11 Venture capital investment as percentage of GDP in the world.
Source: OECD (2015)

- The emergence of specialized investors. In addition to generalist venture capital funds with a wide investment focus, there are an increasing number of venture capital funds that target very specific industries, backed by the operational and entrepreneurial experience of their partners. Examples of this type of funds are OpenOcean in Finland (community-driven software, software-as-a-service) and Notion Capital in the UK (software-as-a-service).

- The emergence of new teams. Either spin-outs from existing venture capital teams, successful entrepreneurs or experienced business angels. This new blood is highly beneficial to the ecosystem, as it brings new investment thesis combined with extensive operational and financial experience. Examples of this new wave of funds include BlueYard in Germany (spin-out from EarlyBird Ventures), Daphni in France (spin-out from Elaia Ventures) and Samaipata Ventures in Spain (created by the co-founder of La Nevera Roja, a food delivery startup).
- Increased activity in the periphery hubs. The decreasing costs of creating a startup (particularly in the ICT industry) and the abundance of strong talent throughout Europe has led to the blossoming of innovation hubs in periphery countries and the emergence of venture capital activity in those hubs. For example, Lisbon has made it to the front page of the specialized media thanks to its vibrant yet emerging startup ecosystem, with strong links to London and several promising startups with Portuguese co-founders such as Uniplaces, Farfetch and Seedrs.
- The rise of European 'unicorns'. The so-called unicorns are startups whose valuation has reached US$1bn. Until recently, these creatures were thought only to inhabit the sunny prairies of the Silicon Valley, but more and more unicorns have been spotted in Europe of late. According to data published by Atomico and Slush,[15] the number of European unicorns has gone from one in 2005 (Skype), to no fewer than 37 in 2016 (companies such as Deliveroo, Unity and Mimecast joined the club that year). The data supports the argument that global technology leaders can be built in Europe given the right combination of ambition, growth capital and talent.

The venture capital industry is a thrilling yet challenging business. The beauty of supporting the next breed of innovative companies contrasts with the difficult decisions that the venture capital managers face in their day-to-day interactions with the portfolio companies, as a large percentage of them will disappear or will not live up to expectations. Yet the rewards are juicy for those who make it. The heterogeneity of fund returns increases the selectivity of the investors in venture capital funds: only those venture capitalists that generate exceptional returns for their investors are able to stay in the business for a long time.

Even though the European venture capital industry still lags behind more developed regions (namely, the USA and Israel), the progress made in recent years is considerable and there are strong indications that European startups will be able to generate the magnitude of returns that the industry requires, closing the virtuous circle of venture capital and thus attracting more private money to the asset class.

15 Atomico and Slush (2016).

KEY TAKEAWAYS

- Venture capital and private equity are similar sources of equity financing and share some important characteristics, but it is the type of companies they're investing in, the sector and the investment stage that determine the difference between the two funding types. Corporates are increasingly providing equity financing for strategic startups. Entrepreneurs need to be aware of the different objectives of equity financing providers to find a good match.
- Equity investors are temporary investors and they generate their returns by exiting the companies they invest in within a defined time frame, most of the time selling the entire business. Entrepreneurs relying on venture capital funds should be ready to sell their businesses.
- Within VC and PE firms we find a diverse pool of professionals with both operational and investment experience. They can also be considered entrepreneurs, as they need to build their own firm and raise capital from other investors, in the same way as entrepreneurs running their own startups.
- The cycle of a venture capital fund is: fundraising; investing in a portfolio of startup companies; supporting the development of the portfolio companies; and finally exiting the companies and returning the money to the initial investors. The economics of equity funds have two main elements; the management fee and the carried interest.
- A successful venture capital strategy must take into account not only the individual selection of startup companies but also the allocation of capital between the portfolio companies and throughout the follow-on rounds.
- Supporting the portfolio companies requires venture capital firms to build operational expertise, either through its in-house team or via external collaborators. This operational support is a powerful selling point for attracting the best entrepreneurs to the fund in competitive deals.
- The most likely outcome for a given portfolio company is failure – successful exits are the exception. On the whole, venture capital involves managing difficult situations in portfolio companies, and from time to time there will be a successful exit.
- Venture capital investments as a percentage of GDP in Europe is roughly one order of magnitude below the leading ecosystems of the USA and Israel. Despite lagging behind the more developed markets, European venture capital is progressing well, although with strong public intervention, which became more intense following the global financial crisis in 2008.

END OF CHAPTER QUESTIONS

1. What are the main differences between VC and PE funds?
2. What is the typical duration of a fund?
3. What is the typical range for management fees in a fund? And the carried interest?

4. How much carry would a fund manager get in normal circumstances if they are able to return 2.5 × a €100m fund?
5. How can you mitigate the risk of having a corporate investor in your company?
6. What are the different types of exit that an equity investor is looking for when selling your company?
7. Why is it so important to diversify the portfolio of a VC fund?
8. What would be the minimum number of portfolio companies you would hold in a portfolio based on the data provided by the EIF report of exits?
9. Explain the concept of 'backing the winners'.
10. You are given the opportunity to invest in a venture capital fund two weeks after the collapse of Lehman Brothers in September 2008. What would your decision be, and why?

FURTHER READING

Metrick, A. (2007). *Venture Capital and the Finance of Innovation*. Wiley.
Gompers, P. and Lerner, J. (2004). *The Venture Capital Cycle*. The MIT Press.
Meyer, T. and Mathonet, P.-Y. (2005). *Beyond the J Curve: Managing a Portfolio of Venture Capital and Private Equity Funds*. Wiley.

REFERENCES

Atomico and Slush (2016). The State of European Tech 2016 Edition. www.atomico.com
Baum, J. A. and Silverman, B. S. (2004). Picking winners or building them? Alliance, intellectual, and human capital as selection criteria in venture financing and performance of biotechnology startups. *Journal of Business Venturing*, 19(3), 411–436.
Cambridge Associates (2017). Global ex US PE/VC Benchmark Commentary Q3 2017. www.cambridgeassociates.com
J. Cassidy (2003) *Dot.con: How America Lost its Mind and Money in the Internet Era*. Harper Perennial.
Chesbrough, H. W. (2006). *Open Innovation: The New Imperative for Creating and Profiting from Technology*. Harvard Business Press.
Chesbrough, H. and Crowther, A. K. (2006). Beyond high tech: early adopters of open innovation in other industries. *R&D Management*, 36(3), 229–236.
Elton, E. J., Gruber, M. J., Brown, S. J. and Goetzmann, W. N. (2009). *Modern Portfolio Theory and Investment Analysis*. John Wiley & Sons.
European Investment Fund (2017). The European venture capital landscape: an EIF perspective. Volume III: Liquidity events and returns of EIF-backed VC investments. www.eif.org

Invest Europe (2016). 2015 European Private Equity Activity. www.investeurope.eu

Markowitz, H. M. (1991). Foundations of portfolio theory. *Journal of Finance*, 46(2), 469–477.

OECD (2015). Entrepreneurship at a Glance 2015. www.oecd-ilibrary.org

Sharpe, W. F. (1964). Capital asset prices: A theory of market equilibrium under conditions of risk. *Journal of Finance*, 19(3), 425–442.

Vanhaverbeke, W., Van de Vrande, V. and Chesbrough, H. (2008). Understanding the advantages of open innovation practices in corporate venturing in terms of real options. *Creativity and Innovation Management*, 17(4), 251–258.

Let's Practise: Case Study

SPACE RETURNS (Part II)

Space Returns, the venture capital firm founded by Mery, John and Mikel, is in the process of preparing the slide deck for the roadshow of the new fund, with a target fund size of €60m, slightly above the size of the first fund. Since fundraising is a time-consuming process, the partners have contacted an external consultant (i.e. you) to prepare parts of the deck. Specifically, the partners want you to model the exit perspectives of the fund under two different portfolio models, since there are differences between the existing partners on how to proceed with the second fund:

1. The first portfolio strategy is to invest the fund equally in 20 portfolio companies at the seed stage, to make sure there is sufficient diversification. No money will be reserved for follow-on rounds.
2. The second strategy will be more conservative in terms of follow-on reserves. Only one-third of the fund will be invested in the initial seed rounds across

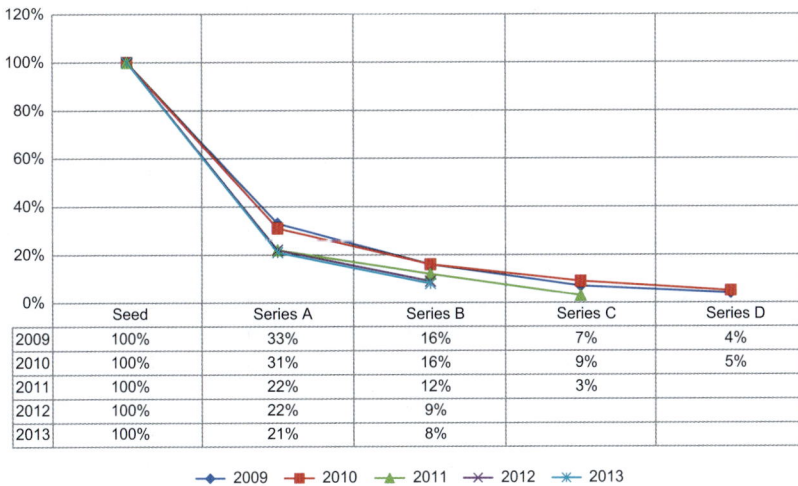

	Seed	Series A	Series B	Series C	Series D
2009	100%	33%	16%	7%	4%
2010	100%	31%	16%	9%	5%
2011	100%	22%	12%	3%	
2012	100%	22%	9%		
2013	100%	21%	8%		

Figure 4.12 Graduation rates for European startups.
Source: Atomico and Slush, The State of European Tech (2016 Edition)

the same number of companies. The remaining two-thirds will be allocated to the follow-on rounds (series A). Not all the seed investments will make it to series A, as Figure 4.12 shows.

Questions for Discussion

What would your advice be to the partners regarding the portfolio model? You will need to make a few assumptions in order to simplify the calculations:

1. all the committed capital from limited partners will be invested in portfolio companies.
2. exit multiples for the portfolio companies are those seen in Figure 4.5
3. seed companies that do not qualify for series A will end up generating the lower exit multiples.
4. initial investments are made on average in the middle of the investment period (year 3), follow-on rounds, if any, are made right after the end of the investment period (year 6), and exits take place in year 10.
   You can structure your answer in three steps:

- Calculate the expected fund return as an absolute figure and as a multiple of committed capital.
- Calculate the expected IRR.
- Compare the expected returns of the two scenarios with other asset classes.

CHAPTER 5

PUBLIC SOURCES OF FUNDING

ISIDRO LASO

Startup Europe, European Commission

This chapter considers the alternative sources of public support and financing available to entrepreneurs both in Europe and worldwide.[1] The European Commission and many EU countries are promoting support programmes, including Startup Europe to develop the ecosystem as well as many financial instruments, to incentivize and support a growing entrepreneurial ecosystem. Does it make sense? And if so, do entrepreneurs know what is available and how to get access to the different sources of public support and financing?

VIEW FROM THE MEDIA

FINANCIAL TIMES   FT

Central and eastern Europe start-ups look beyond EU for finance

Many ventures are dependent more on Brussels than private investors

MAY 12, 2016 BY ANDREW MACDOWALL

From the Estonian software behind Skype through to the Croatian electric supercar manufacturer Rimac Automobili, central and eastern Europe has produced dozens of globally successful start-ups in the past three decades. Leveraging a pool of tech-savvy graduates as well as low costs and geographical location, the region's start-ups have also benefited from generous Brussels financing as the EU has spread eastward. However, developing the scarce supply of private investment in start-ups is a rising priority. A traditional

---

1 The information and views set out in this publication are those of the author(s) and do not reflect the official opinion of the Commission. The Commission does not guarantee the accuracy of the data included in this study. Neither the Commission nor any person acting on the Commission's behalf may be held responsible for the use which may be made of the information contained therein.

emphasis on technical subjects in the education system has made the region particularly fertile ground for start-ups in the field of information and communications technology (ICT). Skype, which provides online chat and video call services, is the most famous example. It was developed by Estonian engineers, backed by Scandinavian entrepreneurs and launched in 2003. ... But many start-ups in the region are highly dependent on various EU funds to develop, whether in partnership with private investors or not. The amounts available across Europe are substantial: In the period from 2014 to 2020, the European Structural and Investment (ESI) Funds are expected to invest €121bn in research and innovation, ICT and support to small and medium sized business across the EU. ... EU funds, then, are an essential component of the start-up environment in central and eastern Europe, supplemented in some cases by government financing. Daniel Tomov, founder of Eleven, an accelerator venture fund in Sofia, says that the involvement of EU agencies has shared welcome experience, helping to reduce the risks involved in early-stage investment and encouraging private investors to join subsequent rounds of fundraising.

Others, though, question the effectiveness of Brussels funding for requiring large amounts of paperwork, and for lacking pressure on recipients to deliver commercial returns. ... Michal Kordaczuk at law firm Dentons, who works with Polish start-ups, says the vast majority of venture capital in the country is backed by the EU or the government's Krajowy Fundusz Kapitalowy, a fund of funds. 'It turns out that start-ups that are taking public or EU money do not have to succeed and they are not that motivated to succeed,' he says. ...

www.ft.com/content/01d8e3ca-0ad5-11e6-b0f1-61f222853ff3

LEARNING OBJECTIVES

After reading this chapter you will be able to:

- Understand which public support and financing programmes are better adapted to the entrepreneur's needs.
- Recognize the main sources of public support and financing available for entrepreneurs in Europe.
- Differentiate between the most innovative ways of providing public financial support to startups.

Where Are We Going Next?

This chapter will first describe the value of public support programmes, the reason for them and the steps that need to be followed to implement them. Some of the most complete European public–private support programmes are described in Appendix 1, namely Startup Delta in the Netherlands, La French Tech, Germany's High Tech GranderFunds and BPIFrance. You will also find cases that have a focus on financing, i.e. Finland's Tekes, Startup Singapore, Spain's CDTI and Red.es, and UK Tech City, in the final section of this chapter.

In addition, you will find a case study of a person possibly like you who wants to set up his own innovative business and how public support programmes can accompany the entrepreneur along its journey.

The chapter next moves to the specific sources of public funding for startups, namely five: (1) grants; (2) loans; (3) guarantees; (4) limited partner; and (5) fund of funds. Details for each source and examples in some countries are provided. The chapter finishes with a section describing the three pillars that the entrepreneur will find in most public support programmes for startups: (1) actions to encourage a bottom-up movement with a strong brand; (2) support activities to strengthen the connectedness and quality of the ecosystem; and (3) funding activities – either direct or indirect.

VOICE OF THE EXPERT: Prince Constantijn van Oranje Nassau (the Netherlands)

Constantijn van Oranje Nassau is special envoy Startup Delta and co-founder and chairman of Startup Fest Europe.

Where do you see the competitive advantage of startups from Europe?
Europe is diverse and the world is diverse. If you manage to market your product in Europe you have a big chance of success in the rest of the world.

What is your advice for (aspiring) entrepreneurs?
Take good advisors on board. focus on market analysis and validation of product market fit. Don't get hung up on the product, technology or specific solution. Focus, focus, focus. Go deep first, capture a market and internationalize before widening the proposition. Keep experimenting and validating through analysing user data.

5.1 The Value of Public Support Programmes

Public support programmes can be useful for entrepreneurs who want to be part of a large entrepreneurial community and to contribute to the creation of a high-quality ecosystem within which they can flourish. First, public support programmes enable entrepreneurs to benefit from networks that include key players, such as investors, at both a local and international level. At the same time, entrepreneurs may also benefit from the financial support that public administrations provide directly or by means of their links with professional investors. Finally, public support programmes are excellent sources of information. They can provide entrepreneurs with useful data to help them assess future strategic actions. Certainly, the effectiveness of public financial support increases when it is not provided in isolation, but within an entrepreneurial community. The last section of the chapter explains in detail the three pillars of a well-designed public support programme for startups.

One of the first steps in the set-up of a support programme provided by a public government is to identify well-connected entrepreneurs or investors who can provide smart money into the ecosystem. Once the key players have been identified, a series of meetings are needed to learn the entrepreneurs' requirements for increasing the amount of smart money available in the ecosystem. The amount will always be limited by the capacity of the investors to provide smart money but also by the amount of high-quality investment opportunities that the ecosystem can generate. Notwithstanding the amount of money that these investors can afford to invest, it is counterproductive to start pumping public money into the ecosystem even if some entrepreneurs consider that there is not enough money. When too much liquidity is available then bad projects get financed and also valuations get inflated. This might end up in money wasted and a potential 'bubble' with all its negative effects for investors, entrepreneurs and the economy in general.

The steps taken to assess the effectiveness of the ecosystem include specific actions to stimulate investment readiness of the entrepreneurs (demand side) and actions to develop the supply side of smart money into the ecosystem. Most public support activity in the area of funding has traditionally been focused on the supply side (pumping public money). Supply side activities are usually provided in combination with mentoring and coaching activities. Supply side activities will not be effective if they are not complemented with actions on the demand side (developing a well connected ecosystem).

5.2   Different Schemes to Provide Public–Private Support

There are a number of public support programmes for startups in many regions across the world, as we will see in this chapter. In most cases, these programmes combine three pillars: (1) actions to encourage a bottom-up movement with a strong brand; (2) support activities to strengthen the connectedness and quality of the ecosystem; and (3) funding activities – either direct or indirect.

The connectedness support activity usually includes face-to-face programmes to increase serendipity between the people that belong to a given ecosystem and programmes to build bridges between them and other relevant people from other ecosystems. Startup Europe is a European Commission initiative that provides precisely connectedness support activities between the EU's local ecosystems and with other parts of the world. Startup Europe is also responsible for bringing stronger coherence to other EU activities that support the ecosystem. The EU uses part of the Horizon 2020 budget (which includes Startup Europe), the Cosme programme, the European Investment Fund and Cohesion Funds to provide financial support to startups throughout their life cycle (although mainly in their early and growth stages).[2] While the total amount is difficult to calculate due to the wide dispersion of the instruments and the participation of many different European, national and local government bodies, it is certain to be a big share of the total funding available for startups in the EU. India has also launched a big startup programme called Startup India, which includes both connectedness activities for the ecosystem and financial support. Another example is the government of Canada (through Canada Business) which provides assistance and grants.

We will now take a closer look at Startup Europe, an international support programme launched by the European Commission in 2010, and we will then consider two national cases (Spain and UK) that take two distinct approaches. While the former focuses on financial support, the latter focuses on taxation benefits.

5.2.1 Startup Europe (SUE)

Startup Europe's mission is to build a startup continent by increasing the connectedness between the players of the European local hubs: 'A startup continent connecting pools of talent.' A startup continent where the density of connections among the players will significantly increase the business opportunities across borders to find investors, customers or partners anywhere in Europe.[3]

Startup Europe (SUE) was launched in November 2010 and it is now seen as a significant player, contributing substantially to the creation of the Digital Single Market for startups and scale-ups. Since its launch, SUE has set out to identify and network clusters of startups across Europe, focusing on branding and providing visible branding for European startups. SUE connects hundreds of startups with financial investors through pitching sessions. It also contributed to the dissemination of the Startup manifesto first of all, and, later, the ScaleUp manifesto. SUE also includes activities that support the international expansion of startups with programmes such as 'SUE comes to Silicon Valley', then to India, Africa and Latin America. SUE sponsored research into startup, scale-ups and cluster development through collaborations with the JRC-IPTS, and Nesta to collect evidence and big data to provide adequate macroeconomic analysis based on real data using big data technologies.

In 2014, SUE launched two flagship initiatives as a response to the Startup manifesto: the Startup Europe partnership (a forum of corporates and startups) and the European Digital Forum (for policymakers). The initial years of SUE focused primarily on creating a movement and developing a strong brand. Later, SUE launched its first call for proposals for the networking of ecosystems of startups, which in 2015 led to the creation of five SUE projects connecting sixteen ecosystems, through a one-stop-shop European platform.

2 See ec.europa.eu/programmes/horizon2020/en/area/smes
3 For more information, see startupeuropeclub.eu/about-us/

SUE has now reached maturity, which means that many of its activities, such as SUE projects and international outreach activities, can become self-sustaining, under the continued political support of the European Commission.

SUE is delivering on its promise, succeeding in creating a vibrant, networked community of startup ecosystems in the EU (European Commission 2017). The next challenge is to export the European ecosystem to the rest of the world, creating two-way bridges with relevant world ecosystems and contributing to the soft landing of European startups in other markets. Target world ecosystems are Silicon Valley (Startup Europe Comes to Silicon Valley initiative), India (Startup Europe India Summit), Africa (Startup Europe Comes to Africa initiative in 2018), Latin America, Eastern European Partnership and China.

SUE will explore ways of involving startups in policy experimentation through actions to mobilize capital and to introduce regulatory sandboxes to enable the scaling up of startups in the early stages. These types of initiatives will leverage the work carried out by Unicorn Forum and Founders Forum for the exploration of a new Startup Single Market, built as a simple, digital, stand-alone, fully fledged corporate legal environment. SUE will forge closer links with corporates, promoting exit via stock exchanges and other instruments. SUE will also contribute to exploiting innovation procurement in the wider policy context of obtaining a first reliable customer for startups and bringing innovation to national public governments.

5.2.2   Example: Spain

While Spain's government provides a plethora of public funding, there is little support in terms of improving the connectedness of Spain's entrepreneurial ecosystem; connectedness both within the Spanish ecosystem itself and connectedness with other parts of the EU and the world. The Spanish government provides financial support in three different forms: (1) non-refundable grants; (2) co-investment with private investors; and (3) grants to hire tech staff. Spain's government programmes are: SME grant for a business plan, Neotec programme providing non-refundable grants to early-stage startups (less than four years old) for the development of their business; co-investment along with private investors by Centro de Desarrollo Tecnologico e Industria (CDTI) organism; and the Emplea programme's grants to hire tech specialists.

While there is no specific programme to strengthen the quality of the ecosystem yet, several organizations (Red.es and CDTI)[4] are stepping up their efforts to work with the ecosystem and provide business assistance.

4 See www.red.es/redes/ respectively. rio.jrc.ec.europa.eu/en/organisations/centre-develop ment-industrial-technology-cdti

5.2.3 Example: Tech City UK. Taxation Benefits: EIS-SEIS

The UK has provided one of the first public–private support programmes with strong branding (Tech City UK), which offers many activities to increase connectedness as well as financial support in the form of taxation benefits, rather than providing funds. The two main taxation schemes we will look at are the Seed Enterprise Investment Scheme (SEIS) and the Enterprise Investment Scheme (EIS).[5] Both schemes look to help smaller, higher-risk companies raise finance by offering tax relief to investors who purchase shares in a company.

The SEIS is specifically designed to support startups in their early stages as reflected in the eligibility criteria: £150,000 maximum amount able to raise; two years' trading history; 25 employees; £200,000 in gross assets.

The EIS is, however, designed to help startups that are already in the growth phase. Its eligibility criteria are: £5 million maximum amount able to raise per annum; must be an unquoted company; 250 employees; £15 million in gross assets.

For both schemes, the company needs to meet HMRC qualifying criteria. For example, property management companies do not qualify.

The schemes are designed to encourage investors to invest in UK companies that may be deemed high risk. The EIS and SEIS seek to remove some of the risk when investing in SMEs by giving investors tax relief of 30 per cent (EIS) or 50 per cent (SEIS) and also exempting them from corporate gains tax if they do not sell within three years.

These schemes have successfully targeted a key barrier to growth, which is access to finance. These schemes also remove some of the risk of investing by providing the investor with attractive tax breaks to compensate for the risks they are taking. The schemes also allow the founders to keep control of their companies, as the scheme restricts the equity in the company. They also restrict how the funding is spent, thus ensuring the funding is directly spent on investing in the company's growth.

5.3 Alternatives for Public Funding for Startups

There are several ways by which public authorities provide funding for startups as the third pillar of their public support programmes (Bruegel 2016). They are: (1) grants; (2) loans; (3) guarantees; (4) limited partner; and (5) fund of funds. Public support programmes for startups usually include a mix of these five different ways of injecting funds into the ecosystem. They should always be thought of as complementary mechanisms for developing a healthy and dynamic ecosystem for entrepreneurs to access capital, mainly from private investors. The last section of the chapter explains in details the three pillars of a well-designed public support programme for startups.

---

5 See www.gov.uk/topic/business-tax/investment-schemes

Tekes (Finland)

Tekes is a publically funded body which supports research, development and innovation in Finland. Although Tekes is publically funded, the body is completely impartial and will only fund companies that its advisors thinks are viable.

All viable companies are given commercial and financial support, and, in some cases, only commercial advice if required.

Tekes will only fund at the early stage and during growth stages. At the early stage, Tekes will provide a maximum grant of €50,000. In the growth stage, the company will offer a non-collateral loan and a maximum of €250,000 will be invested, alongside a private sector funder providing at least the same amount.

The financial support given to each company is detailed online for transparency.

Why is it different?

There is no political bias in the support given to companies. If the idea is good, then funding and commercial support will be given.

Tekes provides commercial support with all funding, and will provide this support even if funding isn't awarded. The advice the companies receive helps to improve the quality of entrepreneurs and in Finland there is a perception that a startup that hasn't been through Tekes is not a 'good' startup.

Tekes has had a direct impact on innovation growth in Finland, increasing both growth and the globalization of Finnish companies.

Tekes has also helped to build international networks and cooperation and expand the customer network for Finnish companies.

Why is it efficient for entrepreneurs?

Lacking political influence, Tekes is able to fund companies on merit rather than through any political bias.

By combining financial support with commercial advice, Tekes has been able to improve the success of the startups it supports.

As Tekes is ultimately a government body, international connections are easier to make through diplomatic channels.

Who have they helped?

- Nokia.
- SuperCell.
- Rovio.
- Applifier.
- Confidex.
- Rightware.
- Transfluent.
- ZenRobotics.

5.4   Grants

Grants are usually used by governments in the early stages of development of the business. They are typically part of a wider support programme that includes mentoring and coaching. There are essentially two types of grants, depending on the level of convertibility of the grant.

The first type of grant is direct funds provided by public authorities as non-refundable grants. The most sensitive part of this mechanism is the selection of the beneficiaries. If the beneficiaries of these grants are cherry picked by the public authorities themselves, with the support of experts, the entrepreneur will need to understand the reasons of the experts for recommending one beneficiary over another. Another more effective way of providing non-refundable grants is by providing the grant to entrepreneurs who have already been able to get funding from a private investor, as a pop-up, or addition, to the money received by the private investor. In the latter case, the selection process has already been undertaken by a private investor who is clearly motivated to identify the entre-preneurs with the highest potential to become successful. In this case, it is essential that the private investment is not conditional on receiving the non-refundable grant. Otherwise, the public grants might act to distort the ecosystem and encourage investments that do not make sense from an economic perspec-tive. If the government decides to make direct investments into areas where there are no interested investors in the ecosystem, it is advisable to work first to invest time in building the ecosystem.[6] Examples of this kind of grants are the SME instrument of the European Commission,[7] the Neotec programme to sup-port early-stage startups created by the CDTI in Spain[8] and the Investments for the Future Programme for startups in an incubator in France.[9] Usually, the more technologically advanced the business, the greater the chance of receiving this type of non-refundable grant.

The second type of grant involves the provision of funds as convertible grants. In this case, if the business is successful, the grant must be repaid, with success criteria fixed when the grant is provided. These grants can be considered as recoverable advances by the entrepreneur, like zero-interest loans, which pro-vide a cash advance without personal liability. It is therefore important to ensure that the entrepreneurs are motivated to succeed, because if they are not there is no financial penalty to be paid. An example of this kind of investment is the DEG Upscaling programme by the German Ministry for Cooperation and

---

6 For example, see Guerrini (2016), retrieved from startupeuropeclub.eu/tag/isidro-laso/
7 For example, Horizon 2020 funds high-potential innovation through a dedicated SME instrument to help them grow and expand their activities into other countries – in Europe and beyond (see ec.europa.eu/programmes/horizon2020/en/h2020-section/sme-instrument).
8 For more information, see www.eif.org/what_we_do/resources/neotec/
9 For more information, see 'French National Reform Programme 2011–2014', on ec.europa .eu/europe2020/pdf/nrp/nrp_france_en.pdf

Development.[10] If the venture fails, the funds will be viewed as a grant and will not need to be repaid. If the venture is successful, the funds must be repaid within five years (with no interest) based on pre-defined financial criteria such as cash flow, revenue or profit.

Programmes That Provide More Than Grants: European Commission's SME Instrument

In 2014, the EU research funding programme Horizon 2020[11] started a new funding instrument called an SME Instrument. In fact, the majority of the beneficiaries have been startups (high-growth, scalable businesses). There was a bit of confusion within the startup community in the beginning because the title of the programme did not include the word 'startup'. And most startups founders do not consider themselves as SMEs. Founders usually say that they are not 'small business people'.

In funding over the period 2014–20, the SME Instrument helps high-potential businesses to develop groundbreaking, innovative ideas for products, services or processes that are ready to face global market competition. Beneficiaries can organize a project in the way that best fits their business needs – meaning that subcontracting is not excluded – and the new scheme has opened a new highway to innovation through phased, progressive and complementary support.

During the first two years of implementation (2014–15), more than 1,200 SMEs were selected to receive funding under the SME Instrument call; as a result, €513 million was invested in the success of innovative SMEs. By the end of Horizon 2020, the SME Instrument will have supported some 7,500 SMEs to get their innovations delivered to the market.

What is different about this programme?

First, this programme is different because it has been able to adapt itself to a changing environment. At the beginning, startups were not particularly encouraged to apply, whereas now there are specific initiatives to sell the programme to the founders of startups. Second, the programme has shown flexibility by clarifying that applicants do not have to apply solely for Phase 1. Now it is very clear that applicants can apply only for Phase 3 if so they wish.

Finally, the programme's Phase 3 provides a set of coaching, mentoring and networking activities to its beneficiaries following the Startup Europe model.

5.5   Public Loans

Public loans to startups take the form of public development loans with favourable interest rates, long maturities and, in many cases, initial grace periods before the repayment obligations kick in. Examples of this kind of funding

10 For more information, see www.bmz.de/en/ministry/
11 See ec.europa.eu/programmes/horizon2020/

include Business Loans provided by Business Development Bank of Canada that provides flexible repayment terms, long amortization periods and capital payment holidays. Similar schemes are the Startup Loan in UK, the Pradhan Mantri Micro Units Development and Refinance Agency Limited (MUDRA) in India. In France, the honour loan (prêt d'honneur), which is similar to quasi-equity, can be taken out with Réseau Entreprendre, Paris Initiative Entreprise, Raise or Total Développement.[12] These are loans to citizens of the respective countries, to be reinvested in the company. The citizen is the personal guarantor of the loan, but the loan is guaranteed up to 70 per cent by the public, thus limiting the risk of personal loss. In France, this type of funding can help to support a company's launch during its first two years. In the EU, InnovFin MidCap Growth Finance offers long-term, senior, subordinated or mezzanine loans from €7.5m to 25m for innovative eligible mid size enterprises, also known as midcaps.[13] Rovio (creator of Angry Bird) has been one of the beneficiaries of this programme, which shows that startups can also benefit from this type of financial mechanism.

Recently, a new type of loan has been developed by government bodies: public loans to investors.[14] These programmes usually offer loans to VC funds at below current market value interest rates in combination with attractive grace periods. These loans are provided by so-called development banks: publicly owned and organized banks which exist at the national and state level.

Startup SG – Singapore SPRING programme – Venture Debt

SPRING is a comprehensive Singapore government programme to support startups. Singapore uses Startup SG as their branding, encompassing all the activities necessary to nurture startups. The programme includes activities aimed at increasing the connectedness of the ecosystem together with grants, vouchers, tax incentives and loans. Together with industry associations and partners, Startup SG aims at building a vibrant and innovative ecosystem of resilient enterprises.

To help innovative, high-growth startups access financing for their business expansion, the Venture Debt Program was launched in January 2016 over a pilot period of two years. Local startups can apply for venture loans of up to S$5,000,000 for the purposes of business expansion.

What is different about this programme?
To help startups access venture loans, SPRING shares the risk of loan defaults with participating financial institutions in the event of company insolvency. Interest rates, repayment structures, collateral and warrant structures will be determined by the participating financial institutions.

---

12 For more information, see ec.europa.eu/small-business/finance/index_en.htm
13 See www.eib.org/products/blending/innovfin/products/midcap-growth-finance.htm
14 See www.eib.org/products/lending/venture_capital/

5.6   Guarantees

Public support programmes for startups may also provide guarantees and counter-guarantees on debt financing in order to improve access to loan finance for innovative startups. Guarantees can mobilize and leverage commercial financing by mitigating commercial default. With public guarantees, a public authority agrees to bear some of the downside risk, typically by assuming a borrower's debt obligation in the event of a default. State-supported guarantee funds emerged in Europe in the aftermath of the Second World War, where they contributed to reconstruction efforts. This mechanism is nowadays used widely across the world in support of innovative startups.

The two main objectives of guarantees are to mobilize financing that would not otherwise be forthcoming, and to lower financing costs. It has been argued that guarantees can catalyse private financing many times the value of the guarantee. However, this is difficult to verify because it is extremely difficult to identify those loans provided to entrepreneurs who would have not otherwise have been given a loan by a commercial bank. These guarantees are expected to mitigate the default risk of high-risk and innovative projects. On the downside, if the commercial banks exploit these guarantees to mitigate commercial default in normal, low-risk loans to businesses, then this public support mechanism becomes a means to support commercial banks and not startups. The level of monitoring to ensure that public guarantees work to support startups is very high. However, it is doubtful whether they have any real impact on improving access to capital for startups. An example of this kind of mechanism is the InnovFin SME Guarantee Facility.

InnovFin Guarantee Facility

The InnovFin Guarantee Facility was established under Horizon 2020, the EU Framework Programme for Research and Innovation. It provides guarantees and counter-guarantees on debt financing of between €25,000 and €7.5 million in order to improve access to loan finance for innovative small and medium-sized enterprises and small mid-caps (up to 499 employees).

The facility is managed by the EIF (European Innovation Fund), and is rolled out through financial intermediaries – banks and other financial institutions – in EU member states and associated countries. Under this facility, financial intermediaries are guaranteed by the EU and EIF against a proportion of their losses incurred on the debt financing covered under the facility. InnovFin is part of the European Fund for Strategic Investments (EFSI).

What is different about this programme?
InnovFin is different because it is not a single financial product. It offers a set of tools that can help the startup along its life cycle from early stage through the growth phase. The assurance provided by the EIF to cover part of the losses of the bank can encourage banks to provide funds to high-risk, innovative startups.

5.7   Limited Partner

Another way to provide funding is for the public authority to become a limited partner together with other limited partners in a venture capital fund (see Chapter 4), or to provide funds to very active business angels (see Chapter 3). This mechanism aims at investing in independent management teams who raise funds from a wide range of investors to provide risk capital to growing startups.

European Angels Fund

EAF is an initiative advised by the EIF which provides equity to business angels and other non-institutional investors for the financing of innovative companies in the form of co-investments. EAF works hand in hand with business angels and helps them to increase their investment capacity by co-investing in innovative companies in the seed, early or growth stage. The activity of EAF is adapted to the business angels' investment style by granting the highest degree of freedom in terms of decision-making and the management of investments.

What is different about this programme?
Instead of granting co-investments on a deal-by-deal basis, EAF enters into long-term contractual relationships with business angels. Co-investment framework agreements (CFAs) are established through which EAF commits a predefined amount of equity for co-investments upfront to each business angel for future investments. For ease and speed, these CFAs are generally standardized, while leaving room for adaptation to the specific requirements of individual business angels. Such elements include, for example, the timeframe, sector focus and number of investments.

Why is it efficient for entrepreneurs?
All investment decisions will be taken by the business angels and their invest-ments will be matched on a *pari passu* basis, i.e. by the same amount, by EAF. With no politics involved in the investment decisions, only the most innovative and feasible businesses will receive the investments. The total volumes available under an individual CFA range typically between €250k and €5m.

5.8   Fund of Funds

Publicly backed Fund of Funds (FoF) are a unique type of fund of funds where the government agency selects a private manager to leverage the initial public contribution of funds to get three or four times that amount of money from private investors. This mechanism is very different from other equity mechan-isms used by governments in the past. In the past, governments were the managers of their funds and allocated the money via Co-investment Framework Agreements (CFAs) directly with the VC funds.

In the case of an FoF, the government agency selects a private manager and this manager will be the one responsible for selecting the VC funds that will benefit from the CFAs. This new mechanism ensures professional management of the funds. The most important FoF that has been launched until now is the Pan-European Venture Capital Fund(s) of Funds Programme.

Pan-European Venture Capital Fund(s) of Funds Programme

The Pan-European Venture Capital Fund(s) of Funds Programme will commit equity financing: (1) on a pari-passu basis with other investors in the fund; (2) preferably at the first closing; (3) at least 7.5 per cent of the fund's total commitments; (4) up to 25 per cent of the fund's total commitments; and (5) within a limit of €300 million. This adds up to total investments in the order of €1.2 billion.

What is different about this programme?
For the first time in Europe, the beneficiaries – VC firms – will be selected by a private manager. This will mean that the VC firms are faced with less bureaucracy and it might also help to attract first-class VC firms to Europe.

The key for success will be the selection of the private manager: it needs to be someone with the credibility to attract other investors into the FoF, and this will be very important if pensions funds and wealth sovereign funds are to be attracted to provide more smart money into the ecosystem.

Why is it efficient for entrepreneurs?
FoF-selected VC firms will provide smart money to the startups. Entrepreneurs should look to get capital from the selected firms because these firms will be able to provide the necessary connections and expertise for the startup to grow.

KEY TAKEAWAYS

- Public authorities must look to provide smart funding to entrepreneurs by partnering with key players in the ecosystem or using new, innovative methods such as Fund(s) of Funds.
- There are five main sources of public financing support. The appropriateness of the source depends on the characteristics and stage of the venture.
- In some cases, the public financing support goes to venture capitalists and business angels who then decide which startups have a better chance of success.
- Public–private support programmes include three main pillars: strong branding; activities to increase the connectedness both within the

ecosystem and internationally; and financial support, including taxation benefits.

- Public support initiatives vary from country to country, but they are now widespread, so searching for those that exist in your country might prove to be a useful investment.

END OF CHAPTER QUESTIONS

1. If you could choose between a €100,000 non-refundable grant from a public authority and a €25,000 investment in exchange for equity from a serial entrepreneur (smart money), which one would you choose? Please give reasons for your answer.
2. Make a comparative analysis between the following public–private support programme case studies: UK, Spain, Startup Europe.
3. Which scheme do you think is more beneficial in terms of increasing the amount of smart money within the ecosystem: guarantees to startups, or guarantees to investors and why?
4. What do you think is the role of international organizations in developing startup ecosystems?
5. How do you see the value of connectedness activities as part of the journey of an entrepreneur from a local ecosystem to becoming global leader?
6. Discuss in teams the value of a grass-roots initiative such as Startup Olé ? to raise the visibility of a local ecosystem at global level.

FURTHER READING

Blank, S. G. and Dorf, B. (2014). *The Startup Owner's Manual: The Step-by-Step Guide for Building a Great Company*. K & S Publishing.
Ries, E. (2011). *The Lean Startup*. Crown Publishing Group.
Senor, D. and Singer, S. (2011). *Start-Up Nation: The Story of Israel's Economic Miracle*. Hachette.
Startup Europe Partnership (2017). SEP monitor. June 2017.
Thiel, P. (2015). *Zero To One. Notes On Start Ups, Or How To Build The Future*. Virgin Books.
For more information on the European Commission support to SMEs, see ec.europa.eu/growth/smes/support_en

REFERENCES

Atomico (2016). The State of European Tech 2016.
Bruegel (2017). From startup to scale-up: examining public policies for the financing of high growth ventures.
European Commission (2017). *Dynamic Mapping of Web Entrepreneurs and Startups Ecosystems Project Report*. ISBN: 978-2-79-65613-2.

European Commission, Horizon 2020 at ec.europa.eu/programmes/horizon2020/

European Investment Bank support SMEs at www.eib.org/products/blending/innovfin/products/midcap-growth-finance.htm and www.eib.org/products/lending/venture_capital/

Guerrini, F. (2016). How building a stronger startup ecosystem could help tackle youth unemployment in Italy and Spain' at www.startupeuropeclub.eu

UK government, Seed Enterprise Investment Scheme and Enterprise Investment Scheme, see www.gov.uk/topic/business-tax/investment-schemes

Let's Practise: Case Study

A new AI startup with multiple EU-country members

On 3rd September 2017 Emilio Corchado is dreaming about setting up his own innovative business. Emilio is a professor from Salamanca University. His subject is Artificial Intelligence. He and his research team have developed a new Artificial Intelligence algorithm that can change the way patients interact with medical devices. Being at the Salamanca University he is in direct contact with other researchers from Madrid universities and from Berlin research institutes. Emilio has always had an entrepreneurial mindset and wants to become the founder of a big startup. Emilio has a global vision and wants to reach high.

Setting Up the Team

Emilio has participated in many of the EU's Startup Europe activities since 2014. As a consequence he knows entrepreneurs, researchers and university professors that can be interested in becoming co-founders of his startups. He decides to organise a series of Skype meetings with the people he believes will be interested in this endeavours.

By the end of September he has a team composed of three co-founders from Madrid, Berlin and Ireland. They have been doing business together before as part of the project Welcome. Welcome was an EU's Startup Europe project that supported the creation of connections between the startups' ecosystems of Salamanca, Madrid, Milano, Berlin and Dublin. They built trust among themselves during more than two years and now they feel they can move to the next level and launch their own startup.

Reaching Out to Investors

The first thing they decide is that they will not create a traditional Business Plan. They will prepare a straight forward pitch supported by an attractive slides deck. Each one of the members of the team is going to prepare a series of meetings with investors in their cities. Emilio and his co-founders will get in touch with the investors through the Accelerators Assembly (part of Startup Europe). Eventually Emilio organises three meetings with investors in Madrid. His co-founders are able to do the same in their respective cities (four meetings in Berlin and two in Dublin). They decide that all the co-founders will attend each and every one of the meetings with the investors. Using low-cost flights they are able to keep costs low.

Where to Set Up

After the first round of contacts with investors, the team close a deal with two investors (one from Madrid and one from Berlin). As the startup is about Artificial intelligence the team decides to set up the company in Madrid as it does provide the company with many tax incentives and, most importantly, Madrid is also the number two city in terms of AI experts according to the latest Atomico-Slush report (Atomico 2016). Emiio had the opportunity to discuss with the author of the report to learn more details on the AI section of the report thanks to the connections that Startup Europe help him to create with Atomico's author.

After doing some research they decide not to have their office in an isolated apartment but rather have an office as part of 'The Cube'. Uber has just decided to set up its office for southern Europe at The Cube with 700 employees. Being at this place will help Emilio and his team to be part of a larger ecosystem.

Getting Visibility

Emilio knows that it is very important to be noticed by the main players of the international ecosystem. As such, the team decides to apply to the different international activities that Startup Europe organises regularly. They are successful and they are accepted to be part of the exclusive group of 20 startups that will fly to Silicon Valley through the "Startup Europe Comes to Silicon Valley".

During the week of intense bilateral meetings with investors and prospective customers in Silicon Valley, they have established good connections that will be developed in the future. They have also appeared in a tech.eu article and the number of downloads of the first version of their app is being downloaded by thousands. The feedback of the users is helping Emilio to pivot the business towards a more specialised software which addresses a particular niche. They are now on their way to become big!

Questions for discussion

1. If you were Emilio, what would you have done differently in the process to set up the business?
2. Do you believe that it is important of a local ecosystem?
3. Are you part of European networks that can help you to get investors and customers? Please discuss how Startup Europe networks have helped Emilio to set up the team, to reach out to investors and to get visibility and customers.

PART II

FUNDING PROCESS

6 DEAL SOURCING AND SCREENING

DIETMAR GRICHNIK

University of St. Gallen

TORBEN ANTRETTER

University of St. Gallen

ALEXANDER STOECKEL

btov Partners AG

The challenges for investors associated with selecting the right investment opportunities are abundant. We might, for example, look at the proper amount of investment in due diligence, the 'do's and don'ts' for term sheets, the nuances of company valuation, the importance of prudent portfolio management and the numerous ways to support a startup in building and, eventually, selling their venture. However, most venture capitalists (VCs) will agree that two aspects determine at least 70 per cent of their final portfolio performance:

- Did the investor have access to the best investment opportunities (deal sourcing)?
- Was the investor able to select the right targets to invest in (deal screening)?

The logic is simple: you can be as thorough as you like with your due diligence or portfolio strategies – in the end, none of this this will help you to reach attractive investment returns if your process is flawed from the very beginning. If the selection process was carried out poorly, then you will most probably either lose some money or lose a lot of money. You will lose some money if you find out in the course of due diligence that your target is not really a target. You may lose a lot of money, however, if you find out after the investment has been made that your portfolio company is unlikely to succeed. Thus, the process of deal sourcing and the screening process is of utmost importance. Let's get started!

VIEW FROM THE MEDIA

FINANCIAL TIMES   FT

What to wear to pitch your start-up

Smart or casual? Investors and entrepreneurs offer tips

AUGUST 2, 2017 BY JANINA CONBOYE

How do entrepreneurs dress when pitching start-ups to investors? It seems like a trivial question, but experts and those who have done it say sartorial codes matter – and there are pitfalls. Founders tread a fine line: they must give the right impression to those with the money their businesses need, but they must also reflect their vision. The key, they say, is knowing your audience – a suit may not always be appropriate. Here, leading venture capitalists – and a few entrepreneurs – reflect on the best approach. Advice from the VCs Suranga Chandratillake, a general partner at Balderton Capital in London, thinks the question of how to present yourself important. 'There's a low bar, but you probably shouldn't wear shorts,' he says. 'In any given week I see people in T-shirts to suits, but suits and a tie are rare.' Presenting to a VC is not the same as a job interview. 'When you're being interviewed by a bank, they're assessing whether they can put you in front of clients,' says Mr Chandratillake, but VCs care less about this. '[An entrepreneur] is building a company and they can do that in their pyjamas.' To him, it is obvious when someone is wearing something they would not usually consider, and this can send wrong signals.

He remembers an entrepreneur who pitched a gaming company wearing a suit two sizes too small – 'He clearly wasn't comfortable'. But some go too far in the other direction. A woman wearing a hoodie – the favoured attire of Facebook's Mark Zuckerberg – kept playing with the pulls. 'At first I thought she was nervous, but it turned out she wasn't, she just wasn't used to wearing hoodies.' ... 'How would you dress if you were meeting with a group of customers?' he says. 'If you are building a VR [virtual reality] game, you would probably have a cool T-shirt with your logo on it. If you are selling enterprise software, you would probably have a sports coat, if not a suit.' But the flip side is dressing to match the VCs' attire. ... 'A young game developer wearing a suit is not at all credible,' says Mr Reichert. '[And] an old fart wearing a T-shirt and jeans is painful to look at.'

... 'Entrepreneurs who present to us are often engineers by background . . . what they say is overwhelmingly more important than how they look,' he says. But he does advise avoiding extremes. 'Don't come looking like you're dressed for the beach and don't come looking like a fashion model,' he says. 'After you leave, you want us to be talking about your product, your team, your technology, your business plan – but not how you looked.' ...

www.ft.com/content/6c14dd88-04ea-11e7-ace0-1ce02ef0def9#0-header-search-primary

LEARNING OBJECTIVES

After reading this chapter you will be able to:

- Understand the principal–agent problem and its effects on venture capital decision-making.
- Understand how venture capitalists generate deal flow.
- Recognize the importance of investment strategies to the overall sourcing and screening process.
- Recognize the impact of psychological biases on the screening decision.
- Comprehend how VCs mitigate the issues associated with the deal sourcing and screening process.

Where Are We Going Next?

This chapter will review principal–agent theory and explain how it affects deal sourcing and the screening decisions made by VCs. It will further show how investors evaluate new ventures based on their fit with their investment strategy and the information provided by the entrepreneurs. As startup investments – especially in the early stages – carry great uncertainty, investors need to find ways to mitigate risk. Therefore, it is important for entrepreneurs to understand how professional investors use different heuristics to balance rational and emotional elements of decision-making.

After setting the stage for how opportunistic and overoptimistic behaviour on both sides of the table influence the entrepreneur–investor relationship, this chapter focuses on how investment opportunities are evaluated by VCs.

6.1   A Review of the Principal–Agent Problem

Principal–agent relationships are prevalent in many business situations as well as in everyday life. They occur when one individual or entity (agent) makes a decision on behalf of, or that influences, another person or entity (principal). The problem in this relationship arises when the two entities have differing interests and asymmetric information, such that the principal cannot be sure that the agent is acting in his best interest or believes that the agent may be acting in an opportunistic manner. Consider, for example, a legal client (principal) hiring a lawyer (agent). The client will probably be wondering whether the attorney is recommending tedious court proceedings because they are truly necessary or because it will increase the lawyer's earnings on the contract.

The same applies to a venture capital setting. The VC (principal) invests in a startup – similarly to a legal client paying for a lawyer – in the hope that the entrepreneur (agent) will best represent the principal's interest in generating a financial return. In this relationship, however, the entrepreneur regularly

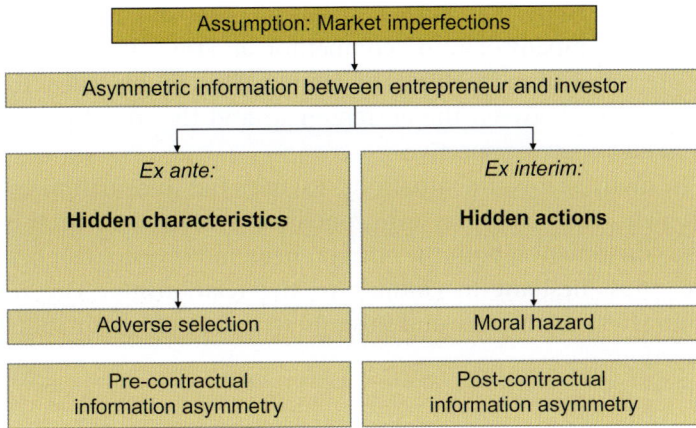

Figure 6.1 The investor–entrepreneur relationship as an agency problem.

chooses actions from a variety of alternatives knowing that it will affect the welfare of both himself and the investor.

6.1.1 Asymmetric Information

Information asymmetries refer to the situation where one party has more or better information than the other. An often-cited example of asymmetric information is the used car market or 'market for lemons'.[1] The seller knows more about the quality of the used car than the potential buyer. The owner of a high-quality car (a 'peach' as Akerlof puts it) is keen to transfer information about the quality of the car to prospective buyers, but cannot do so easily. Merely testifying that the car is a good one will not do the job, because all sellers will ordinarily make comparable claims.

In a venture capital situation, most startups do not have a track record that will allow them to provide 'quality information'.[2] Thus, entrepreneurs are likely to compete for financing by presenting optimistic estimates and withholding negative information. Furthermore, the entrepreneur has superior knowledge about his personal abilities, better known as hidden characteristics. Once a contract has been entered into, parties may act inconsistently with their original intentions. This uncertainty is often referred to as hidden actions. Such problems are known as moral hazard. The different elements of asymmetric information in venture capital are displayed in Figure 6.1.

In combination, these circumstances make it extremely difficult for a VC to judge the attractiveness of an investment opportunity. However, the situation of missing or incomplete information can also present challenges for entrepreneurs. A startup, for instance, does not usually know why potential investors

1 For more information on this topic see Akerlof (1970).
2 As discussed in Chapter 8.

are interested in their particular venture. They might already be involved with a similar company or even a competitor, and thus trying to get close to a startup to prevent it from reaching the market. This double-sided 'lock-in' makes the relationship between the entrepreneur and the investor even more complex from an agency perspective.

In many real-world situations, asymmetric information is only half of the problem. Each party has an incentive to misrepresent what is already known. As a consequence, both the entrepreneur and investor fear being exploited and are, thus, hesitant to commit to the relationship. The result of the pre-contractual asymmetry and misrepresentation of information is called adverse selection.

6.1.2   Adverse Selection

Adverse selection describes the undesired result of market failure due to infor-mation asymmetry. It causes a lack of efficiency and, ultimately, drives good targets out of the market (Akerlof 1970). For example, suppose there are two groups of people to be targeted by a health insurance company. One group consists of heavy smokers and individuals who do not exercise (insurance pre-mium: €200). The other group eats healthily, does not smoke and works out on a regular basis (insurance premium: €100). It appears to be evident that the group of people who live an unhealthy lifestyle have, on average, a higher chance of getting sick, and, thus, cause a financial burden to the insurance company. The insurance company, however, is not easily able to differentiate between the two groups.

Usually, the companies have their applicants fill out questionnaires to iden-tify such characteristics. But the smoker knows that answering truthfully will result in higher insurance premiums. Therefore, he might lie and say he does not smoke and that he exercises regularly. Given this likelihood, the insurance company will price the insurance at an expectancy value of €150. As a consequence, healthy people are not willing to buy an insurance policy at this price and decide to cover the cost themselves. This devious behaviour by individual market participants causes adverse selection, i.e. a result that is not pareto-optimal for both parties.

The same applies to the misrepresentation of ability on the part of the entrepreneur in a venture capital setting. In other words, the investor has insufficient information to effectively evaluate the characteristics of the startup team. For example, the entrepreneurs may try to optimistically oversell their merits and the viability of their venture to secure a more favourable valuation. Additionally, they may think they know more about a particular field or technology than they actually do. From the examples above, we can see that information asymmetries alone do not lead to adverse selection. The problem requires either opportunistic or overoptimistic behaviour on the side of the principal or the agent.

6.1.3   Opportunistic and Overoptimistic Behaviour

Opportunistic behaviour describes one party taking advantage of superior knowledge to promote their personal interests by deliberately failing to disclose information or actively distorting the facts. In venture capital, the potential harm of opportunism is – as described above – a two-way street. On the one hand, entrepreneurs may pitch their numbers as what might be referred to as an 'extended version of the truth'. Venture capitalists, on the other hand, might only engage with a startup because they see an advantage for one of their, eventually more promising, portfolio companies.

Whereas opportunism refers to actions the agent can manipulate (e.g. reporting metrics), overoptimism (also overconfidence) describes misjudging the probability of potentially favourable outcomes that are outside the control of the agent.[3] One example of this would be an overestimation of the future market development. Opportunistic and overoptimistic behaviour are two different concepts. However, they can appear in combination. The important thing to note is that, ultimately, they lead to the same result: the transformation of the principal–agent relationship into a principal–agent problem.

Given the different outcomes of asymmetric information (paired with opportunistic or overoptimistic behaviour) in a venture capital setting, it is important to get a sense of how the principal–agent problem can be mitigated through deliberate actions taken by both the entrepreneur and the investor.

6.2   Remedies for the Principal–Agent Problem: Pre-contractual

The hazard of the principal–agent problem can be reduced through signalling and self-selection, even before the investment decision has been made.

6.2.1   Signalling (Entrepreneur)

In order to arouse interest and display the potential attractiveness of the investment opportunity, entrepreneurs often make claims for the positive future development of their venture. This is why most startups pitching to investors will include at least one slide in their executive presentation with a so-called 'hockey stick growth chart', which signals the (assumed) outstanding growth potential of the business. These predictions are costly or even impossible for the investor to verify and, therefore, rarely build trust. However, in some situations the entrepreneur could disclose competitively sensitive information (such as client contracts) just by showing it to the investors and leaving them to draw their own conclusion. But this can be risky if the venture capitalist decides to exploit the opportunity. In other situations, however, providing confidential information is not feasible. How can an entrepreneur convince the investor that,

3 Landier and Thesmar (2009).

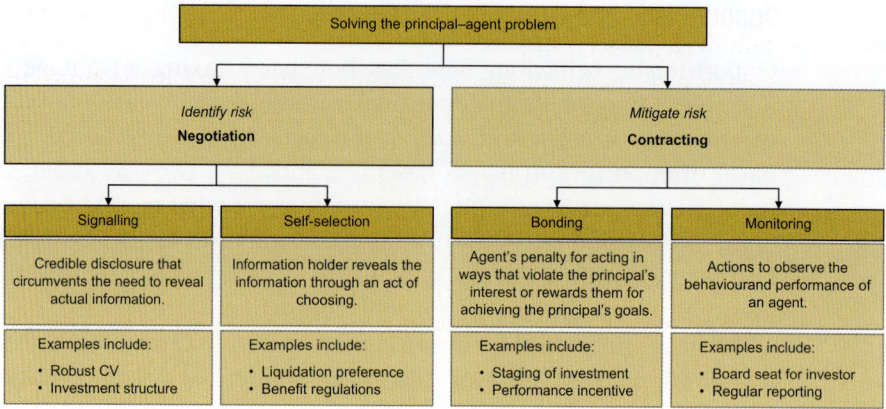

Figure 6.2 Solving the principal–agent problem.

for instance, the technical development of an emotion recognition software has advanced much quicker than expected, without providing corresponding documentation? The challenge in this situation is to do so in a way that is convincing, whilst preserving the value of the information.

One solution for the entrepreneur is to use a signal. A signal is a credible display that circumvents the need to disclose actual information. Sometimes, the entrepreneur offering a certain deal structure can be a reliable signal. Imagine a venture capitalist being anxious about the reliability of the market projections. By proposing a contract that ties his return to specific growth targets, the entrepreneur signals his confidence in his forecasts. Other signals may include the amount of private money invested, industry experience or education.[4] If the entrepreneurs have, for instance, invested significant parts of their own money in the business, it provides a positive message for the investor: The entrepreneurs have their skin in the game. Thus, signalling is a practical way for entrepreneurs to address the problem of adverse selection, as illustrated in Figure 6.2.

6.2.2   Self-selection (Investor)

Self-selection is similar to signalling. But instead of circumventing the disclosure by providing a signal, the party without the information offers a set of alternatives for the information holder to choose from. For example, VCs could provide entrepreneurs with different contract proposals.[5] Those startups that are uncertain about how their venture might develop are likely to seek financing that reduces their personal risk exposure. Startups with low expectations are also likely to prefer terms and conditions that minimize the investor's liquidation preference. The resulting ambiguity is one of the reasons why deal structures

4 Busenitz *et al.* (2005).
5 This will be discussed in detail in Chapter 9 on 'Term Sheets'.

frequently require entrepreneurs to take a significant risk of both success and failure (self-selection).

Hence, the main difference between signalling and self-selection is the identity of the actor. If the entrepreneur e.g. offers certain customer references, then it is considered to be signalling. If, on the other hand, the VC (the party with a lack of information) proposes the deal structure (e.g. in form of a liquidation preference), then the investor is most likely trying to screen the startup based on their confidence about their startup (self-selection). Deal structuring is covered in Chapter 9.

For a successful deal sourcing process, you also need to consider the relationship between the entrepreneur and the investor during and after a decision has been made.

VOICE OF THE EXPERT: Pieter de Jong and Tjarda Molenaar (the Netherlands)

Pieter de Jong joined 3i in 2004 and is Partner, Managing Director of 3i Benelux, based in Amsterdam. He was involved in the buy-outs and growth investments in Refresco, Action, TouchTunes, Basic-Fit, Weener Plastic Packaging Group and Lampenwelt.

Tjarda Molenaar has been Managing Director of the Dutch Private Equity & Venture Capital Association (NVP) since 2002. NVP is the industry body and public policy advocate for private equity in the Netherlands. Before, she was an investment consultant with the Dutch mid-market private equity firm Gilde and a management consultant with A.T. Kearney.

What would be your advice to new entrepreneurs when looking for an equity investor?

Our advice to entrepreneurs is: look for an investor that can be a real partner. Build a relationship with the (potential) investor. So, be open about your ambitions and drives and about the strengths and weaknesses of your plan. Do not hide or postpone set-backs. And be prepared to change your plan: an investor provides capital, but brings also a wealth of experience and expertise to the table. Ask yourself whether you are ready for a partner with an opinion and a say.

At the same time, do your own due diligence on the potential investor: is he or she really a good match with you, your company and your plan? Use your network to find out. Talk to their investee companies, or better, to one that has been sold. Does the investor have the industry knowledge, the network you are looking for among business partners, banks, top management, etcetera. What did he do when things did not work out as planned?

6.3   Remedies for the Principal–Agent Problem: Post-contractual

After making an investment decision, the issues surrounding the principal–agent problem may still prevail. In this situation, various mechanisms can be used to align the interests of both principal and agent, and thereby reduce the adverse effects of information asymmetries under the influence of opportunistic or overoptimistic behaviour. Two of these concepts include bonding and monitoring.

6.3.1   Bonding (Entrepreneur)

Bonding describes arrangements that penalize the agent for acting in ways that violate the interests of the principal (moral hazard) or reward them for achieving the principal's goals. In venture capital, bonding is often performed within financial contracting. One example would be the 'staging' of an investment deal.[6] A staged investment refers to an investment where the entire amount is not capitalized at the time of the initial funding. Instead, only a proportion of the agreed funding is initially invested. The remaining funds are provided over time based upon prior agreed milestones set by the portfolio company. By agreeing to such a bond, the entrepreneurs show that they intend to act in the investor's interests.

6.3.2   Monitoring (Investor)

Another way for the principal to reduce information asymmetry is known as 'monitoring'. Monitoring (as explained in Chapter 10) describes actions taken to observe the behaviour and performance of the agent. Traditional ways of monitoring used by VCs include, amongst others, the limitation of action alternatives through e.g. veto rights, board positions or the request of extensive reporting.

Most VCs follow a structured deal sourcing and screening process in order to handle the principal–agent problem.

6.4   Understanding the Ways VCs Generate Investment Opportunities

Creating high-quality deal flow is critical to the success of a venture capital firm. Because of the time-consuming investment and monitoring process, VCs can only fund a fraction of the deals submitted for their consideration. Still, many companies lose money for investors while others generate only moderate returns. Describing the hazard of venture capital financing, one investor stated: 'If my fund invests in 20 companies, and the first 19 go bust, have I failed? It depends on how the 20th company does.'[7]

If a fund could replace just one loss-making company in its portfolio with a major success, its overall performance would dramatically increase. Thus, the sourcing of the best deals and their proper evaluation is critical to the success of a VC. But how do investors get their hands on the next potential unicorn? Often,

---

6 This is explained in detail in Chapter 9. See Figure 9.1.
7 Hoyt *et al.* (2012: 2).

the deal sourcing process starts with the VC receiving a short email about the company seeking investment. These messages might come from a variety of sources, such as:

- an entrepreneur who was previously funded by the VC firm, who is either starting a new business or referring someone else;
- a founder of an existing portfolio company, who knows about an exciting investment opportunity;
- a friend of a VC member, introducing an entrepreneur;
- a professional, such as a lawyer, who has worked with the VC firm and other startup companies;
- organizations which support startups, such as accelerators;
- other investors who have invested at an earlier stage, such as business angels or pre-seed VCs; or
- a startup or entrepreneur with no previous point of contact with the VC firm.

Not all approaches to the VC are unsolicited. Potential investment opportunities might also result from proactive engagement by the investor. Venture capitalists constantly try to build relationships with interesting people. They network with executives in the field of interest, meet professors and other business leaders and attend conferences or trade shows. They may also participate in campus events to network with outstanding graduates to develop relationships with future entrepreneurs. This network may uncover investment ideas and, thus, facilitate deal flow.[8]

Once a contact is established, it is the task of a VC to distinguish high-potential startups ('peaches') from the 'lemons'.

6.5   Investment Strategy

Before making an effort to screen a potential investment opportunity, a VC should be aware of his investment strategy.[9] It determines what kind of investments the fund is generally interested in. Each strategy has both qualitative and quantitative components as depicted in Figure 6.3.

6.5.1   Quantitative Components

Investment Size

Most VCs have a preferred investment size. It depends on the fund volume, anticipated investments and the prospects of raising future funds. The ticket sizes have to justify the effort put in when staging and monitoring the deal, and should provide the potential for a meaningful return. Besides the individual investment size, a VC will also look for a target number of portfolio companies. For instance, if a fund has five general partners (GPs), it might want to invest in

---

8 Hoyt *et al.* (2012).
9 This is explained in detail in Chapter 4.

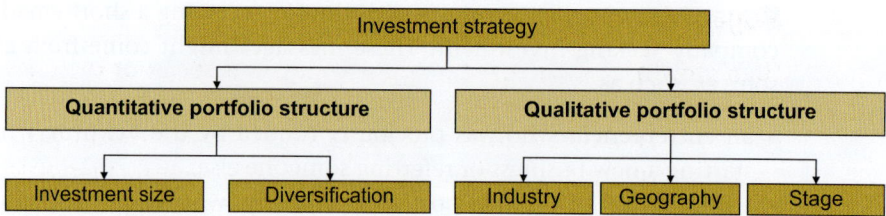

Figure 6.3 Investment strategy.

twenty-five to thirty different companies over a period of four years. After five years, the VC would have raised a new fund. If the first fund volume was €100 million, the firm would invest on average €3–4 million in each company (including follow-on rounds). Therefore, a startup looking for an investment of €1.5 million might be a good match. However, a company looking for €200,000 with a limited need for additional funding fails this criterion. Similarly, a company seeking €10 million would tie up too much of the fund's capital and would, therefore, be screened out.[10]

Diversification

Portfolio diversification is a well-known mechanism for controlling uncertainty by reducing unsystematic risk, i.e. the risk that comes with the startup a VC invests in. However, research shows that maintaining a high degree of specialization might also contribute to controlling risk by building a strong network, expert know-how and a flow of high-quality deals in a given area.[11] So, it remains a matter of choice to what extent an investor diversifies his portfolio.

Industry

In practice, most venture capital firms concentrate on a specific set of industries. Often, they will employ expert partners with experience or interest in each individual sector. For example, the Munich-based VC Holtzbrinck Ventures states that it focuses on the industry cluster 'consumer internet and enablers'.[12] Most of Holtzbrinck's GPs have gained extensive experience in founding or working for ICT companies before becoming an investor.

---

10 It should be noted, however, that most VC rounds are syndicated investments. In other words, they involve several investors.
11 Bygrave (1988); Matusik and Fitza (2012).
12 This information is based on the Holtzbrinck Ventures website, www.holtzbrinck-ventures .com (accessed 23 June 2017).

Stage of Development

High-growth ventures need funding at different stages of their development. At each stage, the level of uncertainty decreases and – in most cases – the amount of desired financing increases. Some VCs make their investments in the early seed or startup stages. This strategy involves a relatively small initial investment and gives investors the opportunity to participate in follow-on rounds as the company grows. Other investors may wait until startups have developed further before they make their first investment.

Geography

One of the central roles of VCs is to provide experienced managerial support to their portfolio companies. This support is easier and more efficient to provide if the company is locally based. Therefore, most European VCs have their focus on European startups. Take, for example, London as one of the venture capital hotspots in Europe.[13] Startups in London have access to extensive technical knowledge and human as well as financial resources. This accessibility allows VCs to build an in-depth expertise of local industries and technologies. When investing in a London-based startup, local VCs can quickly meet with the company and leverage their network of people and suppliers to benefit the portfolio company. For these reasons, a startup from Rome will, ceteris paribus, be less attractive to a London-based VC than a company from the UK.

If an investment opportunity fits the general investment criteria, the next step is to find out whether the startup has what it takes to become a significant business. Most VCs employ a structured screening process to guide the analyst towards a reliable decision.

Let's Practise: Case Study
btov Partners AG Screening Process

btov Partners AG is a venture capital firm and business angel network from Switzerland. The company was established in 2000 and has its offices in St. Gallen, Berlin and Luxembourg. The company employs twenty three individuals, of whom nineteen are investment professionals.[14] btov has about €300 million of assets under management, and about 100 active portfolio companies. As of early 2017, the company had successfully raised three proprietary funds and managed three partner funds for major corporations or family

---

13 Florida and King (2016).
14 The investment professionals have three different roles: (1) Leading the investment activities of the btov funds including organization, screening, due diligence, term sheet negotiation, as well as monitoring and supporting existing portfolio companies. (2) Managing the btov private investor network. (3) Administrating and controlling all investment activities plus reporting.

offices.[15] The firm reviews more than 3,000 startup investment proposals annually, and invests in 15–25 companies per year, not counting follow-on investments in existing portfolio companies.

Venture capital investing at btov is, first and foremost, about people. As Arthur Rock, an early investor in companies like Apple and Intel, once stated: *'Good ideas and good products are a dime a dozen. Good execution and good management – in a word, good people – are rare.'*[16] This quote, however, is not only true for startup companies. It is also true for the VC and his investment team. Since early-stage investors are providing funds to companies with little or no track record, i.e. without much reliable performance data, the investment decision has to take into consideration numerous 'subjective factors'. This means that the intellectual and analytical skills, personalities, and sometimes even the mood of the analysts screening venture proposals, play a crucial role in the selection process. Thus, VCs need people who can:

- analyse business concepts systematically, i.e. without missing relevant strengths or deal breakers on the side of the startup;
- combine industry know-how, technology savviness and entrepreneurial flair to understand the feasibility and potential of a given business concept; and
- put their personality and character to one side during the analysis so that they do not accept or reject business proposals for personal reasons.

btov applies a structured screening concept – as illustrated in Figure 6.4 – to all investment proposals that are submitted to the company and which fall under the scope (overall fit) of the company's investment strategy.[17] The analyst will not only examine ('tick') each topic but also cross-check each aspect with other factors. If, for instance, a product cannot be used intuitively by the customer but requires tutoring, this must be reflected in the business model and financial plans, e.g. in the form of sales representatives who tutor customers and at the cost of scaling the company.

It is important to note that a screening framework should not serve as a scoring algorithm. The structure should only guide the analyst and systemize the examination of the business proposal to ensure that no critical part of the firm's characteristics is left out. It would be dangerous to assign scores to individual aspects during the screening process because this could eventually lead to the selection of ventures not on the basis of strengths that may qualify them as outliers, but because they have few weaknesses and, therefore, do well in an integrated scoring model. So, what are the most important factors to take into account when assessing the attractiveness of an investment opportunity? What

15 Proprietary funds are conceptualized, raised, and managed by btov. Managed partner funds are facilitated in close collaboration with corporations or high net-worth individuals.
16 Sahlman *et al.* (1999: 351).
17 For a detailed explanation of the btov investment strategy, please refer to the website FAQs: http://btov.vc/faq/ (accessed 23 June 2017).

are the rational or subjective factors that an analyst needs to consider and what cognitive biases should they look out for?

Solution: btov Screening Concept

Executive Summary

Rational Aspects

Given that there is an abundance of investment opportunities, and that only a small number of startups will eventually be funded, an executive summary is used to validate the general fit of the investment proposal with the investment strategy as described above. In other words, this short summary provided by the entrepreneurs is probably the only immediate killer criteria for a submitted investment proposal.

Let's take an early-stage investor focusing on financial technology ('fintech') startups. The VC applying this criterion as part of her investment strategy will first of all eliminate all startups focusing on topics other than fintech from their screening process, using the executive summary. The screening process that is guided by the executive summary is probably the least problematic aspect of the selection process, because the analyst can compare the general characteristics of a startup directly with the strategic requirements put forth by her fund or company. There is one potential challenge, namely that some entrepreneurs are not able to summarize their business concept. Either the entrepreneur does

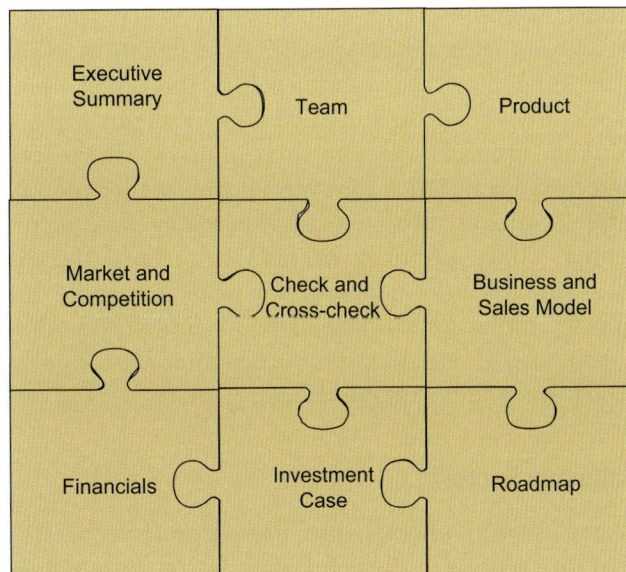

Figure 6.4 btov screening model.
Source: btov (2017)

a poor job at synthesizing the most important aspects of the investment opportunity, or the business model is just too complex. In both situations, the analyst will need to probe further, because an analysis of the executive summary does not result in a clear indication as to whether the business might be a fit with the investment strategy or not.

Subjective Factors

When evaluating the strategic fit, the analyst can easily fall prey to a number of cognitive biases. Consider, for example, the pitfalls of herd behaviour (Scharfstein and Stein 1990; Banerjee 1992). This concept describes individuals gravitating towards similar investments based almost exclusively on the fact that many others are investing in a particular industry or technology. Imagine an Artificial Intelligence (AI) company that fails one criterion of your 'strategy checklist'. Objectively, you would have to pass on the opportunity. In reality, however, your judgement will most likely depend on a reference point (Kahneman and Tversky 1979). So, if currently everyone is investing in AI, you will be more likely to find a way to move it on to the next round.

Team

Rational Aspects

Most private and institutional investors agree that the team is the most important and also one of the most difficult aspects to assess in venture screening. A collective mindset in the VC industry is that you are better off investing in a good team with a mediocre idea than investing in an average team with an outstanding idea. The reasoning behind this is that a good team will most likely succeed anyway. If the initial concept does not work, they will redirect their efforts and eventually become successful. A mediocre team, however, needs luck to succeed. Even if their idea is great, the challenges on the path to success are manifold, and only strong teams will be able to overcome these difficulties and, eventually, take advantage of them. In practice, the analysts will try to get as much verifiable information on the team as possible. Information might come from CVs, professional (social) networks and a review of certificates or references in media articles, etc., to assess the operational (startup) and industry experience of the team (and board) members.

Subjective Factors

The analyst will, however, also make efforts to generate information about the social interactions of the team. How do the entrepreneurs communicate, treat other people and what drives their motivation? One of the main challenges here is that the assessment of such factors is frequently influenced by a number of cognitive biases on the part of the analyst. The individual analyzing the startup may be provoked, impressed, or even positively charmed by the team. These types of perceptions can lead the analyst to be influenced by their positive or negative impressions of the team. Furthermore, rumours reported in the media or by colleagues might unknowingly influence the analyst's judgement of the team.

A successful VC will be able to overlook the fact that the CEO of a startup may be terrible at presenting the business, or may have a difficult personality.[18] The competence of a VC lies in realizing that, in spite of these shortcomings, the entrepreneur's technical know-how and existing network may be more critical to the company's overall success than a good show or an accommodating personality.

As we have said, the entrepreneur's personality can play a major role in the decision-making process. As a consequence, it may lead the analyst to make flawed judgements. He might, for example, fall prey to confirmation bias (Nickerson 1998), which describes the tendency to search for, favour or interpret information in a way that confirms preexisting beliefs or perceptions. As an example, someone who has worked for a top-tier consulting company will be evaluated based, at least partially, on your preexisting opinion about that company. Similarly, researchers found that VCs are more likely to fund individuals who have a comparable background to their own (Franke *et al.* 2006), which makes signalling an even more valuable tool for entrepreneurs.

Product

Rational Aspects

The value proposition of the product or service to be offered by the startup is one of the most important aspects of the screening process. Given that many of the most successful venture-financed startups change their product and business model in the early years, it is important to evaluate the overall potential of the underlying value proposition.

Using rational selection criteria, the analyst will try to get as much verifiable information on the product as he can. For instance, he will try to understand the functionalities of the product as well as its relevance to the problem that is solved for customers. Other criteria used to assess the attractiveness of a new venture's offering include customers' readiness to pay for the product, the unique selling proposition (USP), the product's potential for intellectual property (IP) protection, the unit economics, scalability, possible ways to vary or diversify the product and the make-or-buy (value chain) approach that the startup plans to take.

---

18 Rawhouser *et al.* (2017).

Subjective Factors

Besides these 'hard facts', the analyst will be careful to include soft information on the market's reaction to the product in the assessment. Mistakes often follow, for example, the so-called expert bias of references. An example would be when the analyst talks to an industry expert about a product, but the expert is biased by his twenty-year industry experience and fails to see the disruptive aspect of the product. Another common bias involves the analyst focusing on himself as a potential customer and failing to recognize that the product targets a very different group of individuals. The industry jargon for this misinterpretation is simple: 'The worm must be attractive to the fish, not to the fisherman.' In this context, to invest in strength, not in a lack of weaknesses means that it may be worthwhile investing in a new product category even if the market itself fails to recognize its importance. A prominent example is the (unexpected, from the customer point of view) emergence of the smartphone and the subsequent disruption of incumbent mobile phone manufacturers such as Nokia or Blackberry, which failed to see or were unable to meet a so far unmet need in the market.

Market and Competitors

Rational aspects

The growth rate of the market addressed by a startup is an important indicator of the potential of the firm. Moreover, the competitive landscape in the market targeted by the startup will be of interest to investors, not only regarding the company's potential conflict with competitors but also with regard to under-standing how likely it is that one of its competitors may eventually acquire the startup.

As far as hard facts are concerned, the analysts will try to get as much data on the market and competition as possible through, for example, looking at the present and future geographical scope of the company, the targeted industry segments and the direct and indirect competitors serving the same market. In order to understand industry attractiveness, an analyst will use frameworks such as Porter's Five Forces.[19] The analyst will also research statistics on the market to get a better understanding of the addressable market potential. Where applicable, the involvement of governments or policymakers, as well as the aggressiveness and innovation speed of the incumbents, needs to be understood.

Subjective Factors

Together with the factual information described in the previous section, the analyst will also try to understand the timing of market entry. Moreover, the

19 Porter (1979).

competitive advantages claimed by the startup vis-à-vis its competitors need to be verified (and cross-checked using the product screening). A common argument made by analysts or investors, namely that a competitor could easily copy and implement the same product or service, needs to be investigated carefully in many cases.

One high-profile example of how quickly one can misjudge the competition or product is the 'anti-portfolio' of the leading international VC-firm Bessemer Ventures Partners,[20] which lists 'rockstar' companies (such as Apple, Google, Facebook, etc.) that they had the chance to invest in during the early stages of their development, but whose potential they failed to identify. The anti-portfolio has a very clear message: even the most successful investors don't get it right every time.

As is the case when evaluating a product, market screening is prone to false-consensus bias.[21] This describes the tendency of people to think that others are just like them – although there might be no justification for that. The analyst might reason: 'I would buy that product – so there are probably millions of people out there who want to buy it as well', failing to account for the fact that there will probably not be millions of people 'just like him' in the target market.

Business and Sales Model

Rational Aspects

Many experienced investors in the VC industry claim that, apart from the team, the business model is the second most important aspect of the screening process. Their reasoning is that a team's ability to understand its customers and implement a business model that fits the market needs is a fundamental element of the team's entrepreneurial talent and the potential of the company to excel.

Here, the analyst will try to get a firm understanding of the company's marketing mix (place, promotion, price, product and people) as well as the fit between the business model and its customers' expectations or behaviours. An analysis of the business model is always cross-checked against the review of the product and the financials.

Subjective Factors

As with the product, the analyst will be careful not to listen too much to the feedback about the business and sales model of early customers. Often, those reactions may come from people who, for example, like the product but overlook the business model. Let's consider, for example, a company that provides a marketplace for introducing parents to nannies. A user may easily overlook the fact that the site can monetize the booking only once, because from then on the

20 URL: www.bvp.com/portfolio/anti-portfolio
21 Ross *et al.* (1977).

parents and the nannies will communicate directly, without consulting the platform. Another example is the unleveraged flexibility in the pricing of a product. Suppose, for instance, a team of software developers design a program which saves the corporate user €500,000 per year but the team charges only €250 per customer and installation of the program. Obviously, someone has missed an opportunity here.

In this context, the maxim 'invest in strengths, not in lack of weaknesses' applies to another notorious group of businesses. In Europe, the early-stage funding of companies without business models has proved to be problematic for investors. We are not referring here to biotech start-ups, which rarely pitch business models for their innovations. Rather, this typically involves B2C internet platforms which focus their business on customer acquisition and retention and not on revenues or profits. Famous examples include companies that have never implemented a business model and were very successful none-theless, such as Instagram (sold for about US$1 billion to Facebook, with no business model implemented at all) or Whatsapp (sold for about US$19 billion to Facebook, with a financially insignificant business model). European exam-ples include Spanish Wallapop, rumoured to be worth close to €1 billion in spring 2017.

Here, the curse of knowledge bias often leads better-informed people to find it difficult to think about problems from the perspective of those who are not so well-informed.[22] This may lead investors to consider 'low-tech' or 'simple' business models to be inferior. An analyst might say, 'this is just too easy – it cannot work'. At least, this is what the investors who turned down opportunities Skype, Whatsapp or Spotify might have thought.

Financials

Rational Aspects

Entrepreneurs frequently complain that investors criticize them for being either too aggressive or not aggressive enough with their five-year financial forecast.[23] And the founders are right! No one can design a five-year budget for a startup that will match the eventual reality. But apparently they were talking to unsea-soned investors. Experienced investors will only look at three to five-year bud-gets to get a general sense of the expectations of the startup and its team. They will focus more on the business metrics that the entrepreneurs used to design the budget. The analyst will try to get a deeper understanding of the founders' assumptions on customer acquisition cost (CAC), customer lifetime value (CLV), churn rates, price sensitivities of demand and other unit economics. The analyst will also cross-check the financials with the investment case to see

22 Camerer *et al.* (1989).
23 A more detailed description of the financials can be found in Chapter 7.

how future liquidity plans are reflected in the timing and volume of future rounds of funding, i.e. the financial strategy of the startup.

Subjective Factors

Looking at the subjective factors that influence a financial screening, the VC will try to get as much information as possible about the team's passion for financials and Key Performance Indicators (KPI). Investors, in particular, question how number-driven the team is, e.g. do they meet and discuss the business' performance on a monthly or even weekly basis, do they adjust their activities in the light of significant deviations from the budget figures, and how well do they know their numbers and KPIs to begin with? A common tactic is to ask the founders separately what they believe is the most important KPI for their company. In many cases, the investor will get three different answers from three different founders.

The investor's rationale for challenging a startup's financials is twofold. First, the information will tell the investor something about the business itself. And, second, the answer will inform the VC about how the entrepreneurs are dealing with numbers – and, eventually, their money.

Let us look at an example. Imagine a startup is selling furniture, such as chairs and tables, online. The average basket size (order volume) per customer transaction is €350. The company charges each customer a delivery charge of €30 per delivery. The investor is curious about the delivery fee because he believes it is presumably more expensive in most cases and therefore assumes that a delivery charge of €30 indirectly eats into the company's gross margin.

The entrepreneur, confronted with this question, answers:

'You are correct to assume that this fee does not cover our delivery cost entirely in most cases. However, we tested the introduction of a €50 transaction fee for two months. We then found that customers started complaining about these charges. Consequently, we saw a drop of five per cent in our order volume (while we managed all market channels as usual) and, interestingly, the click-rate on the 'delivery charge FAQ' had almost tripled compared to the time when we charged a lower delivery fee. We then decided that our gross margin was comfortable enough to absorb a €30 delivery fee. Having more transactions and higher revenue is strategically more important to us. Also, we believe that the delivery cost will drop further with increased efficiency, effectiveness and competition in the logistics sector.'

The investor is very pleased because she gets three valuable pieces of information from this statement:

• The entrepreneur knows his unit economics and understands that he is expected to play and experiment with these numbers to identify the best possible business model. Also, he has a fairly detailed management information system that allows him to measure the impact of certain management decisions.

- The entrepreneur does not get lost in details. He acknowledges the need to experiment, but he also understands that it should not take too much of his attention.
- The entrepreneur has an open mindset, i.e. can reflect on his business from a more general point of view and develop reasonable assumptions regarding the future, e.g. in logistics.

This example illustrates why investors are always interested in challenging entrepreneurs on their numbers. By reading between the lines of the financials, they can get much more information than in most other screening or due diligence activities.

Investment Case

Rational Aspects

The evaluation of the investment case[24] is taxing since the information asymmetry between founder and investor is higher in this aspect than in most other areas of the selection process. For the investor, the screening of the investment case is often as important as the screening of the executive summary, because one possible result could be that the deal does not yet meet (too early-stage) or no longer meets (too late-stage) the investor's strategic requirements. However, the main difference from the screening of the executive summary is that the investment case is, in most instances, still negotiable at the time of the application.

On the rational side, the analyst tries to get an in-depth understanding of the venture's previous funding activity. Here, past and current valuations, the shareholder structure, liquidity status, planned execution of the present round of financing, ticket sizes, commitments of existing investors and the background of current investors play a significant role.

Subjective Factors

In addition to the above, the analyst will make efforts to grasp the potential future development of the business (e.g. how many more rounds of funding at what valuation levels will there be, what will the road to exit be, and what is the time horizon of the investment).

In doing so, there are two explicit areas that involve a conflict of interest between founders and investors which the analyst will have to consider carefully.

---

24 This is explained in detail in Chapter 8.

Too-big-a-ticket at Too-high-a-valuation

Some startups try to raise large investment tickets in very early rounds of funding. This scenario frequently occurs when star entrepreneurs with a perceived preference for top-exits start a new venture. The distinct advantage for founders and investors is that the founders may succeed and can then focus entirely on the development of the startup in the following years. An obvious disadvantage for investors (and, consequently, a challenge for founders) is that the investor has to put a lot of money on a horse that he has never seen on the track before – not even from afar.

Moreover, it is also likely that a relatively large ticket comes hand-in-hand with a relatively high valuation, since the founders can then retain their majority share in the enterprise. If that is the case, the investor is also betting on the fact that the founders will be able to develop the company to a very advanced level until all money from the first round is spent. If they fail to reach this level, they fail to justify the relatively high valuation from the first round, and will, thus, most likely fail in trying to get follow-on funding at an even higher valuation.

Too-small-a-ticket at Too-low-a-valuation

Some startups try to raise small tickets of investment in early and very early rounds of funding. This scenario frequently occurs when young first-time entrepreneurs with an apparent lack of experience are advised by well-meaning consultants. The distinct advantage for founders and investors is that the entrepreneurs will struggle less to get this round together since the ticket is small and the incentive, i.e. the share in the company that an investor gets, is relatively attractive. An obvious disadvantage for investors (and, as a consequence, a challenge for entrepreneurs) is that the founders will be forced to raise more money within a short period of time, no matter whether the company is successful or not, because growth is expensive too. Consequently, the founders' focus may be more on funding and less on business development. Moreover, it is likely that a relatively small ticket comes hand-in-hand with a relatively low valuation of the company; again, this will enable the founders to retain their majority share in the company. If that is the case, the investor is also betting on the fact that the founders will be able to develop the company to very advanced levels in subsequent years, because only then will the team be able to justify significant jumps in valuations that are suddenly much higher than in early rounds of funding.

Nonetheless, herd behaviour may lead investors to ignore these conflicts of interest. Just because a famous VC has invested in a company, it does not mean that an unbalanced relationship between the size of the investment ticket and the company's valuation can be justified. The example of Bessemer Ventures Partners' anti-portfolio shows that they do not get it right every time.

Roadmap

Rational Aspects

A screening of the roadmap is undertaken to learn what the company plans to do in the next 12 months (or five years) to reach an exit at some point in the future. Both founders and investors agree that a lot of what is likely to happen in the course of the next few years can only be guessed at by using a crystal ball. However, there is also consensus that all stakeholders should have a common understanding regarding the destination of the journey on which they are about to embark, and that they should, therefore, discuss important milestones.

Looking at the factual information contained in the roadmap, the analyst will assess the entrepreneur's growth plan regarding the team, product, geographic and industry segment expansion, the adoption of new business models, as well as the timing and volume of future rounds of funding. The analyst is also likely to spend some time trying to figure out what his screening results (regarding the team, product, market and competition, business model and investment case) will look like in the next 12, 24, 36, or 48 months.

Subjective Factors

In examining the softer aspects of the roadmap, the analyst will try to understand the entrepreneur's intentions, concerns, doubts, but also the team's feelings about the future. Important questions include: How will the entrepreneurs react to new team members and a different level of professionalization within the company? How will they go from prototype (creative, trial-and-error) to serial production (less creative, more stability and a cost-optimization focus)? How well do they know their future markets or industries? How likely is it that they will be able to optimize the business model? Or how strong are the incentive structures (equity plans) for the necessary team members as part of the investment strategy to keep the relevant people on board?

The roadmap is, some argue, a less important topic, especially for early-stage investors, whose experience has taught them that many aspects of the venture are likely to change in the first two to three years, sometimes even dramatically. However, interviewing the founders about the roadmap remains a popular tool for investors, because there is much to be learned about the operational level of the company and the character of the entrepreneurs the investor is about to engage with.

Working with Findings from the Screening Process

The screening process ends with a presentation of the results by the analyst to other members of btov's investment teams. The selection process also affects the due diligence activities and the term sheet negotiation, i.e.

- the key strengths and weaknesses of a company identified during the screening process are examined in more detail during the due diligence process; and/or
- the key risks identified during the screening process are introduced into the term sheet negotiation process. For example, if the team lacks a key management person with an engineering background, then this will be examined again in the due diligence process. Factors like this can eventually result in a 'condition to closing' in the term sheet, where the founders are forced to recruit an engineer into their team if they want to receive the money from the investor.

Screening and Corporate Governance

In acknowledgement of the challenging nature of the screening process, VCs have introduced different governance policies surrounding the screening process.

Looking at our case company, btov, the screening process is carried out by analysts, associates, investment managers, principals and partners of the firm. There is no investment professional who has not completed a screening process for a variety of startups. Having a high level of engagement increases the level of empathy in the internal discussions about a startup. Every team member knows how demanding this process is. At the same time, all of them acknowledge the fact that the pool of information from which the analysing team member can draw arguments to defend his opportunity against his (critical) colleagues is limited.

btov acknowledges that it is nearly impossible to have enough up-to-date know-how in the team to analyse, assess and select 15 to 25 top investment opportunities from a given deal flow of over 3,000 companies that the fund screens per year. Therefore, it runs two sequential processes to integrate the deal screening process into its corporate governance. The first process runs internally, where analysts review the complete deal flow of the company by applying the screening process described above. The second process involves members of btov's private investor network who get access to the pre-selected deal flow, i.e. about 100 to 130 companies per year. The second process often involves inviting startup teams to pitch their companies live in front of the investors and its network. In the aftermath of the presentation, the btov network members and staff will discuss and analyze the cases together, which is interesting, as members of the network are often entrepreneurs who bring a different perspective and degree of know-how (regarding products, technologies, markets, competitors, etc.) to the table.

btov has also defined a process according to which the analyst who has initially screened an investment proposal is not involved in the actual decision-making process regarding an investment in a given company. The reason for this is that the analyst will have become close to the startup and its team during the screening process. In most cases, the founders behind the promising cases that are pre-selected for the due diligence and term sheet phase are outstanding entrepreneurs with strong personalities and high energy levels. It has often been observed that analysts will, over time, subconsciously 'change sides' and advocate for the founders. In the language of the secret services, one might even refer to them as 'moles', i.e. double agents working for both sides and sometimes not knowing on which side their heart lies. This kind of situation arises because the analysts can grow fond of the companies they evaluate.

At some point, it is possible that an analyst becomes self-conscious about a particular start-up. He has already put in so much effort and energy into this venture that he does not want to see it get cancelled. In this case, colleagues may start hearing phrases as for instance 'I think we need to do (... this and that ...) because otherwise, this will put our company at risk'. It's the 'our' that is discerning in this case because it is not and will never be the VC's company, no matter how attached and close the organizations may become. In the end, the screening process will never be perfect, especially, when it comes down to evaluating human beings and their personalities. However, a screening framework and governance mechanisms as they are applied by the btov Partners AG make sure that process is as deliberate as possible.

KEY TAKEAWAYS

- Venture capital investing is a double-sided principal–agent relationship, which can be influenced by both the investor and the entrepreneur through signalling, self-selection, bonding and monitoring.
- Opportunistic and overoptimistic behaviour transforms the principal–agent relationship between investor and entrepreneur into a principal–agent problem.
- The VC needs to be familiar with his firm's' overall investment strategy in order to make good sourcing and screening decisions.
- The analyst needs to be aware of the interplay between rational and subjective factors as well as cognitive biases in order to make effective screening decisions.

END OF CHAPTER QUESTIONS

1. Why is the sourcing and screening process so important to the overall performance of a VC portfolio?
2. What is a principal–agent relationship in venture capital?
3. What are the factors that cause a principal–agent relationship to become a principal–agent problem?
4. What is the meaning of signalling?
5. What are typical examples of bonding between the investor and entrepreneur?

6. Name three common ways used by VCs to get in touch with potential investment opportunities.
7. If a VC has a fund size of €100 million and is looking to invest in 25 to 30 different companies, what would be the approximate span of investment tickets that the VC is looking for?
8. What rational aspects should an analyst consider when evaluating a start-up team?
9. What is the significance of the false-consensus bias when screening for market and competitors?
10. Which two elements from a corporate governance perspective can a VC use to complement the screening process?

FURTHER READING

Bussgang, J. (2011). *Mastering the VC Game: A Venture Capital Insider Reveals How to Get from Start-up to IPO on Your Terms.* Portfolio.

Cohen, S. (2007). Best practice guidance for angel groups: Deal screening. Retrieved 23 June 2017, from Angel Capital Association.

Draper, W. H. (2011). *The Startup Game: Inside the Partnership between Venture Capitalists and Entrepreneurs* . 2nd edition. Macmillan.

Lerner, J. (2009). *Boulevard of Broken Dreams: Why Public Efforts to Boost Entrepreneurship and Venture Capital Have Failed and What to Do about It.* Princeton University Press.

Mason, C. and Stark, M. (2004). What do investors look for in a business plan? A comparison of the investment criteria of bankers, venture capitalists and business angels. *International Small Business Journal* 22(3), 227–248.

REFERENCES

Akerlof, G. A. (1970). The market for 'lemons': Quality uncertainty and the market mechanism. *Quarterly Journal of Economics*, 84(3), 488–500.

Banerjee, A. V. (1992). A simple model of herd behavior. *Quarterly Journal of Economics*, 107(3), 797–817.

Busenitz, L. W., Fiet, J. O. and Moesel, D. D. (2004). Reconsidering the venture capitalists' 'value added' proposition: An interorganizational learning perspective. *Journal of Business Venturing*, 19(6), 787–807.

Bygrave, W. D. (1988). The structure of the investment networks of venture capital firms. *Journal of Business Venturing*, 3(2), 137–157.

Camerer, C., Loewenstein, G. and Weber, M. (1989). The curse of knowledge in economic settings: An experimental analysis. *Journal of political Economy*, 97(5), 1232–1254.

Florida, R. and King, K. (2016). *Rise of the global startup city*: The geography of venture capital investment in cities and metros across the globe. Martin Prosperity Institute.

Franke, N., Gruber, M., Harhoff, D. and Henkel, J. (2006). What you are is what you like: Similarity biases in venture capitalists' evaluations of start-up teams. *Journal of Business Venturing*, 21(6), 802–826.

Hoyt, D., Ranzetta, T. G. and Strebulaev, I. (2012). Venture capital deal sourcing and screening. Retrieved 22 April 2017 from Stanford University.

Kahneman, D. and Tversky, A. (1979). Prospect theory: An analysis of decision under risk. *Journal of the Econometric Society*, 47(2), 263–291.

Landier, A. and Thesmar, D. (2009). Financial contracting with optimistic entrepreneurs. *Review of Financial Studies*, 22(1), 117–150.

Lounsbury, M. and Glynn, M. A (2001). Cultural entrepreneurship: Stories, legitimacy, and the acquisition of resources. *Strategic Management Journal*, 22(6), 545–564.

Martens, M. L., Jennings, J. E. and Jennings, P. D. (2007). Do the stories they tell get them the money they need? The role of entrepreneurial narratives in resource acquisition. *Academy of Management Journal*, 50(5), 1107–1132.

Matusik, S. F. and Fitza, M. A. (2012). Diversification in the venture capital industry: Leveraging knowledge under uncertainty. *Strategic Management Journal*, 33(4), 407–426.

Nickerson, R. S. (1998). Confirmation bias: A ubiquitous phenomenon in many guises. *Review of General Psychology*, 2(2), 175–220.

Porter, M. E. (1979). How competitive forces shape strategy. *Harvard Business Review*, 57(1), 137–145.

Rawhouser, H., Villanueva, J. and Newbert, S. L. (2017). Strategies and tools for entrepreneurial resource access: A cross-disciplinary review and typology. *International Journal of Management Reviews*, 19(4), 473–491.

Ross, L., Greene, D. and House, P. (1977). The 'false consensus effect': An egocentric bias in social perception and attribution processes. *Journal of Experimental Social Psychology*, 13(3), 279–301.

Sahlman, W. A., Stevenson, H. H., Roberts, M. J. and Bhidé, A. (1999). *The Entrepreneurial Venture, 2nd edition*. Harvard Business School Press.

Scharfstein, D. S. and Stein, J. C. (1990). Herd behavior and investment. *American Economic Review*, 90(1), 465–479.

Entrepreneurial Strategies for Resource Acquisition: The Importance of Having a Good Pitch

By Jaume Villanueva, Assistant Professor, ESADE Business School

For most new ventures, raising capital is a daunting proposition. For every high-profile, high-tech, new venture that secures financing from a prestigious VC – as regularly featured in the news media – there are thousands of less glamorous startups that are unable to attract external resources of any kind. Because of a lack of collateral, a proven track record, or even a validated business idea, most startups face an uphill battle in attracting potential investors. In fact, most new ventures are unsuccessful when it comes to securing the resources they need to pursue their entrepreneurial endeavours. However, some startups do manage to persuade sceptical investors. How do they do it?

Our research[25] suggests that entrepreneurs do not have very many strategies at their disposal to attract potential investors. In fact, we could group all activities that entrepreneurs engage in into two overarching strategies: *projective* and *interpersonal*. While interpersonal strategies focus on capitalizing on entrepreneurs' social networks, the focus of projective strategies is to persuade investors of the merits of the idea as an attractive and worthwhile investment opportunity. It is really about projecting a vision of the future that is so compelling, so attractive, that investors will fall over themselves to get a slice of the action. The name of the game for investors is growth, of course, and that is what the projective idea of the future must focus on . . . a slice of the pie that is worth, say, €50,000 today could be worth a million euros in five years' time. It is this kind of projective vision, of a very attractive future state of the world, that appeals to investors.

When we talk about projective, it is in the sense of conveying a desired vision of the future, not actual financial forecasts. Although financial forecasts will be required, it is not these that will, per se, attract investors. Most investors are quite sceptical by nature, and are likely to have lots of doubts about any given investment opportunity. It is unrealistic to think that one can entirely win them over. What one needs to strive for, as an entrepreneur, is to create a seed of doubt ('maybe it will work out'). Speaking colloquially, the entrepreneur needs to generate FOMO (Fear of Missing Out). Investors may not be fully convinced and may still have doubts about the potential of the venture but . . . what if? 'What if I am missing out on the next Skype, Spotify or Facebook?' It is the fear of missing out on a great opportunity that may help entrepreneurs to overcome the doubts that an otherwise rigorous risk analysis on the part of investors will inevitably raise.

Another means of attracting external resources is by using interpersonal strategies. This type of strategy is based on the relational capital that exists between the entrepreneur and the potential investor, in other words, using one's connections. This does not mean that the quality of the opportunity is irrelevant, or that expectations about the future do not come into play. What it means is that the focus of the strategy is on the relationship of the entrepreneur with the potential resource provider, rather than on the nature of the venture itself. Interpersonal strategies appeal to the investor's sense of obligation and reciprocity toward the entrepreneur based on the nature of their relationship. Projective and interpersonal strategies are not mutually exclusive. Entrepreneurs can simultaneously engage in both.

As regards the tools that entrepreneurs have at their disposal to implement these strategies, the list of alternatives appears to be fairly limited. One of the

---

25 Rawhouser *et al.* (2017).

most common and most effective set of tools involves the use of persuasive communication. In other words, what entrepreneurs say and how they say it, in any given communication form, to influence investors' perceptions regarding the future of the new venture (in the case of projective strategies) or the nature of their relationship with the entrepreneur (in the case of interpersonal strategies). So, even if the majority of entrepreneurs don't have access to a wide arsenal of tools, one thing they all have is the ability to communicate with potential investors in some form or another. For this reason, persuasive communication tools, such as rhetoric or storytelling, are probably among the most useful and readily available set of tools available to entrepreneurs. For projective strategies, in particular, evidence suggests that the way in which entrepreneurs explain their new venture projects to potential investors (how they pitch their ventures to them) influences investors' perceptions and assessments.

It comes as no surprise, perhaps, that rhetorical skills are extremely useful when pitching to investors (rhetoric is, after all, also known as the art of persuasion). What may be more surprising is that storytelling can also be a great tool for influencing investors' assessments. Telling a good story can go a long way. There is increasing evidence to suggest that narratives can affect investors' assessments of many of the elements of a new venture opportunity and that, overall, stories can increase a new venture's legitimacy vis-à-vis sceptical investors.[26]

In any case, what seems certain is that developing a good communication strategy that clearly communicates the business opportunity to potential investors should be a priority for any entrepreneur seeking external capital. It makes sense to develop a pitch (or a set of pitches) that is clear, credible and attractive in order to influence potential investors. We do not fully understand how those who manage to get the money do it, but we do know that having a great pitch plays a significant role.

Let's Practise: Case Study
MOVU Pitch to Investors

On the following pages in Figure 6.5 you will find an early investor pitch deck of MOVU – a Swiss internet platform for moving services. Try to put yourself in the shoes of the investors who could have invested in MOVU in 2015 and answer the following questions.

26 Lounsbury and Glynn (2001); Martens *et al.* (2007).

Figure 6.5 MOVU early investor pitch deck.

Figure 6.5 (cont.)

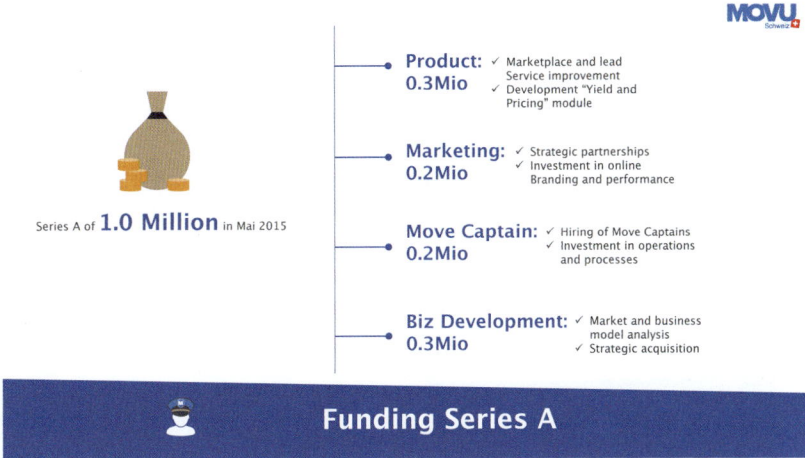

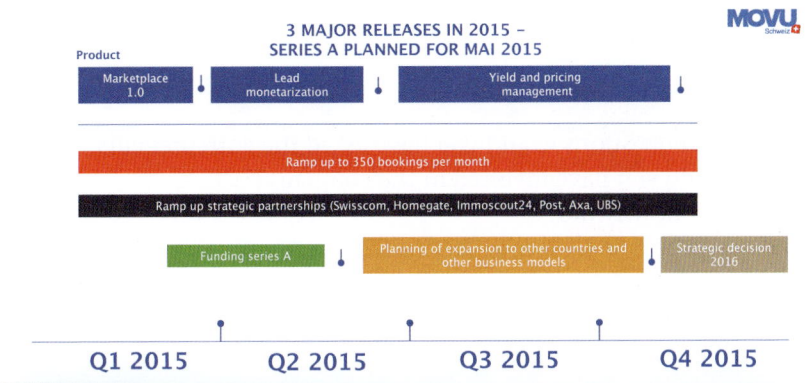

MOVU Schweiz

Series A of **1.0 Million** in Mai 2015

Product: 0.3Mio
- ✓ Marketplace and lead Service improvement
- ✓ Development "Yield and Pricing" module

Marketing: 0.2Mio
- ✓ Strategic partnerships
- ✓ Investment in online Branding and performance

Move Captain: 0.2Mio
- ✓ Hiring of Move Captains
- ✓ Investment in operations and processes

Biz Development: 0.3Mio
- ✓ Market and business model analysis
- ✓ Strategic acquisition

Funding Series A

MOVU Schweiz

3 MAJOR RELEASES IN 2015 – SERIES A PLANNED FOR MAI 2015

Product

| Marketplace 1.0 | Lead monetarization | Yield and pricing management |

Ramp up to 350 bookings per month

Ramp up strategic partnerships (Swisscom, Homegate, Immoscout24, Post, Axa, UBS)

| Funding series A | Planning of expansion to other countries and other business models | Strategic decision 2016 |

Q1 2015   Q2 2015   Q3 2015   Q4 2015

Roadmap

MOVU Schweiz

"Our **Vision** is to be the synonym for movings and cleanings by being the biggest service provider for these needs in Europe.

Business Objectives 2018:

Market leader in Switzerland

Expansion into Europe

25M
Booking revenue
7M
Total earnings
3M
EBIT
(40% EBIT–margin)

20'000+
moves with companies per annum.
25'000
"Do it Yourself" moves per annum

Figure 6.5 (cont.)

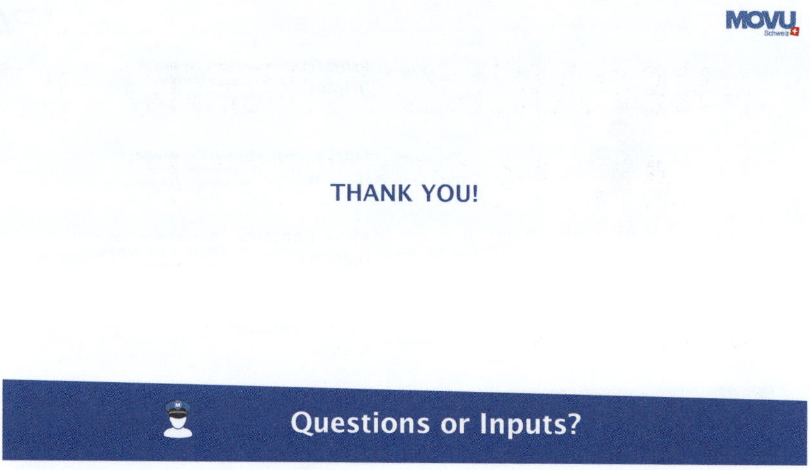

MOVU

THANK YOU!

👤   **Questions or Inputs?**

Figure 6.5 (cont.).

Questions for Discussion

1. What questions would you have asked the entrepreneurs after the pitch?
2. Would you have invested in the company?
3. Why or why not?

PREPARING THE FINANCIAL PLAN: FORECASTING

SOPHIE MANIGART
Vlerick Business School and Ghent University

MIGUEL MEULEMAN
Vlerick Business School and Imperial College Business School

In this chapter, we will delve into the technical aspects of financial planning for a startup. A financial plan is the starting point of any financial strategy. Its first purpose is to understand whether the venture will have an external financing need and, if so, how much financing it will need and when. Next, it will serve as the basis for the valuation of the venture. Third, and probably most importantly, the plan will provide the entrepreneur and potential investors the opportunity to critically assess and optimize the business model.

The first step is to understand the cash flow cycle of the venture, given its business model. Important questions need to be addressed, such as: how much needs to be invested before the business can become operational? When are the first sales expected, and when will customers pay for their purchase? The next step is to translate the business model into a financial model, including the income statement and cash flow statement. Once a comprehensive financial plan has been developed, the uncertainty any startup faces can be modelled through scenario and sensitivity analyses.

VIEW FROM THE MEDIA

FINANCIAL TIMES   FT

Gousto raises funds to take on HelloFresh in recipe kit market
Start-up is competing with dozens of rivals in latest trend for grocery deliveries

NOVEMBER 3, 2016 BY LAUREN FEDOR IN LONDON

Like the sound of rustling up a lemon crab linguine in 25 minutes flat without having to go to the shops? That is the proposition of Gousto, a London-based company set up by former Rothschild bankers, which is trying to compete with Rocket Internet-backed HelloFresh in an increasingly crowded food delivery market. The start-up, which on Thursday said it had secured its latest chunk of funding, is one of a number of companies offering a new take on grocery orders. They prepare the exact quantities of ingredients for at least two meals a week and deliver them, with cooking instructions, to customers' homes. . . .

Gousto does not disclose revenues but said its turnover had grown by more than 200 per cent each year for the past three years and that it delivered nearly 100,000 meals each week to UK customers. Mr Boldt says the underlying business was profitable but the company was 'making an active decision to sacrifice some of the profitability to be able to grow' by investing in acquiring new customers. The latest £10m of funding brings the total amount the start-up has raised to £28m since 2012. That compares with $250m for HelloFresh. Gousto's latest raising was led by London venture capital firm BGF Ventures and involved a clutch of other UK investors including Angel CoFund, which is backed by the UK government, and the venture capital arms of Unilever and Barclays. The company would not disclose its valuation.

Gousto is planning to expand in a market that Technomic, the US consumer research firm, has estimated is worth $1bn worldwide and could reach $10bn of revenues by 2020. The costs of expansion are evident at some of its rivals. In September, Rocket reported that HelloFresh's losses before interest, tax, depreciation and amortisation swelled to €45.7m in the first half, more than double a year earlier. . . . But Neil Campling, an analyst at Northern Trust, says the company's margins were deteriorating as it burnt through cash to acquire new customers and invest in infrastructure. . . . However, Mr Campling says he was sceptical of the long-term growth prospects for HelloFresh and other similar recipe kit start-ups. 'I only see evidence that the scale comes from high investment that doesn't necessarily lead to recurring revenue,' he says, adding that while customers were often wooed to try these services by free vouchers and discount codes, they were unlikely to be consistent, long-term subscribers to recipe kit services. . . . Mr Boldt dismisses concerns that Gousto would face the same difficulties as HelloFresh and others. 'Where we fundamentally differentiate from the competitors is we are not acquiring customers at all costs,' he says. 'We are very much focused on sustainable capabilities.' . . .

www.ft.com/content/97e5eb40-a00f-11e6-86d5-4e36b35c3550

LEARNING OBJECTIVES

After reading this chapter, you will be able to:

- Appreciate the importance of financial planning.
- Understand the cash flow cycle and the underlying drivers of cash flows.
- Determine the external financing need.
- Conduct a pro-forma analysis including the income statement and cash flow statement.

- Understand how scenario and sensitivity analyses help to deal with uncertainty.
- Become familiar with the key concepts used when communicating a financial plan to investors, including important financial metrics such as burn rate and cash runway.

Where Are We Going Next?

This chapter begins by introducing financial planning and explaining why it is crucial for any venture. It continues by briefly outlining the determinants of the financial needs and the distinction between profit and cash flows. Next, we will explain how to conduct pro-forma analyses to assess financial needs, including profit-and-loss statements and cash flow statements. Using the pro-forma analyses, we will provide insights into how to use your plan to define a financing strategy for the venture and how to communicate your financial plan to investors. This chapter concludes with a discussion on how to account for an unpredictable future and how to run sensitivity checks and scenario analyses.

7.1   The Importance of Financial Planning for the Entrepreneur

Cash is king! Money is an important resource for running and growing a startup. Most ventures need money to develop their product or service, to pay salaries and sundries before hitting first sales. Even a company that generates profits may go through periods where internally generated cash is insufficient to finance the investments needed to scale the business. At that time, new external financing is needed to secure its future. Confronted with a rapidly changing and unpredictable environment, most companies will also face unexpected situations that may cause cash shortages and thereby endanger the company's future. Again, external financing may be needed to keep the company alive. Running out of cash is a situation any entrepreneur should avoid, as it may lead to bankruptcy. Additionally, raising new financing with limited funds remaining puts the entrepreneur in an extremely vulnerable position with little (or no) negotiating power, at the mercy of external financiers. A sound financial plan signals when cash is needed, and how much funding needs to be raised to cover periods of cash drought.

Financial planning, therefore, is an essential part of the entrepreneur's planning process. There are several reasons for this. First, given a preferred business model, financial planning helps the entrepreneur to assess *how much* and *when* cash is needed to start and keep the business running. Figure 7.1 illustrates a typical cash flow pattern of a startup company. In the early stage of a venture's life, considerable amounts of cash are consumed in order to develop the business. The rate at which cash is consumed is called the *cash burn rate* and determines the *runway*, or the amount of time left before running out of cash. The time it takes until positive cash flows are generated – the so-called 'valley of death' – may be substantial. For example, it is not unusual for a drug development company to burn hundreds of millions of euros before generating positive

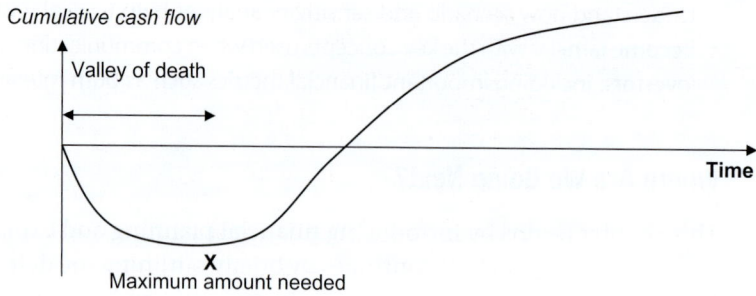

Cumulative cash flow

Valley of death

Time

X
Maximum amount needed

Figure 7.1 Typical cash flow pattern of a startup company.

cash flows, following several years or even decades of product development. It is, therefore, important to calculate from the outset the cumulative cash shortage and the time it will take to get to a position of positive cash flow. If the financial plan indicates that the entrepreneur's funds are insufficient to finance the required investments and operations, the plan will also help to determine when and which financing sources should be targeted.

Second, the financial plan also helps entrepreneurial teams to determine whether they should pursue the venture in its current form, change the business model drastically, or invest their money and time in another opportunity. It enables teams to examine whether the venture is viable or under what conditions it could become profitable. Financial planning, therefore, is an important strategic decision-making tool for the entrepreneur. Furthermore, financial planning facilitates the evaluation of different strategic options and helps the team to pick out the one with the highest expected value-creation potential.

A financial plan further enables the entrepreneur to conduct scenario and sensitivity analyses, helping to translate the venture's financial risks into financial terms. It is advisable to assess the financial needs both in a worst-case scenario and a best case or super growth scenario. Some companies fail, not because they had a bad idea, but simply because they underestimated the amount of funds needed when scaling up a successful initial operation. Finding money can prove to be difficult when the entrepreneur is put in a weak negotiating position, particularly in a recession. Outside investors may then excessively dilute the entrepreneur's stake in the company. The financial plan thus helps to anticipate changing conditions and surprises.

In addition, a good financial plan helps to determine the key underlying assumptions driving the financial metrics, including, for example, gross margins, average customer acquisitions costs, fraction of recurring revenue and average churn. Understanding these key metrics in advance will guide the entrepreneur in developing and managing the business. Also, once the project or the business has started, a good financial plan with sound metrics can be used as a benchmark for performance measurement.

Finally, the plan is an important marketing tool for convincing outside investors of the merits of the project. Moreover, when turning to outside investors, a detailed financial plan is necessary for valuing the business. A well-prepared financial plan will assist the entrepreneur during the negotiating process with outside investors and increases the credibility of the venture. It should be clear to you by now that a good financial plan is of crucial importance.

Let's Practise: Case Study

Assessing the Burn Rate and Runway of Biocartis

Biocartis, a Swiss-Belgian company founded in 2007 by the serial entrepreneur Dr Rudi Pauwels and two co-founders, is an innovative molecular diagnostics company providing next generation diagnostic solutions aimed at improving clinical practice for the benefit of patients, clinicians, funding bodies and industry. The company's proprietary MDx Idylla™ platform is a fully automated, real-time system which offers accurate, highly reliable molecular information from any biological sample in virtually any setting. Idylla™ addresses the growing demand for personalized medicine by allowing fast and effective treatment selection and treatment progress monitoring. Biocartis is developing and marketing a rapidly expanding test menu addressing key unmet clinical needs in oncology and infectious diseases. These areas represent, respectively, the fastest and largest-growing segments of the US$5 billion MDx market, which was expected to grow to approximately US$8 billion in 2018.

Figure 7.2 shows the firm's fundraising history up to the IPO in 2015, in which the company raised €115 million. In a first phase, funding was needed to develop Idylla™; in the current phase, more money is needed to bring the product to the market and to further innovate the diagnostics platform. Before the IPO, the company raised €221 million from different types of investors, including family

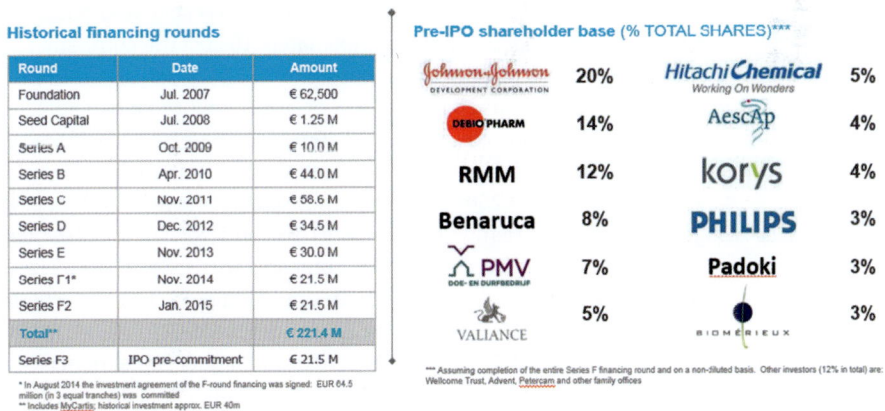

Historical financing rounds

Round	Date	Amount
Foundation	Jul. 2007	€ 62,500
Seed Capital	Jul. 2008	€ 1.25 M
Series A	Oct. 2009	€ 10.0 M
Series B	Apr. 2010	€ 44.0 M
Series C	Nov. 2011	€ 58.6 M
Series D	Dec. 2012	€ 34.5 M
Series E	Nov. 2013	€ 30.0 M
Series F1*	Nov. 2014	€ 21.5 M
Series F2	Jan. 2015	€ 21.5 M
Total**		€ 221.4 M
Series F3	IPO pre-commitment	€ 21.5 M

* In August 2014 the investment agreement of the F-round financing was signed: EUR 64.5 million (in 3 equal tranches) was committed
** Includes MyCartis; historical investment approx. EUR 40m

Pre-IPO shareholder base (% TOTAL SHARES)**

	%		%
Johnson & Johnson DEVELOPMENT CORPORATION	20%	Hitachi Chemical Working On Wonders	5%
DEBIO PHARM	14%	AescAp	4%
RMM	12%	korys	4%
Benaruca	8%	PHILIPS	3%
PMV DOE- EN DURFBEDRIJF	7%	Padoki	3%
VALIANCE	5%	BIOMÉRIEUX	3%

**** Assuming completion of the entire Series F financing round and on a non-diluted basis. Other investors (12% in total) are: Wellcome Trust, Advent, Petercam and other family offices

Figure 7.2 Pre-IPO financing rounds of Biocartis.
Source: Biocartis company presentation (2016)

and friends, angel investors, traditional venture capital investors, family offices and strategic corporate partners.

The financial history of Biocartis illustrates the importance of assessing financial needs given the extended 'valley of death' found in many health-care-related startups. The financial update provided by Biocartis for its 2016 results, as shown in Table 7.1, clearly illustrates the financial challenges of running a healthcare company, even after ten years of operations.

Table 7.1 Biocartis 2016 results

Key highlights

- **Installed base**: Installed base Idylla™ instruments more than doubled in 2016 by adding a total of 224 instruments. Total installed base year end was close to 390 instruments.
- **Cartridge consumption**: Commercial cartridge volume in 2016 increased to over 25,000 cartridges which represents approximately 7.5 times the total commercial volume of 2015.
- **Test menu**: market oncology menu expanded to 7 tests.
- **Revenues**: Total 2016 operating income amounted to €13.8m. Product revenues in 2016 amounted to €6.8m, representing an increase of 88% compared to 2015.
- **Cash position**: Cash and cash equivalents on 31 December 2016 amounted to €83.2m.

Financial highlights

- **Product sales revenues** – Total product sales revenues in 2016 increased by approximately 88% to €6.8m from €3.6m in 2015. This increase was predominantly driven by cartridge sales that amounted to €4.0m in 2016, representing over 3 times the 2015 cartridge sales of €1.3m. System sales increased by approximately 20% from €2.3m in 2015 to €2.8m in 2016.
- **Equity raise** – On 17 November 2016, Biocartis successfully raised €32.7m of gross proceeds by means of a private placement via an accelerated bookbuild offering of 4,058,917 new shares (being approximately 10% of the company's outstanding shares) at an issue price of €8.05 per share.
- **Debt financing** – On 20 July 2016, Biocartis announced it had attracted €55m of non-dilutive financing consisting of a €40m bank and lease financing facility as well as a new subordinated loan of €15m. The bank and lease financing facility consists of €15m lease financing and €25m multiple purpose credit lines (the credit lines are partially guaranteed by the Flemish Government). Biocartis' total debt outstanding amounted to €31.4m as per 31 December 2016, compared to €10.8m as per 31 December 2015.
- **Cash flow** – Biocartis' cash flow from operating (−53.3m) and investing activities (−9.3m) amounted to €−62.7m in 2016, compared to €−32.8m in 2015, mainly driven by increased operational expenses and higher investments for cartridge manufacturing expansion. Given a cash flow from financing activities in 2016 of €41.8m, the total net cash flow of 2016 amounted to €−20.9m.
- **Cash position** – Biocartis' cash position as per 31 December 2016 amounted to €83.2m compared to €104.1m as per 31 December 2015.

Table 7.1 (cont.)

Key figures (EUR 1,000)	2016	2015	% Change
Total operating income	**13,772**	**14,951**	**−8%**
Cost of sales	−5,701	−2,642	116%
Research & Development expenses	−42,091	−36,554	15%
Marketing & Distribution expenses	−10,324	−8,747	18%
General & Administrative expenses	−5,827	−6,662	−13%
Operating expenses	**−63,943**	**−54,606**	**17%**
Operational result	**−50,171**	**−39,655**	**27%**
Net financial result	−586	−790	−26%
Income tax	980	648	51%
Net result	**−49,777**	**−39,797**	**25%**
Cash flow from operating activities	−53,312	−27,335	95%
Cash flow from incesting activities	−9,342	−5,436	72%
Cash flow from financing activities	41,804	125,943	−6/%
Net cash flow	**−20,850**	**93,172**	**−122%**
Cash and cash equivalent[1]	**83,247**	**104,087**	**−20%**
Financial debt	31,407	10,815	190%

[1] Including EUR 1.2m of restricted cash (as a guarantee for KBC lease financing).
Source: https://media.biocartis.com/biocartis/documents/170301-Press-Release-2016FY-Results-EN.pdf

In 2016, the company was still running operational losses of around €50 million and a negative cash flow from operating and investing activities of €63 million, requiring the company to carefully manage its cash needs and to look for additional funding sources.

Questions for Discussion

1. What are the usual main drivers of the financial needs of a healthcare venture such as Biocartis before commercialization starts? What is Biocartis' revenue model?
2. What was the 2016 net operational cash burn (net burn = cash out – cash in from operations)? To what extent is it important to monitor the gross burn rate (cash out)?
3. Assuming that the 2016 net cash burn is a good indication of the future burn rate, what is the runway Biocartis has left? What should the minimum runway be for a startup or scale-up at any point in time?

7.2   Cash Flows, Profits and the Balance Sheet: Putting It All Together

The ultimate goal of a company is to create value by transforming cash today into more cash in the future, in anticipation of meeting the required return. As understanding how much cash is needed and how much cash the operations are expected to generate in the future is key for any startup, the most important part of a financial plan is the cash forecast, or the pro-forma *cash flow statement*. This includes all expected cash income, mainly from sales and from equity and debt investors, and all cash drains, such as salaries, suppliers or service providers, among others. The difference between the cash receipts and cash payments represents the net cash received or paid during a period.

Rather than starting the planning cycle with the cash flow statement, however, it is customary to first forecast the pro-forma *profit-and-loss statement* (P&L) – also known as the *income statement* – which represents all revenues and costs. The difference between revenues and costs is the profit (if positive) or loss (if negative) of the period. The third financial statement is the *balance sheet*, which represents on the one hand the assets of the company, and on the other hand the sources of funding, including equity and debt. While the cash flow and the P&L statement cover a specific period (typically a year), a balance sheet presents a picture of assets and sources of funding at a specific point in time. Hence, the balance sheet is a static representation, while the P&L and cash flow statement are dynamic, and comparable to a movie. A startup's financial plan will typically focus more on the dynamic P&L and cash flow statements, while

Table 7.2 Core components of a startup's financial plan

P&L

	Revenues
−	Operational costs
=	EBIT
−	Taxes
=	EBIT after taxes

Cash Flow Statement

	EBIT after taxes
+	Depreciation and other non-cash expenses
−	Increase in working capital
=	Cash flow from operating activities
−	Cash flow from investing activities
=	Free cash flow (FCF)

the balance sheet will receive less attention, as it is less informative in this context. In this chapter, we will therefore focus mainly on the former.

While there is some overlap between the cash flow and the P&L statement, they are not exactly the same. A company can be profitable and nevertheless run out of cash, or vice versa. Table 7.2 shows how the P&L statement and the cash flow statement are connected.

A startup's financial plan begins with forecasts of the operational part of the P&L, starting from revenues and including all operating costs that are needed to sustain revenues. Revenues minus operating costs give the *Earnings Before Interest and Taxes*, or EBIT, highlighting the fact that EBIT neither includes interest payments, which are financial costs determined by lending decisions, nor taxes. As taxes need to be paid, and hence involve a cash payment, income taxes are estimated as a percentage of EBIT[1] and deducted from EBIT.

Earnings before interest and taxes, however, takes costs into account that do not involve a cash payment, such as depreciations linked to long-term investments or capital expenditures (CAPEX). Therefore, in order to calculate the cash generated by (or consumed by) operations, depreciation and other non-cash costs (e.g. amortizations) have to be added back into EBIT. Further, in order to keep the business operational, most companies have to invest in *working capital*, taking into

---

1 Obviously, taxes are only important if the startup is profitable and pays taxes.

account inventory and the payment terms of customers and suppliers. This clearly affects the venture's cash situation. However, the working capital is not taken into account in the P&L: revenues do not take customers' payment terms into account, costs do not take into account suppliers' payment terms, and inventory does not play a role. Changes in working capital should hence be tracked to capture cash changes. Taking non-cash expenses and changes in working capital into account generates the cash flow from operating activities. A positive cash flow from operating activities shows that the day-to-day operations are generating cash; alternatively, a negative cash flow from operating activities suggests that the day-to-day operations are still consuming more cash than is generated by customers.

Finally, investments in long-term assets, or capital expenditures (CAPEX), negatively affect cash but are not included in the P&L. Hence, net investments (= investments – divestments), or cash flows from investing activities, negatively affect cash and must be included in the financial plan. Cash flows from operating and investing activities together determine the free cash flow (FCF) of the firm. A positive FCF signals that the cash flow from operations is sufficient to cover CAPEX, and the venture is financially self-sustaining.

Note that a startup's financial plan focuses on the operational part of the P&L and cash flow statement and thereby ignores financial flows. Thus, financial flows to and from investors including shareholders (e.g. capital increases, dividend payments) and lenders (e.g. changes in financial debt, interest payments) are ignored in a first phase. This is because the goal of the financial plan is to understand how much financing is needed to run the operations. Hence, cash flows used by or generated by operations have to be estimated, before turning to the question of how to finance potential cash shortages.

How far into the future should the financial plan go when drafting these statements? If the aim of the forecast is to predict future financial needs, you should, as a minimum, forecast the period until the next investment round. When the aim is to estimate the value of the venture, you should ideally extend the forecasting period until the point where cash flows stabilize – or as far as possible, for example, until the expected exit. Another important element in financial forecasting is the periodicity of the forecast. As uncertainty and instability characterize the early years in the life of a business, it is advisable to break the first forecasting periods into short periods of a month or a quarter, and switch to yearly periods when the business becomes more stable. This provides a good benchmark for monitoring the progress of the venture. Making the intervals even shorter is less valuable, since variations in these figures occur too frequently to be meaningful.

7.3   Steps in the Development of a Startup's Financial Plan

This section will take you step-by-step through the development of a full-fledged startup's financial plan. The most important drivers of cash needs are discussed in detail, including:

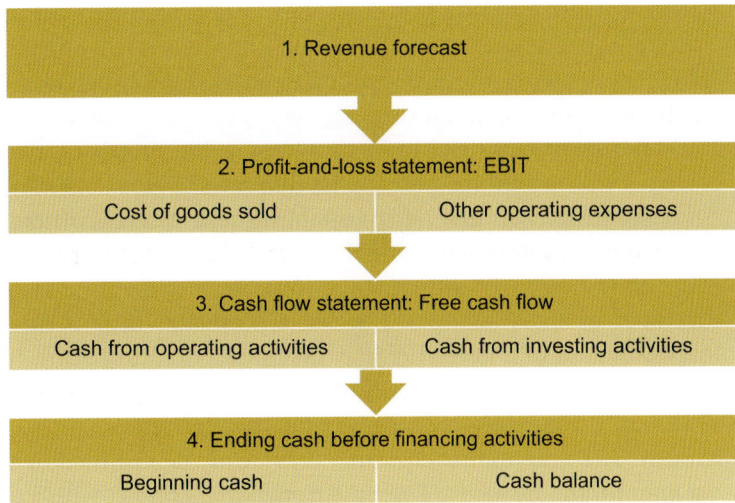

Figure 7.3 Steps in the development of a startup's financial plan.

- the specific characteristics of the business model,
- the time to first revenues and the revenue-generating potential of a startup,
- working capital policies, including customer payment strategies, and
- the efficiency of generating cash i.e. the profitability and the growth prospects of the company.

There are four steps involved in building a financial forecast through pro forma analysis, as illustrated in Figure 7.3. First of all, assumptions must be made regarding revenues. Most importantly, the sales forecast should be determined by considering the level of sales attainable given market demand and available resources. After that, the EBIT can be forecasted as a function of the level of sales, including the assumptions underlying the EBIT such as the costs of products sold and the selling, general and administrative expenses. Once the EBIT has been forecasted, a cash flow statement is computed using input from the P&L statement and the assumptions underlying the working capital policy and capital expenditures. The outcome of the cash flow statement is the free cash flow of the period which, together with the cash at the start of the period, determines the cash position at the end of the period.

Step 1: Revenue Forecast

A reliable estimate of revenues and sales is the main building block of a pro forma analysis. Sales growth is the main driver of the venture's financial needs. Therefore, all financial plans begin with a sales forecast. Due to the uncertain state of the future, forecasts can never be perfect, but a sound plan starts with the most realistic estimate of future sales. The fundamental drivers of a venture's revenue are the price at which products or services will be sold, and the expected quantity thereof. A sound revenue forecast should therefore outline the details of both prices and quantities.

Major questions need to be answered when preparing a sales forecast. First, when will the venture generate its first sales? Some companies sell products or services from their first day of establishment whereas others may need to wait several years before achieving their first sales. For example, companies developing new drugs will anticipate a long development process during which a number of trials take place before a particular drug is finally approved: the development of a new drug may take more than ten years. It is not surprising, then, that these companies often start by offering consulting services so as to generate some early cash flows and thereby reduce their external financing needs. The time to first customer is not only determined by the product development time, however. The time from a first contact with a potential customer to a signed contract, and to first payments from that customer, may take several months or even years when the contracts are significant and crucial to the operations of the target customer. A new company often underestimates this time delay. Therefore, having a realistic appreciation of sales timing is important, as this fully determines the first positive cash flows from operations. Once the company starts to generate sales, it should have a better idea about the growth rate of these sales in order to be able to determine the level of resources that will be required to support their growth.

Second, what is the expected level of sales and sales growth? It is not our intention to discuss all the techniques available for forecasting future sales and sales growth here. Since startups do not have a track record or prior experience on which to base their forecast, making reliable estimates is much more difficult than it is for more established companies. The amount of revenue will depend on a number of different factors including:

- The size and growth rate of the total available market (TAM) and the fraction a company might be able to capture of this.
- The speed to market. For example, will the venture operate and train its own sales force or rely on a third partner to sell its offering?
- The attractiveness of the products and services the startup is selling and the extent to which customers are looking for solutions and prepared to pay for it.
- The revenue model and pricing strategy employed by the startup. For example, a company operating a freemium model (e.g. Spotify, PEAK) will need to subsidize its user base before converting free users into paying customers.
- Additionally, are there opportunities to generate recurring revenue or cross-sell certain products or services?
- The complexity of the buying process. For example, selling a new medical device such as a prosthetic device will require the consent of different parties including   governments,   insurance   providers,   doctors   and   patient

organizations which will often slow down the buying process and the speed at which revenues may be expected.

- The average time it takes for customers to take a buying decision. Selling a new, critical component for an airplane engine will take longer than selling a new type of soft drink to a small retail store.
- The average order size or revenue per customer. Do you need to convince one million customers to pay your company €1 each to buy an app or do you need to sell two contracts worth €500,000 to generate €1 million in sales?

There are basically two different methods of forecasting sales. Many first-time entrepreneurs tend to use a *top-down forecast,* starting from the total available market (TAM). This typically goes as follows, 'if we can capture x% of the XYZ market with a size of €x billion, we will reach €x in revenues'. Even though top-down revenue forecasts might give an indication of the potential size of a company in the future, it fails to account for the barriers, efforts and resources needed to actually reach out and convince customers. Therefore, a *bottom-up sales forecast* is essential for determining the expected revenues. It addresses the following question: given the resources a company has available and the size of the serviceable available market (SAM), what is the expected sales level that can be obtained? Three consecutive steps are needed to perform a bottom-up sales forecast.

1. A first step in the bottom-up sales analysis is to determine the serviceable available market (SAM). The key question to answer is what segment of the total available market will the company address with its products and services. For example, a company producing dog food might decide to only focus on the premium segment of the dog food market, which is around 50 per cent of the total available market for dog food. Additionally, if it sells dry food, it will capture a specific segment of the total premium market which excludes the wet food segment of the market.
2. In a second step, the serviceable obtainable market (SOM) needs to be estimated. The key question to be addressed here is what market share can be obtained by the company taking into account the sales and distribution strategy, the geographical focus and the extent of the competition. For example, the dog food company might initially decide to focus on the UK market and sell through independent pet stores. This strategy excludes supermarkets and pet superstores. Additionally, the available shelf space in these independent stores will influence sales potential.
3. To move to a micro level and make a realistic assessment of the revenues that can be generated in the short to medium term, you will need to outline how quickly you can convince customers to buy into your offering. For example, given the number of sales people the dog food company has available and the average lead time to convince an independent pet store, you might start with twenty pet stores as an initial market test during the first six months after

which sales efforts will be increased to end up with fifty stores at the end of year 1. Based on the initial pilots, the marketing budget and the average amount of dog food sold in an independent pet store, detailed calculations can be made of the expected revenue.

Depending on the type of business, bottom-up sales forecasts will include assumptions with respect to:

- The characteristics of the sales funnel. For example, how many prospects need to be identified to end up with one qualified prospect, and how much resource (e.g. marketing budget, sales effort) needs to be spent during this process? How long does it take to turn a qualified prospect into a paying customer, i.e. what is the length of the sales cycle? What are the conversion rates at different stages of the sales cycle? How long does it take for a new sales rep to ramp up and to become fully productive? These questions are especially important in a business-to-business approach.
- The selling capacity of indirect and direct sales channels. For example, if a company is developing innovative drone systems and uses resellers to distribute its products, it would need an indication of the customer base of its resellers to make a good market forecast. If a company operates a chain of restaurants, it would need to make assumptions with respect to the number of customers that can be served in each restaurant and the average bill per cover.
- The speed at which operations can be scaled. The amount of sales that can be generated within a specific time frame depends on a number of factors including, for example, operational constraints, the speed at which new employees can be hired and trained, the extent to which the back-office can handle customer service, and the ease of expanding into new geographical areas.

Finally, in order to predict future revenues you need good insight into customer behaviour, based on market research, and have a good understanding of the productivity of the sales and marketing engine. Therefore, it is key to collect and benchmark data on the average customer acquisition cost (CAC) and to track the average spending behaviour of customers to calculate customer lifetime value (CLV). Customer lifetime value should exceed the CAC for every customer in order to have a business model that is scalable. Revenue predictions often provide a good indication of the ambition and credibility of the startup team and need to be well grounded to convince investors. Even though revenue forecasts will usually be wrong, it still makes a huge difference by how much they are off target and the extent to which they will threaten the existence of a company.

Step 2: P&L Statement: EBIT after Taxes

Revenues minus cost of goods sold and other operating expenses yield the earnings before interest and taxes, or EBIT.

Cost of Goods Sold and Gross Margin

The cost of goods sold (COGS) includes the direct expenses associated with delivering the products or services. For every additional product or service sold, the cost of goods sold will increase proportionally. These costs may include the products' bill of material, the cost for hosting your solution on the cloud, etc. The difference between the cost of goods sold and the revenue is the gross margin generated by the sales. Comparing the venture's gross margin with revenues yield the gross margin percentage, which typically remains relatively constant over time. An improving gross margin percentage indicates that economies of scale are expected, where output can be generated with relatively lower input values, either thanks to lower input prices or lower input volumes. The gross margin percentage should be benchmarked with comparable companies or with industry standards, and deviations from the benchmark should be clearly understood.

Other Operating Expenses

At startup, ventures may face research and development (R&D) expenses before they are able to launch their products or services on the market. But innovative ventures will continue their R&D efforts to further enhance existing products or to introduce new innovations. Next, launching products or services requires sales and marketing (S&M) expenses. Finally, all ventures are confronted with general and administrative (G&A) expenses, including office rent, accounting, insurance and legal services, communication and travel costs and sundres. All of these expenses are typically made up of a combination of employee and out-of-pocket expenses. For the employee expenses, clearly show the number of employees at each point in time, and their cost to the company per type of employee. Carefully estimate when new employees will be added to the headcount, and do not forget the expenses involved in hiring new employees.

Again, it is important to benchmark expected R&D, S&M and G&A margins (i.e. the percentage of those expenses versus revenues) against those of close competitors, comparable companies or industry averages in order to understand whether your estimated costs are realistic. If your venture's margins are lower than the benchmark, you should carefully consider whether you have overlooked any important cost item. If, for example, your venture's S&M margin is higher than that of your competitors, you should ask why it is that your venture's sales team would be more effective.

Tracking the evolution of these margins over time, as the venture grows, is also important. Chapter 10 covers how investors monitor the actual performance of these margins versus the forecast. A fallacy in many startup financial plans is that these operating expenses are expected to remain constant, even if operations scale significantly. This is obviously not feasible: costs may remain fixed for some time, but as operations grow, these costs will also grow. An obvious example is that sales growth may only be feasible if your venture employs a growing number of sales people. Additionally, your venture may need to move to larger premises, or more administrative staff may be needed to handle increased volumes. At all times, the plan should be consistent: the costs levels should be consistent with the expected revenues and output.

EBIT after Taxes

Gross margin minus other operating expenses yields the earnings before interest and taxes. As long as EBIT is negative and the venture makes losses, it will not pay income taxes. In most countries, losses can be carried over to future years, implying that future profits can be offset by past losses to calculate taxes. Only when all losses are offset with profits will a venture start paying taxes.

At that point in time, taxes are calculated as a percentage of EBIT and subtracted from EBIT. This approach assumes that the company is all equity financed and hence does not pay interest, as it does not use debt. This assumption holds for most growth-oriented ventures. If, nevertheless, debt is important in a venture's funding structure, then interest expenses have to be taken into account before calculating the taxes due.

Step 3: Cash Flow Statement: Free Cash Flows

Non-cash Expenses

The cash flow statement starts from EBIT after taxes, but EBIT is negatively affected by costs that do not (immediately) entail a cash expense. The most important non-cash cost is the depreciation of the venture's fixed assets. Other (less frequent) non-cash costs are amortizations, i.e. the decrease in value of intangible assets. For example, a software tool is created in-house or bought from third parties, and is expected to have a useful life of five years. The investment in the software tool is spread out or amortized over the life of the tool as a cost which affects the P&L during its useful years. Like depreciations, amortizations do not entail a cash payment when they are recorded in the P&L. Hence, both depreciations and amortizations have to be added back to EBIT after taxes to understand the true impact on the venture's cash situation.

Changes in Working Capital

Since most companies are confronted with an uncertain and fluctuating demand, manufacturing and trading companies keep a certain level of inventory in order to generate sales. Inventories may represent a considerable investment, especially when the unit price of the goods is high – for example in the chip manufacturing industry – or the cost of maintaining the economic value of the goods (such as storage costs) is substantial. Then, when the company starts

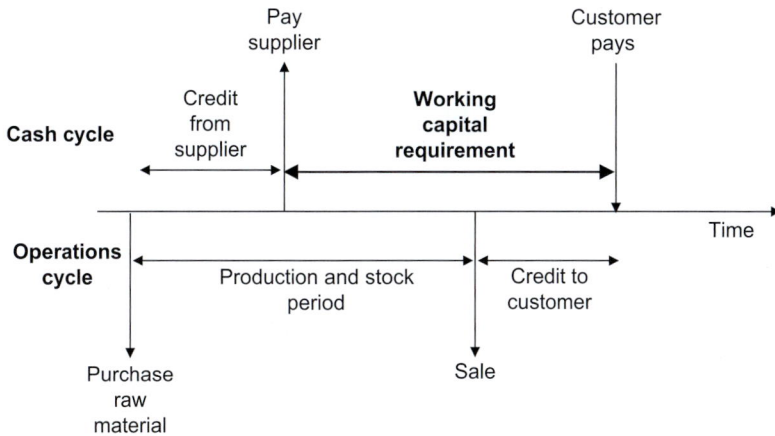

Figure 7.4 Working capital requirement.

selling services or products it can either sell for cash or sell on credit. In the latter case, the company has to wait for its money and runs the risk of not being paid. However, some customers only buy if credit is granted. Alternatively, not all suppliers are paid cash. The difference between the payment to suppliers and payment from customers, including the inventory period, is the working capital requirement of a company (See Figure 7.4). Working capital is important in the cash flow statement, as it takes the timing of the payments of suppliers, customers and inventory into account, but not in the P&L, which focuses on revenues and costs but not on the timing of the payments. The working capital of a venture increases with inventory and customer credit, and decreases with suppliers' credit and other operational liabilities. These elements are briefly discussed below.

Inventory Policy

An important decision a company needs to make regarding inventory is the number of days it wants to maintain an inventory. This choice is a trade-off between two types of out-of-pocket or opportunity costs: carrying costs and shortage costs. Carrying costs involve financial opportunity costs since the money invested in inventory is not available for other purposes. The costs involved in maintaining the economic value of the products in inventory is the second element of carrying costs, for example, the cost incurred for keeping drugs refrigerated. Shortage costs relate to lost customers due to stock-outs or production set-up costs. Keeping large inventories not only reduces shortage costs, but also allows the company to take advantage of volume discounts. It is clear that there is a sweet spot that reduces the combined shortage and carrying costs.

Credit Policy

Most customers demand trade credit when they buy goods or services. Moreover, credit terms are often used as a sales argument and therefore new companies are often obliged to offer credit to their customers. The company needs to decide on the amount of credit it will offer and the length of the credit period as this determines the investment in accounts receivable. The higher the accounts receivable, the higher the net working capital requirements, all else being equal. The length of the credit period varies between industries and geographic regions. Whereas the average collection period in northern Europe is around 30 days, it extends to approximately 80 days in southern Europe. Companies often offer cash discounts to speed up the collection of receivables. While the company has to wait for the money, it has to finance the accounts receivable itself. When offering trade credit, the company runs the risk of not being paid in the event that the trading partner goes bankrupt. Therefore, extending credit should be a well-considered decision.

Payment Policy

By delaying payments to suppliers, companies reduce their working capital requirements. Therefore, it is optimal to defer payment for as long as possible, providing that the price and the quality of the goods remain constant. However, delaying payments to suppliers often implies that the advantages of cash discounts are foregone. The implicit financing cost of not taking advantage of cash discounts may outweigh the costs of alternative means of financing. As a result, most companies pay promptly so as to take advantage of the cash discount. Finally, one should be aware that delaying payments deliberately may harm the customer–supplier relationship.

A cash flow statement tracks the *change* in working capital requirement. An increase in inventory or customer credit, or a decrease in supplier's credit will have a negative impact on a venture's cash situation. A typical growing company will need more working capital (more inventory, more customer credit, which is only partially offset by more supplier's credit). Hence, growth in revenues typically implies a growth in working capital and an ensuing decrease in cash. Ignoring the effects of changes in working capital may lead to a severe underestimation of a venture's cash needs.

Capital Expenditures

Some companies can be set up with virtually no money – e.g. a one-person consulting business – whereas others need huge amounts of investment upfront – e.g. a manufacturing company needing production facilities. Capital-intensive businesses require high inputs of fixed assets compared to other inputs such as personnel. Examples of capital-intensive industries include steel manufacturing, telecommunications and chip manufacturing. These operations are characterized by high up-front investments that are difficult to expand in a gradual way. In contrast, most labour-intensive industries, such as most service industries need less up-front capital expenditures and therefore can be expanded in a more gradual way. As a result, the resources needed up front to start a capital-intensive business are higher than those of a labour-intensive business.

Step 4: Ending Cash

A fundamental goal of a startup's financial plan is to understand how much cash will be needed or generated. The free cash flow generated during a period is the difference between all cash receipts and cash payments. If receipts are higher than payments, the startup is expected to generate cash; if vice versa, the startup is (still) in a cash drain situation, where it consumes more money than it generates.

In order to estimate how much cash the startup is expected to have at the end of the period, the free cash flow of the period has to be added to the cash available at the start of the period – the *beginning cash* – to yield a *cash balance* at the end of the period. A negative cash balance signals that external funding is needed to survive.

Let's Practise: Case Study

NEWTECH (Part I)

NewTech is a company that aims to develop innovative products based on Galileo, the European global satellite-based navigation system that accurately locates moving objects worldwide through satellites. Table 7.3 lists the assumptions underlying the forecast. Given that the expected development time and sales lead-time together are expected to take 21 months, the venture is expected to generate its first sales after 22 months, for a total value of €15,000. After that, the company anticipates a monthly growth rate of 10 per cent for a period of

Table 7.3 NewTech's assumptions under the most likely scenario

1. The entrepreneur invests €50,000 in cash and another €30,000 in kind (a testing machine) when the venture is founded. The machine is depreciated over a period of 5 years. This is the only capital expenditure at startup.
2. The development and first sales process takes 21 months.
3. First sales are expected in month 22 for a total amount of €15,000.
4. Sales will grow at a monthly rate of 10 per cent for a period of two years. After this period, sales growth is assumed to be equal to the growth of the overall economy (3 per cent annually).

Table 7.3 (cont.)

5. The gross margin is 50 per cent of sales revenue.
6. In month 20, a production facility is bought with a total value of €360,000. The facility is depreciated over a period of 30 years.
7. Selling, general and administrative expenses are expected to amount to a yearly fixed cost of €60,000 plus 5 per cent of monthly sales.
8. The company sells on credit. 60 per cent of sales in a given month is collected in the next month, 30 per cent is collected after 2 months and 10 per cent is collected after 3 months.
9. Accounts payable are 20 per cent of costs of sales.
10. The company plans to keep an inventory buffer of 10 per cent of sales expected in the next month.
11. The company is subject to a corporate tax rate of 33 per cent, but losses can be carried forward indefinitely.

two years, given its deployment of sales and marketing resources. The Serviceable Obtainable Market is expected to mature thereafter, with an assumed growth rate equal to the average growth rate of the overall economy (estimated to be 3 per cent). It is assumed throughout the case that the company is all equity financed. This is not a crucial assumption, however, as a startup's financial plan focuses in the first place on the cash from operations.

Questions for Discussion

1. Given the business plan of NewTech, what is its expected monthly EBIT after taxes?
2. What is NewTech's expected monthly free cash flow?
3. Assuming no additional financing is raised, what is the expected cash shortage after four years of operations?

7.4   Use of the Financial Plan

The outcome of the financial plan serves different purposes.

7.4.1   Assessing the Viability of the Business

A financial plan enables an assessment of the conditions under which an opportunity and the overall business model used to implement it has the potential to generate a sustainable profit. For example, the financial plan might indicate that a certain scale is necessary to reach cash flow break-even. It also gives insights into the major revenue and cost drivers and those elements that consume most of the cash.

A good financial plan also provides a sanity check and enables someone to benchmark it against similar companies. For example, if gross margins seem relatively high when compared to close competitors, it might indicate that certain cost items might have been underestimated (e.g. hiring cost of developers or sales efforts) or that the willingness to pay has been overestimated. Additionally, comparing average employee expenses with market standards or revenues generated per employee with similar companies often provides a good reality check. A good financial plan will help to track future performance and will indicate points for attention if reality differs from the plan.

7.4.2   Assessing the Burn Rate

A financial plan shows how much cash is needed to start and sustain the business at different points in time. It indicates the *burn rate* of the business or the amount of money a company is spending (gross burn = cash out) or losing (net burn = cash out − cash in) during a certain time period. The cash balance divided by the net monthly burn rate gives the number of months of cash a company still has (= *runway*). The net burn rate, therefore, will indicate how quickly a company needs to be fundraising, given the amount of cash it still has available. In the NewTech case, the company burns €5,000 per month in the beginning period and starts with €50,000 and, therefore, the company has a runway of 10 months before running out of cash.

Managing the burn rate is important for different reasons:

- The burn rate provides an indication of when a company needs to start raising new capital. It is advisable to have a runway at any point in time that is higher than six months, as raising new funding takes time. Otherwise, the entrepreneur risks ending up in a weak negotiation position as potential investors will know that the company is desperately looking for cash. Additionally, employees also like to have some certainty with respect to their next pay check.
- Money is generally expensive when raising capital in the pre-revenue market fit stage of a new venture's development, as it is not certain yet whether there will be a real appetite in the market for the products or services. Therefore, one wants to keep the burn rate low by adopting a bootstrapper's mindset and by limiting premature investments in scaling up, by, for example, spending heavily on marketing and sales.[2] Whenever product-market fit has been reached and the right sales and marketing

2 Seth Godin (15–06-2017, www.sethgodin.com/sg/docs/bootstrap.pdf) and Eric Ries' book *The Lean Startup* (2011) provide specific guidelines on how to be 'cash efficient' when launching a venture.

approach has been found, the burn rate can be increased to scale up, as outside investors will be more willing to invest at cheaper terms. At that point in time, the efficiency of the invested capital will go up. It's often a trade-off: are you willing to dilute your shares by increasing the net burn with the opportunity to obtain a first mover advantage and become a market leader with a high overall market valuation, or would you prefer to keep the burn rate low, grow organically and retain a high ownership stake, with the risk of being beaten up by faster competitors? Markets characterized by a 'winner takes all' logic often necessitate high spending levels in order for players to reach a dominant position. For example, food delivery companies operating in Europe, including Deliveroo that raised around €500 million and Delivery Hero that obtained over €1 billion in funding, had, by the end of 2016, spent heavily on expanding into the European market given clear first mover advantages including network effects, customer loyalty and scale economies in branding and operating a fleet of drivers. In this type of market, there is little option to stay small unless the venture can carve out a profitable niche.

- It is important to communicate well with existing and new investors on the appropriate burn rate as it will impact their ability to provide follow-on funding. If the burn rate is too high for existing investors given the amount of funds they have available, the company will need to look for new investors who can accommodate a higher level of burn. Current investors also need to accept their future dilution!

People often wonder whether it is more important to track the gross or net burn. The net burn indicates how soon a venture will need to go fundraising. The gross burn is also important, as it gives an indication of the spending level of the company and, therefore, its vulnerability to unexpected decreases in the level of incoming cash. While expenses are largely under the control of the venture, revenues depend on the willingness of customers to buy. For example, if a company loses a big customer that is responsible for a significant percentage of recurring revenue, a company with a high gross burn might end up in difficulties if it cannot easily lower its fixed expenses (e.g. employee costs). Additionally, companies with a high level of gross burn might be vulnerable to an economic downturn or changes in the overall investor sentiment as regards funding of loss-making companies.

7.4.3   Setting a Price on the Shares through Valuation

Many startup companies will need to go fundraising at a certain point in time and, therefore, a valuation will need to be put on the company to determine the price of the shares. Chapter 8 will go into depth in this topic. Additionally, in the event of an exit (e.g. IPO or trade sale), a price will need to be negotiated with potential buyers of the company. A financial plan will provide insights into a number of key parameters that are needed to value a business including:

- The cash flow generating capacity of the business, often expressed as the EBITDA (being the EBIT plus depreciation and amortization).
- The extent of capital expenditures needed to sustain the business.
- The expected performance of the company as indicated by the level of growth in revenues and the gross and net income levels. Is there an increasing or decreasing trend in these numbers?
- The overall stability in earnings – are most of the revenues recurring or project-based?
- What is the overall working capital requirement and cash conversion of the business?
- How much debt can a business carry?

7.4.4   Developing the Fundraising Strategy

The financial plan will indicate how much cash is needed to keep the business going. A key question then is whether all the money should be raised upfront or whether the money should be raised in different rounds as the venture develops. Fundraising typically happens in different rounds to lower the dilution for the entrepreneur and to decrease the overall investment risk for the investors. A financial plan, therefore, will help to determine how much and when cash is raised.

The different funding rounds in a venture are often linked to a set of meaningful milestones. A milestone is an event that indicates that risk has substantially decreased and the company is a step closer to success. In general, customer traction will be the strongest evidence that a business model is working. However, there are often a number of stages to go through before significant customer demand can be created and, therefore, intermediate milestones may be important. For example, a milestone could be developing a first working prototype of your product, signing the first pilot customers, hiring an experienced CTO, running a successful beta test or passing a clinical trial. Each time a milestone is hit, risk decreases and the valuation of the company should go up, which limits the dilution as new capital is raised at more favorable terms (see Figure 7.5). If it turns out that a milestone is not achieved with the current runway, it might be useful to rethink the strategy or show progress against a new milestone to de-risk the business and to make sure a higher valuation is achieved in a next funding round. Alternatively, the burn rate can also be lowered to complete the milestones before running out of cash. Obviously, milestones should be defined in consultation with investors.

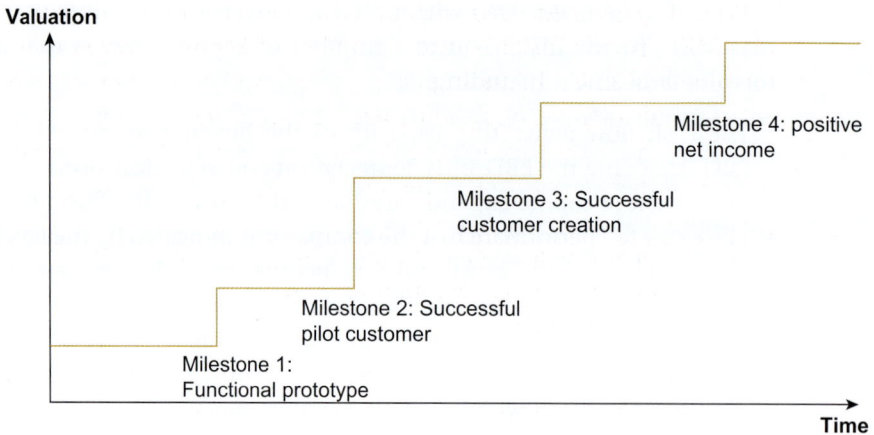

Figure 7.5 Valuation step-ups around milestones.

Let's practice: Case study

NEWTECH (Part II)

Illustration of milestones for NewTech

Returning to the NewTech case, let's consider how the founder might define a first milestone during the development phase at the time a first prototype is completed. Several questions arise at this stage. Can the product be manufactured? How much will it cost to produce the product? How long does production take? What steps are necessary to develop the product? Should the production of the product be outsourced? Having a workable prototype reduces uncertainty considerably and reduces the price to be paid for external financing. Suppose that prototyping is planned to be completed in month 15.

Given that equity is expensive, it is a natural reflex not to raise more than the venture needs. However, raising too little may seriously hamper the development of the venture: it always takes more money than expected to develop a product or service. Additionally, it often takes longer to reach the stage where the first customers sign up and pay. It is, therefore, wise to anticipate a safety cushion and raise somewhat more than the amount forecasted by the financial plan. Even though the inclusion of a cushion will increase dilution in the current funding round, it will help you to successfully obtain a subsequent funding round. You do not want to end up in a situation of having to raise money under time pressure, because the company is running out of cash.

The extra financing needed to fund the venture's growth in a success scenario should not be raised at the start. After all, if the venture turns out to be successful, it will be easier to attract new outside funding. In this case, the price to be paid for outside funding will be lower given the venture's good prospects. The amount of financing needed in a failure scenario should not be considered, as it is often better for both the entrepreneur and the external investor to abandon the venture in order to limit losses.

When should money be raised? Fundraising is a time-consuming process and often involves extensive negotiations, including emotional ups and downs. General advice includes:

- You should start raising capital at least six to nine months before the flame out date or the point at which you will be running out of cash.
- Building relationships with potential investors is something an entrepreneur should do all the time to prepare those relationships for the time when the company needs the money. During these meetings, the progress the company has been making and the challenges encountered can be discussed. By the time the company actually needs to raise funds, it will be hopefully be able to rely on these trusted contacts and it will be able to show that certain barriers have been overcome based on the feedback that was gathered. These meetings will also help the company to decide whether there is a good fit with the investors (e.g. in terms of industry background, available capital, etc.).
- When the time comes when funds are needed in the bank, the entrepreneur will have to spend a considerable amount of time meeting investors. It's a task that cannot be outsourced, and often involves an emotional rollercoaster, with rejections and intense negotiations that will hopefully lead to a fair deal. As an entrepreneur, you will want to make sure you have time available for this and that your business doesn't suffer.

VOICE OF THE EXPERT: Luis Martin Cabiedes (Spain)

Luis has a degree in Philosophy from the Universidad Complutense de Madrid, an MBA from IESE, and is a financial analyst with a charter from CFA Institute. In 1989, he joined the Europa Press Group, where he was co-president for twelve years. In 1998, he started investing in early-stage tech startups. He first operated as a business angel in this investment activity and then set up his own venture capital fund (Cabiedes and Partners), which now constitutes his main occupation. He has invested in more than forty Internet and tech startups, including Ole, Myalert, Acceso, and, more recently, Privalia, Trovit and Offerum. Luis is a part-time lecturer at IESE Business School since 2008 and teaches 'Entrepreneurship' and 'Entrepreneurial Finance'.

What is the best financing for an entrepreneur?
Business angels are fine, VCs are sometimes fine, but as an entrepreneur never ever forget that the best money comes from clients!

7.5   Dealing with Uncertainty

One of the main characteristics of startups or early-stage ventures is uncertainty. Pro forma forecasting may, therefore, seem to be a fruitless task. After all, there is only a small chance that the future will unfold as forecast. Nevertheless, trying to predict the performance of a venture is even more important when its environment is uncertain, compared to a business operating in a stable environment. Including uncertainty in the analyses helps to assess the vulnerability of the venture to unexpected future shocks, or to assess the financial impact of important choices. Failure to do so may cause serious financing problems and put the venture in an adverse negotiating position when turning to outside investors to secure the company's future. For example, a critical trade-off is whether to grow the venture as quickly as possible, incurring further cash drains due to the necessary investments in growth, or to grow more slowly and become cash flow positive and profitable as quickly as possible. In addition, failing to consider the consequences of delays in the development and sales processes, or lower (or higher) than expected sales or profit margins, could place the company in unanticipated difficulty.

Two approaches to modelling uncertainty are discussed in the following sections. First, sensitivity analysis assesses the impact of a small change in one of the assumptions about the cash position of the company. Second, scenario analysis describes different futures states of the economic and technological environment and their impact on financing needs.

7.5.1   Sensitivity Analysis

Sensitivity analysis considers the impact of a change in one of the underlying assumptions of the financial plan holding the other assumptions constant. Key assumptions, for example, include level of sales growth, gross and net profit margins, average customer acquisitions costs, time needed to generate sales, average payment terms, and pricing policies. The critical determinants of the required cash can be identified in this way. Sensitivity analysis is a helpful tool in decision-making as it points to the factors that need special attention and constant monitoring so as to keep the venture's financial position on the right track.

Let's Practise: Case Study

NEWTECH (Part III)

The impact of sales growth on cash is shown in Figure 7.6. The monthly growth rate only applies to the first two years after the first sales are generated. Thereafter, it is assumed that the company grows at the same rate as the overall

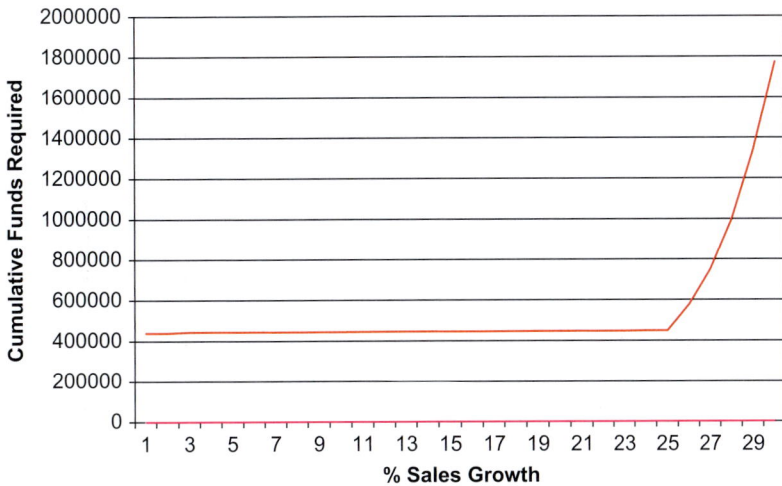

Figure 7.6 Funds required for different levels of growth.

economy. A higher level of growth implies a higher projected cash short-fall, due to the increased working capital requirement. The increase is small for lower levels of sales. Once sales growth reaches 25 per cent or more, the required cash rises exponentially. Note that the time before cash flow break-even is reached will be longer for higher levels of sales. Cash flow break-even is reached when growth falls back to the average growth of the overall economy in most of the high-growth scenarios. Clearly, a high-growth strategy has major consequences for the financial position of a company. Not anticipating this may place the company in serious financial difficulty, especially during times of recession when capital markets dry up.

Comparable sensitivity analyses can be developed for any important assumption in the financial plan, e.g. for different levels of gross profit margin or fixed costs, given the most realistic sales growth, or for a longer time to first sales. These analyses will reveal that for higher profit margins, the decrease in required funding is quite small. When a company is characterized by a situation of rapid growth combined with a low profit margin, however, the need for outside funding may be phenomenal. An entrepreneur pursuing such a strategy should be aware of its financial consequences in order to avoid financial difficulties. It may, for example, be better to raise the price in order to increase the profit margin, even if that lowers growth. As a result, reliance on outside funding may be reduced.

7.5.2   Scenario Analysis

A scenario analysis considers the different options a venture has in terms of business model design and future expansion strategy to assess the likely financial needs of the venture. For example:

- Technology-based firms frequently face the choice between whether to pursue a licensing-based strategy or to manufacture and sell the products in-house. Both strategies clearly impact the funding needs of the company.
- Different revenue models exist which may impact the amount of cash generated and the timing of the cash flows. For example, a software company might decide to offer parts of its software for free to attract customers. Additionally, offering a subscription model (SaaS) versus selling a one-time perpetual licence will influence the timing and quantity of cash flows. As a final example, selling hardware to customers versus offering a rental model will significantly impact the amount of cash needed to run the business.
- A software company might decide to partner up with a third party to commercialize its software rather than developing an in-house marketing and sales department.
- A startup with international activities could use different modes of internationalization (e.g. export versus opening local offices), which will influence the financial needs of the company.
- Many startups face the trade-off between developing certain products and services in-house (e.g. software development, manufacturing) or to outsource. Clearly, this will impact the level of fixed and variable costs, but also the profit margins and, therefore, the cash needs.
- There are different ways to grow a company including franchising models, licensing strategies, exclusive distributor agreements, etc. Each of these models will have implications for the funding needs of a company.

It is vital to think carefully about the implications of your business model design and implemented growth strategy for future funding needs. In many cases, entrepreneurs will need to revise their business model, as the funding required for implementation and expansion might not be available or could lead to excessive dilution. Investors might also insist upon changes to the business model design to facilitate the scaling of the business. Therefore, prototyping the business model and its associated funding needs should be an integral part of the business planning process.

KEY TAKEAWAYS

- Understanding how much and at what stage capital will be needed to start and grow a venture is essential knowledge for every entrepreneur. A fundraising plan is of strategic importance, as it will impact on the ultimate success of the venture and the value the entrepreneur will be able to capture.

- A good financial plan does not need to be complex – it should be transparent, tailor-made to the business model and provide outsiders with the opportunity to undertake sanity checks.
- Understanding the logic of the financial plan and mapping the main underlying drivers of the financials is a key task for the entrepreneur and will provide a good credibility test for outside investors.
- Calculating the cash requirements of a business is a step-by-step process, starting with assessing the revenue expectations, calculating the profitability of the operations, determining the non-cash expenses and estimating the upfront and on-going investment requirements including capex and working capital requirements, to finally arrive at the available free cash flow.
- Fundraising is often linked to milestones to reduce dilution for the entrepreneur and to lower the risk for outside investors.
- Conducting sensitivity analyses and analysing different business model scenarios provide a good understanding of the key parameters driving the financial results and the options available for alternative paths with different funding requirements.

END OF CHAPTER QUESTIONS

1. Why do all startups need a financial plan?
2. What critical insights can you get from a financial plan?
3. Why are both a P&L statement and a cash flow statement needed?
4. Why is it usually impossible to combine high-growth ambitions with quick profitability?
5. How does a startup's payment policy impact its financing needs?
6. Why can a startup expect to be profitable in a given year, but still experience a cash drain situation?
7. Why does a startup's financial plan mainly focus on cash flows related to operations, thereby ignoring its cash flows to and from investors?
8. Why would you raise capital according to a varying set of milestones? What are some examples of milestones in a software-based venture?
9. Why do some high-potential startups (e.g. Dropbox, Uber, Deliveroo, most biotech ventures) need to raise hundreds of millions of euros before turning profitable? How does this make sense?
10. What strategies can a venture apply to reduce its funding needs in an early stage? Why would you do this?
11. What is an investor looking for in a financial plan? What makes a financial plan attractive to an investor?
12. Should entrepreneurs focus on the net burn or the gross burn of their venture? What is the difference?
13. What is the difference between a bottom-up and top-down sales forecast? What do investors generally prefer?

14. What can you do as an entrepreneur when you are running out of cash and you fail to hit the milestones agreed with your investors?

15. Running out of cash is like a heart attack! Running on a low profit margin is like a terminal disease, it will slowly kill your business. Explain.

FURTHER READING

- Janz, C., SaaS Financial Plan 2.0. Url: http://christophjanz.blogspot.com/2016/03/saas-financial-plan-20.html (6 June 2017).
- Mullins, J. (2013). Use customer cash to finance your startup. *Harvard Business Review*, 91(7–8), 19–21.
- Suster, M. (2012). How to develop your fundraising strategy. Url: https://bothside softhetable.com/how-to-develop-your-fundraising-strategy-58c2f0b22d6d (6 June 2017).
- Landström, H. (2017). *Advanced Introduction to Entrepreneurial Finance*. Edward Elgar.

REFERENCES

- Godin, S. (1998). *The Bootstrapper's Bible: How to Start and Build a Business with a Great Idea and (Almost) No Money*. Upstart Publishing.
- Ries, E. (2011). *The Lean Startup*. Crown Publishing Group.

Let's Practise: Case Study

QualiPro: Developing a financial plan for a startup.

QualiPro originated as a life science instrumentation spin-off from a major university and a research institute specializing in microelectronics in 2006. It developed a new medical device, ProSample 16, which enables high-speed quantification of DNA samples in laboratories. This is an important step before labs analyze the DNA itself. Its competitive advantage lies in its patented micro-fluidic ProPlates, through which 16 micro-volume DNA samples can be processed and quantified in a fully automated workflow. It is easy to use, and is expected to appeal to large DNA laboratories for whom it should represent a significant decrease in cost and time for preparing DNA samples for analysis. At startup, QualiPro has a laboratory prototype of ProSample 16 ready, and is developing a beta version of the prototype to be tested in a real-life setting. The ultimate goal is to develop a complete software toolbox for detailed sample analysis and quantification, which can be integrated in any DNA laboratory workflow.

QualiPro is established with capital consisting of €340,000 cash and €200,000 IP rights for the university. The three entrepreneurs received 25 per cent of the shares for their initial commitment. The entrepreneurs' shares carry less rights compared to the investors' shares, however, meaning that they will only benefit if the company performs really well. Further, they are expected to work at below-market salaries to compensate for the shares they received at startup.

More capital was sought at startup from specialized early-stage venture capital investors. They found the project too immature and required further technological development and market testing before investing. It was clear from the outset that considerably more money would be needed. The initial financial plan developed before the startup anticipated that the first products would hit the market in the second semester of 2008, leading to slightly more than half a million euros in revenues in 2008. Given the competitive advantage of the ProSample 16, it was expected that revenues would grow rapidly. In order to get the product on the market, major R&D and marketing spending would be required, totalling more than €2 million from startup to 2009. Nevertheless, it was expected that the company would reach EBITDA break-even in two years' time, at the end of 2009. Capital expenditures were mainly limited to laboratory equipment and tools, but were nevertheless expected to reach a €1.5 million spread over the first three years. Major investments amounting to €417,500 were expected shortly after startup to support R&D, and again in 2009 when production of ProSample 16 and of the ProPlates disposables would have to be organized. This leads to an expected negative free cash flow of €3.7 million to cover QualiPro's first three years.

Based upon the initial financial plan, a €3.5 million financing round was prepared immediately after startup. Very quickly, however, the entrepreneurs realized that it would be impossible to raise this amount of money, given the early stage of development of the company. Investors expected at least a working proof of concept and ideally one or more letters of intent from major customers before committing significant amounts. Therefore, a new and detailed monthly financial plan was developed, covering September 2007 to December 2010. It aimed for a lower spending rate, in order to ease the financing of the spin-off. This would inevitably lead to a slower introduction of the first products on the market.

The New Plan

The **revenue** budget included sales of the ProSample 16 device from July 2008 onwards, and of a new device, ProSample 96, starting from January 2009. The sales budget was based on both a bottom-up and top-down analysis of the market. ProSample 16 would be sold for €10,000, and ProSample 96 for €20,000. In addition to the revenues generated by selling the devices, it was expected that selling the disposable ProPlates would lead to a strong recurring income stream. A ProPlates could only be used once; in order to continue to use the ProSample, new ProPlates must be bought. It was anticipated that laboratories would use two ProPlates per working day for every ProSample installed (both model 16 and 96), for a period of 22 working days in an average month. A ProPlate would be sold at €2 for model 16 and at €8 for model 96. A third income stream would be the maintenance and service of the devices. It was expected that 30 per cent of the customers would pay €1,000 per device per year for maintenance. All sales and services are payable within 30 days.

Expected ProSample Sales, 2008–10

To further develop the devices and the disposables, and in order to develop ProSample 96, more R&D was needed. The monthly cost of R&D employees initially amounts to €10,000, but is expected to increase to €40,000 from 2010 onwards. Other R&D-related costs are the disposables used in the labs, such as lamps, fibres, electronics and biotech consumables, estimated at €7,000 per month. R&D-related subcontracting includes costs for disposable moulding, clean room-related jobs, and the design of electronics, mechanics and software. Based upon a detailed R&D project plan, the following monthly R&D subcontracting costs are forecast: €24,500 in 2007, €18,000 in 2008, €30,000 in 2009 and €32,000 in 2010.

Production of the devices would be outsourced. In order to be ready for the first sales, a fixed production-related cost of €5,000 per month was foreseen from October 2007 onwards, mainly related to quality assurance. This would drop to €2,500 per month from August 2008 onwards, but increase again to €8,333 per month from January 2010. A further fixed production cost of €1,000 per month for electricity, heating, maintenance and so on was foreseen from January 2009 onwards.

Based upon a detailed bill of materials including direct materials, packaging, labour and subcontracting, the variable production cost is estimated to be €5,000 for a ProSample 16 and €7,000 for a ProSample 96 (including appropriate margins for the manufacturer). The variable cost is €1 for a ProPlate 16 and €4 for a ProPlate 96. Finally, it is estimated that the cost of services (maintenance) will amount to 50 per cent of the service revenues.

The manufacturer will require both the devices and the disposables to be produced in batches. Disposables will be manufactured in batches of 50,000; they have to be ordered (and paid for) one month before the disposables are needed. Devices will be manufactured in batches of 100 and need to be ordered three months in advance. The manufacturer requires payment when the order is placed, given that it is risky to work for a startup with uncertain prospects.

From January 2008, a sales manager will be hired costing €8,333 per month for the first year; this salary will increase to €10,000 per month from January 2010 onwards. A monthly sales budget of €5,000 is foreseen for development and maintenance of the website, folders, travel expenses, and so on. This will increase to €8,000 per month in 2010.

General and administrative (G&A) expenses relate to the cost of administrative employees (forecast from July 2008 onwards), costing €45,000 per year and a

CFO (from January 2010), costing €100,000 per year. Other administrative expenses are estimated at €17,000 per month in 2007, increasing by 7 per cent per year. These include office supplies, rental, cleaning, subscriptions to journals, telecom expenses, accounting and other professional services and sundries, but also the fee for the 'management support' provided by the CEO.

Finally, the investment budget is as follows: €16,000 will be spent on R&D lab equipment in September 2007, €200,000 in 2008 (half in January, half in September), €150,000 in 2009 and €210,000 in 2010 (the latter two amounts spread equally throughout the year). All lab equipment is linearly depreciated over five years. There is a major investment relating to the mould for the disposables, estimated at €200,000 for the disposable 16, due early 2008, and €600,000 for the disposable 96, due early 2009. Moulds are depreciated over three years. Other capital expenditures relate to PCs, printers, etc., and are expected to amount to €10,500 in September 2017, and €18,000 annually thereafter (spread equally throughout the year). These investments are depreciated over three years.

All the above costs and investments will be paid in cash, as suppliers will be reluctant to extend trade credit to this startup company.

Questions for Discussion

Based upon the expectations described above, develop a financial plan that answers the following questions:

1. What is the average monthly *burn rate*, i.e. the negative EBITDA before investments?
2. When will QualiPro reach EBITDA-break even? EBIT-break-even?
3. What is the total amount of cash that QualiPro will need to raise? What is the latest point in time that is this needed?
4. How much cash would you advise QualiPro to raise immediately? And later?
5. Which milestones will QualiPro be able to reach with the cash raised initially?
6. What are the most crucial assumptions in the financial plan?
7. Based upon the insights provided by the financial plan, what changes would you suggest to the current business model?

8 VALUATION OF NEW VENTURES

LUISA ALEMANY

ESADE Business School

This chapter considers the challenging, yet exciting world of valuing companies. Valuation has always been a key topic in finance, but it is even more relevant in the case of high-growth ventures because of its impact on raising capital. Equity is the main source of financing for startups, which typically have high potential and few tangible assets. In order to come to an assessment, founders and investors need to determine the value of the business or 'exchange rate' of money for shares.

Valuation is considered an art rather than a science, even when referring to mature, traditional companies. In the case of new ventures, it is sometimes even closer to fortune-telling or searching for new stars through a telescope; you need luck, but it helps if you know where to look. For the entrepreneurial team and those planning to invest in the venture, learning about the process for valuing startups and investing time in understanding the factors that drive value is key. In that way, both the entrepreneurial team and the investors will be in a position to establish a range of values that will improve the negotiating process and make it easier to reach agreement on the price. Let's get started!

VIEW FROM THE MEDIA

FINANCIAL TIMES   FT

European unicorns remain elusive

Investors are concerned about the soaring valuations of private start-ups

JUNE 16, 2016 BY ATTRACTA MOONEY

When Skyscanner, the British flight-search website, raised £128m in financing in January, it joined an elusive club: European unicorns. Since then, just one other European company has managed to become a unicorn, as private start-up companies with valuations of at least $1bn are called, according to PitchBook, a database of venture capital and merger and acquisition deals. That equates to one new unicorn every 2.5 months, compared with one every 1.7 months last year, signalling that investors are becoming more wary of investing in big tech start-ups in Europe. The reluctance to back these companies comes amid concerns about the soaring valuations of private start-ups globally. Recently, many investors were forced to write down investments, including those in Dropbox, the file storage website, and Snapchat, the social media platform where pictures disappear. But venture capitalists and asset managers invested in fledging tech businesses say the reticence in Europe is unwarranted, arguing there is little sign in the region of the overheating North America has experienced. Siraj Khaliq, an investment partner at Atomico, the European venture capital fund founded by Niklas Zennström, the co-founder of Skype, the online telephony group, says valuations for companies in Europe are much more conservative than in the US. 'We are seeing such great companies [in Europe] that we actually have to pace ourselves. We are seeing so many opportunities,' says Mr Khaliq, who set up one of the world's first unicorns, an agri-tech business called The Climate Corporation.

Tim Hames, director-general of the British Private Equity and Venture Capital Association, the industry body, adds: 'The consensus remains that European valuations, while high, [are] not wild and still look more sober than their US counterparts.' . . .

According to PitchBook, the median valuation for these companies in the US has increased twofold to $60.6m since 2010. . . . Early-stage companies in the US that are ready to operate but have yet to begin commercial sales had a median valuation of $8.9m in 2010. By 2016, this number had soared to $22m. In Europe, these numbers are much smaller: early-stage companies have a median valuation of $8m currently, while later-stage companies are worth $21m. The lower valuations in Europe are partly due to the fact that there is less money available to invest in start-ups, says Mr Khaliq, who adds that there is 14 times more capital in

venture capital funds aimed at later-stage financing in the US than in Europe. European investors also tend to be more conservative when it comes to investing in start-up companies, says Manish Madhvani, co-founder and managing partner of GP Bullhound, an investment bank. When European investors invest in a start-up, they like to see strong revenues and the opportunity for these to grow further, he says. . . .

Some investors were spooked by the negative stories surrounding unicorns at the start of the year, but these concerns are now lessening for European companies, he says. 'European unicorns are unlikely to come under the same pressure [as their US counterparts], because they are more advanced in terms of [the] revenues [they generate]. I would expect more of the European start-ups to stay around. In the US, we would expect more failures.'

There are signs that some investors agree with his views. Figures provided by Atomico, using data from Tech.eu/Dealroom, the industry websites, show there were 125 series-A (early-stage) funding rounds where investors provided capital during the first five months of this year, compared with 105 during the first half of 2016. . . . Andy Evans, manager of the Equity Value fund at Schroders, the UK's largest listed fund house, has big concerns about the valuations of Europe's tech start-ups. 'People invest in unicorns on the assumption they will find the next Google or Facebook. But in a basket of unicorns, it is highly likely there will be far more lastminute.coms [which was valued highly, but suffered a precipitous fall in its share price after listing] than Facebooks,' he says. 'Unicorn valuations, in many cases, are a triumph of hope over reality.'

LEARNING OBJECTIVES

After reading this chapter you will be able to:

- Recognize the limitations of traditional valuation methodologies when applying them to new high-growth ventures.
- Understand how investors in new ventures, namely business angels and venture capitalists, approach valuation.
- Apply the 'Venture Capital' method for valuing new startups.
- Understand pre-money and post-money valuation.
- Analyse the use of convertible notes.
- Consider the impact of dilution in future rounds of financing.
- Navigate and weigh additional considerations regarding the value of new ventures.

Where Are We Going Next?

First, we will briefly review traditional valuation methodologies and explain why they are not appropriate for valuing startups. Then, we will look at the way investors in new ventures think. As startups are seldom financed by debt, the equity investor is typically the first person to be interested in valuing the venture. Therefore, it is important to understand how equity investors assess the value and what method they typically apply in the case of a new, high-growth business. We will then review the most commonly used valuation method for new ventures, namely the venture capital method. We will follow the next steps in this method: (1) its expected future value when the investor comes to sell his stake; (2) the percentage of ownership that the investor will request in exchange for his money; (3) the number of shares and price per share the deal will be done at; and (4) the pre-money and post-money valuation of the startup. In the final section, further considerations are added and calculations are reviewed as we assess the effect of dilution on the investor due to additional rounds of financing. Finally, we discuss the difference between value and price, incorporating non-financial aspects into the valuation of new ventures.

8.1   A Quick Review of Traditional Valuation Methodologies

The main obstacles posed when valuing new companies are that they do not have much history (if any), they do not have many tangible assets and their future is uncertain. Traditional valuation methodologies are not helpful, as they rely on the company's history and balance sheet. When valuing an established company, the first step is to analyse the current situation, from both a financial performance and a balance sheet point of view. Second, the growth potential of the company is taken into account, as well as the development of the market(s) the company is operating in.[1] Finally, the degree of uncertainty of that future potential, measured by the risk of the business, is entered into the equation.

What aspects of traditional valuation methodologies make them inappropriate for valuing new ventures? Some of the most commonly used methods include:

- **Net asset value**: in this method, all the company's assets are estimated at their current market value. Total debts, both accounts payable and all other liabilities, are then subtracted from the total market value of the assets to get to the equity value. In the case of new companies, there are not many assets; actually, if they have assets, they are mainly intangible assets or 'work-in-progress', for example, the development of new knowledge, such as software, a new technology or the potential discovery of a new drug. But what is the market value of that research or development which is not yet completed and may still lack market traction? This valuation method is generally not recommended when dealing with companies where most of the value lies in their growth potential, as is the case with many startups.
- **Discounted cash flow (DCF)**: to calculate the value of a company using this method, we need to estimate all its future free cash flows and then calculate their present value by discounting them using an appropriate measure for the cost of capital of the company.[2] Therefore, valuation is determined by two key elements: the future annual free cash flows and the cost of capital.

  As regards the first element, in order to estimate the free cash flows of a company with a certain degree of accuracy, we need to have information regarding:

  (a) the past performance of the company, ideally over five years;
  (b) the evolution and dynamics of the market in which the company is operating; and
  (c) future investment plans.

In the case of a new venture, obtaining this information is a challenge, or sometimes even impossible, for various reasons. First, it could be that there is no history, so we cannot rely on the past to forecast the future. Second, in many cases there is no market, as it is being created by the startup. Or the market is so immature that it is impossible to predict its evolution and future dynamics. Many startups are developed in order to disrupt a market, and that is exactly what will happen. However, we would need a crystal ball to predict the future, although we might look at other disruptive technologies, whose evolution could give us some indication. Third, investment plans will rely

---

1 To learn more about the valuation of established companies, see Brealey *et al.* (2013); Copeland *et al.* (2010).

2 For more detail on the calculation of present values and the time value of money, see Chapter 2 of Brealey *et al.* (2013).

heavily on the evolution of the market, the reaction of competitors or of those being affected by the disruption. New entrants and any changes in the demand and/or supply will force the startup to react quickly.

The second element, the cost of capital, also known as WACC (*weighted average cost of capital*),[3] is a combination of the cost of both elements of the financial structure of the firm: its equity and its debt. For new ventures, it is not possible to estimate the cost of equity (K_e) as we might do for established firms. In general, the cost of equity is calculated using the CAPM model.[4] In order to apply this model, we need to obtain data from public markets for similar listed companies. However, a very young startup is, by definition, very different from a publicly listed company. Therefore, the data we derive from the market cannot simply be duplicated. On the other hand, the cost of the equity of a company is the expected return that the shareholders of this company consider appropriate for the level of risk of the business. In the case of a new venture, the shareholders would be the business angel or the venture capitalist. And, as we learnt in Chapter 4, these investors will request annual returns, measured by IRR (internal rate of return), in the range of 30 to 60 per cent per annum to compensate for the risk that they are taking.

- **Dividend-based valuation**: a very similar method to DCF. Instead of using the free cash flows (FCF), before remunerating the debt or the equity, we consider the cash flows to the equity holders. To do so, interest payments are subtracted from the FCF. And to discount the cash flows to the present instead of using the cost of capital (WACC), we apply the cost of the equity. Basically, using this perspective, we estimate the present value of all future dividends, which are the cash flows to the owners of the shares. And as the cash flows left belong to the shareholders, then the discount rate is the requested return of the equity holders (K_e).[5] This method can only be used in mature companies that are already paying out dividends. This is a distant future for a new startup.

- **Multiple-based valuation**: using this method, we can estimate the value of a company using ratios that relate financial or non-financial variables to the value of the company. The advantage of this method is that it is very easy to apply and thus often used when looking for a quick valuation. If this is the first time you have heard about this type of valuation, you can compare this method to the way in which the value of real estate is determined. For example, if you know that the price per square metre of real estate in the Barceloneta neighbourhood, by the beach in Barcelona, is around €3,500, and you are looking to buy an apartment of 100 square metres, then the value of

---

3 For more information on the WACC and its calculation, see Chapters 8 and 9 of Brealey *et al.* (2013) or Chapter 11 of Copeland *et al.* (2010).

4 CAPM stands for Capital Asset Pricing Model. See note 3 for ways to learn more about the subject.

5 For more information on Dividend-based valuation, see Chapter 4 of Brealey *et al.* (2013).

the apartment should be €350,000.[6] Well, this is the theoretical average value. Of course, if the apartment has been renovated, or is on the top floor, or has a fabulous view of the Mediterranean Sea, you will need to adjust for that. And finally, there is always supply and demand. If there is only one apartment and a large number of buyers in the market, the final price, most likely, will be well over the theoretical value of 350,000 euros.

Two different types of multiples can be used:

(a) Similar companies. We look for comparable firms that are listed in the market based upon, for example, industry, size or development stage. Typically, we would need to identify at least four or five similar companies in order to produce an average. A quoted company has a 'market' value, which allows us to estimate ratios of that value to some key variables. For example, we can estimate how many times a company is worth its sales (EV/Sales or Enterprise Value/Sales) or its EBITDA, or even some non-financial variables, such as number of subscribers, number of square metres for a retail business, or number of downloads for an app.

(b) Similar transactions. Instead of using information from publicly listed companies, we might consider information that is available about previous transactions in the sector, and, if possible, in the same or a similar country. Again, if the information is available, it can be estimated how many times the buyer paid the sales of the company (that is the price divided by the most recent sales figures of the business), or its EBITDA, or its number of subscribers. When using multipliers from similar transactions, the value will, in general, be higher, because the buyer might be paying a 'control premium' in order to buy the majority of the acquired company.[7]

It is almost impossible to use the comparable method to estimate the value of a startup. First, as far as comparable companies are concerned, a new venture is, by definition, dissimilar from a publicly listed company, which is large, already successful and most likely operating in several markets. Second, the number of transactions for very young companies is negligible and, even more challenging, this information is unlikely to be in the public domain. For a startup, a similar transaction would be the deal agreed for another new venture. However, as this type of deal often happens in private, between the founders and some angel investors or a seed venture fund, it is hard to identify a reference point for determining the average price paid.

So, the shortcomings of traditional valuation methods, for the large part, relate to a lack of historical information, difficulty in estimating future cash flows, and the fact that a new venture does not have comparable companies to reference.

---

6 Here is the calculation: 3,500 euros/ square metres × 100 square metres = 350,000 euros.
7 The 'control premium' has been estimated by academic research to be in the range of 20 to 25%.

Given these challenges, a new approach to valuation is needed. Venture capitalists have used different techniques to get a 'feel' of where the value of a startup might be. These investors are more concerned with the size of the company in the future, assuming that all goes well. 'Are we looking at a €10 million business in three years, or is this more a €100 million or even €500 million company?', a venture capitalist would ask. Getting a sense of value is more important than doing calculations that attempt to arrange an uncertain future into a predictable model. Seasoned venture investors are well aware that their business is about taking risk. In the next section, we review investor constraints and objectives for startups.

8.2   Understanding the Way Equity Investors in New Ventures Think

Venture capital investors have certain limitations when it comes to deciding in which companies to invest. As explained in Chapter 4, venture capitalists raise funds from different sources, such as the financial sector, corporations, government funds, university endowments or wealthy individuals. The capital providers in the fund are referred to as *Limited Partners* or 'LPs'. The venture fund managers, or *General Partners* (GPs), contractually agree to a certain type of investments with their LPs,[8] and these agreements are recorded in the contract of the fund and establish the type of companies it can invest in. These contractual arrangements define the scope of the investment and may include:

- Maximum/minimum amount of money invested per (portfolio) company.
- Activity/sector: the fund can be more generalist, like an investor in 'technology', or more specific, for example, an investor in 'apps' or 'mobile apps'.
- Geography: a city, a region, a country or continent.
- Stage of the company: pre-prototype; with prototype; first customers (maybe given free access to test the prototype); sales over a certain amount (for example, €1 million); market position; expanding internationally, or pre-IPO.
- Target stake in the venture (percentage that they will consider, for example, 20 per cent to 30 per cent).
- Type of deal: seed; series A, B, C, or late stage.

For example, the strategy of venture capital fund ABC could be '*investments in software companies in the south of Europe, with a proven prototype and a first beta tester, looking to raise between €2 and €4 million, for a 20 to 35 per cent share in the company*'. That means that ABC can only invest in companies that meet these characteristics. Even if the partners of the ABC fund find an interesting opportunity that they would love to invest in, if it is outside the defined scope, they are not allowed to do so.

8 Venture capitalists present the details of the investment proposal to the limited partners in a document called a 'Private Placement Memorandum'. Once the limited partners agree to commit capital to the fund, they sign a 'Limited Partnership Agreement'. To learn more, see Chapter 4.

The contract between the GPs and the LPs also includes specific conditions:

- Time horizon: venture capital investment should be returned within a specific (relatively short) period. This might prove to be very challenging, given that these investments are in unlisted companies that need time to mature. Depending on each fund, the average period would be between three to seven years (with a maximum of ten years). The way to return capital to the LPs is by selling shares that were bought in the startup. Having an 'exit strategy' is always a must.[9]
- Return required: these investments have a higher risk profile than companies that are listed in the stock market or mature businesses that are privately owned. Providers of capital see this asset class as a high-risk/high-return bet, expecting an IRR high enough to compensate for the higher risk carried. Additionally, venture capitalists usually add value to portfolio companies. They do so by providing support on strategic and financial matters, in the hiring of key personnel, or other key activities.[10] The value added should also be reflected in a higher return. Depending on the stage at which they invest, the younger the startup, the greater the risk. The more innovative the sector, the higher the risk. And so they may expect a different IRR in terms of the level of risk. For example, investing in early biotech bears greater risk than investing in late-stage cleantech. In general, equity investors in startups expect a return in the range of 40 to 60 per cent for early-stage deals and more technology-based companies, and a lower range, of between 30 and 40 per cent, in later-stage and less disruptive companies.

The expected return and time to liquidity are not fixed contractual commitments; rather, they are based on the fund managers' targets. However, venture capitalists' reputations and success in raising future funds is at stake, so they will do their best to ensure that these conditions are met.

These conditions also play a key role in valuation. They allow investors to calculate how many times their initial investment must be multiplied in order to be successful. Let's consider an example:

If Elena, a venture capitalist, demands 40% IRR and expects to sell her shares in BravoTech in five years from the investment date, how many times will she have to multiply each euro invested to be successful? Suppose that Elena invests €1 million in BravoTech. (Try to do the calculation before looking at the solution. Hint: imagine you are investing €1,000 in a bank's

---

9 In general, a venture capitalist will make a profit by buying at a low price and selling when the value of the company has increased, as already explained in Chapter 4. The return comes from the capital appreciation. Dividends are not used very often because in most countries receiving dividends means paying taxes, and investors are trying to maximize their net return. The increase in value of the shares for venture capital funds is tax-free or taxed at a very low rate. See Chapter 17 for more information on 'exits'.

10 See Chapter 10 for more information.

deposit account that is giving you 4% annually, over five years. Now change the 4% for 40% and the €1,000 for €1 million).

Solution:
C_0 = *Capital invested at time zero*
C_5 = *Final capital in time 5 (after five years)*
$C_5 = C_0 (1 + IRR)^5$
$C_5 = €1m (1 + 0.4)^5 = €5.38$ *million*

For every euro invested in the startup, Elena should multiply it 5.38 times. That is to say, if her investment in BravoTech is €1 million, and the exit will be in five years, when Elena sells her stake in the company, it should be worth €5.38 million.

The calculation in the example is very typical of the process followed by early-stage investors when valuing a new venture. It begins with the end in mind, which may sound strange. Certainly, it is very different from a traditional valuation, where the goal is to value the company today.

A venture capitalist will consider, 'How much money do I need to make at exit?' and once she has identified the amount, she will try to work out whether that level of return will be possible in the case of the company that she is currently analysing for a potential investment. Many investors don't need to make these calculations, as they specialize in a particular type of investment requiring a specific IRR and will be aware of how much time they will have to wait before selling their stake in the business. See Table 8.1 for a calculation of 'time required to multiply your money'.

Continuing with the example, Elena's stake in BravoTech should be worth €5.4 million at exit. Therefore, the full value of the startup should be much higher, maybe four or five times that amount, as our venture capitalist will have only a minority stake in the company. In order to work out how much her stake is worth, she will need to do the valuation of the startup at the time of exit. We will explain how to do that in the next section. After estimating the likely

Table 8.1 Time required to multiply your money based on number of years and expected return on the investment (IRR)

IRR	Year 2	Year 3	Year 4	Year 5
30%	1.69	2.20	2.86	3.71
40%	1.96	2.74	3.84	5.38
50%	2.25	3.38	5.06	7.59
60%	2.56	4.09	6.55	10.48

Calculation: $(1+IRR)^n$ = times investment

value of the company in the future, we will be able to assess the number of shares that the investor will be buying and the price per share.

8.3   Valuation: Looking to the Future

As we saw in the previous section, equity investors in startups will be far more interested in the future value of the company, rather than its current value. They will estimate its value at exit, and then they will calculate the implied value of the venture today. Their goal is to make money, so from the entrepreneur's perspective this might seem counter-intuitive. Entrepreneurs – well, most entrepreneurs – are not thinking of selling the company they are about to start or have recently started. They are focused on growing the venture, being successful and – why not – making this world a better place. The Venture Capital (VC) valuation method, illustrated in Figure 8.1, can be applied to new ventures, and is based on the assumption that the investor will be a temporary partner and that they will be planning to make a substantial return in exchange for money and value added.

VALUATION IN THE FUTURE: STEPS IN THE PROCESS

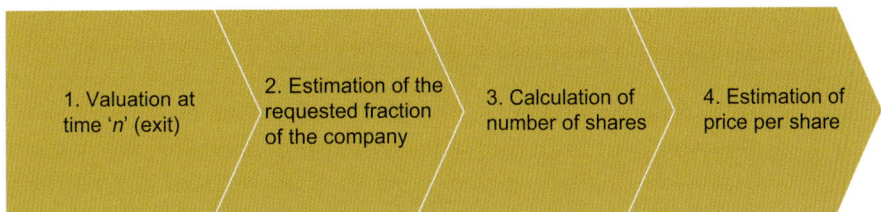

1. Valuation at time 'n' (exit)

2. Estimation of the requested fraction of the company

3. Calculation of number of shares

4. Estimation of price per share

Figure 8.1 The VC method of valuing startups.

8.3.1   The Venture Capital (VC) Method

There has been a great deal of academic research on valuation in the field of traditional corporate finance, including by famous Nobel laureates,[11] and many books that explain the process and 'rules' of valuation. However, there is no agreement on the definitive method when trying to value a new venture. If you ask three venture capitalists, you might get three different answers, as each of them might follow the VC method with some variations. However, the main objective is to get an idea of the value that the company could achieve at the time of the investor's exit. We will refer to this moment as year 'n'. Year 'n' will be different for each company, depending on many variables that we will discuss later in the chapter.

11 If you are interested in learning about the origins of valuation see Miller and Modigliani (1961).

Venture capitalists will sell their stake in the company in year 'n' to another corporation (for example, a strategic buyer), to a financial investor like a private equity firm, or at the time of an initial public offering (IPO).[12] The value obtained at 'n' could be used at a later stage to calculate the present value of the startup. This is known as a 'pre-money' or 'post-money' valuation. We will review these calculations later in this chapter.

The VC method acknowledges that the startup will be 'burning cash', and will have negative cash flows during its early years. This is why it focuses on the future when, even if the startup is still losing money, it will have increased in size, making it attractive to an acquirer who is willing to pay a high price for it. The key question the venture capitalist needs to answer is:

How much of a stake should I hold in this company at the time of selling my stake, given the value that I believe it will have at exit, in order to obtain the expected return (IRR)?

To answer this question, which is the underlying motivation for the VC method, we need more information about the venture and the expectations of the venture capitalist. This information will allow us to estimate the value at exit. The percentage that the investor will need to hold on exit is determined by data regarding the investor's desires in terms of exit time and return.

Information Required from the Venture

Investing time in getting the best information available or best estimates for the company will pay off. Obtaining data for the valuation involves a process of learning about the fundamentals of the business. Obviously, as the VC method is pretty simple in terms of the calculations needed, having the wrong figures will result in an inaccurate valuation. This also happens with traditional valuations, although having a firm's history and past financial accounts to rely on helps considerably in getting more accurate estimates.

- **Income/Sales (I_t):** Current income (I_0) and forecasted growth rate (g) would be one way of estimating future income by exit time. For many startups, especially those which are at the stage of raising money from business angels or seed funds, there is no sales data. In that case, there are two main ways of estimating future sales:

  1. Bottom-up approach: Understand the selling process and start building from zero. For example, in an internet B2C business, key variables would be: investment in online ads, number of click-throughs, number of potential customers, number of buyers, average shopping basket, repeat customers, and so on. Basically, it is about following the sales funnel. For a B2B

---

12 Exit routes are discussed in detail in Chapter 18.

business, the focus could be on the number of sales people in the company, calls per day, visits per week, successful visits, time to close a sale, average sale per customer, and so on. Again, each business is different, but we need to do some homework in order to get an idea of how the sales figure is built.

2. Top-down approach: Alternately, if we know the size of the market, we could try to estimate the market share that the company will own in year 'n'. Investors prefer to treat this approach as complementary – as a reality check. For example, a business angel might ask one of the founders, 'according to the figures that you are presenting today, what would your market share be by year 5?' With this question, the investor is trying to understand whether the numbers make sense. Of course, if your venture is a 'copycat', or it is an innovation within a well-established market, then this approach alone might be appropriate.

Vueling, the leading Spanish low-cost airline based in Barcelona, was founded by Carlos Muñoz in 2004 and backed by the venture capital fund Apax. The Spanish airline market was mature and well-understood at the time. Vueling was going to be the first Spanish low-cost airline to enter the market. Carlos and his investors could estimate the potential income of Vueling three or five years ahead by looking at similar players in other European countries, like Ryanair or Easyjet. The question was how the airline market would grow thanks to the new player. For example, the new low-cost airlines had encouraged many people to fly instead of taking the train or staying at home for the weekend. Both entrepreneur and investor would need to combine the forecast change in market size with an assessment of the market share the new entrant would assume in three to five years in order to calculate future income.

It is important to note that some investors specialize in one or more vertical sectors, such as mobile apps, cleantech or business software, and so they are experts in those fields. They know the size of the market, the growth rates, the evolution of players and the key challenges ahead. If you are an entrepreneur approaching one of these investors, be it a business angel, seed fund or venture capitalist, make sure to do your homework and be as well prepared as possible. Naturally, your focus is on your individual business, your 'baby'; for them, it represents one out of a dozen businesses they will consider every week.

- **Time of exit ('*n*'):** When will the investor sell his stake in the company? In other words, when will the company be sold? This depends on several factors, such as the sector and the strategy followed by the company. For instance, as regards sector, software companies or mobile apps tend to be sold faster than biotech or industrial companies.

The chosen exit route also affects timing. If the plan is to sell to a strategic investor, the company will normally be sold before it becomes too large.

The buyer will be interested in the technology, the products or maybe in the leadership position of the startup in one particular market. However, a strategic buyer, usually a larger company operating in the same sector, might be interested in integrating the acquired business. The smaller the startup, the easier the integration. The goal of merging the two companies is to create synergies. If the plan is to take the company public and list it on the stock exchange, the process might take longer. In many countries, especially in Europe, the regulations for listing companies impose conditions such as minimum revenue or even require the company to be in profit.[13]

- **Profit margin after tax at time '*n*' (EAT/Sales):**[14] At this stage, we might be in a position to estimate how much money the company will be making at the time of exit, assuming we have a detailed financial plan. However, investors rarely review the financial plan as part of their first analysis of the company. Some of them might have a quick look. Many of them will totally ignore it until a later stage. So, how can we establish what a reasonable profit margin would be for the venture at time '*n*'? One solution is to look at the current margins for more 'mature' companies in the same sector. For example, software companies, internet business, biotech, games, platforms, telecom, etc.

- **Price/Earning Ratio (PER or P/E):**[15] We need to work out a multiplier or an average of similar companies listed on the stock market. The PER is easy to find, as it is shown on most finance websites, where you will also find the evolution and historical data of the stock of a company. Of course, today's startup is far less mature than these listed companies. However, as we are looking forward to the time of exit, providing that everything goes according to plan, we can expect the venture to be similar to those referent companies.

With all this information to hand, we are now ready to proceed to a valuation of the startup at time '*n*'. The process of calculation is as follows:

i.   *Estimate Income (I_t) at year '*n*':*
     $I_n = I_0 \times (1+g)^n$, '*g*' being the average growth rate. If current sales are zero and we are using a top-down approach, then:
     I_n = Total market size ×market share at '*n*'

ii.   *Calculate earnings after tax at '*n*' (EAT_n)*
     $EAT_n = I_n \times EAT/Sales$

iii.   *Work out the value of company (EV_n) using the multiplier from similar companies*
     $EV_n = EAT_n \times PER$

---

13 Information on legislation for the key European Alternative stock markets can be found in Chapter 18.

14 EAT stands for Earnings After Taxes. In the case of a startup which is still losing money at the time of exit, the method can be also applied using gross margin, or EBITDA margin, or any other measure that is relevant for value.

15 If working with a different financial margin, like gross margin or EBITDA margin, then the appropriate multiplier should be used, like EV/gross margin or EV/EBITDA.

Given the small number of calculations involved, this is a fairly simple method. And that is its main strength. You can do a valuation of a startup in three minutes if you have all the necessary numbers, which is also its main drawback. If the numbers used are flawed, then the valuation will be too. The time invested in getting accurate financial information will pay off.

8.3.2 A Couple of Variations of the VC Method

There are two main variations of the VC method. The first is known as the 'First Chicago' or 'Golder' method.[16] The second is referred to as the 'Fundamental' method.

The First Chicago or Golder Method

This is a commonly used adaptation of the VC method. The procedure followed for the valuation is to start with three scenarios, typically one that is optimistic (best case), one that is reasonable (base case) and one that is pessimistic (worst case). In fact, the optimistic scenario is the one we used in the VC method, as this represents the 'best case', where everything goes well, the company grows and there is a succesful exit. In the 'base scenario', the company will reach break-even and will survive. However, under this scenario the startup does not grow as expected, does not become a market leader in a country or industry, and no party is interested in buying out the investor. Basically, there is no exit. Still, the second scenario (base case) can be good for the founders; it does not mean that the venture has failed. It just means that the investor, venture capitalist or business angel, cannot sell his stake in the company and, therefore, there is no return. In some cases, the startup will pay back the money invested at a low interest rate. In the final scenario, the 'worst case', the company goes bankrupt. Game over. Nothing is recovered. For each scenario, the VC method is applied, using multiples at the time of exit. Therefore, we end up with three valuations.

After assessing the valuations of all the scenarios, probabilities are applied to each scenario, reflecting the likelihood of it materializing. The question is, how can you establish the probabilities for each scenario? If you are an investor, you probably know from experience what proportion of investments will be 'home-runs', with a higher than expected return, how many will be write-offs, where everything is lost, and, finally, how many lie in the middle.[17] The ones in the middle, those that survive but can't be exited, are known as 'walking deaths'. Not a very nice term, but it represents the investor's sentiments, as they still have to sit on the board of the company, review the monthly financial statements and make sure things are under control. The investor knows that this particular

---

16 Scherlis and Sahlman (1987).
17 More information about the success rate of investors can be found in Chapters 3 and 4.

investment will, at best, only recover the money invested, and putting in time and effort feels like a waste of time.

For the entrepreneur, finding information on these probabilities means researching statistics on the VC sector. In general, it is quite easy to find data on the percentage of companies that are successful and those that fail. Those that remain are the 'walking deaths'. It is important that an entrepreneur looking for data tries to focus on the same sector as her startup. The percentages differ by sector, and are not the same for software, mobile apps, gaming, biotech or cleantech, to mention a few. Finally, the value of the company is the expected value of the three scenarios times their probability.

In the following example (see Table 8.2), a startup is expected to be worth €500 million at exit under the best-case scenario (a very good case, indeed). The probability of the best case is only 20 per cent, so we need to consider the remaining eight out of ten cases where the startup will not attain such a high value (the base and worst-case scenarios). Having considered all three scenarios and their expected probabilities, the weighted value of the startup will be €105.4 million, rather than €500 million.

The Fundamental Method

This method combines the VC method with the traditional discounted cash flow (DCF) method. Basically, it consists of forecasting the future income of the startup in order to arrive at its free cash flows. The future cash flows are divided into two periods, a high-growth period, where the company is still a startup and is growing very fast, and a mature growth period, where the firm is growing in line with the market. In the first stage, the startup is high-risk, and the cash flows are discounted at a very high rate. In fact, during the early years, the company will be mainly financed by equity, and the cost of that equity is the required return by the investor, something in the range of 30 to 60 per cent annually. During the mature stage, a typical cost of capital (WACC) for that sector should be used.

The main issue with this method is that it takes more time than the VC method and, as the quality of the numbers in general is low, reliable forecasting

Table 8.2 First Chicago valuation method, example

SCENARIO	VALUATION AT EXIT (EV_n)	PROBABILITY (%)	EV_n * PROBABILITY
Best Case	€500 m	20%	€100.0 m
Base Case	€12 m	45%	€5.4 m
Worst Case	€0 m	35%	€0.0 m
WEIGHTED VALUE			**€105.4 m**

Where EVn is enterprise value at year 'n', which is the exit year.

is difficult, making the outcomes no better than the ones obtained using the VC method. Consequently, this method is seldom used by business angels or venture capitalists. However, some corporate VCs apply this method and in the second stage of the valuation they assume that the startup is incorporated in their own company already.

Other Methods

Finally, in some cases valuation can be carried out using options or decision trees. This is particularly relevant for some biotech startups, where the team is developing a new drug that has to pass several milestones, mainly different approvals, as the different tests are performed.[18] The value of the venture can be assessed after every milestone.

8.3.3   Estimating the Percentage Required by Investors

Once the value of the company has been estimated, we can calculate the percentage required by the investor, taking into account his target IRR. It is important to note that for new ventures the value of the company (enterprise value or EV) in most cases equals the value of the equity (EqV), as most startups do not have any financial debt.[19] For mature companies, with debt in their balance sheets, we need to subtract their financial debt in order to get from enterprise value (EV) to equity value, or the value of the shares (see Figure 8.2).

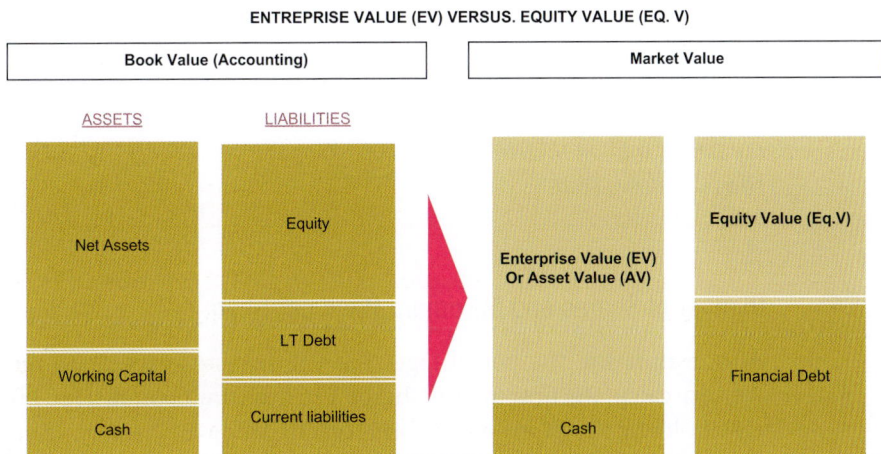

Figure 8.2 Enterprise value versus Equity value: accounting and market perspective.

18 To learn more about options or decision trees, see Chapter 32 of Copeland *et al.* (2010).
19 Enterprise Value (Value of the assets) = Equity Value + Net Financial Debt; in the unlikely case that the startup has debt, it should be subtracted from the enterprise value to get the equity value.

The process of calculation is as follows:

i. Calculation of the money expected by the investor at the time of exit, *value of the investment at time 'n'* (VI_n). Two variables are needed for the calculation: (1) time to exit; and (2) expected return (*IRR*). The formula used is the one for calculating the value of an investment using compound interest, but in this case the interest rate (I) is substituted by the IRR:[20]

$VI_n = VI_0 \times (1 + IRR)^n$ where VI_0 is the money to be invested.

ii. Estimation of the percentage, or fraction required (F_R), knowing the value of the company at exit. To assess this, we need to divide the future value of the investment of the VC (VI_n) by the value of the equity of the company (that in most cases is the company value, EV_n):

$F_R = VI_n / EV_n$.

We return to the example of Elena, the venture capitalist, with a 40 per cent target IRR, looking to invest in BravoTech. She thought she could sell her stake in the startup in five years (n). From the previous calculation, we know that her investment of €1 million (VI_0) has to become €5.38 million (VI_5).

After gathering some data on BravoTech's software-as-a-service (SaaS) market, Elena has estimated that the value of BravoTech at exit will be €20 million (EV_n). What percentage of the company will need to be exchanged for the invested €1 million?

Solution:

$VI_5 = VI_0 \times (1 + IRR)^5$

$VI_5 = €1m \times (1 + 0.4)^5 = €5.38$ million

$F_R = VI_5 / EV_5$

$F_R = 5.38m / 20m = 0.269$ or almost 27%

For her €1 million investment in the startup, Elena should get 27 per cent of the total shares of BravoTech.

8.3.4   Number of Shares and Maximum Price per Share

After estimating the percentage that the investor expects to receive at exit, we can calculate how many shares the venture capitalist or business angel will hold in the startup. One important thing to bear in mind is that, in most cases, the company will be issuing new shares for the equity investor. There are two types of shares that the investor can buy: existing shares (old

---

20 The formula to calculate the future value of an investment using compound interest rate is: $C_n = C_0 \times (1+I)^n$.

shares) and new shares. When the venture capitalist invests in the startup, he receives shares in exchange for his investment. In this case, the company issues new shares.

A very different situation occurs when the venture capitalist buys out previous investors, such as friends, family or business angels, and therefore receives 'old' shares. This only happens in later rounds of financing, when the investor's funding provides early liquidity to former investors or to the founders. In this case, the company itself does not receive any money, or only receives part of it.[21] However, this does not happen very often, as venture capitalists have little interest in making other people rich, but wish to support the future growth of the company.[22]

The information needed to calculate the number of shares that the investor will buy is:

- Number of shares already issued. This includes the founders' shares and any other shares that earlier investors in the company, such as friends and family, equity crowdfunding, business angels or previous venture capitalist, have.
- Number of stock options granted. Employee stock options are common in technology startups. It is a form of salary top-up, allowing the startups to access great talent at lower than the market rate. A stock option gives the owner the right to buy shares in the future at a price fixed today. As the startup increases in value, so does the stock option. More detail on employee stock option plans (ESOP) can be found in Chapter 13.
- Number of additional stock options needed in the future in order to recruit key personnel to support the expected growth.

Existing shares plus all stock options (granted and future) will be identified as 'S_{pre}', where 'S' stands for shares and 'pre' for pre-existing shares. Stock options are not shares, but if things go well for the company, stock options will convert into shares in the future.

With that information, we calculate both the number of shares and the price per share.

21 Venture capitalists in later rounds (third or fourth round) are sometimes interested in 'cleaning' the balance sheet, i.e. simplifying it and getting rid of some small investors. Remember that every time a shareholder agreement is signed, or there are changes to the company by-laws, all existing shareholders have to go to the notary to sign. And some founders can have many friends and many cousins and uncles . . .

22 In the case of private equity (PE), the investor is typically buying 'old' shares. This is the case in all buyouts, such as leveraged buyouts (LBOs) or management buyouts (MBOs). In fact, the term 'buyout' refers to a situation where the PE investor is buying out a former shareholder.

The calculation is as follows:

i. Calculation of number of shares of this round (S_M) equivalent to the percentage required by the investor (F_R):
    $F_R = S_M / (S_M + S_{pre})$, from which we obtain
    $S_M = (F_R \times S_{pre}) / (1 - F_R)$.
    where S_{pre} = number of shares pre-round (old shares)
ii. Knowing the number of shares that the investors will get and the value of the current round ('M', from 'money'), we can calculate the maximum price per share (P_M):
    $P_M = M / S_M$.

Let's Practise: Case Study

CRYPTO (Part I)

It was January 2017, and Paul, one of the partners of the venture capital fund Johnson & Smith (J&S), was assessing whether or not they should invest in the firm Crypto. The company's business was the development and commercialization of cryptographic software. The cryptographic market was in a process of rapid expansion, given its many applications, and the fact that both enterprises and government departments were moving their operations from paper to online. The expected market growth was 55 per cent annually over the next five years.

In the previous year, 2016, Crypto's revenues were three million euros. The company had contacted J&S because they were looking to raise two million euros in financing in order to expand across Europe. For the year 2019, Crypto's business plan forecasted an after-tax profit margin of approximately 30 percent of sales. Paul thought that if they were to invest, they would be able to sell their shares in the company in three years' time. Similar companies' stock was quoted at 15 times their earnings after taxes (*PER* or *P/E* ratio of 15×).

Crypto was founded at the beginning of 2015, issuing 1,000,000 shares at a price of €0.01/share. In addition, the company's employee stock option plan implied that they would need an additional 100,000 shares to help recruit a management team to take charge of the European expansion.

Questions for Discussion

Paul, the partner of J&S responsible for the analysis, was trying to prepare some numbers for a Monday call. What might the value of Crypto be at the time of J&S' exit? What percentage of Crypto's capital should J&S request in exchange for the two million euros of venture capital financing? J&S' target internal rate of return for a project with Crypto's current risk profile was 40 per cent annually. How many shares would the venture capital fund be getting with their two million euros? How much would they pay per share?

8.4   Valuation in the Present: *Pre-money* and *Post-money* Valuation

Once you have valued the new venture using the VC method and have estimated the percentage that the investor would receive in exchange for their investment, the implicit valuation given to the startup can be determined. In fact, pre-money or post-money valuations are not methods, but inferred values. These values are very important, as they are the ones that will be put on the negotiation table. The VC method reveals the future value, but that value is not the outcome of the negotiations but merely an input. Both the investor and entrepreneur will have their view on the value of the venture. The negotiation will centre on coming to an agreement on the value of the venture today.

Pre-money or post-money valuation allows the investor to conduct a reality check and see if the valuation makes sense. Should the valuation today not make sense, the investor will need to revert back to the assumptions used in the VC method and try to understand why the valuations differ.

8.4.1   Pre-money Valuation

This is the value of the startup today, right before the round that is being negotiated closes. To calculate the pre-money valuation, the existing shares (including stock options) are valued at the new price. The new price is the one that the investor will be paying to buy shares in this round of financing.

Pre-money valuation = Number of existing shares × Price / share of current round.

For example, in the Crypto case the original price of the shares is 1 cent. This is the price that the founders fixed when they incorporated the company: this price is the nominal price of one share. However, as the investors recognize that Crypto has increased in value since its creation, they are now willing to pay €14.83/share. Therefore, the pre-money valuation for Crypto is €16.3 million (price/share * number of shares before the round).

8.4.2   Post-money Valuation

This is the value of the company once the money from the current round is invested in the company. The startup has new cash, and so its value is the pre-money value plus the additional cash.

Post-money valuation = Pre-money valuation + Money of the current round.

Note that the post-money valuation can also be estimated by dividing the money that will be invested by the percentage given in exchange. For example, if €2 million is invested in exchange for 25 per cent of the company, then 100 per cent of the company is worth €8 million (€2m / 0.25 = €8m). In the Crypto case, its post-money valuation is €18.3 million, which is calculated as follows:

Post-money valuation = €16.3 m + €2 m = € 18.3 m or

Money of the current round / Percentage for the investor =
€ 2 m / 0.1091 = €18.3 m

There is no right or wrong value for these valuations and here, more than anything else, common sense and rule of thumb applies. Venture capital investors and business angels apply varying valuation scales or ranges for a startup depending on multiple factors, such as: when it was founded, number of people in the team, background and experience of founders, stage of development, sector, patents and 'hotness' of the market/sector.

For example, in angels' rounds the post-money valuation of the startup is, in general, in the range of €1 million. Prior to the involvement of business angels, when the founders only have a business plan, the post-money valuation can range from €100,000 to €300,000. Series A of VC financing starts in the region of €3 million in value, and can go as high as €10 million. From there the valuation can leap up, and it is difficult to predict specific amounts, but at any given moment in time, for each specific market and sector, there are specific numbers that investors have in mind based on similar transactions or comparable companies.

Finally, it is very important when negotiating the valuation that the entrepreneur and the investor clarify whether they are talking about pre-money or post-money valuation. It can lead to a very awkward situation if, for example, there was an agreement that the value was €2 million in a round of €500,000 and the entrepreneur thinks this is the pre-money valuation whereas the investor thinks it is the post-money value. The entrepreneur is planning to give up a 20 per cent stake for half a million euros, while the investor is expecting a 25 per cent stake!

Entrepreneur: Pre-money = €2 million, therefore post-money = €2.5 million.

Venture Capitalist: Post-money = €2 million, therefore pre-money = €1.5 million.

8.5   Convertible Notes

There are many issues that arise when valuing a new venture. First, you need to devote some time to getting information on the market, the business model, the key value drivers, its sales model or the potential cost structure. All this information will help you to produce a good estimation of value when using the VC model. Second, as there are at least two parties involved,[23] different views on the

---

23 A valuation involves the current owner (entrepreneur) and the future partner (the investor). However, in some cases the entrepreneurs might be talking to a group of business angels,

future, and therefore on the value of the startup, will lead to a considerable amount of time spent in negotiation. Delays incurred whilst the entrepreneurial team focuses all its attention on fundraising will inevitably affect the development of the startup. Additionally, without the money the startup cannot implement its plan, and this can also have an effect on value. Third, the negotiation process can lead to disagreements between the investor and the entrepreneurs. The investor may challenge the entrepreneurial team's assumptions, and some entrepreneurs might take this personally. The investor may also question the team's abilities and whether they know what they are doing, which will be even more irritating to the founders. All these issues are related to the agency problem and the subjective factors that come into play when the venture capitalist (or business angel) is analysing the investment (see Chapter 6 for more information). Finally, if the investor buys shares in the startup, a *Shareholders' Agreement* will be needed, and that means negotiating a *Term Sheet,* with all the issues that this involves (see Chapter 9).

One way of solving this issue is by using convertible notes or convertible debt.[24] Convertible debt is a type of loan that includes an option for the owner to convert the debt into equity at a specific time. The time when the owner of the convertible debt makes the final conversion from debt to equity is called 'maturity'. Maturity is negotiated by both parties, but is either a fixed period of time[25] or the next round of equity financing, whichever comes first. At maturity, either the debt remains as a debt, repayment of the principal starts and the option loses all its value, or the debt becomes equity at an agreed amount, called a conversion ratio. Generally, the owner of the convertible debt (the investor, or in this case the 'debt holder'), will wait until the last minute to decide whether to convert the debt into equity or not. Her decision will be based on the value (or expected value) of the equity at that time. If the expected value of the equity that she will receive using the conversion ratio is higher than the current value of the debt, she will convert. Otherwise, she will ask for the debt and the interest to be paid back. The longer the time that this decision is deferred, the higher the value of the option for the holder of the debt. Why might that be? Because she will have had time to observe the evolution of the startup, and the uncertainty and the risk will be reduced.

As regards the interest to be paid on the convertible debt, there are several options that may be agreed between the parties. The first option relates to the interest rate. In some cases, the convertible debt will pay an interest rate based on the reference interest plus a spread (for example, euribor plus 3 per cent). In other cases, the interest rate will be based on the results of the startup, so the better the results, the more interest is paid. This is known as participating

raising funds through a crowdfunding platform and even approaching some seed venture capitalists at the same time.

24 To go into detail in convertible bonds see Brennan and Schwartz (1988).

25 For the period of time to maturity 18 or 24 months is used often for startups although there is no standard.

interest (or participating debt). The parties will agree on a minimum rate, which, in general, is lower than the base rate, and a maximum rate that comes into play when the startup starts to make big profits.

The second option relates to whether the interest will be paid in cash from the start, or whether it will be accumulated with the debt, meaning that the debt will be higher at maturity. With all startups, as cash is king, the best solution is for the interest to be generated, but for payment to be deferred.

In traditional corporate finance, there are several reasons for using convertible debt.[26] From the point of view of the company: (1) it is cheaper than equity; (2) it sits on top of more senior debt, so allows for more leverage; and (3) it delays the negotiation and issues related to valuation. From the point of view of the investor: (1) debt is always safer than equity (ok, in the case of a new venture it is almost as risky as equity because if the venture fails no one will get anything); (2) the interest rate is a bit higher than that applied to more senior debt, to cover the additional risk; and (3) the upside is much higher, as the investor has the option to convert the debt to equity if things turn out well.

There is another motivation in the case of an early-stage investor looking to invest in a new venture that is even more important: time. By using convertible notes, the founders and the investor can skip the long, and sometimes tedious, step of negotiating a valuation. The investor's cash will be paid into the bank account of the startup very promptly and the entrepreneurs will be able to focus on creating and growing the business. On top of that, the fact that the valuation stage has been skipped helps devloping the relationship, as the parties have no need to put forward arguments to support their own view of the valuation or to disagree over this. By using convertible debt, the principal–agent issue that arises in the agency problem[27] (explained in detail in Chapter 6) is solved, or at least deferred. By moving the decision to buy equity into the future, the principal (the investor) will have time to observe the behaviour of the agent (the entrepreneur) and take a better-informed decision.

Convertible notes are widely used by business angels, some accelerators/ incubators and may also be used by seed venture capitalists. The standard procedure is to agree on the amount that the company needs now to move on to the next stage. That means raising enough funds to move from idea to prototype, or from prototype to first customers and metrics, and so on. The idea behind it is that the startup will then be ready to raise funds from the next investor in the value chain. Once the amount of investment has been agreed upon, the option on the convertible note will reach maturity when the next round of financing take place. At that time, the investor (a) will have the option to convert to equity at a fixed conversion ratio; or (b) will have an obligation to convert under certain conditions, such as a minimum amount raised and/or a minimum valuation

---

26 To learn more about convertible debt and its uses see Lewis *et al.* (1998).
27 If you are interested in the 'classical' articles on the agency problem see Jensen and Meckling (1976) and Jensen (1986).

(automatic conversion). The second option is a bit different from the traditional convertible debt, where the debt holder has the right to decide, but not the obligation to convert. However, in the case of startups, as the key to the conversion is the value of the equity when the decision is made, the raising of a new round provides a good indication of value. To avoid converting when the value of the startup is too low, the investor has the right to define the minimum pre-money valuation for the conversion to happen. Therefore, it is an obligation, but only when the investor considers the valuation to be fair.

This obligation to convert is key for the entrepreneur, as investors in the next round (for example Series A) will be unwilling to put money in the startup to pay back debt owed to previous investors. Also, by not converting, the first investor is signalling that the startup is not performing, so new investors will beat a hasty retreat.[28]

Currently, conversion ratios are mainly based on the valuation of the next round minus a discount premium. The discount premium takes into account the time to the next round, as well as other factors such as the minimum amount to be raised and range of the valuation. In several cases, a step-type discount can be used. The standard range of discount is between 30 and 20 per cent of the future value. Also, some convertible notes will have a cap on the maximum valuation to be used in the conversion. In this way, the owner of the convertible note is protected against getting a too small stake in the company.

Let's look at an example:

Pablo and Sophia are raising 300,000 euros for their startup, Moontrip. They need the money to finish the prototype and get some initial customers to test the product. If everything goes as planned they will be raising 1 million euros in nine months.

A business angel approaches them after participating in an investors' forum in Madrid, and proposes to invest in Moontrip using a convertible note. They like the proposal, as they do not need to discuss a valuation now, when most likely the valuation is going to be pretty low (they only have half a prototype).

The conditions of the convertible note are:

a. *it will convert automatically with a 30% discount if the entrepreneurs raise the funds within a year, with a minimum pre-money valuation of 2 million euros and a minimum amount of funds raised of 500,000 euros,*

b. *if the valuation is lower than 2 million euros pre-money or the amount raised is lower that 500,000 euros the investor will have the option to convert,*

c. *if the entrepreneurs raise the funds in 6 months or earlier, with same conditions as shown in point (a), the automatic conversion will be at a 20% discount of the valuation of the next round, and*

d. *the valuation for conversion is capped at 5 million euros pre-money.*

---

28 For more in-depth information on the signalling effect see Chapter 6, Section 6.1 'A Review of the Principal–Agent Problem'.

Before signing, the business angel is working on some numbers in order to estimate what his stake would be in Moontrip in three different scenarios:

1. Moontrip is valued at 2 million euros pre-money and raises 500,000 euros in nine months.
2. Moontrip is valued at 1.5 million euros pre-money and raises 500,000 euros in eleven months.
3. Moontrip is valued at 8 million euros pre-money and raises 2,000,000 euros in six months.

Can you estimate the percentage that the business angel, the entrepreneur and the venture capital fund will own after the round under the three scenarios?

Solution:
Let's do the calculation for the first scenario:
   In this case, the business angel has automatic conversion with 30% discount of the valuation of the round. The business angel will convert right before the round. Therefore, the pre-money valuation for the business angel is 1,400,000 euros. By dividing his 300,000 euros investment by the post-money valuation (€1,400,000 + €300,000) of 1,700,000 euro we can calculate his stake right before the round. His stake would be 17.65% and the entrepreneurs will hold the remaining 82.35%.
   However, the venture capitalist is about to invest 500,000 euros in this round. Therefore, the post-money valuation for her is 2,500,000 euros (€2,000,000 pre-money + €500,000 investment). The venture capitalist will get 20% of the startup, and previous investors will get their share diluted by 20%. Therefore, their respective stakes in the startup will be:

Entrepreneurs:	65.88%
Business Angel:	14.12%
Venture Capital Fund:	20.00%
TOTAL:	100.0%

For scenarios 2 and 3, see the calculations in Table 8.3 We have also included scenario 3 without a cap at 5,000,000 euros.

As we can see in Table 8.3, the final stake of the business angel, once the shares of the venture capital fund have been issued, can be as high as 16.67% or as low as 5.58%. You may think that scenario 3 is the worst for the business angel, as he gets a really small stake in the company. But is that really the case? What would you prefer if you were the business angel? To be investor in a company with a current post-money valuation of €10 million or €2.5 million?
   What about Pablo and Sophia? What would their final stake in the company be? Can you do the calculations? Of course, under scenario 3 they would be very happy indeed.

In conclusion, convertible debt is a good solution for early-stage investors as it postpones the challenges of valuation to a later stage and passes the responsibility of negotiating a sound valuation and favourable terms on to the next investor.

8.6 Dilution Effect Due to Additional Rounds of Financing

The process we have followed so far for the VC method is:

1. estimate the value of the company in the future,
2. calculate the future value of the VC investment at exit to get to the target IRR, and
3. estimate the percentage of the startup that the investor should own at exit.

One basic assumption underlying all of this is that there has been only one round of financing. Why have we made this assumption? What would happen if, two years after the initial round of investment, the startup needed more money and raised another round of funding? Imagine that our VC needed to take a 20 per cent share of the company to get to his target 45 per cent IRR. Now, if the company issues more shares, let's say in two years' time, to get more financing, the 20 per cent stake in the hands of the VC is going to be diluted. By how much depends on two factors:

a. how much money the startup would be raising in the second round, and
b. the valuation in that second round.

Certainly, given the current number of shares the VC holds, his percentage in the company will be less than 20 per cent once the new shares have been issued. And, if that happens, he will not achieve his target IRR of 45 per cent.

The question now is whether that is a realistic scenario. Would there need to be another round of financing? The answer most likely is in the affirmative. If the startup is growing fast, it is going to need cash to finance its growth. Two or even three rounds are the average for successful startups. And we are presuming that the startup we are looking at, from both an entrepreneur's and investor's perspective, is going to be a success!

Companies normally receive more than one round of financing in their early stages. The first round allows the founders to build a prototype, to start operations and maybe reach their first customers. So, this initial round of funding merely serves to prove the model. If everything works out well, the investors will see the potential of the company more clearly, and the founders will review their business plan and decide what to do next. It is likely that the company would then need a second round. That second round could provide the team with the financing for a launch at a national or international level, or allow them to further develop or improve the product line.

It makes a lot of sense for the parties involved, both the entrepreneurial team and the investors, to receive the funds in more than one round. Venture capitalists or angel investors prefer staged financing because it minimizes the

Table 8.3 Stake in Moontrip for the business angel after converting debt to equity

	Pre-money valuation (VC) (000)	Amount of round (000)	Conversion Discount (%)	Pre-money for BA (000)	Post-money for BA (000)	Stake of BA (Pre-VC) (%)	Post-money for VC (000)	Stake of VC fund (%)	Stake of BA (Post-VC) (%)
SCENARIO 1	2.000	500	30	1,400	1,700	17.65	2,500	20	14.12
SCENARIO 2	1.500	500	30	1,050	1,350	22.22	2,000	25	16.67
SCENARIO 3	8.000	2.000	20	4,000	4,300	6.98	10,000	20	5.58
SCENARIO 3 without cap	8.000	2.000	20	6,400	6,700	4.48	10,000	20	3.58

amount of money invested at the maximum level of risk. Additionally, in most cases, the entry of other investors in the future means an increase in the value of their stake (at least on paper). Staged financing allows investors to force the entrepreneur to focus on reaching milestones and thereby place 'controls' on the business or on the founders. The next round of financing will only take place if certain milestones are achieved.

From the point of view of the entrepreneur, staged financing also has its advantages. By getting less money when the startup is worth less, the dilution of the founding team's stake will be reduced. Clearly, raising €500,000 at the very beginning might mean that the founders have to relinquish their majority stake at that point, whereas if they raise €50,000 or €100,000 to finish the prototype or a beta test and maybe get some customers (in some cases, these are not paying customers, but at least somebody is using the product or service and giving feedback), they can then raise the remaining amount needed for further development. By then, the valuation of the company has gone up, as it is no longer merely an idea. The team has proved that they can carry out their plan and that there is some interest in the market. Raising half a million euros in a second round, perhaps involving venture capital, will be much cheaper.

Therefore, the calculations used for the VC method need to take into consideration the fact that the investor's stake will, most likely, get diluted, and 'adjust' for that. To calculate the new number of shares, taking into account later dilution, we will consider a situation where there are several rounds of financing, which we shall call M_1, M_2, etc. For each of these rounds, there will be a new injection of capital and the number of shares of each issue will be S_{M1}, S_{M2}, and so on. The price of each round will be identified by P_1, P_2, etc. Additionally, the company has a number of shares issued at the moment of foundation (S_F) and a Stock Options plan S_{SO} ($Spre = S_F + S_{SO}$).

The calculation is as follows (let's assume two rounds of financing):

i. From the valuation obtained using the VC method, or another alternative method, we obtained the percentage required by the investor at the time of exit. Now we are going to adjust for future dilution, so even if the final percentage is the same, the number of shares that the investor will get in this round has to be greater. So, let's return to calculating the number of shares for the first round:

$F_R = S_{M1}$ / Total number of shares
$F_R = S_{M1} / (S_F + S_{SO} + S_{M1} + S_{M2})$
Although to calculate S_{M1} we need to know S_{M2}.

ii. We work out the number of shares that will be issued in the second round. Normally, we will know the size of the investment in the second round and we will have an idea of the price multiple to be applied in the second round, that is, P_2 as a function of P_1.

$$S_{M2} = M_2 / P_2 = M_2 / (P_1 \times \text{price multiplier 2nd round})$$

iii. We know that the price per share in the first round will be a function of the money raised in the first round (M_1) and the number of shares bought (S_{M1}).

$$P_1 = M_1 / S_{M1}$$

iv. Finally, we can substitute P_1 in equation (ii) for equation (iii). Thus, we have:

$$S_{M2} = M_2 / ((M_1 / S_{M1}) \times \text{Price multiplier 2nd round})$$

Now we know all the numbers except for S_{M1}, but we can plug equation (iv) into equation (i) substituting S_{M2}, and estimate S_{M1}. And that's it!

By following these steps, we will have a new number of shares for S_{M1}, higher than our initial calculation, and a new price for the first round, which is lower than the first time we did the calculation. Now, we have taken the dilution into account and we have corrected for it.

Let's Practise: Case Study

CRYPTO (Part II)

After the Monday call, the partners at venture fund Johnson & Smith (J&S) were seriously thinking about investing in Crypto. Paul, the partner presenting the deal did a good job in terms of summarizing the key figures, and now was the time to put a good analyst to work to look at the company in more depth.

One of the first things that J&S usually did when they were interested in a company was to hire external consultants specializing in the company's market to carry out a business due diligence. With the information provided by the consultants, the J&S analyst prepared Crypto's detailed financial accounts for the next three years. From the forecasted statement of cash flows it was clear that, to support 55 per cent annual growth, they would need more money, or they would be running out of cash in two years. A second round of financing of around €3 million was needed to provide working capital investments and capex. The analyst asked Paul what the price of the shares might be in the second round of financing. Based on Paul's experience, a twofold increase in price would be more than acceptable, taking into account the fact that the company would be larger and a less risky proposition in two years' time.

According to J&S' policy, they would not be investing in the second round of financing. Therefore, any future financing round would imply a dilution of their stake in Crypto. This could have an effect on the previous numbers presented by Paul to the committee. The analyst was reviewing the numbers to make sure that

J&S would be the owners of 10.92 percent of Crypto stock at the time of exit. Otherwise, they would not reach their planned IRR of 40 percent, and this was a serious matter for Paul and his partners. How many shares should J&S ask for in respect of the €2 million invested in the first round? What would the price offered be?

Everything was looking good, but an investment manager told the analyst right before the meeting that he was sure the partners would be asking for pre-money and post-money valuations.

8.7   Price versus Value

It is very important to note that value is not the same as price. Often, we mix the two concepts although their meanings differ. In general, a business is valued when its owner is interested in selling it and another party, being a person or another company, is interested in buying it. The valuation will differ depending on who is looking at the company (for example, the buyer or the seller), which method is used (one that only considers the present versus one that takes the future into account) or even the time when the valuation is performed (for example, valuing a business when the economy is booming rather than during the financial crisis). Therefore, there are several 'values' for a company. However, there is only one price. And that is the one that the buyer and the seller agree upon. It is exactly the point at which supply meets demand. This happens for all type of businesses. Theoretically, value and price should be close, but again this depends on many factors. For example, imagine that somebody really needs to sell their company and there is only one potential buyer. In this case, the buyer could profit from the situation and offer a very low price for the company. *C'est la vie!*

In the case of high-growth ventures, the valuation of the company is performed in its very early years, sometimes in its early months. The company needs financing and equity financing is the only option, as discussed in Chapter 1. In order to exchange money for equity, we need to have a valuation. However, the value obtained using the VC method discussed in this chapter might end up being amended by several factors before the final price of the deal is agreed. This happens during the negotiation stage. Some of the factors that will be on the negotiating table are:

- *Number of investors interested in the venture*. The greater the level of interest, the higher the valuation. Entrepreneurs are advised to approach several investors, but not to shop around too much or to mislead investors. This is a small world. Investors know each other; they meet regularly at different events, such as conferences, networking parties or gala dinners. As an example, if the entrepreneur says to a business angel that VC XYZ is interested, in an attempt to put pressure on the business angel, the latter might call XYZ to check this and to find out the results of the venture capitalist's analysis. If it is not true, the entrepreneur will lose both investors.

- **Serial entrepreneur versus first time founder**. Clearly, an entrepreneur who has already started a business and is proven to be successful will have some leverage. For example, if the founder of Skype, Booking or eDreams decides to start a new venture, most investors will be highly interested to talk to him.
- **Hot market**. Valuations in markets that are 'hot' can be inflated. For example, if the next new thing is machine learning, or fintech, a valuation premium may be incurred just by the very fact that a company is operating in this market, as investors will be willing to pay more just to get a slice of the next 'unicorn' (this point is further developed in Chapter 6).
- **Difficult to measure (no sales).** Some companies will not have made sales and do not expect to make them in the near future. In this case, investors or entrepreneurs might try to convince themselves that the value lies in the number of users, time of use or any other metric, and that some multinational corporation will pay big money for it. Let's think about Whatsapp or Barcelona based Wallapop.
- **Network effects**. In some business models, the value lies in the power of becoming the market leader or the reference so that everybody has an incentive to use it. Perhaps you have some examples in mind, especially if you think about social networks or platforms. For example, if you are a small hotel you could feature on the Booking website, or you might be listed on a new hotel platform that charges you lower commission, half the rate charged by Booking. But where would the majority of customers go to find hotels?
- **An impressive CV**. Some entrepreneurs have worked for well-known consultancy firms, investment banks or have an MBA from a top 10 business or engineering school. This is not a guarantee of entrepreneurial success, although it is perhaps a guarantee that the person has worked very hard up to now. Most likely it also means that the entrepreneurs are good at preparing investors' decks and pitching at investors. Having 'star' names in a résumé can increase the valuation significantly (see also Chapter 6).

As famous investor Warren Buffet said 'Price is what you pay. Value is what you get.'[29] And that, in the case of a new venture, you will only discover in time.

---

29 Warren Buffet's *2008 Chairman's Letter*

VOICE OF THE EXPERT: Frank Maene (Belgium)

Frank Maene has been working with software startups for the past twenty-five years, both as investor, coach and executive. Frank currently sits on the board of Awingu, BitSensor, Flavr, VAMP, Sentiance and SweepBright. Prior to Volta Ventures, he was a managing partner at Hummingbird Ventures and Big Bang Ventures. Notable transactions include exits to Western Digital (Amplidata), Clarabridge (Engagor), SUN (Qlayer) and Symantec (DCT). Currently focusing on startups with HQs in the Benelux, he has operational experience in Silicon Valley and Turkey. Frank holds Master's degrees in Applied Economics and Accountancy from the University of Gent-Vlerick, Belgium.

How do you agree upon the percentage in the venture as return for your investment?

Through negotiation. Advanced valuation methods such as discounted cash flows are useless to value a pre-revenue startup since there simply aren't any cash flows to apply a discount rate on. As a seed and early stage venture capital fund we don't seek a majority stake in the company. We believe that the founders should remain in control of their company to make sure that they are fully engaged and motivated. On the other hand, an equity stake of less than 15% has become insignificant for a VC and not worthwhile the time and effort. Based on the equity stake (15–30%) and the amount that is being raised you can quickly determine the valuation of the company. The exact equity stake will depend upon elements such as quality of the team, value of the product/solution, size of the market, competitors and the associated terms such as liquidation preference and other preferred terms.

KEY TAKEAWAYS

- New ventures are difficult to value due to the lack of historical information, the anticipated high growth and the uncertainty of the markets in which they operate.
- A valuation can be carried out, but rather than looking at the present value, investors prefer to estimate the value of the venture at the time of their exit.
- The Venture Capital (VC) method is the preferred method when dealing with high-growth startups. It is based on the way that venture capitalists think about new investments.
- Investing time in researching the market, its dynamics and the way value will be created will pay off. Very few numbers are needed for the VC method.
- Pre-money and post-money valuations represent the present value, which is calculated from the VC method and the value at exit.
- Convertible notes are a good tool for early financing rounds.
- Price is not the same than value and it is affected by many factors.

END OF CHAPTER QUESTIONS

1. Why is it difficult to value new ventures?
2. What are the main valuation methodologies? Why are these not useful when valuing startups?
3. What is the key question that investors in new ventures ask themselves when thinking about investing?
4. What information do we need to have in order to estimate the future value of the money invested by the venture capitalist or the business angel?
5. What is the meaning of IRR?
6. What is the typical IRR demanded by early-stage investors?
7. If an investor is looking to get 50 per cent IRR from investing in a company for four years, what is the money multiplier that he needs to get?
8. A venture capitalist invests €1.5 million in a new startup that she estimates will be worth €100 million in five years. If her expected IRR is 60 per cent, what percentage of the company would she be asking for?
9. In the previous example, what would be the post-money valuation? And the pre-money?
10. The company BravoTech issued 200,000 shares for its Series A round. The price per share was €3. If the company was incorporated a year before and 600,000 shares of €0.05/share were issued: (a) what was the money raised in Series A?; (b) what was the pre-money valuation?; and (c) what was the percentage left for the founders after the Series A round?

FURTHER READING

Damodaran, A. (2006). *Damodaran on Valuation: Security Analysis for Investment and Corporate Finance*. 2nd edition. John Wiley & Sons.

Gompers, P. and J. Lerner, J. (2001). *The Money of Invention: How Venture Capital Creates New Wealth*. Harvard Business School Press.

IPEV (2010). *International Private Equity and Venture Capital Valuation Guidelines*. Edition August 2010, IPEV Board. The European Venture Capital Association, formerly EVCA and now called 'Invest in Europe', is a founding member of the IPEV Board together with AFIC (the French VC Association) and BVCA (the UK VC Association).

Lerner, J. (2000). *Venture Capital and Private Equity: A Casebook*. Wiley.

Timmons, J. A. (2008). *New Venture Creation: Entrepreneurship for the 21st Century*. 8th edition. McGraw Hill.

REFERENCES

Brealey, R. A., Myers, S. C. and Allen, F. (2013): *Principles of Corporate Finance*. 11th Global edition. McGraw Hill.

Brennan, M. J. and Schwartz, E. S. (1988). The case for convertibles. *Journal of Applied Corporate Finance*, 1, 55–64.

Copeland, T., Koller, T. and Murrin, J. (2010). *Valuation: Measuring and Managing the Value of Companies*. 5th edition. Wiley.

Jensen, M. C. (1986). Agency costs of free cash flow, corporate finance, and takeovers. *American Economic Review*, 76(2), 323–329.

Jensen, M. C. and Meckling, W. H. (1976). Theory of the firm: Managerial behavior, agency costs and ownership structure. *Journal of Financial Economics*, 3(4), 305–360.

Lewis, C. M., Rogalski, R. J. and Seward, J. K. (1998). Understanding the design of convertible debt. *Journal of Applied Corporate Finance*, 11(1), 45–53.

Miller, M. H. and Modigliani, F. (1961). Dividend policy, growth and the valuation of shares. *Journal of Business*, 34(4), 411–433.

Scherlis, D. and Sahlman, W. (1987). *A Method for Valuing High-Risk, Long-Term Investments*. Harvard Business School Note 9–288–006.

Let's Practise: Case Study

Fibra Optica Express

Maria Garcia, founding partner of leading venture capital firm *Garcia & Martinez Venture Partners* (G&M), was pretty happy that Friday. The weekend was looking good, sun was forecast for both days and, on top of that, she had just received a very interesting business plan recommended to her by a well-known professor. The entrepreneurial team was composed of three ESADE MBA students and two engineers from Barcelona Polytechnic University (UPC). A quick read-through of the executive summary was enough for her to realize that *Fibra Optica Express* (FOE) was a promising venture. Additionally, it fitted well with G&M's investment criteria and was within its area of expertise. She thought that maybe by working a little bit over the weekend, she could present a preliminary report on the company for the Monday morning Investment Committee.

The Opportunity

After reviewing in detail FOE's Business Plan, and being impressed by the CVs of the founders, Maria decided to start with the valuation of the business. It was the type of venture she liked to analyse: early stage, with a prototype ready and some initial sales. Best of all, FOE's technology was protected by a national and international patent.

An early-stage company brings with it a high risk to investors; however, it was the type of investment G&M were looking for. In fact, high risk means high return. For this type of company, the target IRR was 40 per cent and the investment would last for around four years. The IRR was high, but it needed to compensate for the risk involved and the probability of the startup not surviving at all.

FOE's valuation

After a careful analysis of the financial plan and its main assumptions, Maria had a better understanding of FOE's full potential. In order to estimate the value of the company, she slightly modified some of the assumptions. Maria thought that FOE could be making a profit of between €4 and €6 million after tax by the expected exit year. Additionally, she had just read a market report from some well-known investment bankers that indicated that 15 to 20 times was the average PER (price-earnings ratio) for this type of business.

The amount of capital that the entrepreneurs were trying to get in this round was €3 million. Maria was sure that this money would only last for the next 12 months. Therefore, she forecast that in one year's time, if FOE was performing according to its business plan, the entrepreneurs would need to raise more funds to grow the company internationally. According to her experience of working with similar startups, FOE would need an additional €5 million one year from now. She thought that the second round multiplier would be around three times the price of the first round. G&M only invested in seed and startup rounds. Much of the value of their investments came from the increase in value in the second and later rounds of financing. In fact, they knew that if the current business plan was not met, the maximum price for the second round would be twice the current round.

The MBA students had already incorporated the company. Its equity was divided into 5,000,000 shares, one million per founder, and the book value of the equity was €50,000. The founder team had also reserved 500,000 shares for the employee stock options plan. Some of these shares were to be assigned to the ESADE professor who had been helping with the venture.

Monday Morning's Investment Committee Meeting

Maria was pretty satisfied. She had not enjoyed the sunny weekend as much as she had hoped given the arrival of FOE's business plan. However, she would be surprising her colleagues at the Investment Committee meeting with an excellent investment proposal.

She had anticipated some of the questions she would be asked after her presentation of FOE's investment proposal: 'What would be the price range per share that G&M should be negotiating with the entrepreneurs?' 'How many shares should G&M be getting to ensure its IRR target?' Maria could not miss this wonderful opportunity, so even though it was Sunday evening and she was tired, she decided to prepare two cases; an 'optimistic case', where everything went well, and a 'negative case', where everything went badly.

THE TERM SHEET AND NEGOTIATING WITH INVESTORS

STEFANO CASELLI

Universit Bocconi

Equity investment involves a partnership and is temporary, since from the outset the investor and entrepreneur know it will eventually come to an end. Although the term sheet is the key document to be negotiated, the parties will first define and exchange various pieces of information and reach an agreement about both day-to-day and medium to long-term behaviours. Second, they must commit to working together and to complete transparency when managing any agency problems that arise. The end goal of the investor and the share-holders of the company is always the same: the creation of value. This issue divides successful operations from failures, allowing the investor and the startup to achieve the expected returns. Although they have a common goal, they may have differing views on many aspects of the business. Conflict typically arises, for example, over the duration of investor involvement, the strategies used to increase company value, financial and industrial alliances and new opportunities that modify the pre-investment situation. Both the investor and the entrepreneur will try to solve all potential disagreements before the decision is taken to invest and to partner together; however, it is impossible to forecast the future and legislate for every eventuality. Conflicts may also arise because the investor has his own portfolio to manage with constraints arising from the IRR objective, the residual maturity, the regulatory capital and covenants settled between the fund's originators. On the other side, the venture-backed company and the founders will have their own strategic, financial and personal goals that may differ from those of the investor.

VIEW FROM THE MEDIA

FINANCIAL TIMES   FT

When VCs get two bites of the apple

APRIL 6, 2017 BY KADHIM SHUBBER

There are a million ways to do over the investors in your company, but the simplest is to sell the business at a valuation lower than the one they invested at.

Take £10 m from someone at an £100 m valuation – giving up just 10 per cent of your venture – spend the money on lavish hotels, flights and anything else you can claim as a business expense, and then sell the company to anyone who'll buy it for ... let's say £10 m again.

You walk away with a bunch of fun memories plus another £9 m in your pocket from the sale. Your investor, on the other hand, gets back just £1 m – 10 per cent of the new, much lower valuation. Most of their money has disappeared.

This is the scenario venture capitalists describe when they explain why 'preferred' share structures are justified. They arrange their investments in such a way to give them first dibs on a certain amount of money – typically the same sum they invested – when a company is sold.

If everything goes well and a business has a big sale or stock market float, then the structuring becomes all but irrelevant. However, in tougher times, as we discussed a couple of weeks ago, these arrangements can be a disincentive for entrepreneurs. (Why bust your gut if your investors are going to get most if not all of the proceeds of a sale?)

But this is finance and that means things inevitably get even more complicated. This time we're going to look at the way venture capitalists have structured their investments in two of the UK's rising fintech stars: Funding Circle and Transferwise.

The way preferred investments are commonly structured is as a "non-participating preferred" structure. This means the investors either get their money back in a sale, ahead of anyone else, or they get a share of the overall cash pile as if they were an ordinary shareholder.

That's how Transferwise's shareholdings seem to be structured ...

Relatively straightforward.

Funding Circle, on the other hand, seems to have a more complicated setup called a 'participating preferred' structure. This means the investors get their money back in a sale, ahead of anyone else, and they get a share of the cash that's left over. They basically get to have their cake and eat it too.

... While 'non-participating' structures are common in venture investing, several London-based VCs told us "participating" structures are relatively rare.

When do they occur? Fred Wilson from Union Square Ventures, which is a long-time investor in Funding Circle, wrote about two scenarios back in 2010:

'First, it is a great way to bridge a valuation gap with an entrepreneur. Let's say we feel the business is worth $10m but the entrepreneur feels it is worth $20m. We could bridge that valuation gap by agreeing to pay $20m with a participating preferred. If the Company is a big winner, then it won't matter if we paid $10m or $20m. But if the Company is sold for a smaller number, say $50m, then having the participating feature gives us a return that is closer to what it would have been at our target valuation of $10mm.

The other place a participating feature is useful is when the entrepreneur might want to sell the company relatively soon after your investment. In that case, there is a risk that not much value will be created between your investment and an exit. A participating preferred works well in that situation as well.'

LEARNING OBJECTIVES

After reading this chapter, you will be able to:

- Understand the goal and the main characteristics of the term sheet, the document which is most commonly used to support the negotiation phase.
- Recognize the most important points contained in the term sheet and understand which aspects relate to the entire negotiation phase and fall outside the scope of the term sheet.
- Perform a detailed analysis of the contents of the term sheet.
- Understand the role of covenants and the appropriate usage of them, according to the specific profile of each deal.
- Coordinate all relevant aspects of the investment (i.e. business planning, company valuation, due diligence, etc.) with the term sheet and the negotiation process.

Where Are We Going Next?

This chapter will briefly define what a term sheet is as well as other key legal documents. Then, it will review the main issues surrounding the negotiation which will form the basis of the document lawyers will use to write the contract of investment. Finally, the chapter discusses the topic of rights and reviews major covenants and mechanisms used to regulate the relationship between the investors and the founders of the venture-backed company.

9.1   Definition of Term Sheet and Other Key Documents

A **term sheet** is a document that outlines key financial aspects, such as number and category of shares to be bought and their price, as well as a long list of terms for a proposed investment. The term sheet can be known also as the 'Letter of Intent' (LoI), 'Memorandum of Understanding' (MoU) or 'Agreement in Principle'. Investors use it to make a proposal to the entrepreneur and it is the basis for drafting the final investment documents. With the exception of certain clauses (commonly those dealing with confidentiality – i.e. company can't disclose terms or even existence of term sheet – exclusivity – i.e. company can't shop the deal, usually within 30–60 days – and sometimes the costs of performing a due diligence or similar expenses), the provisions of a term sheet are not usually legally binding. That means that even if you have received a term sheet from a famous venture capitalist, you should not start celebrating the round yet, because the round is not closed until the final document (of a very long list) is signed. The term sheet is bona fide, which means that the investor has the intention to invest in the company, and that the negotiation and the due diligence process that will follow is intended to finish in a satisfactory investment. But bear in mind that things can change in the weeks, sometimes months, that it will take from preparing the term sheet to closing!

The term sheet is at the core of the negotiation with investors, and although it is not binding, because it is subject to final documentation, due diligence and other closing conditions, such as legal opinion or audited accounts, practically speaking, it is very unusual for the actual deal to vary significantly from the term sheet itself. For this reason, in this chapter, and in the real world too, we consider the term sheet as equivalent to 'the contract' around which the entire negotiation process revolves.

Once the term sheet has been negotiated, using the exact legal taxonomy, the documents that need to be signed for an investment round are a 'Subscription Agreement' (also known as 'Sale and Purchase Agreement', or SPA) and a 'Shareholders' or Investors' Rights Agreement'. Frequently, these two documents are combined into a single 'Subscription and Shareholders' Agreement' or 'Investment Agreement and Articles of Association'. All the provisions, conditions and rights of the term sheet will be included in these documents. You will find examples in Appendix 3 and Appendix 4.

The **Subscription Agreement** will usually contain details of the investment round, including number and class of shares subscribed, payment terms and representations and warranties about the current condition of the company. These representations and warranties (investors refer to them as "Reps & Warrants") will be qualified by a disclosure letter and supporting documents that specifically set out any issues that the founders believe the investors should know prior to the completion of the investment.

A **Shareholders' Rights Agreement** will usually contain investor rights and protections. These include economic rights, political rights, such as board representation, and non-compete restrictions. The provisions or terms in this shareholder agreement will, hopefully, be used as the basis for subsequent funding rounds. Therefore, it is important for the entrepreneurial team to negotiate well in the first instance and to have good legal advisors.

Some of the protective provisions in the Shareholders' Agreement may instead be contained (or indeed repeated) in the **Articles of Association**. The decision to include terms in one or both of these documents may be jurisdiction-specific, based primarily on company law restrictions (some Continental European jurisdictions limit the rights that can be attached to clauses in the Articles of Association), enforceability concerns (investor protections can be difficult to enforce in some Continental European jurisdictions) and confidentiality concerns (Articles of

Association typically must be filed as a public document with a relevant company registry while the other investment documents can often be kept confidential).

However, the entrepreneurs will first of all deal with the term sheet, and then, once everything has been agreed upon, the lawyers will come in to draft the final documents (the name used for these documents will vary according to the country in which you are based). The more detailed the term sheet, hopefully, the fewer the issues which will need to be agreed on during the drafting of the contract. The process can be complex, and it is recommended that, in order to minimize both timeframe and costs, you work with lawyers who are familiar with venture capital transactions. It may be that one of your best friends is a very good lawyer. But the fact that she is the top specialist in divorce law or labour law will not be very helpful when it comes to dealing with raising capital and negotiating with early-stage investors.

One venture capital firm usually leads a venture capital investment round. The venture capitalist leading the round is known as the 'lead investor'. He will put together a syndicate of investors (before or after the Term Sheet is agreed) and then he will coordinate the syndicate until the round is completed. The syndicate will usually comprise some or all of the existing investors and some new ones. The lead investor is the one investing more money in that round. The new investors can be invited to the syndicate by the lead venture capitalist or brought by the entrepreneurs.

9.2 The Main Challenges in the Negotiation with Investors

The term sheet documents the agreements made between entrepreneur and investor. The negotiation with investors aims to define the commitment of the investor to the venture. It impacts and sustains value creation and allocates duties and rights between the investor and venture. The term sheet (which will be transformed into a contract as mentioned) facilitates management and control of the process and allows both parties to identify the proper balance of risk and return. Governance of the venture plays a key role and will be analysed separately in Chapter 11.

The typical challenges in completing the term sheet pertain to balancing the control between investor and entrepreneur and their role in the allocation and monitoring of investments. More particularly, three types of issues can be distinguished: (1) the type of shares, (2) the use of funds, and (3) the rules post-investment (i.e. monitoring and adding value).

9.2.1 Type of Shares

The key financial issue to be defined within the contractual package is the level of engagement. The first step involves choosing which categories of shares or share class to buy, with the aim of ensuring that the investment and management can be fully guaranteed. As there may be many rounds of financing, each round of shares is labelled with a different capital letter: series A will be the first one (i.e. 'A' shares), series B will follow, and so on. Series B and subsequent series will usually piggy-back off the terms formulated for the previous rounds: entrepreneurs should be aware that they will have to live with the investors involved in earlier rounds. As a rule, after Series A, terms can only deteriorate because of further dilution and control issues. At every round, there is a complex balancing act in order to preserve the rights of the previous rounds' investors and to create incentives to attract new investors. To that end, the investor has the option to choose from several different types of shares, all having their own associated rights and duties:

- **Common shares** are securities representing equity ownership in a corporation, providing voting rights, and entitling the holder to share in the company's success via dividends or capital gain. The holders receive one vote per share which can be used to elect the company's Board of Directors and to decide on company matters such as stock splits and company objectives.
- **Preferred stock** does not usually include voting rights, or provides at least limited rights in extraordinary matters. This is compensated for by offering priority over common stock in the payment of dividends and upon liquidation. Their dividend is paid out prior to any other dividends. Preferred stock may be converted into common stock.
- **Convertible preferred stock** is a preferred stock that can be also converted, if the shareholders wish, into common stock. This status gives the investors the option to choose whether to take their returns on liquidation event or through the underlying common equity position.
- **Participating convertible preferred stock** is a convertible preferred stock that has got an additional characteristic, which is that in the event of a sale or liquidation event the investor has the right to receive the face value and the equity participation as if the stock were converted.
- **Shares with embedded option** provide rights entitling the holder to buy company stocks issued at a predefined price due to an attached option. It is not traded by itself, and it affects the value of the share of which it is a part.
- **Tracking stock** is a security issued by a parent company related to the results of one of its subsidiaries or lines of business. Financial results of the subsidiary or line of business are attributed to the tracking stock. Often, the reason for issuing this type of stock is to separate the high-growth division from a larger parent company. The parent company and its shareholders remain in control of the subsidiary or unit's operations.

There is also convertible debt or notes (See Chapter 8). However, strictly speaking, they don't represent 'shares', at least not in the traditional sense. Convertible notes are popular for very early venture capital/seed investment and are offered together with shares. A convertible credit note represents a credit the investor holds, which can be converted into common stock at a certain date (or in a certain time window). The conversion rate is agreed at the outset (1:1, 1:1,5, 1:2, etc.) and may be subject to certain conditions. The rationale for using these convertible notes is to protect the investor until the conversion date. The holder of the convertibles can choose to remain a creditor or become a shareholder. The choice made is determined by the development of the venture. In the event that the venture does not perform well, it might be preferable to be a creditor, whereas, if the venture surpasses all expectations, converting the debt into shares (at a favourable price, as dictated by the conversion rate) is more lucrative.

One important and more general caveat: having a preference (i.e. a preference for the venture capital investor) between different types of shares is normal practice, but it is best to focus on trying both to minimize participation and accrue dividends. Moreover, it's important to understand how the various preferences interact so that everyone's incentives are aligned. It can get very complicated when multiple rounds are stacked up. In some cases, there may be flat spots or even drastic jumps of multiple that create divergent incentives. The early rounds set a precedent for later rounds, so that early investors that are too greedy on terms may live to regret it. Sometimes a preference can be used to bridge a valuation gap, but again, worry about the precedent in that case.

9.2.2   Use of Funds

Another key challenge during the engagement stage concerns the paying policy (use of funds), which involves the technique of issuing shares and the relationship of management within company corporate governance.

To ensure an effective and satisfactory paying policy, three basic questions need to be answered:

a. What is the source of the money? The investment can be obtained through new shares issued by the company or old shares sold to the investor by the entrepreneur/owner.
b. What are the entrepreneur's reasons for issuing the shares? The two main reasons are: the entrepreneur simply wants to generate cash for him/herself or because the entrepreneur feels he needs financial or strategic support to sustain the activity and growth of the venture.
c. What does the relationship with the other/existing shareholders look like? The venture capitalist could invest in the company and keep total control of the risk capital, or retain all or part of the existing shareholders and negotiate the exit of those fired.

Answers to these three questions provide an insight into why the funding is needed and how it will be allocated. Whatever the occasion/choices made, investors will need to be triggered to invest.

9.2.3   Post Investment Monitoring

The role of the term sheet and the aim of the negotiation, once the deal is closed, is also to facilitate the managing and monitoring of investors (as previously discussed in Chapter 6), to ensure the creation of value and the control of any opportunistic behaviour by the venture.

There are two completely different areas of focus during the post-investment phase for creating and protecting value: how to create and measure value, and how to live together as a team. The first one involves the setting of strict contractual rules, where the goal is to enhance the liquidity event and the performance of the business. The second aim is to agree upon the package of behaviours, mechanisms and tools the venture capital investors will offer and deliver to the venture-backed company, even if most are incapable of being expressed in contractual terms but represent per se the core values of equity investment. For these reasons, they could be called 'soft factors'.

These obligations are qualified as contractual covenants and help both the entrepreneur/founder and the venture capital investor to:

- Set standards – once goals have been identified they must be translated into standards to become effective.
- Use as motivators for the venture-backed companies – the main tools to motivate employees are money, status and recognition.

9.3   The Term Sheet in Action: Reducing Risks

Venture capitalists and business angels provide money and value added to the portfolio companies. This is why it is known as 'smart capital'. However, the participation and involvement of the equity investor in the venture-backed company requires rules. The goal is to reduce conflicts and mitigate agency problems between the investor and the entrepreneurs. A detailed discussion of agency problems is included in Chapter 6. The investment period is defined as a 'temporary marriage' and is a time when both the investor and the founders have very specific risks to avoid.

New ventures are founded in many different countries and industries. They have different goals and are at different stages when looking to raise new funds. As a result, each deal is different in terms of the type of investor, number of participants, deal structure and amount of funds needed. Consequently, the number and the nature of risks that could arise makes it impossible to forecast and cater for all the possible conflicts. This is the main role of the term sheet. During the term sheet negotiation process, the contractual covenants (i.e. the different points negotiated) will be used to help reduce and mitigate all anticipated risks. Each party will be worried about different risks. Let's look at it from both perspectives.

9.3.1 The Investor's Perspective

The investor will become a partner in the company. However, they will not be present during the day-to-day operations of the business to ensure that things are done in the best interests of the shareholders. Therefore, the investor is interested in avoiding the following risks:

- Poor operational, industrial or marketing decisions by management that affect the firm's performance and thus reduce its value in the medium to long term.
- Lack of commitment from the entrepreneurial team and key personnel that might reduce the effectiveness of the business plan.
- Divergence of opinion on the right timing for creating value. Founders might be aiming to create long-term value, but remember that venture capitalists need to exit in the medium term to cash out and return the money to their investors. Certain decisions can directly impact the IRR for the investors.
- Entrance of new shareholders that can generate conflicts between parties.

9.3.2 The Entrepreneurs' Perspective

The founders have created the startup with a vision and a mission in mind. Some of them may plan to stay in the company for the long run. Others may be even thinking about passing it on to the next generation. Most of them see it as their 'baby'. For all these reasons, the entrepreneurs are interested in mitigating the following risks:

- Lack of involvement and commitment from the investor that reduces the available financial resources or the advantages connected to the investor's network or expertise and knowledge.
- New shareholders entering into the equity which may impact on the balance between the entrepreneur and the investor (for example, by leaving the entrepreneurs as minority shareholders). Additionally, depending on the profile of the new investor, this may affect the company's strategy.
- The investor exiting at the wrong time, which may impact the overall result of the investment. The negative effect can involve fewer financial resources than expected (if the venture capitalist exits too soon) or excessive meddling from the financial partner, if the venture capitalist adopts a late exit strategy when the entrepreneurs want to sell.
- Exiting surprises interrupting the investment cycle and negating the realization of value for management and the entrepreneur.

9.4   The Term Sheet in Action: Key Terms

Mutual trust and patience is the best way to manage risks. However, when things do not go as planned and start looking ugly, trust and patience disappear very fast. For this reason, venture capitalists, with lots of experience in the topic, use specific contractual rules that will help to sustain mutual trust and patience in the bad times. These rules (the 'covenants', 'terms' or 'clauses') are usually designed to fit the deal. However, many of them are pretty standard, and are used worldwide by financial investors and entrepreneurs.

Covenants fall into two broad categories: positive and negative. **Positive covenants** are the list of things the entrepreneurial team and the company agree to do, including producing audited reports, holding regular board meetings and paying taxes on time. **Negative covenants**, usually included in the preferred equity agreement, serve to limit detrimental behaviour by the entrepreneur. Thereby, certain actions are expressly forbidden or require the approval of the investors (known as 'veto' power). Covenants may also include **ratchets** which are contractual agreements that provide the option to change duties or rights should specific conditions occur. For example, if the entrepreneurs meet the business plan, they will get additional shares.

Each covenant is de facto a stand-alone agreement, with pros and cons that clearly identify the rationale for its usage. However, the main concern during the negotiation process is not to select the right covenant, but to identify a group of covenants that will in conjunction mitigate the risk of conflicts while maximizing shareholder value (including ensuring a timely liquidity event for the investors). The following section describes the most commonly used covenants. They can be classified into four groups according to the rights that they entitle: economic, political, team commitment and other rights.

9.4.1   Economic Rights

The owner of preferred shares is entitled to some specific economic rights which, in the case of venture capital and private equity deals, are related to the liquidity event (i.e. the exit of the investor). The most commonly used economic rights are: (a) liquidation preference; (b) anti-dilution provision; (c) transfer of shares; and (d) call and put options.

Liquidation Preference

This is a provision that grants the preferred stock preference over common stock with respect to any liquidity event, dividends or payments in the event of the liquidation of the firm. In venture capital, the most common application is not related, of course, to dividends (as venture capital is mostly based on capital gains) but to the moment the company is sold (the liquidity event). The intention is to lead to an exit price for the venture capital investor which is in line with its IRR expectations. The way it works is that preferred stock (that held by the venture capitalist) has the right to get its money back before the common stock gets anything (i. e. the 'preference'.). Sometimes, the investor gets his money back more than once. To calculate the amount, 'multiples' are used ($1\times$, $2\times$, $3\times$ the investment amount) and sometimes accrued, but not paid; dividends are also included. This is essentially like adding an interest rate component to the preference (range of between 4 and 9 per cent).

After the investor gets their money back, the remaining amount of money (if any) will be distributed between the entrepreneur and the investor. There are three main options (ranked in increasing order of severity): (1) Non-Participating Preferred, (2) Capped Participating Preferred, and (3) Uncapped Participating Preferred. Let's see how it works (and remember this applies for any 'liquidity' event, not only for the liquidation of the company):

- Non-Participating: First pay the original purchase price on each share of Series A Preferred (i.e. the total amount invested by the venture capitalist). Thereafter, the balance of any proceeds shall be distributed pro rata to holders of common stock. In this case, the venture capitalist will only get his money without interest (maybe more than once). The remaining proceeds will be distributed between the entrepreneurs, friends and family and business angels.

- Participating with cap: First pay the original purchase price of each share of Series A Preferred (total amount invested). Thereafter, Series A Preferred joins with common stock on an as-converted basis until the holders of Series A Preferred receive an aggregate of x times the original purchase price. This is known as double dipping (with a cap).
- Participating without cap: First pay the original purchase price of each share of Series A Preferred. Thereafter, the Series A Preferred joins with the common stock pro-rata. No limit in this case, so double dipping (without a cap).

Calculating Final Outcome with Different Types of Liquidation Preference

Let's assume a €5m Series A investment at a €20 pre-money valuation (resulting in the Series A investors owning 20 per cent of the company). The company ends up being sold for €40 without any additional shares being issued after the Series A investment.

A '1× Non-Participating Preferred' means Series A get the greater part of their €5m preference, or what they would receive if they converted to common stock (i.e. 20 per cent of €40m, or €8m). Result: €8m goes to Series A (20%); €32m goes to common stock (80%)

A '1× Participating Preferred with a 2× Cap' means Series A get their €5m preference plus 20 per cent of the remaining €35m up to a total 2× cap (€10m). Result: €10m goes to Series A (25%); €30m goes to common stock (75%)

A '1× Participating Preferred without a cap' means Series A get their €5m preference (the 'preferred') plus 20 per cent of the remaining €35m, or €7m (the 'participating'). Result: €12m goes to Series A (30%); €28m goes to common stock (70%).

Anti-dilution Provision

In a preferred stock agreement, the anti-dilution provision is the mechanism that adjusts upwards the number of shares (or the percentage of the company) held by venture capital investors (holding of the preferred shares) if the firm subsequently undertakes financing at a lower valuation than the one at which the preferred investors purchased their shares. The rationale is to protect investors in a future 'down round'. This happens when new money is invested at a pre-money valuation (or price per share) that is lower than the previous round's post-money valuation. Best practice provides for two main types of provision: full ratchet and weighted average (broad-based and narrow-based). A full ratchet anti-dilution provision compensates investors in earlier rounds for a lower price in a subsequent round based on the difference between the price of each round, ensuring that the investors' ownership percentage remains the same as if it had occurred at the new lower price. It's important to note that even a small round of financing at a lower price could lead to an adjustment. Weighted average anti-dilution is a mechanism to compensate venture capital investors in earlier rounds for a lower price in a subsequent round based on the average price of each round weighted by the number of shares held.

The conversion price for investors is automatically adjusted downward if the company issues new shares (i.e. series B) below the share price that investors have originally paid (down round). The adjusted conversion price for investors will be set to the lowest conversion price of any later stock issue (full ratchet protection). Given:

PB = price paid by Series B investors
$CP2$ = adjusted conversion price for Series A investors
OPP = original purchase price for Series A investors
$n(A)$ = number of shares subscribed by Series A investors.

If:

$PB < OPP$.
Then $CP2 = PB$ and $n(A)$ is adjusted according to the following formula:
$n'(A) = [OPP \times n(A)]/CP2$.

Where $n'(A)$ is the new number of shares held by Series A investors. The anti-dilution provision will not apply for any capital increase made in conjunction with employee participation programmes.

As a reference example, suppose that Series A investors pay €3 million for one million A shares at €3/share (OPP) and that founding shareholders hold two million shares (€1 per share). If the Company issues three million Series B shares at €1/share (PB) so that $PB<OPP$, then the adjusted conversion price ($CP2$) is set at PB = €1 and the number of shares held by Series A Investors ($n'(A)$) becomes 3,000,000/ €1 = 3 million shares. In this way, total shares outstanding after Series B financing are eight million, Series A investors hold 37.5% of the total shares like Series B investors, and founders retain a stake of 25%. Post-money value is €8 million and pre-money value is €5 million (€8 million – €3 million).

Transfer of Shares

There are several terms that relate to the transfer of shares (buying or selling shares). The following are the most common:

- **Right of first refusal (ROFR):** If one shareholder wants to sell their stakes, this provision allows the venture capital investor to avoid including undesirable new shareholders in the company. The venture capitalist has the right to refuse the new shareholders' entrance, but he must acquire the stake of the outgoing shareholders under the same terms offered by the potential buyer.

- **Right of first offer (ROFO):** This is a contractual obligation of a shareholder (i.e. it applies to both the founder/entrepreneur and the venture capital investor) to a rights holder to negotiate the sale of the equity with the rights holder before offering the equity for sale to third parties. If the rights holder is not interested in purchasing the equity or cannot reach an agreement with the seller, the seller has no further obligation to the rights holder and may sell the equity. A right of first offer is closely related to a right of first refusal, but the former is considered to favour the seller, while the latter is considered to favour the prospective buyer. A right of first refusal gives the holder of the rights the capacity to match an offer that has been received by someone wishing to sell equity.
- **Tag along right**: An agreement to protect the minority shareholder in the startup (i.e. the venture capitalist or the business angel). If the majority shareholders (the founders) sell their stake, the investor has the right to join (pro rata) the deal, so he can sell his minority stake in the venture-backed company at the same terms and conditions to the same buyer.
- **Drag along right:** If the venture capitalist wants to sell his stake, this mechanism provides the right to ask (i.e. force) all other shareholders to sell their stake under the same terms and to the same buyer. This clause was introduced to ensure that venture capitalists can sell a minority stake and maximize the selling pricing by forcing the sale of the majority stake (or even 100 per cent of the company).[1] This allows the buyer to purchase the entire company in one go. It's probably the clause that favours the equity investor the most, because through this mechanism the equity investor – whatever the size of their stake, even a minority one – is able to sell one hundred per cent of the shares of a certain company, significantly enhancing the liquidity event. However, this clause is very unlikely to be agreed to by the entrepreneur – who has to be prepared to lose his/her company – and for this reason it occurs only in two very different circumstances: the sale of the company is an accepted outcome; the sale of the company is the consequence of the breaking of other covenants, such as the put option, when the entrepreneur doesn't have sufficient liquidity to buy back the shares.
- **Call and put options**: This mechanism represents the presence of a call option and a put option, which are embedded into the shares. More precisely, these are part of the financial agreement according to which the existing shareholders have the right to buy the stocks from the private equity investor ('callable') and the private equity investor has the right to sell the stocks to the existing shareholders ('putable'). In both cases, the option agreement can be executed with or without a specific date on which to exercise these options. These securities can be single or combined; that is, only call or put or both call and put together. In both cases, the strike price could be fixed, floating with

---

1 A minority stake, in general, means that you do not control the company. It is for this reason that a majority stake is worth more. This is referred as the 'control' premium.

a fix multiple, or floating with a fix multiple and with a price floor. The fact that the entrepreneur (or the existing shareholders more generally) has a call option indicates the preferred means of exit for the entrepreneur is to fire the equity investor. From the investor perspective, this mechanism enhances the liquidity event significantly and it helps to fix ex ante the IRR (when the strike price is fix) or the minimum value of the IRR (when the strike price is calculated on a fix multiple and a price floor). The presence of a put option is the most fully developed covenant for enhancing a liquidity event. However, as the put option is exposed to liquidity risk, it is very common for the equity investor to require a partial liquidity guarantee, having a pledge on securities inserted in an escrow account. In the event that the put option is exercised, the equity investor can use the pledge for the missing liquidity; should the entrepreneur be unable to pay, multiple scenarios could happen: a discount of the price of the buy-back; a renegotiation of the date of the exercise of the put option; the arranging of a bridging finance to generate the liquidity; a further renegotiation based on the concept of PIK (i.e. payment-in-kind), where the equity investor receives free shares of the venture-backed company and the lack of liquidity is compensated for by the chance to have a higher IRR in the future because of the larger amount of shares held; or, as an alternative to PIK, the use of a drag along right, giving the equity investor the option to sell 100 per cent of the company, which is much easier than to sell a percentage lower than the 100%.

9.4.2 Political Rights

Political rights are designed to provide control rights to the venture capitalist. She might be a minority investor, but 'de facto' has majority powers. The entrepreneurial team may believe they control the company, but the moment venture capital becomes a shareholder in a company, the rules of the game change. The most common rights are: veto rights; information rights; seats on the board of directors and voting rights. The venture capitalist will need to approve certain key matters, of which the following are the most relevant:

- **Asset sales covenants**: these are restrictions placed on selling assets above a certain value or assets representing a certain percentage of the firm's book value. This prevents the entrepreneur from increasing the risk profile of the company and changing the firm's activity from its intended focus, and also from making 'sweetheart' deals with friends.
- **Merger or sale covenants**: limitations preventing a merger or sale of the company without the approval of the investor. Transfer of control restrictions are important because venture capitalists invest in people and, if the management team decides to remove its human capital from the deal, venture capitalists would want to approve the terms of the transfer. Controlling transfers

may harm the position of the private equity investor if the terms are unfavour-able to earlier investors.

- **Asset purchase covenant:** restrictions placed on the purchase of major assets above a certain size threshold that may be prohibited without the approval of the venture capitalist. These restrictions may be expressed in absolute terms of value or as a percentage of the book value of the firm. These covenants may help prevent unwanted changes in strategy or wasteful expenditure by the entrepreneur.
- **New securities restrictions:** these limit the issuance of senior securities without the approval of previous investors and prevent the transfer of value from current shareholders to new security holders. Approval for this must be obtained by the super majority consensus of the shareholders.

Information Rights

Information rights define the quantity and periodicity of financial and qualitative information to be provided to the investors. In early-stage deals, this might be monthly. When the company is a bit more mature, this can be changed to quarterly reporting information. Normally, the periodicity relates to the date of the meeting of the board of directors. The information that is requested is used to monitor and control the investment. See Chapter 10 for more detail on this topic.

Board of Directors

Corporate governance rules also provide a set of dispositions that dictate the structure and operation of the company's main functions. Usually the venture capitalist has a representation on the Board of Directors proportional to the dimension of the capital subscribed. Rules for the Board of Directors should grant veto power to the venture capitalist representatives on the most important matters. For the Board of Directors to function effectively, it is advisable to appoint at least one independent member who does not have any type of personal relationship, such as affinity or family relationship, with the other members of the board or with the shareholders, who does not participate, directly or indirectly, in the risk capital of the company, and who has no power to influence the autonomy of the other members, for example, by his own economic resources. The Board of Directors should meet at least quarterly, if not monthly. The quorum provided for should be higher for all topics relevant to the existence of the company's, for example, dividends and reserves distribu-tions, changes to the articles of association, and for all extraordinary operations, such as a merger and acquisition or an initial public offering. The previously mentioned veto power should cover annual budget approval, the appointment and firing of the Chief Executive Officer (CEO) and Chief Operations Officer (COO), stock option plans approval, restructuring and turnaround plans, delegations of authority and remunerations of the directors, financing operations (debt issuing), capital expenditures operations and putting up collateral. To ensure on-going dialogue between management, the entrepreneur and the venture capitalist, the company should produce monthly communications that allow the venture capitalist to verify the management team's skills and to exercise his deliberation power during the shareholders' meeting. The company should communicate all information regarding risks that may affect: (1) the investment performance; (2) shareholders, directors, and employees; and (3) financial and operation data such as balance sheet reclassified, monthly financial plan, yearly budget and capital expenditures.

9.4.3 Team Commitment

The key element for a successful venture capital deal is the trust that the financial investor has in the expertise and management skills of the founders. Thus, it is reasonable to adopt a mechanism to ensure the stability of the property and the ongoing commitment and involvement of the entrepreneurs and key personnel. The most common terms are: stock options; lock up; permitted transfer clause; earn-out agreement; and exit ratchet.

Stock Options

Stock options can be assigned both to the management and to the founders to motivate and increase their desire to maximize the company's value. This is especially key when the venture capital investors together have the majority and need the full commitment of the key personnel working for the company. As stock options strictly fall within the compass of governance issues, a detailed analysis can be found in Chapter 11.

Lock Up

An agreement between the investor, existing shareholders and/or the management that prohibits them from exiting by selling their stock to third parties. It is wise to adopt a series of agreements connected with the transfer of the shares starting from the end of the lock-up period. The most important and frequent clause is the pre-emption clause, which gives the exiting partner the right to buy shares from an existing party. To ensure this clause is upheld, all parties assign their shares to an escrow agent, usually a trustee company, who will act according to the agreement signed by the parties so any opportunistic behaviour is avoided.

Permitted Transfer Clause

A provision between the investor and existing shareholders that prohibits both existing shareholders and private equity investors from selling their shares without the approval of the other party. This rule protects the stability of the parties' commitments and as such it could be considered a more sophisticated and flexible lock-up mechanism.

Earn Out Agreement

This is used mainly in private equity deals. It is a payment system consisting of a postponed payment of a part of the original acquisition price. This is done at the realization of defined performance indicators which are fixed a priori by a common agreement between the seller and the venture capitalist. This happens within a year or two after acquisition of the shares, and reduces the financial investor's economic risk.

Exit Ratchet

The exit ratchet provides an incentive for the entrepreneur (and manager). It allows to entrepreneur to obtain a part of the capital gain realized by the venture capital or private equity investor when the company's shares are re-allocated between the entrepreneur (and manager) and the venture capitalist. This ratchet is based on the periodic evaluation of the increasing value reached by the venture-backed company. It is a technique frequently adopted in leveraged buyout operations (especially in case of a management buyout or management buy-in, see Part IV of this book) combined with management objectives.

9.4.4   Other Terms

Staging Technique

This technique allows for financial resources to be invested in the firm in several staged instalments. The instalments are paid after specific business targets are hit (see Table 9.1). This provision ensures that the money is not squandered on unprofitable prospects and is also known as a 'tranched' investment. It is very common within venture capital investments where the venture-backed company doesn't need the injection of the whole amount at the beginning (e.g. to buy a plant or a machinery). It is common in investments in sciences-based companies for payments to be tranched, each tranche being measured against the achievement of agreed KPIs. These KPIs are measured against, for example, the different stages of development of one or more products, the company agreeing to take on new developments or the results of pre-clinical or clinical trials. It is common for the investors to be able to waive milestones or other completion conditions in the event of these events not being achieved.

Table 9.1 The content and the functioning of staging technique agreement

Tranches	Completion conditions	Completion mechanics
Initial tranche	The investors will stipulate that certain conditions must be satisfied before the initial tranche of the investment can proceed to completion. These conditions may include the following: • completion of any necessary due diligence in respect of the company; • the delivery of a satisfactory business plan and management accounts; • obtaining any required tax clearances; and • having the necessary authorities (board and shareholder) in place to issue the new shares to investors as part of the investment and adopting the new articles of association. The latter will likely require the passing of shareholder resolutions (whether by written resolution or by the holding of a general meeting) which may impact on: • when the investment can be completed, depending how quickly these resolutions can be passed; • the founders and key management having being issued shares or options; • the assignment in full of the necessary intellectual property rights owned by the founders or other persons to the company; • and appropriate insurance, such as keyperson and directors' and officers' liability insurance, being put in place.	These are the actions that need to be taken on the completion of the initial tranche of investment: • approval of the investment agreement and, if applicable, the disclosure letter; • issue of subscription shares and related certificates to the investors; • appointment of the investor director(s) to the board of directors; • an obligation on the investors to pay the subscription monies to the company's bank account; • approval and execution of service agreements if the founders are to become executive directors of the company; • and adoption of or commitment to adopt a share option plan. The investment agreement will stipulate that the proceeds of the investment (whether in the initial or subsequent tranches) must be used for achieving the agreed milestones and the realization of the agreed business plan or budget.
Subsequent tranches	It is typical for completion conditions to be attached to each subsequent tranche of investment. These would commonly include: • completion of the initial investment/ previous tranche; and • no material adverse change occurring (i.e. a negative event which impacts	These are the actions that need to be taken on the completion of the subsequent tranches of investment: • issue of new shares and related certificates to the investors; • and an obligation on the investors to pay the subscription monies to the company's bank accounts.

Table 9.1 (cont.)		
Tranches	**Completion conditions**	**Completion mechanics**
	significantly on the business, the result of which may otherwise affect an investor's willingness to invest in a company); • the achievement of the agreed milestones related to the tranche in question; • there being no material breach of the investment agreement, the new articles of association or a director's service agreement; • the continuing employment by the company of the founders/certain key employees; • and the company not having entered into an insolvency event.	

Exclusivity and Confidentiality

The parties agree that the venture capital financing round shall exclusively be negotiated with the investors within the time window defined in the term sheet. As a consequence, within this period neither the company nor the holders of common shares may negotiate with other interested parties nor conclude any agreements with such parties concerning the financing of the company. With the consent of the investors, additional investors may accept this term sheet. If the negotiations cannot be completed within the time period set out in the term sheet, then the parties are no longer bound by this term sheet. The company and founders also agree to treat the term sheet confidentially and will not distribute or disclose its existence or contents outside the company without the consent of the lead investor, except as required to its shareholders and professional advisors.

Business Angels term sheets for startups

By Vincenzo Capizzi, Full Professor, Università Piemonte Orientale

The aim of this section is to clarify the most commonly proposed terms and conditions that are negotiated and signed when entering into a business angel investment (Chapter 3 goes into depth on this type of investor). These terms and conditions are usually included in a 'term sheet' or 'letter of intent' prepared by the startup or the business angel. Most of the terms are non-binding, with the exception of certain confidentiality provisions and, where applicable, exclusivity rights (see below).

Though, at a first glance, you may see little difference between an angel or seed investor term sheet and a venture capital term sheet, the investment structures and founder covenants required by angels are less constrained by standardized institutional practice. In fact, business angels use term sheets that offer less protection than venture capital term sheets, relying instead on their close relationship with entrepreneurs. They use term sheets that are not too detailed, costly or time consuming to design and negotiate. Angels' term sheets are typically quite short and may even be presented as a so-called 'one page term sheet', with provisions that are easier for the entrepreneur to digest and are based on alignment and fairness (See example in Appendix 2).

This brevity can be a mixed blessing. It allows founders and angels to reach tailored arrangements that suit the individual circumstances, even if the terms from an angel can sometimes omit to cover a number of potential future governance issues.

Angel Groups or Business Angel Networks (BAN) differ from this, in that they have put angel investing on a more professional footing, with more formal protection methods for risk, information asymmetries and agency costs. As a consequence, their contractual provisions and term sheets more closely resemble those of venture capitalists.

Key Provisions in an Angel Term Sheet

Startup founders should be familiar with the following five key provisions of an angel term sheet.

1. Investment Structure

Angel investment structures vary, but angels generally invest in one of three types of securities:

- Common shares;
- Convertible preferred shares; and
- Convertible debt.

Common and Preferred Shares

Common shares are residual value shares of the same class of those previously subscribed by the startup's founders. Convertible preferred shares (so-called 'Series A stocks') are shares that include a liquidation preference over common shares (with business angels' transactions, usually this is the original investment price), and are convertible into residual value common shares.

With common and convertible preferred share transactions, the parties will fix a valuation for the startup before investment (pre-money value, see Chapter 8), and this sets the price of the investment.

Convertible Debt

Angel investors often invest through convertible debt. This involves the investors lending money to the company, with the loan amount being convertible into equity shares of the startup.

The principal advantage of this structure is that the parties can defer fixing a valuation on the enterprise until a future financing round. When the future round is complete, the debt converts into equity shares at the purchase price determined at that time, sometimes subject to a discount of between 10 per cent and 25 per cent to reward the angel for investing early (see Chapter 8 for detail in convertible debt).

2. Key Economic Terms

Essentially, the key economic terms consist of:

- quantifying the preferred return of the investment; and
- quantifying any accruing earnings on the investment

Preferred Returns

Preferred returns represent an amount that the startup must return to the business angel before it distributes any assets (or payments) to other stakeholders. With business angels' deals, this amount should generally not exceed the original investment amount, and founders should negotiate any term sheet that proposes a different formula.

Accruing Returns

Accruing returns take the form of accrued dividends on equity shares, or of an accrued interest rate on convertible debt. It is rare in angel deals for this interest to be payable in cash. Rather, such amounts accrue and are converted into equity shares at the same time as the principal amount of the loan. The industry has no set standards for accruing return rates, but commonly the rates vary between 5 per cent and 12 per cent.

When negotiating these arrangements regarding convertible debt structures, founders should keep in mind the discount rate (if any) for the future purchase price. Angels typically do not ask for both a discount rate and accrued returns.

3. Board Structure and Reporting

While the practice is not uniform, angels often require some degree of formal representation on a startup's board of directors (either as a board member or appointed 'observer'), but they typically don't require control. Some will require certain reporting procedures (such as monthly sales or product development updates).

Generally, founders will agree to provide angels with reporting rights proportionate to the nature of their investment, provided that satisfying the obligations does not materially detract from the pursuit of the startup's objectives. Naturally, if a startup finds the right kind of angel investor capable of adding value to the business, the founders will willingly engage with those angels.

4. Corporate Governance and Shareholder Agreements

Angel investing almost always requires a shareholder agreement between the founder group and the new investors. When reviewing or crafting any proposal, there are some fundamental points entrepreneurs need to keep in mind:

- *Most angels are in your corner*: if you choose them wisely, most of the legal details that you negotiate will carry little significance. If you stumble, but communicate clearly the reasons for failure and the steps you have taken to address them, most angels will stick by you. (They wouldn't have invested in the first place if they didn't believe in the entrepreneur.)
- *Look forward to the next transaction*: notwithstanding the basic need to trust one another, founders should have a clear understanding of what it will take to change the shareholders' agreement and the share capital structure in the future. Consider carefully the pre-emptive rights provided to investors, or any consent rights over future financing rounds. If you have multiple angels, you can create a corporate governance regime that includes an independent evaluation of available alternatives and offers some protection against investor misfeasance or opportunism.
- *Regular, honest communication matters*: your conversation with angels (even passive ones) does not end at the closing. Whatever the actual terms of the shareholder agreement, it pays to recognize that the quality of a founder's personal relationship with his or her investors drives the tone of the company's governance. Considering all the other challenges a startup will face, adding unnecessary drama to the decision-making process amounts to bad management practice.

5. Due Diligence

The term sheet should define the timeline and process from the date of signing the term sheet to the closing date, as well as the conditions for closing, including

due diligence. Most angel term sheets include some basic confidentiality obligations (especially if the proposed investors have not signed a non-disclosure
agreement). Exclusivity covenants that require the startup to cease investment
discussions with anyone else are less typically found, but some of the more
organized angel syndicates do include these provisions in their standard term
sheets. (If so, founders should aim to limit that period to no more than 30 to 60
days.)

See appendix for two term sheet examples.

KEY TAKEAWAYS

- The term sheet is the most crucial element in the negotiation between the
  entrepreneur (or shareholders) of the company and the equity investors.
  Its goal is to regulate their temporary partnership, leading to a successful
  exit.
- Within the negotiation process, choosing between the different categories of
  shares is a key contributory factor in finding the right balance between
  a venture capital investor's aims and the goals of the founders/
  entrepreneurs.
- Major covenants and mechanisms which, through their functioning and
  effects, help to regulate the relationship between the investors and the
  shareholders of the venture-backed company, play a fundamental role in
  the term sheet.
- Covenants can be classified into four main areas represented by economic
  rights, political rights, team commitment and other issues.
- Each covenant has a complete and effective status per se, with pros and
  cons that clearly identify the rationale for its usage. However, one of the
  main tasks of the negotiation process is to identify the group of covenants
  that, when taken together, mitigate the risk of conflict, enhance the
  liquidity event and the performance of the investment for the equity
  investor.

END OF CHAPTER QUESTIONS

1. What is the relationship between the negotiation process, the term sheet and
   the contracts underlying an investment of an equity investor into a venture-
   backed company?
2. What are the main areas of the negotiation process? In which ways are they
   linked together?
3. What are the main characteristics of shares involved in the negotiation

process? Why is it necessary to establish a hierarchy giving different rights or preferences to different capital investors?

4. Why is the equity investment defined as 'a temporary marriage'? What are the most sensitive areas when analyzing risks and potential conflict for the investor and the venture-backed company?

5. What is the main purpose of covenants and what is the rationale behind them? Can they help to completely eliminate risks and conflicts in an equity investment?

6. How are covenants classified?

7. What do we mean by liquidation preference? And what are the options available to regulate it?

8. What is the rationale for employing an anti-dilution mechanism? How does it operate and in favour of whom?

9. How does lock-up differ from permitted transfer? In what ways can they be considered similar?

10. Does a put option guarantee the liquidity event? If yes, why? If no, how can an equity investor sustain the liquidity event?

11. Which covenants maximize the opportunity for the equity investor to sell the company in the market? Why might the entrepreneur be in favour of these covenants?

12. What are the pros and the cons of combining a put option with a fixed strike price? How might this mechanism be improved from the perspective of the equity investor?

13. Do stock options allow the entrepreneur to have greater control of the company, or do they have a different aim?

FURTHER READING

BVCA (2014): *Model Documents for Early-stage Investments*. British Private Equity and Venture Capital Association.

Caselli, S., Garcia Appendini, E. and Ippolito, F. (2013). Explaining returns in private equity investment. *Journal of Financial Intermediation*, 22(2).

Caselli, S. and Negri, G. (2018). *Private Equity and Venture Capital in Europe. Markets, Techniques and Deals,* 2nd edition. Elsevier Academic Press.

Constantinides, G. M., Harris, M. and Stulz, R. M. (2013). *Handbook of the Economics of Finance*. Elsevier Academic Press.

Gompers, P. A., Kovner, A. and Lerner, J. (2009): Specialization and success: Evidence from venture capital, *Journal of Economics and Management Strategy*, 18(3), 817–844.

Gompers, P. and Lerner, J. (2000). *The Venture Capital Cycle*. MIT Academic Press.

Gompers, P. A. and Sahlman, W. (2001). *Entrepreneurial Finance: A Casebook*. John Wiley & Sons.

Invest in Europe (2015): *Professional Standards Handbook*. Invest in Europe.

Kaplan, S. N. and Stromberg, P. (2004). Characteristics, contracts and actions: evidence from venture capitalist analysis. *Journal of Finance*, 59(5).

Lerner, J., Leamon, A. and Hardymon, F. (2012). *Venture Capital, Private Equity, and the Financing of Entrepreneurship*. Wiley & Sons.

Lerner, J., Leamon, A. andHardymon, F. (2012). *Venture Capital and Private Equity: A Casebook*, 5th edition. Wiley & Sons.

Let's Practise: Case Study

MONTE DEL VINO

It's October 2017. In a world excited by the promise of fintech startups and big data, Robert Barrel, a very bright guy, decides to launch a startup, buying an old-style brand name located in Tuscany that has produced fantastic wines for many years. 'Monte del Vino' has disappeared from the market and Robert wants to demonstrate that it is possible to sell a glamorous and traditional product – such a great Tuscan red wine – using new concepts and leveraging the power of the net to enhance the visibility and the awareness of the brand. Moreover, Robert wants to demonstrate to himself and to the world that he's a successful entrepreneur. He's also respectful of the traditions of the label, and despite wanting to buy the company, he wants to keep the son of the founder of the company and his brother on the board, as experts in growing grapes in Tuscany. He loves Tuscany and he decides to live there, to become a real hands-on entrepreneur.

Robert has got great ideas, but he needs an injection of cash, even though he has some million euros in his pocket from his last job as an investment banker. He decides to give his old MBA classmate, now partner at Alpha Investor, John Cash a call. John's reaction is positive – he likes Tuscany and wine as well – and he will provide Robert with feedback in a couple of weeks.

Two Weeks Later

John is smart and he understands that the potential is huge, and he knows Robert is the right person to do it. After dinner in a nice restaurant, they meet in the Alpha office in Milan the next morning and they start going through the deal. Facts and figures are on the table: the value of the company is €30 million and Robert is able to invest €12 million, i.e. everything he has got. John is ready to invest the missing €18 million and he declares he could stay as a shareholder in the company for three years, or four years at the most. Robert is familiar with the exiting requirements of equity investors; he also knows that Alpha is looking for a minimum return of 18 per cent (IRR). This is an existing business, and therefore not so risky as a new startup. Both know that he cannot give any guarantee to enhance liquidity.

The key figures of the business plan are the following, starting from 2017 (i.e. the year +1) in thousands of euros:

€000	2017	2018	2019	2020	2021	2022
Sales	37,000	41,000	45,000	45,000	48,000	52,000
Operating costs	31,000	33,000	35,000	35,000	37,000	40,000
EBITDA	**6,000**	**8,000**	**10,000**	**10,000**	**11,000**	**12,000**
Net income	3,564	4,917	6,917	6,617	7,284	8,117
Net Financial Debt	**5,000**	**4,500**	**4,500**	**4,000**	**4,000**	**3,500**

The Term Sheet

A week later, John is going to meet Robert to discuss the term sheet. Robert is ready to listen to what John is going to propose based on a €12 million investment (i.e. 40 per cent of stake) and a €18 million investment for Alpha (i.e. 60 per cent of stake). When he starts reading, the key conditions are:

- expected holding period for the investor: three years;
- put option with expiry date of three years and strike price and multiple of six; and
- in the absence of liquidity, use of a drag along mechanism.

Governance mechanisms haven't yet been written into the term sheet and John asks Robert to put forward a proposal on that issue. Robert wants to first evaluate the rules set out in the term sheet, and he's worried about the liquidity issue after three years. He goes home and he starts thinking about different alternatives to suggest to John, trying to find a balance (he was an investment banker, after all!) between the investor's expectations and his own expectations.

After a Long Night

Robert barely sleeps, and after a long night he's ready to meet John again to discuss alternative options, keeping the same amount of money on table: €12 and €18 million respectively. The first option is to try to reduce the percentage of John's stake: but will it be high enough for John? If the first option doesn't work for John, an alternative would be to postpone the drag along and to suggest a PIK mechanism where the equity investors increase their stake by 20 per cent more and agree to move the drag along to year four. Would that be a reasonable option for the equity investors? Another alternative would be to keep the status quo and just simply to postpone the same mechanism to year four. Again, would this be acceptable to the equity investors?

The puzzle isn't an easy one to solve, and you will have to help Robert to work out the results of each solution, to find other solutions and to be ready to discuss these with John, bearing in mind the 'marriage' must be convenient and effective for both partners.

Questions for Discussion

1. The case is based on different hypotheses to enhance private equity IRR. Please comment on the thinking expressed in the case.
2. Calculate the IRR with the three years put option.
3. Calculate the IRR with PIK mechanism.

PART III

GROWING THE VENTURE

10 MONITORING TACTICS AND KEY METRICS

JAN BRINCKMANN

ESADE Business School

MIGUEL MEULEMAN

Vlerick Business School and Imperial College Business School

PETER WITT

University of Wuppertal

Investors in startups need to know what is going on in the companies. They engage in monitoring activities to find out whether a portfolio company is developing well, it needs support or corrective action. However, monitoring is only possible if the startup provides relevant information. Monitoring requires regular reports from the entrepreneurs, because they are the ones who know how the startup is doing – at least they should know. A business report is the lens through which investors understand the progress. Monitoring by investors will succeed or fail based upon the quality of the reporting. This chapter will explore what characterizes good reporting, i.e. which key metrics investors need for effective and efficient monitoring and which qualitative information entrepreneurs should provide.

Reporting is not only of value to investors. It helps the entrepreneurs to find out if their company is still on track and helps to enforce discipline. It allows founders to base important decisions on facts. Preparing regular reports is advisable, even without external investors, as the reporting system is the natural continuation of the business plan. Every core component of the business model should be subject to monitoring. Founders must regularly compare their business plan's assumptions with the actuals. In doing so, they will find out which assumptions were true and which ones were false. We have witnessed many startups who have changed their business model multiple times after incorporation, because their reporting showed the initial business model was ineffective or hopelessly optimistic.

VIEW FROM THE MEDIA

FINANCIAL TIMES   FT

Venture capital is about avoiding losers as much as picking winners

APRIL 11, 2017 BY KADHIM SHUBBER

Venture capital is full of contradictions. The men who dominate it claim to be prophetic pickers of winning startups, but they also spread their bets in the hope that one win will prove to be a runaway success. The question, then, is whether there is a knack to venture investing, and what is it?

Unfortunately for the public, but luckily for venture capitalists (VCs), the industry is very opaque. VCs invest over long time horizons, meaning their success, failure or mediocrity is not immediately obvious, and there are few public figures about the relative performance of one VC against another.

But there are some institutions who have had a broad exposure to many VC funds over many years. The European Investment Fund is one of them and on Monday it released a report analysing the performance of two decades worth of European VC activity. They examined thousands of startups funded by 355 EIF-backed funds between 1996 and 2015.

One unexpected discovery they made is that VCs working on their first fund, who were new to the venture investing game, performed basically as well as more experienced VCs, at least when times were good.

The EIF offer a rather mundane potential explanation for this, which is that they're skilled at selecting VCs, so even the newbies they back perform well. But that doesn't explain another conclusion they came to: 'Investments carried out by first-time teams perform worse during market downturns, where experience turns out to be key in shaping the investment outcome.'

That points to a different story of venture investing than one typically told by the industry. Picking winners in a calm market is something first-timers do just as well as old hands, but avoiding losers is where skill and experience matters.

https://ftalphaville.ft.com/2017/04/11/2187263/venture-capital-is-about-avoiding-losers-as-much-as-picking-winners/

LEARNING OBJECTIVES

After reading this chapter, you will be able to:

- Understand the main goals of monitoring and reporting in startups.
- Appreciate current reporting practices in startups and understand their main shortcomings.
- Evaluate business models and derive key performance metrics for different types of startups.

- Understand how key performance indicators measure the dynamics of a new venture as it develops.

Where Are We Going Next?

This chapter will explore business planning as the starting point for all planning and reporting activities in startups. Investors can only monitor a new venture effectively if entrepreneurs provide them with the right qualitative and quantitative information. However, a brief overview of the existing reporting practices in European new ventures reveals some serious shortcomings. While experienced professional investors will have clarified their reporting needs in their investment contracts, many other investors fail to obtain adequate information on the performance of their portfolio firms. We have also found that many startups waste precious time in board meetings reporting to their investors, rather than using this time for a critical discussion of key performance indicators. Thus, this chapter will take a systematic look at which key metrics are required to monitor a startup effectively and efficiently. We will investigate several different business models and propose sets of appropriate metrics for each. We will also learn how to measure the dynamics of new ventures, i.e. reliable metrics for growth.

10.1   Business Planning as the Starting Point for All Monitoring and Reporting

The main goal of all planning and reporting practices is to create confidence. First, writing plans and comparing these plans with real outcomes helps entrepreneurs themselves to gain confidence in their business model. Second, these activities allow investors, suppliers, senior employees and other stakeholders of the new venture to become confident in the future success of the company. The starting point of all reporting activities are the business planning documents. The business planning documents are a systematic survey of a startup in its entirety over a planning horizon of three to five years. In the business planning documents, entrepreneurs formulate their idea comprehensively, prepare financial plans and set targets for the development of their venture. The business planning process fulfils two purposes, which are both equally relevant. On the one hand, it forces entrepreneurs to translate their business idea into a business model. The term 'business model' refers to the way in which the new company will try to make money and includes the structure of revenues and costs. Typical questions to be answered are: Who will our customers be? Who will pay for which offerings? What will it cost us to provide the products or the services? Without proper business planning it is difficult for entrepreneurs to judge the viability of a business idea.

On the other hand, the business planning documents are marketing documents used to get support from stakeholders. One of the most important stakeholders in the early stages of a new venture's development are investors, i.e. external providers of financing. The outcomes of the business planning activities, such as the investors' slide deck, sales planning material or detailed financial calculation sheets are the point of departure for prospective investors to begin the evaluation of a venture. They will later guide their due diligence and help to ascertain the potential risks of the venture. These documents determine investors' expectations, which makes later interactions between investors and the management team much easier. Every startup is different, but a common set of factors lies behind every successful business. The business planning documents should help to highlight those factors. They should also state the assumptions made by the founders, so that investors can form their own judgements on their viability. Finally, the business planning documents should openly discuss the various risks faced by the new venture. Investors are prepared to take risks, but they will want the entrepreneurs to identify and communicate the risks, to address those risks and put an appropriate risk management system in place. There is a nice saying in the world of entrepreneurial finance: 'Investors can take a lot of bad news, but they hate surprises.'

Later on, when the company has established itself in the market, the business planning documents form the basis of an ongoing controlling and reporting system to be established. Again, both the entrepreneurs and the investors will benefit from this system. The controlling system allows founders to constantly check their assumptions, measure target fulfilment and adapt the plans to new market conditions. It also provides investors with information about the progress of the implementation of the plans. They will be able to see if the business model turns out to be viable and profitable. If it does not, both entrepreneurs and investors can aim at trying to make changes.

10.2 Reporting Practices in European Startups

10.2.1 Some General Observations

Depending on the legal form of a startup, some degree of reporting to shareholders is mandatory in all European countries. Unfortunately, these reporting requirements are typically limited to an annual report, the annual shareholder meeting and, usually, to accounting numbers. Let us look at an example. A German limited liability company needs to prepare financial statements and send them to its shareholders once a year. These financial statements consist of a balance sheet, a profit and loss statement and a cash flow statement, all on an annual basis. The shareholders' meeting then approves the financial statements. As far as the monitoring needs of investors are concerned, this type of reporting comes too late. It is also presented in an inappropriate form, because all the information stems from accounting data, which, in turn, follow national accounting standards. The dominant principle behind formal reporting along the lines of corporate law is compliance. Managers are supposed to fear the consequences of non-compliance. The focus is not on forecasting future performance but rather on the documentation of past performance. The object of interest is the company as a legal entity, not a business unit, a product or a customer segment. Therefore, it is frequently almost impossible to derive information on the success of individual products, business models or strategies from accounting data.

Surprisingly, many startups do not report to their investors beyond the legal requirements. Although most of the entrepreneurs involved are convinced that good communication with investors is important, they still do not feel that formal and regular reporting e.g. on a monthly basis is necessary. Even some very successful and rapidly growing startups, like Micromax, a mobile handset company from India, for a long time did little to standardize market and employee information in reports, or to use those reports to communicate with investors (Gulati and DeSantola 2016). There are many reasons for this unwillingness to report on a regular basis. Some entrepreneurs simply do not know that their investors expect written reports on a monthly or even weekly basis. Others feel that standardized reporting takes up too much of their precious time, and that a telephone conversation with investors every now and then will fulfil the same purpose. Some entrepreneurs shy away from regular reporting, because they do not know which metrics and what type of qualitative information investors need. Finally, some entrepreneurs mistakenly believe that investors only want to hear good news. Therefore, when the startup is not going well, they wait, and report nothing until there is some good news to communicate.

Whenever professional investors, for example business angels or venture capital firms, are involved, standardized reporting practices become the norm (Kaplan and Strömberg 2004: 2186). Typically, the investment contract will specify the guidelines for reporting, i.e. the form, the timing and the content. Monthly reporting in written form is a standard practice agreed on in most venture capital contracts. Business angel associations across Europe provide their members with guidelines and principles of good practice on reporting (for the UK, see KPMG 2014). These guidelines are voluntary, and aim to encourage entrepreneurs to provide angel investors with thorough reports in their own best interests, rather than due to a fear of non-compliance. Monthly reporting in written form is also the norm in business angel contracts. However, effective reporting does not just mean reporting obligations for the startup. Interestingly, the reporting guidelines of business angel associations also require investors to give feedback to the entrepreneurs. In this sense, reporting entails a process of two-way communication, which stimulates interaction between entrepreneurs and investors.

Reporting does not only happen in written form. In many of the startups that we have worked with, additional verbal reporting is also common. Entrepreneurs typically utilize meetings with investors, or monthly or bimonthly board meetings or calls, to report about the state of their company. However, verbal communication cannot and should not replace written reports.

Board time is valuable. Therefore, reporting should not take up an entire meeting. Nor should it take the form of entrepreneurs reading out bullet points from a presentation. Our own personal experience as members of the boards of several startups indicates that communication with investors and board members is more effective if the reporting happens outside of the board meeting. Ideally, the entrepreneurs should send out a written report before the board meeting takes place so that the directors have read it when the actual meeting starts. The focus of the meeting can then be a discussion about the report, i.e. answering questions or digging deeper into those parts of the report that need further clarification.

10.2.2 Quantitative Reporting Practices

All reporting needs to contain quantitative information, i.e. the so-called metrics or key ratios measuring the company's performance. We will explain them in detail later for three different business models:

- Brick-and-mortar retail store.
- e-Commerce.
- Software as a service.

Some key performance indicators are input-oriented. Investors may want to know how many people the company employs, how much money is still available or what the cost projections for different expense categories such as salaries, marketing spending, the cost of goods sold or shipping costs are. Other quantitative measures look at the output of the startup. One of the most prominent and most important sets of output metrics involves sales, including the number of customers, the number of orders and average order values. Investors need to see whether the business is scaling well. An extended measure for sales success is the revenue run rate, which measures how sales are developing over time. This helps investors to judge whether the company meets its forecasts, if there are seasonal patterns in sales and if the sales growth rates remain stable. The average revenue per user (ARPU) is another classic output ratio. It measures a customer's average contribution to revenue. A rising level of ARPU means that on average the startup is achieving more sales from each customer. To get more information on the sales per individual customer group, or per distribution channel, the ARPU ratio can be broken down by channel and by segment. Investors place special focus on the net revenue, which excludes not only value added tax payments (VAT) but also discounts and returns that will not result in income streams for the firm.

Some metrics provide information on the costs associated with generating revenue. A key metric is the customer acquisition cost. This shows how much a startup is currently paying to attract a new customer. It helps entrepreneurs and investors to monitor how efficient the sales process and sales team are. Over time, with better brand awareness and improving sales processes, the customer acquisition cost may come down, which will help to improve the profitability of the company. Another important measure is the churn rate, which measures the percentage of customers a company loses per month or per year. Some ventures report the percentage of retained customers as retention rates. Given that the percentage of retained customers plus the percentage of churned customers together equal 100 per cent, it is easy to determine the respective values. Customer retention or customer churn are core metrics as they show whether a startup is able to keep the customers it has acquired. The lower the churn rate, the better. Low churn rates indicate that customers are satisfied and loyal. They make repeat purchases. Here again, the absolute values for churn rates matter as much as the trend. In startups that are growing successfully, churn rates should descend over time. Another customer-related ratio, which investors always like to see in start-up reports, is customer profitability. Although it may not always be easy to get a reliable figure from the cost accounting system, its importance is undisputed. Customer profitability indicates that the startup is not only success-ful in attracting and keeping customers but that it is able to make money from them.

Quantitative reporting also includes financial success measures, some of which are important for the valuation of the company. Others are more rele-vant when evaluating the venture's chances of survival. Most financial metrics apply to both of these dimensions. A first classic measure is cash flow. For entrepreneurs and investors alike, cash is king. While cash flows may be nega-tive in order to finance the growth of a company, negative cash flow needs to be externally financed and requires that the entrepreneur obtain this funding in good time. Positive cash flows will be a delight for entrepreneur and investor alike. A related measure is the burn rate of cash. The burn rate describes a negative cash flow situation. It indicates that the company's money outflows were greater than the money inflows in a given month. It also informs inves-tors how much time remains before the startup's current funds are spent and the company runs out of money. Absolute profits and profit margins per product or service are of similar importance. Low margins may be an indicator that the startup's administrative costs are too high, that it is spending too much on scaling the business, that prices are too low, or that, in general, there are challenges involved in operating profitably in a particular industry or type of business. It may be insightful to compare the startup's profit margins with industry benchmarks, and benchmark the numbers against other young ventures in similar domains. However, investors should be aware that ventures tend to have specific characteristics, and hence the way metrics are defined, developed and interpreted may vary.

10.2.3   Qualitative Reporting Practices

Reporting and monitoring is not only about numbers and ratios. In general, qualitative information helps the investors to interpret the quantitative statements and it more comprehensively describes the situation of the company. The qualitative description usually included in the monthly email sent to the investors, will commonly describe the progress of the venture, its challenges, the current focus and potential contingency plans. Following on from this general outline, a description of the different areas may be included, covering topics such as strategic considerations, competition, sales, marketing, technology, product, human resources, operations, finance and accounting. Frequently, reports present the highlights for each respective domain in a concise, bullet-point format. Entrepreneurs will typically focus on the positive aspects and progress made to impress investors or convey their enthusiasm for the venture. However, it is better to provide a balanced picture and, in particular, to highlight challenges that the investors could help to address. For instance, entrepreneurs could include a section at the end of the qualitative description that addresses areas where they need support.

Qualitative reporting is especially valuable because some success factors of a new venture do not readily translate into metrics. A good example is the startup's strategy. Some strategic goals lend themselves well to quantitative monitoring, such as market share, growth rate of sales or customer retention. Other aspects are equally important but may be more difficult to measure. Examples include strategic considerations arising from informal discussions with market participants, qualitative and general trends in the market not captured by KPIs, the quality of leadership, progress on innovation projects or customer insights. The same is true for business functions, like human resource management or operations. Investors and entrepreneurs will need to know if the startup is doing well in these areas, but they do not always have reliable metrics. Employee satisfaction is an example, here. While the company can conduct surveys to measure employee satisfaction directly, it will typically only do so once a year or every two years. Numerical proxies for employee satisfaction exist, e.g. the fluctuation rate or rates of absence, but they may not be very accurate measures of the metric. Qualitative reporting is also essential when it comes to assessing competitive threats. If a new competitor has entered the market, a new technology serving the same customer need is available or an existing competitor has succeeded in raising the next round of financing, investors need to know. The report should not only indicate what is happening in the competitive landscape around the company, it should also comment on potential counter-measures.

10.3 Key Metrics

10.3.1 Measuring Performance as the Ultimate Goal

As an entrepreneur, you need to keep track of your progress and the ultimate success of your venture by monitoring key metrics for a number of different reasons. First, keeping track of the performance of your company will guide you in your strategic decision-making and will show whether your business model is working. Early performance data might indicate that you need to change the direction of your venture by pivoting the business model, or that the business you had envisioned might not be viable. Second, keeping track of the success of the different business functions will help you in monitoring the performance and effectiveness of your employees and the actions they perform. Measuring the outcomes of your employees' activities will enable you to manage the business in a more objective way. Additionally, by making performance data more visible within a company a sense of urgency and commitment can be created for the various stakeholders. Lastly, clearly tracking the success of your activities will help you communicate with investors, strengthening the relationship with them and, in the process, assist you in subsequent fundraising rounds. The availability of objective performance data creates transparency, helps the entrepreneur to define a clear set of goals, and establishes the progress made towards achieving these goals.

However, given the abundance of data available and the many options available for reporting specific metrics, it is important to understand which metrics will be important at what stage in the life of the venture. The choice of metrics will depend on the profit-making logic of the business model. For example, a software company operating a SaaS business model will require a different set of metrics than a traditional bricks-and-mortar retail store. The stage of development of the company will also necessitate a different approach when reporting metrics. In the early stage, when the entrepreneur is still searching for a product–market fit, the types of metrics reported on will be different from those used by a company that is post product–market fit and has started to scale the business by investing heavily in sales and marketing. In the initial start-up stage, the available data will often be more difficult to quantify. Nevertheless, entrepreneurs should from the outset collect qualitative data in a rigorous way to provide meaningful insights. Agreeing with investors on which set of metrics should drive business decision-making is, therefore, of crucial importance at every stage of a company's life cycle. Above all, the set of metrics should be (Ries 2011: 143–147):

1. *Actionable.* The key question to ask when reporting metrics is how decision makers can change their behaviour or actions in order to influence the metric. For example, measuring the click through rate on a webstore by running A/B testing with different page set-ups may clearly indicate which actions to take. It's important to make a distinction between *leading* and *lagging* metrics. Lagging metrics are typically output-oriented (e.g. sales, profit, churn) whereas leading metrics (e.g. viral coefficient, bounce rate, number of customer complaints, qualified leads) are mostly input-oriented and easier to act upon. As a lagging metric reports on the past, it is more difficult to influence by taking immediate action. For example, when the churn increases, e.g. the number of customers that

decide to abandon a subscription goes up, you may only discover problems late in the day. Conversely, a leading metric is rather predictive in nature and will provide early indications that performance might drop. For example, the number of customer complaints handled within a specific time range might well be a good predictor of future churn. Additionally, to make metrics actionable it is essential that the feedback loop between taking the action and obtaining the resulting data should be as short as possible.

2. *Accessible.* It should be relatively easy to collect the data and to make it available to the right people at the right time in the right format. This implies that a good metric should be commonly understood by the people involved and that there should be no ambiguity with respect to the calculation method.

3. *Auditable.* To ensure that metrics are reliable and objective there should be transparency and consistency in the way in which they are calculated. For example, in order to compare metrics over time, one needs to be sure that everyone uses the same calculation methods. This also requires a good definition of the data sources. As metrics are there to evaluate actions, including the performance of people, there should be no ambiguity about how they were generated.

Given all the data that might be available, the challenge will be to pick a limited number of metrics that are of crucial importance for the stage the startup is operating in and the kind of challenges the venture is facing. Having a well-defined set of metrics will increase focus and align the actions of the entrepreneurial team and the investors.

VOICE OF THE EXPERT: Gianluca Dettori (Italy)

Gianluca is founder and chairman of Primomiglio SGR, an investment company operating in early stage venture capital that launched Barcamper Ventures, its first technology venture fund. In 2006 he founded dpixel, technology venture capital advisory firm that develops advisory and consulting projects in the area of startups collaborating with partners such as ERG, QVC, Cisco or Microsoft. He started to operate as an angel investor in 2003, funded and co-founded several startups. As investor he is active with over twenty investments in the Internet and software sectors. He started as Marketing and Commercial Director in Italia Online (Olivetti), then General Manager of Lycos Bertelsmann in Italy, launching the first Internet search engine in Italy. In 1999 he founded Vitaminic, digital music startup that developed the largest legal online download platform. As CEO of Vitaminic raised over 20 milion Euro in venture capital and IPOed the company on the Italian stock exchange. Graduated in business at the University of Torino. Gianluca is advisor of the European Commission in the Future Internet Accelerators project.

How do you stay in control/up-to-date throughout an investment in a venture?

We apply the standard venture capital terms: tag along, drag along, liquidation preference, anti-dilution and the ordinary governance of a venture invested company. We are actively involved with investors and normally lead invest so we normally have the right to have a board member and in any case a board observer. Normally a partner of the firm takes the board position and supports entrepreneurs and the company in achieving their objectives. In any investment we have certain information rights that allow us to monitor portfolio companies.

10.3.2   Business Model Logics and the Use of Appropriate Metrics

In order to select the key metrics to monitor in a venture, it is essential to understand the business model's logic and, more specifically, to understand how key metrics will capture how the implemented business model will grow, achieve profitability and ultimately generate cash. One system which captures the *growth* of a business is the popular A-A-R-R-R pirate metrics, as developed by Dave McClure (2007). The initial letters refer to customer acquisition (A), customer activation (A), retention (R), referral (R) and revenue (R):

In the digital domain, *customer acquisition* metrics sometimes refer to how many unique visitors a website received and how many of those visitors stayed, for example, more than 10 seconds or made more than two clicks. Frequently, those numbers are further broken down to distinguish between new and repeat visitors. Of course, an acquired user who visits a website or signs up for a newsletter will not necessarily generate revenue, but it is important to influence this initial user to make a first time or repeat purchase decision. Hence, *activation* metrics could include completion of additional data or further website usage. The first 'R' stands for *retention* and captures the previously-discussed retention or churn of customers. Metrics that enhance an understanding of customer retention include usage behaviour, for example, usage frequency. Here, it is important to understand the usage patterns of a product in a respective category to determine its performance. For instance, in the fast-paced, competitive mobile app business, retention is measured after 1, 7 and 30 days, while B2B software subscriptions are frequently purchased and repurchased on an annual basis, hence annual retention rates are measured. Other retention metrics can capture the average interval between purchases, the number of purchases per period and/or the order value development of a retained customer.

The second 'R' captures customer *referrals*, which is an important customer acquisition channel, especially if offerings have been perceived as positive. Metrics that fall into this domain capture the percentage of customers that recommended a company's offerings, the number of recommendations they made or the number of new customers that were brought in on average per customer recommendation. Ways of tracking customer recommendations include running 'member get member' campaigns and using technology to track customer recommendation behaviour. The final 'R' stands for revenues generated by the business. In this regard, it is important to focus on net revenues excluding discounts, cancellations and returns. It is generally helpful to break out revenue by new and retained customers to get a better understanding of what is driving the revenue growth of the firm. Other metrics that help in understanding revenue growth are the number of orders and the average order value. Overall, the A-A-R-R-R metrics framework helps the venture to assess whether a particular business model is able to attract customers, convince them of the value of the product or service and ultimately succeed in growing and monetizing the customer base.

Generating revenue is not the only factor involved in becoming viable as a business. Ultimately, entrepreneurs want to develop a sustainable and profitable business venture. Key questions relating to the *profitability* of the venture are: (1) How many customers or users are needed for the business to become profitable? (2) How can customers be attracted in a cost-efficient way? (3) What is the average revenue generated per customer and the expected customer lifetime value? (4) What is the gross and net margin generated by the business? (5) What are the main drivers of the variable and fixed costs and how do they evolve with turnover? (6) How much cash is needed to run and grow the business?

In order to provide answers to these questions, we need to understand the underlying financial logic of the business model. A business model describes how an organization creates, delivers and captures value from customers. Common patterns of business models with similar profit-making characteristics can be observed. Examples include freemium models (e.g. Dropbox, PEAK, Spotify, Placed), marketplaces (e.g. AIRBNB, Bol.com, AutoScout24, BlaBlaCar, Deliveroo, Lending Club), Software as a Service or SaaS business models (e.g. Salesforce.com, Showpad, Wix), traditional retail models (e.g. Zara, Sissy Boy, SuitSupply, Pret-a-manger, Action), franchising models (e.g. Pizza Hut, Century 21, The Body Shop, Leonidas), open source business models (e.g. Drupal, Joomla, Wordpress) and the traditional pharma blockbuster model (e.g. Lipitor by Pfizer, Singulair by Merck).

In the following section, we describe several metrics that use the unit economics of a business model to assess profitability. These metrics are relevant for all business models. We will then provide some examples of metrics used within specific types of business models. The business model patterns we describe are by no means exhaustive. They represent just a small sub-sample of an ever-growing set of business model archetypes.

10.3.3   The Unit Economics of the Business Model

Unit economics starts with the observation that every business has at least one core unit with which respective revenues and variable costs can be associated.

Unit economics answers the fundamental question whether selling or operating that one unit can be profitable. If a unit's variable costs are smaller than the revenue the unit generates, unit profitability is achieved and a positive contribution margin is generated. This contribution margin multiplied by the number of units sold can help in covering the fixed expenses that the business has and which are excluded when determining unit profitability. The basic unit will depend on the type of business model and can be expressed, for instance, at the customer level, the product level, the transaction level or even the geographical level. Unit economics is an essential analysis for the calculation of break-even points and helps the business owner to assess under what conditions a business will ultimately be viable or should be further optimized or scaled.

Let's Practice: Case Study
Modelling Unit Economics in Car Sharing

Many players with different types of business models (e.g. peer-to-peer services) operate in the European car sharing market, including Cambio, Snappcar, Avantcar, Car2Go, GoMore, Mobizen, DriveNow, Zipcar and Buzzcar. In the most popular car sharing model a company puts a fleet of cars in geographically convenient locations close to where customers live and enables its customers to rent a car on a minute, hourly or daily basis. Companies using this model include Car2Go and DriveNow. Customers of such a service typically pay a small membership fee in addition to charges for the actual usage of the car. Using the following steps and employing fictitious data, we illustrate how to calculate unit economics for a popular car sharing model like Car2Go which was introduced by Daimler in Germany in 2008 as an independent business:

Step 1: The first question to answer when calculating unit economics is what is the relevant unit of analysis. The *unit of analysis* reflects the operations of the business model and can be a customer account, a user, a single buyer, an operating unit (e.g. a vending machine, a store, a seat in a plane), a transaction (e.g. selling property), a product or even a piece of infrastructure (e.g. a windmill, a charging station). In Car2Go's business model, the unit of analysis could be a customer account or one individual member. It could also be the car that Car2Go operates or the Car2Go activities in specific locations. Often it is advisable to calculate the unit economics of a number of core units to determine their respective profitability levels and identify ways to improve the respective unit economics.

Step 2: The second question to be answered is what are the underlying drivers of the economics of one unit. Key questions include: (1) what revenue does one unit generate? (2) how much does it cost to operate one unit or provide products or services at the unit level? and (3) how much does the company need to spend to acquire and service one user or customer at the unit level?

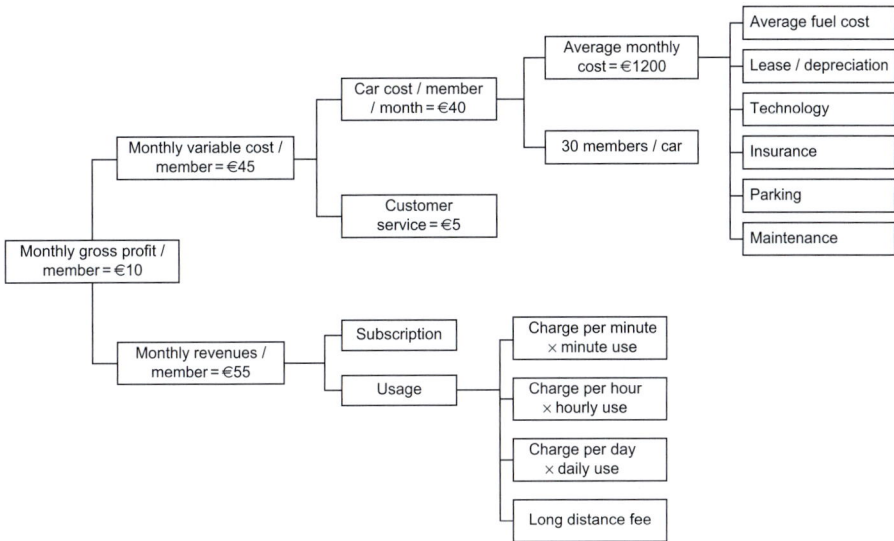

Figure 10.1 Car2Go's monthly gross profit per member.

On the revenue side, a business model might generate different types of revenue streams (e.g. subscriptions, advertising, commissions, volume or unit-based pricing, service charges, interest fees). Additionally, revenue streams can be a one-off (e.g. perpetual licence) or recurring (e.g. service fee, subscription fee, insurance fee). The total revenue generated per unit will depend on the price charged, the average transaction size, the frequency and duration of purchase and the extent of cross-selling or upselling opportunities. In Car2Go's business model the revenue streams per member consist of three parts which, however, might vary in the future: (1) a small subscription fee for gaining access to the service; (2) a rental fee per minute, per hour or per day; and (3) a long-distance fee if you drive over 50 kilometres (see Figure 10.1). When initially launched some of the parameters were known in advance (e.g. hourly charge) whereas others were unknown and dependent on actual customer behaviour (e.g. average hours used per member).

On the cost side, a business model will have different cost drivers, some of which will be *variable, semi-variable* and *fixed* in nature. Questions to be answered include whether the business model's major cost drivers are variable (e.g. wholesale business), semi-variable (e.g. car fleet provider) or fixed (e.g. semi-conductor producer)? Additionally, what level of sales can be supported with the level of fixed costs? To calculate the unit economics in the case of Car2Go it is useful to distinguish the variable (e.g. fuel) and semi-variable costs (e.g. cars) from the fixed costs of running the Car2Go platform (e.g. app, website, technology platform, administrative support, management). In Car2Go's business model, the main semi-variable and variable costs relate to the cost of providing the car fleet. On the level of one car, this includes:

- the leasing fee or depreciation cost to provide one car,
- the insurance,
- the cost of installing the technology for members to open the cars and to log the driving statistics,
- the average fuel costs,
- the rental fee to be paid for having access to parking spots, and
- the costs to maintain and clean the car.

To calculate the unit economics, you will need to know the average semi-variable and variable cost spent to serve one unit or, in Car2Go's case, to provide car access to one member (shown in Figure 10.1). To derive this number, insights are needed on the average number of members that can be served by one car or, differently stated, at the aggregate level the number of cars needed to serve a specific customer base. Even though assumptions can be made on these numbers before launching the venture, actual usage data will reveal what these numbers are. These numbers will heavily depend on the operations of Car2Go including the level of customer service Car2Go wants to provide (the more cars are available, the easier it will be to book a car at any point in time) and the timing and frequency of the use of cars. In Car2Go's business model, these operational metrics will need to be closely monitored as they will heavily influence the average car cost per member and the overall contribution margin generated per member. This resembles the load factor in the airline business, where airlines closely monitor the percentage of empty seats in order to assure profitability per flight. Overall, it will often be key to track *operational* metrics as they affect average cost levels. Examples of operational metrics in other businesses include the amount of time needed to serve a customer, the number of units produced per machine per hour, and the number of stops a delivery van can make in one hour.

As well as the direct variable cost of providing the product or service, the variable costs incurred by the company to *acquire* and *retain* customers should also be taken into account as shown in Figure 10.2. This will include

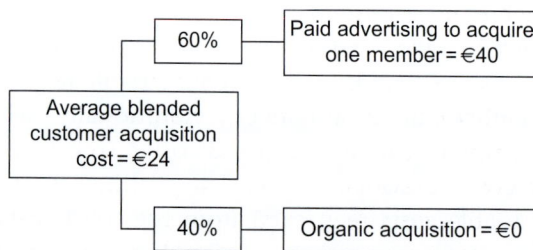

Figure 10.2 Car2Go customer acquisition cost.

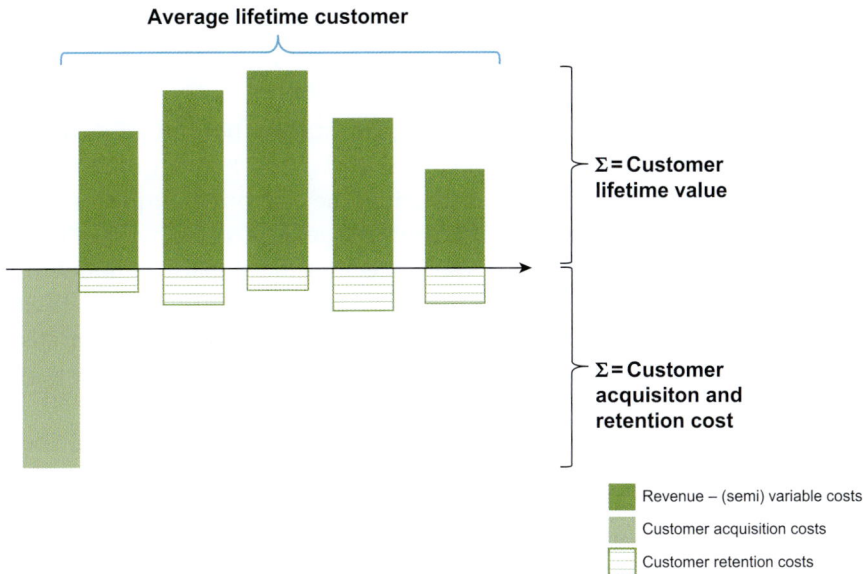

Figure 10.3 Average customer lifetime value versus customer acquisition cost.

the variable cost of selling, marketing expenses and other variable costs that can be directly attributed to actions deployed in recruiting and convincing potential customers or retaining existing customers. We call these measures the *cost to acquire a customer* (CAC), the customer retention or account management costs.

In software companies, selling and marketing expenses often make up the bulk of all the variable costs. The higher the CAC, the higher the overall gross profit per customer should be in order to recover the initial marketing and sales expenses. In Car2Go's case, it is clear that the gross profit generated per member over the lifetime of one member should be higher than the average customer acquisition and retention cost in order to end up with a positive contribution margin, and ultimately a viable business. As illustrated in Figure 10.2, the average customer acquisition cost in Car2Go's business can be calculated as the average advertising budget spent to generate one customer and the percentage distribution between customers that come in organically versus paid channels.

One essential metric in many business models, including Car2Go's, is the profitability per customer over the lifetime of a customer, or the customer lifetime value (LTV). The LTV equals the gross profit generated over the lifetime of a customer. Figure 10.3 illustrates this idea. We compare the LTV to the CAC incurred when acquiring the customer. The higher the ratio of LTV to CAC, the more profitable it becomes to invest in marketing and sales. It is a good indication of whether the selling and marketing approach works well. Another related core metric is how long it takes to recover the CAC through the cash flows generated from a customer. Typically, this period should be of less than a year. If it takes several years to recover the initial customer acquisition cost, the startup becomes a credit-giving operation, which has very high capital costs, and hence might face problems in scaling the venture and financing the customer acquisition costs. In our fictional Car2Go's model, customers generated on average €10 gross profit a month. If a customer's average lifetime equals 24 months, their total lifetime value will be €240, which is significantly higher than the initial CAC of €24. The average customer lifetime will depend on customer satisfaction levels and alternative offerings in the market. It is measured by tracking churn in the customer base.

Step 3: Based on the previous calculations, we can derive the *contribution margin* generated per member. The contribution margin represents the revenues minus the (semi)variable cost per unit, including the CAC. The contribution margin, therefore, represents the portion of sales revenue that is available to cover the fixed costs and gives an indication of the break-even level of the business. A small contribution margin will indicate that a business model at low volumes might not be viable, and typically signals substantial financing needs. A negative contribution margin means that for every unit of sales generated the company is incurring a loss. Contribution margin is often confused with gross margin. Whereas gross margin is an overall measure of the profit a company generates after subtracting those costs directly associated with production (i.e. cost of goods sold), contribution margin is generally expressed at the unit level and includes variable costs unrelated to production (e.g. CAC). For example, in software companies the gross margin might easily be higher than 80 per cent. However, selling and marketing expenses often constitute the most important chunk of the costs in software businesses and, therefore, contribution margins will be significantly lower. The break-even point is the number of units needed for the business to become profitable. It can be calculated as follows:

- break-even point in units = fixed costs / contribution margin per unit.
- break-even points in sales = fixed costs / contribution margin ratio, with contribution margin ratio = (sales – variable cost)/sales.

Overall, the key metrics to monitor on the cost side will include the absolute amount and percentage of variable, semi-variable and fixed costs compared to sales and the average customer acquisition costs. In the example of Car2Go, we assumed that each member contributes on average €9 per month in terms of contribution margin (i.e. profit of €10 per month minus €1 average CAC over lifetime) and that the fixed costs of running the business on a monthly basis equal $80,000. In this example, Car2Go will need 8,889 members to reach break-even and achieve profitability. Though all these estimations have to be considered as guesses if there is no operational history established, it is still a very useful calculation, as it provides an indication of the viability of the business given the predicted size of the market.

In summary, unit economics are important for assessing the overall viability of a specific business model. They provide insights into the minimum efficient scale required to run a business and the overall attractiveness of the profit engine of a business model. Even if some of the parameters are unknown at the outset when modelling the unit economics, building a good model will provide an understanding of the main cost and revenue drivers and the major underlying assumptions that will drive the firm's overall financial performance. As such, it is an essential tool for driving strategic decision-making and will guide discussions with investors. Unfortunately, there is no blueprint for mapping unit economics. Therefore, each entrepreneur will need to build their own model reflecting their venture's underlying business model economics ideally with the help of experienced entrepreneurs. For an investor, this is often a good test of whether the entrepreneur actually understands what she is doing from a business and financial point of view.

10.3.4   The Business Model of a Traditional Brick-and-mortar Retail Store

Brick-and-mortar stores are traditional businesses that host customers in a physical office or store. Even though e-commerce has increased considerably at the expense of physical brick-and-mortar stores in recent years, traditional retail stores still generate a significant part of consumer spending. For many consumers, physical stores represent the preferred retail format, especially when buying products or services with a strong emotional connection. E-commerce channels and brick-and-mortar stores are often complementary as they serve different customer needs, as illustrated by Amazon. com setting up traditional brick-and-mortar stores and H&M, a Swedish fashion chain, adding e-commerce to its traditional shops. Examples of categories of popular brick-and-mortar retail stores include health and personal care stores, bakeries, groceries, electronic appliances, car dealerships, speciality apparel retailers, restaurants and fast food outlets and home decoration businesses.

Even though metrics are often associated with business models operating in a digital setting, traditional brick-and-mortar stores can also track a number of metrics, and the availability of new digital technologies (e.g. beacons) and more sophisticated loyalty cards (e.g. Joyn) today enables a wider variety of metrics. At the customer acquisition level, for example, key metrics that capture traffic and conversion include:

- the outside potential (e.g. traffic in front of the store),
- the number of unique visitors,
- the number of bookings,
- the number of new versus repeat visitors,
- the average time spent by each visitor in store,
- the number of paying customers, and
- the ratio of paying customers to number of visitors.

To track the average lifetime value of customers, the following metrics can provide useful information:

- the average amount spent per paying customer per visit or over a certain period,
- the average amount spent per visitor (i.e. shopper value),
- the average number of items per transaction and the average selling price per item,
- the percentage of visitors willing to join a loyalty programme,
- the customer satisfaction level,
- the average spent on certain product categories, and
- the percentage of items sold at a discount.

To assess the overall profitability of one individual retail store, investors and entrepreneurs track the following metrics:

- the amount of turnover generated per staff member,
- the percentage of staff costs as compared to revenues,
- the total contribution margin generated per outlet,
- product and service margins,
- year-over-year percentage changes in sales and profit,
- the inventory rotation, and
- net revenues per square metre of sales space.

Measuring some of these metrics will help the business to figure out which strategies are working to attract and monetize customers. For example, when running a restaurant one might want to set up an experiment to assess the impact of the layout of the menu and the pricing display technique on the average amount spent per table and per customer. Clearly, each individual brick-and-mortar retail outlet will have specific challenges and, therefore, will need to define metrics that reflect the core of its profit engine that can be tracked over time.

10.3.5   The e-commerce Business Model

In an e-commerce business model, customers buy goods and services online. There are a number of different models, such as online shopping websites, online marketplaces and business-to-business web portals. Examples of traditional e-commerce retailers active in Europe are Amazon, Zalando, Bol. com, Ebay, VistaPrint, Made.com, Vente-privee.com and Otto. E-commerce companies generate revenue by selling products or services which they deliver either electronically (e.g. streaming music through Spotify) or deliver physically (e.g. food delivery through Hello Fresh). The most important cost drivers typically include the cost of goods sold and the customer acquisition cost. Given the digital nature of an e-commerce platform and the many tools and techniques that are currently available to track data, there is a wide range of metrics available to track the success of an e-commerce platform. To track customer acquisition, the following metrics are useful:

- Visitor and website traffic including number of (new) visitors, bounce rate, time spend on website, number of searches on site, number of product pages visited, frequency of visit and source of traffic (e.g. organic search versus paid ads.),
- Advertising and search engine-related metrics including search volume, average ranking position, number of impressions, open rate (e.g. mail marketing), cost per click, click-through rate and coupon redemption rate,
- Conversion-related statistics including number of registrations, shopping cart conversion rates, number of visitors who buy something, marketing spending per average order value and drop-out rates, and
- User-related statistics including geography and demographics and characteristics of specific segments and cohorts over time.

To track customer lifetime value, key metrics include:

- Revenue-related statistics including number of orders, average order value, purchases per year and value per visit.
- Churn rate, customer satisfaction rate (e.g. net promotor score), return rate, shopping cart abandonment rate.

In addition, there are a number of operational metrics available when running an e-commerce platform which might influence customer acquisition costs and lifetime value including:

- Average delivery time.
- Stock availability.
- Product return rate.
- Payment methods used.
- Downtime and connection time.
- Customer support activity levels.

Tracking these metrics will help the business to assess the effectiveness of a website and allow it to determine the outcome of experiments. For example,

A/B testing will help to assess how different search engines implemented on a portal lead to different levels of conversion.

Let's Practise: Case Study

Suitcase

In the following example, we will use the story of Suitcase to illustrate the use of metrics in an e-commerce setting. Suitcase, launched by Anthony De Wit and Jonathan Wanten in 2014, offers a personal online retailing service for men. After subscribing online and consulting their personal style advisor via a quick phone call, outfits are handpicked based on given preferences and budgets. Suitcase then delivers a personalized box filled with two to three outfits to the customer's doorstep free of charge. Customers of Suitcase have a seven-day fitting period before returning the items. Members of Suitcase do not have to pay a membership fee nor are they obliged to buy these boxes on a regular basis. Customers only pay for the items they keep. Suitcase was the first organization to introduce the concept of curated shopping for men in Belgium, and had built a customer base of nearly 4,000 customers by 2017. Similar players in the European market include, for example, Outfittery (Germany), The Chapar (UK), The Cloakroom (NL), Zalon (Germany), Modomoto (Germany) and House of Einstein (Germany). The metrics used within the Suitcase business model consist of: (1) revenue-related metrics and (2) cost-related metrics. These metrics are necessary for predicting future cash needs, to support negotiations with investors and to measure the business' overall operational performance.

Revenue-related metrics within Suitcase's business model stem from the main revenue drivers. The metrics driving the total revenue depend on two main factors (1) volume of suitcases sold and (2) the retention value (the average spend per unit or suitcase). Each of these metrics in turn depends on several drivers; so-called leading metrics. For the first driver of total revenue, which is *volume*, leading metrics track the inflow of inputs: the number of leads generated via advertising channels (for new leads) or by mailing campaigns (for existing customers). This is illustrated in Figure 10.4. The volume of suitcases ordered will depend on the effectiveness of the company's marketing activities, i.e. the ability to generate traffic to the website and convert those visitors into paying customers. The churn rate reflects the number of recurring customers that no longer want to use the service.

Pushing online advertisements or sending out specific mailing campaigns may boost the total volume of suitcases sold. The effectiveness of these actions immediately affects the cost to acquire a customer (CAC). Given the illustration above, this measure refers to the cost of converting one person to a sale. In the clothing retail industry, the CAC will typically vary depending on the actual

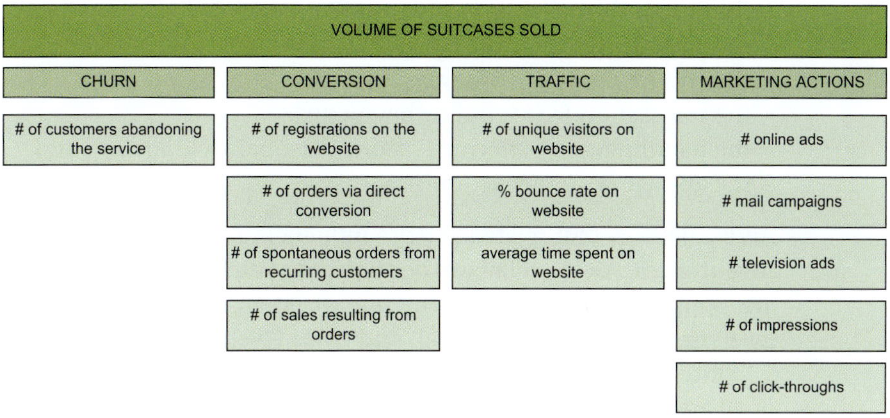

VOLUME OF SUITCASES SOLD			
CHURN	**CONVERSION**	**TRAFFIC**	**MARKETING ACTIONS**
# of customers abandoning the service	# of registrations on the website	# of unique visitors on website	# online ads
	# of orders via direct conversion	% bounce rate on website	# mail campaigns
	# of spontaneous orders from recurring customers	average time spent on website	# television ads
	# of sales resulting from orders		# of impressions
			# of click-throughs

Figure 10.4 Marketing metrics for Suitcase.

customer's needs and seasonal patterns. For example, the customer acquisition cost is generally higher in low seasons, while it decreases in high seasons.

The second driver of the total revenue, the *retention value* or average spend per box, consists of a number of drivers which are more difficult to manipulate. One should consider this as less actionable in the short-term (for new customers) and more actionable in the long-term (for recurring customers). Increasing the retention value means influencing the spending behaviour of the customer. Within Suitcase's business model, the insights on customer preferences derive from the customer profiling analysis, which is done when welcoming the customer, the beginning of the customer journey. The accuracy of the customer profile is improved, based on returns, feedback and repeat purchases. The more information the company has on customer preferences and their overall profile, the more likely the sales order for each box sent will increase. Increasing or decreasing sales prices will follow a certain price elasticity, and will influence the average retention value. Additionally, the net promoter score also provides a good indication of the future retention value per box.

In summary, the order value of a repeating customer is the bread and butter of Suitcase's business model. Capturing customer data increases the level of intelligence held in the complete customer profile, which gradually improves with every new suitcase ordered, prolonging the customer life cycle journey. The eventual goal of gathering this intelligence is, therefore, to increase the average spend per customer or ARPU.

Cost-related metrics are metrics which influence semi-variable and variable costs, which influence the overall profitability of the organization and contribution margin. Variable and semi-variable costs in fashion retail business models such as Suitcase and The Chapar include:

- the cost of the clothing items (cost of goods sold, defining the margin),
- the packaging cost of the boxes,
- the cost of shipping both ways,
- the transaction fee for online payments,
- the handling cost performed by one personal style advisor, and
- the average customer acquisition cost.

An example of cost-related metrics influencing the COGS are *inventory metrics*. Inventory metrics in retail can be analysed at different levels of detail. Examples are 'supplier level' (name of the brand), 'item level' (type of clothing), 'type level' (seasonal or non-seasonal) and 'style level' (classic versus leisure).

Continuously evaluating stock levels and the overall desirability (via metrics) of all articles on hand is crucial to managing the contribution margin and total COGS in retail. The percentage of goods that need to be liquidated at the end of each season (also defined as *dead stock*) negatively influences the gross margin. Liquidating stock means selling articles at a price that is lower than the original purchase price of the items. For example, any leftover stock of the non-seasonal type will be easier to carry over to subsequent seasons, as it can be sold both in winter and in summer time. Seasonal items, on the other hand, are harder to sell throughout the year. These articles will be more likely to end up as dead stock, so the company will promote them at a discount or, eventually (as the least favourable action), will liquidate the remaining stock. As previously mentioned, liquidation will have a direct negative effect on COGS and on overall profitability.

Dealing promptly with articles which are most likely to end up in dead stock will lower the number of items that need to be liquidated and help to keep the margin safe. Possible actions to dispose of these items include swapping, returning or discounting. The first two actions are dependent on the relationship with the supplier and the purchasing conditions. Good data analysis will therefore become a powerful tool when assessing brand strength within a brand portfolio. To track inventory performance in retail, the following key metrics should be monitored:

- The amount purchased versus the amount sold, also referred to as the 'sell-through percentage'.
- The comparison of slow-turning items versus high-turning items, based on the amount of days that items are held in inventory or the amount of times they are shipped versus sold.
- The percentage of returns, indicating the attractiveness of the items. This also indicates the service level provided by the personal style advisor. The company can compare this with customer feedback to obtain a clear understanding of the underlying problem.
- Overall stock availability of items on hand (what is 'present' in our inventory) versus number in transit (stock on its way to the customer or back to our office).

- The number of days in inventory since purchase date gives an indication of possible items to liquidate, discount or swap.

Some of these operational metrics are also helpful for assessing employee performance. Using the example of Suitcase, the following metrics can be tracked per style advisor on a weekly and monthly basis:

- the number of items returned versus customer feedback on price, colour, fabric, fitting, style, budget and initial demand (qualitative),
- the number of boxes made, and
- the average retention value per customer.

These metrics should be visible internally to the organization via dashboards in order to stimulate joint accountability in achieving company goals and to maintain clarity on the key objectives. Analysing, evaluating and assessing budgeted versus actual targets should therefore be done on a weekly and monthly basis, both by management and by the whole team. This provides both parties with control over the status of the organization and gives the decision-making power to management so that they are in a position to influence the leading metrics described above.

10.3.6 The Software as a Service (SaaS) Business Model

A company operating a Software as a Service business model delivers software on a demand basis, commonly through the cloud. Examples of businesses operating a SaaS platform include Dropbox, Google Drive, Collibra, Teamleader, Amazon Web Services, Wix, Zendesk, Algolia, Showpad, HubSpot, Salesforce.com, and Doctolib. Different types of revenue models are used, including subscriptions, usage fees (e.g. for storage), freemium and advertising. In many cases, SaaS providers offer tiered pricing models with different pricing options depending on the type of services users want. As the marginal cost of adding one user is small (e.g. providing free storage), users are often attracted by an offer of certain basic services for free. The company may then withdraw services after a specific time period with the hope of ultimately converting users into paying customers when they require more features or become used to the service. Finding the optimal tipping point to convert freemium users into paying customers, therefore, is one of the key challenges for freemium SaaS businesses.

As mentioned, a significant number of SaaS businesses generate revenue over the lifetime of the customer through a subscription or licensing model. The longer the customer stays on board, the higher the possible profit. However, SaaS businesses may face significant losses in the early years, as they need to invest heavily in customer acquisition. Therefore, SaaS companies need to find a good balance between the costs incurred for attracting and retaining customers and the revenues and net profits generated over the lifetime of the customer through recurring revenue and exploiting upselling and cross-selling opportunities.

Table 10.1 Evolution of Hubspot's LTV to CAC ratio

HubSpot	Q1'11	Q2'11	Q3'11	Q4'11	Q1'12	Q2'12
LTV:CAC	1.7	1.9	1.9	2.6	3.5	4.7
CAC	$6,025	$7,876	$8,541	$7,809	$6,880	$6,793
MRR CHURN	3.5%	2.7%	2.8%	2.3%	2.0%	1.5%
AVG MRR	$429	$507	$548	$560	$583	$577
SOFTWARE MARGIN	83%	81%	80%	82%	81%	82%
LTV	$10,074	$14,964	$15,919	$20,325	$23,775	$31,806

Source: Forbes (2012)

To be financially viable, the customer lifetime value has to be significantly higher than the customer acquisition cost. Only when the LTV to CAC ratio indicates that the customer acquisition and monetizing strategy is working does it becomes viable to scale the business in a profitable and sustainable way.

Table 10.1 below illustrates how the CAC and LTV of HubSpot, a software company facilitating inbound marketing and sales founded by Brian Halligan and Dharmesh Shah in 2006 at MIT, evolved over six quarterly periods to eventually become very attractive in quarter 2 of 2012. The reduction in monthly recurring revenue churn from 3.5 per cent in Q1 of 2011 to 1.5 per cent in Q2 of 2012 was the main factor in an increase in customer lifetime value. By breaking down the LTV to CAC ratio into different components, it becomes easier to see how the company increased its performance. Oftentimes, it makes sense to calculate these numbers for different customer segments as some might be attractive whereas others might be loss making.

To track how well an SaaS business performs in terms of customer acquisition cost, the business needs to track number of metrics related to the sales funnel:

- Visitor and website traffic including organic versus paid traffic rate, number of new and unique visitors.
- Marketing costs including cost per lead (for different channels or ad campaigns), average time needed to convert a lead.
- Viral coefficient (i.e. number of invitations the average user sends × the percentage of invitees who convert to customers).
- Conversion rates at each stage of the sales funnel including bounce rate, signup rate, free to paying customers conversion rate.
- Number of qualified leads.
- Sales productivity.

In order to understand customer lifetime value in an SaaS setting, the following metrics will be key:

- (New) monthly recurring revenue (MRR) from new and existing customers.
- Lost MRR from lost customers and from retained customers (i.e. revenue churn).

- Customer churn.
- Average revenue per account (ARPA) and total contract value.
- Number of customers.
- Customer engagement including number of active users, frequency of usage and average session length.
- Lifetime value.
- Lifetime value to customer acquisition cost ratio.
- Months to recover customer acquisition cost.
- Net promotor score (NPS).
- Support tickets created and average response/resolution time.

Overall, it will be important to select a reasonable number of metrics that clearly drive performance and that are adapted to the stage at which the company operates (e.g. pre- versus post-product/market). Furthermore, it is important to track how the different customer groups develop over time, e.g. by comparing the behaviour of customers who adopted the service in different months and their behaviour as a group over time which is called cohort analysis. Making these metrics visible by developing a dashboard that the management communicates to employees and investors can clearly help to define action and priorities and to track progress.

10.4 Towards a Dynamic Understanding of KPIs

As startups develop, the focus of the founders' attention typically changes. Following methodologies that focus on creating high-growth, high-potential ventures, such as the Lean Startup Methodology (Ries 2011), the focus moves from Product Market Fit (PMF) related metrics, to growth related metrics and a later focus to business profitability-related metrics. In growth-focused ventures, overall profitability and positive business cash flows are usually not so important in the early years. Early-stage entrepreneurs focus more on revenue growth and gaining market share. The valuations of high-growth firms depend on the revenue run-rate they generate. Additionally, the unit economics are important from a profitability point of view. Frequently, short-term overall business profitability is traded off for greater investments in technology and sales efforts in order to generate even stronger revenue growth, oftentimes with annual growth rates in excess of 100 per cent per year, while assuring that unit economics are controlled or are improved as the startup scales. In the following section, we describe how the focus of such startups typically evolves as they grow.

10.4.1 KPIs at the Product Market Fit Stage

In the early stages of a startup, the core focus is on achieving Product Market Fit (PMF). PMF captures whether a specific target customer has an important, high-priority pain point, and which value proposition best addresses these pain points. At this stage, the founders should focus on ensuring a good fit between the target customers' needs, the value proposition offered by the startup, and the product and service attributes to deliver on the value proposition. Though this is still a somewhat fuzzy stage where qualitative indicators dominate, the founders could focus on metrics such as number of target customers to do co-development with, number of direct target customer interactions, percentage of potential clients agreeing to commit relevant resources to the development of the offering, etc. However, rather than driving up these numbers, it is important to ensure that there is high-quality interaction and learning. This implies a minimum number of actively engaged and critical target customers that the startup can handle. It also implies that a large enough number of target customers exists to avoid developing only customized solutions for a small number of customers as this in consequence may mean that the company cannot sell a more standardized product to a larger market.

By working with an increasing number of target customers, the founders can obtain more information and validate the information previously obtained from other target customers. When the founders observe that the marginal information per additional target customer decreases, they will know that their initial customer base is sufficiently large for the initial product development and creation of PMF. The number of target customers a startup is interacting with at this stage is typically small. For example, startups in in B2B contexts might focus on around twenty to thirty customers, with five to ten customers being more closely involved in product development. In B2C settings, startups may work with 100 customers or more. Still, it is advisable to start using some benchmarking to assess the PMF quantitatively. Here, metrics such as the Net Promoter Score or a 10-point scale to assess customer satisfaction can be helpful to track changes month by month. Rather than looking at the absolute numbers resulting from these scales, it is important to monitor the improvement of the numbers over time. At this stage, the founders try to identify which segments experience high satisfaction with the initial product. The founder also focus on finding out what the needs of these customers are, how well the target customers understand the product and which value proposition is most compelling for them. In doing so, the founders will obtain important insights on which target customers to focus on and how to further develop the product.

An early-stage Product Market Fit metric suggested by Sean Ellis who managed marketing efforts for companies such as Dropbox and LogMeIn asks the target customers, after they have had sufficient exposure to the startup's offerings, how dissatisfied they would be if they could no longer use the startup's offerings (Ellis 2017). He considers startups to have Product Market Fit if more than 40 per cent of the target customers state that they would be very disappointed. In addition to capturing this quantitative feedback, it is important to collect additional qualitative information about the respondents to learn what target customers with high overall ratings like about the offerings, how they use the offerings and in which situations, and where these customers see opportunities for improvement. As a specific target customer group becomes increasingly satisfied with the startup's offerings, these customers may show repeat purchase behaviour or start making recommendations to other customers. These are important, positive signs of a PMF, and can indicate that the startup is building the foundations for a scalable, attractive business. However, if the startup is not able to retain a core group of customers, questions arise whether the startup has PMF. In this case, further iterations and learning on a small scale, or even a fundamental pivot towards other target customers, another market or other offerings might be required. At this early PMF stage, it is important to document the target customer interactions in an Excel-type document or start using customer relationship management software (CRM), as it helps to professionally document the activities and communicate the status, the progress and the challenges to investors. Furthermore, entrepreneurs can use a summary of this information in their communications with potential investors. This early information and regular updates on progress can help potential investors to get to know the founders and their venture over time, which builds trust and can substantially increase the likelihood of receiving an investment from them.

10.4.2   KPIs at the Growth Stage

As the startup moves towards initial PMF, the strategic focus shifts. During the PMF stage, first sales were generated to get a better understanding of the target customers' pain points and customers' responses to the value proposition, as well as to potentially observe repeat purchase behaviour. The focus at the PMF stage was on learning and the optimization of the PMF with a reduced number of target customers as outlined before and less on driving a large number of customers through a professional sales funnel. This changes when the startup moves towards PMF. The entrepreneurs now know the characteristics of specific target customers. They also know customers' main pain points and have a plan for how to address them. Thus, they can start to focus their attention on laying out the sales process and optimizing the sales approach. This helps to establish an effective and more efficient sales process and sales funnel and to reduce CACs, which are commonly very high initially. Further, a standardized and effective sales funnel allows for scaling of the venture without squandering a large amount of resources in the sales domain. Hence, KPIs relating to sales funnel dynamics become more important during this stage. In the B2B domain, commonly used metrics relate to the number of leads generated, the number of qualified and nurtured leads, the number of advanced or closed customer accounts, the economic value of those leads as they move through the sales funnel, the sales cycle time, the conversion ratios from one step to the next and overall closing rates. In the B2C space, the amount of advertising and marketing budget spent on the different customer acquisition channels, the click through rates, customer traffic derived on the different channels, the number of orders obtained and the cost per order can capture the effectiveness of the sales funnel of digital internet or mobile customer acquisition funnels.

In addition to these revenue or growth-focused metrics, the profitability of the startup's business is important. Here, the unit economics are of special importance. It is important to ensure that over time unit economics are improved. Before scaling up the venture, the unit economics should generally be profitable in order to avoid scaling loss-making unit sales, which would imply, overall, increasing losses as the startup grows. Thus, close observation and reporting of metrics relating to unit economics, such as the different CACs per main sales channels, the payback time of CACs, different contribution margins, the churn rate and the Customer Lifetime Values broken down by the main sales channels and customer segments are of increasing importance at this stage. If unit economics are very profitable and the payback times for CACs are short, the startup can become a very attractive investment case for the investors. Documenting and regularly reporting these numbers to the existing investors can prompt them to invest more money in the subsequent financing rounds. Further, these metrics can offer persuasive arguments for new investors to provide funding to the startup, and help in obtaining an attractive valuation of the firm. In consequence, the additional investment benefits the startup's development as the new firm can then spend even more funds on acquiring customers and further developing the technology and product, which further increases the revenue growth, leading to a virtuous circle of development. Thus, there is an important relation between achieving, documenting and communicating unit economics and the subsequent opportunities to grow the startup's revenues and firm valuation.

Taken together, the KPIs relating to the revenue growth of the startup and the unit economics should provide a detailed picture of the growth the startup is experiencing, and will indicate whether these generated growth numbers will lead to an economically sound, profitable business. Oftentimes, startups have problems both in generating strong revenue growth and in ensuring unit profitability. If this is the case, it is advisable that the founders report these challenges to the investors so that joint decisions can be taken on how to best address these challenges. Moreover, whilst unit profitability might be difficult to achieve initially, there should be a clear rationale for how to improve unit economics and how to achieve unit profitability. During this stage, entrepreneurs and investors should closely monitor unit economics and make any necessary improvements. Frequently, it is a challenge to maintain positive unit economics as the startup scales. This, for example, can happen to startups in the e-commerce space, because the CACs might increase as these startups and their competitors spend bigger advertising budgets and hence compete for the same customer traffic, for instance, on Facebook or Google's advertising platforms. Hence, collecting, documenting and communicating these metrics to investors is important as they can assess the growth potential and the risks of the startup as it scales.

10.4.3   KPIs at the Profitability Stage

As we have seen, founders and their investors typically prioritize firm growth over profitability in the early years to increase revenues, gain market share and increase the firm's valuation. This comes from the observation that the startup's valuation is predominantly tied to revenue and revenue increases as well as its relative market share, assuming that the business can be profitable as indicated by the unit economics. Investors, employees and the public are frequently shocked to learn that many startups purposefully incur substantial losses and a high cash-burn based on this trade-off between revenue growth and profitability. Thus, successful startups often show strong revenue growth operating at substantial losses. However over time, achieving annual revenue growth rates of over 100 per cent usually becomes harder if the revenue base and the company size is substantial. Hence, the relative revenue growth rates tend to decrease over the years. As the startup matures into an established firm, business profitability and positive cash flow often gain in importance. After several years of operations, investors may want to see that the firm is capable of generating profits and positive cash flows. In addition, the founders may want to avoid taking on more investment, which will lead to a dilution of their equity stake, and aim for firm profitability.

As the focus shifts towards profitability, firms normally reduce their investment in marketing and sales spending, or focus more on the returns from their marketing and sales activities, drawing on unit economics considerations. Similarly, the management may reduce the recruiting and human resources increases, which tend to be the biggest expense category for firms. Here, it is important to achieve a balance between a continuation of solid firm growth, for instance, by ensuring revenue increases by more than 50 per cent per year, while being able to achieve that the overall business is profitable and cash-flow positive. As growth is managed at a more moderate pace and future revenue-related expenses are considered more carefully, the firm's profitability and cash flows improve.

The reporting metrics and the type of business analysis employed at this stage is normally much more sophisticated and differentiated than in the early years. With a substantial operating history, entrepreneurs generally have better analysis systems in place. For instance, the firm may have a separate business intelligence team that tracks unit economics in a highly differentiated way by channel, product group, geography and customer segment. Frequently, there will be detailed data on sub-segments per customer acquisition channel and a detailed understanding of the behaviour of these sub-segments over time. Increasingly, multivariate systems, advanced algorithms and machine learning are suitable for determining the profitability of sub-segments, or even individual customers. Cohort analysis shows how customer segments and sub-segments behave over long periods, and the algorithms can predict the likelihood of customer churn, the customer lifetime, as well as the CLV. On the sales and marketing side, entrepreneurs and investors will have a better understanding of the customer journey, which describes how the company acquires a customer. The management will typically spend marketing and sales budgets more effectively to ensure profitability and the highest return on these investments. These positive advances should result in better overall business performance and profitability. Key Performance Indicators documenting these improvements are, for example, a decreasing CAC, increasing CLV and an improving ratio of CAC to CLV, as well as a reduction of major expense categories as a percentage of revenues.

10.4.4   Venture and Market-specific Considerations

The considerations discussed in Section 10.4.3 are relevant to growth-oriented, externally financed firms. However, different factors reflecting the goals of the founders, the firm's business model, the industry or the market the firm operates in and additional contextual factors such as the general funding environment may result in diverging approaches. For instance, in markets with strong first mover advantages, network effects, economies of scale and customer lock-in effects, early and massive scaling without a proven product market fit might be preferred. At the other end of the spectrum, founders of a venture may choose to focus on achieving overall business profitability and positive cash flows first, to then use the operational cash flows to fund firm growth and avoid having external investors altogether. Moreover, many founders commonly choose to remain a micro or small firm with no or very few employees. Hence, the approach outlined above is dependent on the specific venture. Founders and investors must determine the approach that best fits their goals and situation. Then, based on the approach chosen, they should determine the respective KPIs. They should also discuss how the KPIs might change as the venture develops. As the startup evolves, the entrepreneurs and investors should regularly review the chosen approach and adjust the KPIs and their respective reporting as necessary. The most successful founders and investors are frequently not those who got everything right from the start, but the ones who learned the fastest and adjusted as needed.

KEY TAKEAWAYS

- Monitoring is essential in order for investors to evaluate the performance of their portfolio firms and to take corrective action if necessary.
- Business planning activities represent the first stage in monitoring. Investors need to be able to understand the startup's business model from the outset.
- Investors should apply those metrics which best fit the startup's business model.
- Qualitative reporting (KPIs, metrics) should be used in combination with qualitative information on the development of the startup.
- The importance of KPIs and metrics will evolve as the venture develops.

END OF CHAPTER QUESTIONS

1. Why do entrepreneurs tend to report only very little information to their investors?
2. What should entrepreneurs base their reporting on?
3. What is the ideal form of reporting?
4. What characterizes good metrics?
5. What does the term 'unit economics' of a business model mean?
6. What metrics should brick-and-mortar retail stores report to their investors?
7. How can an e-commerce startup measure the lifetime value per customer?
8. What are the essential metrics for a startup using the business model 'Software as a Service'?
9. Why is it important to consider the dynamics of metrics in reporting?
10. Are there venture-specific recommendations for monitoring and reporting in startups?

FURTHER READING

Croll, A. and Yoskovitz, B. (2013). *Lean Analytics: Use Data to Build a Better Start-up Faster*. O'Reilly Media.
Hamermesh, R. G., Marshall, P. W. and Pirmohamed, T. (2002). *Note on Business Model Analysis for the Entrepreneur*. Harvard Business School, 9–802–048.

REFERENCES

Colao, J. J. (2012). In defense of the lifetime value (LTV) Formula, *Forbes*, www.forbes.com/sites/jjcolao/2012/09/13/a-dangerous-seduction-revisited-in-defense-of-the-lifetime-value-ltv-formula/#535ee21b4c71 (28 April 2017).
Ellis, S. (2017). Using Survey.io, www.startup-marketing.com/using-survey-io/ (21 April 2017).
Gulati, R. and DeSantola, A. (2016). Start-ups that last. *Harvard Business Review*, 94(3), 54–61.
Kaplan, S. N. and Strömberg, P. (2004). Characteristics, contracts, and actions: Evidence from venture-capitalist analyses. *Journal of Finance*, 59, 2177–2210.
KPMG (2014). *Angel Reporting Guidelines and Principles. A Practical Guide for CEOs and Executives of Angel-backed Businesses*. KPMG / UK Business Angels Association.
McClure, D. (2007). Startup metrics for pirates: AARRR!!!, www.slideshare.net/dmc500hats/startup-metrics-for-pirates-long-version (21 April 2017).
Ries, E. (2011): *The Lean Startup*. Crown Publishing Group.

CORPORATE GOVERNANCE

STEFANO CASELLI

Università Bocconi

This chapter considers the challenges and benefits of developing a proper corporate governance structure and policy while growing as a venture. Although the public debate over corporate governance seems to focus on public companies, an effective governance structure is equally important for startups and private companies, especially given the stronger link between the financing and investment decision in startups as compared to public companies.

Corporate governance is not simply about the board of directors and their activities. It is a more complex set of rules, regulations and etiquettes that regulate the responsibilities and authority of shareholders and management, directed towards the achievement of the goals in the business plan and agreement on how to deal with business strategy.

Topics to be decided upon include the legal structure of the firm, its board size and structure, share remuneration, veto rights. More generally, in the case of startups, the challenge is to strike a balance between allowing investors to benefit from their investment, allowing them to secure that somehow, while, at the same time, preventing them from appropriating the entrepreneurs' venture and role.

The different approaches to corporate governance found in the various countries across Europe make this is an interesting area to consider, revealing the different cultural and historical traditions of those countries and reaffirming the challenge of addressing governance properly. Looking to the future, however, investments and new ventures will keep on growing and get more international, revealing the benefit of investing in proper governance for both investors and entrepreneurs.

VIEW FROM THE MEDIA

FINANCIAL TIMES   FT

Boss of troubled tech unicorn Ve Interactive steps aside

MARCH 3, 2017 BY KADHIM SHUBBER

The boss of troubled advertising technology startup Ve Interactive has resigned.

David Brown, who launched the business in 2009, stepped down as CEO of the £1.5bn business on Friday, just days after it failed to meet payroll on time.

His resignation may clear the way for new funding that will help stabilise the company, which has around 850 employees and is one of just a handful of billion dollar startups in Britain.

. . . Over the past seven or so years, he has built it up into a global business with hundreds of employees, offices in 28 countries and a string of awards that belie the fact the startup has failed to ever turn a profit. The company trades in the competitive world of digital advertising, helping brands place ads online and offering them web tools that encourage shoppers to spend more.

After an unpleasant experience with his venture capital backers at Serious, Brown chose a different fundraising strategy at Ve. He received over £50m in funding from around 500 high net worth investors, who believed they were investing in the next Facebook, Google or Snapchat.

The funding structure allowed him to run a board made up entirely of close associates and the company's management. Last year, he told us there was no legal need for independent oversight.

'We have a complete ban on venture capitalists – don't like them,' he was reported as saying in the Evening Standard in 2015. Those allowed to invest were also given short shrift. 'It is a case of give us your money and bugger off,' the newspaper quoted him saying.

But this year, the company is intending to raise money from institutional investors for the first time. It needs the funding. Ve is still burning more cash than it brings in, according to accounts filed in January.

. . . In the meantime, there was a clearout of the Ve board, with four directors leaving in January, and problems paying staff on time as the company struggled with cash.

A person close to the company said the plan now is to 'regularise' the business and put it on the path to profitability.

LEARNING OBJECTIVES

After reading this chapter, you will be able to:

- Understand the impact of different country perspectives and frameworks on corporate governance practice.
- Assess the key activities to manage and monitor in relation to the potential divergence of interest between investor and entrepreneur.
- Understand the impact of formal and informal rules on the interaction between the entrepreneur/management and investors.
- Appreciate how the development phases of a venture affect the governance relationship.
- Recognize that even minority shareholdings can be leveraged to influence the direction of the venture and address specific challenges.
- Review the impact of standards and European harmonization guidelines on practice across industries and countries.
- Establish market proof of the benefit of proper corporate governance methods and practice for all parties involved.

Where Are We Going Next?

This chapter will begin by establishing a definition of corporate governance, its role in the relations between investors and entrepreneurs and assessing the key variables that determine the corporate governance practice. The subsequent sections deal with the key activities to manage and monitor as well as formal and informal rules. The formal rules reflect the duties and rights of shareholders, the functioning of the board of directors and the information flow, which together form the backbone of the decision-making process of the venture. The informal rules assess the importance of 'soft factors and qualities' through which an investor can support the entrepreneur and the venture. Both formal and informal rules are intended to provide an understanding of the general scope of corporate governance practice. Typical challenges for startups pertaining to the founders' dilemma, structure and process are reviewed to provide context for the corporate governance challenges that may be experienced within a (new) venture setting. In this respect, the changing role of governance practice is also discussed. The chapter concludes with a discussion of harmonization attempts within the Eurozone and the benefits of corporate governance for the venture, the investor and the entrepreneur.

11.1 Defining Corporate Governance and Cornerstones for Analysis

Intuitively, it might seem odd to discuss the topic of corporate governance within the context of the startup, as the topic is often more commonly associated with large corporations dealing with issues of compliance and the need to unite a wide range of goals and expectations. Indeed, academic studies often focus on such firms.[1] However, corporate governance also proves to be critical to startups, as it represents the means of enhancing the 'marriage' between the investor and the venture. Moreover, corporate governance is a very effective tool for communicating the venture's DNA and investment purpose both within and outside the company.

Traditionally, the governance of private companies focused first on protecting investors and creditors from managerial opportunism, second on paying attention to the relationship between shareholders, i.e. the protection of shareholders from the misconduct of other shareholders.[2] But the area of corporate governance is concerned with more than the relation between management and shareholders or shareholders amongst one another, and determined for a large part by the country perspective and analytical perspective chosen.

---

1 McCahery and Vermeulen (2008).
2 McCahery and Vermeulen (2008).

11.1.1   Definition

In line with the OECD, Corporate Governance is defined as:[3]

Corporate governance involves a set of relationships between a company's manage-ment, its board, its shareholders and other stakeholders. Corporate governance also provides the structure through which the objectives of the company are set, and the means of attaining those objectives and monitoring performance are determined. Good corporate governance should provide proper incentives for the board and management to pursue objectives that are in the interests of the company and its shareholders and should facilitate effective monitoring

Corporate governance thus considers the relationships between a company's management, its board, its shareholders and its other stakeholders. This see-mingly straightforward definition allows for an initial assessment of corporate governance, insofar as a particular country's perspective on the interests a company should serve is concerned, and on the role of corporate governance in society.

11.1.2   Country Perspective

Ventures or companies in general play an important role in society. This role pertains to both their economic value as well as their responsibility to society at large.[4] Their economic value relates to the importance of making a profit as a primary goal, while the responsibility to society emphasizes the consequences of their actions within a certain environment. In some instances, these roles reinforce one another, while in others they may come into conflict. The country tradition and perspective indicates the nation's perspective on this role of companies. Two key perspectives emerge from Academic studies:

- Stakeholder (continental European) perspective.
- Shareholder (Anglo–Saxon) perspective

The stakeholder perspective emphasizes the firm's societal responsibility role over and above its economic role. Companies are perceived as coalitions of parties working towards a shared goal. The company should protect and strive to satisfy the interests of all contributors, i.e. stakeholders. These stakeholders consist of many parties, such as employees, customers, suppliers, government, interest groups and shareholders. This perspective thus envisages a broad role for the company in society, a role that goes beyond merely making an economic

3 OECD Principles of Corporate Governance (2004), the EU corporate governance framework includes legislation in areas such as corporate governance statements, shareholders' rights and takeover bids as well as 'soft law', namely recommendations on the role and on the remuneration of companies' directors.
4 Eurostat (2015), indicating that SMEs represent 99% of all enterprises in Europe and employ an increasing number of persons.

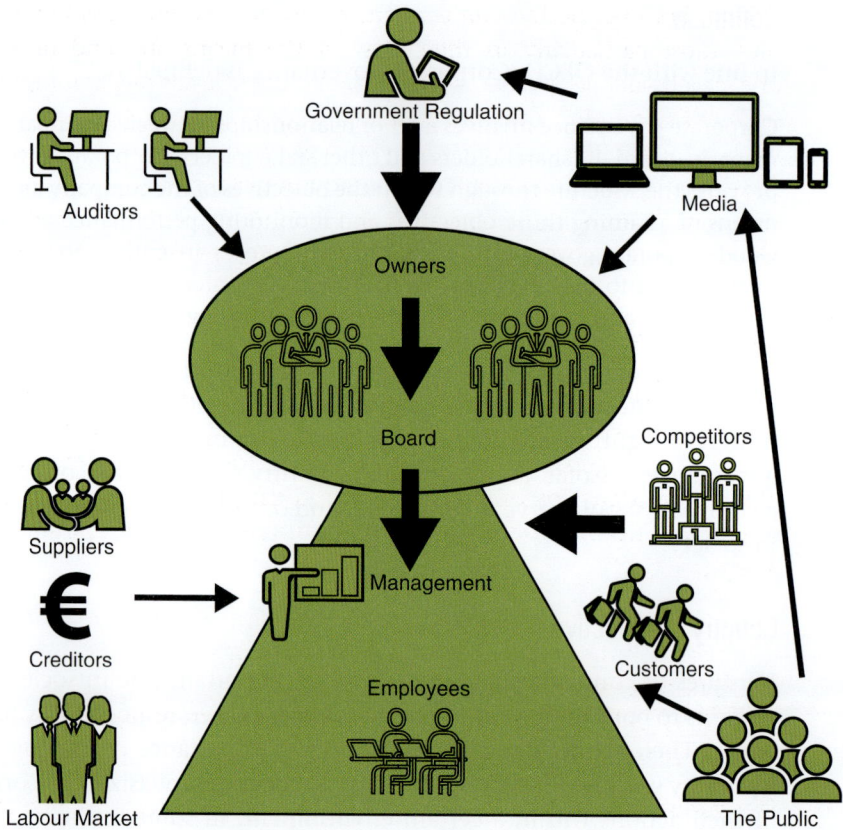

Figure 11.1 The company and its stakeholders.
Source: adapted from Thomsen & Conyon (2012)

profit. This makes the measurement of its performance more diffuse, as it involves addressing the satisfaction of all its stakeholders.

The shareholder perspective views the organization as instrumental for its shareholders, emphasizing the company's role in being economically profitable over and above its social responsibility. At the core of this view is that society at large is best served by companies pursuing their self-interest and aiming to maximize shareholder value. Other parties, i.e. individuals and government, are responsible for making sure that stakeholders' interests are being served. This focus on shareholder value makes the measurement of the company's contribution less ambiguous, as all the variables of success relate to the economic share value.

Figure 11.1 depicts a typical solution to the corporate governance challenge, in which a board is selected to monitor managers. The owners are a diverse group, from the founder to a larger group of private investors, possibly even institutional investors. The figure also reveals that the company is influenced by its stakeholders. The country perspective (shareholder/stakeholder) largely determines the degree of formal pressure that these stakeholder groups can apply.

Thus, both perspectives differ in their view of the prime orientation of companies, most particularly in their view of the means and end of a company. The stakeholder perspective regards shareholder value as one amongst many constituents in creating stakeholder value, whereas the shareholder view considers social responsibility merely a means to creating shareholder value. In Europe, the stakeholder perspective is the dominant view, with the exception of the United Kingdom, where the shareholder view is adopted. Exactly how each perspective translates into specific rules and regulations differs from country to country.[5]

11.1.3   Common Theoretical Frameworks

Typically, when reviewing corporate governance frameworks, the monitoring role of boards is stressed. Adopting this as the prime function of the board leads to the use of agency theory as a framework for analysis. However, it is also possible to argue for other roles to be given prime importance, such as its service and networking function. These different roles can be summarized as 'the three Cs':[6]

- the Control role (i.e. the monitoring function, as stressed in agency theory),
- the Consulting role (i.e. the service function, as stressed in stewardship theory and resource dependence theory), and
- the Contract role (i.e. the networking function, as stressed in resource dependence theory).

The traditional view is the one expressed in agency theory, which emphasizes the monitoring role of boards when there is a separation of ownership and control. The key question is how to make sure that agents (the employees or management) work in the best interest of the principals (the owners) given asymmetric information. In line with its view of mankind being opportunistic and focused on its own interest, this requires active monitoring and the setting of proper incentives to make sure that the agents work to accomplish the goals of the principals.

The conflict of interest signalled applies to the corporate governance of both public and private companies. However, there are some key differences in a private setting. These differences further complicate the relationship between principal and agent, namely:

- the lack of an exit for investors, as there is no market in which the shares are being traded;
- the lack of a formal price, again because of not having a market in which the shares are being traded; and
- the lack of formal authorities to regulate the market and create a level playing field.

5 IFC World Bank (2015).
6 Thomsen and Conyon (2012).

Stewardship theory emphasizes the service role. As such, board members are mainly called upon to contribute to value creation through their wealth of experience and the advice they provide. According to this theory, the core view of mankind is that it is intrinsically motivated to perform well, meaning that controls are not necessary and may even hamper individuals from delivering well.

The consulting and contracting role of boards can be traced back to resource dependence theory, according to which companies aim to develop external ties by creating ownership ties and board connections. This perspective stresses the role of the board members' connections, access to external information and their provision of legitimacy for the company. It is because of the links with external parties that board members provide, that the company can flourish further.

These three views on the function of boards are not mutually exclusive but are distinct, stressing different aspects of the reason for having a board and setting different expectations for the contribution made by the board. As will be apparent, the dominant view on board necessity will lead to the setting of very different tasks and expected benefits.

11.2   Board Structure

From an agency theory perspective, boards are only necessary when there is a separation of ownership and control. The investors hire representatives to control the management for them.[7] The need for such a board is also less when ownership is concentrated and the owners can do their own monitoring. The larger the company becomes and the more shareholders a company has, the more apparent the need for a board becomes. These boards can be structured according to either the one-tier or two-tier model:

- **One-tier model** combines the managing (executive directors) and supervisory (non-executive directors) roles in one board of directors. This structure is more typically found in Anglo-American companies.
- **Two-tier model** (or dual boards), in which the managing and monitoring boards are separated. This structure is more typically found in North European companies.

In the two-tier model, the shareholders select a supervisory board. The role of the supervisory board is to appoint members of the managing board, monitor this board and advise them on the strategic direction or planning of the company.[8] The supervisory board often contains directors elected by the investors as well as, in larger companies, representatives from the employees. All operational tasks are done by management. In the one-tier model, insiders and outsiders form the board together and jointly run the company.

7 Fama and Jensen (1983).
8 Mallin (2013).

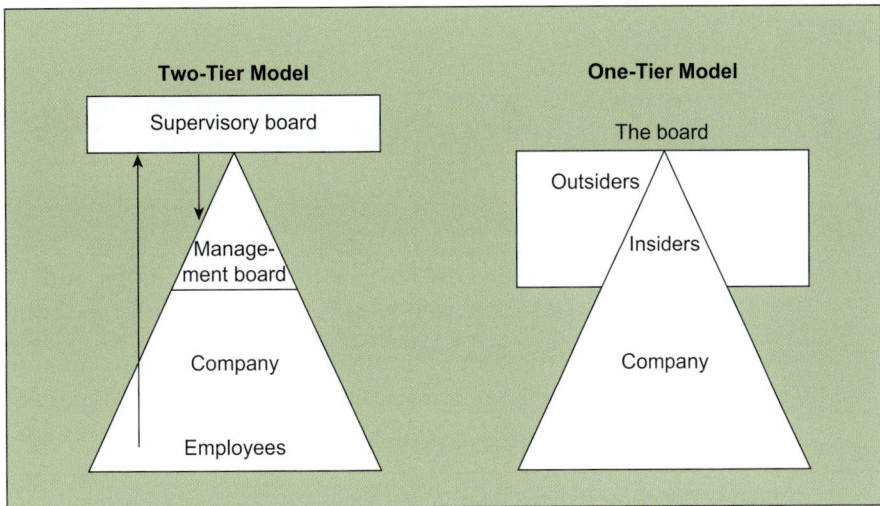

Figure 11.2 One-tier versus two-tier board structure.
Source: adapted from Thomsen and Conyon (2012)

Both advisory boards and supervisory boards will have an impact on the strategic direction of ventures. However, when mentioning a board in the formal sense, this refers to the board of directors (one-tier structure) or supervisory board (in a two-tier structure). Supervisory boards have rights that are determined by law, while advisory boards are more informal by nature.[9] The specific characteristics of these different types of boards are given below.

A Board of Directors/Supervisory Board

- protects the interests of the investors by formally monitoring the CEO and approving all key decisions of the company,
- finds board members that are supportive of the venture's vision and have its best interest at heart,
- sticks to a manageable number of board members to make meetings practicable
- brings the number of representatives in line with equity interest,
- has an odd number of board members, of which one is a non-biased third party to avoid a voting tie,
- makes sure that all members truly add value, whether through knowledge, experience or connections, and
- strives to only have members that are truly engaged, i.e. not just be present at meetings but also contribute.

9 Deeb (2014).

An Advisory Board

- consists of an informal group of mentors who support the venture with industry-specific knowledge and expertise as well as building credibility with potential investors,
- results from a voluntary decision to set up this board,
- has tasks/expectations that are dependent upon the management and investors of the venture,
- similarly, has its size governed by practical considerations, and
- is often set up to associate well-known individuals with the venture.

As will be apparent, there are various guidelines for deciding upon the structure of the board, but there is no 'one size fits all', as the exact governance depends on so many different factors.

Bianco and Rosso is a high-quality Italian family-owned startup company with a board consisting of four members: the founder, his two sons and his wife. The board isn't effective, as the founder manages the company and many decisions are shared and taken in the day-to-day life of the family. When a private equity investor decides to invest in the company with a minority stake, if the status quo is maintained, the equity investor could claim a seat on the board as one of four, firing one of the existing members. The solution could be to establish ex ante some principles, e.g. to enlarge the board from four to seven seats, and to accept the fact that at least one board member must be independent. The result is a board where the four family members keep their seats and the founder retains the chairmanship; the equity investor appoints two members; the equity investor and the family together identify an independent board member with a CV appropriate to the business.

11.3   Formal and Informal Rules

The key corporate governance regulations are set in individual country law. As we saw in Chapter 9, specific corporate governance arrangements are laid down in the term sheet. This is one of the key means of avoiding conflict between the investors and the entrepreneur, from, for example, a potential divergence of opinion about how to take decisions and how to react to unforeseen events.

But corporate governance must also take into account a wider perspective represented by a broad array of formal and informal rules that ensure:[10]

1. the effective and pragmatic application of duties and rights as written in the term sheets pertaining to investors and entrepreneurs, and

10 Smith and Walter (2006).

Table 11.1 Corporate governance rules	
Key rules	**Description**
Shareholder duties and rights	› Discipline of activities shared between shareholders' meeting and board of directors (who decides what) › Setting the number and the profile of independent directors, CEO and chairperson › Setting the numbers and the role of committees (if any) › Special quorum rules
Board of directors' activity	› Power(s) of CEO and of executive directors › Inner rules of board of directors' functioning and voting › Independent directors' expected activity and contribution
Information flow	› Content of info flow from the board to shareholders and from the management to the board › Scheduling of info flow (year, semester, quarter) › Auditing activity to monitor the information flow

Source: Caselli (2010)

2. the ways in which investors can support the venture and/or entrepreneur by transferring knowledge, making suggestions and enhancing the process of taking decisions when faced with market challenges.

11.3.1   Formal Rules

Formal corporate governance rules assign responsibilities and regulate the activity between shareholders and the board of directors. More particularly, these rules relate to appointments, duties and rights, policies and processes, key controls and auditing staff.[11]

The investor and entrepreneur both hold shares in the venture and have to carry out their duties and rights in line with the legal framework of the relevant country and the particular agreements made in the term sheet.

In many cases, the investor, irrespective of whether they have a majority or minority interest, might want to play a decisive role in certain decisions. This may lead to conflict that could become a deal breaker in the term sheet negotiation. Let's consider, for example, a case where the founder is also the CEO of the company and the minority investor wants to have the power to fire and to select a new CEO. Partially related to this is the issue of special quorum rules (or veto power) used to avoid the minority shareholder (who could be the venture capital investor or the entrepreneur) from being excluded from critical decisions.

11 Caselli (2010).

The decision about the number of directors appointed by a new venture always comes down to a trade-off between: (1) a broad level of representation and the presence of the right people, and (2) having the agility to take decisions. Although large boards – while not enormous – may make sense for listed companies, for startups they might feel excessive, particularly in terms of costs. The key parameters and suggestions for best practice on the creation of an effective board of directors is to focus on competences and know-how, rather than 'names'. In a startup company in particular, the level of risk and uncertainty is very high and only certain people will be in a position to help the company to take the right decisions. The use of independent directors is fundamental, not only to create a 'buffer' between the investor and the entrepreneur but also to bring qualified competences to the venture.

Besides the duties and rights of shareholders, the role of the board in the decision-making process is considered critical. The presence of a strong CEO could reduce the role of the board to merely a body that complies with regulations and advises the CEO. Such a model, in consultation with the shareholders, would be particularly beneficial in the early phases when decisions need to be taken fast. In the later development phases (i.e. startup and early-growth), a more collective action/decision-making model is recommended, with input from skilled independent directors. This model emphasizes the importance of the contributions made by the independent board members.

Another issue relating to board activity concerns the internal rules that apply to board of directors' functions and voting, as well as the quorum mechanism (if any) at shareholder level. If all crucial decisions are to be determined by the shareholders, no special voting system is required. However, if some particularly sensitive aspects are left to the board (e.g. new financing decisions, management recruiting, salaries, etc.), the investors will want to make sure that their interests are taken into account. This is where special voting rights come in.

For the purposes of checking that the day-to-day activities of the venture accord with the long-term strategies identified in the business plan, a proper information flow should be set up. This reporting system will need to facilitate communication between managers and directors and between directors and shareholders. The characteristics and the timing of reporting are often addressed in the term sheet because of its crucial role in venture performance and timely adjustment. These data pertain to both lagging (i.e. output-oriented, conclusive) and leading (i.e. input-oriented, predictive) indicators.

11.3.2   Informal Rules

As we saw in Chapter 9 the relationship between VCs and growth firms is largely determined contractually in the term sheet, which includes clauses relating to control measures, responsibilities and incentives. Term sheets and formal agreements, however, have their limitations. Governance rules may be formal and documented in the term sheet but they involve something much more complex and 'soft', related to the style of the relationship between investor and entrepreneur. We might see this as the lifestyle of the 'marriage' they are entering into.

The degree to which informal processes are developed depends upon the following factors:[12]

- style of investor and nature of investment agreement, with profiles varying from i) a hands-on approach (with serious involvement in governance, strategic and financial decisions) to a ii) hands-off approach (mere presence in governance processes and involvement limited to financial decisions);
- the venture development stage: earlier stages typically see more strategic involvement of the investor, while in later (expansion and replacement) stages the investor support is more advisory, dealing with financial and legal issues;
- duration of the investment: as investor and management spend time together, the basis for trust improves while decreasing the need for control;
- geographical distance, impacting the number of meetings between investor and management; and
- expertise of investor and type of risk and the kind of challenges faced by the venture, some of which rely more on the particular knowledge of the investor.

The soft factors come in the form of:[13]

- mentoring, consisting of technical and process support;
- involvement of specific experts from the investor's network; and
- supporting the process of finding investors for additional funding.

Attitudes, expectations, fears and motivations are beyond the remit of the term sheet. These last aspects emphasize the importance of a proper fit between investor and entrepreneur, as a potentially bad atmosphere or any kind of antagonism between investor and entrepreneur could seriously affect the success of any deal, irrespective of the quality of the term sheet and the firm's corporate governance. As in a marriage, people matter.

11.4   Governance Dynamics

Corporate governance is a much-discussed topic, both in the academic and business world. While a larger part of this discussion focuses on the governance of public companies, the challenges experienced in early-stage and private business are also addressed. This section will review two key contributions to this debate, relating to a key choice that founders will have to make and to changes in the governance function over the life cycle of a venture.

---

12 Smith and Walter (2006).
13 Caselli (2010).

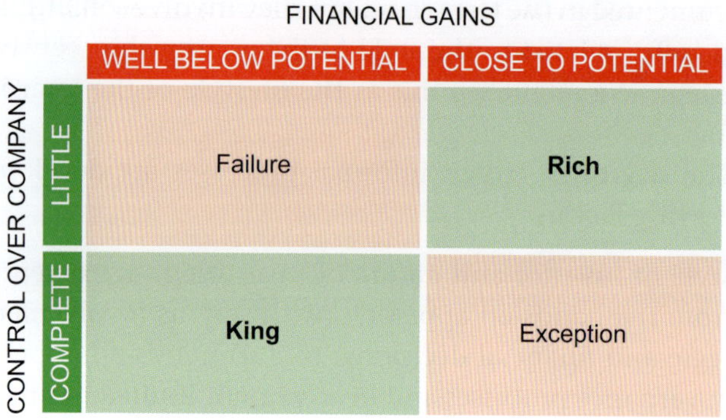

FINANCIAL GAINS

Figure 11.3 The trade-off entrepreneurs make.
Source: Wasserman (2008)

11.4.1   Founders' Dilemma

The key question for the founders when setting up a venture is whether their primary motivation is to make money or to manage their venture. This question is key as it determines to a large extent the choices that founders make when they need more resources. Research shows that being open and honest from the outset about this natural, primary drive is best for the venture, especially when those loyal to the venture oppose it.[14] Often, however, the entrepreneurs themselves are unclear about this and are convinced that they are the only people capable of leading the venture to success. Aside from the overconfidence that many entrepreneurs share and their naivety about the potential problems they might face, they may also become emotionally attached to their venture in the process of setting it up.

As Figure 11.3 shows, having no financial gains constitutes a commercial failure, while combining both financial gains and control are an exception. The rationale behind the diagram is that very different skills are needed for setting up a venture as opposed to growing a venture. Investors appreciate this difference, and will therefore push for their candidate of choice when in control.

The question for founders is, therefore, whether they aspire to be 'king' or 'rich'. They may be king of a venture in which they retain control but have a limited investment as result of the limited amount of equity they are willing to give up, or rich by allowing significant investments and sacrificing an equivalent degree of control in the venture. Ultimately, for the entrepreneurs, being aware of their personal motivation and choosing between money and power will provide focus and clarity about what success actually means for them.

14 Wasserman (2008).

The choice that the founder makes between 'king' or 'rich' will also have a significant impact on the value of the venture itself.[15] While the founder is still in control (as CEO or otherwise controlling the board of directors), the value of e the pre-money valuation of the venture is reduced by 17 to 22 per cent. While a founder's vision and capabilities prove to be essential in the early stages of a venture, holding on to that control may harm the value of the venture in later stages. This reaffirms the concept of a company's 'best owner', how it changes over time and evolves throughout a venture's development.[16]

11.4.2   More Dynamics in Governance

As ventures develop and go through different stages of the venture financing process, the governance of the venture will change as well. While research on corporate governance in general is abundant, there has been only a limited amount of research on this relationship. The available research generally confirms this perception about the relationship between the venture life cycle and corporate governance mechanisms.

Overall, governance creates value and governance practices tend to improve the more mature ventures become.[17] This finding is not surprising, as the more a venture grows the greater the impact of its decisions will be, the larger its number of stakeholders and, accordingly, the more significant the level of interference of government and legal provisions.

On the other hand, ventures tend to be more transparent and accountable when they are in their earlier development phases, in order to attract external capital and increase their profitability. Combining these findings indicates that the explanatory value of the different theoretical frameworks (Section 11.1) is impacted by the venture development phase, i.e. the resource/strategy perspective and monitoring/control functions are both relevant but at different stages in the life cycle.

The changes in governance mechanisms over time can be explained by the wealth creation and wealth protection functions of corporate governance.[18] While corporate governance codes are largely focused on wealth protection in mature companies, these directives may come at the expense of the degree of wealth creation needed in earlier stage ventures. For this reason, an analysis of the changing nature of the role or contribution of corporate governance in relation to venture maturity stages, as shown in Figure 11.4, provides useful insights.

Filatotchev *et al.* (2006) analysed the changing emphasis in governance in relation to the transition of the venture from one stage to another in its life cycle (called 'strategic thresholds'), thereby rejecting the existence of a universal governance template. Figure 11.4 provides their key framework, linking

15 Wasserman (2017).
16 For more information on this topic, see 'The Best Owner' in Koller *et al.* (2011).
17 O'Connor and Byrne (2015).
18 Filatotchev *et al.* (2006).

		Governance Objectives	
		Wealth creation	Wealth protection
Strategic Environment	High 'Velocity'	Quadrant 1 Founder/IPO threshold Governance functions: • Monitoring: low • Resource: high • Strategy: high	Quadrant 2 IPO/maturity threshold Governance functions: • Monitoring: medium • Resource: medium • Strategy: high
	Low 'Velocity'	Quadrant 4 'Re-invention' threshold Governance functions: • Monitoring: low • Resource: medium • Strategy: medium	Quadrant 3 Maturity/decline threshold Governance functions: • Monitoring: high • Resource: low • Strategy: low

Figure 11.4 Strategic thresholds and the roles of corporate governance. *Source: Filatotchev et al. (2006)*

governance objectives to environmental dynamics, revealing a concomitant change in governance functions. The 'governance objectives' focus on either 'wealth creation' (enabling managerial entrepreneurship and allowing shareholders to benefit from the upside) or 'wealth protection' (ensuring the accountability of management to minimize shareholder risk). The 'strategic environment' reveals the dynamism in the environment, either rapidly changing and difficult to predict ('high velocity') or slower and more predictable ('low velocity').

The startup or small company, generally founder-owned with a narrow resource base, allowing management to move quickly and have little managerial accountability to external stakeholders, is situated in Quadrant 1. As the venture grows and its need for external funding and expertise become apparent, the governance system needs to expand and provide more transparency and monitoring and control options to investors (typically business angels or venture capitalists). In Quadrant 2, the venture has grown into a public company with a fully developed governance system. In Quadrant 3, the company exploits strategic opportunities and may over-diversify where the governance is insufficient to prevent managerial opportunism. In response, the scope is narrowed again by taking the company private again through buy-outs and private equity, moving to Quadrant 4.

Each of these four quadrants shows a different combination of governance functions. These functions are in line with 'the three Cs' mentioned in Section 11.1, all of which have a role to play throughout the life cycle of the company, although there is a change of emphasis.

11.5   Leveraging Ownership

Although the role of governance varies according to the stage of the company, in literature the agency theory perspective tends to prevail.[19] The desire to cope with the potentially opportunistic and self-serving behaviour of management places an emphasis on the role of monitoring and control in governance over and above its resource and strategic contributions. Shareholdings can help to address these challenges, as means of control and as means of incentivizing profit-oriented behaviour.

11.5.1   Controlling shares

When a venture is still in the opportunity phase, decision-making is easy as the power to do so is in the hands of the entrepreneur. As soon as external investors get involved, decision-making becomes complicated because of the large number of people or parties involved and because of the separation of ownership and control. An investor might reduce the level of complication by acquiring all shares and thereby restricting the extent of the deliberations.

Obtaining a significant portion of shares allows an investor to have a stronger influence over the direction of the venture. The challenge for the investor, however, is how to make their voice heard when they do not hold the majority of the votes. This challenge is not merely dichotomous – not having a controlling share does not mean that the investor can merely 'enjoy the ride' without having any impact on the venture's future direction.

In practice, the tools that protect investor rights when they do not have a majority typically pertain to the ability to block certain predefined and impactful decisions, as a 'foot on the brake'. Some of these mechanisms have already been discussed in relation to the term sheet (Chapter 9). These mechanisms, which refer to both financial and operational limitations that are agreed upon by the issuing company, are referred to as 'negative covenant' (most often found in bonds or loans), veto rights (*veto* is Latin for 'I forbid') or blocking rights. It forces the venture to meet or sustain certain ratios or activities or refrain from certain activities and allows the (minority) investor to have a say in areas or actions that this investor deems to be material.

Another means by which the investor can have a say in the direction of the company is through the use of 'dual class' shares. This means that shares deviate from the proportionality principle (one share = one vote). The dual class shares assign differential voting rights to shares of different classes, while all shares have the same dividends, or cash flow, rights.[20] For example, the venture might issue A-shares and B-shares, with the A-shares being for the founders while the B-shares are provided to the investors. The B-share might only be given one-tenth of the voting power of A-shares.

19 For more information on the Agency Theory and its origin, see Fama and Jensen (1983).
20 Thomsen and Conyon (2012).

The function of dual class shares is different from that of common and preferred shares, which relate to different rights in relation to a company's assets and earnings as well as to the size of dividend payouts.

While the former mechanisms (negative covenants etc.) can be provided by the venture on a deal-by-deal basis and tailored to a particular deal, the latter have rights and obligations that are defined for all the owners of those shares. The challenge for the entrepreneur is to keep corporate governance manageable while having different rounds of investments with possibly different share mechanisms and classes. While this will always remain a challenge, the best advice is to keep it simple from the start, that is, limit the options from the beginning when attracting investors.

11.5.2   Shares as an Incentive

Providing shares and stock options to management represents a very popular and effective corporate governance tool for aligning the interests of the entrepreneur with those of the investor. Their use is regulated via term sheet and covenants and the rationale is to make the shareholders' interests more relevant to the venture's key personnel (i.e. directors or management). By providing them with stock options, the importance of 'steering for shareholder value' becomes of interest for them too and they are 'locked in' to the venture. This topic has been discussed in more depth in Chapter 9, together with other types of covenants.

While the use of stock options seems to be more straightforward in a public company (as the share is publicly traded and, as such, has a market value), they are also used in private companies. In the latter case, specific adjustments will have to be made. It is common to set operational and managerial goals for each function, but the parameters surrounding these goals can easily be manipulated. Therefore, the use of stock options is typically linked to the final value of the company at the time of exit, utilizing the IRR realized with the investment as the key parameter.

Several challenges surrounding stock options remain, however, such as:

- How to define key personnel?
- When to give out the stock options?
- How many stock options should they receive?

Let's Practise: Case Study

How to motivate Mr Pietro Rosso?

It's almost midnight and Alpha Investors' team is preparing to sign the term sheet with Mr Rosso, the entrepreneur/inventor of a company operating in the fintech sector. But the facts and figures are crystal clear: the post-money valuation of the company leads to €40 million in the hands of Alpha (and Mr Rosso's company needs €40 million) and

€20 million in the hands of Mr. Bubble, i.e. 66.67 per cent shares for Alpha. The Alpha team is worried: Mr Rosso is the asset (in fact, the only asset) of the company and despite owning the majority and the lock-up mechanism for three years, the risk of Mr Rosso not being committed is too high. 'Majority of what?', 'majority of nothing!' says one of the managers at midnight.

But the next day, some new ideas are on the table. The solution is to create a common pool, with a fixed three-year stock option for Mr Rosso, for €10 million (i.e. representing 14.28 per cent of equity) leading to a post-money valuation of €70 million, with Alpha ready to agree to owning 57.14 per cent of the shares but gambling on a higher upside because of the commitment of Mr Rosso, with the requirement of a drag along as well. For the year +3 Alpha Investors identify four different scenarios based on expected earnings and P/E ratio:

	Expected earnings year +3 (million euros)			
P/E ratio	5	6	10	12
x10				
x11				
x12				
x13				

Taking into account the fact that at year +3 Alpha is going to use the drag along which will easily generate the liquidity event, when will he use the option to buy the shares? What are the expected returns for Mr Rosso in the different scenarios if the option is used? What's going to happen if the option is not used?

11.6   Standards and Harmonization

There is a wide variety of legal structures and regulations within Europe. In addition, at sector level there are different governance challenges to be addressed. With a view to decreasing the many hurdles for doing business within the internal market, national standards and European guidelines have been developed to address these challenges and to identify best-practice principles.[21] European Union (EU) reforms have contributed to the convergence of governance policies in member states.

---

21 ICF World Bank (2015).

11.6.1   Practical Standards

Every member state in Europe has regulations and codes for effective corporate governance for public companies. There is also a growing interest in standards and codes for private companies, but this is more difficult to achieve because of the many different kinds of non-listed companies and the particularities of their requirements, making it very difficult for regulators to define corporate governance principles for these companies. Moreover, government intervention is often not appreciated.

As a result, corporate governance for non-listed companies is largely regulated through professional and industry standards. These guidelines or codes of conduct are not legally enforced but build upon the commitment of its participants to achieving the goal of transparency and growth.

The industry standards are largely regional. Examples include the codes for family businesses in Belgium and Germany, the code of conduct of the NVP (the association of PE and VCs) in The Netherlands and the Corporate Governance Code for Unlisted Companies (2016) in Slovenia.

Despite accounting for more than 75 per cent of European GDP and the acknowledgement that their shareholdings need better protection because of their illiquidity, non-listed companies have received less attention in corporate governance reforms. There are various initiatives at a European level, aiming to improve the management and governance by providing guidelines that transcend national laws. Invest Europe and the EcoDa are two of such initiatives promoting growth through better management and governance.

Invest Europe

Invest Europe (formerly known as EVCA, the European Private Equity and Venture Capital Association) is the guardian of professional standards, promotes a long-term approach to investing in privately-held companies, from startup to established firm.

Invest Europe emphasizes the role of good corporate governance as a key element in improving economic efficiency and growth as well as enhancing investor confidence. The key role is for integrity. For this purpose, to help its members decide what 'acting with integrity' means, guidelines are developed promoting the highest ethical and professional standards.

The Invest Europe 'Professional Standards handbook' (2015) promotes the attainment of sustainable growth, bringing together key elements of governance, transparency and accountability. In this handbook, the importance of governance is stressed as to be able to make informed decisions. Core in this handbook is the Code of Conduct.[22] Compliance with this code is mandatory for all Invest Europe members.

---

22 Invest Europe (2015).

Table 11.2 Code of conduct	
1	Act with integrity
2	Keep your promises
3	Disclose conflicts of interest
4	Act in fairness
5	Maintain confidentiality
6	Do no harm to the industry

Source: Invest Europe (2015)

EcoDa

The European Association of Directors' Associations (EcoDa) is a voice of European board directors. It acts as a discussion forum to share national experiences and promote high standards for directors, in hopes to promote economic development in Europe. In its Corporate Governance Principles it lays out fourteen principles of good governance.

In these principles, the development of the company is taken into account as well, recognizing the importance of corporate governance evolvement over the life cycle of a company. The principles are split into two parts, Phase 1 applicable to all unlisted companies, and Phase 2 only the larger and more complex unlisted companies.

11.6.2 Harmonization Directives

The European Commission (EC) has been actively involved in corporate governance practices through action plans, recommendations and directives since 2003. In '*Europe 2020 – A strategy for smart, sustainable and inclusive growth*', the EC restated its interest in aligning more closely governance practices between member states to increase competitiveness and develop sustainability among European companies.

Their aim is to increase consistency and decrease the regulatory burden for companies operating cross-border.[23] It is a process of ascertaining the permissible limits of international unification, but does not necessarily amount to a vision of total uniformity.[24]

23 European Commission (2011).
24 Menski (2005).

Table 11.3 Principles of good governance

Phase 1 principles:
Corporate governance principles applicable to all unlisted companies

Principle 1:	Shareholders should establish an appropriate constitutional and governance framework for the company.
Principle 2:	Every company should strive to establish an effective board, which is collectively responsible for the long-term success of the company, including the definition of the corporate strategy. However, an interim step on the road to an effective (and independent) board may be the creation of an advisory board.
Principle 3:	The size and composition of the board should reflect the scale and complexity of the company's activities.
Principle 4:	The board should meet sufficiently regularly to discharge its duties, and be supplied in a timely manner with appropriate information.
Principle 5:	Levels of remuneration should be sufficient to attract, retain, and motivate executives and non-executives of the quality required to run the company successfully.
Principle 6:	The board is responsible for risk oversight and should maintain a sound system of internal control to safeguard shareholders' investment and the company's assets.
Principle 7:	There should be a dialogue between the board and the shareholders based on the mutual understanding of objectives. The board as a whole has responsibility for ensuring that a satisfactory dialogue with shareholders takes place. The board should not forget that all shareholders have to be treated equally.
Principle 8:	All directors should receive induction on joining the board and should regularly update and refresh their skills and knowledge.
Principle 9:	Family-controlled companies should establish family governance mechanisms that promote coordination and mutual understanding amongst family members, as well as organise the relationship between family governance and corporate governance.

Phase 2 principles:
Corporate governance principles applicable to large and/or more complex unlisted companies

Principle 10:	There should be a clear division of responsibilities at the head of the company between the running of the board and the running of the company's business. No one individual should have unfettered powers of decision.
Principle 11:	Board structures vary according to national regulatory requirements and business norms. However, all boards should contain directors with a sufficient mix of competencies and experiences. No single person (or small group of individuals) should dominate the board's decision-making.

Table 11.3 (cont.)	
Principle 12:	The board should establish appropriate board committees in order to allow a more effective discharge of its duties.
Principle 13:	The board should undertake a periodic appraisal of its own performance and that of each individual director.
Principle 14:	The board should present a balanced and understandable assessment of the company's position and prospects for external stakeholders, and establish a suitable programme of stakeholder engagement.

Source: EcoDa

The purpose of EU rules in this area is to:[25]

- enable businesses to be set up anywhere in the EU;
- provide protection for shareholders and other parties with interest in specific companies;
- make business more efficient and competitive; and
- encourage businesses based in different EU countries to cooperate with each other.

Europe 2020, EU Actionplan 2012 and other EU corporate governance reforms have succeeded in bringing about convergence in corporate governance regimes between member states. However, the EU still faces significant challenges in ensuring that corporate governance initiatives are properly implemented.

On a worldwide scale, there is increasing convergence in corporate governance practices. This seems to be a global shift, in which both the Continental European model has converged with the Anglo-American model and the Anglo-American model has converged with the European model.[26] Various arguments on shareholding, corporate law and behavioural corporate governance are mentioned in connection with this converging process.[27]

11.7 The Benefits of Corporate Governance

The efforts that are being made to improve corporate governance not only involve limiting the risk for investors and improving their returns, they also protect the interests of other stakeholder groups, especially in Europe. Improving corporate governance practice impacts on the effectiveness of decision-making and the attainment of each of the constituent's goals. This final

---

25 European Commission on company law and corporate governance, http://ec.europa.eu/justice/civil/company-law/index_en.htm, retrieved 18 June 2017.
26 Thomsen and Conyon (2012).
27 For more information, see Hansmann and Kraakman (2002).

section considers the benefits that result from corporate governance improvement for the company itself, its founders, management, investors and other stakeholders.

Although not the sole driver, many studies have revealed the value of corporate governance in economic performance.[28] Besides improving competitiveness in general, the following benefits of good corporate governance across Europe are cited:[29]

- increased access to external financing, because of the fostering of trust between investors and founders/managers;
- lower cost of capital, through disclosure that decreases the risk and increases the willingness of investors;
- improved operational performance, following more efficient management and better asset allocation;
- increased company valuation and improved share performance, formulated as a 'corporate governance premium', indicating that investors are willing to pay a premium for well-governed companies;
- improved company reputation, through increased job satisfaction and higher staff retention; and
- reduced risk of corporate crises and scandals, by means of having an effective risk-management system in place.

All companies in Europe are also required to have a high level of transparency and to be accountable for their way of doing business towards all stakeholders. The OECD also complements this by emphasizing the importance of financial and non-financial information for comparing the performance of companies between countries.[30] To this purpose, an integrated reporting model (see Figure 11.5) has been developed and adopted by many companies across Europe.

As has been shown, many variables determine the corporate governance challenges for any venture. These ingredients include aspects such as the venture development phase and legal structure, number, concentration and kind of investors, nature of investment agreement (hands-on or hands-off), geographical distance, country perspective and board structure. Although less attention is given to privately held companies than to public companies, guidelines for creating a setting that is prosperous for the investor and venture have emerged from director associations and the European Committee. Both recognize the importance of corporate governance for sustainable economic growth and consider it to be a contributing factor to the development of ventures and for obtaining investments. Integrated reporting helps in complying to the guidelines and help increase transparency taking into account stakeholder interests.

28 Claessens and Yurtoglu (2012).
29 IFC World Bank (2015).
30 For more information, see 'Principles of Corporate Governance' by OECD (2015).

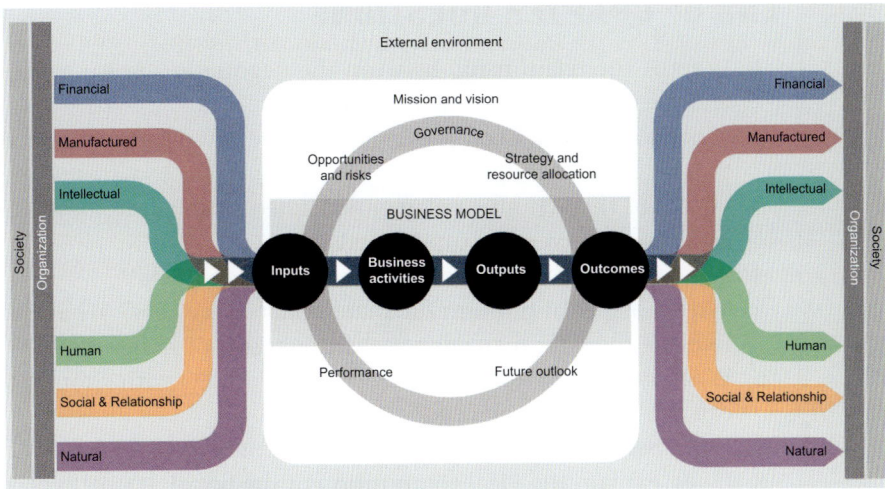

Figure 11.5 The Integrated Reporting Model.
Source: IIRC (2013)

KEY TAKEAWAYS

- A venture's corporate governance is established during the negotiation stage of the term sheet but at the same time it plays a significant, independent role, as it represents the legacy of the relationship between the venture capital investor and the company.
- Corporate governance is more than a system of rules and a mechanism for managing a business; it is something much more complex, which is based both on formal issues/processes and on informal processes.
- Soft factors are a key element of corporate governance and while they cannot be written down in a term sheet, they represent the way in which the venture capital investor sustains and supports the entrepreneur.
- The formal process of corporate governance aims to define the decision-making process and is based on the definition of duties and rights of shareholders, the functioning of the board of directors and the information flow.
- The contribution and focus of governance changes with regards to its controlling, consulting and contracting role throughout the life cycle of a venture.
- Investors in a venture can, even when holding only a minority stake, make a decisive impact on the direction of the venture.
- The use of stock options is a key covenant that helps the venture capital investor to motivate the entrepreneur to generate value.
- There is a noticeable convergence of governance practices, both within Europe and on a global scale.

END OF CHAPTER QUESTIONS

1. What is the relationship between the negotiation process, the term sheet and the corporate governance of a venture?
2. What do we mean in corporate governance when we say that investors need to have a 'foot on the brake'?
3. What are the actions or elements defined as soft factors within corporate governance in venture capital deals?
4. What are the main duties and rights of shareholders'?
5. Why is a special quorum for shareholders necessary? What other alternatives are there for managing the voting rights of shareholders?
6. What are the pros and the cons of having a CEO with strong powers? How can this power be balanced?
7. Is it possible to define a 'perfect' number of board members?
8. If yes, explain the ideal composition of the board; if not, explain the main guidelines for identifying an effective number.
9. Why are independent directors so important for venture capital deals? What is their role?
10. What are the main elements to consider when setting the voting system for a board?
11. Explain the characteristics of information flow within a venture. Why is it relevant for corporate governance?
12. Do stock options allow the entrepreneur to have greater control of the company or do they have a different aim?

FURTHER READING

BVCA (2014). *Model documents for Early-stage Investments*. British Private Equity and Venture Capital Association.

Galloway, T. L., Miller, D. R., Sahaym, A. and J.D. Arthurs, J. D. (2017). Exploring the innovation strategies of young firms: Corporate venture capital and venture capital impact on alliance innovation strategy. *Journal of Business Research*, 71, 55–65.

Gompers, P. and Lerner, J. (2000). *The Venture Capital Cycle*. MIT Academic Press.

Hansmann, H. (1996). *The Ownership of Enterprise*. Harvard University Press.

Hellmann, T. and Puri, M. (2002). Venture capital and the professionalization of startup firms: Empirical evidence. *Journal of Finance*, 57(1), 169–197.

Invest in Europe (2015). *Professional Standards Handbook*. Invest in Europe.

Kaplan, S. N. and Strömberg, P. (2003). Financial contracting theory meets the real world: An empirical analysis of venture capital contracts. *Review of Economic Studies*, 70(2), 281–315.

Koller, T., Dobbs, R. and Huyett, B. (2011). *Value, the Four Cornerstones of Corporate Finance*. Wiley.

REFERENCES

Caselli, S. and Negri, G. (2018). *Private Equity and Venture Capital in Europe. Markets, Techniques and Deals,* 2nd edition. Elsevier Academic Press.

Claessens, S. and Yurtoglu, B. (2012). *Global Corporate Governance Forum Focus 10.* IFC.

G. Deeb (2014). How to structure your board of directors or advisory board. *Forbes,* 11 October.

European Commission (2011): *Green Paper: The EU Corporate Governance Framework.* 5.4.2011 COM (2011) 164 final.

Eurostat (2015): Statistics on small and medium-sized enterprises, retrieved September 2015.

Fama, E. F. and Jensen, M. C. (1983). Separation of ownership and control. *Journal of Law and Economics,* 26(2), 301–325.

Filatotchev, I., Toms, S. and Wright, M. (2006). The firm's strategic dynamics and corporate governance life-cycle. *International Journal of Managerial Finance,* 2(4), 256–279.

Hansmann, H. and Kraakman, R. (2002). Toward a single model of corporate law? In J. A. McCahery, P. Moerland, Raaijmakers T.L. Renneborg, (eds.) *Corporate Governance Regimes: Convergence and Diversity.* Oxford University Press.

IFC World Bank (2015). *A Guide to Corporate Governance Practices in the European Union.*

International Integrated Reporting Council (2013). *The International IR Framwork.* IIRC.

Invest Europe (2015): *Professional Standards Handbook.*

Lerner, J., Leamon, A. and Hardymon, F. (2012). *Venture Capital, Private Equity, and the Financing of Entrepreneurship.* Wiley & Sons.

Mallin, A. (2013). *Corporate Governance.* Oxford University Press.

McCahery, J. A. and Vermeulen, E. P. M. (2008). *Corporate Governance of Non-Listed Companies.* Oxford University Press.

Menski, W. (2005). *Comparative Law in a Global Context.* Cambridge University Press.

O'Connor, T. and Byrne, J. (2015). *Governance and the corporate life-cycle. International Journal of Managerial Finance,* 11(1), 23–43.

OECD (2004). *Principles of Corporate Governance,* 2nd edition. OECD Publication Service.

OECD (2015). G20/OECD *Principles of Corporate Governance.* OECD Publishing.

Smith, R. C. and Walter, I. (2006). *Governing the Modern Corporation.* Oxford University Press.

Thomsen, S. and Conyon, M. (2012). *Corporate Governance: Mechanisms and Systems.* McGraw-Hill.

Wasserman, N. (2008). The founder's dilemma. *Harvard Business Review,* 86(2), 102–109.

Wasserman, N. (2017). The throne vs. the kingdom: Founder control and value creation in startups. *Strategic Management Journal,* 38(2), 255–277.

Let's Practise: Case Study

Corporate Governance Challenge: e-Food Case

It's May 2017: Paul and Robert Wash are very nervous because they are waiting for John Cash, a partner at Alpha Investor to discuss the term sheet of the deal. Robert is 29 years old, he's got an MBA from SDA Bocconi, he's very creative, generous but also aggressive and he had the idea of e-Food and he invested all his money and time to promote it. Paul is his uncle, 69 years old, who spent the entire life in the food sector, with a lot of passion and competence but he never got to the top. The duo seems not so sparkling but John Cash considers e-Food has a lot of potential to scale up even at international level: the first test launched in many cities in Italy gave an amazing response indicating the success of the idea. The idea is bright: you can order in couple of minutes all the ingredients to cook whatever course you like and even the cocktail to prepare aside, only squeezing the content of a nice sachet in the cold water. And Paul never reached the top but he's a serious professional and he knows very well suppliers in the slow food sector. After thirty minutes John Cash arrives at the meeting starts.

After the Meeting

It's almost 8.00 pm and the meeting with Paul and Robert was very long. John is happy because he feels the deal will happen and he sees a lot of potential in e-Food. And he's thinking about the two entrepreneurs: Robert is a bit arrogant but his energy is genuine and he's a great worker; Paul is perfect to balance Robert and he's knowledge of the food sector with a special touch for healthy ingredients is unbelievable. John is thinking about the many requests he received in the largest cities in Europe to launch an initiative like that but also in the Gulf area and in China and India. Yes, we can scale up very quickly.

The term sheet is ready but it's completely open on the issue of corporate governance. Alpha is going to invest 5 million euros and will receive 40% of shares but perspectives sound very interesting. e-Food doesn't have any governance because Paul and Robert have got 50% each and they have a board they never used because it's on paper and is made up of the two of them. Post-money shares are 40% for Alpha and 30% each Paul and Robert. But there's room to elaborate more. John wants to discuss the deal with other partners of Alpha and the only concern is related to Robert: he's really entrepreneurial but he seems to change his mind continuously not on the content of the business but for the strategy. In three hours he was talking about the idea of acquisitions, he turned to the need to stay in Italy and he suggested also the hypothesis to go to Asia . . . But John is not surprised as he has met in his life many entrepreneurs and startuppers like him. However, he wants to sleep and to organize a report to share the day after with other partners.

The Report to Face Corporate Governance Issues

The day after John is ready to highlight the key issues of the corporate governance, having crystal clear in his mind the (successful) story for the next years.

Alpha is ready to invest 5 million euros and to support e-Food to enter the market in the main European capital cities; after 2/3 years maximum a new round of financing to move towards an expansion outside Europe, moving to China. And later . . . a very beautiful exit. The topics to face and to manage are the following:

- shareholders agreement about duties and rights;
- the board structure;
- the presence and the role of the CEO; and
- the usage of stock option mechanisms.

As usual John has to discuss pros and cons of every solution and to decide together with other partners to move towards another meeting with Robert and Paul to talk about the corporate governance settings. For the first topic, John wants to avoid the two entrepreneurs taking the wrong decisions because of the nature of Robert, ready to change his mind continuously. For the second one, the size of the board is always a risk as well the selection of components, in term of number, skills and independence. For the third one, the issue is the choice of the CEO: Robert expects to be the CEO – or probably he doesn't have any doubts about it – but he hasn't international experience in the food sector and Paul hasn't got the standing to do that. Last, stock option could be a right solution – but for both of them? – as a new capital increase will happen and Paul and Robert can be diluted.

But now it's time to move from doubts to proposal. Which frame for the governance will John set? Let's go through the main items he's going to discuss with other partners:

1. Identification of the balance of duties and rights for Alpha (40%) and for Robert and Paul Wash (60%).
2. Composition of the board: number of members, number of independent directors and their profile, name of the chairperson, voting system.
3. Name of the CEO and definition of the powers.
4. Content of stock options plan.

The partners meeting at Alpha is ready to start.

12 | MANAGING YOUR INTELLECTUAL PROPERTY

PETER HISCOCKS

Judge Business School, University of Cambridge

This chapter introduces you to the concept and practicalities of intellectual property: what it is and why it can be of importance to your new business venture. Intellectual property (IP) will be at the heart of most businesses and it is a key element in achieving competitive advantage, enabling cash flow and justifying value. Sometimes it takes considerable financial investment to develop IP; some types of IP protection can cost a great deal of money; some types of IP protection are very low cost. All in all, IP is a very important element in the finances of a new and growing business and management needs to understand the key issues surrounding the decisions that will need to be made.

There is no guaranteed right way or wrong way to address intellectual property. For some businesses, this is one of the most important issues whilst for others it has little commercial importance and can be a costly distraction. You will have to decide the right approach for your business based upon your differentiation in the marketplace, the value-add that you bring to your customers and the basis for your long-term competitive advantage.

Intellectual property protection is a complex and legalistic matter and there are many different ways that this can be undertaken, as described in the chapter. If the intellectual property of your business is critical to its competitive position and growth then it is strongly recommended that you seek professional advice, help and support so that you make the right decisions.

VIEW FROM THE MEDIA

FINANCIAL TIMES   FT

Why you can trademark a Toblerone but not a KitKat

JUNE 28, 2017 BY SCHEHERAZADE DANESHKHU, CONSUMER INDUSTRIES EDITOR

... The value of a trademark lies in its longevity. This is in contrast to patents, which are for new inventions that are capable of industrial application. Their exclusivity in the UK for example expires after a maximum of 20 years, to encourage competition among manufacturers. A trademark however 'can be renewed every five, 10 years, depending on your jurisdiction, ad infinitum, which gives you quite a monopoly,' says Kate Swaine, partner at law firm Gowling WLG. ... A string of failed attempts by consumer goods companies to trademark shapes and colours have highlighted both the complexities of intellectual property law and the value to brands of at least seeking the virtual monopoly of trademark protection.

As Mary Bagnall, a partner at law firm Charles Russell Speechlys, explains, trademarks are usually 'logos or names registered in relation to specific goods or services, so you can have businesses with the same name but operating in different spaces, such as Polo for Ralph Lauren clothing, for Volkswagen cars and for Nestlé's mint with a hole'. The Apple trademark coexisted quite happily as The Beatles' record label and as the computer business but the two companies become embroiled in a legal fight after these once-distinct areas converged with changes in technology including the rise of digital music. To qualify for registration, trademarks have to be distinctive, the most uncontroversial being invented names, such as Kodak. ... Last month Nestlé was unable to replicate in the UK its success elsewhere in trademarking the shape of its KitKat four-fingered chocolate wafer. Christian Louboutin, the shoe designer, has also been successful in some countries in trademarking the signature red colour of his soles. For companies that invest heavily in their brands, a trademark makes it easier and cheaper to prevent copycat imitations, though the English law of Passing Off can still be used to protect unregistered trademarks.

Nestlé was thwarted in its attempts to trademark the KitKat shape after a judge in the UK's Court of Appeal last month ruled that the rectangular bars with breaking grooves was not distinctive enough. The Swiss group said: 'We will explore other avenues to protect our famous KitKat® 4-finger shape.' Yet Toblerone, the bar belonging to US chocolate rival Mondelez, does have a trademark for its triangular shape. Coca-Cola also managed to trademark its fluted, curvy glass bottle in 1980, but failed with a more recent design. Why the difference? Both the Toblerone shape and the original Coca-Cola bottle were central to the groups' advertising, says Ms Bagnall. Toblerone's advertisements talked about using triangular honey from triangular bees and Coca-Cola featured its bottle so prominently in its ads that people were able to identify it as a Coke bottle without labelling. Gowling's Ms Swaine says: 'Coca-Cola was able to show what Nestlé couldn't – the bottle itself was distinctive. Moreover when you buy Coca-Cola, you see the bottle but when you buy a KitKat, you don't see the bar – it's in a wrapper.' ...

www.ft.com/content/16351d98-46d9-11e7-8d27-59b4dd6296b8

LEARNING OBJECTIVES

After reading this chapter you will be able to:

- Understand what intellectual property is and why could it be important to your business.
- Appreciate the different ways that intellectual property can affect the value of your business and what you need to take into account when developing an intellectual property strategy.

- Understand the importance of protecting intellectual property and some of the key principles for doing this.
- Recognize that you need to be aware of other people's intellectual property and not infringe their intellectual property rights if they have protected them in some way.
- Acknowledge that there are different ways of protecting intellectual property, that these are relevant in different situations and that they provide different types and levels of protection.
- Understand that *registered* intellectual property protection can have significant associated costs, particularly patents, and that it is important for new ventures to evaluate carefully whether such protection is needed in their business.
- Recognize that *unregistered* intellectual property protection can be very important for a business and can (under certain conditions) provide adequate protection.
- Be aware that you and your business will be responsible for policing and prosecuting anyone infringing your intellectual property and to do so can be expensive.
- Understand that you need to develop an intellectual property strategy for your business and determine the cost/benefit of protecting the intellectual property on which your business is based.

Where Are We Going Next?

This chapter will enable you to evaluate the ideas and intellectual property on which your business is based and determine whether you need to protect it and, if so, what will be the most appropriate method. It will describe what you need to do to develop an intellectual property strategy for your business and how this can help enhance the value of your new business venture.

The chapter will start at the beginning with ideas, and how ideas are your intellectual property (IP). We will discuss how ideas are formed and how they add value to your business. The concept of quantifying the value of IP is discussed as well as the ways in which it can add value to your business. Next, we discuss IP protection and review the different types of IP protection available under the two different types of IP; *registered IP* and *unregistered IP*. In this chapter, the processes for enabling these different types of IP protection are explained, and we look at the level of protection that is provided and estimate the costs for undertaking IP protection. The importance of developing an IP strategy for your business is explained and the principal steps that are needed to achieve this are described. Finally, it is recommended, before undertaking any IP protection, that the costs and benefits of such a step are considered. Two case examples are provided; one describes a business where IP protection has been at the core of the business's success; the other describes a new business venture where IP is important but fewer resources have been expended on their protection.

12.1   Background

Ideas are wonderful things. They are a critical step in the journey of development for the products and processes that have changed our world since the birth of mankind. They come from nowhere, they cost nothing, and they weren't there (in their fully developed form) a few seconds beforehand. And the changes that they have made help to make us healthier, warmer, better clothed, more able to travel, to be entertained, to access information, etc. In fact, ideas have changed the world, mostly for the better, although there are probably some things that we wish could be 'unmade'.

Focusing on the positive side, we can see that ideas have not only resulted in the development of new products, processes and services that help make our modern world work the way that it does, but that ideas are also at the heart of many of the businesses that employ thousands of people and are the engines of growth in our modern economies. Ideas are essential for the formation of new businesses and also for the survival and growth of existing businesses.

We are used to the concept of property and owning things. My shirt and my wallet are mine; so is my house, and many other things. They belong to me and people can't take them away without my agreement and permission, and this may involve them paying me money in exchange for the item of property. Do our 'ideas' belong to us in the same way that our shirt and shoes do? Yes, they do, and we describe this characteristic of ideas as 'intellectual property'. The ideas that you have are yours, at least to start with.

And this brings us to another characteristic of ideas: once they are shared then the genie is out of the bottle. We can't unmake an idea. This means that your property, your intellectual property, may need some mechanism to protect it to prevent other people from stealing it or using it in ways you did not intend. We will come back to intellectual property protection in a later section, to explore alternate ways of protecting intellectual property, and we will study the advantages and disadvantages of different approaches.

12.2   How Can Intellectual Property Add Value to My Business?

Firstly, let's review how intellectual property can help a new business venture to grow and become successful and how it can add value to that business. The success of a business relies on customers and/or clients being very satisfied with the products or services offered by the business to the extent that the customers keep coming back (maybe encouraging more customers) and the business can charge a premium for its products. Successful businesses will have products or services that are better in some way when compared with their competitors' products. The mechanism for 'better' may be that the product works better but it could equally be that it is cheaper or works more effectively or has fewer faults, etc. This capability of the product being better usually results from someone having had an idea for developing a better product. That idea, especially when it has been developed into a successful product that customers want to buy, is a key part of the intellectual property that your business may own. The intellectual property that you have developed within the business is an important element in gaining competitive advantage in your marketplace; that is, being better than your competitors. A useful review of intellectual property from a legislative perspective can be found on the European Patent Office.[1]

The intellectual property (IP) that we have developed within the business can add value to the business in a number of ways. The most obvious is that if the IP is the core to making our product or service better than competitive products, then this is at the heart of our business's competitive advantage, thereby enabling the business to sell more products, possibly at a higher price. If our IP makes our product very much better than all the competitors and most of the customers in the market come to buy our product resulting in high levels of sales and possibly high profit margins, then the IP will have a very significant value to the business. Furthermore, if our competitors can't copy this IP or find a way to make their own products better than ours, then this IP may provide competitive advantage for our business for some considerable time. This is what Michael Porter calls 'sustainable competitive advantage'.[2] This is the most important use of IP within a business and we can look at expected future cash flows from products and services that are based on our IP and can make estimates of the value of the IP based on these future cash flows. This analysis will give us some idea of the value that our IP brings to the business. However, we do need to remember that our competitors will always be trying to develop new products that will overtake our IP – we will never have a monopoly on inventiveness in our industry sector.

Another way that IP can add value to the business is when we are estimating the value of the business because we are seeking investment funding or we are considering the sale of the business, either in whole or in part. In such situations, IP will be an important consideration when calculating the value of the business and, in certain cases, IP will represent the largest part of the value of the business. However, protected IP is usually given a higher value by professional investors, such as VCs, as this makes it more difficult for a competitor to copy the business's products and services. Protected IP may be one of the main sources of our 'sustainable competitive advantage', which provides us with the ability to defend our market position and our profit margins. The type of protection that we can use to protect our IP will also affect the value of that IP since some methods of protection are more effective than others and some last longer.

1 For more information see the website of the European Patent Office at www.epo.org/apply ing/basics.html. Information relating to patenting in national countries can also be found; an example is the UK government website: www.gov.uk/intellectual-property-an-overview /what-ip-is
2 Porter (1980).

In general, IP, and particularly, protected IP, will make a significant difference to the value of your business. As such, it is important to identify this in your business plan and to propose a well-thought-through IP development and protection strategy. If you have been able to register a strong brand as a trademark, protect inventions through patent(s) or have important copyright material relating to your business then this can be important, not only for making the business become more successful but also because it can increase the valuation of the business should you be raising investment finance or possibly selling the business.[3]

12.3   Using Other People 's IP

We tend to focus our IP thinking on 'how we can protect our own IP'. In addition to this, we should always consider whether we are likely, in any way, to infringe other people's IP. Our idea for a product or service may be new, but if it relies on some knowledge or activity that has been protected by another business we need to be aware of this and take appropriate action. You may ask 'How will I know if we are infringing someone else's IP?' Well, this is an important thing for you to determine and will require you, or a patent attorney employed by you, to undertake a search of the registered intellectual property. If you find that you are infringing someone else's IP, it is usually advisable to discuss this matter with the owner of the IP and try to reach an agreement. If you infringe their IP, they have a number of measures that they can take against you and your business. Firstly, they can demand that you cease making, importing, using and/or selling the products or services that infringe their IP. They can sue you for damages and require you to pay them the profits that you have made on selling the product that infringes. If you continue to infringe, then they can sue you and take you to court. This is certainly not advisable: it is usually very costly and could have a very bad effect on your business. If you are going to be using videos or music or other examples of unregistered IP, then again it is advisable to check carefully that you are not infringing the IP of another business. Unregistered IP, such as music, videos, published material or software, is likely to be the intellectual property of the creator. If you are using this material without gaining their permission, you will be infringing their rights and you could have to stop selling your product and possibly have to pay damages.

If your business is dependent on the IP of another firm, then you should probably discuss the matter with them and negotiate a licence to use their IP. You should almost certainly get your lawyer involved in such an arrangement, as you need to be sure that you will continue to have access to their IP into the future and possibly have some 'pipeline rights' to any further developments they make to their technology or products. Pipeline rights represent an

---

3 A more in-depth analysis of how to value a patent and how it can affect the value of a business can be found in Pitkothly (1997).

agreement from the person licensing the IP to you that they will give you the first rights of refusal of new inventions that they make in this field of innovation. The reason you want pipeline rights is to ensure that if you have taken a licence on their first innovation, they do not then license a second (and, presumably, better in some way) innovation in the same field to a competitor, thereby reducing the value of your licence. The person selling you the licence in the first place may be persuaded to give you pipeline rights because you pay extra for them and/or you encourage them in some other way, such as research collaboration or joint marketing.

12.4   Intellectual Property Protection

There are basically two types of intellectual property protection systems: **registered** and **un-registered.**

Table 12.1 Registered IP protection

Type of IP	Requirement	Time of protection	Costs
Patent	Novel innovation	20 years	Could be €100ks over patent lifetime
Registered design	Novel design	25 years	€350 for Europe
Trademark	Distinctive design	As long as you continue to use the trademark	€850 in one class

Source: European Patent Office (2017)[4]

Table 12.2 Unregistered IP protection

Type of IP	Requirement	Time of protection	Costs
Copyright	Your own composition	70 years beyond death of author	None
Un-registered design	Novel design	15 years	None
Trade secret	Keep it secret	As long as you can keep it secret	None

Source: European Patent Office (2017)[5]

4 Note: the data quoted above are for the European Patent Office; the terms will be different in different jurisdictions.
5 Note: the data quoted above are for the European Patent Office; the terms will be different in different jurisdictions.

Intellectual property protection systems do not prevent other people from copying your product or infringing your rights in other ways but they do enable you to sue the person or business who is infringing your IP. However, you need to understand that the legal process to prevent someone copying your IP and to gain financial redress for their infringement of your IP may be expensive, may take a long time and you may not win.

12.4.1 Registered Intellectual Property Protection

Patents

A patent grants an absolute right of monopoly on an invention for a limited period of time, usually 20 years, if the patent is kept alive that long by paying renewal fees; however, most are not. This monopoly right means that you can sue anyone who makes, uses, sells or imports a product based upon or using your patented IP within the territories where your patent is registered and valid. In exchange for this protection, the patent will be published, showing other people how the invention works and in a way also giving them insight as to how to circumvent the patent and invent something better. Even if someone independently and subsequently invents the same thing, then the original patent holder will have priority on the invention and can stop the second inventor from exploiting the idea for the duration of the patent. Traditionally, when there are different parties who have granted patent rights that are dependent on each other, then cross-licensing has been used to allow all parties to continue to operate, but this must be agreed explicitly by the businesses and the appropriate cross-licence agreements be drawn up and agreed. In very crowded areas of patent rights, so-called 'patent pools' have been established to allow the technology or standard to be established and prosper (rather than have everyone fight each other and no-one be able to exploit this field of innovation). Under the patent pool arrangement, inventors all share the rights to exploit the innovations, often without having to make explicit cross-licensing agreements.

For an idea to be patentable it must be novel, which means that no-one can have filed a patent, written about it, described it in a learned paper that has been published or made it available to the public – for example, by incorporating it into a product – before the filing date of the patent. The idea cannot have been well known beforehand or be based on 'prior art', which means that this idea was widely understood and used before the patent was filed.

To be valid a patent must also be a 'non-obvious invention to someone skilled in the art', which means that you cannot just transpose one or two elements from another existing invention. It must be practicable, feasible and useful.

To file a patent, the inventor must describe the invention and file this with the appropriate Patent Office. In Europe, this is the European Patent Office (EPO). You will find a great deal of information about applying for a patent in Europe at www.epo.org/applying/basics.html. This website describes in detail the process that you need to go through to file your patent and also the thinking that you need to do.

You will need to decide the geographical areas you wish to cover with your patent, understanding that the wider your coverage the higher the cost of filing your patent and getting it granted. When selecting the geographic areas to cover with patent protection, you need to consider the industry in which your business is operating. In those industries where IP is critical for protecting your product and discouraging competitors, such as the life science market, it is important to have wider geographical coverage. In these circumstances, you should probably file in more countries, securing the main markets of the United States, Europe (often with a selection of key countries) and possibly China.[6]

When you file your patent application this sets the 'priority date' for your invention. This is the 'start date' for the patent protection of your IP. This means that you have priority over anyone who invents exactly the same idea after you and you can also utilize this to file the patent in other countries up to 12 months from the priority date. Since the United States has also moved to 'first to file' (through the America Invents Act [AIA] on 16 March 2013), the way to establish the priority date is from the date the Patent and Trademark Offices such as the IPO receives your patent application. Previously, in the United States, it was possible (under certain circumstances) to gain agreement on an earlier date if you could show from laboratory records, books and computer files that the invention was made at an earlier date; this may still be relevant to some extent as patent filings transition to conform with 'first to file' rather than 'first to invent' legislation. This law was changed in the United States from first to invent to first to file in September 2011 and first to file should be good for all patents filed after September 2011 in the United States.[7]

What can and cannot be patented is currently in a stage of transition. Until recently, only actual products, technologies and technical processes could be patented. Mathematical formulae, genes and purely based software algorithms could not be patented (but could possibly be protected by other less 'strong' IP protection methods like copyright). However, this situation is changing rapidly and a global debate is underway regarding the extent to which software and business processes can be protected by a patent. It is possible to get a patent for an algorithm, software code or business process in Europe, as well as in the United States, if there is a technical effect linked to the software; that is to say, the software IP causes a physical change to happen. The United States has in recent years moved closer to the European interpretation on software-related

6 Details about applying for a patent in Europe can be found at www.epo.org/applying/basics .html or if you are applying in the United States look at www.uspto.gov/patents-getting-started/general-information-concerning-patents. For other jurisdictions, look up the relevant government websites.

7 However, there are still some cases coming forward where the invention is claimed before September 2011 and the case law in these circumstances has yet to be resolved.

inventions. There are significant recent changes in the 'case law' about the level of protection that can actually be achieved by software patents; it is still not clear how 'strong' such patents will be in litigation or during invalidity proceedings.

When filing your patent application, it is strongly recommended that you get help from an experienced professional patent agent. This is more costly than doing it yourself, but the chance of protecting the critical elements of the invention and of getting the patent office to grant your patent are increased significantly compared with the outcome if you write the patent application yourself. The whole process is expensive and time-consuming, taking up to two or three years, or even more, to get a patent granted. That said, there are now developments such as the Patent Prosecution Highway that allow fast-tracking prosecution for inventions in fast-moving industries. As a result, it should be possible to get patents granted in around a year from filing if early publication is requested. The process can cost tens of thousands of euros, when professional fees are included, for patenting in just one country. And even then your monopoly is not guaranteed. Competitors may challenge your patent in the courts, and this too will take time and cost money. Furthermore, it is up to you to check for infringement of your patents and then to prosecute the law case; again, considerable time and money is involved. Also, do remember that your patent will be published 18 months from the earliest priority date, which means competitors will see what you have included in the patent application. This means that in some cases it is worth withdrawing your pending patent application to keep information for your company secret and confidential if you are uncertain about the success or strength of your patent application.

If you are applying for a UK patent, for example, when it is granted it will only provide you with cover in the UK: should you require protection in other countries then you must apply in each country or jurisdiction. Fortunately, there are now offices that provide patenting services Europe-wide and, after a long wait, the Unitary European Patent system with a Unified Patent Court could soon be fully implemented. The Agreement for a Unified Patent Court was signed by twenty-five members of the European Union in 2013, but this has to be ratified by the national law in at least thirteen countries including France, Germany and the United Kingdom before it comes into force. At this point in time (May 2017), only twelve countries have signed. Also, to keep your options open it is often recommended to use the International PCT patent application which allows for worldwide patent pending coverage for up to about 30 months from the first priority date. The Paris Convention (1883) allows for international agreements to recognize the date of the first filing in any country as the priority date.

Design Rights

If you have developed a new product that does not have any patentable technology or characteristics but is novel, and this novelty means that customers want to buy it, then you will want to protect your design so that competitors can't copy it. You can do this by 'unregistered design rights' or, preferably, by 'registering your design'. An example would be a business such as Joseph Joseph that designs and makes high-end chopping boards (and other products) for use in the kitchen. The design of the Joseph Joseph chopping board makes them much more convenient to use than existing chopping boards and, therefore, by registering the design the business can stop competitors from copying it.

Design rights may be registered or unregistered and provide different levels of protection accordingly. Design rights protect the shape of both three and two-dimensional designs that have either been drawn or have been made, either as a finished item or as a representative model. Black-and-white line drawings are preferred in most jurisdictions but photographs showing all sides of an object also work well. Design rights can be claimed only on an original, i.e. new design. There is a grace period of up to twelve months in Europe to register your design after you have made it. Registered design rights, known in Europe as Registered Community Designs (RCDs) last for twenty-five years and can be registered on a Europe-wide basis. Unregistered design rights last for ten years and are conferred on the design of a product in a similar way to copyright. Design rights as a mechanism for the protection of intellectual property are relevant only to physical objects such as cars or vacuum cleaners, trainers or handbags, but will not cover services or software or products that do not have a physical form. Design protection is a very cost-effective way to protect your creation and costs a few hundred euros. The current fee from the EU IPO is €350 to register a design for the whole of Europe. Once you have filed the first design filing to get a priority date, you will have six months to file internationally. This is why it is recommended to file your EU design registration before making it public, as other jurisdictions do not always have a grace period. Renewal fees are payable every five years. For detailed information on applying for design rights in Europe it is recommended that you look at https://euipo.europa.eu/ohimportal/en/designs.

Design rights can be important to the profitability of a product and, therefore, can be of significant value to a business, both in terms of being able to charge a premium price for the product and by claiming a higher value for the business as a whole due to its ownership of the design. In the UK, there are no damages for 'innocent infringement' of a design but the designer can claim profits back from the infringer. The offence of knowledgeable and unauthorized copying of a design can result in criminal sanctions with fines and a possible prison sentence. Some examples of law cases around design rights are: *Pepsico* v. *GrupoPromer Mon Graphic* on the design of pogs and tazos; *Procter & Gamble* v. *Reckitt Benckiser* on the design of an aerosol spray; and *Samsung* v. *Apple* over the shape of their tablets. In the *Samsung* v. *Apple* court case, the court made a damages judgement of $399 million against Samsung. However, this damages judgement was appealed by Samsung and in December 2016 the judgement was reversed, proving that the people who win in IP cases are the lawyers.[8]

Trademarks

Trademarks can be very important for some businesses, particularly as they get large and have a high-end consumer presence. A registered trademark may consist of any signs capable of being represented graphically provided that such signs are capable of distinguishing the goods or services of one business from those of another. A registered trademark cannot be copied by other businesses without your agreement and can, therefore, be used to identify and differentiate your products from your competitors. As a small (but growing) young business with only a small number of customers, you are probably not a recognized 'brand' yet, and it may not seem important to register your trademark. However, businesses like Adidas, Guinness, Coca Cola, Nike, etc. all started small but now have a huge amount of value linked to their trademark, and so it is recommended that you register your business logo or identifier and make sure that it is suitable as a trademark. A trademark must be able to distinguish the goods and services of one company from another. However, it can't be descriptive of those goods, it can't be a generic term for those goods, and it must have an inherent distinctiveness.

As with all registered IP protection methods, trademarks are territorial and therefore you have to register your trademark in the countries where you want it to apply. You register the trademark with the European Intellectual Property Office (EU IPO) and with equivalent government offices in other countries. The current costs are €850 for one class (industry sector) of protection.[9]

Once you have a priority date for your initial trademark filing, with e.g. the EU IPO, you should file internationally within six months to maintain the earlier filing date. If you do not file within the priority period, you can still do so for trademarks (something that is not possible if you miss the priority period for patents and designs), but it becomes a first-come first-served case, just as we have with some other areas of IP, e.g. domain names. The application will be examined by the relevant IPO and will be published if it meets the criteria for a registered trademark. Third parties can challenge the application, and the challenge will be reviewed and a decision made by the EU IPO. Furthermore, the trademark must be used in the marketplace; if the trademark is not used for a period of time (typically three to five years depending on the territory) then it is consider as 'abandoned', and other businesses can challenge and adopt the trademark.

8 Further information on common design rights problems can be found at www.albright-ip.co .uk/2013/12/six-registered-design-disasters-and-how-to-avoid-them/
9 Further information can be found at https://euipo.europa.eu/ohimportal/en/trade-marks

12.4.2   Unregistered Intellectual Property Protection

There are some types of intellectual property protection that you do not need to register with a government or trade office. The best known of these is copyright, but 'trade secret' is probably used as much in the real world of business.

Copyright

Copyright is exactly what it says it is: it is a right that prohibits copying. It does not grant a monopoly or prevent independent invention. It can't be used for names or phrases that are used commonly but it can be used for complete designs. It was first developed to enable music composers to gain financially from their work and prevent other people taking the music and performing it without giving any payment or recognition to the composer. The area of application of copyright spread to books, films, videos and computer programs, including databases. Copyright is still widely used as protection for software and is therefore of great importance to many new age businesses. Copyright does not protect the idea, only its expression, so you cannot protect the idea for your new software model but only the expression; the actual code that defines the computer actions that will make up the software product. Indeed, some software systems have been deliberately re-implemented as 'clean-room copies' by teams with no original knowledge of, or access to, the original code; such an outcome would have its own copyright.

Copyright is self-declarative, and so the author automatically owns the copyright of work that they may have written, although in the case of most employees this ownership will be automatically assigned to the business (employer) as set down in the employee's employment contract. This is a good time to remind you, as a potential business owner, that you need to ensure that your employment contract does address intellectual property ownership and assignment so that you own the IP that your employees develop in the business, rather than them retaining ownership.[10]

At one time, it was considered necessary to include the word 'Copyright' or the copyright symbol © together with the name of the author and the year of publication on your material. This is no longer required, but it is very simple to do and it does show others (especially potential copiers) that you have a clear presumption of ownership. This presumption can still be challenged and refuted, and there have been many long, complex and expensive legal cases involving claims and counter claims on copyright issues. An example would be Ryanair's claim that their customer databases were protected under the European Parliament's 'Database Directive'. Ryanair sued and won protection. In this case the following judgment was made: *on 15 January 2015, the Court of Justice of the European Union (the '**CJEU**') gave a preliminary ruling in the case of*

---

10 Further information on copyright can be found at https://www.eucopyright.com/

*Ryanair Ltd v PR Aviation BV (Case C-30/14), which could have a significant impact on both website database operators and websites that carry out 'screen-scraping' activities (such as price comparison websites). The CJEU held that website operators should be able to rely on the Database Directive (96/9/EC, the '**Directive**') to prevent screen-scraping and also they might potentially be able to use their website terms and conditions in order to make a breach of contract claim.*

The Directive provides two forms of protection in respect of databases:

(i) Article 3(1) states that the structure of the database may be protected by copyright; and

(ii) Article 7, otherwise known as the '*sui generis*' or 'database' right, protects the actual contents of the database.

At present, copyright lasts for seventy years beyond the death of the author, although this may be different in some jurisdictions and for some classes of materials. Under the Berne Convention of 1886, which has most important countries as signatories (the United States joined in 1988), copyright is recognized internationally, although the conditions of application and the standards of enforcement vary considerably. Copyright is incremental so, for example, the translation of a work carries both the original copyright and the copyright of the translator. This can be particularly important for aggregation of material such as a database, where the original information may have its own copyright as well as the aggregated database. There is also an entirely separate European database right that is analogous to copyright, but exists for the protection of databases (see above). The individual items may not be original or protected, but the database as a whole is considered as an original work.

'Fair use' of copyrighted material is permitted. For example, limited use of works may be possible for research and private study, criticism or review, teaching in schools or the not-for-profit playing of a sound recording. Fair use normally applies only to text, although hyperlinks seem to be OK. There is a limit to fair use of copyrighted text, which is normally about 300 words or, in different conditions, making a small number, up to twenty-five or so, photocopies. The case law around this topic is long and complex dating back from 1703 and still developing new case law today.[11]

Detection and prosecution of copyright abuse is the responsibility of the copyright owner, although organizations such as the PRS (Performing Rights Society) and FAST (Federation Against Software Theft) are starting to become more effective in support of policing. It can be quite difficult to prosecute infringements of copyright, as direct copying must be shown and it is essential to prove that the material copied is yours. One way to help against this problem, particularly with software, is to use steganography to introduce (hidden) signatures in your original. For example, you could include a few lines of harmless but nonsensical code in your software program which would be unlikely to be

11 A good overview and analysis is provided at https://en.wikipedia.org/wiki/Fair_use

included in any possible reinvention. The presence of this code in another program would then indicate that copying has occurred. However, with such a high incidence of copyright infringement the issue is often not so much whether copying has happened as whether it is feasible or economic to prosecute.

Copyright may seem a bit of a 'flabby' or weak method for protecting your important intellectual property, but there are many large businesses and even industries that rely upon copyright for their profitability. Examples are the music industry, films, computer games, software and publishing. However, this is of most help to the larger companies as they have the resources to police and prosecute copyright infringement, which is often more difficult for the smaller or new business to undertake.

Trade Secrets

One of the simplest ways of protecting your intellectual property is by not telling anyone else how your product or service works. It is often surprisingly difficult for competitors to 'reverse engineer' your innovation, and the costs of this approach to intellectual property protection are very low.

There are several definitions of what makes a trade secret, but the most common are:[12]

- It is not generally known to the public.
- It confers some sort of economic or commercial benefit to your organization.
- Reasonable efforts have been made to keep the intellectual property from being divulged.

Some important businesses use trade secret to protect their intellectual property; Coca Cola is probably one of the best known. The story is that there are only two people in the world that know the complete formula and they are not allowed to tell anyone; and it is written down in only one place and is kept secret in a very large and imposing safe. This story is probably as much a publicity stunt as an actual method of intellectual property protection, but it is interesting that in the last 125 years no other soft drink manufacturer has been able to exactly replicate the flavour.

A related approach to trade secrets can be for an organization to keep their intellectual property secret but also to continue to innovate to make the product or service better. This approach of keeping the IP secret but continuing to invest in innovation can enable a business to maintain long-term competitive advantage over its competitors.

Should it be necessary to divulge the intellectual property (possibly to a customer or a supplier) then the protection can be maintained by getting them to sign an NDA (Non-Disclosure Agreement). Such agreements are usually

---

12 Definition is taken from US law: 18 U.S.C. § 1839(3) (A), (B) (1996).

mutual and allow the exchange of specific information that may be a part of (or all of) your trade secret IP. NDAs impose important obligations on the parties involved to keep the matter confidential and, in some cases, to record a complete list of the people within the business who have had access to the information.[13] NDAs should be worded so that they cover any casual information obtained, even if this is an overheard conversation or the sight of a document. Companies should put in place a register of NDAs that they have signed, and should track these to ensure they keep any related documents in appropriate storage and destroy them at the time required by the agreement.

Some companies refuse to sign NDAs on the grounds that they are more trouble than they are worth, and that their business has sufficient trustworthiness in the marketplace to make such an agreement unnecessary: these are usually larger companies. For a small company, an NDA is of doubtful value as such a business is unlikely to have the resources to sue a major corporation for infringement with any chance of success. Large companies will often require you to sign their standard form of NDA and will not accept any other format. If this is the case, it is advisable to read the document very carefully as there may be clauses that could impose difficult or impossible burdens on your new business.

Let's Practise: Case Study

Important Intellectual Property, but Limited Protection: Pod Point Ltd

Pod Point was founded in April 2010 by Erik Fairbairn and Peter Hiscocks. The mission of the business is to 'contribute to transportation that does not harm the world' and its business objective is to become Europe's leading electric vehicle (EV) recharge business.

Erik originally had the idea for EV recharging in April 2009 and he set up a company called Infracharge with other investors. An EV recharging unit was designed and developed and the first sales were made. The product was not patented, but 'unregistered design rights' existed on the product. In March 2010, differences in strategy between Erik and the other investor resulted in Erik buying out the other investor with the assistance of Peter Hiscocks. The other investor wanted to stay in the EV recharge marketplace and there was a negotiation over the IP rights in Infracharge, specifically the IP relating to the 'design rights'. Infracharge changed to become Pod Point, and the other investor started a competitive company.

Why didn't Infracharge or Pod Point apply for a patent for the EV charger? Because Pod Point had a non-executive director who was a qualified patent attorney and he reviewed the technology and 'prior art' and determined that

13 Further information can be found at www.iprhelpdesk.eu/sites/default/files/newsdocu
ments/Fact-Sheet-IP-Management-H2020-Proposal-Stage.pdf

there was nothing novel about the EV chargers that were being developed. The core principles of charging electric vehicles were well understood and documented, and there was little scope for novelty and/or the novelty would not bring much value and would therefore not be worthwhile patenting. However, Pod Point did register all of its product designs, registered its trademark and has made sure to copyright the software used to run the back-office networks that manage the charging systems.

In 2012, Pod Point received a letter from a competing EV charge company claiming that they had patented the concept of charging EVs and that Pod Point had to stop making their chargers or had to pay for a licence to use the competitor's technology. The ex-patent attorney studied the 'prior art' and reviewed the patent literature extensively, and prepared a letter explaining to the competitor that the patent filing they had made had no validity as there was clear prior art. The competing company withdrew their claim against Pod Point.

This illustrates that 'holding a patent' does not always win the day, especially if your technical team has not carried out their IP reviews thoroughly. A weak patent is usually a waste of money and management time, as experienced and professional business teams will study the case carefully, will find the weaknesses in the patent and will refute it. In the case of Pod Point, the most effective ways of maintaining a competitive position in the marketplace is by using low-cost IP protection systems such as design right, trademark and copyright, maintaining trade secrets where necessary and continuing to innovate new products faster than the competition.

Questions for Discussion

1. If you were the senior management team at Pod Point, what are the issues that you would consider and use in the development of your IP strategy?
2. Is the current strategy suitable for the long term and if not, how should Pod Point evolve its strategy?
3. In an industry sector where there is little opportunity for 'novelty' (or at least, for novelty that provides sustainable competitive advantage) what are the most effective mechanisms to protect intellectual property and why?

12.5   Developing an IP Sstrategy

Intellectual property arises as a result of ideas, and ideas can be rather random. However, your business should not be random in its approach to IP and IP management; you need to develop a strategy. Firstly, you need to be clear about your overall business goals and objectives; these will drive your business strategy. This business strategy will also guide your IP strategy which will, in turn, be determined by the pace and effectiveness of your business's innovation activities.

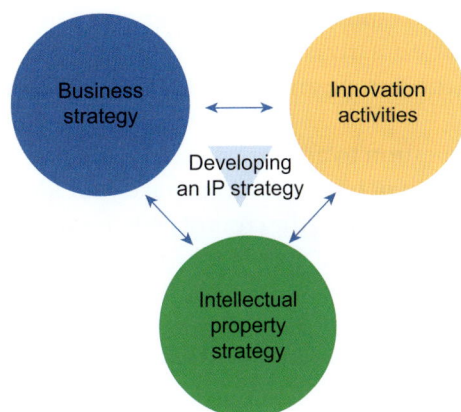

Figure 12.1 Developing an IP strategy.
Source: Derived from Seiko Epson business strategy planning

Your IP strategy should provide clarity on many important issues:

- How important is IP in your marketplace and how will you use it for competitive advantage in your business?
  - To prevent (or discourage) competitors from copying your products/services.
  - To license your technology to other companies.
  - To continue to develop innovations thereby keeping ahead of competitors (and providing a 'pipeline of licences' to current customers).
- Whether you need to protect the IP and, if so, the best method and approach.
- The costs likely to be incurred in achieving this IP protection and whether this is cost effective.
- Competitive IP analysis: what do your competitors have and how effective are they at developing new and better IP.

An effective IP strategy is also a good bargaining tool when it comes to negotiating the value of a business when raising funds (or possibly when selling all or some of the business). An effective and well thought-through patent strategy will show investors that a key element of value in the business has been reviewed and plans for the future development and exploitation of innovation have been made. In most businesses, this will correlate with an increase in the value of the business.

12.5.1 Should You Protect Your IP or Not?

It can cost more than €100,000 to patent a single invention with coverage in most major jurisdictions. As your business grows, there may be a number of products that you want to protect from copying and IP infringement. But do you want – or need – to spend that much money, particularly as those costs do not include policing costs for the IP and the renewal fees of the IP protection? It is often the case that smaller companies look to patent in too many countries at an early stage of development rather than securing the key markets like the Europe and United States, which are often sufficient for most industries.

It is a difficult question to answer, as each business will have to make its own assessment of the risks of having someone take your ideas and copy them versus the costs of protecting your IP, the costs of policing your IP and then the possible costs of a legal battle that you may or may not win.

There are some businesses where IP protection is very important: biochemistry and biotechnology; software; high end fashion items; computer games; film, video and music, although even here in some markets, such as music, there is a new move to make materials open source and to find other ways to generate revenue, such as holding gigs or selling merchandise. An example of this is the rock band Nine Inch Nails with Trent Reznor that releases its music on open source and earns money from gigs and selling band memorabilia. There are some businesses where IP protection is sometimes important but you will need to take a clear risk-versus-cost decision. Engineering or consumer products may fit into this category, as will many service-based businesses. You should draw up an analysis of where the potential risks are and then an analysis of the costs, both at the outset and of the ongoing renewal and policing costs.

Finally, there are many businesses where IP protection is not very relevant and can be a costly distraction. This includes most retail businesses, distribution, food, restaurants, gym clubs, etc. As before, think carefully: is there some intellectual property that is critical or important to my business and how much sense would it make to protect it. You need to ask yourself 'do I really need to do this and can I afford the costs?' If you want to protect your IP, review the methods described above and select the most appropriate one for your products and your business. It is also recommended that you take professional advice.

KEY TAKEAWAYS

- Ideas that are novel and that have the potential to create value for your business can be considered as intellectual property (IP). Your IP will enable you to differentiate your products and services from those of your competitors, allowing you to charge higher prices and generate more revenue. It will also add value to your business, should you wish to sell it at a future date.
- An IP strategy will be a useful tool for your business, and should include your overall business strategy and innovation activities. IP protection can be expensive, and you should only file a patent on your innovation if the benefits clearly outweigh the costs.

- There are many different ways to protect the intellectual property of your business. There are two broad classes of IP protection; registered IP and unregistered IP.
- Patents are granted for innovations that are novel and that have a practical application. They can provide up to twenty years of IP protection, but are expensive to obtain and uphold. Design rights offer a low-cost means of protecting the novel designs of physical products, and can offer up to twenty-five years of IP protection, when registered with the relevant patent or IP office.
- A trademark is an image used to signify that a particular product or service is supplied by your company. It is relatively cheap to register your trademark which must be distinctively different from other companies' trademarks. Trademarks and brands are more valuable for larger companies, but remember, large companies were all small once.
- Copyright is an unregistered form of IP protection and is used by many industries to protect their profitability. It can be difficult to police and you will have to undertake and pay for any legal action to prosecute offenders and to recover any lost profits. Complex and costly legal battles are not uncommon in this area.
- Trade secret is an unregistered and low-cost means of limiting the number of people who are party to information about how your product or service is made. It relies on the honesty and integrity of your employees; you may also ask people to sign non-disclosure documents (NDAs) to reduce the likelihood of the secret getting out.

END OF CHAPTER QUESTIONS

1. What steps would you take to determine the importance of intellectual property in the marketplace (and technology) where your new business is situated?
2. Make up a list of the characteristics of the main product or service of your new business and write against each function/characteristic whether this has novel IP. What are the alternate methods you could use to protect this IP?
3. What are the characteristics of a new idea that would enable you to patent it?
4. … and what are the first steps you would need to take to enable you to file a patent?
5. When you are developing your new idea, which is the foundation of your new business, what are the checks on IP that you should undertake?

6. What are the different methods for protecting your intellectual property and how should you select the most appropriate method for your product or service?
7. What are the issues you need to consider when making a decision about whether you should apply for a patent?
8. What are the key issues you need to consider in the development of your IP strategy? Why is it important for you to develop an IP strategy?
9. What are the issues that you need to consider to ensure that you have protected your business's IP in your various contracts; e.g. employment contract, terms of business, licence agreements, joint venture agreements, etc?
10. Prepare a list of ten new products or services that have been launched in the market recently. Determine which method of IP protection you would have recommended if this had been your product. Then check with the business (you will probably find the necessary information on the company website or product datasheets) to see what type of IP protection the company actually used.

FURTHER READING

Bergman, B. (2014). *The Intangible Investor: Profiting from Intellectual Property*. Close-up Media.
Palfrey, J. (2012). *Intellectual Property Strategy*. MIT Press.
Tormey. P. and Tormey, J. (2014). *Start-up Guide to Intellectual Property: Early stage protection of IP*. Create Space Publishing.
Witte, K. (2009). *Wertkonzeption Einer Nutzenbasierten Bewertung Von Patenten: Konzeptualisierung Eines Handlungsrahmens Zur Separierung Patentspezifischer Cash Flows*. (European University Studie) Peter Lang.

REFERENCES

Ferriani, S., Garnsey, G. and Lorenzoni, G. (2015). *The Intellectual Property Business Model: Lessons from ARM plc*. IfM University of Cambridge.
Pitkothly, P. (1997). *The Valuation of Patents*. Oxford Intellectual Property Research Centre, published by Cambridge Judge Business School WP 21/97 University of Cambridge.
Porter, M. (1980). *Competitive Strategy*. Free Press.
Copyright. www.eucopyright.com/
Design rights. https://euipo.europa.eu/ohimportal/en/designs www.albright-ip.co.uk/192013/12/six-registered-design-disasters-and-how-to-avoid-them/
Intellectual property overview. http://europa.eu/youreurope/business/start-grow/intellectual-property-rights/index_en.htm
Patent. Europe www.epo.org/applying/basics.html and UK www.gov.uk/apply-for-a-patent

US Patents www.ustpo.gov/patents-getting-started/general-information-concerning
    -patents
Trademark. https://euipo.europa.eu/ohimportal/en/trade-marks

Let's Practise: Case Study

Building a Business Based on the Strength of IP: ARM Holdings Ltd

In the 1980s, a UK computer hardware company called Acorn Computers developed a new technology for computer chips called RISC (Reduced Instruction Set Computing). RISC chips are much smaller than equivalent capability traditional chip designs and this makes them cheaper. Even more importantly, they use a lot less electrical power meaning that battery-powered devices, such as mobile phones and PDAs, last much longer between recharges. This new technology was spun-out from Acorn as a new business venture in 1990 called Advanced RISC Machines Ltd (later to become ARM Holdings Ltd). Acorn retained about 25 per cent of the equity whilst funding for the new business was raised from a corporate investor (Apple Inc. invested £1.75 million and computer chip manufacturer, VLSI Inc. £250,000). In the late 1990s, with Steve Jobs gone and Apple teetering on the brink of insolvency, Apple sold its ARM shares for $800 million (representing a growth multiple of 'times 285' on their investment) and was saved from going into bankruptcy. ARM was acquired recently by Japanese company Soft Bank for $24 billion, showing the value that IP can generate in a business.

This case study illustrates the importance that IP can deliver to the growth of a business and to its overall value. IP strategy has been core to the development and success of ARM, as one of the few European major computer chip companies. ARM, from the very beginning in 1990, decided that their business would be based on the development and sale of intellectual property as they did not have the resources to develop their own chip foundry and worldwide marketing and sales activities. Instead they sold licences to their IP to other computer chip manufacturers such as Intel, NXT, TI, and, of course, TSMC. These licences were not exclusive and so ARM could license the same technology to a number of different businesses. ARM has been very diligent in developing an IP strategy, and this includes developing a 'pipeline' of new IP so that companies that have licensed one generation of technology from ARM are then enticed to license the subsequent generations in order to keep up with developments in technology.

ARM protects its technology by a combination of patents, copyright and trade secret. ARM has protected its core technology with a series of strong patents, but it does not have a huge number of patents. ARM has also used copyright to protect software that is embedded in the computer chips and used trade secret to prevent competitors from sharing application knowledge about the chips. This type of 'layer approach' to IP protection can be very effective at protecting IP, as well as being cost effective.[14]

Questions for Discussion

1. If you were the senior management team at ARM, what are the issues that you would consider and use in the development of your IP strategy, and how would this impact the overall business model for the company?
2. How could the IP strategy for ARM influence or guide the business model that has enabled the extensive use of ARM technology?
3. Is the IP strategy that ARM has adopted suitable and appropriate for the long-term development of the business? If it should change then, why and how?

---

14 Ferriani *et al.* (2015).

PART IV

ALTERNATIVE ROUTES TO ENTREPRENEURSHIP

ENTREPRENEURSHIP THROUGH ACQUISITION (1): MBOS AND MBIS

MIGUEL MEULEMAN

Vlerick Business School and Imperial College Business School

HANS VANOORBEEK

Vlerick Business School and INSEAD

This chapter will provide insights on an alternative path to entrepreneurship, i.e. entrepreneurship through acquisition. Rather than starting a company from scratch, you can become owner-manager of a company by acquiring an existing company through a management buy-in or management buyout and use that company as a platform to pursue your entrepreneurial ambitions. Given the number of companies that change ownership every year and the risks involved in starting from scratch, for many individuals this might be a worthwhile route to consider when aspiring to become an entrepreneur. The process of buying a company requires a special skill set and mindset that differ from the traditional startup approach. The main goal of this chapter is to provide you with a step-by-step guide to the key questions to consider when buying a company.[1]

1 We would like to thank Professor Sophie Manigart (Vlerick Business School, Ghent University) and Professor Mathieu Luypaert (Vlerick Business School) for having provided access to some of their teaching material in this chapter.

FINANCIAL TIMES   FT

Lessons on buy-ins as well as lessons on start-ups are needed

Entrepreneurship teaching is too often limited to an academic exercise on business plan writing

AUGUST 21, 2012 BY SOPHIE MANIGART AND MIGUEL MEULEMAN

Jumping on the bandwagon set in motion by prestigious business schools, many business schools have embraced entrepreneurship as a core area in which they want to excel. Most of these programmes focus on how to set up and grow a new business. The ultimate goal, they claim, is to see a sizeable fraction of their graduates opt for a career as an entrepreneur and start a new venture. This goal, however, is hard to achieve. The route to starting and building a successful new venture is fraught with difficulties. Finding a value-creating business opportunity is not easy, especially for non-technical individuals operating outside technology clusters. And it is common knowledge that most of these ventures never achieve the growth hoped for in their business plan. Some may survive, others will be killed off due to lack of customer interest, finance, or the impossibility of delivering at acceptable costs. As a result, for many MBA graduates, entrepreneurship is limited to an academic exercise on business plan writing. But is this the only way to teach entrepreneurship? More and more MBA students aspire to be independent, rather than spending their professional career as managers in large companies being accountable to numerous layers of bosses. Another way to realize their entrepreneurial potential is to take over an existing company through a management buy-in. Given the huge number of company founders and owners who will retire in the coming decade, focusing on management buy-ins might prove a more fruitful route to put business students' entrepreneurial skills to work, for the students as well as the economy at large. In many business schools the course focus on start-up entrepreneurship and related business plan competitions has led to too little attention being placed on this fruitful avenue to entrepreneurial success. The risk in this type of operation is much lower than setting up a business from scratch: the company has already a product or service, there is a customer and supplier base, organizational routines have been developed, and so on. Business schools might teach their students how to take over companies as an alternative route to pursuing their entrepreneurial aspirations. This would include topics such as how to target a take-over candidate, how to perform due diligence, how to finance the deal, how to define a new strategic course to create value and how to replace the previous management. Focusing on entrepreneurial buy-ins is not only beneficial for students, but also from a wider economic perspective. Research has shown that mature companies largely benefit from this kind of change. New owners come with a new vision for the company. They often use the existing operations as a platform to develop new products and services and address new markets. In particular highly educated MBA graduates could develop new strategies to bring the companies to higher levels of efficiency and economic value. Moreover, hundreds of thousands of current company owners will be retiring in the coming years in both Europe and the US. Whereas company owners hitherto expected their sons or daughters to take over their family business, succession within the family is less and less assured. Finally, more and more private equity investors embrace these transactions compared with investing in high-risk start-ups. Hence, equipping MBA students with the skills to acquire an existing company may be especially valuable for students and companies alike. Additionally, this would provide an MBA programme with the opportunity to give a more realistic perspective on entrepreneurship and a business school a relevant route to differentiate itself from its peers.

www.ft.com/content/8a952a7e-c778-11e1-a850-00144feab49a

LEARNING OBJECTIVES

After reading this chapter you will be able to:

- Understand the advantages and disadvantages of buying an existing company as compared to taking the traditional start-up approach to entrepreneurship.
- Identify the different steps to take when buying a company.
- Understand different value-creation levers in a buyout transaction.
- Ask the key questions when assessing the attractiveness of a target.
- Understand how to value a target and structure a buyout transaction.
- Gain insights on how to leverage limited personal funds when buying a company.
- Have some basic understanding of the key contractual terms included in a share purchase agreement.

Where Are We Going Next?

This chapter will start with an introduction to entrepreneurship through acquisitions as compared to traditional startup entrepreneurship. It will continue by briefly outlining the different steps in the buyout process. Next, we will discuss how value can be created in a buyout transaction and how your due diligence should focus on value-creation levers. We will continue with the deal structuring process including the valuation and financing of a transaction. We will conclude with a brief overview of the main contractual terms to be considered when signing an agreement with a seller.

13.1   The Rationale for Buying Your Own Company

13.1.1   Becoming an Entrepreneur: A Make or Buy Decision

Many people consider the option of becoming an entrepreneur at one point in their career. Entrepreneurship is often represented in the popular media as the heroic act of starting a business from scratch with limited financial means and a high probability of never becoming profitable, as exemplified by the entrepreneur operating from a garage. However, have you ever considered buying an existing business and running it as a CEO in order to realize your entrepreneurial ambitions? If you have the managerial skills to lead and manage an organization and you prefer an organizational setting that is radically different from a traditional multinational company, buying yourself into a small or medium-sized business might offer a radically different career path. This entrepreneurial pathway has been referred to as 'entrepreneurship through acquisition'. We use the term 'entrepreneurial buyouts' to describe how individuals seek to acquire a majority stake in a company with the main goal of running the company on a day-to-day basis, often facilitated by funding provided by banks or other investors. A management buy-in (MBI) involves an outside manager or outside management team acquiring a stake in a target company thereby replacing the existing management, whereas a management buyout (MBO) involves the existing management team buying out the shareholders.

We use the Case Study of Frank Verschuere on page 366 and his acquisition of LS Bedding to illustrate the advantages of buying an existing company as compared to starting a business from scratch, which are:

- The probability of success is higher when compared to starting a business from scratch.
- You will start with an existing base of products and services, employees and customers which helps to generate immediate cash flow, enabling you to pay salaries, attract debt and invest in future opportunities.
- You may be more qualified to manage an existing company given your former experience in leading an existing company.
- You will have some existing cash flow and are therefore able to pay yourself some compensation.
- In some markets, the entry barriers might be too high to start from scratch as an individual.
- Overall, the financial returns of investing in existing, later-stage businesses has proved to be more attractive than investing in early-stage startups.[2]
- In most developed countries, there is a well-developed market supporting the process of buying and selling companies, including different funding options

However, there are also some disadvantages in buying an existing company:

- You buy a company with a history that might not be perfect.
- Changing the strategy and reputation of an existing company takes time and effort.

---

2 EVCA, (2013) Pan-European Private Equity Performance Benchmarks Study, Url: www .investeurope.eu/media/199202/2013-pan-european-private-equity-performance-benchmarks-study-evca-thomson-reuters-final-version.pdf (15–06-2017).

- You will often need a significant amount of your own financial resources to buy a company. Your own capital might be supplemented by capital provided by professional investors.
- As you will have spent a large amount of your personal wealth, your stress levels and risk profile are high.
- It takes time and effort to buy your own company. On average, it might take twelve to twenty-four months to succeed in buying a target. You clearly need perseverance.
- You will often be competing with other buyers, including strategic buyers who can realize synergies when buying a specific target and, therefore, are often willing to pay a premium.

In the European Union alone, business transfers affect up to 450,000 SMEs and 2 million jobs every year.[3] There are many reasons why thousands of companies change hands every year, offering an opportunity for an entrepreneurial buyout. Firstly, many owner-managers want to retire at a certain age and lack internal successors. Secondly, owner-managers might be forced to sell their business at a certain point for a variety of reasons, including illness, financial issues or conflicts with business partners. Thirdly, some entrepreneurs who have launched a business become bored of managing a business or lack the skill set to grow and professionalize it. Finally, existing companies often sell divisions or business lines that no longer fit the strategy of the parent company.

There is significant variety in terms of the businesses that come up for sale every year, and many of those businesses aren't as glamorous as the fast-growing tech companies the business press covers on a daily basis. However, some of them are quite unique and offer much-needed products and services in a B2B and B2C context. For example, did you ever consider buying one of the following companies: a balloon printing company, a specialized moving company, a metal box gift packaging company, a cleaning products production company, a specialized software company, a fish-smoking business, an elevator servicing company, an electrical part manufacturer, a certification company, a specialized engineering company in aircraft composite material or a glass transformer? These firms often go unnoticed but can generate annual revenues in the range of €2 to €20 million, with healthy cash flow margins. Overall, they can provide attractive returns to different type of investors.

Let's Practise: Case Study
Frank's dream

Frank Verschuere, CEO and owner of LS Bedding, looked back at the decision he had taken almost twenty years earlier to buy the company LS Bedding. LS Bedding designs, manufactures and commercializes high-quality mattresses

3 Van Teeffelen *et al.* (2016).

and bed bases and has been operating from 1946 onwards. In 1999, Frank's brother presented him with an opportunity he had heard of through his business club, as the former owner of LS Bedding was considering retirement. The company had a good reputation and was located near to where Frank lived. The company had a turnover of €7.8m and generated an EBIT margin of 2.4 per cent.

Frank had been considering buying a company after he had gained an MBA from Vlerick Business School in Belgium. He had pursued an international career, beginning at Johnson Wax then at ICI Paints in the UK, where he later became general manager for the Benelux business. However, by 1999, Frank realized he wasn't satisfied with his current job, as he started to get frustrated with the structure of a large multinational. He wanted to be his own boss with the freedom and autonomy to run a business as he saw fit. However, he wasn't sure how easy it would be to buy a company. Before he set out on his search to acquire a company, he drew up a list of acquisition criteria he would use to evaluate potential targets. He came up with the following list:

- potential to personally lead,
- possibility of understanding customers and products,
- ability to build up a brand,
- organic growth potential,
- easy to understand business operations,
- quality reputation and products that live up to certain ethical standards,
- close geographical proximity or easy travel access,
- stable industry with 'controllable' revenues and expenses, and
- mature company with stable cash flow.

While he was still working for ICI Paints, he started to meet with potential sellers, bankers, accountants and brokers to find targets. It was a time-consuming process that took almost fourteen months to come to fruition. Before he ended up buying LS Bedding, he had looked into more than 100 acquisition opportunities, around 15 of which he spent a couple of hours' work on, analyzing the details of the investment opportunity. Finally, he signed two letters of intent (LOI), one of which ended up in a successful acquisition. After a long journey, he bought LS Bedding together with an insider, Peter De Meyer, who had been the financial and operations manager at LS Bedding for a decade.

By 2015, LS Bedding was generating a turnover of €21.5m with a healthy EBIT margin of 12.5 per cent, and employed 113 employees. Frank and his team had succeeded in leveraging the initial brand awareness and created one of the most recognizable and reputable brands of mattresses and bed bases in the Belgian market. Additionally, they managed to turn the company around from being barely profitable to generating a steady and healthy profit and cash flow margin.

In 2012, Frank attracted private equity funding to invest in international expansion and to cash in part of his initial investment. Clearly, LS Bedding had enabled Frank to realize his entrepreneurial ambitions and financially he had earned more than what he probably could have earned in a corporate career. He was proud of his achievement and was often invited to share his story with aspiring entrepreneurs.

13.1.2   The Process of Buying a Company

Buying a company involves a number of different steps, as described in Figure 13.1. Steps 1 through 3 are covered in detail in Chapter 14. As a first step, you will need to decide as an individual how you will tackle the search process. Some individuals give up their job to fully concentrate on

Preparing your search
- Determine your search strategy
- Develop your acquisition criteria
- Develop your personal pitch

Identifying companies
- Activate your network and contact intermediairies
- Approach potential targets
- Perform preliminary due diligence

Proposing an offer
- Start early negotiations with the seller
- Make a preliminary valuation
- Make an offer and sign a letter of intent

Structuring the transaction
- Prepare a detailed valuation of the company
- Arrange bank financing
- Arrange equity financing (if needed)

Due diligence
- Prepare a detailed business plan
- Perform confirmatory due diligence
- Verify main assumptions underlying the business plan

Preparing the legal documents
- Prepare share purchase agreement
- Prepare shareholder agreement
- Close the deal

Managing the company
- Communicate with the employees
- Become familiar with the company and its stakeholders
- Manage the financial and operational dashboard

Figure 13.1 Buyout process.

this. One major advantage of doing this is that it enables you to scan more targets and act more quickly should an opportunity arise. Additionally, potential sellers and intermediaries will take you more seriously if you show such a high level of commitment. Finally, if you decide to give up your job, you won't need to worry about your current employer becoming aware of your search and, therefore, you will be able to communicate your intention to buy a company more openly. Rather than giving up their job, some people decide to act as an interim consultant, or to keep their existing job while looking for targets. Clearly, this pathway poses less risk as it enables you to generate a steady stream of income. However, this may hamper your search process, as you cannot devote your time to examining acquisition targets. Which road you will take clearly depends on your risk preference.

During this first step, you will need to think carefully about the search criteria you will apply when identifying targets: size of the company, industry, location, minority versus majority position, active versus passive involvement, investment horizon, stage of the company, willingness to team up with others, etc. Obviously, these search criteria will help you to filter the large number of prospects you will encounter and help you to determine which prospects deserve more attention. An additional reason for having search criteria is that it will help to define how you sell yourself vis-'a-vis a potential seller. As you will be competing with other buyout candidates and other buyers in the market, you want to get on the radar of intermediaries. Having a clear and well-defined profile might help you to be at the top of the list when they look for buyout candidates.

The second step involves identifying acquisition targets by approaching a diverse set of players in the market: brokers, corporate finance advisors, business networks, accountants, matching platforms, bankers. You will also need to activate your network in order to get introduced to potential acquisition targets. For most buyout entrepreneurs, this process proves to be the most challenging and frustrating part of the journey. As an individual entrepreneur, you will often find yourself at the end of the food chain in the takeover market. The most attractive companies often end up in the hands of either strategic buyers or private equity investors with deeper pockets and strong, well-established networks. Your best chance might be to identify proprietary deal flow or deals that have not yet been advertised as being for sale. Given the importance of the search process, Chapter 14 will provide more detail on the tips and tricks of finding companies for sale.

The third step, after having identified a company that is for sale and carried out a positive preliminary due diligence, is to draw up a first indicative offer by proposing a letter of intent (LOI). The LOI includes a number of terms that describe your proposed acquisition offer and outlines the concrete steps needed to come to a final agreement.

These include:

- a price indication, often expressed as a range,
- 'assumptions made', outlining all the assumptions where the price is based on such as the given historic and projected profit and loss, the latest balance sheet, etc.,
- a 'subject to' clause outlining conditions such as satisfactory commercial and financial due diligence, obtaining appropriate debt funding, receiving normal reps and warranties, etc.,
- a 'good and prudent housefather' clause which requires the current owner to run the business as normal without doing crazy things (e.g. raising the salaries of the key managers) after signing the LOI,
- a plan for conducting due diligence, describing what data you would like to consult and who you would like to talk to (e.g. company employees, suppliers),
- if possible, an exclusivity agreement for a couple of weeks or even months to exclude other candidate buyers,
- some initial guarantees (e.g. guarantees with respect to taxes),
- a description of your future intentions for the business and your post-transaction relationship with the seller,
- confidentiality agreement,
- the timing and next steps, and
- termination stipulations or how you will terminate the agreement if no final agreement is reached.

The LOI is the basis for further negotiations and the drafting of the final share purchase agreement. In most cases, you should be able to draft your own LOI based on a template. However, if you feel uncertain or lack experience in drafting an LOI, you should seek appropriate advice. A lawyer can at a little cost always take a look at it. From a tactical point of view, the LOI is equally a sales tool: you don't want to make it too detailed or be too harsh on the seller as it might scare sellers away. At all times, you should keep the door open by staying flexible. Signing a well-drafted LOI will significantly increase your chances of getting a deal done. You will also want to avoid spending money on different types of advisors (e.g. financial due diligence) before you have a signed LOI. Otherwise you risk ending up with no money left in your pocket before actually having to pay the acquisition price.

As a fourth and fifth step, you will start to structure the transaction and conduct the confirmatory due diligence. Both steps will run in parallel and in an iterative way. The key questions to be addressed when structuring the deal are what is the final price that you are prepared to pay and how will you finance the transaction. Even if you have done some preliminary work when drafting your LOI, you will need to have banks and other investors (if needed) lined up to provide the necessary funding under acceptable terms and conditions. This stage will, therefore, involve negotiations with multiple banks and, potentially, discussions with equity investors such as business angels or private equity investors should your personal budget be insufficient to provide the necessary equity. At this stage, you might also want to negotiate with the vendor to help you finance part of the acquisition price by providing a vendor note, which is a delayed payment in the form of a credit. Another element of the structuring phase is to think about how, in legal terms, you are going to acquire the target, for example, via a holding company specially set up for this purpose.

During the confirmatory due diligence, you will check whether your initial assumptions with respect to the acquisition target were correct and you will draw up a detailed business plan enabling you to verify your valuation and outline your post-implementation action plan. This phase is clearly time-intensive, and generally requires the involvement of specialist advisors to check specific assumptions. During the confirmatory due diligence, you will have the opportunity to gain access to detailed documents, contracts, employees, suppliers and managers. You clearly want to learn as much as possible during this stage to verify your underlying investment hypotheses. Often, issues will arise that fundamentally alter your perception of the company and impact on your willingness to pay the initially agreed price in the LOI or, in some cases, even lead you to terminate the deal.

As a sixth step, you will appoint lawyers to assist you in the final negotiations with the seller and to draw up all the necessary contracts and documents that are required to legally close the deal. It's clear that you will need to protect yourself as a buyer from hidden liabilities, and to make sure that the seller is legally accountable if certain information has been misrepresented or comes to light after the deal has been signed.

Lastly, when the deal is finally closed you will become the new owner of the company and your long and exhausting journey will finally be rewarded. Now the real work starts, and it becomes your responsibility to manage the company and turn it into a sustainable business for the future. You will want to learn as much as possible about the day-to-day business of running the company and you will want to become familiar with its employees, suppliers, customers and other stakeholders to provide for continuity. At the same time, you will need to closely monitor your financials and other operational key performance indicators, as you will require cash to repay your debt and other obligations.

13.1.3   Understanding Value Creation in a Buyout Transaction

Before starting your buyout journey, it is important to understand how you can create value in a buyout transaction or how you can realize a return on your invested capital. There are different levers for creating value in a buyout transaction and ideally you will have identified different value-creation levers during your due diligence to lower the risk when buying a company. To understand how to generate value in a buyout transaction, you should be familiar with the following formulae (as seen in Chapter 8, figure 8.2) describing the value of a company:

$$\text{Total Enterprise Value} = \text{Equity Value} + \text{Debt} - \text{Cash} \tag{1}$$

As an owner, you will invest in the equity (i.e. the shares of the company) and, therefore, you are interested in the equity value. We can state Equation (1) as follows:

$$\text{Equity Value} = \text{Total Enterprise Value} - \text{Debt} + \text{Cash} \tag{2}$$

The total enterprise value is often calculated as a multiple of EBITDA, as described in Chapter 8 on traditional valuation methodologies. Therefore:

$$\text{Total Enterprise Value} = \text{EBITDA} \times \text{multiple}$$

With EBITDA = (Revenues × EBITDA margin) and Net financial debt = (Debt – Cash).

Therefore, we can rewrite Equation (2) as follows:

$$\text{Equity Value} = (\text{Revenues} \times \text{EBITDA margin}) \times \text{multiple} - \text{Net financial debt.} \tag{3}$$

The formula expressed in Equation (3) outlines the different value levers you have when buying a company:

- the valuation multiple,
- revenues,
- EBITDA margin, and
- net financial debt.

If you want to enhance the equity value, you will need to change one of these components. Figure 13.2 illustrates the return on equity in a buyout transaction using these different components. The internal rate of return on the equity equals 38 per cent in the example. Given the risk, the involvement of the buyer and the illiquidity of the investment, a normal expected return on investment in smaller buyout transactions should be at least 25 per cent annually. A higher return is, of course, a surplus.

Based on these relatively simple accounting principles of creating value in a buyout transaction, Berg and Gottschalg (2004) outline a framework that practitioners can use to understand the structure of value generation levers. This framework is illustrated in Figure 13.3 and explained below.

Value-capturing Mechanism

The first lever to create value is related to changes in the multiple valuation, which will be the difference between the multiple you pay to acquire the target and the multiple valuation you receive when selling the target. There

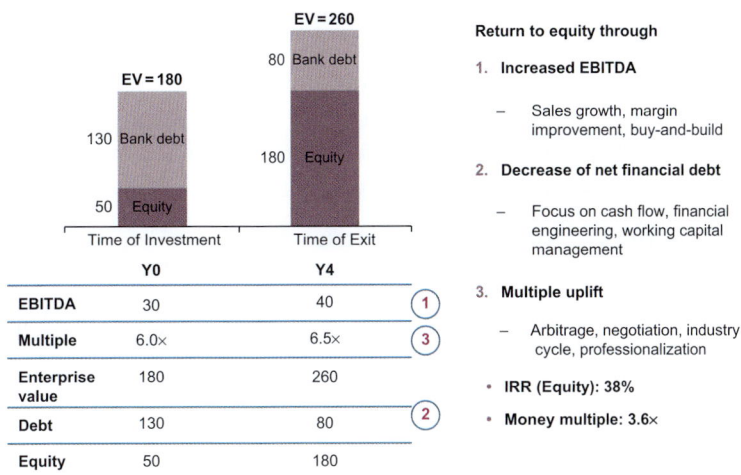

Figure 13.2 Return to equity in a buyout transaction.

Return to equity through

1. **Increased EBITDA**
   - Sales growth, margin improvement, buy-and-build

2. **Decrease of net financial debt**
   - Focus on cash flow, financial engineering, working capital management

3. **Multiple uplift**
   - Arbitrage, negotiation, industry cycle, professionalization

- **IRR (Equity): 38%**
- **Money multiple: 3.6×**

	Y0	Y4	
EBITDA	30	40	(1)
Multiple	6.0×	6.5×	(3)
Enterprise value	180	260	
Debt	130	80	(2)
Equity	50	180	

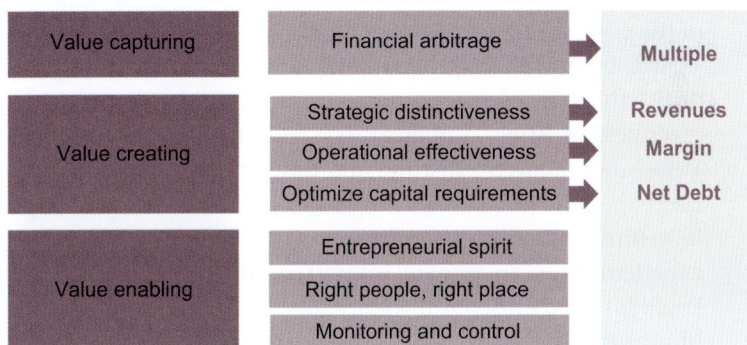

Figure 13.3 Value generation framework in a buyout.
Source: Adapted from Berg and Gottschalg (2004)

are several factors that will influence a multiple uplift, i.e. buy low and sell high:

- To what extent did you negotiate a good price when buying the target? Maybe you had superior information with respect to the underlying target or you dealt with an unsophisticated seller. Additionally, there might have been limited competition for the target company as you identified the deal through proprietary deal flow or few buyers were interested in the target.

- By professionalizing or even strategically redirecting the company and improving the financial health of the company, you can increase the valuation multiple potential buyers are willing to pay.

- By making some strategic complementary add-on acquisitions, you will be able to benefit from possible synergies and cause your company to become larger. In general, higher multiples are paid for larger companies.
- You might benefit from an overall uplift in multiples paid for similar companies because of general economic conditions or an improved outlook within the industry the company is operating in.

Clearly, a lot of value can be destroyed if you overpay when buying the target. The price you negotiate with the seller and the buyer at the time of the acquisition and divesture is therefore essential. Given the fact that you can potentially increase the value of the equity without any underlying changes in the underlying financials, this type of value generation has been described as 'value capturing'.

Value-creation Mechanism

The second source of value generation refers to actions you take as a manager to change the underlying financial performance of the company by increasing the revenues and operational margins or by lowering the net financial debt position of the company.

First, by optimizing the strategy of the company and changing the strategic distinctiveness of the company you might be in a position to increase the revenues of the company. To take the example of LS Bedding, Frank Verschuere created a distinct and unique brand position with a focus on customer experience for one of the bedding brands. Additionally, he improved relationships with a number of retailers that enabled him to create a unique selling experience for customers interested in buying products from LS Bedding. Finally, he expanded internationally into France and Germany which enabled him to target a significantly larger market. These strategic actions clearly take time and effort and need a long-term perspective to come to fruition.

Increased revenue can either happen through an organic growth strategy or through a buy-and-build strategy. For example, Mark Vandecruys, a Belgian buy-in entrepreneur and currently owner-manager of Fedrus International NV, created a construction material group specializing in roofing material with a turnover of around €650 million and an EBITDA of €50 million through a buy-and-build strategy, starting from an initial buy-in of a company with €4.2 million turnover and having made twelve add-on acquisitions over a period of twelve years.

Second, by enhancing the operational effectiveness of the target company you can improve the margins and the operational cash flow the company is able to generate. Frank Verschuere of LS Bedding achieved several quick wins by installing a cost-cutting programme, given that the company wasn't always professionally managed by the previous owner. For example, he outsourced several non-core activities, including transportation. He also decided to cut the number of unprofitable small customers who were unwilling to pay higher prices. Additionally, he hired a professional purchase manager to renegotiate contracts with key suppliers. These interventions enabled LS Bedding to improve its operational efficiency in a relatively short period of time.

Third, by minimizing the capital requirements of the business and paying off debt you can lower the net financial debt position and increase the equity value. One key element for lowering the capital requirements of the underlying target is to optimize the working capital requirements. For example, Frank Verschuere of LS Bedding installed a professional inventory management system that lowered the required inventory. Together with his financial partner, he more strictly managed the accounts receivable. These interventions enabled him to free up hidden cash from the operations of the business and to lower the net financial debt position of the company. Additionally, by renegotiating debt with banks, they obtained more favourable interest terms which again increased the available cash and hence the net financial debt.

In summary, value-creation mechanisms refer to actions you can take as a manager to enhance the value of the company. Many small businesses offer opportunities to create value, as the former owners might not have been very professional in running their business or might not have had the energy or insight to put the company onto a new growth trajectory. In general, you will often discover during your due diligence opportunities to enhance the value of a small business by implementing simple management techniques.

Value-enabling Mechanism

The third lever of value generation in a buyout transaction which enables value creation concerns the managers and the employees and the incentives provided to them to run the business in a professional way. By introducing new ownership, new energy will often flow into the business. The entrepreneurial abilities of the buyout or buy-in manager combined with the incentive of ownership often leads to the exploitation of new opportunities. For example, a subsidiary of a large company might not have been viewed as strategic to the parent company or might not have received the financial resources it needed to stay competitive. In such a case, a divisional buyout will often provide the impetus to put the former subsidiary on a new growth path.

An important value enabler in many buyout transactions is the monitoring and control imposed by banks (Jensen 1989), outside investors or the new owners entering the company (Cumming *et al.* 2007). Banks will typically include covenants when granting debt which will push the company to work efficiently. Outside investors, such as professional private equity companies, will regularly meet with the managers of the company, require detailed reporting, and exercise control through board membership which will discipline managers to work hard and follow previously agreed objectives (similar to entrepreneurs' milestones with venture capitalists, as seen in Chapter 10). Finally, when a buyout happens, this often provides the new owners with an opportunity to replace ineffective management or employees and to offer revised employment contracts which include better performance incentives, or even to offer some key employees the opportunity to have some equity participation in the transaction. For example, when Frank Verschuere acquired LS Bedding he hired a new production manager and even increased the salaries of a significant number of employees, given that the previous owner was underpaying them.

13.2   Deal Structuring

13.2.1   Introduction

The key questions in any buyout transaction are how much are you willing to pay to buy the target company and how will you finance the transaction. When you are writing the letter of intent, you will need to give an indication of the price you are prepared to pay. Determining a reasonable price for buying a small company is often not an easy task. Different valuation methods often produce different results, and small changes to the underlying assumptions can significantly impact your valuation. Many experts have stated that valuation is as much a science as it is an art. It is a science because there are well-established methodologies to rely on, including discounted cash flow analyses and multiple valuation. It is an art because you often will need to adjust your valuation according to the specificities of the underlying target (e.g. real estate) and prevailing economic conditions. Overall, it's important to model different deal structures and to study the impact of changing key underlying assumptions.

We will use the case of SeaSmoke to illustrate how an entrepreneurial buy-in of a small company can be structured.

Let's Practise: Case Study

The Entrepreneurial Buy-in of SeaSmoke

After a long career in banking, and having occupied a top position in a major French bank, Philippe Lepoutre decided to pursue one of his dreams and become an entrepreneur through acquisition. One of the brokers in the area where he lived presented him with the opportunity to buy a fish smoking company, SeaSmoke,[4] just before the summer of 2012. SeaSmoke was founded in 1875, and is one of the last traditional fish smokeries in Calais, France. The main owner wanted to sell as he was retiring. The table below contains key data describing the SeaSmoke investment opportunity as provided by the broker in the investment memorandum.

---

4 The name and the location of the company have been disguised as some of the data is confidential.

SeaSmoke Investment Opportunity

Basic information

- Active since 1875.
- Focused on smoking pelagic fish such as sprat, sprat fillet, herring and herring fillet, mackerel and mackerel fillets. Specialties like slices of hot smoked salmon, salmon Belle Vue, trout, halibut, dogfish, curled strips of smoked dogfish, freshwater eel and claresse complete the product portfolio.
- Former owner acquired the company in 1996. In 2005, the son-in-law of the main owner joined the management team.
- In 1997, a new production unit was built.

Customers

- SeaSmoke has a strong focus on retail with a market share of 90% in the niche and region (Northern France) in which it operates.
- Types of customers.

  - Retailers   +/− 20   +/−90% Turnover.
  - Wholesalers   +/− 10   +/−10% Turnover.
  - Industry (producers of salads, . . .).

- Number of customers.

  - Currently the company serves approximately fifty customers.
  - 83 per cent of the total turnover is realized by ten customers.
  - In 2011, a total of 3700 invoices were issued.
  - Almost all customers are repeat buyers who order on a regular basis.

- Regional focus

  - +/− 90% of the total turnover is realized in the north of France, +/− 10% is exported to Belgium and Germany.

People

- CEO is responsible for:

  - Daily direction, budgeting with internal accountant, purchasing, selling, contracting with clients, cost/price calculations.

- Four white-collar staff.

- One full-time person being responsible for production, production planning, inventory management – 6 years seniority.
- One full-time person who assists the production leader – 4 years seniority.
- One part-time person responsible for administration, invoicing – 30 hours/week, 15 years seniority.
- One part-time person taking care of accounting, cash planning, budgeting and HR – 26 hours/ week, 10 years seniority.

- Twenty-two labourers active in production on a fixed contract.

Operations

- SeaSmoke fulfils the highest quality standards.
- Transportation is outsourced to a specialized company.
- Machinery and car fleet.

  - Modern production process with continuous investments.
  - New investments were made (700k EUR) in a new filleting machine and a packaging station.
  - The new packaging machine enables a variety of packaging choices depending on the client's wishes.
  - Future investments limited.
  - Car fleet: two leased cars (BMW, Citroen) and one hired car (Ford Transit).

Key P&L Figures

€ amounts	31/03/2011	31/03/2012	Forecasted 31/03/2013
Turnover	7,035,000	7,475,000	7,900,000
EBIT	261,000	234,000	450,000
Depreciation and amortization	192,000	249,000	278,000
EBITDA	453,000	483,000	728,000

The accounting year of SeaSmoke historically always closes at the end of March. The most recent available published data reflects the 12 month period ending at 31 March 2012. The strong increase in expected EBITDA in 2013 reflects high expected cost savings as a result of recent investments in filleting and packaging machines. This amount should capture the impact of increased productivity and a reduction in salary costs.

Key Balance Sheet Figures

€ amounts	31/03/2011	31/03/2012
Equity	1,544,000	1,738,000
Financial debt	1,125,000	1,264,000
Cash	66,000	218,000

Note: the company still has tax losses carried forward equalling €2.4 million.

Real Estate

- The company owns the following real estate:
  - Land: 7892 m^2.
  - Offices: 394 m^2.
  - Production hall: 1666 m^2.

- The property is up-to-date and is part of a modern industrial zone in a strategic position with good connections with suppliers and customers – industrial zone in Calais.

  - There is an opportunity to expand – the land next door is for sale.

- An assessor has estimated the value of the property to be worth €1,614,340.
- The environmental and operating licence runs till 22/08/2016.

SWOT Analyses

- Strengths.

  - Market share of 90 per cent in retail market.
  - Strong product (sprat fillet) with high gross margin.
  - Oldest fish smoking company in north of France with well-established reputation.
  - Fulfils highest quality standards.
  - Large portfolio of smoked products.
  - Modern production facilities with limited future investment needs.
  - Modern property on industrial zone with strategic location.

- Weaknesses.

  - Dependent on fish supply with considerable price fluctuations – however, strong market position enables SeaSmoke to pass on price increases to customers.

- Opportunities.

  - Increased efficiency because of continuing investments.

- Potential to further internationalize in Belgium, Germany and Russia.
- Sprat is recognized as regional product, European recognition under way.
- Possibility to increase current product portfolio.

Purchasing Offer

- The purchasing price for all outstanding shares which are owned by the family equals:

  - €2,200,000 based on a weighted average corrected EBITDA of the year running from 31/03/2011 to 31/03/2012 multiplied by 6.9; cash and debt free from 31/03/2012.
  - + an earn out equal to the realised EBITDA on 31/03/2013.

- Guarantees offered by seller.

  - Standard guarantees.

Questions for Discussion

1. Would you personally be interested in buying this company at a fair price? Why? Why not?
2. What research would you undertake to assess the potential of this company?
3. How could you contribute to increasing the value of the company?
4. Suppose you are interested in buying this company, do you personally think the price asked to acquire the shares is too high, fair or too low?
5. What is the maximum price you would be willing to pay to acquire the shares in this company?
6. How will you finance the transaction? Outline your sources and uses of funds.

13.2.2   Valuation of a Buyout Target

Many valuation techniques exist for valuing a company, as discussed in Chapter 8 on valuation. In practice, practitioners often rely on the multiple method when valuing a buyout target. More specifically, the price of a small company is often stated as a multiple of EBITDA. In the smaller deal segment, the EBITDA multiple typically ranges between 3 and 6 times EBITDA. Therefore, a company with an EBITDA of €500k would be priced between €1,500,000 and €3,000,000. In Figure 13.4 you will find an overview of average EBITDA multiples paid in M&A transactions for different deal ranges in the Belgian market over the period 2013 through 2016.

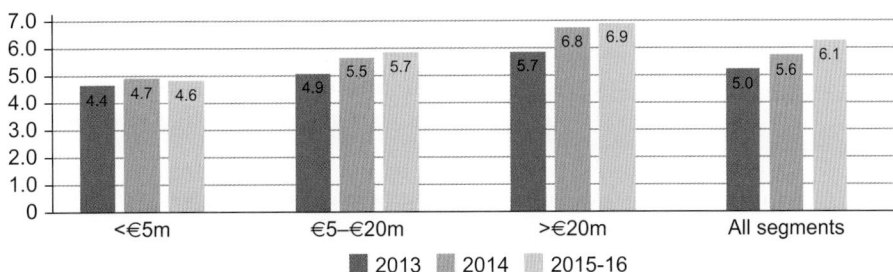

Figure 13.4 Evolution Enterprise Value / EBITDA multiples for different deal ranges.
Source: Luypaert (2016)

It is clear from these figures that multiples evolve from year to year depending on market conditions. More specifically, the availability of cheap debt, the level of dry powder in the private equity market and the overall economic outlook have a major impact on the price that needs to be paid to buy a company.

Even though most valuations of small companies will fall in a range of 3 × to 6 × EBITDA there is still a difference between paying 3 × EBITDA and paying 6 × EBITDA. Therefore, you will need to make an assessment of where the company fits into the range. Factors that will influence the valuation range include:

- The future growth potential of the company and the industry in which it operates. The higher the future growth of the company, the more cash flows the firm will generate and the higher the price you might be willing to pay today.
- How uncertain are the future cash flows of the company? Are you buying a company with recurring revenue and long-term contracts with customers or are you buying a project-based company with significant fluctuations in cash flows? Clearly, the more predictable the future cash flows, the less risk and the higher the price one should be prepared to pay.
- How professionally has the business been run and how easy will it be to take over as a new owner? In small companies, the company often depends on a few key people, including the previous owner, to run the business and generate sales. This clearly increases the risks when acquiring the business and hence the price one should be willing to pay. Larger companies are on average more professionally managed and less dependent on a few individuals to be successful.
- As the EBITDA does not take into account capital expenditures (e.g. machinery) and working capital requirements (e.g. inventory, accounts receivable), companies that need significant capital expenditures or high levels of working capital to run and scale the business will generally be priced lower, as cash flow conversion will be lower. It is therefore always a good sanity check to compare

the EBITDA multiple with an 'EBITDA minus expected future capex' multiple. The latter takes into consideration the impact future capital expenditures have on the cash flow. If this multiple is much higher than the EBITDA multiple, you should be careful that you do not pay too high a price.

Using the example of SeaSmoke, one could look at trading multiples of companies active in food processing and wholesale food supplies to get an early indication of the multiple range. In 2012, food processing companies and food wholesalers on average traded at an EV/EBITDA multiple of 9.70 and 6.11 respectively, giving an average EV/EBITDA of 7.91. However, one should apply a size and illiquidity discount of at least 25 per cent,[5] which leads to a multiple of 5.93.

Bureau Van Dijk's M&A database[6] provides a list of comparable transactions under 'Processing, preserving and wholesale of fish, crustaceans and mollusc'. Even though it's difficult to find a similar transaction, given that most deals are in other geographies and are on average larger, there was one reported transaction in Poland with a multiple of 5.6. Overall, a multiple of around 6 seems justified. In Table 13.1, we look at the valuation outcome for a multiple analysis with EV/EBITDA multiples ranging between 5.5 and 6.5, and use both the 2012 reported EBITDA and the forecasted figure for 2013. As the due diligence exposed some items that justified a discount, the price was adjusted by €53,000. This discount reflected some of the inventory that had exceeded its expiry date.

Table 13.1 shows that there is still significant variation in the equity value you obtain depending on the multiple used and whether you use the 2012 cash flow or the predicted 2013 cash flow. The key question, therefore, is whether you believe that the company will be able to generate a cash flow of €728,000 in 2013, which is a 50 per cent increase over 2012.

As the SeaSmoke case illustrates, there might still be considerable uncertainty with respect to the underlying cash flows the company will be able to generate in the future. There is a significant risk that the seller has been creative in 'dressing up the bride', and has, for example, managed earnings to look more promising than they really are, or manipulated working capital to lower the net financial debt position of the company. Additionally, the cash flow of the buyout target might have been impacted by non-recurrent transactions (e.g. exceptional expenses) or non-business-related expenses, including the private expenses of the owner. Therefore, during the confirmatory due diligence the quality of the cash flows (normalized EBITDA), the quality of the net working capital (normalized net working capital), the required level capital expenditures going forward and the overall net financial debt position of the target will need to be assessed.

In the SeaSmoke case, the significant increase in cash flow from 2012 to 2013 could be explained by the installation of a new filetting machine and packaging station in 2012, as mentioned in the investment memorandum. These new

5 Damodaran (2009).
6 www.bvdinfo.com/en-gb/home

Table 13.1 SeaSmoke multiple valuation

€ *amounts*	31/03/2012			Forecasted 31/03/2013		
Multiple	5.5	6	6.5	5.5	6	6.5
× EBITDA	483,000	483,000	483,000	728,000	728,000	728,000
= Enterprise Value	**2,656,500**	**2,898,000**	**3,139,500**	**4,004,000**	**4,368,000**	**4,732,000**
– Financial debt	–1,264,000	–1,264,000	–1,264,000	–1,264,000	–1,264,000	–1,264,000
+ Cash	218,000	218,000	218,000	218,000	218,000	218,000
– Due dil corrections	–53,000	–53,000	–53,000	–53,000	–53,000	–53,000
= Equity Value	**1,557,500**	**1,799,000**	**2,040,500**	**2,905,000**	**3,269,000**	**3,633,000**

investments lowered the need for manpower, and early data in 2012 indeed showed that the EBITDA had increased considerably following this investment. As Phillipe Lepoutre (the buyer) and the former owner still disagreed on sustainability of these improvements, they decided to include an earnout in the deal structure. In an earnout, the buyer and the seller agree that a certain percentage of the acquisition price will be variable and depend on future results. In the case of SeaSmoke, the following was agreed in the earnout provision based upon the EBITDA realized in 2013:

- No earnout would be paid if EBITDA < €483,000 (=EBITDA of 2012).
- Full pay out of EBITDA above €483,000 (with maximum of €350,000).
- Half of the EBITDA realized above €833,000.

Based on this, Philippe Lepoutre agreed on an equity valuation of €2,926,000, which included the earnout provision and a discount for the expired inventory of €53,000. Given that the 2013 EBITDA turned out to be much better than expected, i.e. €997,000, an earnout of €432,000 had to be paid. This can be calculated as follows:

- Tranche 1 = €833,000 − €483,000 = €350,000.
- Tranche 2 = (€997,000 − €833,000)/2 = €82,000.
- Total extra payment = €350,000 + €82,000 = €432,000.

Therefore, the final price paid to acquire the equity equalled €3,358,000. As the net financial debt position of the target was equal to €1,046,000 in 2012, the total enterprise value was equal to €4,404,000 (= 3,358,000 +1,046,000). Based on this number, we can calculate the multiple that was actually paid in this transaction:

- Based on EBITDA 2012 = €4,298,000/ €483,000 = 9.1 × EBITDA.
- Based on EBITDA 2013 forecasted = €4,298,000/ €728,000 = 6 × EBITDA.
- Based on EBITDA 2013 actual = €4,298,000/ €997,000 = 4.4 × EBITDA.

Overall, the price Philippe Lepoutre paid to acquire SeaSmoke seems reasonable and ultimately, given the actual results in 2013, he paid a relatively low price to acquire this small company.

13.2.3   Financing the Transaction

Agreeing on an appropriate price with the seller is the first step in signing a letter of intent. However, the seller will also want to have an indication of how you will pay for the transaction and where you will obtain the necessary funding. After all, the seller wants to be sure that you will be able to put the money on the table. When signing a letter of intent, you should already know what sources of funding you will use to close the deal. Figure 13.5, sources and uses of funds, outlines the different sources of funding and how you might use them in a transaction.

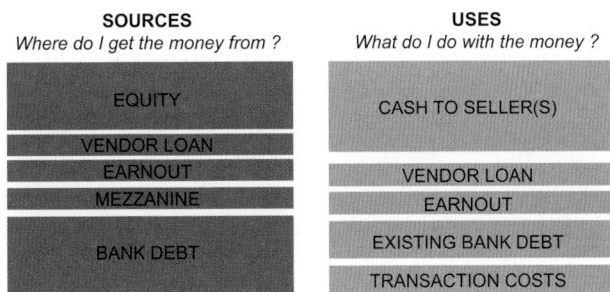

Figure 13.5 Sources and uses of funds.

Equity Component

The first source of funding will be your own capital. Debt providers will need to see a significant equity injection into the company before they are willing to provide loans to finance the acquisition. The equity or semi-equity (e.g. vendor loan) component will on average lie between 25 and 40 per cent of the total transaction value depending on the prevailing market conditions, the cash flow predictability of the underlying target and the amount of collateral the firm can provide.

The equity will be composed of the amount of capital the entrepreneur or the co-investors (e.g. private equity investor or business angel) bring in. It's important for you to be able to easily provide this initial amount and, as an individual buyer, you should try to stay within your budget. A frequent mistake made by individual buyers is that they spend all the cash they have on paying for the transaction price without having any buffer should the target perform below expectations or should there be any unexpected cash needs. Depending on the specific situation of the individual buyer and the status of his or her career, an investment of 1 × to 2 × gross annual salary should be the absolute minimum in order to 'put your money where your mouth is', and be taken seriously by other investors like private equity firms. You need to be prepared to lose this if things turn out for the worst. Based on a survey of potential buyout candidates conducted by the authors, individual buyers are on average willing to put in €150,000 to €300,000 to acquire a target.

Should the individual savings of the entrepreneur be insufficient to put together the equity component, other investors can be invited to join the deal. Depending on the amount required, these investors can include:

- Family members and friends, who might be easily called upon to provide the required funding. However, are you willing to risk personal relationships if thing go wrong?
- Members of the existing management team or key employees, who could be invited to join the deal. Alternatively, you might want to bring in outside

team members. A key question to answer is whether you are willing to share control and whether you are well aligned in terms of values and future vision for the company. Additionally, in small companies the number of senior managers is often limited and cash flows might be insufficient to provide a decent return if the management team becomes too big.

- Wealthy individuals or business angels. In many countries, wealthy individuals and business angels are increasingly investing in small buyout opportunities, given the attractive returns this asset class has offered in the past.
- Private equity players. For larger deals, traditional private equity players might be the only option to put together the necessary amount. They often contribute more than money and bring strategic and operational expertise to the deal. However, private equity players will often require a majority position and, in many cases, will have vetoes in place to replace the management team (i.e. yourselves) should they underperform.
- Family offices. There is a worldwide increase in the number of family offices. Increasingly, they are considering investments in smaller buyout targets as a means of diversifying their portfolio. One advantage family offices offer is that they often take a longer-term perspective and they might be more flexible in the way that they structure a transaction.
- In some countries, investment funds sponsored by the government might be available to facilitate the transfer of businesses.

These different options offer both advantages and disadvantages. As a buyout candidate, you clearly want to have a good overview of what's possible and leverage your personal network to get access to funding.

Vendor Loan

Small buyout transactions are often partially financed by the seller of the company through the provision of a vendor loan or seller's debt. This is a loan granted by the seller to help the buyout or buy-in manager buy his company and, therefore, represents a form of delayed payment. Ideally, as a buyer you try to maximize this amount. A vendor loan clearly provides an incentive for the seller to remain involved after the buyout transaction to help the business to succeed. There is some flexibility in the way that a vendor loan is structured. The main features of a vendor loan include:

- Amount: 15–30 per cent of the total transaction value.
- Usually at a higher interest rate when compared to bank debt e.g. 5–8 per cent p.a.
- Mostly relatively short-term maturity (as the seller will argue that the longer time goes on, the lower his impact on the business) i.e. 2–4 years.
- No or limited guarantees except for a share pledge (i.e. the seller gets his shares, the company, back if you are not able to repay the vendor loan).

- Ideally this loan is fully subordinated to bank debt, as the bank will consider it as (quasi)equity which allows you to increase your leverage. Fully subordinated implies that the maturity is later than the bank (e.g. bullet repayment) and there are no or limited cash interest payments (e.g. PIK – payment in kind or rolled-up interest).
- Sometimes the repayment of the vendor loan is made conditional on achieving certain financial targets.

Earnout

In an earnout agreement, the seller and the buyer agree to make a certain part of the sales price conditional on future company performance. As with a vendor note, it is a deferred payment. As illustrated in the SeaSmoke case, an earnout often helps to resolve differences in opinion (e.g. a hockey stick forecast in sales) with respect to the valuation of the company. The seller will only receive a higher sales price if the company achieves certain results, while for the buyer an earnout helps with the management of the downside risk. Clearly, an earnout aligns the interest of the seller with the buyer in reaching a successful transition. Key features of an earnout include:

- The amount: on average 10–30 per cent of the total transaction value.
- The most popular metric for determining the earnout payment is EBITDA, while revenue is also often used in smaller transactions.
- An earnout payment generally takes place between 1–3 years depending on for how long and how intensively the seller remains involved.

Mezzanine

Mezzanine debt is a hybrid form of financing that falls in between senior debt and equity or semi-equity (e.g. vendor loan or shareholder loan) and comes in different shapes and formats as illustrated in Figure 13.6. It is subordinated to bank debt and generally is not secured by collateral. Investors or banks providing mezzanine finance will generally base their investment decision on the future cash flow generation of the underlying target. Mezzanine fills the gap between the senior debt provided by the banks and the equity provided by the entrepreneur and other investors and, therefore, can be considered as a long-term source of unsecured risk capital with debt repayment characteristics which lowers the pure equity component.

There is quite a lot of flexibility available in the way that mezzanine debt is structured. Key features of mezzanine include:

- The amount: on average $1 \times$ to $1.5 \times$ EBITDA depending on the size of the transaction, the cash flow variability and the prevailing economic conditions. Minimum amounts start at €500,000 to €1,000,000.

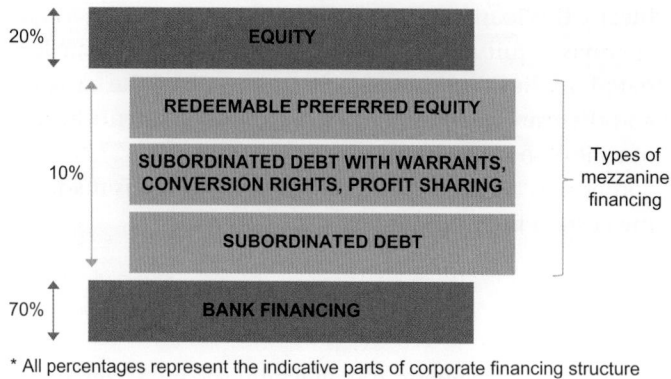

* All percentages represent the indicative parts of corporate financing structure

Figure 13.6 Where does mezzanine financing fit in the capital structure?

- The maturity: mezzanine debt generally expires after the senior debt has expired, i.e. after 7–8 years, with a bullet repayment of the principal amount.
- Interest payments in cash or a PIK interest[7] or a combination of both. The overall interest charged on mezzanine debt in small transactions ranges on average from between 8 to 12 per cent.
- Mezzanine debt might include an equity kicker through the inclusion of warrants or a conversion feature where the debt might be converted into common equity, similar to a convertible bond. These provisions will typically only result in value if an exit happens. For the mezzanine investor, it helps to boost the internal rate of return on the investment.
- The mezzanine debt generally includes a covenant package with more flexible terms and conditions.

In recent years, mezzanine investors have become more prominent in the smaller deal segment of the buyout market and offer additional opportunities to limit the equity contribution by the buyout entrepreneur and boost the return on buyout transactions.[8]

Bank Debt

Traditional bank debt plays a key role in the acquisition of smaller firms. On average, 50 to 60 per cent of the total transaction value is paid by raising bank debt. Traditional banks offer different types of bank debt, including

7 A Payment In Kind (PIK) loan is a type of loan which typically does not provide for any cash flows from borrower to lender between the drawdown date and the maturity or refinancing date, not even interest or parts thereof, thus making it an expensive, high-risk financing instrument. PIK is to be interpreted as interest accruing until maturity or refinancing (Wikipedia, 15-06-2017, url: https://en.wikipedia.org/wiki/PIK_loan).

8 An example of a mezzanine player active in the smaller segment of the buyout market is Capital@Rent with a focus on the Benelux (www.mezzaninefinanciering.be/en).

acquisition term debt, straight loans and commercial finance (for working capital purposes) and even mezzanine debt. As a buyer, you will need to decide on the type and amount of bank debt you would like to raise. The debt needed for the acquisition, the so-called acquisition term loan, is always amortizing. Your financial plan should indicate how much debt the underlying target can carry. Key considerations when setting the amount of bank debt include:

- What is the debt capacity of the underlying target? On average, banks will limit the net financial (senior) debt position to $2 \times$ to $4 \times$ EBITDA, depending on the collateral provided, the size of the company, the cash flow characteristics, and the prevailing debt conditions in the market.
- Based on the underlying operational and financial model of the target company, what is the amount of bank debt needed to run the company (e.g. working capital) and to provide funding for future necessary investments (e.g. capex), while at the same time amortizing the acquisition term loan?

Your financial and operational model might indicate that the underlying target cannot support the amount of bank debt needed to pay the purchasing price. In this case, you will either need to increase the equity or semi-equity component (e.g. vendor loan) or negotiate a lower price. It's extremely important to run different scenarios in your financial model and assess the fit of different financial structures to be sure the target can fulfil its payment obligations. Leverage has been shown to be one of the key contributors to bankruptcy in buyout transactions and, therefore, caution should be applied when using debt.

Different types of bank debt exist including:

1. (Senior) amortizing bank debt which is generally secured by the assets of the company and is the most senior claim against the cash flows of the business. As such, this debt is always amortizing and repaid first, with its interest and principal payments taking precedence over other, junior sources of debt financing. This type of debt is often called 'acquisition term debt' or 'term loan', mostly with a term between 5–8 years.
2. A revolving credit facility ('revolver' or straight loan) is designed to offer the target firm some flexibility with respect to its capital needs. It serves as a line of credit which the company can draw upon as its working capital needs dictate (e.g. due to intra-year fluctuations or growth) to cover working capital increases without having to seek additional debt or equity financing. This debt is not amortizing and can be drawn in equal tranches of, say, €100k or €250k.
3. Commercial finance is a generic term for a range of asset-backed finance services. The most important form is factoring or invoice discounting, in which a certain percentage of the invoices, usually between 70–90 per cent depending on the type of business, is automatically financed by the bank at a certain fee. These loans are secured by the receivables of the company. Commercial finance is attractive for growing businesses that will need working capital to grow but which lack existing assets to attract traditional debt.

It is often imposed by the banks as an alternative to revolving credit facility as it is better for their own capital ratios.

Overall, it might be good to use a mix of these debt instruments and keep the way in which you structure the overall debt package quite simple. Make sure that you obtain the appropriate financing for the foreseeable future to avoid having to go back to renegotiate the debt package.

When approaching banks, be careful to prepare a sound business case to raise the chances of successfully raising debt at favourable terms. You will have only one opportunity to make a good first impression. The bank will want to see the following items:

- detailed financial statements for the past three years including year to date figures.
- business plan (and strategy) of the buyer: P&L, balance sheet and cash flow statement for future years.
- the proposed deal structure.
- recent real estate (and other assets) expert assessment.
- other items: order book, licences, capital expenditures, and
- resumé of the acquirer and details of his or her financial situation.

Questions for Discussion

Philippe Lepoutre needs to find the money to pay for the acquisition of SeaSmoke. He is willing to personally invest a maximum of €800,000 of his own savings. As previously discussed, he and the existing owner initially agreed on a payment for all the outstanding shares of €2,873,000, including an earnout based on the EBITDA achieved in 2013. Additionally, the net financial debt position of the target equalled €1,046,000 on the closing date. He believes he can raise a senior loan from the bank to finance the acquisition. Now answer the following questions:

1. What are the various terms of the senior loan that will need to be negotiated with the bank?
2. What are your priorities in your negotiation strategy with the bank? What are the nice-to-haves? What are the must-haves?
3. What amount of senior debt can realistically be raised to finance the SeaSmoke acquisition?
4. Given Philippe Lepoutre's investment of €800,000, how should the potential gap in funding or the difference between the acquisition price and the amount of own funding and the funding provided by the bank be financed?
5. Show the sources and uses of funds table that describes the financial deal structure of your proposed transaction.

13.2.4   Negotiations with Banks to Raise Acquisition Debt

Loan Terms

When raising acquisition debt from the bank, you will need to negotiate the terms that will be included in the legal financing documents. Terms that need to be negotiated include:

1. the amount of the loan, or the overall leverage the bank is willing to provide,
2. the repayment schedule of the loan, including the maturity of the loan, the frequency of principal repayments and prepayment possibilities,
3. the interest rate charged on the loan and other fees,
4. the covenants (e.g. a maximum leverage ratio or senior debt / EBITDA ratio), and
5. personal or other guarantees.

Priorities when Negotiating Loan Terms

When negotiating with the bank, it helps to set some priorities before entering discussions. First, the most important item to be discussed will be the principal amount of the loan the bank is willing to provide. As a buyer, you want to make sure that the loan amount is sufficiently large to finance the transaction in order to limit the equity component in the deal. Therefore, within safe limits of the debt repayment capacity of the underlying target, and taking into account the net financial debt / EBITDA multiples applied by banks, one should aim to maximize this amount. In general, the banks are willing to provide amount of debt ranging between 2 × and 4 × EBITDA in this small type of transaction. The more debt that can be secured with assets the better and the higher the debt multiple. In the case of SeaSmoke, Philippe Lepoutre was able to negotiate a loan of €2,872,000, which represents 5.9 × the 2012 EBITDA and 3.9 × the forecasted 2013 EBITDA. From a debt/EBITDA multiple perspective, it is clear that bank debt is slightly high in this transaction. However, SeaSmoke could offer some collateral in order to secure the transaction. The collateral included fixed assets worth €2.2m (of which €1.6m is real estate), receivables of €1.4m, and an inventory of €0.4m. The bank usually takes a haircut on the collateral, depending on the type of collateral. For example, a stock of perishable food will attract a more severe haircut than a stock of easily saleable chemical commodities. Even the fixed assets are generally valued by the bank at a 'forced sale' value (mostly 70 per cent of market value). In the case of SeaSmoke, the bank decided that it had sufficient security in the deal.

Second, it is best to obtain some flexibility when structuring the loan. This includes negotiating loan covenants that are not too stringent and flexibility in the payment terms.

A covenant is a condition attached to a loan that requires the borrower to fulfil certain conditions, usually stating limits or thresholds of certain financial ratios that the company may not breach (e.g. net financial debt/EBITDA <4, net after tax cash, low/total principal repayment and net interest costs>1.1). Banks will seek to impose loan covenants that reflect your financial projections and will want you to operate in a bandwidth somewhat close to these financial projections. Negotiating this bandwidth is important. For example, if your senior debt/EBITDA ratio drops below a certain pre-specified amount, the bank could charge additional fees or might even require the full repayment of the loan. Therefore, as a borrower you will want to negotiate covenants with a sufficiently large margin in case the business performs below expectations.

Additionally, when negotiating the loan, the bank will propose a repayment schedule or amortization table. This schedule stipulates when and over what time period the principal amount of the loan needs to be repaid. The longer the maturity of the loan, the less pressure there will be on your cash flows to repay the loan, and the more freedom there will be to allocate free cash flows. Banks will generally require the borrower to repay the loan in five to seven years. A maturity of seven years will clearly provide more flexibility versus a maturity of five years. In some cases, it might even be possible to have a non-linear repayment schedule (i.e. the repayments are lower at the beginning) or to postpone the repayment of the principal amount for a certain number of years, which offers even more flexibility once the acquisition has been realized.

Third, you will want to avoid providing personal guarantees or personal collateral when signing a loan with the bank. However, in many countries banks will require personal guarantees when granting loans to finance the acquisition of a small business. By all means, try to avoid signing personal guarantees if you cannot afford to lose the money. It will significantly increase the risk of a transaction, and might even lead to personal bankruptcy if the buyout target defaults. Well-prepared buyout candidates who propose attractive and sensibly structured buyout acquisition opportunities to their banks will often succeed in having these guarantee requirements waived. This will require good negotiation skills and some shopping around between different banks. In some countries, governments also offer guarantee schemes to banks where the borrower can buy a guarantee at a small fee to secure the loan provided by the bank.[9]

Finally, you will want to negotiate reasonable and competitive rates and fees. The cost of a loan is generally expressed as a variable base rate (e.g. EURIBOR, LIBOR) and a fixed margin or spread expressed in basis points (100 basis points = 1 per cent). Additionally, the bank will charge fees, including an arrangement fee, a commitment fee and documentation fees. You will want to be sure that you have read and understood all these different fees when signing the final loan contract and that those fees are reasonable. Overall, your final return on your personal investment in the buyout target will only be marginally impacted by those fees if they are priced competitively. Therefore, we've put them last in the priority list.

9　For example, in Belgium, PMV provides guarantees on loans provided by banks active in Flanders. More info can be found here: www.pmv.eu/nl/financiering-voor-ondernemers /waarborgen/waarborgen-tot-15-miljoen-euro. The European Union is also active in this space: https://ec.europa.eu/growth/access-to-finance/funding-policies/loans-guarantees_en

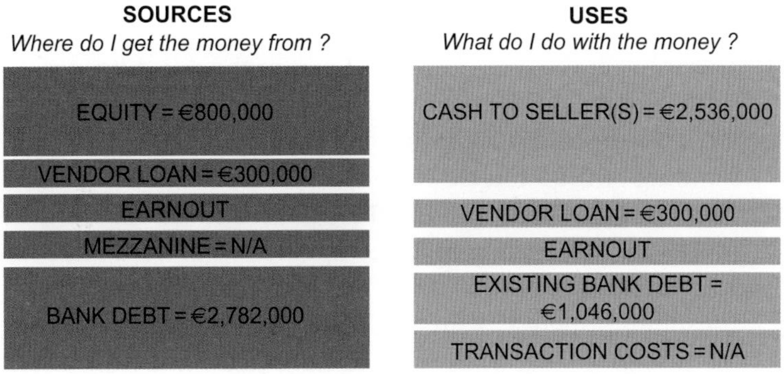

SOURCES	USES
Where do I get the money from ?	*What do I do with the money ?*

EQUITY = €800,000	CASH TO SELLER(S) = €2,536,000
VENDOR LOAN = €300,000	
EARNOUT	VENDOR LOAN = €300,000
MEZZANINE = N/A	EARNOUT
BANK DEBT = €2,782,000	EXISTING BANK DEBT = €1,046,000
	TRANSACTION COSTS = N/A

Figure 13.7 Sources and uses of funds in SeaSmoke transaction.

Final Deal Structure SeaSmoke

To finance the initial acquisition price, Philippe Lepoutre had to find €3,972,000, excluding the earnout payment. This total enterprise value is composed of an equity value of €2,926,000 and a net financial debt position of €1,046,000.

As the bank was willing to provide €2,872,000 in senior debt and Philippe had €800,000 available in personal savings, there was still a gap in funding of €300,000. To bridge this gap, Philippe negotiated a small vendor loan of €300,000 with the seller. Figure 13.7 shows the sources and uses of funds in the SeaSmoke transaction. The investment capital raised by Philippe Lepoutre is used to pay cash to the seller and to refinance the existing bank debt. Detailed information on the transaction costs was unavailable, but clearly these also need to be paid for advisors. The final earnout based on the EBITDA realized in 2013 that had to be paid equalled €432,000. An agreement would have to be made with the bank before signing the deal to provide this extra funding, or the financial plan should indicate that sufficient internal cash flow would be available to pay for this.

13.3 Confirmatory Due Diligence

From the moment an agreement has been reached with the seller and the letter of intent has been signed, confirmatory due diligence will begin. The purpose of confirmatory due diligence is to validate your understanding of the essential elements of the target's business by carrying out a cross-check of the company's internal and external documentation with the advice of experts such as accountants and lawyers. It allows the purchaser to decide whether to proceed and at what price.

There are different types of confirmatory due diligence, as discussed below.

13.3.1   Commercial Due Diligence

This is by far the most important part of the due diligence. If you are wrong on this one, the chances that you are buying the right company and have made a good investment are rather low. The goal here is to get a thorough understanding of the strategic positioning of the target. The market environment of the target, the drivers behind this market and the main trends in this market, as well as the positioning of the competitors, will need to be analyzed.

While for larger deals such work will be performed by (expensive) strategy consultants such as Bain & Co., McKinsey, Booz Allen or Roland Berger, in the case of smaller deals you will have to do this work yourself. As every company is different, there are no standard due diligence tick lists that you should follow. However, a thorough strategic and commercial due diligence should focus on:

- The company: An overview of the company including the business economics and the capabilities of the target. The following should definitely be performed:

  - An analysis of the value chain and the target's position therein.
  - An analysis of the different products and activities of the company and their historic contribution to turnover and margin. What is the current and future strategy with respect to the product portfolio?
  - Detailed information about customer needs and behaviour, including the strengths of the relationships. An analysis of customers should be part of this: Who are they? How has the relationship been evolving? What is their contribution to the bottom line? What are their key purchasing criteria (e.g. price, quality, service, the importance of personal relationships)? Are they satisfied?
  - An analysis of the key suppliers and the risk associated with this. Are there alternatives?
  - The advantages or disadvantages of the site location in terms of labour, proximity to customers and/or suppliers, access to transportation, state and local taxes and laws (including zoning and environmental impact regulations), and so forth.
  - An analysis of the facilities, including plant and office space, storage and land areas, special tooling, machinery and any other capital equipment currently used to conduct the company's business. What are the future equipment needs and likely capital expenditure in the coming years?
  - An analysis of the existing management. Who are the key managers in the company and what are their strengths and weaknesses, their track records and their future roles? Make an organization chart of the company.

- Market: A thorough analysis of the market, with historical and future volume/value developments of the market. What is the size of the target's addressable market? How has this market grown (in volume and price)? What are the major factors affecting market growth (e.g. industry trends, socioeconomic trends, government policy, environmental impacts, population shifts)? How resilient is the market to the economic cycle? What is the risk of substitution? What are the different scenarios for future market growth?

- Competition: An analysis of the target's competitors including insights into strengths and weaknesses versus current and potential competitors. What is the degree of competitive rivalry? Where are the sources of competitive advantage? Does the target have a sustainable competitive advantage? How do competitors perform against customers' key purchase criteria? Is there a threat of a new market entry?

- Strategy and business plan: An evaluation of the existing and future strategy and business plan, given the external environment and the target's capabilities. What are the key underlying assumptions in the plan? What are the key risks and opportunities in the business plan? What are the vulnerabilities and sensitivities of the plan?

In practice, you will collect any internal company data – financial and operational – that the company has in its IT system. Very often you will have to process the raw data coming out of the system into readable and interpretable data. It may even be the case that you have to sit for hours with the accountant in order to extract this data.

Regarding the market and competitive data, once you have carried out an exhaustive search of the Web for information about the business, the best way to proceed is to purchase market studies, if they exist, to check the officially published annual accounts of competitors, and, more importantly, to try to speak to all the relevant players in the industry. It is amazing how much interesting information you can obtain by having simple conversations (i.e. interviews), ideally via a physical meeting, with customers, suppliers and competitors of the target. Having long, in-depth and repeated interviews with the employees of the target, or even with the seller, are a must as they will be able to explain better than anyone else how the company get its job done. Triangulating these interviews with customer and supplier interviews will really get you on the learning curve of your potential future business. Due diligence is always an iterative process.

This analysis can all be done in a relatively cheap way: outsourcing here is not recommended. Besides, it is often too expensive to pay advisors for this kind of work. More importantly, you should always perform this kind of analysis yourself as it is by far the best way to get an understanding of the business you want to purchase. Good investors do not usually delegate or outsource the commercial due diligence to external parties.

Take, for example, the case of Budget Butcher, a Belgian low-cost butchery chain with forty butcher's shops, often located adjacent to an Aldi (food retail discounter) shop. The investors decided to withdraw from the deal after doing some confirmatory due diligence performed on a shoestring. They took the top ten best-selling products from Budgetslager (minced meat, veal sausages, etc.) and compared the prices of those products with similar products sold by the competition (the main food retailers and other independent butcher shops). The conclusion they reached was that the Budget Butcher's shops were the most expensive butchers in the market after the local independent butcher, who typically serves more quality-focused customers and that they were not 'budget' at all.

13.3.2   Financial Due Diligence

The goal of financial due diligence is to enhance the purchaser's understanding of the financials of the target. The financial due diligence enables the acquirer to decide whether to proceed and at what price. It also helps the purchaser in his negotiation with the seller and when deciding on representations, warranties and indemnities in the legal contracts. The key question relates to the quality of the cash flows, as they will drive the valuation and the final price will be the one the purchaser is willing to pay.

As this is a rather technical area, often requiring detailed knowledge of book-keeping and financial statements, it is recommended that you are assisted by specialized accountants. Most of the larger accountancy firms have specialist teams who do this kind of work almost exclusively. Very often, smaller firms do not have audited financial reports or robust internal financial reporting systems. One should therefore start by looking at any inconsistencies, fluctuations or inaccuracies in the numbers across the historic accounting data. In general, official accounts (as shown to the tax authorities) are always on the conservative side, as nobody declares a higher income to the tax authorities than they actually generate.

The financial due diligence will use the financial statements of the company and its internal management information systems to focus on the following main topics:

a.   Quality of Earnings (QoE)

Is the historic profitability, often expressed in terms of EBITDA, correctly translated in the accounting reports? What is the real recurring EBITDA at stand-alone level (i.e. what will the future performance of the business be)? This 'normalization' analysis takes place via a (very) detailed assessment of the revenue and cost drivers of the company. Some of the adjustments are hard and undisputable (such as truly private or one-off expenses) whilst others are of a softer nature, and subject to discussion.

Examples of hard EBITDA normalizations include:

- A potential buyer has to add Euros? to the EBITDA given the fact that the owner had a gardener maintaining his private garden paid for by the company at a salary of Euros? per annum.

- A potential buyer should add 50k to the company's EBITDA as there was a one-off payment of 50k due to the loss of a court case against a disgruntled ex-employee.
- A potential buyer needs to subtract 50k from the EBITDA as the current owner only pays himself a salary of 25k while a normal salary in such a position should be at least 75k.

Examples of soft EBITDA normalizations include:

- The seller adds bad debt write-offs (provision for doubtful debtors) in the P&L of 35k to the EBITDA, as he considers it exceptional. Is this correct? What has been the average bad debt write-off over the previous years? Is 35k the right number?
- The seller has added 100k related to a technical quality problem to the EBITDA, as he considers it exceptional? Is this correct? Doesn't every company have some technical problems every year? What were the costs relating to this problem in previous years? Is 100k the right number?
- Timing errors in revenues and associated costs are always tricky, in particular in a multi-year project business. To what extent do you recognize the revenues and costs in a particular year?

b. Quality of Net Working Capital (QoNWC)

Is the historic working capital a normal average working capital? As the level of net financial debt has a direct impact on the price paid for a company, it is important that, when you make an offer, your bidding price should be based on 'an average normalized working capital' level. Simply put, when the seller 'forgets' to pay the suppliers for a while and at the same time pushes customers to pay promptly, the cash position of the company will be much more positive, and hence the net financial debt will be lower. Using the formula where the price paid for the equity is the enterprise value minus the net financial debt (see Chapter 8, Figure 8.2), the purchaser will have to pay more for the same company. Many smart sellers will try to do this in order to boost their selling price, as they are able to steer, to some degree, the level of suppliers, customers and stock of the company, at least temporarily.

Another reason why calculating the average normalized working capital is essential is seasonality. To give an example, the cash position of an ice cream company in October (holds a lot of cash as most of the ice cream has been sold during the summer) (see scenario 2 in Figure 13.8) is fundamentally different from its cash position in April (little cash in hand as all the raw materials have been purchased and little ice cream has been sold yet) (see scenario 1 in Figure 13.8). If a purchaser looked only at the net financial debt position, he ought to buy the company in April, as the price would be lower. To avoid this kind of distortion, an offer should always assume an average normalized working capital.

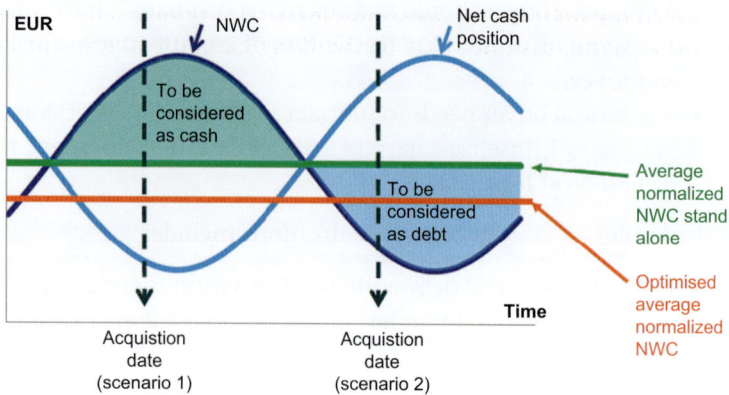

Figure 13.8 Net working capital evolution.

c.   The Quality of Net Financial Debt (QoNFD)

Is the calculation of the net financial debt position correct? As net financial debt has a direct impact on the price paid, it is crucial that this number is correctly calculated.

As mentioned above, net financial debt can be influenced by working capital manipulation. To a certain extent, QoNFD and QoNWC are communicating vessels. Often, corrections in the net working capital will be mirrored in the net financial debt normalizations.

Examples of net financial debt normalization include:

- A liability for a litigation in the balance sheet is a 'debt-like item' and needs to be added to the net financial debt position.
- Corporate income tax payable is a debt and should be added to the net financial debt, while corporate income tax receivable is a 'cash-like item' and should be subtracted from the net financial debt.
- An amount payable owed to a supplier of capex does not belong to the normal working capital and needs to be considered a 'debt-like item'.

d.   The Feasibility of the 'Stand-alone' Business Plan

While the commercial due diligence analyses the business plan from a market perspective, the financial due diligence will analyse the business plan from a financial perspective, i.e. what is the recurrent EBITDA going forward? What are the working capital requirements going forward? What are the capex assumptions going forward?

For example, if the business plan assumes a 5 per cent growth rate going forward, the commercial due diligence will have to assess whether this is possible given the market and the competitive environment. If the business plan, on the other hand, assumes that the working capital will grow in line with sales, the financial due diligence will have to confirm this.

e.   An Analysis of the Historic Capital Expenditure (Capex) and the Recurrent Capex Going Forward

As mentioned above, the financial due diligence will have to analyze, based on the historic capex needs and the underlying business plan, the capex needs going forward, often making a distinction between maintenance capex and expansion capex.

f.   Other Potential Risks Covered by 'Representations and Warranties'

The financial due diligence will expose certain issues that need to be covered in the legal contracts and which could lead to representations and warranties made by the vendor. Issues like large customer claims, litigation, exit costs, deferred tax assets and many others all have an impact on the ultimate valuation of the company and need to be taken into consideration in the legal contract.

13.3.3   Legal Due Diligence

The legal due diligence makes an evaluation of the company's contractual and litigation risks. You need to read all the company's major contracts and make sure they are consistent with your plans for the business. Most of the contracts will be common sense. If there is any doubt about the legal impact of certain contracts, do not hesitate to have your lawyer review it. For example:

- Certain contracts could have change of ownership clauses (i.e. the contract can only be transferred to the new owner if the other party gives its consent), which are important to know, as you want to acquire the business.
- Certain personal guarantees have been given to certain suppliers. Do you have to give similar guarantees?

Another part of the legal due diligence is analysing the risk of pending, ongoing and future litigation proceedings. Typically, most of the findings of the legal due diligence find their way into the legal contracts.

13.3.4   Tax Due Diligence

The purpose of the tax due diligence is an analysis of the target's tax treatment in respect of its compliance with national, provincial or local tax laws and to uncover significant potential tax exposures. It covers not only income taxes but also VAT, payroll and employment taxes, property taxes, etc. In the case of smaller companies (with, for example, no international subsidiaries), a good accountant should be able to perform this type of due diligence. Typically, most of the findings of the tax due diligence find their way in the legal contracts.

13.3.5   Specialized Due Diligence

For these type of due diligence, you should hire an expert.

* Machinery and equipment. If they are the key assets of the business, it is important to know their condition, their remaining useful life, etc.
* Environmental due diligence to make sure that the company complies with all the environmental regulations and has the necessary permits.
* IT due diligence to assess the performance of the IT system and the possible need for additional investments.
* Regulatory compliance due diligence; particularly important if the company operates in a highly regulated field.
* Pension and insurance due diligence, in order to see whether pension liabilities or possible risks are adequately covered.
* Human resource due diligence to get an understanding of the company's culture and work ethics.

It is generally advisable, given that all external advisors are costly, and should be costly ('if you pay peanuts, you get monkeys'), for you to start doing as much due diligence yourself as you can, in order to avoid incurring costs at an early stage in the process, before you even have made your mind up whether you are going for it or not. Always try to use advisors towards the end of the process.

In summary, after the confirmatory due diligence and depending on the outcome of the due diligence:

* You can close the deal as agreed in the LOI assuming that the due diligence has confirmed what you were expecting (i.e. your assumptions in the LOI).
* You can ask for an adjustment of the price if the due diligence has shown that you were too optimistic in your LOI, or you can ask to shift part of the price into an earnout.
* You can change the contract terms if the due diligence has indicated specific liabilities or risks for which you require a warranty.
* You can walk away if the due diligence has given you reason to lose your faith in the company ever being able to realize its business plan, or even a more modest version of it.

13.4   Closing the Transaction

If the due diligence progresses satisfactorily and you have confidence that the deal will eventually be closed, you will have to start spending money on a good lawyer. A company only changes legal ownership if a share purchase agreement gets signed on the dotted line.

Before you engage a lawyer, you should have discussed all the potential deal breakers – as far as you are aware – with the seller and made sure that you are happy with the compromises you have made. It is a costly affair if you have issue anxiety, avoiding discussing your concerns about the deal, which could lead to a lot of work and effort for nothing.

The lawyer you choose should be an experienced lawyer acquainted with this kind of M&A transaction. These lawyers are often more expensive. However, their experience will provide you with the necessary guidance and steer you through the minefield of the legal aspects of acquiring a company.

By far the most important legal document is the Share Purchase Agreement (SPA), the legally binding document that regulates the change of ownership of the company you want to acquire. Although an SPA is different for every company, given that each company has its own specific characteristics, issues or circumstances, every SPA for every company in the world contains similar provisions and uses a similar template. An SPA always contains:

- Definitions. Every SPA has always a couple of pages of legal definitions. Although these definitions are often written in boring legal mumbo-jumbo, it is worthwhile reading them carefully with the help of your lawyer. The devil can be in the detail. Some definitions have a direct impact on the valuation (e.g. the definition of EBITDA) or on your legal position when things go wrong later (e.g. the definition of taxes, latest accounts, etc.).
- A chapter describing the purchase and sale of the shares. This part of the SPA states that the purchaser will become the legal owner of the shares at closing, describing the purchase price in detail, such as defining the amount(s), the timing of the payment(s) and the payment method. The closing procedures will also be described, such as whether there will be a signing first and then a closing, the time and location of the closing, the procedures for the closing (such as the approval of the seller's board of directors, the dismissal of board members of the seller, etc.).
- Representations and warranties ('R&W') of the seller and buyer. This is a very important part of the SPA and limits the risks to the purchaser of a company, as the purchaser takes over all the assets, liabilities, as well as the social, legal and fiscal risks of the company. By providing the buyer with the so-called R&W, the seller is giving some assurances so that the buyer can rely on the seller to provide a true account of all information and supporting documents involved in closing the transaction. Although every company is different, and sometimes specific R&Ws are needed, most R&Ws are the same for all companies, e.g. the fact that the seller is the legal owner of the shares, the fact that the accounts are true, the fact that all taxes have been paid, etc. However, the seller is allowed to provide the buyer with some disclosures, in fact confessions, which are exceptions to the R&W.

- The indemnification. Should the purchaser encounter – after the transaction – a violation of the R&W, she has the right to an indemnification from the seller for the damage she has suffered. However, the seller will try to limit his responsibility in the contract by including an indemnification in time and in amount (a minimum threshold to allow for a claim and a cap on the amount that can be claimed). Often, the seller is required to provide a bank guarantee or to deposit money in an escrow account to prove to the buyer that the money the buyer could claim in case of such a violation of R&W, is there and the buyer does not have to worry about the ongoing creditworthiness of the seller. If you have negotiated a vendor loan in the transaction, this amount can be used as a kind of security for the buyer, as he already 'possesses' the money.
- A chapter on the closing documents, procedures and timing and miscellaneous topics such as post-closing cooperation and transition between the seller and purchaser, a non-compete clause and non-solicitation clause for the seller, etc.

The second most important legal agreement is the shareholders' agreement (SHA, discussed in Chapter 9). If you have more than one shareholder, i.e. you are not buying 100 per cent of the shares yourself, you need an SHA in order to regulate the relationship between the different shareholders. Although certain specific situations can occur, every SHA for every company in the world contains similar provisions and has a similar template.

First, an SHA determines the corporate governance rules of the company. It addresses questions such as number of board members, who sits on the board and who can appoint board members, who decides what (board vis-à-vis management), who can legally represent the company, etc. Second, the SHA will regulate share transfers within the company. It describes the procedure and it can grant different rights to shareholders, the most commonly used being:

- a pre-emption right (the right of existing shareholders to acquire shares that come up for sale),
- a tag along right (if the majority shareholder sell his shares, the minority shareholder(s) has the right to equally sell their shares under the same terms and conditions), and/or
- a drag along right (if the majority shareholder sells his shares, the minority shareholder(s) is forced to sell his shares under the same terms and conditions).

Third, the SHA can also provide options for shareholders to buy each other out, and conflict resolution mechanisms in case of conflict. The SHA has many other miscellaneous provisions.

Besides the SPA and the SHA, which are the two main documents governing the sale of a company, there are several other legal documents to take care of, such as the banking legal documentation, the appointment and dismissal of directors documents, the labour or management agreements with the new managers, etc. Again, it is important that an experienced lawyer advises you in these matters. Not even very experienced investors will do this without a lawyer.

13.5   Managing the First 100 Days

After signing the legal documentation and drinking a glass of champagne, you are now the legal owner of the company. Although your due diligence may have been very thorough, for the first time you will be able to see the company from the inside. Not surprisingly, you will discover further upsides but also unexpected downsides.

While each company will have different priorities, there are six essential priorities you should focus on after closing the transaction:

1. Communication. You will want to introduce yourself first to all your managers and employees and reassure them that they aren't going to see any immediate changes. It is important that you prepare a (consistent) story line and this is a perfect opportunity to share your plans and goals with the company. Your employees will have the chance to ask questions and to build their confidence in you. They will have three main questions which you should address: Is my job safe? Will my job change? Will I still report to the same person? However, it is important to remain vague when explaining your future plans, as you do not yet know the company well enough. Make sure that you do not preach about revolution, but rather continuity and evolution. After you have communicated with the personnel, you should make a similar announcement to the other stakeholders in the company, such as your customers, suppliers, the (specialized or general) press if needed, your competitors, external advisors, etc.

2. Transition period with the former owner. You will want to make sure that the former owner's knowledge, expertise and relationship network remains within the company. Although the former owner may stay on board for a certain period, everyone should know who does what after the sale. It is important to maintain a good relationship with the former owner, as he is probably the cheapest and most experienced advisor you can imagine.

3. Take control of the cash, and make sure you have the dashboard working. Given that the company bears a debt load, it is crucial that you track your cash flow at all times and that you have early warning indicators in place. Most small companies will have limited or insufficient reporting systems in place. It is therefore crucial to install the dash board as soon as you can, in order to track the company's cash generation. Two quick

examples of simple reporting tools to implement immediately after the purchase are:

a. A weekly net financial debt statement (showing on one sheet all the existing bank debt minus the cash) is helpful for understanding whether the company, in particular in the medium term, is generating cash or not, as the bank account never lies. It is a kind of very simplified cash flow statement.

b. A weekly sales report also is a good indicator of how the business is doing. Every IT-based bookkeeping system should be able to produce such a statement.

Equally, setting up a process whereby you approve all payments before they go out and review your accounts receivable balances on a very regular basis, ideally with an ageing analysis tracking by how many days each customer is overdue, should be done in the short term. At a slightly more sophisticated level, you should have a 90-day rolling cash flow forecast, forecasting your cash receipts and expenditures for the next three months. It will certainly help you to avoid cash crises by identifying early on when cash is likely to get tight, so you can take actions such as redoubling collections efforts, slowing payments of accounts payables or even arranging a line of credit at a bank.

Finally, after a couple of months, a basic monthly reporting package should be in place, providing you with a (consolidated, if needed) profit & loss statement, a balance sheet and a cash flow statement. In particular, the latter tends to be overlooked, but it is crucial for understanding where your cash is going. If your company has specific KPIs to monitor, you should supplement this financial reporting with some operational reporting whereby you can follow the performance of the KPIs of the company. All this reporting should be produced by your IT system. It is therefore crucial that you are sure that you have the proper IT system in place. Very often, a renewal of the IT system will be needed and this is probably the best investment you can make.

4. Understand and respect the existing culture. Very often, small family companies have a strong SME-like family culture, where a pater familias would govern all the decision-making. As a newcomer, do not charge in like a bull in a china shop. It is important that the changes that are needed happen with respect for the existing culture.

5. Understand the business. Although you may already have developed a strategy for the business before you made the acquisition, by being involved from the inside, you should be able to verify the assumptions underlying your planned strategy and modify the strategy when needed. Certainly, don't rush into big decisions in the first few months. Most of these can wait. Notwithstanding your thorough due diligence, you still have much to learn about running your new company and you will make

better decisions with a few months' experience under your belt. However, always remember you have leveraged the company and the repayment of cash flows is a must.

Now you are the owner of the company, you have unlimited access to everything and everyone, and it is key that you familiarize yourself with the business from the inside. Make time to meet all the employees individually and allow them to speak freely. Second, go and meet your (main) customers and suppliers, obtaining useful insights why they do business with your company. These meetings will certainly give you plenty of ideas about how to improve the service you provide, the business and how to sell or buy additional or alternative products. Third, make equally sure you meet the other stakeholders in the company, such as auditors, banks, accountants, insurance brokers, tax advisors. Your knowledge of the business will improve immeasurably after all these meetings.

6. Understand the staff, their motivation and capabilities. After you had your meetings with all the employees, draw up an organizational chart showing clear tasks and responsibilities. A good financial person, on your right hand, will allow you to focus on the business, while having accurate information and reporting to further develop the business. It is important to learn who are the 'keepers' and who are the people who will have to go. Very often, a family has kept people on board even if they were underperforming. It is important to motivate high-performing individuals through financial incentives or, even better, through other means of recognition.

In conclusion, entrepreneurship through acquisition will undoubtedly be an exciting journey, comparable with a roller coaster: 'it is fun but has its ups and downs'.

KEY TAKEAWAYS

- Entrepreneurship through acquisition is an alternative way of developing an entrepreneurial career. It has both advantages and disadvantages as compared to starting a business from scratch.
- There are different ways of creating value in a buyout transaction, including margin improvement, revenue increase, multiple uplift and reducing the net financial debt position. Whenever you undertake a buyout opportunity, you should try to identify multiples of these levers to manage your risk.
- The price you pay to acquire a company will have an important impact on your final return. Make sure you assess different scenarios to come up with a valuation and check your underlying assumptions through different types of due diligence.
- There are many ways to finance a buyout transaction. Familiarize yourself with all the funding options available, including your own capital, business angels, family offices, private equity investors, mezzanine investors, banks

and other players active in this market. Look at different ways to structure your transaction.

- Beware of a debt overhang! Always model your future cash flows taking your financial structure into account and include a buffer for unforeseen circumstances.
- Involve good advisors at certain stages to guide you through the process.
- Make sure you understand the different terms and conditions of all the contracts you will need to sign and never forget that some level of trust will be needed to successfully close a deal.
- Don't preach revolution when you finally get to running the company. Make sure you can provide continuity and get to know the company and the people. Get the dash board working to track your cash flows and your performance and make sure you can repay your debt.

END OF CHAPTER QUESTIONS

1. What are the advantages of a management buyout as compared to a management buy-in?
2. How would you describe the ideal buyout acquisition target?
3. What are the key sources of value creation in a buyout transaction? How can you add most value as an individual buyer?
4. What factors do you need to take into account when determining the pricing multiple?
5. What are the advantages of debt financing? What are the disadvantages?
6. What sources of external equity funding exist to finance a buyout transaction?
7. What are potential alternatives for traditional equity funding?
8. Would you consider mezzanine as expensive debt funding or cheap equity funding?
9. Do you agree that you should try to maximize the financial leverage (debt/equity ratio) in your deal structure?
10. Why do you need to 'normalize' the earnings, net working capital and the net financial debt? What are examples of normalizations for each category?
11. What sources of data can you use to conduct commercial due diligence?
12. What are the main contracts used in a buyout transaction? What type of risk do you try to cover in each contract?
13. What contractual terms facilitate the exit of your investment in a buyout target?
14. What are the main reasons for the failure of buyout acquisitions?
15. What would you stress in your first speech to the employees of the buyout target you have just acquired?

FURTHER READING

Gilligan, J. and Wright, M. (2014). *Private Equity Demystified: An Explanatory Guide*, 3rd edition. ICAEW Corporate Finance Faculty, url: www.icaew.com/en/techni cal/corporate-finance/financing-change/private-equity-demystified-an-explanatory-guide-160216

Hunt, R. A. and Fund, B. (2012). Reassessing the practical and theoretical influence of entrepreneurship through acquisition. *Journal of Entrepreneurial Finance*, 16(1), 29–56.

Rickertsen, R. and Gunther, R. E. (2006). *Buyout: The Insider's Guide to Buying Your Own Company*. AMACOM.

Ruback, R. S. and Yudkoff, R. (2017). *HBR Guide to Buying a Small Business*. Harvard Business Review Press.

REFERENCES

Berg, A. and Gottschalg, A. (2004). Understanding value generation in buyouts. *European Venture Capital Journal*.

Cumming, D., Siegel, D. S. and Wright, M. (2007). Private equity, leveraged buyouts and governance. *Journal of Corporate Finance*, 13(4), 439–460.

Damodaran, A. (2009). Valuing young, start-up and growth companies: Estimation issues and valuation challenges. Available at SSRN: https://ssrn.com /abstract=1418687 or http://dx.doi.org/10.2139/ssrn.1418687

EVCA (2013) Pan-European private equity performance benchmarks study, url: https://www.investeurope.eu/media/199202/2013-pan-european-private-equity-performance-benchmarks-study-evca-thomson-reuters-final-version.pdf (15–06-2017).

Jensen, M. C. (1989). The eclipse of the public corporation. *Harvard Business Review*, 67, 61–74.

Luypaert, M. (2016). M&A monitor: Shedding light on M&A in Belgium. Vlerick Business School, url: www.vlerick.com/en/research-and-faculty/knowledge-items /knowledge/strong-growth-in-belgian-mergers-and-acquisitions-market (15–06-2017).

Van Teeffelen, L., Weesie, E., Depelssemaker, M., Alba, O., Pirotte, N. (2016). *Quality of SME Business Transfer Matching Platforms: Research Outcomes of 12 European Countries*. EU4BT.

CHAPTER 14

ENTREPRENEURSHIP THROUGH ACQUISITION (2): 'SEARCHERS'

TIMOTHY BOVARD

INSEAD and Columbia Business School (United States)

This chapter will go deep into the process of searching for a business to acquire and run as an equity-owning CEO, as a way of becoming an entrepreneur in an existing business, similar to what we saw in Chapter 13. However, in the case of a 'searcher,' the company to acquire has not yet been identified, and a good deal of effort is devoted to the search for the 'dream' company. As we have seen for startups looking for financing from external investors, the idea is to search for a business, acquire it, run it for some years and then sell it, allowing the investors and the searcher to have a healthy IRR of around 30 per cent.

Entrepreneurship through acquisition (ETA) has reached a level of awareness never thought possible among top business school students. From a little-known phenomenon that attracted only a handful of recent graduates each year since the early 1990s, starting in 2012, the numbers started climbing significantly. In 2017, there are more than 50 per year following the traditional search fund model, and well over a hundred per year if one takes into account all forms of ETA. While the vast majority of searches takes place in the United States, there is an increasing number of searchers in other countries around the world. ETA is slowly becoming a global phenomenon as MBAs and other graduate students weigh up their options of becoming equity-owning entrepreneurs: starting a company, joining an early-stage business or buying a company.

VIEW FROM THE MEDIA

FINANCIAL TIMES   FT

Entrepreneurs use business school tool to buy companies globally

Business school graduates find US financial tool pays off worldwide

MARCH 30, 2015 BY JONATHAN MOULES

Starting your own business is risky, so why not buy one that someone else has already steered through the perilous formative years? That is the logic behind the search fund, a specialist vehicle in which investors back a promising individual rather than an existing start-up team. In the first stage, money is raised to pay the individual a nominal salary and expenses, sometimes for several years, while they hunt for an acquisition target in which they believe they can add value. Further funds are used to manage and grow the company. The concept was developed at business school more than 30 years ago, led by Irving Grousbeck, a professor at Stanford Graduate School of Business in the US, who started teaching the concept to his MBA students. Now, like that other Californian creation, the venture capital-backed model for high-growth tech start-ups, search funds are being tried in countries around the world. ... Europe should be ripe for search fund entrepreneurs because it has so many family businesses with succession problems. Recent years have also seen a more risk-taking culture among investors, encouraged by the emergence of start-up hotspots in cities such as London, Berlin, Stockholm and Barcelona. However, understanding of the concept remains limited largely to those who have been through business school. ... Yet despite the success stories, expansion of the search fund market looks like a slow-burn activity. While there are now at least three private equity funds in the US dedicated to the model and some investors backing more than 100, it remains a niche concern even among business students. ... Marc Bartomeus, an MBA graduate from MIT Sloan, returned to his native Spain to set up one of Europe's first home-grown search funds. 'I knew I wanted to be an entrepreneur, and I had thought of doing an MBA as a break that would enable me to think about my next move,' he says. ... 'It made a lot of sense because starting a business on your own is so risky,' Mr Bartomeus recalls. ... In 2011, Mr Bartomeus created his search fund Ariol Capital with the backing of a dozen investors, mostly from North America. ... He was concerned that his US backers might balk at the idea of putting money into his troubled home market. In fact the reverse was true. 'Many were actually attracted to the idea because they have made some of their best gains in times of crisis,' he says. Ariol Capital has since acquired a plastic packaging distributor with more than €15m in revenues.

https://www.ft.com/content/dc677e6e-a31d-11e4-9c06-00144feab7de

LEARNING OBJECTIVES

After reading this chapter, you will be able to:

- Understand the various routes to entrepreneurship through acquisition
- Prepare for the search process.
- Understand search strategies.
- Identify potentially good businesses and contact company owners.
- Select good acquisition prospects and engage with business owners.
- Make an offer to buy a business.

Where Are We Going Next?

In this chapter, we will first examine four paths to entrepreneurship through acquisition. The rise of interest in search funds has spawned several options for searchers other than what is now known as the 'traditional search fund model', as popularized by the Stanford Graduate School of Business and its Search Fund Primer. We will then focus the bulk of our attention on the search process itself, which, while somewhat impacted by the path chosen, is largely the same for all searchers. The overall aim is to provide a comprehensive view, from making the very personal choice to pursue a search to learning how one goes about finding a company to buying a business with the goal of becoming an equity-owning CEO.

14. 1   Financing the Search: Four Paths to Entrepreneurship through Acquisition (ETA)

Prospective searchers must determine not only if ETA is right for them, but also which of the paths available is the most appropriate. Part of this decision is financial and part of it is more a question of personal preference. Regardless of the path chosen, the search period needs to be financed. Naturally, the searcher needs to pay for their living expenses, but in addition, they must also cover all the search expenses that will be incurred. Finding a business to buy and completing its acquisition can take anywhere from twelve to twenty-four months or more, as will be explained later. Therefore, the choice of which path to follow is important.

There are four main paths to entrepreneurship through acquisition: (1) the traditional search fund model; (2) the self-funded search; (3) the accelerator model; and (4) other single sponsors. Prospective searchers are encouraged to research each of these paths to determine which, if any, is most appropriate for their search. It has become a tradition for prospective searchers to reach out to those in the search 'community' of past and present searchers, CEOs and investors to inform themselves about the pros and cons of each path. In fact, most investors, regardless of the path, expect that those seeking to raise capital will have conducted a thorough investigation, speaking to fifteen or more members of the community prior to contacting them. This due diligence process is highly recommended regardless of the path chosen.

14.1.1   Traditional Search Fund Model

The traditional search fund model is covered in depth in literature available online written by the Center for Entrepreneurial Studies at the Stanford University Graduate School of Business.[1] In a nutshell, a searcher prepares a Private Placement Memo (PPM),[2] contacts dozens of potential investors and eventually raises search capital from a group of fifteen to twenty of them. Ranging from $450,000 for a single searcher to roughly $700,000 for a team of two searchers, this capital covers the searcher's salary, office and administrative expenses, and travel and data costs for two years. In return, the investors have the option to invest significantly more capital in an eventual acquisition. Should the investor not wish to invest in the deal, their initial capital is rolled over into the acquisition vehicle. If no company is acquired, the search capital is lost.

If a single searcher succeeds in buying a business, they will get up to 25 per cent carried interest (30 per cent for duos) on the gains generate by the acquisition. They will invest time and effort in finding a company to buy and acquiring it, but are not required or even expected to invest any money in the deal. Therefore, their 'equity' is structured as carried interest with the initial search capital, the acquisition capital and a preferred return to investors all being payable to investors before the searcher participates in the split of capital gains. The right to carried interest, or capital gains, is split into three parts: one-third awarded at the time of acquisition, one-third vesting over four years, and one-third at a valuation or exit event that is pro-rated on a sliding scale of IRR from 20 to 35 per cent. This last tranche incentivizes the searcher to maximize returns to investors.

While most serial search fund investors are based in the United States, there is a growing number of non-US investors as well as an ever-increasing number of non-US search funds. Typically, a non-US searcher brings onboard a few local or regional investors to back their search and then the doors are opened to US-based search fund investors seeking portfolio diversification by investing internationally. For prospective searchers seeking more information on non-US searches, a team at IESE in Barcelona cooperates with Stanford GSB to study and promote search funds internationally.[3]

---

1 The most relevant documents include the Search Fund Primer and the bi-annual Search Fund Study: Selected Observations (Center for Entrepreneurial Studies, Stanford Graduate School of Business).

2 PPMs in the search fund world are massively standardized, some 85% is similar, the remaining 15% includes information on the searcher's background and motivation to do a search, and three industries that he/she finds attractive (author experience).

3 www.iese.edu/en/faculty-research/research-centers/eic/search-funds

The advantages of the search fund model include: a salary for the searcher(s), a pool of knowledgeable investors (individuals and funds of search funds) who are primed to consider the deals the searcher finds, mentorship by experienced investors, and a codified set of investment parameters and documentation. The constraints searchers accept by choosing this path include: capped equity participation, lower levels of mentorship from investors than is generally believed, and high reported failure rates: 27 per cent of searchers fail to acquire a business and 35 per cent of the businesses acquired fail to return full investor equity.[4]

14.1.2   Self-Funded Search

As its name implies, a self-funded search requires the searcher to live off their savings while searching for a business to buy, rather than being backed by a group of investors from the start. This gives self-funded searchers the opportunity to handpick their investors once a deal is found, and to engage with those investors on market-clearing terms proposed by the searcher.

Self-funded searches have the advantage of allowing searchers the autonomy to search as they like. In contrast to the more institutionalized models, self-funded searchers can focus on a particular geography or industry, target smaller companies, or look at companies in industries that are generally shunned by search fund investors. Typically, self-funded searchers also aspire to having a greater stake in the equity or capital gains generated by the acquisition, even to the point of having majority control. Obviously, this is an advantage to those who have personal or family wealth, or privileged access to investment capital through their network. Depending on the searcher's needs, the main disadvantage of a self-funded search is not having the credibility that comes from having a base of investors who can provide capital, and the mentorship those investors can offer. Finding both is the responsibility of the searcher.

14.1.3   Accelerator Model

In the last two years, 'search accelerators' have emerged in the United States to provide a more structured environment for searchers, with the aim of improving 'searchers' and investors' odds for success and overall returns.[5] While it is too early to speak of concrete results, they are getting more attention from searchers and investors alike. Typically, there is some form of initial training on search methods and best practices. This is followed by mentorship from the accelerator's principals and varying levels of collaboration among the searchers themselves. Depending on the accelerator's model, investment capital is either provided from funds raised by the accelerator itself or sourced ad hoc by the

4 Kelly *et al.* (2016).
5 Note: Search accelerators have generally applied many of the techniques deployed by startup accelerators (see Chapter 2), but they are distinctly different given that the goal is to acquire an existing business. There are no such accelerators in Europe to date (July 2017).

searcher with assistance from the accelerator's staff from among interested investors. Finally, the economic benefits to searchers vary according to each model.[6] Searchers should conduct their own due diligence to understand the advantages and disadvantages of each as compared to other accelerators and the other paths to ETA. But generally speaking, these accelerators were conceived to correct perceived weaknesses in the traditional search model and help searchers to succeed.

14.1.4 Other Search Sponsors

As the search fund model has proliferated, and concomitant with the appearance of search fund accelerators, other sponsors have emerged to support and fund entrepreneurs searching for companies to acquire and run. Investors who have seen the returns historically generated by the search fund model (as reported in the Stanford studies)[7] have decided to invest more actively in searchers by creating their own investment vehicles. Some of these vehicles are backed by one or two individuals or a family office, while others have larger investor bases giving access to the asset class to a wider range of investors. Some of the vehicles have their roots in one particular MBA school and may or may not be restricted to graduates of that school. The advantages and disadvantages of each of these options are intrinsically variable and will hold different appeal to different searchers. But it is interesting to note that as interest in ETA grows, more and more new models are appearing to appeal to the growing demand from searchers and investors alike.

14.2 Other Considerations before Choosing an ETA Path

Before discussing how searchers can best organize and execute their search to find a company to acquire, there are two other topics that prospective searchers must consider: (1) conducting a solo or partnered search, and (2) having single or multiple investors. There are many viewpoints on these two important issues. Before making a decision, searchers should do their own due diligence by speaking to a wide variety of searchers, CEOs and investors.

14.2.1 Solo versus Partnered Searches

Up to 50 per cent of traditional searchers decide to partner with another searcher. Often seen as a way to combat the loneliness of searching, the logic is also that two

---

6 Search Fund Accelerator, the first such accelerator (founded by the author) offers searchers the same potential as in the traditional search fund model to earn 25% of the capital gains created, but searchers benefit from unlimited coaching, mentoring and advising; lower overall search and acquisition costs; and no preferred return to investors (typically 8 per cent of invested capital compounding annually).

7 Kelly *et al.* (2016).

heads are better than one, that two searchers can be more productive and screen more companies, and that they can help maintain each other's motivation and support one another emotionally. Searchers who decide to partner also emphasize the complementarity of their skill sets, which will be valuable during the search and post-acquisition, when managing the business. While some partners are childhood friends and have a longstanding desire to work together, which is perfectly understandable, most search partners meet while getting their MBA and really do not know one another all that well.

Searchers need to be honest with themselves when considering a partnered search, and answer a number of key questions. Are their skill sets truly complementary? How differentiated are the skills of investment bankers, private equity professionals and consultants? Do either of them have operational experience? Who will be the CEO once a company is acquired? Or can they both be co-CEOs?

Then there are the economics. In the traditional search fund model, single searchers can earn up to 25 per cent carry. But partnered searchers split 30 per cent; i.e. 15 per cent each. This means that each partner gives up 40 per cent of their potential gains from day one. The question to answer is, is it worth it? And while many prospective searchers focus on the search phase, that is only the tip of the iceberg. Most value is created while running the business, and having two inexperienced MBAs may be both redundant and costly. Obviously, there is no way of knowing beforehand whether the management team of the company they will eventually acquire will be solid or not. But one can legitimately ask if the searcher, once CEO, would hire their search partner to reinforce the team. Arguably, a more optimal solution would be to hire someone with industry experience, lower salary expectations and no requirement for equity ownership.

14.2.2   Single versus Multiple Equity Sponsors

While the private equity-backed Leveraged Buy Out (LBO) market has almost exclusively been built on the principle of a single control investor, the world of search funds is based on a vastly different model. In a private equity-backed LBO, particularly when doing deals in the lower middle market size range, all deal equity is typically provided by a single fund that then controls the board. CEOs involved in management buyouts have readily accepted this structure of financial sponsorship and governance, and profited from it.

Perhaps taking their lead from startups, where entrepreneurs raise seed capital from multiple angel investors, in the traditional search fund model, searchers raise their initial search capital from between twelve and twenty investors, the majority of whom invest if and when the deal is closed. This leaves the searcher with a considerable number of investors in the acquisition, three or four of whom comprise the board.

During the search, having multiple, experienced investors, who are invariably listed on the searcher's website, lends credibility to the searcher. The investors also serve as mentors. Searchers can reach out to them and seek their opinions and guidance on a variety of topics. Having multiple investors also gives search-ers (and sellers) the confidence of having a broad group of investors from whom they can seek investment capital once they find a company to buy, and, at least theoretically, near certainty that they can get a good deal financed. Post-com-pletion, the board members are drawn from the pool of investors and they have the benefit of having followed the searcher, the search process and the transac-tion. Finally, many searchers reason that they will have the largest equity stake of any of the investors in the deal and will thus have considerable autonomy as CEOs.

On the other hand, most search fund investors are involved in several dozen searches and investments at any one time (to build a portfolio), and have demanding professional and personal lives. Time is their scarce resource. And given that most investors are already high net worth individuals, no single deal is likely to make any meaningful difference in their wealth. Accordingly, many traditional search investors have little economic incentive or time to devote to their searchers. Therefore, mentorship may be much more limited than expected. There is also the potential for searchers, who control the information provided to investors as they decide to invest or not, to exploit the passivity of their investors and strategically win investor approval for less than perfect deals. Finally, it can be far more difficult than expected to manage the varying and sometimes divergent interests of multiple investors and their board representatives. It can be argued that these mechanisms could partially be to blame for the high levels of failure in the traditional search fund model.

Using a single source of equity also has its advantages and disadvantages. On the plus side, the searcher can carefully choose their partner and the resulting close personal and professional relations can result in a strong, effective partner-ship. This can lead to enhanced mentoring, greater engagement and better governance from the investor that can be beneficial to the searcher. A fund or family office that provides all the equity needed for the acquisition have a clear fiduciary responsibility to closely follow what is then a sizeable investment. Searchers can profit from close, professional oversight to the extent that inter-ests are well aligned. And finally, it is relatively easier to work with a single equity sponsor with known objectives, rather than working with multiple sponsors with potentially diverging agendas.

On the negative side, searchers are reticent about putting all their eggs in one basket. They are rightly concerned about the negative consequences of a professional or personal conflict with their single equity sponsor. They are also often worried that their autonomy as CEO will be diminished: it could be better to divide and conquer with multiple investors. In fact, autonomy is often raised as one of searchers' primary objectives in pursuing ETA. The question that needs to be raised, and answered, is when can too much of a good thing, be bad.

Marc is the CEO and Board Director of Repli, the largest distributor of rigid plastic packaging in Spain. Marc acquired Repli via his fund Ariol Capital. Prior to founding Ariol Capital, he worked for a middle-market private equity firm in Boston. Marc holds a Degree in Industrial Engineering from the Universitat Politècnica de Catalunya (UPC) and an MBA from MIT Sloan School of Management.

What is your experience with developing the search process? What is your advice to entrepreneurs on the search process?

Search Funds have historically provided superior returns and offer an excellent opportunity for recent MBA graduates to become equity-owning managers. However, this is no easy path and prospective entrepreneurs should be aware of the many risks associated with buying small and medium companies. If you are 100% committed, get surrounded by experienced people and go for it!

14.2.3 A Final Word on Choosing Your Path to Entrepreneurship through Acquisition

The choice of which path to follow is a very personal one. Some searchers rather superficially investigate the options, while others take their due diligence very seriously. Given that the search phase lasts about two years and, if successful, the searcher manages their business for an average of seven years, the decision is an important one that will potentially span a decade. However, most MBAs are accustomed to viewing their careers as a succession of two-year stints as consultants or investment bankers, rather than as a ten-year professional commitment. Outside of the decision to marry – and most searchers have not yet made that leap – committing to ETA will be the single most important, long-term decision an individual, at their stage in life, has ever made. It should be taken seriously. Prospective searchers should thoughtfully and maturely investigate the options, weigh the pros and cons, and dig beneath the myths and folklore. Searching for, buying and managing a business is a serious, long-term pursuit that can lead to considerable self-fulfilment and wealth. It can also lead to frustration, unhappiness and failure. That is the lure of entrepreneurship and entrepreneurship through acquisition is no exception.

Let's Practise: Case Study

HANDS-ON SEARCHER CHALLENGES

One California-based searcher from a leading business school established a traditional search fund backed by a group of seasoned search fund investors. After twelve months of searching, he signed an LOI with a company owner and began working on due diligence, deal financing and the legal documentation. With everything in the final stages, two weeks before closing he moved his family halfway across the United States to the town where the company was located. A week later, the seller backed out of the deal. Rather than move back to their previous location, the searcher continued to search from his new hometown, but affected emotionally by the deal failure and hitting the twenty-four-month time limit, he closed his search fund. He was burned out, disappointed and needed to reset his life. Searching had been much tougher than he had imagined and he never thought he would be one of those searchers who fails to buy a business. Two months later he began working for a prestigious global consulting firm in a role that would be the envy of most MBA graduates. The firm clearly valued his search experience, the knowledge he gained and the grit he exhibited. While he knew the search experience had been as valuable as it had been disappointing, the external validation of getting an outstanding new job, confirmed it.

Questions for Discussion

1. What is 'failure' in the search world?
2. Imagine yourself conducting a two-year search without buying a business. What skills and experience do you think you would gain that could be marketed to a potential employer?
3. Given the risks associated with search, why would someone want to pursue this career path? Why are you considering it?

14.3   Searching for a Business to Buy

There is no one recipe for finding a business to buy. Different searchers use different methods and often change methods midstream as they continuously learn and adapt following their successful and unsuccessful experiences. In this aspect alone, ETA is very entrepreneurial.

Consider the challenges. A newly minted searcher, who has never bought a company before and who has not previously been a CEO, embarks on their most important professional exploit with little preparation. Over the course of the search, the searcher will contact thousands of business owners to engage them in a discussion about selling their most precious and most valuable asset. And this will be set against a background of competition from other searchers, investment funds and strategic buyers all trying to accomplish the same thing. The odds should be daunting, and yet we know that dozens of searchers succeed each year.

The rest of the chapter will be devoted to preparing for and executing the search. It is a process. Therefore, one can describe the steps, techniques and best practices searchers have used in the past. Searchers can select from among these techniques.

14.3.1   Preparing to Search

There are a number of administrative and preparatory steps most searchers take when launching their search. While none of these preparatory activities get the searcher any closer to finding a company to buy, they are generally advised in order to have an appropriate base on which to run the search and to build credibility with company owners. These steps include:

1. Choosing a lawyer and establishing a legal search entity to collect investment funds, and codify the ownership and rights of the investors. While a necessity for funded searches, even in self-funded searches, a legal structure enhances the searcher's credibility with company owners.
2. Hiring an accountant to follow the financials, set up payroll and benefits and to prepare annual reports and tax documents.
3. Leasing office space, connecting utilities and establishing data lines.
4. Building a website targeted to company owners as a means of enhancing the searcher's credibility.
5. Selecting an email-marketing platform for outreach and a CRM or other contact tracking system to manage contacts with company owners.

While the legal, accounting and office considerations mentioned above are relatively straightforward, selecting the name of the search entity, creating an appropriate website and choosing email and contact tracking systems merit further discussion.

Search Entity Names

The legal entity created serves to enhance the searcher's credibility, and the name chosen for that entity should reinforce that as well. Many searchers choose names that evoke professionalism, investment experience and access to capital, along with references to building for the future and growth. Some searchers create names that 'tell their story': their motivation for buying and running a business. And many names are akin to those used by private equity funds. While this is obviously a personal choice, searchers should put themselves in the shoes of their 'customers' and think through how the name will resonate and what image it will convey to company owners.

Examples of search fund names include:

European-based search funds	US-based search funds
Leela Capital	Silver Field Capital
Hemera Partners	Pacific Oak Partners
Kronos Kapital	Valent Capital Partners
ARP Capital Partners	Wright Equity Partners
Continuum	Servan & Co.

Websites

Searcher websites lend credibility to their undertaking in the eyes of the most important constituent, company owners. Sellers will consult the website either before responding to an initial email or prior to a first telephone conversation. The purpose is simple: 'tick the box'. It should reassure the viewer that the searcher is a serious candidate to take over their business.

Searchers can find a wide variety of styles on the Internet by looking at the websites of current searchers. These examples can provide inspiration for the structure and content of the websites. However, there seems to be a tendency to craft the image of a private equity firm, rather than that of an entrepreneur seeking to buy and run a business. At the end of the day, the website should reflect the personality of the searcher while conveying professionalism, entrepreneurial spirit and seriousness. Best practice also suggests that they should be simple and follow the adage that 'less is more'.

Email Marketing Platforms

There are numerous email marketing platforms that searchers can use to drive their outreach programmes, to the extent that they choose email over postal mail.[8] Without delving into too technical a discussion, there a few key considerations that must be weighed when selecting a platform. The system should allow for adequate email volumes, personalization, scheduling, drip campaign staging, email tracking and integration with CRM platforms to name a few. It is also useful to be able to run statistics on different campaigns and to be able to conduct A/B testing. While the system need not be overly sophisticated, search is a direct marketing effort and the proper tools can make all the difference.

Contact Tracking Systems

Professionally following leads that result from email marketing campaigns requires a solid yet easy to use tracking system. Most sales organizations use one of the

8 Examples of such platforms include Quickmail, PersistIQ, Yesware and ToutApp.

many customer relationship management (CRM) platforms on the market.[9] Again, simplicity is important. Sales organizations seek to track detailed client relationship information over long periods of time, creating a deep database of all client interactions. Search is quite different. Company owners are not long-term clients. They are only interesting to the searcher to the extent that they engage in discussing the potential sale of their business. Therefore, there is no need to track volumes of client history. At a minimum, searchers should be able to easily import contacts to and from their email-marketing platform. They should also have the ability to manage leads that are in various stages of discussion, from setting up a call, to requesting an NDA, to waiting for financials, to making an indicative offer. In short, the platform should help the searcher manage their sales pipeline. Many such platforms are available as SaaS software.

14.3.2   Building an Outreach Programme

The many pages it has taken to reach the point where we can now focus on how to conduct the search illustrates the preparation time searchers need to raise funds and launch the search. Unfortunately, the process does not accelerate from this point forward. Searchers begin with remarkably little concrete knowledge of how to execute the search. Even after extensive discussions with current and previous searchers, the keys to an effective and efficient search can remain elusive. This highlights one of the major issues searchers face: every searcher is required to reinvent the wheel.

Learning to search efficiently is a lengthy process. While research shows that it normally takes a searcher between nine and twelve months to become truly efficient, some investors believe it can take as long as fifteen months. Considering that a search is supposed to last twenty-four months, this represents a large proportion of the total time. One can therefore easily understand why, according to Stanford research,[10] 44 per cent of search deals are completed in month 21 or later. It just takes time, not only to learn how to search, but also to find the 'right' company to buy.

In the rest of this chapter, we will discuss the search process up to the point of making an indicative offer on a business. We will cover defining and applying search criteria, selecting and executing a primary search strategy (proprietary or brokered), understanding the impact of geography, recruiting and using interns, qualifying sellers, evaluating opportunities as an investor, and making the initial offer.

14.4   Defining Search Criteria

There is broad consensus among searchers and investors as to the types of businesses searchers should be seeking to acquire. However, not only can these

---

9 Examples include Insightly, Zoho and HubSpot.
10 Kelly *et al.* (2016).

criteria vary by individual, but also as a function of the ETA path chosen. For example, a searcher looking only at businesses within one hour of a single, large city would be unlikely to be able to attract investors to join a funded search. However, a self-funded searcher could easily do this. But regardless of the specificities that define an individual's search, there are commonly accepted search criteria that define the characteristics of the companies searchers, as untested CEOs, should seek to acquire.

In a nutshell, searchers should target solid, unbreakable businesses. When most people think of buying a business, however, they usually think of buying a bad business and making it better. But the world of turn-arounds (see Chapter 15) should be left to experienced managers, not first time CEOs. Searchers should be seeking to buy good businesses. Their challenge will be to make them better by increasing revenues and EBITDA, paying down debt and positioning them as a long-term hold, or preparing them for eventual sale.

The commonly accepted search criteria denote companies that are good, profitable businesses, well-positioned strategically in their industry, and poised to grow in the future. These criteria include:

- **Transitioning owner who is motivated to sell and who cares about their legacy**: selling their 'baby' is often not easy for company owners, so owners should have credible reasons, such as retirement, and should be motivated to sell and demonstrate that they care about the future of their company and their employees. This makes them sensitive to exactly who acquires the business, and how the new owner will run it, to the point of accepting a lower price than a strategic buyer would offer.
- **History of profitability**: a consistently profitable business will be easier for a new CEO to manage and grow. It is interesting to look for evidence of profitability through downturns such as in 2008 to 2012.
- **Recurring (or repeat) revenues**: revenues that are contractually recurring (i.e. monthly maintenance contracts) or revenues that can be counted upon to repeat with a high degree of certainty (i.e. product reorders) provide a level of certainty that does not come from project-type revenues (i.e. construction).
- **Strong EBITDA margins**: companies with strong EBITDA margins are ones that create enduring value for their customers and therefore do not principally compete on price.
- **Stable cash flows**: companies with cash flows that are predictably stable are both easier to manage and easier to finance. Volatility is a sign of underlying problems with the business model.
- **Growing industries**: it is generally easier to grow a business when the industry it plays in is itself growing.
- **No customer concentration**: it is highly risky to acquire businesses where a single customer represents over 10 per cent of total revenues, or a small group of customers represent over 25 per cent.

- **Low capital expenditures**: free cash flows should be available to service the acquisition debt rather than being used to sustain the business through capital expenditures. Searchers should also evaluate capex and working capital required to grow the business going forward.
- **Fragmented industries:** it is easier to compete in an industry where there are no dominant players that pose a competitive threat to the target company.

At first glance, it may seem nearly impossible to satisfy all of the above criteria. In fact, it is not all that infrequent, since many of them are inherently correlated. Again, searchers should be looking to buy good, solid businesses, and there are many companies that meet these criteria. However, searchers must be both patient and unwavering in their search.

Part of the post-acquisition failure identified in searcher-acquired companies can be attributed to searchers failing to adhere to the above-listed criteria.[11] Searching for a company to buy can be incredibly frustrating. As time passes, it becomes easier and easier for searchers, when looking at an acquisition target, to rationalize that one or more of these criteria are not that important, to relax those criteria, and then buy the company. For example, searchers regularly dismiss customer concentration (i.e. one client representing 25 per cent of sales), saying that once they become CEO the business will grow substantially and thus diminish the risk from potentially losing its largest customer. But what happens if, unbeknownst to the searcher, there was a special relationship between the seller and that customer and the customer left shortly after the deal closed? There would be no recourse to the seller, and the business, now run by an inexperienced CEO, would immediately be in serious difficulty having suddenly lost a quarter of its revenues. Let this example serve as a warning: adhering to search criteria is a matter of the utmost importance.

14.5   Defining the Search Strategy

There are two main search strategies used to find companies to acquire: proprietary and brokered searches. The proprietary strategy involves contacting company owners directly to see if they are interested in discussing a potential sale of their business. In a brokered strategy, the searcher focuses on reaching out to business brokers or other M&A advisors who are mandated to sell a company on behalf of its owner. These two strategies differ in two major respects: the methods that each implies and the deal parameters that are likely to result. While some searchers choose one strategy or the other, most use a mixture of both strategies.

14.5.1   Brokered Searches

Many business owners reach out to business brokers for help with marketing and selling their company. In many cases, the owner's shares in the business are their

11 Kessler and Ellis (2012).

most valuable asset. It is, therefore, normal that an owner would want to max-imize the value of that asset at the time of sale, and this is even more true of retiring sellers, since the proceeds of the sale are likely the last large payday they will have in their lifetime.

From the searcher's point of view, there are numerous advantages and dis-advantages of using brokers that vary considerably depending on the engage-ment and professionalism of the broker. A major advantage of having a broker involved is that the seller, having signed an exclusive 'sale mandate', is much more likely to follow through with the sale. One of the most difficult chal-lenges every searcher faces is determining the likelihood that the seller will actually sell the company. Another advantage of having a broker involved is that the broker can be a useful source of information and can help smooth communications during negotiations. Brokers, particularly small brokers who may only sign one or two deals each year, need to sell companies to earn their living. They would rather achieve lower fees with greater certainty by selling a company at a lower price, than trying to maximize the sale price at the risk of the deal not happening. Often, these same brokers lack the talent, experience or drive to adequately market the business. This is immediately visible in the quality of the *Confidential Information Memorandum* (CIM) and the existence – or not – of a properly structured auction process. Many brokers underperform on all aspects, and this is where a professional buyer, such as a searcher, has an advantage over other possible buyers. Professional buyers will see through a broker's shortcomings and view this as an opportunity to be seized in the discussions.

There are also important disadvantages of using brokers. To begin with, searchers may be generally and rightfully concerned that, given their relative inexperience, brokers will first show them the unwanted, picked-over deals to see if they can unload them. Beyond that, the main drawback of working through a broker is price. If the broker organizes a sale process, competitive bidding can drive up the price considerably, often beyond the means of most searchers. Avoiding competitive bidding processes is one of the tenets of the search fund world, as searchers invariably seek to buy a business from an owner who has other priorities than just maximizing the sale price.

Every searcher must weigh the advantages and disadvantages of using brokers. But even if the searcher opts for a proprietary search, using brokers to see deals early in their search and gaining practice can be very useful. Likewise, looking at deals with brokers can provide ideas on potentially interesting industry niches in which to search. In the end, it is not an either/or decision.

Brokered Search Techniques

The brokered search process begins with the searcher establishing lists of brokers and contacting them. But who are these brokers, how do you find them, and which ones should be contacted? In its broadest definition, a broker is anyone who facilitates transactions on behalf of buyers or sellers. It is not uncommon for 'buy side' brokers to contact searchers and try to offer to help them, for a fee, find a company to buy. Searchers would be wise to reject these requests altogether. Searchers should focus on 'sell side' brokers who are mandated by, and ultimately paid by, the company owner.

Brokers come in many shapes and sizes, ranging from one-man shows to Goldman Sachs. Those dealing with companies in the size range searchers are looking for are obviously at the lower end of the spectrum. For illustrative purposes, these brokers can be put into three buckets: individual brokers that do one or two deals each year, brokerage firms that do numerous deals each year, and online deal marketplaces.

Finding and Selecting Brokers

The first reflex of any searcher is to scour the Internet for 'business brokers'. This will yield results, but the listings will require considerable vetting. Among the most prolific entries will be online marketplaces and deal listings. Searchers should mostly avoid contacting these, since they tend to focus mainly on small companies such as bars, restaurants, retail stores, etc. Some larger, more professional online marketplaces exist, but the companies found in them will be among the most picked-over of all broker listings. Though there are, of course, exceptions, the companies still listed will often be ones that have been for sale for quite some time and have attracted no buyers.

Instead, searchers should seek business broker associations and focus on their members. This added level of professionalism is a small but perceptible hurdle that will reap rewards in terms of quality and seriousness. But there are still significant differences between one-man shows and larger brokerage firms. Brokerage firms will be more professional and, on average, have more deals under mandate to present to searchers. But they are also more likely to run structured sale processes that will increase competition and, therefore, prices. Despite this, they are good, solid sources of deal flow and should definitely be targeted. Smaller brokers, ones that do only one or two deals per year, are highly heterogeneous in terms of quality. But it is safe to say that the average broker in this category is less likely to run a true sale process and is more concerned with selling the business and collecting their commission. The deals they represent tend to be those of company owners in their network. And while searchers will have to be more discriminating, if they find an interesting deal, they can often proceed with little or no competitive pressure.

Dealing with Brokers

Searchers need to cultivate relationships with the brokers they contact in order to successfully find an interesting deal. After an initial contact by email, searchers should reach out by phone and speak with the broker. During the call, the searcher has four primary objectives: (1) establish credibility and rapport, (2) vet the broker in terms of professionalism and deal flow, (3) explain their search criteria, and (4) see what deals the broker currently has in hand that could be of interest.

Most searchers, at least early on, approach these calls in a defensive posture since they see themselves as inexperienced searchers who have never before bought or run a company. Through the eyes of the broker, however, the searcher is a highly-qualified potential buyer for the companies the broker is trying to sell. So searchers should approach these calls with confidence, and focus on vetting the qualifications and experience of the broker and learning about the deals they currently have. For deals that are potentially interesting, the broker will send the searcher a *teaser*. A teaser is a one or two-page document that succinctly describes the business without revealing its name or location. The broker will hide the company's identity until the searcher signs a *Non-Disclosure Agreement* (NDA) in order to protect the broker's relationship with the seller and, above all, preserve their commission. Upon signing the NDA, the searcher will receive a CIM that describes the company in detail.

Confidential Information Memoranda are marketing documents prepared by the broker for the sole purpose of selling the business. While they are for the most part truthful, since buyers will have ample time during due diligence to verify the veracity of the contents, they will position the company in a positive light. They can range in length from five to fifty pages, and in quality from excellent to poor. Unfortunately, there is no correlation between the quality of the CIM and that of the business, as it is more a reflection of the seriousness, experience and professionalism of the broker than the quality of the company being presented.

Searchers use CIMs to quickly understand the scale and nature of the business and determine whether they want to pursue it further, first with the broker, and eventually with the seller. The first interactions with the broker should enable the searcher to clarify issues and be in a better position to make an initial offer on the company. To this extent, the broker serves as a positive buffer to the seller. But once the searcher has decided that the company merits further attention, the searcher's objective should be to speak directly with the seller. At this stage, the broker can either be a facilitator, helping the two parties build a productive relationship in order to reach an agreement, or be an obstacle, creating problems that can ultimately undermine the chances of a deal being signed. Either way, the searcher must be concerned with and deal with the psychologies of both broker and seller. From this stage forward, the deal, if it progresses, will follow the stages outlined below for proprietary searches.

14.5.2   Proprietary Searches

Most searchers heavily weight their strategy in favour of proprietary searches. The objective is to enter into one-on-one discussions with a willing seller, without the competitive pressure – and therefore the uncertainty – of having other bidders involved. This approach necessarily requires the searcher to continuously evaluate the probability that the seller will actually sell.

Unlike brokered strategies, where searchers may contact several hundred brokers or other deal intermediaries to create deal flow, in a proprietary search, the number of contacts is well into the thousands, sometimes up to 20,000 or more over the entire search. It is a numbers game. This is the most glaring drawback of proprietary searches. Whether the contacts are made via mail, email or telephone, they are unsolicited approaches ('cold calls') and, as a result, produce relatively low positive response rates, hence the need for a high volume of contacts. The challenge is fairly daunting. It is the proverbial search for a needle in a haystack. Searchers are looking for a company that not only corresponds to all the criteria enumerated earlier, but also that the searcher identifies and contacts at the exact moment of the owner's life when a discussion about the potential sale of their business is of interest. Two windows of opportunity – the searcher's and the owner's – must align simultaneously.

While there are no studies that quantitatively compare brokered and proprietary searches, anecdotal evidence suggests that proprietary searches lead to better deals. This approach obliges the searcher to build a significant pipeline of quality deals, which is constantly being culled and supplemented, in order to succeed. It also requires discipline and fortitude, because the expected levels of rejection and failure are high.

A proprietary search is essentially a direct marketing campaign aimed at the owners of companies that are a likely fit with the searcher's criteria. While this campaign can be conducted via telephone calls, letters or emails, the latter is increasingly the medium of choice. Having said that, the efficiency, or even appropriateness, of each approach is highly dependent on the culture of the country in which the search is taking place. But before discussing the methods of outreach, we must first understand how to build a list of contacts.

There are two basic proprietary search strategies: (1) an industry niche-focused search, and (2) a geographically focused search.

Industry Niche Focus

Of these two approaches, the industry-targeted strategy has a greater probability of success, though both are perfectly valid approaches. Why is an industry-focused search more likely to succeed? By targeting companies in a relatively small-sized industry niche, searchers can more easily identify and target interesting businesses. The searcher can evaluate the business model of the niche and then, if it proves to be interesting, identify all the companies in that niche and contact them. They can more easily and efficiently personalize the emails they send, tailoring them to the specificities of the targeted industry, thereby rendering the emails more appealing and effective. Searchers can also more readily gain credibility with business owners by quickly learning the inner workings and vocabulary of businesses in that niche. This can also allow the searcher to network among companies in that niche. Finally, the industry niche approach is generally nationwide which, in turn, by virtue of sheer numbers, further increases the odds of success.

Geographic Focus

It is clear that some searchers will have strong geographic preferences or constraints and will therefore conduct a geographically focused search. However, searchers should be aware that by limiting their search to a small geographic region, they automatically reduce their chances of success. This, in turn, significantly reduces the probability of raising capital for a funded search. Why would a third-party investor accept the higher risk of a geographically constrained search when they have many opportunities to back searchers looking nationwide? For that reason, searchers who need or want to focus on a region or metropolitan area usually opt for self-funded searches. In addition to severely limiting the population of potential targets, there is another major disadvantage to this approach. To compensate for the limited number of companies in a geographic area, most searchers conduct a search that is industry agnostic. Since the contacts are by definition heterogeneous, each discussion with an owner is about a company in an entirely different industry, making it relatively harder for the searcher to build industry knowledge and gain credibility, both of which are important to company owners considering selling their business.

While the risk of limiting the number of potential acquisition targets is clear, there are some advantages to being geographically focused. If the searcher already has extensive personal and professional networks, these can be leveraged to source deals. Even if a particular company owner is not part of a searcher's existing network, it is usually much easier to connect with them. And when that connection is made, there is a hometown advantage that is built from shared experiences, such as going to the same high school or college, knowing the same people, or other commonalities. All things being equal, many company owners prefer selling to someone who is equally attached to the area where the company is located. Finally, this approach allows the searcher to meet the owner in person more easily and cheaply, which is an obvious advantage for building a solid relationship.

Proprietary Search Techniques

When conducting a proprietary search, there are a number of techniques and best practices that will enhance a searcher's chances of success. In this next section, we will identify and explain these considerations.

Identifying Industry Niches

The first step in a proprietary search is to identify interesting industry niches. Unfortunately, this is much more of an art than a science. And since it is the key to an industry-focused search, it can be a major stumbling block for searchers. While there is no magic formula, there are a number of 'tricks of the trade' that searchers employ. Once ideas surface, it is up to the searcher to think through the business and economic characteristics of the niche to validate or invalidate it as one on which to focus. Some tactics for identifying niches include:

- **Analysing industry codes**: most governments have a classification system for businesses that groups them under industry codes. For example, in the United States, there are SIC and NAICS codes, and in France there are NAF codes. These codes enable a searcher to search databases for companies in the same sector.
- **Reviewing private equity acquisitions**: searchers often look at recent acquisitions by private equity firms or at the portfolio companies of private equity firms to get ideas for interesting industries.
- **Scouring broker listings**: searchers will often turn to broker listings as a source of inspiration for industry niche ideas.
- **Keeping your eyes open**: while it sounds amateurish, searchers are constantly on the lookout for potentially good service businesses by reading the sides of service trucks and looking at advertisements.
- **Working with interns**: searchers who use interns often task their interns with coming up with industry ideas. While they generally lack the business experience of the searcher, the challenge is interesting for interns and they often come up with compelling and less conventional ideas.

Typically, searchers work on two or three industry niches at a time. Like gold mining, if they come across interesting leads and have fruitful conversations with company owners, they dig deeper. If not, they move on to another niche in the hopes that it will yield better results.

Identifying Companies, Owner Names and Contact Details

Once a niche has been chosen, the searcher and the searcher's interns can use a wide variety of databases and other online tools to find companies in that niche and assemble contact lists for mailing or emailing. One approach is to search generalized company databases using industry codes and keywords to find potentially interesting businesses in the identified industry niche. Another method is to find existing lists of companies, such as memberships in industry associations and exhibitor lists from trade shows. Finally, tech savvy searchers are able to develop scraping tools to automate the gathering of large amounts of qualified information from Web-based sources. Regardless of the method employed, it is a tedious task, but one that is crucial to building the outreach programme.

In addition to identifying potential targets, most searchers try to qualify the contacts, particularly in terms of size. To the extent possible, searchers should try to screen out companies that are either too big or too small. To achieve this, in some countries, detailed data is publicly available because companies are required by law to file accounts and other company information annually with government entities. Where these data are not readily available, there are commercial databases that often include revenue figures, number of employees, and other metrics, for a fee.[12] Though these are generally imperfect estimations, it may be the best data available. Some of these same databases also list owner names and sometimes email addresses. Otherwise, owner names can often be found on the company website or other online sources. While postal addresses are fairly straightforward, and are readily found on websites and databases, email addresses are more complicated. If the email address is not available on the website, there are numerous email finding tools that use the individual's first and last names, plus the domain name of the company, to work through the possible combinations and identify the correct one.

Owner Outreach

Most prospective searchers, when they imagine contacting a company owner, think of cold calling. In reality, most searchers use postal mail or email, the latter now being the preferred method in most countries. Regardless of the means, this is a direct marketing campaign, much like those used by companies to reach prospective clients and sell their goods or services. In this case, the prospective client is the company owner. And like most prospects, what is unknown is whether or not the person contacted will be receptive to the message. In the particular case of searching for a company to buy, the 'product', or the owner's business, is a very peculiar one that probably represents that person's most valuable asset, to which they may have a strong emotional attachment. Furthermore, selling one's company is often tied to retirement, which can also be a very emotional decision.

As with any direct marketing campaign, there are numerous variables that come into play. Reaching out to company owners and trying to engage them in a conversation about selling their business is no exception. The most basic component is the message itself. At a minimum, the message must identify and convey a positive image about the searcher, and clearly ask if the owner would be interested in discussing the sale of their company. Careful consideration

---

12 Most notable example in the UK is Companies House. Bureau van Dijk offers its Diane service in France and Dafne in Germany; also in France there is Infogreffe.

should be given to how the typical owner, if there is such a thing, will react to it. Beyond this, there are numerous other considerations when constructing the campaign in terms of drafting the message itself and setting other parameters of the outreach:

- **Message length**: it is as easy to write too much as it is to write too little. It is important to strike the correct balance.
- **Searcher background**: searchers often include certain information about their personal and professional background to connect with the owner, gain their confidence, and build credibility.
- **Search criteria**: some searchers include some of their key search criteria to act as a screen to prevent owners of companies that do not meet the basic characteristics from replying. Size requirements in terms of sales or EBITDA are often cited.
- **Personalization**: searchers regularly include 'hooks' that will create a link to the owner and give the impression that the message was written especially for them. These can include mentioning the company name (in long or short form), the geographical location, information on the industry, etc.
- **Considerations for emails**: attention must also be given to the subject line (content and length), the day of the week and hour of the day when the emails are sent, and the content and timing of follow-up emails.
- **Considerations for postal mail**: searchers should sign the letter and can optionally add a handwritten comment, envelopes can be hand addressed, 'personal and confidential' stamps can be placed on the envelope, and considerations of timing also apply.

Tracking Outreach Metrics

Throughout the process, searchers should record detailed metrics on the number of contacts generated, messages sent, total responses, positive responses, bounce rate, phone conversations, NDAs sent, financials received, etc. By tracking these data, searchers can track their progress and improve their campaigns over time. Many searchers also conduct A/B tests on messages in order to increase the efficacy of their outreach. They test different messages, different content and different timing, making slight variations to see what works best. This obviously requires consistent data tracking and analysis. Though time is limited, it is important for searchers to have some objective, quantitative gauge by which to measure their effectiveness.

In addition to tracking search data to identify potential improvements, these data can also be used for goal setting and performance tracking. Searching for a company to buy is a numbers game. It will require a large, often very large, number of messages sent, to generate a sufficient quantity of seller phone calls that lead to a reasonable number of financials received, etc. This is known as a funnel.[13] Some searchers, by the time they acquire a business, will have sent over 20,000 messages, talked to hundreds of owners, and investigated, in some depth, dozens of companies before they succeed in making an acquisition. Searchers need to be prepared for a long and tedious process.

Using Interns

Most, but not all, searchers use interns to help with company and owner research during the search process. Their tasks usually include finding company names and screening them to develop contact lists, then finding owner names and contact details to create mailing lists. Their role can also be broader. It can include helping identify interesting industry niches, researching industries, researching companies and helping with commercial and strategic due diligence.

Most search fund interns, usually college juniors and seniors, are looking for business experience that will enhance their resume when applying for jobs in private equity, banking or corporate finance. Most interns are recruited through general online internship postings or postings directly at targeted colleges and universities. When interviewing candidates, searchers should not only verify their qualifications and motivations, but also honestly describe the unglamorous side of interning for a searcher. Interns are not always easy to manage. They have many other demands on their time, and often lack the professionalism that only comes with years of work experience. But properly managed, they can not only provide a huge boost to the search, but also help with the loneliness that comes with it. Many searchers and interns enjoy relationships both as friends and mentors. Searchers obviously train their interns on the search process, but also on LBOs, due diligence, deal financing and other aspects of acquiring a company. Searchers also generally provide career counselling, review résumés, help with cover letters and assist in interview preparation. The ideal searcher–intern relation is professional and productive, but also friendly and mutually beneficial.

14.6   Engaging with Owners

The primary objective of the outreach process is to have a first conversation with a company owner. However, this is really just the beginning. This is the first truly concrete step that can lead to an eventual acquisition. This is the point where the 'selling' begins in earnest.

---

13 The funnel starts with raw contacts that searchers find, but no one really counts those. 'Official' numbers start with the number of emails (or letters) sent out during the search, say 5–10,000; positive responses to those mails lead to calls with company owners, say 400–600; this leads to about 30–50 initial offers (IOIs), then to 2–5 LOIs, and hopefully 1 company gets acquired (based on author experience).

The probability of any one seller call resulting in acquiring the company is low. And yet, each call has to be treated as though it were 'the one'. There is, however, an interesting information dissymmetry at play. The searcher knows that they have never bought a company before, and has not only never run a business, but may have only had limited team management experience. This knowledge tends to push searchers to spend too much time introducing themselves and trying to justify their aptitude to buy the company. This lack of confidence can result in the conversation centring around the searcher, instead of focusing on the seller and the seller's company. On the other hand, company owners know little or nothing about the searcher. The information they have will be limited to whatever the searcher has on their website, LinkedIn profile, the outreach letter and, though less likely, information that is generally available on the Web. A quick glance at the searcher's background probably leaves a predictable impression: the searcher appears to be a very smart person, a little young maybe, but with impressive credentials. And remember, the call is only taking place because the seller responded to the outreach message. The seller chose to have this conversation.

To be effective and, paradoxically, to avoid drawing attention to their comparatively limited experience, searchers should keep their introductory comments to a minimum. This requires a level of confidence that will only come with the experience of having had numerous seller calls. Instead of centring excessively on the searcher, the conversation should focus on qualifying the business, qualifying the seller, establishing rapport, and, if the aforementioned points are all positive, asking for financials. If, on any of the previous dimensions, the results are not positive, the searcher should quickly, but politely, end the call. In a search, time is the scarce resource. Too many searchers waste time chatting with company owners even though the business is obviously not interesting or the owner is not serious about selling.

14.6.1   Qualifying the Company

The searcher should ask if the business has revenues in the range of what the searcher is seeking. Some sellers will respond by simply stating their approximate revenues. Others will be more reluctant to give a number and instead give an indication of size with respect to the range the searcher is targeting. Asking about EBITDA, net income or cash flow will be trickier, since most sellers will regard this information to be more confidential. Regardless, the searcher needs to quickly determine whether it is useful to continue the conversation.

14.6.2   Qualifying the Seller

The good thing about company owners is that they usually love talking about their companies and themselves. In addition to determining fit, searchers should also try to assess whether or not the owner is genuinely interested in selling their company. The easiest way to find out is to simply ask. Often, the reason is retirement. But even owners of retirement age often have difficulty selling their business. Some owners are reluctant to sell because of their emotional attachment to the business. Others are reluctant because they have no idea what they would do each day if they were no longer managing their company. Searchers need to listen carefully to decode the answer they hear to determine if it sounds plausible and sincere. Again, this requires experience, though fortunately searchers gain it relatively quickly.

14.6.3   Building Rapport

As the searcher qualifies the company and seller, they should also build rapport with the owner as the conversation progresses. This rapport will put the company owner at ease and allow them to open up and share more information about the business. At some point, the owner will likely shift into 'sales mode'. Concomitantly, the searcher will be more and more at ease in the conversation, boosting their confidence and making it easier to ask for more and more information. While being mindful of the time spent on the call, and not trying to go too far too fast, the searcher will quickly see whether there is sufficient mutual trust and respect to take the conversation to the next level.

14.6.4   Asking for Financials

Assuming the conversation progresses positively, the searcher should ask the seller if they would be willing to share recent financials. In order to further build credibility, demonstrate professionalism, and to allay the seller's fears of sharing sensitive information, the searcher should propose to sign a NDA with the seller. Searchers should explain that it is only by reviewing the financials that they will be in a position to confirm interest in the company and make an initial offer. The seller's willingness or lack thereof to share financial information is a key test of the seller's mindset and true intent to sell. But even eager sellers will often take time to sign the NDA, pull together the financials and send them to the searcher. This process often requires patience and frequent follow-up, but searchers must remember that even willing sellers are usually still grappling with the reality of selling their 'baby' and transitioning to a new lifestyle in addition to the constant demands of running their business.

14.7   Discussing Price

The initial investigation of the company's financials will invariably lead to a multitude of questions, which will in turn lead to further discussions between searcher and seller. As the searcher becomes more and more comfortable with the past performance of the company and its future prospects, there comes a time when the parties will want to determine if a deal is possible. While there are many components of an offer, price is the elephant in the room, and searchers should approach that discussion professionally. This requires preparation, thought and a bit of psychology.

Searchers, and their investors and bankers, generally think of price in terms of EBITDA multiples, except when working in sectors that have specific valuation metrics such as multiples of sales or multiples of recurring monthly revenues. Discounted cash flow valuation methods are neither appropriate nor used in small transactions. And while multiples are the most frequent method by which companies are valued, they are at best indicative. There are no formulas for calculating the multiple for a transaction. Rather, there are historical averages and tendencies that can inform appreciations of what range of multiples would be appropriate.

Multiples are a function of the intrinsic characteristics of the company. These include: size, level of profitability, cyclicality, volatility of earnings and/or cash flows, recent and future growth, etc. For example, the higher the growth rate, the higher the multiple. They also reflect the nature of the transaction: is the buyer taking a minority or controlling stake. Finally, though it is somewhat less true for smaller transactions, multiples vary with markets. When equity and LBO debt is readily available, multiples tend to rise as competition for deals increases. This is yet another reason to target smaller firms that are well below the level at which most strategic and financial buyers would find them interesting.

In both the US and Europe, if searchers stick to buying companies that have EBITDAs in the range of €1.0–2.5 million per annum, in today's market, searchers can find companies for which the market clearing price will be in the range of 3.5–5.0×EBITDA. While this is not universally applicable, as there are many counter-examples, it is a good starting point. Companies with EBITDAs above €3m but less than €10m can be expected to trade in the range of 5–7×EBITDA, whereas above €10m of EBITDA, multiples can quickly rise into double digits. The step change in multiples is linked to the nature of buyers in the market. Markets dominated by individual buyers exhibit lower multiples. But above a certain threshold, strategic and financial buyers are active and multiples rise as they seek to deploy their capital. These principles hold roughly true in other economies as well. Having said that, in other geographies with smaller economies, investment funds are likely to scale down in size and may end up competing with searchers for smaller deals.

How do sellers think about the value of their companies? Sellers sometimes reason in multiples, but in general, they are thinking much more in terms of euro amounts. Searchers, therefore, are well advised to present their offers in a manner that is readily understood by company owners who may not have any prior experience selling a business. The offer should be expressed in monetary, not multiple, terms. Since sellers' understanding of company valuation techniques and metrics is highly variable, the price, arguably the most important component of the offer, must be clear. Searchers should attempt, from the very first call onwards, to understand how the seller thinks about the value of their company. But searchers should be prepared for surprises. Non-analytical valuation 'methods' are far more common than one would imagine. For example, it is not unusual for a seller to value the business as a function of how much money the seller needs to retire comfortably. These notions, while reflecting the charm of buying smaller businesses, are obviously difficult to reason with, and make it much harder for the searcher to reach an agreement with the seller on price. Sometimes, it is impossible to reach a price level that seasoned practitioners would find acceptable. Searchers should expect this, and be prepared to walk away from the deal, knowing that on occasion this act in itself will bring the seller to reason.

14.8   Making an Offer

When there is a broad agreement on price, or at least a bridgeable difference, and the searcher has verified, to the extent possible, that the company meets the established search criteria, the searcher should submit an initial offer. This early-stage, non-binding offer is generally known as an *Indication of Interest (IOI)* or *Letter of Intent (LOI)*. Searchers should submit offers sooner rather than later to test the seller. Again, a searcher's most precious asset is time, and it is very easy to waste many hours, days, even weeks on deals that will never close. A written offer puts the seller face-to-face with the reality, both in psychological and economic terms, of selling their company.

An IOI is a relatively simple letter the searcher sends to the seller. It is generally so simple that a lawyer does not need to be involved in redacting the letter. In fact, the only truly legal clause that an IOI should absolutely contain is a statement that the offer is 'non-binding' and that it is 'Subject to Contract'. From a business point of view, an IOI should, as a minimum, stipulate the price being offered and the underlying financials communicated to the searcher by the seller on which the offer is based. Tying the offer to known numbers will allow the searcher to objectively revise the offer at a later date if the numbers change, notably from due diligence. Beyond that, and to the extent that it has already been discussed with the seller, the IOI can also mention seller financing (amount, interest rate, payment terms), a working capital adjustment, escrow account, seller transition, etc. The IOI should also point the seller to the future and give them confidence that the deal is real by laying out the need for and timing of due diligence, as well as a date or estimated numbers of days until the deal could be completed.

An LOI is generally a more definitive version of the offer with more detail and defined, negotiated terms. The LOI should essentially contain all the deal terms that will be drafted into the final deal documentation. The searcher's objective should be to discuss every topic to make sure there is a true agreement before committing time and money to conducting confirmatory due diligence. The LOI should include:

- **Deal structure**: most jurisdictions provide for two basic types of acquisitions: stock deals and asset deals. In stock deals, the buyer acquires the equity of the company, buying the entire legal entity along with any potential contingent liabilities that may exit. In an asset deal, the buyer acquires the assets of the business, though it can also include operating liabilities such as accounts payable. The seller retains ownership of the legal entity that previously owned the business. While stock deals are most common in the overall LBO market, search deals tend to be mostly asset deals, to avoid potentially fatal problems with entities that have previously been owner-operated. It is important to note that there are tax considerations for both buyer and seller that need to be taken into account and for which tax advice should be sought.

- **Price**: it sounds simple to put a price on a business and yet, in reality, price is often split into numerous components. Searchers commonly give an overall Enterprise Value as a headline price, though they sometimes include other payments – such as interest on seller financing – to get closer, on an aggregate basis, to the number the seller has in mind. Searchers should always clearly identify the financial data and assumptions on which the offer is based, in case those assumptions change following due diligence reviews.

- **Seller financing**: sellers often agree to defer payment of a certain portion of their total consideration in order to facilitate the deal. It is also an obvious vote of confidence in the future of the company that gives comfort to buyers. Seller financing generally ranges from 10 to 50 per cent of the amounts due. In return, the seller will earn interest payments that are usually above typical bank rates. While the deferred amounts are typically unsecured, they are backed by the future performance of an asset the seller knows well. If a searcher is also using bank debt, the seller debt will typically be junior or subordinated to the senior debt. This means that while interest payments can be paid quarterly or annually, the principal is not returned until the bank debt has been fully repaid. The principal is often returned as a bullet payment four or five years after the transaction closes.

- **Representations and Warranties**: searchers should stipulate that they will seek 'Reps & Warranties' that are customary for the type of deal under consideration. Reps & Warranties act as an insurance policy to financially protect the buyer against any event that occurred under the previous owner, that the owner knew or should have known, but of which the buyer was unaware.

- **Escrow**: it is typical for buyers to negotiate that a small portion of the seller's total consideration be placed in escrow, a bank account controlled by a lawyer or escrow agent, in the event of claims under the Reps & Warranties. An escrow account gives the buyer access to a relatively quick cash remedy (versus suing under the Reps & Warranties) should an event occur that is covered by the seller, but that has an immediate cash cost to the buyer.
- **Seller Transition Agreement**: searchers generally want sellers to remain in the company for a certain period of time to help transition the business to the new CEO. This can include introducing clients and suppliers, transitioning management functions, teaching the new CEO technical aspects of the business, etc. Sometimes this is done as an ongoing employment contract. Sometimes there is an external consulting agreement. Either way, the agreement should clearly define responsibilities, term of the transition and remuneration.

At this stage of the deal, the LOI should also contain an exclusivity clause. Exclusivity means that for an agreed period of time, typically 90 to 120 days, the seller will neither solicit nor engage or continue discussions with any other potential buyers. This gives the searcher a clear runway to conduct due diligence and engage lawyers, both of which are costly, in order to close the deal without competition from other parties.

Finally, the offer should outline the steps to closing, such as financial and legal due diligence, securing senior debt financing, and obtaining final approval from the equity providers. This shows the seller, especially when the seller has accorded exclusivity, that there is a clear path to completing the deal.

Unfortunately, when making offers, many searchers try to avoid conflict by not discussing those deal points that are potential sources of disagreement. They often favour a more simplistic agreement on price alone. While they may think they have a deal, as we have just seen, there are many more potentially contentious points that need to be discussed. The erroneous logic that many searchers adopt is that it will be easier to discuss the more difficult points once the due diligence has been completed and the seller is 'on the hook'. Searchers would do well to remember that the seller can back out at any moment up until the final signatures. Rationally speaking, it is far better for the searcher to find out if the seller has strong objections to any of the deal points sooner rather than later, and especially before spending significant amounts of time and money on due diligence and drafting legal documents. Again, the point of the exercise is to provoke a reaction, even if it is a negative one. In short, if the seller is going to back out, it is better to back out early in the deal discussions. Like startup entrepreneurs, searchers should seek to fail fast and move on.

Depending on the nature of the prior discussions, the seller will almost certainly react to the searcher's offer. There may be disagreement on price. There may be other points or issues the seller rejects or wants to discuss or negotiate. Or the seller could reject the offer purely from a change of heart from seeing the offer in writing, forcing them to really think through the implications of selling their business. From this point on, the searcher will need to rely on their negotiating skills and relationship with the seller in order to progress.

14.9   Completing the Transaction

In many respects, reaching agreement on the terms of a deal is just the beginning. There is still a long road ahead to complete the deal. Due diligence is a detailed and lengthy investigation of the company's accounts, legal structure, contracts, commercial relations, employees, technology, etc. Due diligence can take two to four months and often reveals issues that are deal killers. Drafting and agreeing to all the legal documents and exhibits is also very time consuming. Contacting banks (sometimes as many as eighty) and raising senior debt can take two to three months. There will also be discussions with banks over security, including personal guarantees, and the relation to the seller debt. As the deal progresses, lawyers on both sides will raise other issues that will cause blood pressures to rise and potentially put the deal in peril. And even if everything goes well, the seller may ultimately get cold feet. This is all part of the emotional roller coaster that characterizes entrepreneurship through acquisition.

KEY TAKEAWAYS

- Entrepreneurship through acquisition is an interesting path to becoming an equity-owning CEO and entrepreneur.
- Buying and improving an existing business is a less risky route to entrepreneurship than starting a startup.
- There is a small but easily identifiable and growing number of investors interested in backing searchers in the search for and acquisition of a business.
- Searching for potential acquisition targets is a lengthy, time-consuming process that takes time to learn, mostly through trial and error, but it works.
- Searchers can successfully find and acquire a good business, typically from a retiring owner, at a reasonable price.

END OF CHAPTER QUESTIONS

1. Do you want to be the equity-owning CEO of a small or medium-sized business?

2. Do you feel you have the management experience and entrepreneurial spirit to buy and run a business? If not, what steps could you take to prepare yourself?

3. Have you ever thought of buying an existing business? Do you know anyone else who has bought a business?

4. Do you know or have access to potential investors who could also provide you with mentorship in addition to the capital needed to acquire a business?

5. How comfortable do you feel with setting up a search and reaching out to company owners to discuss the idea of them selling you their business?

6. Do you have the experience necessary to manage a transaction, value a business, conduct due diligence and close a deal, or have access to advisors who can help you along the way?

7. Do you fully understand the time, effort and patience that is required to source good companies? Are you comfortable with the idea of screening thousands of businesses over a period of twelve to twenty-four months?

8. Do you feel comfortable evaluating businesses objectively and avoiding the problems of confirmation bias when making the distinction between 'good' and 'bad' investment opportunities?

9. Is this the right time, professionally and personally, for you and your family to pursue entrepreneurship through acquisition? Will you have the support of your family and friends?

FURTHER READING

IESE Business School (2016). International Search Funds – 2016: Selected Observations. www.iese.edu/research/pdfs/ST-0415-E.pdf

IESE Business School. Search Funds: What has made them work? www.gsb.stanford.edu/sites/gsb/files/st-0357-e.pdf

Stanford Graduate School of Business. Search Funds: Best Practices for the Search Phase. www.gsb.stanford.edu/sites/gsb/files/ces-search-funds-best-practices-search-phase.pdf

Stanford Graduate School of Business. Search Funds: Death and the Afterlife. www.jimsteinsharpe.com/wp-content/uploads/2015/02/120907-Search-Funds_Death-and-the-Afterlife_Benjamin-Kessler_9.7.2012–1.pdf

Stanford Graduate School of Business. Search Fund Primer. www.gsb.stanford.edu/faculty-research/centers-initiatives/ces/research/search-funds/primer

Paul Thomson (2011). Search Fund Manifesto. www.jimsteinsharpe.com/wp-content/uploads/2015/09/Paul-Thomson-Search-Fund-Manifesto-2011–09.pdf

REFERENCES

Kelly, P., Dodson, D., Irving Grousbeck, H., Pohlmeyer, S. and Rosenthal, S. (2016). *2016 Search Fund Study: Selected Observations. Center for Entrepreneurial Studies.* Stanford Graduate School of Business.

Kessler, B. and Ellis, J. (2012). *Search Funds: Death and the Afterlife. Center for Entrepreneurial Studies*, Stanford Graduate School of Business.

Let's Practise: Case Study

SEARCH FUND: AltEquity[14]

My name is Sean O'Neill. I graduated INSEAD in December 2013, and was going through interview rounds for PE firms when I decided to take a leap of faith and go the entrepreneurship route instead. More specifically, I decided to raise a search fund. This is my story.

Deciding to Raise a Search Fund

Having worked at Alinda Capital Partners for six years, I was pretty familiar with both the transaction and the operations side of a PE firm. Yet, I couldn't get myself to choose between the two and, as a result, was having a hard time finding a firm that fit my aspirations.

That's when I started thinking about buying and running a business of my own. Then I heard about the search fund model, and ended up discussing it at length with my wife. This was especially important since this decision had the potential to substantially change our life together.

Two reasons led me to choosing that path. First of all, it was a way for me to 'de-risk' the process of finding a business. In other words, I would have a salary for the next two years, which would enable me to properly conduct a search without worrying about feeding my family – I had a wife and daughter with another one on the way. Had I had sufficient capital, I might have considered a self-funded search, but this wasn't an option for me – which made the decision relatively simple. Another reason for going the search fund route is that I felt excited about the community of investors and searchers involved in search funds. I wanted the relationship with investors, having them as a sounding board and learning from them over the course of the search and subsequent operation period. I'd be able to leverage their experience, and would gain in credibility when talking to buyers, as I would introduce my backers as successful entrepreneurs and business leaders – instead of a distant

---

14 This case was written by Lauren Bovard, under the supervision of Timothy Bovard, Adjunct Professor of Entrepreneurship at Columbia Business School. It is intended to be used as a basis for class discussion rather than to illustrate either effective or ineffective handling of an administrative situation. The authors gratefully acknowledge the assistance of Sean O'Neill with the development of this case study.

nebulous group. Current searchers were more than willing to speak with me and share with me their experience raising their fund and getting their search underway. Both groups comprised fascinating people with whom I readily felt comfortable.

The next step was talking about it with my wife, Julia. Her immediate reaction was that it sounded incredibly risky, but that the end result of operating a business was ideal. We both thought the process of getting there was a bit far fetched, but agreed to test the waters and think about it some more. That's when I began asking around for my friends' opinions. Most knew what a search fund was, and those who didn't quickly caught on. The problem was that 100% of my classmates were 110% supportive. Though it was incredibly comforting at first, it was actually an issue because their perspectives weren't necessarily objective. Some said that this was an amazing experience and encouraged me to go for it, asking me to update them along the way as a means of living vicariously through me from the comfort of their stable job at a top firm. Yet, I appreciated their support.

The first 'adult' I spoke to was my REP professor at INSEAD. I wrote down my thoughts on a post-it, putting on paper the main reasons for which I wanted to do this, and explaining not only why this was the right opportunity, but also why I was the right person for this. I put a lot of thought into it and met with him for a beer. Instead of the ten minute conversation I was expecting, we sat down for ninety minutes and he was exceedingly receptive – after which I asked him if he minded being my advisor. This was a strong signal and was my first turning point.

The second turning point was my mock interview at INSEAD. We were left to choose the type of questioning we wanted to run through, and I ended up practicing a PE interview alongside one of my good friends. And then, the woman running it asked a question I'd been grappling with for a while: "What would you choose, the transaction or operations side?" She pointed out that though my experience had covered both facets of a PE firm, I was going to have to make a decision as most companies generally split out their deal and their portfolio teams. Unable to answer it in my head, I tripped over my response. At the end of the interview, she gave us feedback and told us we had both gotten the job. However, she continued: "Sean, I think you're kidding yourself here. Sitting across the table from me is an entrepreneur." I then explained to her what my actual post-graduation plan was and she supported me as well.

The last people I spoke with about my decision were my former colleagues and work buddies. I expected honest feedback and most likely some pushback, but they were incredibly supportive too.

So, Julia and I set out on this path together. I emphasize the 'together' because it is very important that your spouse or significant other be fully aware of what their signing on for. In fact, it is a good idea to have your partner talk to other searcher partners to ask questions firsthand.

Getting the Funding

I gave a long hard look at the obstacles I was facing, the most important of which was uncertainty. Uncertainty financially: would I be able to raise this fund? I'd left my job and it would have been two years without an income and an expensive MBA, eating away at our savings. Uncertainty of where we would end up. And uncertainty of whether this would be successful – and of what we would do if this wasn't.

I had lined up a string of PE interviews on my own and each time, I was asked the same question I had been asked by the mock interviewer. I struggled with having to choose between the transaction and operations role because, having done both, I valued the relationship building and learning which takes place during the transaction period, along with its vital role during the subsequent operations. I had a really difficult time having to pick one or the other and really couldn't find a firm I wanted to work with. I'd never set foot in INSEAD's career center and didn't go to any recruiting sessions. It definitely didn't help looking at the salary statistics either; I'd be taking a huge haircut doing a search fund.

However, I'd made up my mind, and began my first search . . . for investors. I had identified a number of search fund investors that had come to INSEAD for a search fund conference, including some of the leading US investors. I began researching other search funds' websites and saw that they all listed their investors as Limited Partners. I wrote down the names, noted the repeats, and developed a network of who knows whom, etc. At one point, my wife realized that one of the names sounded familiar – she had gone to high school with him. Julia messaged him on Facebook, telling him that while they hadn't spoken since high school, she was currently at INSEAD with her husband and daughter and that I was interested in raising a search fund. Would he mind speaking with me? He immediately wrote back, and we had an hour-long Skype discussion the following day. He was extremely receptive and became a valued advisor. I felt comfortable enough to ask him a question I'd been having some trouble figuring out: when does one officially consider their search fund launched? He answered that as I had already mentally committed, I had therefore already launched.

I had put a lot of thought into working with a partner, but didn't have the right candidate in mind. If you choose not to go it alone, it is just as important – if not more so – to find the right partner as it is to find the right company. It also made it more challenging to find one since most of my classmates were moving to different hemispheres after graduation. I spoke to some people I knew that had heard about my project and were interested in teaming up, but I eventually decided that I wanted to go at it on my own. The main reason for my choice was that anyone I would consider working with would have needed to go up the same learning curve as I in terms of operating a business. I also knew I could just hire someone to fill the gaps and help me through situations I had had less experience with. Eventually, I felt comfortable enough in my skills and experience to navigate these waters alone. Because of those reasons taking primacy, I didn't even take into account financial considerations in deciding whether or not to team up with a partner.

While all my friends were traveling to Greece and other warm countries during the P4–P5 break, I stayed at INSEAD working on my Private Placement Memo (PPM). I had booked several meetings with investors, all of whom asked to see my PPM – which I hadn't written at the time. I began reaching out to them with short, punchy emails explaining my background and telling them I was involved in the operations and growth of a portfolio of companies we had acquired over the years, and that I'd appreciate hearing about their experiences in the search fund space. These emails were two-pronged: to connect, and fundraise. Many agreed to set up a call. Having gone through the fundraising process in the PE world and seeing what it takes to raise a fund – along with the vetting process that goes on – this was a night and day difference. It all went much faster.

One of the biggest fundraising challenges was to execute on the strategy of finding the right investor group on day one. At the outset, you have very limited information and don't know who has worked with whom or if you're going to succeed in raising the fund. As you gain momentum, traction and start testing the market, you then begin to develop a better understanding and refine your strategy. The fundraising process was very exciting but tough to navigate, as I sought a diverse and complementary group of individuals with whom I would develop long-term relationships. Instead of setting up a mass email blast to all the search fund investors I'd heard about, I researched each potential investor individually so as to understand his background, unique skillset, industry expertise, level of involvement and network. Also, it was important to me to have investors I liked and respected. This was the start of an incredibly important and long-standing relationship and I wanted to make sure that all of the odds were stacked in my favour to the maximum extent possible.

I had some difficult decisions along the way. There was a point when I stopped and assessed my position, being near the end of my raise, when I had to turn down a few investors I had heard great things about, but who needed more time to decide. When push came to shove, I had to begin my search process without them, though we agreed to stay in touch. However, while I felt that I had made the right selection, this was definitely a leap of faith!

Setting Up the Search Process

Though it may seem unconventional, my wife and I pulled out a map of the US. We could have just as easily looked on Internet, but I loved the idea of using a real map. The question at the time was: where should we move? We started calling our friends. I had a close friend from India who was very familiar with the research triangle in Raleigh, Durham and Chapel Hill, which he suggested as a great place to live. Above all, we were looking for an urban area where we had a network of friends and family, where we would enjoy living, and where there was a good access to an airport – especially since we knew that after those two years, we could end up anywhere in the US and might not have a chance to travel and visit family as much. We crossed New York off the list because it was too expensive. My sister-in-law was in Philly, halfway between my family in New York and Julia's in DC. It was affordable, with a great access to students for internships. It had a great transportation network and was on the East Coast. The second location we considered was DC, and the third was the Bay area – which we eventually crossed off as it was too pricey for us. We eventually chose Philadelphia. Strangely, I felt that calling from Philly gave me leverage with business owners compared to calling from New York. As a New Yorker, I identified completely with the city but understood that many saw it as the home of private equity guys and fancy bankers. Calling from Philly would set me apart from that stereotype and would get business owners to see me through a different lens.

The challenge that arose was clearly to work against the clock without a guidebook on what to do. How did you find companies for sale? I had a good sense of what needed to be done, but executing it was the hard part. The first hurdle was identifying different industries and figuring out how to uncover interesting companies in them. The industry niches had to fit the criteria for the search fund model as did the companies in them. Through trial and error I found information on a number of sectors, drilled down into them to develop qualified lists of companies, and further drilled down to get owner names and contact details. It took a while to get the hang of it, but eventually it became much easier.

I chose to reach out to business owners through direct mail rather than cold calling, as I felt it was a better use of my time. I didn't want to engage non-interested sellers over the phone. However, it took me some time to write a letter template that I thought was worded just right. I was well aware that business owners receive many such letters each week, and I wanted mine to stand out. Interestingly, one of the hardest parts was the act of sending the letters themselves, without telling myself that if I just researched things a bit longer, I would produce a better output. It's hard to know when to stop. In the end, you just have to go for it.

Another decision I had to make was how I would keep track of the data gathered through company identification and emailing business owners. After twelve years in finance, I felt pretty confident in my Excel skills. I told myself I could hold my own, and wouldn't need to invest in fancy CRM software. But after talking to some fellow searchers, I realized that I would need something more robust for the purpose. I started researching the different CRM systems out there and quickly I realized how easy it was to get lost. I did some of my learning through conversations with searchers who were ahead of me in the process, but most of it came through trial and error. Finally, I found a CRM that fit my purpose. However, I felt like I had lost precious time selecting the software and even more learning how to use it properly, which is a common sentiment among searchers.

Then I began reaching out to business owners. It went pretty smoothly, even though I occasionally hit some bumps in the road. For instance, I'd made a point to reach out to business owners using their nickname – if I could find one – in order to make it seem more personal and less like the mail merge it was. One day, I received a call from a woman asking me if I knew her husband, since she had noticed I used his nickname. Upon replying that I had not had the pleasure of meeting him, she started yelling at me, informing me that her husband had passed away two years earlier. I felt horrible and explained that I found his name on the company's website. Thankfully, we cleared everything up and she forgave me. But that taught me the importance of doing proper research and that I was working with imperfect information.

Another thing I learned to watch out for were crazy people. Two separate individuals told me that the devil was pointing me to their industry. After the second such conversation, I decided to create a CRM category for them. I also learned the hard way not to jump on a plane and meet someone without having the detailed financials. On one particular occasion, I had been in talks with the CEO of a company and I received verbal confirmation that his firm met all of the criteria that I had established. He explained that he had no faith in NDAs and didn't want to send me the financials, but that we would review them in person and that it would not be an issue. When I flew down to Texas to meet him, it turned out that all he had was a pipeline. He had barely an excel sheet populated with some financial information. I made sure he knew he had misled me and that I didn't appreciate it, and flew back home. He admitted to me that he had hoped my seeing his twenty-year old business and its potential future would make up for the lack of financials. I could have definitely done without that trip, but it served as a good lesson.

Using Interns

Hiring interns was another challenging part of the search process – and this is where one of my mentors talked me off a ledge. I had a first failed round of interviews, during which I brought in potentially smart, interested people. However, they just weren't the right fit. I felt that I had a pool of candidates from which I was forced to choose, even though none of them were the right person. I called my mentor for advice and he told me to do it again; start the whole process from scratch. But first he suggested I get advice from other searchers on recruiting techniques and that I get in the weeds with the search process myself before bringing interns on board. I then went out and found my next group.

I went through the cycle myself first so that I could figure out the pitfalls, before teaching the process to my interns. I also wanted to show them that I wasn't above this, and that I had done it for an even larger industry than the one I assigned them. I wanted to be there for them as a safety net, but let them go through it on their own. I found Luke early on in the process, and he did an amazing job of learning the ropes and passing down his learnings to future interns. It was key for me to find someone who understood what I was doing and who wanted to train others; this also provided Luke with the opportunity to gain management experience, which is not normally the case in most internships. At the end, we had a group of three interns in charge of the emailing process along with industry research.

The early days of the search process were definitely a challenge. Going up the learning curve was a long and laborious process. I found it important to constantly make sure everyone was kept in the loop as to where we were, what we were doing and why. It's definitely an investment of time, but I believed it would pay off in the coming months.

Tracking Time

Time is your worst enemy over the course of the search fund process. It works against you and the clock starts ticking before you feel you've even begun searching. The scariest part – and the easiest pitfall – is crossing off items from checklists. Especially when you derive the same satisfaction of accomplishment from crossing off 'buy new CRM software' as you do from 'send letters to 200 business owners'. There are so many opportunities to waste precious hours all the while feeling productive, engaged in 'false activities'. It's easy to feel productive spending hours tweaking the presentation of your quarterly letter to investors because in your previous job as a consultant or an investment banker, you were taught that an impeccable presentation was primordial. However, these things become superfluous when you are a searcher; you need to learn to focus on the essentials and prevent yourself from losing time on activities that don't matter.

Thankfully, one of my investors was constantly on my back to get letters out. It was worth me delaying the closing of my fund and spending so much time and energy getting this person to commit. I wanted someone to push me to be a better searcher. I needed someone to call me and ask how many emails, NDAs, IOIs and LOIs I'd sent that month. It is very challenging to be a solo searcher and keep yourself on track at all times. Especially once you've found a company and aren't gauging your productivity through easily tracked measurements – and yet still need to continue searching even while advancing with one opportunity.

To be honest, my actual search did not begin until a full month after I launched AltEquity. And even more honestly, the only real grasp I had on the time that had passed was every two weeks when I had to submit my payroll. It was a moment of reflection, a moment of truth. And those two weeks constantly felt like a fleeting twenty-five seconds apart.

Another point of adjustment was getting used to living on a very tight budget. As I've mentioned before, launching a search fund meant taking a huge salary haircut. Instead of my former comfortable PE income, I was now forced to living a rather basic, frugal lifestyle, riding my bike to work to save on gas. And yet, in a very perverse way, I think that this is part of the process. When you're making good money, you're not forced to track every penny, but I do now. And that's a great training for when I run a business of my own!

Valuable Advice from Investors

Over the course of my search, I have gotten some pretty useful advice from my investors. Here are the main lessons I've learned:

1. Just because I can raise the capital to buy a business doesn't mean I should buy it. Investors have a diversified portfolio and can more readily weather a loss. Therefore, their support should not be misinterpreted as a complete vote of confidence that this is the right business. Their risk appetite differs from mine due to being a portfolio. On the other hand, I am placing all of my eggs in one basket and can't afford to make a bad investment.
2. Get to 'no' quickly. That one's tough. If you talk to someone in a new industry, any intel you get is welcome. However, though time is of the essence, it is sometimes tricky to keep a conversation short. Try to limit yourself to twenty minutes and cut to the chase. This means quickly getting the financial and other information you need to make a 'go/no go' decision as fast as possible.
3. It's not a done deal until you've signed the papers. We've all heard the horror stories of some sellers backing out at the eleventh hour. Keep your search active even if you are going through the due diligence process and hoping to close with a company. I have been working on a deal for months and while it could close, the deal could also die at any moment.

The relationship with investors is absolutely critical as a way to augment a searcher's frame of reference and comparable data points. However, just like any relationship, there are at times differences in understanding between searchers and investors. Searchers are closer to and more informed about the specific details of the deal, but investors have the perspective and objectiveness searchers often lack. As such, even if investor input may be oversimplified – or sometimes factually incorrect – there's a valid reason for the investor's reaction. It is up to me to reflect on the nature of the feedback and message being conveyed instead of stubbornly defending my point of view.

Finding 'The One'?

On 1 June 2014, I sent out a first round of letters to the security industry. Shortly after, I received a call from the CEO and founder of one of the companies I contacted. We had a fantastic conversation and he immediately offered to put me in touch with his lawyer to vet me as he was a respected industry insider. He was getting older and was interested in pursuing another venture, which is why he had been considering disposing of his current business. It took the lawyer a long time to get in touch with me, but we then arranged an in-person meeting and after many back-and-forths, eventually signed a LOI on November 10th. I liked the industry. I had done a series of investments in this field in my previous job, which gave me further comfort. I knew that I would be able to add value to the company. It was also exactly what I was looking for in terms of being able to take a traditional business and take it to a new level. At $11 mil in sales, it was the right size and it appeared that I could get it for a good price.

But the hardest part of the search is the part I am confronting right now: taking the decision that this is the business I want to buy and run for the next five to seven years. Is this the company for me? It's tricky to remain objective while simultaneously approaching my backers with a proposal to move forward with this investment. I think it is a great opportunity, but there are still a lot of unknowns. And getting comfortable with the unknowns is the trickiest part. Is the seller really a seller? Am I the right person to run this company? And is this the one I should buy? Sharing my thoughts and questions with Julia, it made me think of when I was deciding to ask her to marry me. It's exhilarating, but it's also nerve wracking at the same time.

Questions for Discussion

1. How did Sean decide whether doing a search was the right path for him? What would you do to validate your choice?
2. Like most searchers, Sean went through a trial and error learning process. How could you get up to speed more quickly?
3. Sean's experience shows that investors can provide valuable advice and guidance. How should you think about finding the right investors to back your search?

15 TURNAROUNDS, WORKOUTS AND OTHER RESTRUCTURING: REINVENTING VALUE

BENOÎT F. LELEUX

IMD

Restructurings, whatever their colour or hue, have never been as glamorous and shiny as most other types of ventures. Fallen angels often carry a deep stigma of failure. A business story has already been played out … and failed for the most part, leaving many stakeholders shaken and disheartened. And from this bitter experience, someone hopes to salvage another value-creation opportunity. Needless to say, turnarounds are among the most difficult forms of ventures. Because of that, they carry a rather sulphurous reputation, for the most part undeserved. There is no denying the value these transactions can add to an economy, giving second and third opportunities to initially unsuccessful attempts at creating or capturing markets. Most ventures do not succeed at first, so the ability to regroup and try again is essential to any entrepreneurial culture. In this chapter, we argue that these transactions, while requiring very specific approaches, also offer fantastic opportunities to generate value. We review the evidence on turnaround funds and provide some guidance on rules of engagement, taking the example of the Stelton transaction, a famous Danish tableware brand that was acquired and successfully turned around.

VIEW FROM THE MEDIA

FINANCIAL TIMES   FT

Restructuring specialists staff up

JULY 15, 2012 BY ROBIN WIGGLESWORTH IN LONDON

Restructuring and turnround specialists are staffing up and poaching from rivals in expectation of rising corporate distress across the world, particularly in Europe. 'We've been hiring and growing consistently, as have our rivals,' said Peter Briggs, managing director at Alvarez & Marsal, a turrnround firm. 'The restructuring market is growing as companies get more used to using outside advisors and interim managers.' Alvarez & Marsal, which worked on Lehman Brothers' bankruptcy, has grown from less than 75 people in 2002 to over 1,800 people today, and earlier this year opened offices in Athens and Mexico City. Some of the 'big four' accounting and consulting firms – KPMG, Deloitte, Ernst & Young and PwC – have been hiring particularly aggressively at their restructuring, insolvency and business turnround divisions. KPMG recently hired Lukas Fecker, a former director of Alvarez & Marsal, as a restructuring partner, and three directors from AlixPartners, another turnround-focused firm, in response to 'huge demand from companies for assistance in underperforming and distressed situations'. The restructuring advisory arms of larger investment banks, or advisor-focused investment banks, have been hiring more cautiously, as the number of larger companies forced to restructure – which often require their more specialised advice – is still relatively muted compared with historical averages. However, most experts predict that the default rate of larger companies will also continue to rise steadily. Moody's global trailing 12-month default rate on companies rated below investment grade, or junk, inched up to 2.6 per cent in April, up from 2.5 per cent in March.

The rating agency's models indicate that the default rate will rise to 3.1 per cent by the end of the year, but many analysts argue that this is too sanguine – particularly if Europe's sovereign debt crisis continues to worsen. 'We are cautiously increasing staff levels,' said Joseph Swanson, managing director at Houlihan Lokey, one of the larger investment banks that specialise in restructuring advice. Houlihan Lokey is hiring 'senior advisers across Europe', including a senior banker to focus on the Nordic countries, and will open a Madrid office later this year, according to Mr Swanson. Similarly, Martin Gudgeon, head of European restructuring at Blackstone, does not expect a 'tidal wave of restructurings', but expected activity to grow at a healthy clip. 'You cannot deleverage in a flat economy, so there's going to be plenty to do.' Blackstone's restructuring arm opened a Frankfurt office this year. Michael Hampden-Turner, a strategist at Citigroup, predicts that the European corporate default rate will climb rapidly in the second half of the year to 6 per cent by the end of 2012. Investment banks are also shifting or seconding some resources from their underworked mergers and acquisitions departments to their restructuring advisory arms, where the work prospects are somewhat brighter. 'There is new blood coming into the restructuring industry from M&A and leveraged finance bankers,' Mr Briggs said. 'They're following the flow of work and fees.'

www.ft.com/content/92f51e54-cd09-11e1-92c1-00144feabdc0

LEARNING OBJECTIVES

After reading this chapter you will be able to:

- Identify the symptoms and true causes of failure.
- Determine which failure situations offer prospects of revival.

- Work out a turnaround plan, focusing on the key drivers of success.
- Understand the various phases of a turnaround, and the critical determinants of positive outcomes.
- Recognize the challenges of implementation.

Where Are We Going Next?

This chapter will briefly review the key issues surrounding turnarounds, workouts and other forms of restructuring. The focus throughout is on the value-creation potential of such interventions, not only for the instigators of such transactions (who we would like to think of as entrepreneurs) but also for many other stakeholders, from employees to lenders, former shareholders and ultimately society as a whole. Clearly, such transactions do not have the emotional appeal and 'sexiness' of startups, with their untested and thus mostly untainted promises, however unrealistic. Nor do they exhibit the boring predictability of most classic buyout stories, where mature targets, i.e. profitable and cash-generating, are given a new lease of life. In turnarounds, the target companies have often experienced hard times, some self-inflicted, some the result of external conditions not entirely managed or manageable. Stakeholders will have grown disgruntled, and will have left in despair. At the same time, these companies will have been battle-tested, their shiny armours sandblasted to reveal the cracks and structural weaknesses. Which of these embattled ventures deserves a second shot? How should the transactions be engineered to ensure the best chances of success? What are the areas to focus on? And finally, how can these interventions make sense for investors?

15.1   A Private Equity Industry Perspective

Before moving to a micro perspective on turnaround and restructuring transactions, i.e. the how-to-do-it with a reasonable prospect of success, it can be useful to look at this asset class within the larger private equity world. Indeed, for many institutional investors, turnarounds, workouts and other restructuring transactions fall into a sub-class generically referred to as 'distressed private equity', i.e. any form of intervention where the starting point is a firm in some stage of financial distress.

The period 2013 to 2016 was nothing short of stellar for the private equity industry as a whole. Following the disastrous financial crisis of 2007–08 and the ensuing deep recession, recovery was relatively swift and enthusiastic, with funds benefiting from the healthy appetites of investors, as illustrated in Figure 15.1.

In 2016 alone, private equity firms globally raised $589 billion in capital, just 2 per cent less than in 2015. With more than $500 billion raised each year since 2013, it has been a banner period, with capital pouring into every private equity

Global PE capital raised (by fund type)
$800B

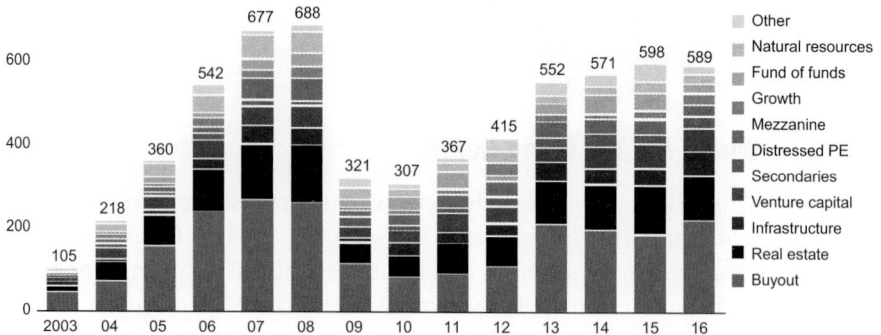

Notes: Includes funds with final close and represents the year in which funds held their final close; buyout includes buyout and balanced funds; distressed PE includes distressed dept, special situation and turnaround funds; other includes private investment in public equity and hybrid funds

Figure 15.1 Global private equity raised by fund type (2003–2016).
Source: Bain & Company (2017)[1]

sub-asset class. Buyout funds had an even better year than the whole of private equity, with $221 billion in raised capital, a 20 per cent upswing. Distressed private equity came in sixth position in the fund-raising league, behind buyout, real estate, infrastructure, venture capital and secondaries, but ahead of mezzanine, growth, fund of funds and natural resources.

In Europe, the investment picture is grimmer, with only 0.5 per cent of 2015 private equity investments going into rescue / turnaround situations, representing only 0.9 per cent of the private equity deals. The European investment statistics for 2015 are presented in Figure 15.2.

The pure fundraising perspective hides a more interesting reality, as highlighted in Figure 15.3: the distressed private equity sub-class generated the strongest performance over the period 2000–15, easily outperforming the buyout category.

When a risk–return profile is constructed, as in Figure 15.4 which shows median net IRRs (in per cent) against standard deviations of these net IRRs, the distressed sub-class again outshines all other private equity sub-asset classes, except secondaries. While the class remains small (represented by the relative sizes of the bubbles in the figure), it has clearly delivered superior risk-adjusted returns in a rather consistent manner.

Most turnaround specialists are service firms selling turnaround consulting advice or providing interim management teams, financial restructuring, etc. Companies falling into this category include *Alix Partners, LLC* (from

1 Used with permission from Bain & Company. www.bain.com/publications/articles/global-private-equity-report-2017.aspx

% of Amount

Seed Startup
0.2% 4.2%

Later-stage venture 3.5%

Growth capital
13.6%

Rescue/
turnaround
0.5%

Replacement
capital
1.2%

Buyout
76.6%

% of Number of companies

Buyout
18.6%

Seed
8.5%

Replacement
capital
1.6%

Rescue/
turnaround
0.9%

Startup
35.8%

Growth
capital
21.9%

Later-stage
venture
12.7%

Venture Capital	€3.8bn	Venture Capital	2,836 Companies
Buyout	€36.3bn	Buyout	944 Companies
Growth	€6.5bn	Growth	1,108 Companies

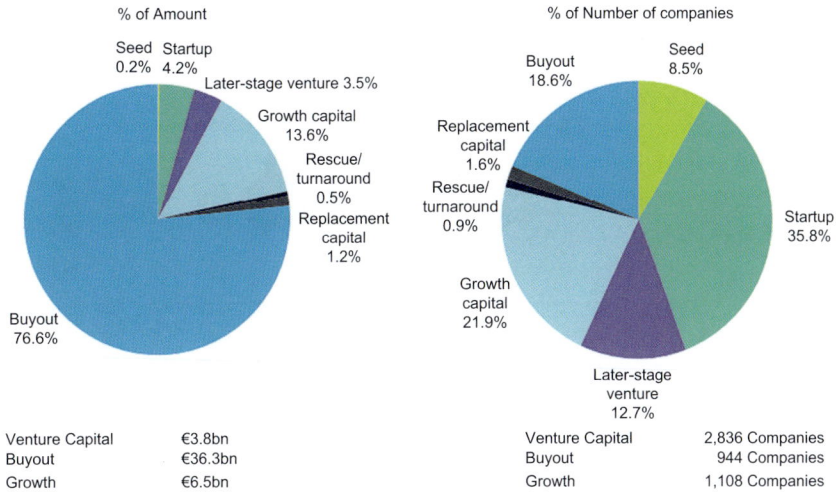

Figure 15.2 European private equity investments by deal type (2015).
Source: Invest Europe (2015) / PEREP_Analytics

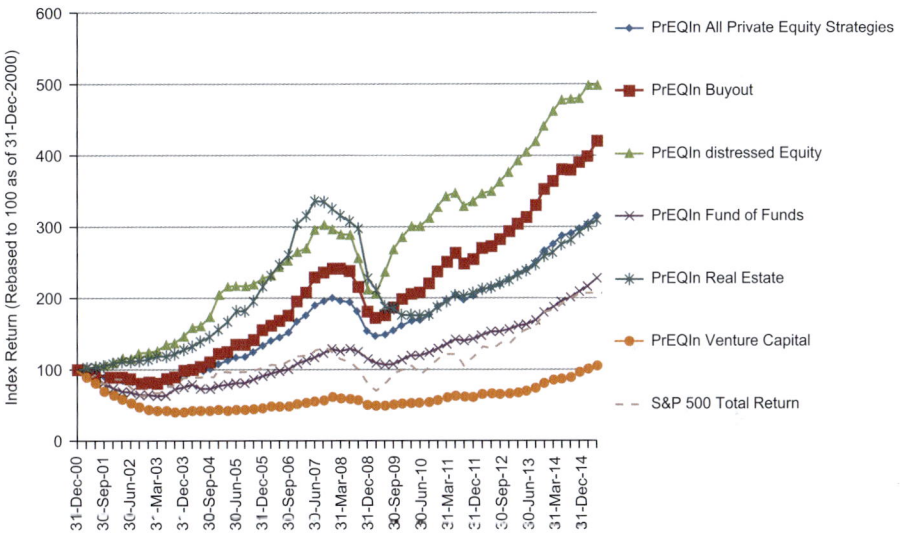

Figure 15.3 Global private equity index returns by fund type (2000–2015).
Source: Preqin (2016)

Southfield, Michigan, formerly known as Jay Alix & Associates, www
.AlixPartners.com). A few players have evolved fully fledged investment vehicles to actively invest in turnaround situations. One of the best-known players
in that category would be *Alvarez & Marsal, Inc.* (from New York, New York,
www.AlvarezandMarsal.com). Its Alvarez & Marsal Capital entity is a separately capitalized organization offering alternative asset investments, often

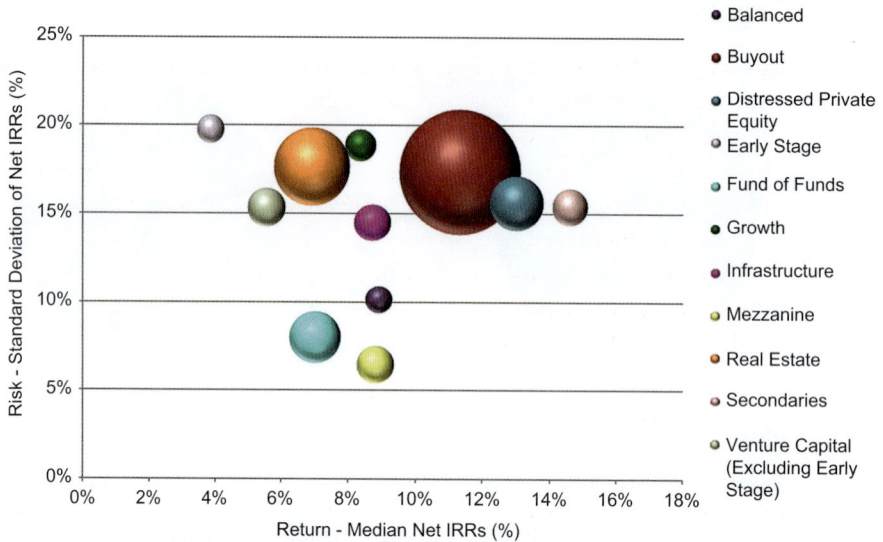

Figure 15.4 Global private equity risk–return profiles by fund type.
Source: Preqin (2014)

connected to its restructuring activities. Its first fund, A&M Capital Partners, with $600 million under management, principally made control investments in the range of $20 to $75 million in businesses with enterprise values between $75 and $750 million and EBITDA between $10 and $75 million, mostly in middle-market companies undergoing a management or ownership transition, seeking capital for growth or that could benefit from access to world-class operational expertise in the areas of corporate carve-outs, consolidation, special situations or businesses seeking to address specific operational issues or management needs. Its second fund, A&M Capital Opportunities, principally took minority investments in the range of $15 to $45 million in growth-oriented businesses with enterprise values of between $25 and $150 million and EBITDA of between $5 and $25 million. It focused on investing alongside entrepreneurs and management teams looking for a partner with performance improvement resources and experience that promote increased operational scale and efficiency.

15.2 Identifying the Crisis Level

A first important step in a turnaround is to identify the actual stage of business decline or crisis that the company is facing. The earlier the intervention, the higher the chances of returning the firm to adequate performance. Typically, there are four major stages of underperformance: Stagnation, Underperformance, Performance Impairment, and Crisis. These are reviewed briefly below.

15.2.1 Stagnation

In a way, this is the early infancy stage of the crisis, where crisis signals are still weak but converging. Typically, early signs of impending trouble include flat or slightly declining revenues (often attributed initially to outside, temporary forces), margins and other key parameters falling below industry averages, inventory write-downs, portfolio mix issues and reported management dissatisfaction. This phase can incubate for years as minor 'patches' are applied one on top of another, preventing a swift descent into crisis but never providing a true long-term solution. This is the denial phase, where arguments can still be made for the non-existence of a crisis.

15.2.2 Underperformance

When revenues and key profitability metrics (EBITDA, fixed costs, etc.) start to dip materially, plant utilization rates drop, working capital becomes overextended (especially receivables and inventories) and lines of credit are pushed to the limit, the crisis is starting to play out at full strength, even though management may still not be willing to accept its severity. The speed of decline tends to accelerate, and each new (inadequate) measure taken further precipitates losses. But the company remains operational, with customer and supplier relationships very much intact.

15.2.3 Performance Impairment

By this stage, the level of underperformance is undermining the company's ability to continue operating. Shortages occur throughout the supply chain, creditors degrade trade terms or refuse to ship, bank relationships suffer as a result of repeated covenant violations, and key personnel, customers or suppliers move on. The company's ability to operate is challenged. Denial is often replaced by panic about the looming insolvency. Action needs to be taken immediately.

15.2.4 Crisis

When payables are overdue and key obligations (social security payments for employees, salaries, major loan covenants) can no longer be met, insolvency becomes unavoidable and legal measures have to be taken. At this stage, the company's legal obligations and turnaround options will vary considerably depending on the country and what measures are in place to protect the shareholders' capital, the creditors' interests or employees and the continuation of the business activities.

15.3   Staging the Turnaround

Turnarounds are naturally difficult business transformations for various reasons. First and foremost, the starting point is an organization at different stages of distress. Distress often implies that the historical track record reveals an organization heading in the wrong direction. That track record does not offer a sound basis on which to raise leverage to facilitate the transaction, so turnaround transactions rely disproportionally on creative equity financing techniques rather than debt financing. Assets may also have been compromised by the progressive descent to distress: re-investments in equipment may have been deferred for years, maintenance may not have been performed adequately and R&D may have been sacrificed in favour of short-term profit boosts to salvage key covenants on existing loan agreements. Finally, the most important assets, employees and management teams, may have been weakened by years of frustration and lacklustre performance; key personnel always tend to leave the boat before less business-critical employees. The bottom line is that the target company has often fallen into a negative spiral and is left with even fewer resources to tackle the fundamental problems that caused the underperformance in the first place. In summary, these companies fall into a form of *negative halo effect,* in the sense of Phil Rosensweig's popular business book,[2] i.e. a cognitive bias in which the perception of one's quality is contaminated by more readily available attributes. In the context of a business, observers' views about a firm's lack of customer focus, poor leadership or unguided strategy may be contaminated by indicators of the company's past poor performance, such as a declining share price or profitability.

Breaking the death spiral and the negative halo effect requires drastic intervention, where time will be of the essence. Practically speaking, a typical restructuring often includes four stages:

1. Evaluate and assess.
2. Stop the bleeding.
3. Restructure.
4. Create sustainability.

These phases are reviewed below.

15.3.1   Evaluate and Assess

This critical first phase can be broken down into several elements. First is the recognition and acknowledgement that the company has effectively 'peaked' and is heading for decline. Psychologically, there are many hurdles to early recognition of the symptoms of decline. They can remain hidden for a long time by the cash that continues to be generated during the period of low growth that often precedes a period of decline. This can blind leaders to what is actually starting to happen.

2 Rosenzweig (2007).

Second is the identification of the factors that contributed to the decline, some external (the introduction of innovations by competitors, a downturn in demand, shifting regulations, etc.) and some internal (slipping working capital practices, runaway R&D budgets, uncontrolled growth, etc.). All of them destabilize the company's performance. In this phase, it is crucial to assess which factors are structural and will permanently affect performance and which are subservient, i.e. can be controlled rapidly through corrective actions and/or will not last.

Finally, one can assess the likelihood of a turnaround. Many distressed companies will never qualify as potential turnaround targets because the underlying factors are pervasive and permanent and cannot be modified sufficiently or quickly enough to return the firm to profitability. The key exercise in this first phase is thus to identify the true causes of distress as well as credible interventions to redress the situation. The objective of this phase is therefore to rigorously evaluate the severity of the situation and whether it can still be turned around. Typical questions are: Can the business survive? What will it take to turn it around? What is needed to ensure its sustainability, i.e. so that it does not fail again? The analysis culminates in the formulation of a short intervention plan listing what is seen to be wrong, how to fix the issues, key strategies to point the company in a positive direction and a cash flow forecast to cover the immediate intervention period (see Section 15.3.2 below).

Effective turnaround strategies typically combine operational interventions with new strategic initiatives and fresh manpower. Operational interventions include increasing revenues, reducing costs, selling and redeploying assets and a radical competitive repositioning. Strategic initiatives might include a new positioning, new value propositions for different sets of customers and novel approaches to the market. Manpower needs to be addressed early on, since many of the best employees will probably have already left the company, leaving behind mostly dedicated but 'second-string' personnel.

This phase is primarily conceptual and is, in effect, the due diligence for the intended turnaround. A new business plan has to be created, validated and stress-tested, focusing in particular on making sure the key resources (often people and capital) will be available to effect the firm's transformation. The phase is completed with the actual closing of the deal.

15.3.2   Stop the Bleeding

Once a deal has been finalized, the new owner needs to make things happen rapidly. The most critical step is to stop the negative cash-flow spiral as quickly as possible. That often requires deep cuts into the flesh of the organization, killing 'sacred cows' and refocusing energies and capital on the two or three most impactful items. The objective here is primarily to 'buy time', i.e. to make sure that the resources raised for the reorganization will be sufficient to implement it. It is usually conducted in less than 90 days.

The primary objective is to regain control of the situation expeditiously, particularly in stopping the cash bleed. Time is the enemy, and the only way to protect the asset value is to show quickly that things are under control and that the transition to a better future is underway.

The phase usually requires raising cash rapidly, usually through the company's own balance sheet by, for example, improving collections on receivables, renegotiating payments on payables or selling non-operating assets, such as unrelated real estate or under-utilized assets. New business models may also free up resources, for example, outsourcing more of the supply chain. Human resources will have to be adjusted to the new reality. Right-sizing often means laying off employees quickly and fairly; this is better done in one major swoop than in repeated little cuts. It is essential to rapidly re-establish a sense of job security for those remaining so that they can focus on the job to be done. To attract new and motivated employees, it is also important to offer performance-incentivized remuneration that will make it worthwhile considering joining a firm with a tainted past. But with a clean slate, a stabilized patient and a simple game plan, the downside is better calibrated and manageable.

15.3.3   Restructure

Having stopped the bleeding and stabilized the patient, it is time to take the company to the operating room and perform the structural changes required by its new strategy and competitive situation. The objective now is to move rapidly to profitability through the remaining operations. This is usually achieved through a combination of activities, including: new product mixes stressing profitability; new target clients and revised supply chains offering higher margins; improved reporting systems offering finer understanding of costs and revenues; and stronger performance-based incentives with objectives that are better aligned with the new strategy.

15.3.4   Create Sustainability

Once the new strategy has been put in place, it is essential to ensure that the company does not go back to its old habits. The objective in this phase is to institutionalize the changes and construct a new corporate culture focused on profitability and return on assets. New opportunities for profitable growth should be regularly identified and captured. Competitive advantages need to be continuously strengthened. Management and employees need to be developed to improve the overall quality of the human capital.

Early indicators must also be put in place to provide warning signs of any deterioration in the company's competitive position, should it happen again. Competitive advantages are fleeting in a fast-evolving global economy, and maintaining an edge requires a pro-active stance and ongoing adjustments and interventions.

Let's Practise: Case Study

STELTON: Turnaround Opportunity?[3]

MARCH 2004. Michael Ring took a deep breath. The temperature was arctic and the wind off the sea made it even worse along this stretch of Danish coastline. Somehow these extreme conditions were just what he needed at the moment. But, although he knew this beach and shoreline so well, today he was not enjoying the view as much as usual. He had a momentous decision to make: Should he acquire Stelton?

Ever since he had lost his position as managing director at Georg Jensen, he had been searching for that special opportunity to continue doing what he enjoyed most – working with great designers, passionate handcrafters and a well-known brand. Only this time, he wanted to be in charge. He kept hearing the voice of his teenage daughter saying:

Dad, you can lie on the sofa for the rest of your life and feel sorry for yourself – or you can get up and actually do something about your situation.

But did that *something* mean taking out a huge mortgage on his house and risking everything he and his family owned?

The hurdles were not insignificant. The current owner was approaching retirement age but felt under no compulsion to sell. Turning him into a willing seller, or at least persuading him to relinquish a controlling ownership, would require a lot of diplomacy. Even though Michael had a potent track record in the industry, the transaction was clearly a buy-in and would require a detailed due diligence. For the very same reason, bankers might feel reluctant to lend money to the transaction. The company had not been doing too well lately, adding a layer of uncertainty. This deal was also the first one of its kind for Michael, and starting with a turnaround buy-in seemed a bit ambitious at best. But then again, opportunities like these were clearly not going to show up every day. This was a once-in-a-lifetime chance to regain control of his future . . .

The Entrepreneur

Michael had built himself a solid reputation, the result of an impressive corporate career which started with the East Asiatic Company,[4] a very old and reputable Danish company with global activities. Equipped with that solid first experience and a good deal of foreign exposure, he went on to earn his MBA

3 The case study is based on the original IMD case study; see Leleux and Agersnap (2008a).
4 www.eac.dk

from one of the most selective programs (IMD, in Switzerland) before moving to Hilti, the global professional tool company based in Lichtenstein, where he worked as managing director in Denmark and Germany for five years.

In 1999, Michael was hired by Royal Scandinavia as managing director for the Georg Jensen and Royal Copenhagen divisions.[5] When the private equity firm Axcel acquired Royal Scandinavia in December 2000, Michael was kept on as managing director for Georg Jensen, but a new person was put in charge of the Royal Copenhagen division. Then, out of the blue, in August 2003 he was fired. His dismissal came as a total shock since he was convinced that he had consistently delivered good results, solid progress and a visionary yet realistic strategy for the company's future. He had just returned from a trip to Asia, where he had negotiated significant deals with some of the biggest department stores there, including one with Takashimaya which would dramatically improve the company's sales in the ever-important Japanese market. One of the board members took over his position. Michael felt stabbed in the back:

It struck me like a bolt of lightning. Georg Jensen was the only division which was profitable at the time. I felt ill-treated, and promised myself that I would never, ever, end up in such a situation again.

Michael had little idea about his next move. He had given enough to the roller coaster of corporate politics; maybe it was time to seriously consider alternatives where he would not have to answer to a board or be subject to opaque outside forces. Since starting a greenfield project seemed a bit far-fetched, he started to look for existing companies he could acquire and improve.

Relatively quickly, Stelton appeared on his radar screen. On many dimensions, the company was very similar to Georg Jensen. It was a well-known Danish brand with superb craftsmanship and design. The founder was nearing retirement age and Michael thought he would be willing to consider various options to guarantee the future of the company, one of which may be a buyout that he could orchestrate.

Stelton

Stelton was founded in 1960 by Peter Holmblad to sell stainless steel hollowware, such as platters, salad bowls and serving dishes. In 1963, Stelton started to work closely with world-famous designer and architect Arne Jacobsen, who helped to formulate the company's trademark design formula – a comprehensive line of tableware whose matching designs would always ensure harmonious table settings. The result was the now-famous Cylinda-Line, which was launched in 1967 and, with its serene and functionalist design, immediately

---

5 www.royalscandinavia.com

attracted considerable attention. The company grew rapidly thanks to the success of the Cylinda-Line in Denmark and in export markets.

After Arne Jacobsen's death in 1971, a young designer, Erik Magnussen, well known for his work for Danish porcelain manufacturer Bing & Grøndahl, began to work with Stelton. His first creation was the stainless steel vacuum jug with the unique rocker stopper, which was introduced in 1977 – the best-selling article so far in the history of the company. Since then, Erik Magnussen and Stelton have gone on to develop an extensive range of table-top items, in stainless steel and ABS plastics.

This early work with reputed designers led to numerous other collaborations with a whole generation of up-and-coming Scandinavian designers. Stelton would define the product categories, the market needs, as well as the technologies and materials to be used; the designers would then come up with original shapes and colours. The collaboration proved immensely powerful, and many pieces won coveted design prizes around the world. Stelton products were even exhibited at leading design museums, such as the Museum of Modern Art and the Cooper-Hewitt Museum in New York, the Philadelphia Museum of Art, the Victoria & Albert Museum and the British Museum in London, the Staatliches Museum für Angewandte Kunst in Munich, the Kunstindustrimuseet in Copenhagen, and the Louvre Museum and the Pompidou Centre in Paris. This was no small achievement for a tableware company ...

However, the pace of innovation and creativity was difficult to maintain. Only one totally new product had been released since 2001. By 2003, the company employed almost 100 people, the majority of them working at Stelton's production plant and about a dozen at the headquarters in an old-fashioned villa in one of Copenhagen's wealthy suburbs. The number of staff dedicated to a specific job reflected its importance in the company's strategy; naturally, the largest headcount was found in production, since production and production techniques (operational improvements) were critical for the company's development and survival. Stelton mastered a unique production technique called 'flow', whereby the products were melted and shaped from one single piece of metal. The technique allowed for some exceptional designs and quality, and was ideal for producing cylinder-shaped products. Stelton also relied on more traditional metal-working techniques for other hardware ranges. Ninety-five per cent of the products were made at the plant, with roughly 70 per cent of the plant's production used by Stelton directly with the remaining 30 per cent sold as components to third parties.

When Michael pored over the figures for the company, he noticed how quickly its financial situation was deteriorating. Sales had been stagnant over the last five years; turnover in 2002 actually showed a marked decline over the 2001 numbers. Return on equity, return on assets and other liquidity ratios showed equally disturbing declining trends (see Figures 15.5 and 15.6 for Stelton's financial statements from 1998 to 2002). In 2002, the company

Profit and Loss	2002	2001	2000	1999	1998
Sales, net	82,189	87,198	82,246	81,632	81,362
Cost of sales	46,099	50,071	45,222	48,390	46,812
Gross profit	36,090	37,127	37,024	33,242	34,550
Distribution	17,807	18,315	14,047	15,318	13,704
Administration	14,375	15,150	14,701	13,608	14,087
Other operating costs	1,861	2,197	1,508	1,244	1,316
Operating profit	2,047	1,464	6,768	3,072	5,443
Other income	(20)	(21)	241	(33)	163
Extraordinary expenses*	–	–	–	4,383	–
Financial income	2,263	975	897	855	1,594
Financial expenses	2,095	560	597	1,304	899
Taxable income	2,195	1,858	7,309	(1,794)	6,301
Taxes	731	564	2,830	793	2,075
Net income	1,464	1,294	4,479	(1,000)	4,226

* A major recall of defective products took place in 1999.

Figure 15.5 Profit and loss statements for Stelton, 1998–2002 (DKK thousand).

generated a turnover of some DKK 82 million (around €11 million), not significantly different from its turnover in 1998. Net income approached DKK 1.5 million[6] (about €200,000) for the year – less than a 2 per cent net profit margin. The company was clearly in trouble, and turning that tide would require a great deal more than financial savvy.

The Market and Industry

Stelton primarily served the Nordic markets, broadly defined to include Denmark and its neighbouring countries in Scandinavia, Germany and the Benelux countries. Consumers in these countries shared a strong attraction to four basic decoration styles: Scandinavian, International Minimalistic, Country and Romantic. Stelton's 'pure' designs appealed more to customers decorating their homes in the Scandinavian and, to some extent, the International Minimalistic style. Customers who preferred Romantic or Country styles were less attracted to Stelton designs.

6 At the end of 2002 DKK 1 = $0.1412, €0.1347 and CHF 0.1959.

Balance Sheet	2002	2001	2000	1999	1998
Property	10,735	11,538	12,431	12,166	12,768
Machinery, tools etc	6,870	7,469	6,997	8,096	5,961
Other equipment	730	1,231	1,642	2,018	2,531
Property plant & equipment	*18,335*	*20,240*	*21,070*	*22,279*	*21,260*
Investments in associated Co.	0	373	421	218	272
Marketable securities	315	266	241	202	181
Deposits	4	4	6	9	9
Net investments	*319*	*644*	*668*	*430*	*462*
Other assets	**18,654**	**20,884**	**21,738**	**22,709**	**21,722**
Raw materials	6,643	6,166	4,533	3,767	4,834
Goods in process	4,139	2,381	2,230	2,449	1,685
Finished goods	5,930	3,476	3,183	2,089	1,617
Total inventories	*16,712*	*12,023*	*9,946*	*8,305*	*8,136*
Trade receivables	12,229	16,746	17,119	15,446	7,798
Stelton USA receivables	0	0	0	0	1,054
Other receivables	930	1,016	1,324	1,145	1,045
Tax receivables	0	477	19	575	912
Total receivables	*13,159*	*18,239*	*18,462*	*17,167*	*10,809*
Cash	3,904	969	4,247	2,114	10,967
Bonds	21,015	6,341	5,994	5,827	11,044
Cash and cash equivalent	*24,919*	*7,310*	*10,241*	*7,941*	*22,011*
Current assets	**54,790**	**37,572**	**38,649**	**33,413**	**40,956**
TOTAL ASSETS	73,444	58,457	60,387	56,122	62,678
Company capital	7,200	7,200	7,200	7,200	7,200
Retained earnings	28,548	24,788	33,494	29,014	30,014
Shareholders equity	*35,748*	*31,988*	*40,694*	*36,214*	*37,214*
Deferred Taxes & Liabilities	2,705	1,960	3,051	4,036	2,606
Long-term debt	*24,939*	*3,960*	*4,443*	*4,920*	*6,290*
Current portion of LT debt	2,579	484	477	1,370	1,363
Debt to Stelton USA	0	373	367	167	0
Accounts payable	2,641	2,957	5,600	2,400	3,814
Other debt	4,822	16,734	5,755	7,015	11,391
Short-term debt	*10,052*	*20,549*	*12,199*	*10,952*	*16,568*
Total debt	**34,991**	**24,509**	**16,642**	**15,872**	**22,858**
TOTAL LIABILITIES	73,444	58,457	60,387	56,122	62,678

Figure 15.6 Balance sheets for Stelton, 1998–2002 (DKK thousand).

The markets in which Stelton operated were far from static. Among the major trends that could be identified were: (1) the increasing importance of an older customer group; (2) the increasing availability of cheaper products thanks to globalization; and (3) the development of a wealthier middle class who could afford more luxurious homes and travelled more.

The product markets were customarily segmented into four generic categories: (1) table top; (2) products for the home; (3) gourmet and kitchen; and (4) personal accessories (mainly bought as gift items). Eighty per cent of the market (measured by volume) was priced relatively low, with products costing less than DKK 300 (around €40) in retail shops. The majority of the products fell in the DKK 150–200 range. With an existing gross margin of 52 per cent, Stelton had to sell high volumes in this segment to create a viable business. For a leaner Stelton, this segment could be a potential growth area. As an industry reference, retail prices were roughly seven times the cost of production.

Looking at the market potential, Michael knew from experience that, as a rule of thumb, a brand in the medium- to high-end segment could capture up to 10 per cent of market share of the potential market, at which level a natural 'saturation' would start to kick in. Moving beyond that natural limit would require shifting to a completely different business model, as market penetration essentially self-destructed the high-end positioning of the product. Similarly, Michael believed that if a brand was grown too fast, it ran the risk of overexposure, which would lead to the market tiring of the products quickly. Certainly, new growth areas for the company could be identified later on, and the brand further developed, but, with the current brand and set-up, Michael believed it was probably wise to stick to a controlled growth agenda.

The industry had become global. Three types of companies could easily be identified. First, the old 'national institutions', with strong but not necessarily very lucrative brands, including such prestigious companies as Wedgewood in the UK, Orrefors in Sweden, Rosenthal in Germany and Royal Copenhagen in Denmark. Highly respected, they had slowly become complacent. Second, were the 'local and regional gift brands', with fairly limited value chains but the ability to make money, if only on a local scale. They built on strong regional loyalties and were relatively better at responding to regional changes. Finally, and the most diverse, were the 'design brand' houses (to which Stelton belonged) which offered very strong and original designs. Profitability was highly variable in this category.

The value chain was also different for the three strategies. The institutions maintained a longstanding tradition of doing everything themselves, from production to retailing. The local and regional gift brands (also known in the trade as 'followers' or 'early adapters' because they copied trends and simply found ways to produce them more cheaply) had practically no research and development and only variable production costs. Good supply chain management and a strong sales and marketing culture largely accounted for their profitability. The brand design houses often looked more like the institutions but without captive retail houses and with fewer fixed production costs. However, design and R&D were more in focus.

The Industry Segments

Four major segments could be identified in the kitchen and table top business-to-business distribution system. The top segment, the branded shops, represented less than 1 per cent of sales in the industry. These captive stores sold exclusively the product of a single brand, usually in luxury outlets targeting a very high-end clientele. The second segment was made up mostly of department stores, usually carrying multiple brands, sometimes in a store-in-store concept. A third segment included specialty stores in hybrid markets, with players such as IKEA, Carrefour, ICA (in Sweden), Tchibo (in Germany) and Bilka (in Denmark). At the bottom of the pyramid, sales were mostly made through supermarkets and discount stores. Margins were highest in the top segments.

Stelton sold mostly in the second segment. For Michael, these top segments were where the action was in Scandinavia, since these department stores had been slow to enter these markets. But to be successful in those segments, it would be critical to properly align all the elements of the Stelton offering: pricing, branding, quality and design.

The Brand

While Stelton enjoyed solid brand recognition, at least in Denmark, this had never been properly quantified. So, Michael decided to carry out a more scientific test to explore not only how *well-known* the brand was but also its *status*. To test these elements, he used the classic AITR framework: Awareness – Interest – Trial – Repeat. Based on a representative sample of potential customers, he was able to put some numbers on the brand (see Figure 15.7 for details of the brand perception and value):

- 72 per cent of the Danish population were familiar with Stelton,
- 18 per cent expressed interest in the brand,
- 41 per cent had tried it, and
- 35 per cent were repeat customers.

While Michael found it encouraging that 35 per cent of respondents were repeatedly shopping for Stelton's products, the fact that only 18 per cent of the respondents were interested in the products was a serious cause for concern.

Early Assessment

Michael believed that a successful design brand needed to master the following key ingredients:

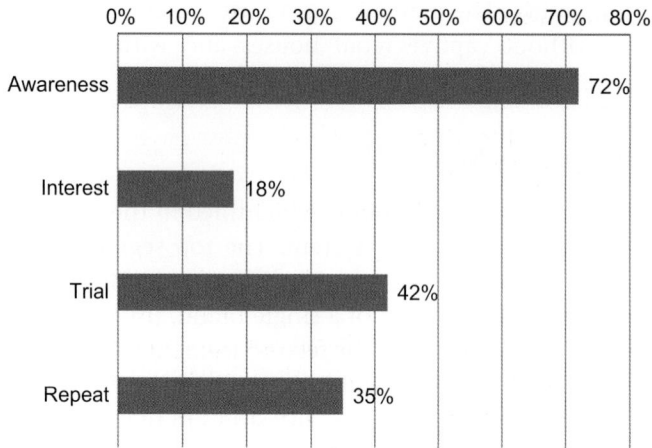

Figure 15.7 Results of the brand tests (AITR) for Stelton, March 2003.
Source: Company information

1. a consistent brand value,
2. a continuous new product stream,
3. an optimized marketing mix,
4. an aggressive sourcing policy,
5. innovative shop-in-shop solutions,
6. an efficient distribution system, and
7. a manageable geographical focus.

When he looked at Stelton's strategy, brand issues appeared to be its only successful element. The other success factors had not been taken care of for a long time. Clearly, the focus had been on Stelton's own production system. This was further confirmed by the financials: only 10 per cent of costs went into R&D and less than 2 per cent was spent on marketing, while some 50 per cent went into production!

Stelton products were largely retailed through stores that carried multiple tableware brands. The stores were often crowded with products, and it was hard for any individual brand to stand out. The shop owners did not have sophisticated cost accounting systems, and thus often did not know their profit margins on individual products or brands. In Michael's experience, no shop – irrespective of whether it belonged to a larger chain – was better than the guy behind the counter. A shop would only do well if the owner was behind the counter. To make things happen, it would be critical to develop a strong sales force to regain shelf space and the respect and cooperation of these shop owners.

Competition

The two most obvious Danish competitors were Rosendahl and Menu[7] (see Figure 15.8 for financial information on these competitors). Menu was founded in 1979 and developed table and giftware in a Scandinavian style. It sold a mixed range of products but under a single brand. The products were sold via shops and agents in more than twenty countries, primarily in Europe but also in Australia, the United States and South Africa.

Rosendahl was established by Erik Rosendahl who had designed the very first products and had been the CEO for a generation. Rosendahl developed several design 'languages', and offered not only products in the gift, table and kitchenware markets but also watches. Rosendahl was sold in more than forty countries, with noticeably strong exports to Japan.

Now What . . .

Michael turned around and started to walk home – his family's home. Did he really dare bet everything he owned on Stelton? Could Stelton become a first-class brand with lucrative products, in Denmark as well as abroad? Was the market just too fluid for a single brand to dominate, or had the company simply failed to find a way to export Danish design as its competitors had managed to do? Why had Stelton stopped growing and how could he turn it around? Without a solid business case, he would not be able to convince bankers to back him in the transaction. Somehow, the deal was already about much more than just money. It was a challenge he could no longer really say no to. But he still needed to build the case to convince others . . . many others!

Questions for Discussion

1. What is Michael looking for – in a company and for himself?
2. What do you think of Stelton as a traditional buyout opportunity? Identify and list all factors that are pros and cons for a buyout.
3. What are the special challenges posed by a target company in urgent need of a turnaround? Compare this to the traditional buyout situation, where you are buying a company in decent shape. What are the major hurdles faced by Stelton?
4. As part of the due diligence, you will need to figure out what you will need to do to the company once you own it. What would be the urgent items in your action plan? How would you prioritize these items?
5. If you were Michael Ring, would you jump at the opportunity and acquire Stelton in March 2004?

---

7 www.rosendahl.com and www.menu.as

	Menu			Rosendahl		
	2001	2000	1999	2001	2000	1999
Turnover	n/d	n/d	n/d	199,365	160,866	n/a
Materials	n/d	n/d	n/d	86,243	72,445	n/a
Gross profits	45,879	34,953	26,389	113,121	88,421	40,790
Salaries etc.	14,162	10,677	8,580	11,806	13,234	9,022
Other external expenses	17,807	12,850	13,836	27,240	19,206	-
Depreciation	2,196	1,680	1,190	4,018	3,548	2,128
Subsidiary results	-	-	85	296	296	144
Financial income	154	71	169	2,150	607	996
Financial expenses	2,757	2,930	1,481	2,738	2,661	1,715
Extraordinary income*	–	17,000	–	–	–	–
Result before tax	9,111	23,887	1,556	69,765	50,678	29,065
Taxes	2,875	8,040	153	21,350	16,910	9,021
Results after taxes	6,236	15,847	1,403	48,415	33,765	20,044
Extraordinary income**				7,000	-	-

* Sold property n/d: Not disclosed
** Sales of Goodwill n/a: Not available

	Menu			Rosendahl		
	2001	2000	1999	2001	2000	1999
Assets, selected figures						
Property	23,249	20,859	1,932	14,564	–	–
Inventories and materials	3,492	2,835	2,875	9,665	11,228	8,484
Financial assets	–	–	510	10,943	9,020	7,125
Stock	22,095	15,936	17,309	30,244	21,402	19,640
Outstanding from sales	24,863	23,749	16,891	50,182	54,855	32,737
Total assets	84,353	87,278	45,877	147,569	108,241	79,811
Liabilities, selected figures						
Equity, company capital	11,152	8,034	4,154	66,130	12,815	4,050
Retained earnings	4,864	5,188	0	2,000	2,000	0
Long-term debt	20,642	21,905	5,130	39,062	38,564	31,152
Short-term debt	39,695	44,151	28,593	40,377	54,861	44,609
Total liabilities	84,353	87,278	45,877	147,569	108,241	79,811

Source: Company website and public information

Figure 15.8 Stelton's major competitors in the Danish market: Menu and Rosendahl.

Implementing the Turnaround at Stelton

STELTON: Turning the Company Around[8]

For Michael, signing the final documents completing the acquisition of Stelton had been both a nerve-racking and a sobering experience. Yes, he had wanted the company – it had all the features he had been looking for since making the decision to go it alone: it was renowned for its phenomenal design work and superior craftsmanship, and was popular the world over. However, despite the quality of its products, it was going nowhere fast ... and the idea of risking everything he had invested in over the years, not to mention the well-being of his family, was a big negative.

In spite of this, having thrown himself into the project and the challenge of turning around this Danish design jewel, he had reached the point of no return. He had realized that if he did not go through with the acquisition and try to make his dream come true, he would always regret it:

At some point, you have to stop dreaming your dreams, and start living them ...

Doing the Deal

Putting the deal together had not been easy. For one thing, Michael did not have sufficient resources to buy the company outright. Peter Holmblad, the founder and owner of Stelton, was still running the company, and even though he was keen to find the right successor, he was not prepared to settle for just any offer. The company represented his life's work and, while he was aware that its performance had been less than stellar in the last few years, that did not mean it was in danger of immediate bankruptcy.

Michael approached the company directly and the two men immediately hit it off – they shared similar values, both loving pure design and great products. They were both dedicated to the human dimension of business and the need to treat everyone involved with respect:

You take care of all stakeholders so that ultimately they take care of you. You cannot build something sustainable on someone's slumping back!

For Peter, the idea of complete separation from the company was still difficult to digest. On the one hand, he understood that the new owner would want free rein to do whatever was necessary to put the company on solid ground for the future. On the other hand, he had sown the seeds for that future and was really keen to see how it developed.

For Michael, the key factors surrounding the deal were as follows: (1) he wished to acquire full operating control, and a majority ownership stake;

---

8 The case study is based on the original IMD case study; see Leleux and Agersnap (2008b).

(2) the seller wanted to realize some of the value he had created over the years with the company but was anxious to retain a stake in the business going forward; (3) Michael would need to find other investors to put in the equity he could not bring to the deal; and (4) banks would probably be willing to chip in with loans, but these would have to be kept at very manageable levels, since the operational risks were already significant. After all, this was really a turnaround situation ...

Keeping the founder on board made a lot of sense. Since most investors were looking for 100 per cent ownership, showing some flexibility would definitely soften the seller's stand on price. So, Michael made an offer for 80 per cent of the company: 50 per cent for himself and 30 per cent for a partner. While that put him in full control of the company, it also meant that he was financially over-stretched. He recalled:

I pledged everything I owned – except my boat! Well, to be honest, I am not sure they would have taken it as collateral anyway. It was a calming thought that I could always sail away, should everything go really wrong ...

Day 1 in the Office: Hatching the 3-Stage Plan

On Michael's first morning as new majority owner and CEO, one of the customer service employees showed him a letter she had received from a woman in the Netherlands complaining that the white vacuum jug she had bought some ... 22 years ago was becoming slightly discolored. She wondered if this 'defect' would entitle her to a discount on the new jug she intended to buy. Michael commented:

That was beautiful. Right there, I knew we had something to build our future on. That brand was as strong as the metal we were using for the jugs!

He saw his job as both a challenge and a privilege. His turnaround plan consisted of three phases: (1) getting the right structure in place; (2) investing where necessary to rebuild the brand; and (3) creating sustainability.

The first phase was the most urgent. Only with a leaner, more focused company could he create the platform and results needed to find the investors and make the investments required to build a sustainable future. Michael had already done a great deal of the necessary analysis to create the right structure. He believed in refocusing Stelton on the areas in which it had the strongest competitive advantage: design. It should primarily be a *design brand*, and only get involved in production when absolutely necessary.

To be successful as a design brand, it would have to build the brand and bring much-needed discipline to its product development, marketing and distribution systems. It was also critical to develop a world-class sourcing organization as a substitute for the in-house production facilities, where possible. Similarly, the geographic focus had to stay manageable, at least in the beginning. Stelton had been selling in the United States, for example, but clearly was not able to control development in that market. So, the focus would be on selling Stelton as a *brand* in its primary European markets, but as a *product* in other countries.

The New Product Strategy

Two key words dominated the new product strategy: *visual identity* and *brand*. Michael explained:

The design is an overall experience. It's about your behaviour, processes, how you develop new products, about the product itself, marketing, shop-in-shop solutions, packaging, handling of customers' requests, after sales, etc. Everything you do has to breathe and shine 'design and brand'.

The same holistic approach had to be applied to design:

Design is not a process to solve specific tasks or issues in the production system. Design never stands alone – it should be created around a specific need and function. All elements must work together, and all elements must be indispensable. The trick is to build functionality into the aesthetic.

Stelton had a tradition of functional designs and products, and Michael insisted on continuing that tradition. A good example of that strategy was Stelton's USB memory stick. While these had become ubiquitous electronic storage devices, it was difficult to find one that was anything other than a purely functional device. Stelton decided to create one that would not only be functional but also something that would stand out at your workstation or on your laptop. Michael remarked:

Design principles are not stuck in time: they are organic, dynamic. They live with the times. Design belongs to every aspect of your daily life, and the computer is now an important part of people's lives.

In order to achieve this, Michael was willing to sacrifice short-term profits to build a durable brand and new products with staying power to carry the company into the future. There should be no cutting corners in these areas in the first phase: this was make or break.

    With the strategy clearly spelled out, Michael focused on putting the right structure in place to roll it out. Cost-cutting, he explained, was an unavoidable part of it:

It is the most unpleasant job for a manager: You have to cut right to the bone. Sometimes you might even have to cut into the bone, and that hurts. You are dealing with people and emotions – and that is why I believe you have to do it quickly. At Stelton we did all the surgery within the first 30 days. People knew immediately if they were going to be part of the future team or not.

The new team was focused on the key competencies required for the future: marketing, product design and development, and sales and distribution. New staff were hired when no in-house expertise was present. It was important to recruit people who understood the retail business and who could get the products over the counter once the structure was in place.

The New Supply Chain

With the renewed focus on innovative design, marketing and sales, production was no longer at the heart of the company. Michael's analyses indicated that the market for industry products would continue to decline. The factory had to be downsized. This was a tough decision and a direct challenge to Stelton's historical culture. Michael opted for the 'honest, in your face' approach: he delivered a speech to the whole company in which he outlined the future – how Stelton would have to adapt and change if it wanted to survive. He did not attempt to hide the changes that would have to take place, even though they would seriously affect people on the production floor, people who had previously been seen as the 'princes' of Stelton.

The unique flow technique was preserved and the factory was kept running, but more than 30 per cent of the workforce had to be laid off during the first year, and numbers had halved within two years (see Figure 15.9 for the evolution of employment at Stelton). New people were hired to set up and manage a high-quality sourcing department with smooth processes and firm control over contractors and deliveries.

Another cost-cutting and culturally challenging exercise was moving from the big villa in a smart suburb of Copenhagen to an old warehouse. The warehouse was more suited to creative minds than the villa; it was more central, and the location was more lively and fashionable.

Marketing and Distribution

Although Stelton already had a great brand, the new marketing manager still had his work cut out. The new strategy was rooted in the results of the AITR test that Michael had done before the buyout, which illustrated a clear need for decisive action. High brand awareness but low purchase interest indicated that customers' price elasticity was probably fairly low. Interest had to be raised by means other than discounts and price reduction campaigns.

First, the communication strategy was refocused around the customer experience: products had to be distinctive, in a way that signalled innovation and quality. It quickly became clear that part of the new strategy would have to include in-store promotion, since that was the best place to attract customers' interest.

A careful study of retail stores' display and sales efforts revealed that Stelton products were often losing the shelf war – ending up lost amongst competing

Job Area	2003	2004	2005	2006	2007
Product development	0	2	2	2	2
Marketing	0	0.5	1.5	1.5	2
Sales	5	5	8	10	13
Management	2	1.5	1.5	1.5	1.5
HR + finance + admin	3	3	3	3	3
Customer service	4	4	4	4	4
Technical support of prod	5	1	1	1	1
Production administration	10	5	4	3	3
Distribution	7	6	6	7	10
Production	86	54	42	36	30
Total no. of employees	**122**	**82**	**73**	**69**	**69.5**

Source: Company information

Figure 15.9 Evolution of employment at Stelton.

products. They did not stand out in any particular way. Moreover, sales staff generally were unknowledgeable about Stelton products and were neither capable nor interested in pushing the product further. An urgent campaign needed to be targeted at sales staff to show them the current sales figures for Stelton products and how those figures could be increased.

To help the product stand out, an innovative shop-in-shop concept was developed. Exclusive display units were designed which presented Stelton products separately from other brands. Since they were often bought as gifts, it was important for the packaging to have the same 'luxury' feel as the product inside. The box, illustrating the product and its features, served both to display the product in the store and as attractive packaging when purchased. It was a simple but effective idea – the display box framed the product and attracted customers' attention. It also guaranteed uniformity of the shopping experience: Stelton's products were displayed in the same way in all stores (see Figure 15.10 for an example of a Stelton display box).

Advertising material was also completely revamped, again focusing on the customer rather than the product, since Stelton was already well-known (see Figure 15.11 for examples of the new advertising cues). Michael knew that different advertising challenges required different approaches, as exemplified by Rolex and Cartier's different strategies. Rolex enhanced its image with adverts featuring celebrity ambassadors doing exceptional things with their Rolex watches on, such as climbing mountains, sky- or scuba-diving and playing in classical concerts. For Cartier, retaining customer interest was not as much of an issue, so it could focus its advertisements on the products and their features.

Figure 15.10 The Stelton display box.
Source: Company information

Figure 15.11 Stelton's new advertising material.
Source: Company information

For Stelton, the campaign was built around the 'Stelton State of Mind' theme. Core values were established and embedded in every aspect of the company's communication strategy. Clear vision and mission statements were also developed to provide a common red thread to the messages.

Vision
Stelton is the most innovative, trend-setting, ahead-of-its-time brand / design house based on the Scandinavian design philosophy, in which the best designers in the world aspire to work.

Mission
Stelton wants to be the first choice for consumers who actively seek good design to enrich their way of living.

The new campaigns were launched in synch with the new product mix. Two angles were addressed on that front. First, Michael's analyses revealed a sweet spot in the gift segment in the DKK 150–300 price range, a range in which they were historically not well represented. With the new organizational structure, and its resultant lower production costs, gross margins had improved dramatically, reaching at least 69 per cent, making the traditional 'gift segment', for example, quite appealing from a financial perspective. Within that category, Stelton launched its *i:con* product range, including items such as business card holders, money clips and luggage tags. Second, Stelton refocused on the historic Stelton products such as the traditional vacuum jug, which was completely updated to provide a more modern interpretation.[9]

In total, 25 per cent of revenues were dedicated to sales and marketing. Of this, 50 per cent went into external activities such as PR, customer branding and brochures, 35 per cent was earmarked for internal activities (salaries, trade sales, etc.), and the final 15 per cent went on in-store promotions to cover rent for the space that was occupied, decorations, etc.

Product Development

A strong sustainable brand could only be built on the basis of a continuous flow of new products to the market. Some products had taken on iconic status, such as the vacuum jug, and had very long product life cycles; others stayed on the shelves for a year or two at most. It was always hard to predict which of the new products would become long-lasting winners and which would never take off. So, as in many other industries, it was necessary to develop a large range of products – all true to the Stelton design, irrespective of category and price. Out of 10 new product launches, the objective was to get two 'home runs' and six 'base load' sellers. The company could definitely withstand two disappointments.

9 Products can be seen on www.stelton.com

The target was to develop twenty to thirty new products each year. It typically took 9 to 12 months from the initiation of research to the new product hitting the shelves. The time to market was longer for products sold to industry, where it often took 24 to 36 months to meet the more stringent requirements of business customers.

Michael and the product development manager made the final decisions on every product proposal received from in-house and external designers. When making those decisions, they relied on a series of pre-conditions: the product needed not just a strong design that would fit with the Stelton brand but it should also be well made, from excellent materials and with high functionality. Functionality would drive everything else, with every superfluous attribute removed in the redesign. For Michael, this was the key to classic products: minimalistic, functional chic.

The Cylinda-Line by Arne Jacobsen, which had been a Stelton classic for over forty years, was an example of this design philosophy. Creating a series of products in which each product could stand out individually, but where the complete collection created a harmonious ensemble, was revolutionary. Many splendid designs had followed in the footsteps of the Cylinda-Line, and the legacy was so strong that Michael decided to launch a special 'Arne Jacobsen Heritage' project. He invited designers closely involved in past developments to re-interpret the Arne Jacobsen design cues and construct a brand new line of products involving the same features. The new line would utilize its own design language and be able to establish its own space within the Stelton collection. Designers were given a four-year timeframe to create the new collection.

Building Momentum

There was so much that could go wrong, in spite of all the carefully laid plans. First and foremost, the huge investments in marketing and product development did not guarantee success. Clearly, an aggressive marketing and advertising campaign was essential, but there was no way of knowing if it would really fly. It could succeed in attracting the customers who had proved so elusive in the past, or the company could end up undercapitalized and in no better shape to face the future. Failure was not really an option ... The vision and mission statements were ambitious, but was the strategy really aligned behind those grand statements? Finally, Michael was also worried that he may have missed something critical in the rollout of the turnaround plan. On paper, it seemed to make sense. He thought he had dealt with all the 'emergencies', but had he overlooked other priorities? He would no doubt find out soon enough ...

Stelton case study Epilogue[10]

By January 2008, Michael's turnaround plan had been fully implemented. Stelton's new structure was firmly in place, with a renewed focus on design and marketing, and increased reliance on external suppliers for production.

10 The epilogue is based on the original IMD case study; see Leleux and Agersnap (2008c).

The new strategy was well under way, the required investments had been made and the results were beginning to be seen. It was now time for Michael to create truly sustainable growth going forward (see Figure 15.12 for financials 2003–07). The full year estimate for net sales in 2007 would approach DKK 142 million, with estimated earnings after tax of around DKK 20 million.[11]

Over the last couple of years, more and more companies had been capitalizing on the Scandinavian design trend. The competition was toughest in Denmark itself, where many well-known brands vied to represent Scandinavian design, many of them also developing attractive shop-in-shops concepts in very much the same locations as Stelton. Several of these brands were also targeting the same export markets, especially Scandinavia and Germany.

Other limitations to Stelton's organic growth were starting to materialize too:

- The Scandinavian countries were the biggest markets for the 'Minimalist International' style. Not all countries favoured this style, and demand would therefore not be the same in new markets.
- Distribution in Sweden and Germany was undergoing a period of change. With big chain stores beginning to squeeze out the specialist shops, the role of sales representatives was becoming increasingly important. If the brand was relatively unknown, the design had to be strong enough to attract the customer.
- Customers had not proven very responsive to brand communication in general.

However, Michael believed there was still some space to capture in the current markets. The core markets represented a total sales value of around DKK 250 million, and Stelton was nowhere close to saturating it.

Growth was not a luxury for a small player like Stelton: it was fundamental to reaching the critical size at which Michael would start to have more negotiating power vis à vis the suppliers and the distributing stores. Suppliers had become a more critical component of his value chain as he progressively shifted production outside the company. Similarly, the battle for shelf space was in full swing; gaining distributors' attention or negotiating advertisement campaigns with media agencies also required size and scale. The current scale of operations also created problems internally since many sales and administration costs were fixed. The relative costs of marketing and distribution activities were high, and Stelton was not necessarily a priority for the sales agents. A larger turnover would certainly help with the heavy investments needed in the core markets and to reach higher efficiencies in supply and distribution. However, larger volumes would have to come from the current geographical focus and via the same channels.

---

11 On 7 January 2008, DKK 1 = $0.1981, €1.343 and CHF 0.2194.

PROFIT AND LOSS	2007 (E)	2006	2005	2004	2003
Net Sales	142,095	95,897	79,221	72,751	74,236
Cost of goods sold	61,471	43,797	37,086	38,748	47,896
Gross profit	80,624	52,100	42,135	34,003	26,340
Distribution	40,275	36,173	29,083	19,510	18,483
Administration	9,804	7,782	7,843	11,345	11,925
Other operational costs	3,639	2,920	2,688	1,090	1,730
Operational profit	26,913	5,234	2,520	2,058	(5,798)
Other income	100	96	58	0	33
Financial income	370	455	592	700	495
Financial expenses	1,361	970	1,160	1,271	2,028
Pre tax profits	26,022	4,815	2,010	1,487	(7,298)
Taxes	6,505	671	473	510	2,088
Net income	**19,516**	**4,143**	**1,537**	**977**	**(5,210)**

CASH FLOWS	2007 (E)	2006	2005	2004	2003
Operations	–	6,086	6,959	2,483	1,279
Investments	–	(2,642)	(3,241)	5,755	(1,371)
Financing	–	(2,265)	(11,632)	(3,252)	(17,186)

KEY FIGURES	2007	2006	2005	2004	2003
Employees (FTE)	72	68	69	77	94
Stelton sales to third parties	2.8%	6.2%	7.6%	16.6%	
ROA		10.0	6.3	4.6	(10.8)
Equity ratio		46.6	42.3	40.3	35.5
ROE		16.6	6.9	4.7	(18.7)

Figure 15.12 Financial Statements (2003–2007).

Building a More Efficient Structure

Michael now had to consider new options to better leverage the current cost structure, the core competencies and the brand. Three directions seemed to be open to him: (1) a strategic partnership for sales or distribution; (2) acquiring another company or product line and; (3) acquiring new competencies.

BALANCE SHEET	2006	2005	2004	2003
ASSETS				
Property	6,402	7,010	7,605	16,396
Machinery & tools	2,911	2,890	2,725	4,669
Other material	2,932	3,116	2,414	1,187
Plant, property and equipment	*12,245*	*13,834*	*12,744*	*22,252*
Investments	243	296	338	338
Deposits	537	522	507	4
Financial assets	*780*	*818*	*845*	*342*
Long-term assets	13,025	13,834	13,589	22,594
Raw materials	4,642	5,417	4,611	6,720
Goods in process	1,403	1,385	1,646	1,653
Finished goods inventory	11,087	7,434	4,813	3,336
Inventories	*17,132*	*14,236*	*11,070*	*11,709*
Accounts receivables	24,853	20,513	15,000	13,508
Other receivables	892	694	510	884
Tax receivables	50	70	0	270
Receivables associated companies	18	0	237	0
Receivables	*25,813*	*21,277*	*15,747*	*14,662*
Cash	1,336	3,296	9,782	2,756
Bonds	715	1,521	2,949	4,885
Cash and cash equivalents	*2,051*	*4,817*	*12,731*	*7,641*
Current assets	44,996	40,330	39,548	34,012
TOTAL ASSETS	**58,021**	**54,164**	**53,137**	**56,606**
LIABILITIES				
Company capital	7,200	7,200	7,200	7,200
Retained earnings	19,851	15,708	14,171	12,870
Shareholders equity	*27,052*	*22,908*	*21,371*	*20,070*
Deferred income tax	1,495	1,977	1,748	2,556
Long-term debt	*5,838*	*8,268*	*19,565*	*22,793*
Current portion of long-term debt	2,344	2,180	2,515	2,539
Bank debt	5,664	9,609	104	-
Accounts payable	8,534	4,478	1,618	2,574
Other debt	6,013	4,737	5,698	6,074
Debt of associated company	1,081	7	0	0
Short-term debt	*23,637*	*21,011*	*10,453*	*11,187*
Total debt	29,475	29,279	30,018	33,980
LIABILITIES & EQUITY	**58,021**	**54,164**	**53,137**	**56,606**

Source: Company information

Figure 15.12 (cont.)

A strategic partnership would strengthen sales and distribution. A joint sales force could, for example, carry two brands at the same time. This would reduce the need for sales agents: dedicated salesmen, even if shared, could create better results than agents. The problem, of course, was to identify a partner that would not be competing directly with Stelton but would be compatible in terms of values and prices. A dedicated kitchen brand could be interesting, or a brand anchored in a specific material.

An acquisition would have to provide strong synergies and strengthen Stelton's core competencies. It could be opportunistic (although none had appeared so far) or Stelton could start a dedicated search to look for a company representing a certain product category in the core markets, such as cutlery.

Another option would be to acquire new product competencies, either in markets with little competition, to build a new line within the Stelton brand, or to acquire an already existing strong brand.

Of course, none of these options was mutually exclusive, and it seemed possible to combine some of them for the benefit of Stelton.

The Strategic Alternatives

Michael felt that the following options were plausible for Stelton going forward:

A: Organic growth up to 10 per cent p.a. with primary markets in Denmark, Norway and Sweden

These markets looked promising and could generate the new growth that would be needed to compensate for stagnation or losses in other markets. All other markets would remain 'export markets'. Following this strategy meant it would not be necessary to pursue other new markets for at least three years. Product development would focus on fewer and safer introductions. Ninety per cent of the marketing budget would go to the primary markets. Michael believed this strategy would lead to an increase of the yearly result (before taxes) of around 10 per cent and a company free of debt by 2008.

B: Double-digit organic growth p.a. with the current product range but in more markets

Besides the primary markets in Denmark, Norway and Sweden, investments would have to be made to win greater market shares of the German and Benelux markets by developing the current sales force in Germany and supporting new agents in Benelux. All other markets would remain 'export markets', and would still be allocated the same resources. Product development would continue within the usual categories. Marketing costs would increase to 12 per cent of the turnover. Michael expected an increase of around 5 to 10 per cent of revenues but the company would not be free of debt by 2008.

C: Double-digit organic growth p.a. with an expanded product portfolio

This plan would rely partially on the B strategy but with redefined product categories. For example, Home Products could be extended to include a cordless phone; Personal Accessories could include a computer bag. Financially, an EBIT margin before tax of 10 per cent would be expected, but in the long term Stelton would have a greater growth potential due to the higher level of innovation and the new products.

D: Distribution of another brand

Certainly, the financial impact of this strategy would depend on the exact product(s) and brand(s) that Stelton would distribute, but the estimated improved sales contribution in Denmark was DKK 4–5 million, with added costs of around DKK 1 million. This would facilitate access to the big wholesale shops, but there was a risk that the Stelton products would receive less attention.

E: Acquiring branded companies but retaining a stand-alone strategy

This approach would involve identifying a company with a strong brand but in need of better management. Through active board members, Stelton would transfer its turnaround experience. There could be synergies between Stelton and the new company but that would not be a goal on its own. The financial outcome of this strategy was hard to predict since it would depend, to a large extent, on the company acquired.

F: Acquiring branded companies and integrating them fully

This strategy would require identifying candidates within the region and making investments in the sales force to support the new combined entities. Distribution and management resources would be used more efficiently across the combined entities. In some instances, one could even envision a net inflow of competencies into Stelton, and there would also be administrative synergies, in areas such as IT and finance. The companies would be fully integrated into Stelton, with the possibility of keeping their own brand names (if strong enough) and organizations.

In fact, Michael relished being forced to make these choices. Having to grow was the best thing that could have happened to him. It was less than four years since he had acquired Stelton. All in all, things had gone very well and he felt privileged to be confronted with these problems. While it had not been entirely smooth sailing, it was also important to take stock of the impressive progress that had been made so far. These decisions were the natural next steps for the successful company. But being natural did not make them any easier to take. Things had just started to stabilize and the post-buyout stress had finally disappeared: was it necessary and appropriate to inject a new dose of stress into the system so early by acquiring other companies or developing new markets? What should Michael's priorities be: increase profitability, build long-term prospects or reduce the debt, even it meant sacrificing short-term earnings?

KEY TAKEAWAYS

- Early identification of declining performance is key to ensuring rapid intervention and to prevent a 'death spiral', where the speed of decline accelerates and the chances of stopping the negative dynamic drop.
- Interventions, in general, need to be decisive and fast, involving significant reductions in costs and changes in personnel. Some legal environments support these interventions, others make them very difficult to implement. In the latter case, liquidation is often the only alternative.
- Too many investors end up doing turnarounds when the original intention was simply to orchestrate a buyout or buy-in. Lack of financial resources lead them to focus on 'cheaper' targets, often companies that have already entered the death spiral.
- It is usually appropriate to assume that management teams are not incompetent and will have already implemented the easy fixes. Therefore, a company that is still showing signs of declining or impaired performance is usually in need of stronger interventions.
- Short-term fixes to stop the bleeding are not permanent solutions: they only buy time to implement a more sustainable solution. In a turnaround, it is essential to first determine what that new sustainable business model will look like, and then identify the steps to take the company from where it is today to that long-term situation.

END OF CHAPTER QUESTIONS

1. What tools or steps would you use to identify early signs of declining performance, especially when sales or margins are still healthy?
2. What are the financing challenges of funding turnaround transactions, particularly with respect to leverage and debt financing?
3. How can you create a sense of urgency in a target company that is still in the early stages of crisis, in order to implement the necessary but radical measures?
4. How would you suggest dealing with sagging morale in a declining or underperforming company?
5. Seller financing is often a key component of the turnaround financing package. What are its pros and cons?
6. Cash management is a the heart of the turnaround operation: first stop the

bleeding then find ways to generate more cash. What action points would you recommend?

7. How would you incentivize your workforce and key players to engage fully with your turnaround plans when you know it will take time for results to materialize and resources will remain constrained in the meantime?

8. How do you handle external stakeholders (e.g. suppliers) who are key to supporting your turnaround but who have often already been antagonized by the company's difficulties?

9. Customers also need to nurtured back to the company, after a protracted period of uncertainty. What measures would you recommend to rebuild customer confidence?

10. Underperformance occurs for many reasons, some external but many internal. It is often difficult to separate their respective contributions to the end results and yet this is key to ensuring the potential success of a turnaround. What recommendations would you make for conducting a thorough strategic due diligence in those situations?

FURTHER READING

Altman, E. I. and Hotchkiss, E. (2006). *Corporate Financial Distress and Bankruptcy*, 3rd edition. John Wiley & Sons.

DiNapoli, D., Sigoloff, S. C. and Cushman, R. F. (1991). *Workouts and Turnarounds: The Handbook of Restructuring and Investing in Distressed Companies*. Irwin Professional Publishing.

Gilson, S. C. (2010). *Creating Value Through Corporate Restructuring: Case Studies in Bankruptcies, Buyouts, and Breakups*, 2nd edition. John Wiley & Sons.

Nesvold, H. P., Anapolsky, J. M. and Reed Lajoux, A. (2011). *The Art of Distressed M&A: Buying, Selling, and Financing Troubled and Insolvent Companies*. McGraw-Hill Education.

Foster Reed, S., Reed Lajoux, A. and Nesvold, H. P. (2007). *The Art of M&A: A Merger Acquisition Buyout Guide*, 4th edition. McGraw-Hill Education.

Rosenberg, H. (2000). *The Vulture Investors*. John Wiley & Sons.

Sloma, R. S. (2000). *The Turnaround Manager's Handbook*. Beard Books.

Turnarounds & Workouts, published monthly by Beard Group, Inc., P.O. Box 40915, Washington, D.C. 20016.

Turnaround Management Association, https://turnaround.org/

Whitman, M. J. and Diz, F. (2009). *Distress Investing: Principles and Technique*, John Wiley & Sons.

REFERENCES

Bain & Company (2017). *Global Private Equity Report 2017*. Bain & Company.

Invest Europe (2015). *2015 European Private Equity Activity*. Invest Europe.

Leleux, B. and Agersnap, B. S. (2008a). *Stelton (A): Buyout Opportunity?* (IMD-3-1963), IMD.

Leleux, B. and Agersnap, B. S. (2008b). *Stelton (B): Turning the Company Around.* (IMD-3-1964), IMD.

Leleux, B. and Agersnap, B. S. (2008c). *Stelton (C): When Competition Awakens.* (IMD-3-1965), IMD

Preqin (2014). *Preqin Data Pack 2014.* Preqin.

Preqin (2016). *2016 Preqin Global Private Equity and Venture Capital Report.* Preqin.

Rozenzweig, P. (2007). *The Halo Effect.* Free Press.

16 | IMPACT INVESTING: FINANCING SOCIAL ENTREPRENEURS

LISA HEHENBERGER

ESADE Business School

JOHANNA MAIR

Hertie School of Governance

SARA SEGANTI

European Venture Philanthropy Association

This chapter will provide an overview of impact investing and how to finance social entrepreneurs. Social entrepreneurship provides innovative solutions for social needs that are not adequately dealt with. Social enterprises can adopt various legal forms and can be characterized by pursuing a social mission while competing in the market economy.

Putting their social mission first, social enterprises often lack stable funding, organizational capacity or access to partnerships to build sustainable and scalable business models. Impact investing and venture philanthropy are investment approaches that seek a societal impact combined with different degrees of financial return by investing in social enterprise. Impact investing uses innovative financing mechanisms, capacity-building support and impact measurement and management. Impact investing is also characterized by a long-term and high-engagement/hands-on approach to investees and an intentionality in producing positive and measurable societal impact at both investor and investee levels.

In many ways, the impact investing process is similar to that of venture capital, but there are important differences that we will explain in the chapter.

Impact investing is an emerging field of practice that evolves as we speak. As such, we are all still in a learning mode, and practitioner networks such as the European Venture Philanthropy Association (EVPA) with research functions, as well as academic institutions and researchers, play an important role in facilitating this learning. In this chapter, we build on existing research, and make recommendations based on what we consider 'best practice', although we acknowledge that impact investors use a spectrum of approaches.

VIEW FROM THE MEDIA

FINANCIAL TIMES   FT

The drive for a social purpose

We may peg 2017 as a breakthrough year for the concept of impact investing

MARCH 9, 2017 BY STEPHEN FOLEY

What if that bond in your fixed income portfolio not only paid you a decent interest rate but also saved a giant forest from succumbing to wildfires? What if your latest venture capital investment not only earned you a fat return but also provided jobs for former prisoners who otherwise would find it tough to get employment? The idea that you can be more ambitious for your investments than simply earning a good financial rate of return has rapidly been gaining ground. In fact, for many wealthy millennials the question is, why would you not aim to invest for good? But until recently it has been hard to find solid investments that can also demonstrate a measurable impact on problems such as climate change, poverty, access to clean water, inequality or any of the other big challenges facing the globe. That may be changing and we may even peg 2017 as a breakthrough year for the concept of impact investing … There is so much activity coming down the pike … The financial returns from which will depend on the social impact of the programmes they fund. Schemes such as preventing former prisoners reoffending or to cut hospital visits for asthma in children. There is a whole Global Innovation Lab for Climate Finance, backed by the UK department of energy and former New York mayor Michael Bloomberg among others, to test new capital structures for green energy projects. Meanwhile, so-called 'double bottom line' companies are mushrooming. B Labs now certifies more than 1,800 so-called 'B Corps' that are committed to producing a measurable positive social impact as well as profits, everything from manufacturers of organic body care products to mobile money transfer agencies in Africa … The entrepreneurs and others streaming out of business schools are increasingly driven by a social purpose as much as by the desire to make money. And there is the demand from investors themselves … Wealthy individuals can take a dual role in this fizzing ecosystem. They can use their philanthropic resources to back the development of the impact investing space more broadly, by funding projects and platforms designed to bring the non-profit and investing worlds together. Most of all though, they can jump in as pioneering investors in experimental projects such as the forest resilience bond, taking on the proof-of-concept work that conservative investors never could. Using a bit of your fortune to prove that you can do good and make money? That might just be the best investment anyone can make.

www.ft.com/content/b438e132-f9bd-11e6-bd4e-68d53499ed71

LEARNING OBJECTIVES

After reading this chapter you will be able to:

- Recognize impact investing and venture philanthropy as investment approaches in social enterprise.
- Understand how impact investors define their organizational structures and funding models.
- Develop the key components of an impact investing investment strategy.
- Grasp the basics of how to measure societal impact and how to develop a Theory of Change.
- Understand how the investment process in impact investing differs from that of a regular investment.

In this chapter, we will use the term 'impact investing' to refer to both early-stage and later-stage investment in social enterprise. We will use the term 'impact investor' to refer to investment fund managers that seek a societal impact combined with different degrees of financial return – by investing in social enterprises, thus including venture philanthropy as well. The social enterprises are the 'investees'.

Where Are We Going Next?

This chapter will introduce the concept of impact investing and related terms such as venture philanthropy, and will provide some useful market data. It will explain how impact investing differs from venture capital and other forms of entrepreneurial finance. It will then describe how an impact investing fund is set up and financed, and explain the components of an impact investment strategy. Impact measurement is an integral practice of impact investing and an important factor distinguishing it from regular investing. Therefore, the chapter will explain the basics of how to measure impact. Finally, we will highlight the key steps in the investment process.

16.1   An Introduction to Impact Investing and Venture Philanthropy

We define impact investing and venture philanthropy as investment approaches that seek a societal impact combined with different degrees of financial return – by investing in social enterprises. In this chapter, we will use the term 'social enterprise' to depict an organization that has a primary social mission, but operates in the market economy. Social enterprises need different types of financing at different stages in their evolution. Venture philanthropy can be seen as the type of financing that social enterprises need at seed stage, normally implying smaller ticket sizes and higher risk, whereas impact investing kicks in at startup and growth stages when there is a proven business model and some track record. Due to the risky nature of venture philanthropy, investors are often philanthropic ones who

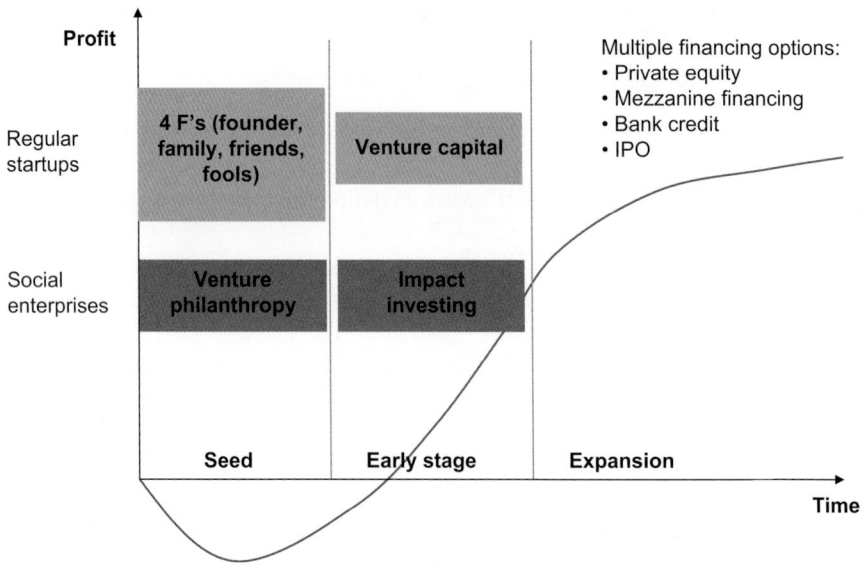

Figure 16.1 Social enterprises need different types of financing at different stages in their evolution.
Source: Vecchi et al. (eds.) (2016)

do not demand a financial return, and sometimes grants are used – alone or in combination with other financing instruments that seek a positive financial return. Impact investing, on the other hand, does not include philanthropic financing instruments. Both venture philanthropy and impact investing aim to achieve a societal impact, whereas the expectation of economic returns varies from case to case. Figure 16.1 provides a schematic overview of the different types of financing that social enterprises need at different stages in their evolution.

It is difficult to obtain a clear understanding of the overall size and financial return of the impact investing market due to the fragmented nature of data collection efforts. The OECD expert group on social impact investment is working on streamlining and standardizing data collection so that data can become more comparable.

The European Venture Philanthropy Association (EVPA) survey provides an yearly update on the European venture philanthropy and 'social impact investment' sector every two years. It includes organizations based in Europe that invest domestically or all over the world using a venture philanthropy approach. The survey excludes organizations with a 'finance first' investment strategy, i.e. where financial returns are maximized and social impact is of secondary importance. The survey report,[1] published at the end of 2016, reported that 97 organizations invested €756 million in a total portfolio of 3,121 social enterprises during 2015.

---

1 Boiardi and Gianoncelli(2016).

The Global Impact Investing Network (GIIN) publishes an annual survey on impact investment. It has a global scope and also includes the 'finance first' part of the investment spectrum. The latest survey,[2] published in 2016, accounts for US$15 billion in investments made during 2015. The sample used is clearly different from the EVPA survey and represents much larger investment amounts.

Several studies have attempted to assess the financial returns expected and achieved in impact investing. As in the studies of market size, the financial return achieved depends on the scope of the study. For example, EngagedX calculated financial returns on about 400 individual deals closed by three UK-based impact investors, invested in between 2002 and 2014, reporting an overall return of negative 9.3 per cent.[3] In contrast, Cambridge Associates and the GIIN reported an overall internal rate of return (IRR) of 6.9 per cent for the sample of 51 funds making investments between 2000 and 2014.[4] The latter includes data from finance-first, private equity funds. Until the impact investing sector develops more standardized measures and asset classes, benchmarking across funds is not very helpful.

The ambition to achieve societal impact is clearly a distinguishing factor in impact investing, and the concept of impact measurement is, therefore, important. Measuring the impact is a fundamental practice in impact investing and is compulsory both at the fund level and at the level of the investee. The ultimate objective of impact measurement should be as a tool to help both investor and investee steer their organizations towards greater societal impact. We will explore impact measurement in more detail later in the chapter.

16.2   The Investment Process in Impact Investment

As in venture capital, impact investors follow an investment process as outlined in Figure 16.2. The impact investor should handle this process to maximize the achievement of the social and financial return and make the most impactful use of its resources. The final aim of the impact investor is to plan, oversee and

Investment Process

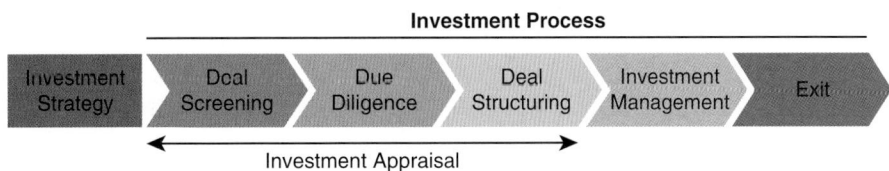

Investment Strategy → Deal Screening → Due Diligence → Deal Structuring → Investment Management → Exit

Investment Appraisal

Figure 16.2 The impact investment process.
Source: Balbo et al. *(2016)*

2 Mudaliar *et al.* (2016).
3 Richter (2015).
4 Matthews *et al.* (2015).

execute the investment and the exit while leaving behind a social enterprise with a stronger business model and organizational structure capable of attracting and managing the resources required to achieve its social impact mission in the long term.

After considering the key elements of its investment strategy, the impact investor assesses the investment opportunities available (deal flow). Following a first screening, a detailed analysis (or due diligence) supports the impact investor's investment decision in choosing which social enterprise to invest in and how to structure the deal (deal structuring). The investment management comes after the investment appraisal phase. The exit will be conducted when the impact investor can no longer bring value to the social enterprise, when the objectives have been achieved, or when the predefined duration of the investment has come to an end.

16.2.1   Investment Appraisal

As in venture capital, the effort of the impact investment needs to be proportionate to the potential benefits that may result – both at the social and at the financial level. The key elements of the investment appraisal process are *deal screening, due diligence* and *investment decision and deal structuring*. The impact investment appraisal is different from the process undertaken for venture capital as each element will include an assessment related to the impact measurement practice, the non-financial support needed and the consequences of the exit strategy at the social level.

Deal Screening

The first phase of the appraisal process is a preliminary screening of the investment opportunities available (the deal flow) in order to eliminate applicants that do not fit the basic standard requirements (first screening). This first step requires initial application documents only. Impact investors often have to create the market when getting started and may need to contribute at an earlier stage than initially anticipated by engaging in market-building activities and even setting up their own incubators.

The Deal Flow

There are many ways of identifying potential impact investment targets[5]; among these, the impact investor should consider networking activities related to the field of interest, speaking at sector-specific conferences, desk research and connecting with other traditional funders that have dropped deals that may be suitable for the impact investor. Open competitions for

---

5 Hehenberger *et al.* (2014).

social business plans can be an interesting option to raise interest about impact investor activity. However, the impact investor has to consider the considerable effort in terms of time and resources related to such a procedure.

First Screening

The impact and financial objectives of the impact investor will guide the deal screening in the investment process in order to select social enterprises that will fit the overall investment strategy. The impact investor will evaluate the expected outcome of each investment in a social enterprise, which is the result of the expected outcome of the social enterprise and of the impact investor's expectations to contribute to achieving this outcome.

At the impact management level, the impact objectives set by the social enterprise – which is the social issue to be solved and its theory of change (inputs/activities and expected outcomes) – must match the impact investor overall strategy to pass the preliminary screening. This phase corresponds to Step 1 of the impact measurement process outlined further in this chapter.

The impact investor also has to assess the needs of the social enterprise (light assessment) from the non-financial support point of view in order to ensure that the general needs of the social enterprise can be efficiently and successfully addressed by the impact investor's core non-financial support strategy. Finally, in this first screening, the impact investor will have to look at the exit strategy, assessing how the key elements of its investment strategy relating to an investment opportunity are going to influence the exit and its results.

Due Diligence

Detailed screening is usually performed through analysis and validation of a business plan. The investment proposal is thus presented to the investment committee to make the final investment decision. The stakeholder analysis that corresponds to Step 2 of the impact measurement process should be a fundamental part of the due diligence phase. This includes defining who the direct and indirect contributors and beneficiaries are and setting up a system to verify and value expected results. To avoid wasting resources, the impact investor can progressively increase the intensity and the number of stakeholders involved as the prospect that the investment will be realized grows. Key stakeholders should be consulted to double-check the impact objectives, and any major change related to impact goals must be properly shared.

The detailed screening process will cover all the traditional elements of the venture capital screening process at the financial sustainability level plus the following items focused on assessing the social impact, peculiar to the impact investing due diligence:

- Theory of Change – The impact investor should, first of all, have a detailed understanding of the current and expected social impact of the social enterprise. For this reason, it is helpful if the social enterprise has already developed an impact measurement process that is sufficiently solid to prove the social outcome has been achieved. For younger, less mature social enterprises, the impact investor may need to provide the necessary expertise to help the potential investee articulate its theory of change and impact objectives.
- Impact measurement systems – The impact investor should check whether the social enterprise has an impact monitoring and assessment system that works sufficiently well; if not, it should include the development thereof in the budget.
- Organizational Resilience – The impact investor should analyse the management and governance of the potential investee. Impact investors report that investments have failed due to inadequate attention to the power of the board and an overestimation of the capability of a charismatic management team[6] (common mistakes in venture capital also).

The impact investor should develop an in-depth assessment of the social enterprise in order to understand the organizational capacities needed in subsequent years and to decide whether the impact investor will be able to provide adequate non-financial support.

Investment Decision and Deal Structuring

This phase corresponds to a set of terms and conditions that specify how the agreement between the impact investor and the social enterprise invested in is to be defined. The impact investor should ensure that the social enterprise leadership is truly and deeply committed to the social mission of the organization, is on top of the business plan and its future needs, and is prepared, in term of skills and expertise, to execute its plans effectively. In many cases, impact investors will support the social enterprise in developing and reviewing a business plan only in the fields in which it can add value. In all cases, joint development and ownership of the business plan is recommended as cooperation in business planning fosters commitment and buy-in from both sides.

It is riskier to invest in social enterprises with an undeveloped product/service, focusing on sectors or countries that the impact investor is not familiar with and where it cannot add strategic value, or in social enterprises that are not yet ready for the impact investing approach.[7] In order to minimize the risk of failure in deal structuring, the impact investor can start with stepped investments in

6 Hehenberger and Boiardi (2014).
7 Hehenberger and Boairdi (2014).

target social enterprises; for example, by completing small investments in multiple social enterprises to get to know the organization and build mutual trust.

The financial considerations are similar to those affecting for-profit deals, although there is a wider variety of financial instruments (as presented in Section 16.4 on Investment Strategy). Once the deal is structured, the impact investor and the social enterprise should work jointly to develop a non-financial support plan and an exit plan.

Non-financial Support Plan

The development needs of the social enterprise must be assessed and identified before signing the deal and defining a non-financial support plan. The impact investor and the social enterprise should then agree on for each development area, the priorities to address. The non-financial plan includes the baseline, goals, milestones and target outcomes to be reached by the social enterprise. The objective is to monitor the progress made on the three dimensions of financial sustainability, organizational resilience and impact objectives. The plan should refer explicitly to the support that the impact investor will provide to the social enterprise to boost its capacity to achieve the planned goals and concrete deliverables. However, the resources of a social enterprise are always limited, and impact measurement is an essential tool. The core of the impact investing approach relies on impact measurement, and although the rigour and depth of the impact analysis can differ from case to case, the impact investor plays a fundamental role in convincing the investees of the value of impact measurement. Before structuring the deal, the impact investor should ensure that, at the social enterprise level, an impact measurement system is set up to measure results: outputs, outcomes, impact and indicators related to the objectives of the investee. It is also important to decide who is responsible for collecting what type of data. Decisions need to be made about the amount of time and resources that a social enterprise should dedicate to impact measurement. The costs of supporting and maintaining a social enterprise's impact monitoring system (including personnel time and costs) should be part of the social enterprise's budget and hence part of the negotiation with the investor in order to decide how costs should and/or could be split.

Exit Plan

Before the investment is finalized, the impact investor should co-develop an exit plan with the social enterprise. The plan should consider the expectations of both parties and define a scenario based on the key points related to the exit, including the need to preserve the capacity of the social enterprise to pursue its social mission, the general goals of the investor related to the financial, organizational and impact outcomes to be achieved, and the timing of the exit. Both investor and investee should ensure openness and transparency in aligning their expectations.

The key elements to define in an exit plan are:

1. Investment goals of the overall investment strategy of the impact investor;
2. Goals to be achieved by the social enterprise as defined in the non-financial plan that determine when exit readiness is reached.
3. Timing of the exit that should be determined in relation to the financial instrument used.
4. Mode of exit that influences the how and to whom to exit, both of which elements are largely influenced by the financing instrument used.
5. Resources available and included in the non-financial support plan to monitor the investment and execute the exit plan.
6. Exit market scenarios that envisage to whom the impact investor will exit and what the market context will be at that time.

16.2.2   Investment Management

The impact investor manages the investments made both at the level of each investee social enterprise and at the whole portfolio level.

Goal Monitoring and Reporting

The monitoring of the advancement of the social enterprise in achieving the goals set in the non-financial support plan is an integral part of the investment process. Not all indicators will be monitored at the same time and with the same rigour; data collection has to be adjusted to the reporting objective and the resources available. As a general rule, for the impact measurement system, the impact investor should assess output indicators more frequently than outcome indicators. The social enterprise should report on the progress in achieving the indicators every quarter, every six months or every year throughout the investment period. It is advisable to agree on reporting requirements upfront with the investee and co-investors to eliminate the burden of multiple reporting on the investee.

At the social enterprise level, it is important to verify and value impact for key stakeholders. Stakeholder analysis should be regularly repeated either at prearranged times, or when significant changes occur that may adjust the outcomes to be achieved, including obtaining new funding, developing new business opportunities, or following a relevant policy innovation. Key stakeholders should be regularly involved, at least once during the investment period, in order to verify that their expectations are met. Verifying and valuing results and impact involving the key stakeholders are the best 'reality checks' to assess the value created by the investment. The impact investor should never forget that the main objective of monitoring is to build knowledge from the experience.

The data collected and analysed should be used to implement any necessary changes and develop corrective actions.

Non-financial Support Delivery Models

The impact investor delivers non-financial support through a variety of delivery modes, including one-on-one coaching, taking a seat on the social enterprise's board, offering training and access to networks. Each of these options should be assessed by both the social enterprise and the impact investor in order to define priorities and a common strategy to achieve them. The delivery of the non-financial support is subject to change following the development of the social enterprise and should be adjusted to its needs. The non-financial support plan must include information about when the relationship between the impact investor and the social enterprise will end. Both parties should clarify at the outset to what extent the impact investor will be involved in the social enterprise's management and set the targets that will define whether exit readiness has been achieved. The non-financial support should continue until the impact has been achieved or until the impact investor believes its services no longer add value to the social enterprise.

Determining Exit Readiness

The impact investor monitors the achievement of the goals of the social enterprise based on the exit plan and assesses when the social enterprise is exit ready. It is very important that the social enterprise provides full cooperation by providing information on the progress made in achieving the goals previously agreed upon. The monitoring phase is essential, and it allows both the investor and the investee to make corrections and take action should there be any deviation from the agreed exit plan. Monitoring can reveal whether exit readiness is achieved at the planned date of exit.

In managing the portfolio, the following aspects, which are peculiar to the impact investing approach, should be taken into account:

- Flagship investments: as impact investing is a new and not yet well-defined practice, the impact investor may be advised to begin by investing in well-recognized and credible social enterprises.
- Leverage: the positive leverage between investments made in organizations that complement each other rather than compete against each other will enhance the impact investor's mission. In this way, leverage effects will enhance the sharing of knowledge, experience and economies of scale.
- Competition for resources: social enterprises within the same portfolio will compete for the impact investor's resources at the funding and the non-financial support level. Such competition is inevitable, although good account management at the investor level is fundamental to managing it.

- Cost efficiency: tracking how efficiently the investor uses its resources is critical in any investment management. However, the impact investing approach involves high engagement in the investees, often at a high cost – a reality that needs to be communicated to the funders.
- Impact management: impact investors should first measure impact at the social organization level and then assess their own impact achieved in supporting the investee.
- Facilitation: portfolio managers should favour synergies between the social enterprises in their portfolio that show some alignment. For example, social enterprises can share the same client base or the same suppliers. Portfolio managers should encourage regular meetings between portfolio organizations in order to exchange experiences and opportunities.

16.2.3   Exit

At a certain point in time, the impact investor can no longer add value to the investee, and at this point the relationship should be ended. An impact investor will aim for the social impact to be either maintained or increased after the exit, and tries to avoid exiting under such conditions that the impact decreases. Depending on the type of financing instrument used, the impact investor will have some influence when deciding whom to exit to and the mode of exit. The stage of development and the legal status of the social enterprise will also influence the exit. Independent of all these considerations, the decision needs to be primarily guided by the main objective of preserving the social mission of the social enterprise.

In order to safeguard the social impact of the investee after the exit, and consequently of the impact investor itself, the impact investor should assess whether the potential new investors have a positive interest in the investee's social mission and what their expectations are on financial returns.

16.2.4   Evaluation and Post-exit Follow-up

Once the exit is executed, an evaluation of the investment should take place, including the degree of achievement of both investor's and investee's objectives and lessons learnt from the process.

The impact investor appraises the results of the investment after the exit in terms of both financial and social return. The impact investor should also ensure how well it has succeeded in offering support to the social enterprise to achieve its objectives. The non-financial support satisfaction level should be assessed using independent studies, and a comparison should be made between the cost of the non-financial support provided and the impact obtained. The impact investor should measure the social return by comparing the outcome of the investment against initial objectives. The information that results from outcome verification will be used by the impact investor to show its success as a 'high-engagement' investor and takeaway lessons learnt for future investments. This detailed information should be put together in a meaningful document to report the results to donors and investors.

The social enterprise evaluates to what extent the objectives were achieved alongside the three dimensions of social impact, financial sustainability and organizational resilience. Impact management from the social enterprise point of view includes the final evaluation of the impact achieved and the delivery of meaningful information, based on data collection, for its key stakeholder groups.

The follow-up includes all the activities that the impact investor develops to maintain a relationship with the social enterprise after the exit, such as offering additional non-financial support or networking opportunities. The purpose of such activities is to monitor and preserve the social impact achieved through the investment phase after the exit. The idea is to reduce the risk of mission drift, once the investment process comes to an end, by assessing the commitment of the social enterprise to the achievement of its impact goals.

16.3 How to Set Up an Impact Investing Fund

16.3.1 Organizational Structure

In Europe, venture philanthropy and impact investing have largely been implemented by independent investment funds. Examples include PhiTrust and Oltre Venture, as an entity within a foundation, for example, King Baudouin Foundation's VP fund; as charities, for example Impetus-PEF; or as foundations operating entirely using the VP approach, as in the case of the Shell Foundation. There are also examples of mixed structures, with a fund and a foundation, as in the case of BonVenture. Although the growth of for-profit impact investors has led to an increase in investment fund structures, according to the latest EVPA Survey,[8] non-profit structures still dominate the organizational set up of venture philanthropy and impact investing organizations in Europe. A large majority of these organizations are structured as non-profits, such as foundations (either independent, 38% or linked to a corporation, 8%), charities (16%) or companies with a charitable status[9] (10%), 19% of the ventures are companies while 7% are funds. Around 30 per cent of the respondents reported that they managed social impact funds.

For-profit impact investors tend to be set up as investment funds. Country-specific legal and cultural norms need to be taken into account when

---

8 Boiardi and Gianoncelli (2016).
9 When it comes to 'companies with a charitable status' adjustments depending on the country of origin should always be considered, as legal system might define it in different ways.

establishing the legal structure of an impact investment fund. In Europe, it is possible to register as a EuSEF – a European Social Entrepreneurship Fund. The objective of the EuSEF Regulation is to support the provision of finance to social business in the EU by facilitating fundraising activities by funds that are specialized in this type of business. The Regulation promotes social funds in two ways:

- these funds may benefit from a marketing passport, and
- the Regulation creates an exclusive pan-European fund label that identifies these funds as 'social' (EuSEF).

Decisions taken about legal structure will influence the financial instruments used and the type of investments sought by the impact investor. According to the latest GIIN survey,[10] 59 per cent of the organizations surveyed identified themselves as fund managers. A further 13 per cent identified as foundations. A greater proportion of respondents headquartered in emerging markets are fund managers (77 per cent) compared to the proportion of fund managers among all respondents headquartered in developed markets (53 per cent).

16.3.2   Management, Governance and Funding

The quality of the founder, who defines the vision and sets the objectives of the venture, will be a key factor for success in achieving both financial return and social impact. In the impact investing market, the founder typically comes from either the venture capital world and/or from the social sector. The founder needs to attract the right start-up management team – and the right CEO – who fit with the fund's social mission and build the organization's knowledge and expertise in a rapidly evolving industry.

Motivation is a fundamental quality when recruiting a management team: ideally the founder should look for open-minded individuals who share the founder's vision and passion for social change. Attracting and keeping the talent is a challenge for a sector that often offers lower remuneration levels compared to the private sector – the intrinsic motivation of generating social impact must be part of the equation.

The board of an impact investing fund can fulfil both external responsibilities, including being in charge of fundraising and public relations, and internal obligations such as offering expertise and support to the management team. In the start-up phase, a highly engaged hands-on board is crucial to achieve success for a new venture. Decision-making practices in the impact investing field do not differ significantly from venture capital practices, involving, at various degrees, the investors in the investment decision through the investment committee.

Fundraising is a key issue for an impact investing fund. Usually, the prospective funders in a first round of funding belong to one of the following groups: the

---

10 Mudaliar *et al.* (2016).

founder's personal network, existing trusts and foundations, high-net-worth individuals, corporates and government agencies. There must be a strong alignment between the investors' and the founder's vision regarding the investment model and goals for achieving both social impact and financial return. When raising a second fund, a positive track record and proven investment success stories are useful assets. After the first five years of operation, and depending on the results achieved, the impact investor should revise its entire strategy and consider whether any of its main objectives should be changed. Changes in strategy could involve adopting a narrower sector focus on areas that have delivered the most social impact, or changing its financial return objectives to attract a different type of investor – taking into consideration that the financial return sought may have implications for the type of social enterprise it can invest in. Recently, European impact investors have been able to attract institutional investors, including the European Investment Fund's Social Impact Accelerator, by promising higher financial returns, and targeting social enterprises with a proven track record (see the Oltre Venture case study at the end of the chapter for an illustrative example). We will now turn to look at the main components of the investment strategy.

16.4   The Components of an Impact Investment Strategy

16.4.1   Theory of Change and Financial Return Expectations

Impact Investment funds are vehicles that channel funding from donors and investors to selected social enterprises. We sometimes refer to the vehicle as the 'impact investor'. Their impact investment strategy is the result of a set of choices that determines their focus and their objectives, and that consists of specific combinations of social and financial expectations. The balance between the social and financial return goals represents the most important decision for the impact investor.

Social Expectations

First, the impact investor needs to define its social objectives. The methodological framework most commonly used in this sector to develop an understanding of the impact an organization wants to achieve is the 'theory of change'[11] (developed further in Section 16.5 on impact measurement). In this context, a theory of change is essentially an explicit and comprehensive description of the causal pathways that lead from the activities to the long-term outcomes that contribute to achieving the final intended impact. An impact investor achieves impact by investing in a number of social enterprises dealing with a particular

11 www.theoryofchange.org

social problem. However, it is important also for the impact investor to define the overarching impact it aims to achieve through its investment strategy.

In practice, defining its theory of change means that the impact investor needs to determine:

- The wider social problem that the impact investor will address – e.g. youth unemployment in Spain (including an analysis of the dimension of the problem as the base case).
- The specific objective the impact investor wants to achieve – e.g. reducing youth unemployment in Spain by investing (financial and non-financial support) in social enterprises with innovative solutions to bring youth into the labour force (including an assessment of what the greatest needs of such social enterprises are and how the impact investor can help them).
- The expected outcomes that the impact investor must achieve to be considered successful (the milestones against which the investors will be measured). For example, a specific number of young people who found stable and quality jobs in Spain as a result of the activities promoted by the social enterprises (the investees).

Achieving a positive social change means improving people's lives. Impact investors should look at outcomes (quality and stable jobs for young people) rather than just measuring successful outputs (numbers of young people who attended a training programme) in order to assess the social impact of their investments. In practice, however, many impact investors are not yet that sophisticated in their impact measurement approach.

An impact investor needs to define its social impact objectives and embed them in the overall impact management system of its investments. A sufficiently well-articulated theory of change is a necessary framework for choosing appropriate investments in social enterprises that will contribute to solving the social issue that the impact investor is addressing. The impact investor should consider involving its key stakeholders (donors/investors, staff/human resources, social enterprises, etc.) in the definition of its impact objectives so that their expectations are managed and their contributions are aligned.

Financial Expectations

The financial expectations of an impact investment fund may be similar to those of a traditional fund, but they have to be balanced against the social objectives (including whether they are of equal importance or whether financial expectations are secondary to the social objectives). The financial expectations can be aligned with or be below average market returns depending on the general strategy of the impact investor. For impact investors who deliberately place social impact objectives above financial expectations, capital repayment may be sought. The targeted financial return will determine the types of financial instruments used as well as the type of investments targeted.

The theory of change and the financial return expectations are the key elements of the investment strategy, and will help the impact investor to further refine its investment strategy.

Broadly speaking, there are six further elements that define the investment strategy of an impact investor:

- Investment focus.
- Type of investment targets.
- Type of financial instruments.
- Co-investment policy.
- Non-financial support.
- Exit strategy.

16.4.2 Investment Focus: Social Sector and Geographic Scope

The investment focus includes the geographical and social sector focus of the impact fund operations. These choices will determine the preferred models of intervention of the impact investor and the type of social enterprises that will be supported.

Impact investors are becoming increasingly specialized in terms of their investment focus – some are clearer about the social impact they want to achieve and choose to invest in social enterprises that are clearly in line with their impact objectives. The high-engagement nature of the investor–investee relationship requires a close proximity between investment managers and social enterprise management, implying that impact investors either invest in domestic markets, or have local teams on-site if they invest in multiple countries. They will also have understood the value of connecting portfolio companies for networking and knowledge sharing. Furthermore, focusing on specific impact areas enables the impact investor to better manage and communicate impact achievement at the portfolio level.

Social Sector Choices

The choice of a specific social issue on which to concentrate the investment strategy depends on the theory of change adopted by the impact investor and on the pipeline of potential quality investment opportunities existing in their field. If the market is too small, then the investors will have to broaden their scope, as is often the case in smaller, less mature markets.

According to the latest EVPA Survey,[12] with data from 2015, Figure 16.3 shows the top social sectors targeted by European impact investors in terms of funding:

12 Boiardi and Gianoncelli (2016).

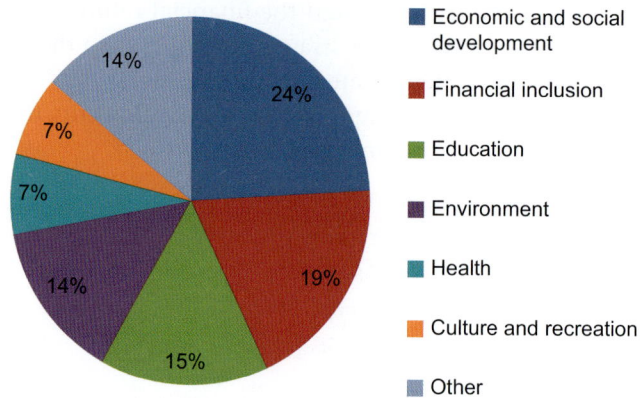

Figure 16.3 Target sectors by € spend.
Source: EVPA Industry Survey 2015/2016

Geographic Focus

Impact investors also need to define the geographical scope of their activity.

European impact investors tend to operate either in their own domestic market or in developing countries. According to the latest EVPA survey[13] on the European-based venture philanthropy and social investment organizations, 67 per cent of the respondents invested in western Europe, of whom 64 per cent invested in their own country (domestic investments) and 3 per cent across European borders; while 14 per cent invested in Africa, 10 per cent in Latin America, 6 per cent in Asia (see Figure 16.4).

According to the latest GIIN survey[14] organizations were headquartered mainly in developed markets as follows: 44 per cent in North America, 32 per cent in western, northern and southern Europe and 20 per cent based in emerging markets.

Investments are managed in the following geographical areas: 28% in North America, 19% in sub-Saharan Africa, 11% in Western, Northern and Southern Europe, 10% in Latin America and the Caribbean, 9% Eastern Europe, Russia, and Central Asia, 13% in East, South and South East Asia (see Figure 16.5).

The choice of investing at an international level may bring interesting opportunities, even when additional costs and management complexities are considered. Impact investors will need to perform a prior market analysis to assess whether there is a sufficient investment pipeline and to understand the quantity, quality and size of potential investment targets. As with any other kind of investment, the number of opportunities should significantly exceed the total number of investments necessary to fill the portfolio.

Investing in developing countries is one of the first strategies adopted by impact investors, providing direct support to social business initiatives to

---

13 Boiardi and Gianoncelli (2016).
14 Mudaliar *et al.* (2016).

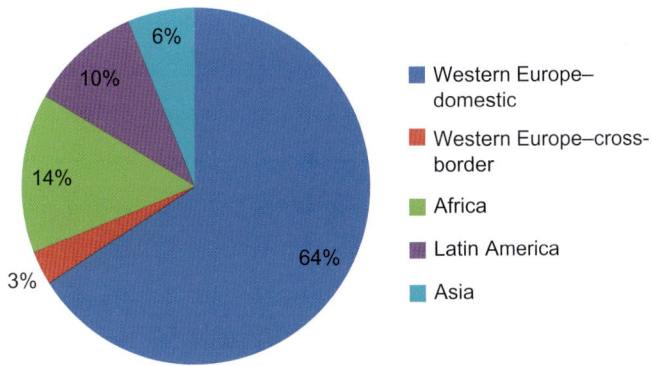

Figure 16.4 Geographic focus by € spend.
Source: EVPA Industry Survey 2015/2016

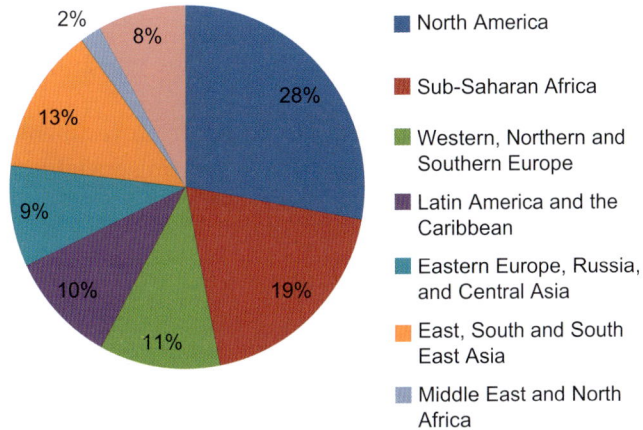

Figure 16.5 Geographic focus by $ spend.[15]

answer the needs of those who are usually defined as the 'bottom of the pyramid'.[16]

Impact investments are increasingly being used in partnership with traditional international aid interventions and/or private corporates to develop innovative solutions targeted to the needs of local populations, with a strong emphasis on financial self-sustainability. In developing countries, achieving

---

15 Based on GIIN 2016, sample excluding outliers: n = 153; total Assets Under Management = USD 49.5 billion.

16 The 'bottom of the pyramid' refers to the segment of the global population that lives on less than 2.50 dollars a day. The definition is taken from: Prahalad (2004).

social goals has a different meaning compared to the developed world context, as stronger attention is paid to increasing access to basic services such as health, energy efficiency, access to water, financial services, rural development and education for the largest number of people.[17]

An impact investment strategy focused on developing countries should, however, carefully consider what are reasonable levels of social and financial returns, as there are many cases where particularly high financial returns leave room to doubt whether the impact investor's goal is to create positive social impact (in combination with financial sustainability), or just to develop a business strategy addressing new markets and new consumers.

16.4.3   Type of Investments Targeted

Impact investing's products address social enterprises. As previously explained, we use a broader definition of social enterprises taking into account all the social purpose organizations that have a societal related mission and a sustainable business model (see Figure 16.6).

The impact investor will define the size, type and stage of development of the investee(s).

Those that are typically considered for investment by impact investors will generally fall into the revenue-generating social enterprise and the socially driven business categories, collectively referred to as social enterprises in this Chapter.

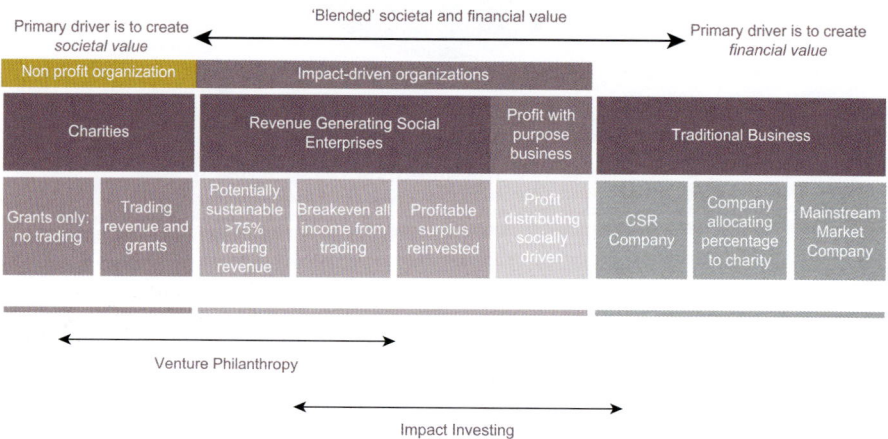

Figure 16.6 The Investment Spectrum.
Source: Balbo et al. *(2016)*

---

17 Numerous scholars and institutions have studied social impact investing in developing countries, including: Whitley *et al.* (2013); Power *et al.* (2012).

Impact investing is not appropriate for all social enterprises, just as venture capital is not the best form of financing for commercial businesses at all stages of their life cycle.

In general, the venture philanthropy approach is best suited to those ventures that do not yet have the capacity of being sustainable in the market whereas impact investing is addressing social enterprises that may already be financially sustainable, but require an injection of capital to grow and scale up their business.

Early-stage investments are more risky and better suited to venture philanthropy, often backed by philanthropic capital. Impact investing is more suitable for focusing on fewer and larger investees that can achieve disruptive impact with a potential to scale, and in partnership with entrepreneurs who are willing to do so. Both venture philanthropy and impact investing aim at boosting the capacity of the social enterprises to generate a positive social return.

16.4.4   Types of Financial Instruments Used

The types of financial instruments used are clearly a distinguishing factor between impact investing and venture capital. Impact investors employ a wide range of investment instruments that range from debt instruments to mechanisms that establish an ownership title over investees (including equity). However, venture philanthropy often combines grants with other instruments as early-stage social enterprises are sometimes not able to repay a loan, and the organizational structure (for example, in the case of non-profits or cooperatives) may inhibit equity investment. Impact investing uses a tailor-made approach in designing the financial instruments and the relation with the social enterprise. The following list provides an overview of the most common financing instruments used:

- *Guarantee:* Social enterprises may be supported by impact investors through a guarantee on bank loans. The financial support in this case is indirect: the investors do not supply cash upfront but the guarantee takes over some or all the risk that the lender would otherwise incur. In this way, the social enterprise has access to a source of funding that would have been otherwise precluded.
- *Debt:* Impact investors can provide traditional loans to social enterprises, charging interest at the same level or below market rates. The loan may carry a higher risk compared to commercial policies or it may be characterized by a particularly long-term repayment scheme. The interest charged varies also in relation to the securitization and repayment priority of the loan (senior versus subordinated loan). An impact-related loan can also imply a variation of the interest rate according to the social performance achieved. For example, a discount on the interest rate can be linked to the achievement of certain predefined social outcomes.

- **Mezzanine finance (also known as quasi-equity):** This financial instrument bridges the gap between debt and equity/grant through some form of revenue participation. It may involve offering a high-risk loan, repayment of which depends on the financial success of the social enterprise. For example, a loan that is repayable only through royalties based on the future sales of a product or service; or a royalty-sharing agreement that can become effective only once an agreed profitability threshold has been reached. These instruments can offer an original and appropriate balance of risk and return.
- **Equity:** Equity is the most high-risk financial instrument in the venture capital framework and there is no difference in the impact investing scenario. Impact investors can acquire part of a social enterprise's business. This option is considered when a loan repayment doesn't seem credible. But it's important to underline that an equity investment is a hands-on approach to the business case; the investors step into the social enterprise and take part, in different ways, in the strategic management. Equity investment offers the possibility of a financial return in the form of dividend payments. In addition, it allows for the possibility of a transfer of ownership to other funders in the future, although exits are more difficult in the impact investing experience.
- **Hybrid Instruments:** These mix together different elements of other financing instruments such as grants, equity and debt capital. We have provided some examples below. There is also a possibility that investors in the same financing deal use different financing instruments (such blended structures go beyond the scope of this chapter).

The most common examples of hybrid financing instruments are:

- *Convertible grants*: the social impact investor provides the social enterprises with a grant that is convertible into equity in the case of success.
- *Convertible loans*: unsecured loan or subordinated loans, with the option (either to the debtor or the lender) to convert into an equity stake. This converting option is appealing when financial return perspectives unexpectedly rise and the investors have the opportunity to generate additional return on the investment by converting a loan with limited financial gains to an equity stake with upward potential. The other scenario for which this instrument can be used is when the prospect of loan repayment may drop below earlier expectations, hence offering the social enterprise an opportunity to get rid of a liability and convert it into a form of funding that cannot be reclaimed.

The matrix shown in Figure 16.7 describes the organizational structure of the social enterprise on one axis and the return expectations of the impact investors on the other axis. This graphic representation shows very different scenarios; on the left-hand side we find charities and socially oriented organizations which can be funded using grant-related instruments, as these ventures do not involve a financial return, whereas on the right-hand side the funder invests in the equity of a hybrid or corporate vehicle, expecting a social as well as a financial return.

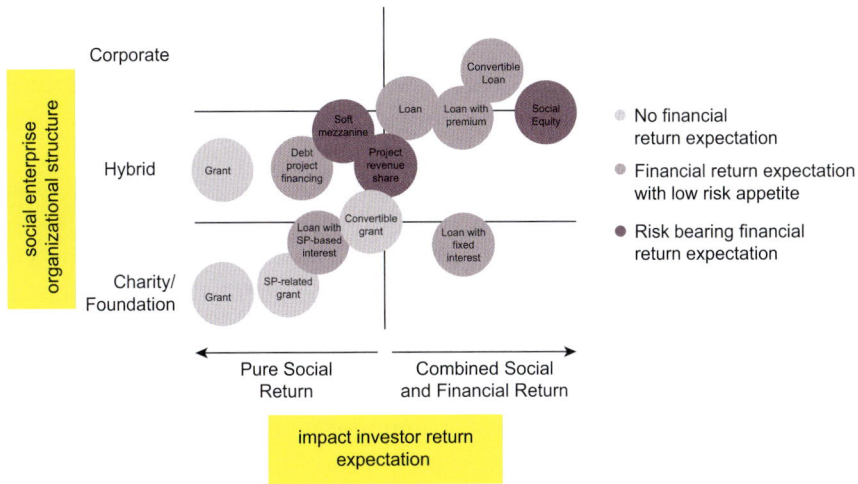

Figure 16.7 Financing instruments: social enterprise organizational structure and impact investor return expectation.
Source: Balbo et al. *(2016)*

As in venture capital, the key in impact investing is to select the tool that offers the best fit. However, impact investing's peculiar approach is unique in mixing grant-related instruments with traditional ones and this can generate some critical issues for impact funders, such as the difficulty in controlling what grant money is used for. To overcome these challenges, investors can request a matching grant and structure the financing in such a way that cash disbursement is done in tranches depending on the achievement of predefined milestones to assess the social enterprise's achievements.

As part of an investment strategy, the impact investor will have to define which kinds of instruments to deploy, and how to tailor these to the needs of the specific social enterprise's business case.

16.4.5 Co-investing Policy

Co-investment is used to reduce transaction costs, as in the case of venture capital. Additionally, co-investing can bring additional funds to the deal, promote the impact investor's activities among a wider audience and spread the risk. Sharing the costs related to managing the investment may be a difficult negotiation. However, impact investing differs from venture capital in some key aspects in relation to co-investing. For impact investors, it is very important to align objectives with co-investors, considering the social and the financial expectations and the theory of change of the impact investor (investment strategy and exit plans). If co-investors don't share a similar framework regarding their expectations and mission the risk of divergence increases. In the worst case scenario, during an investment period a purely financial co-investor would opt out of an investment that is doing well from a social impact perspective, but without generating the desired financial return. This would force the investee out of business and the social impact investor to fail.

16.4.6   Non-financial Support

Non-financial support is a key characteristic of impact investing's approach to investment. Impact funders usually have a high engagement approach to their investees that goes far beyond the financial support they provide.

The funders can provide the non-financial support themselves or hire or appoint pro-bono consultants to offer value-added services, such as strategic planning, marketing and communications, executive coaching, human resources advice, access to other networks and potential funders. Importantly, non-financial support in impact investing includes helping the social enterprise develop its social impact goals, and build an impact measurement and management system. Impact investments are those that 'intentionally target specific social objectives along with a financial return and measure the achievement of both'.[18] According to the impact investing paradigm, the impact investor is, by definition, aligned with the social enterprise in protecting the social impact of the business they invest in. As previously discussed, impact measurement and management are the strategic tools used to support the social enterprise in strengthening its societal impact.

Non-financial support is particularly important as the investees may not be used to dealing with an investment approach. A capacity-building process is thus necessary to mitigate the risk of the investment. The non-financial support provided must be be consistent with the goals of the impact investor in terms of financial return and societal impact, as defined in its theory of change, and tailored to the needs of the investee.

The non-financial components of an impact investor's support can be as significant as the financial support. Figure 16.8 provides an overview of the types of non-financial activities that an impact investor can provide to its investee. The activities are mapped according to the areas of development: *societal impact, organizational resilience* and *financial sustainability*. The impact investor also provides generic support that contributes to all three areas of development. The impact investor should work with the social enterprise in order to enhance:

- *Societal impact*: helping the investee better understand its social impact – including both measuring impact and managing towards greater social impact
- *Financial sustainability*: helping the investee become financially sounder, less dependent on external funding, and grow in revenues/income.

18 Social Impact Investment Taskforce (2014a).

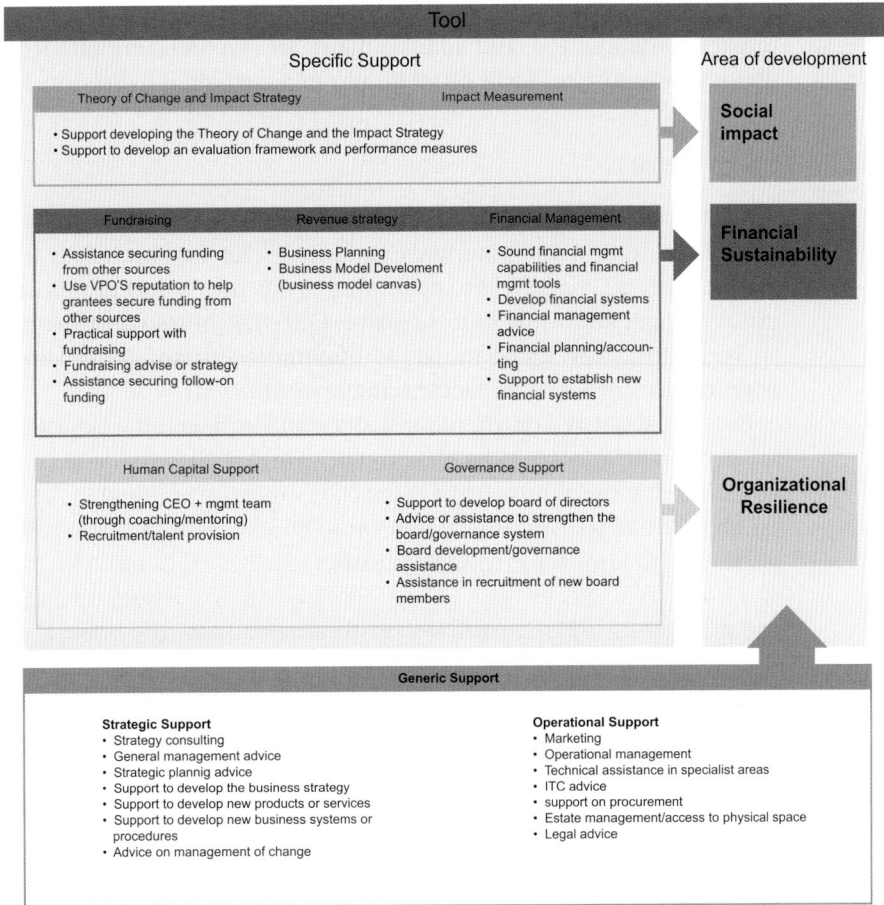

Figure 16.8 A mapping of non-financial support.
Source: Balbo et al. (2016)

- *Organizational resilience*: helping the investee become stronger as an organization, notably with a more developed management team and governance structure.

It is recommended that the impact investor controls the costs of such added services by mapping its own assets and expertise and assessing who will provide the core and non-core support. The impact investor should have a clear view of what are the actual costs of the non-financial support it is providing and how these will be financed.[19] There are different models of providing non-financial support. Some impact investors provide the core support through its own internal team and outsource the provision of technical skills that lie outside the

19 For details on how to manage non-financial support services refer to: Boiardi and Hehenberger (2015).

competences of the internal team to paid, low-bono or pro-bono consultants. Impact measurement and management are a core component of the non-financial support, and will be addressed in more detail in Section 16.5 below.

16.4.7   Exit Strategies

Impact investors need to design how they will exit their investments bearing in mind the duration and potential exit routes.[20] An exit strategy is an action plan (as outlined in Figure 16.9) to determine in advance whether an impact investor can no longer add value to its investee. Once the investment relation comes to an end, either the social impact is maintained or amplified; either way, the potential loss of social impact should be minimized.

The impact investor should consider the exit as an essential part of the investment strategy and be attentive to the fact that the exit strategy should guarantee the social mission of the social enterprise invested in. The fundamental objective is that the social enterprise continues to pursue its social impact goals after the impact investor has exited.

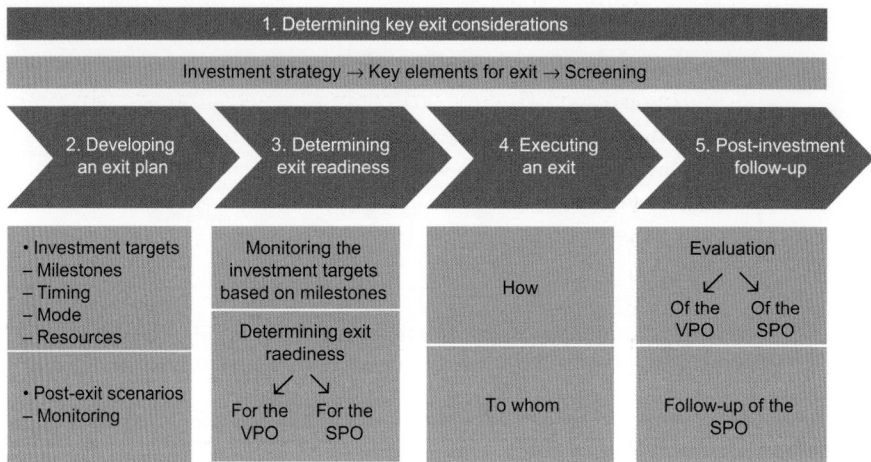

Figure 16.9 The five-step exit strategy process.
Source: Balbo et al. (2016)

20 Boiardi and Hehenberger (2014).

Social impact can be secured and locked into the social enterprise in different ways:

- Develop new legal forms that best suit the mission-related activity.
- Design a business plan aligned and strictly related to the social impact.
- Ensure that the social mission is ingrained in the organizational culture.

The key elements of the investment strategy that affect the exit strategy are the following:

- **Context**: the sector and the geographical focus of an impact investor both influence the setting in which both the social enterprise and the impact investor operate and, consequently, the exit strategy. In some scenarios, depending on the geographical background or the social sector, exit options may be reduced.
- **Type of investee**: there are different types of investees that can be funded. The stage of development, the legal structure and the organization's governance can determine how, when and to whom the impact investor will exit. The impact investor and the social enterprise should commonly agree on some milestones that will define exit readiness at the very beginning of their partnership.
- **Type of funding**: each investment instrument (debt, equity, grant, etc.) has different benefits/features and places different constraints on the exit strategy. Some investment structures will define the exit strategy, while others will pose more challenges for both the investor and the investee when planning and executing an exit.
- **Co-investing**: co-investors may bring with them a broad network which can be a very important resource, typically when executing the exit. At the same time, co-investors can also be a challenge, if strategies and impact and financial return expectations are not aligned. The impact investor should therefore assess the co-investors' investment strategy and objectives, the financial/impact trade-offs and the exit strategies before engaging. A mismatch between the investment strategies of the co-investors will create problems throughout the investment period.
- **Relationship with the impact investor's funders**: the fundraising history of the impact investor will influence the investment strategy and the key exit considerations.

The overarching social and financial objectives of the impact investor determine the investment strategy, including the exit strategy that will be a consequence of all the key elements mentioned above.

VOICE OF THE EXPERT: Andreas Ernst (Germany)

Andreas Ernst is Managing Director of Impact Investing at Anthos Asset Management. Andreas has fifteen years' experience in impact investing. Prior to joining Anthos Andreas was Global Head of Impact Investing at UBS. At UBS he was responsible for defining a strategy for the impact investing team, for the whole value chain from origination to fundraising. Prior to joining UBS, Andreas worked for IJ Partners, a family office in Geneva. As Head of Direct Investing Emerging Markets and Impact Investment he was responsible for the investment strategy and for securing several impact investing deals. Andreas has lived and worked in various European and Asian countries. He holds a Master's degree in Business Administration and a Bachelor's in both Economics and Political Science from the University of Hamburg, Germany.

What do you consider to be the importance of focus and impact measurement for the success of impact investing?
Focus is instrumental for the professionalization of the impact investing market. The impact investing market has been very focused since inception. As the impact market matures we see managers and investors increasingly taking sector and geographical lenses, and building on that constructing impact portfolios.

On the other hand it is important that impact is not seen in its narrow idiosyncratic niche; investors must understand the broader context and repercussions on other markets and populations produced by unintended consequences. Measurement is important but there has been too much focus on accuracy of data, which in our view is even at high costs unattainable. Instead of accuracy the impact investing market should seek for precision of the data as well as coherence in the manner data is collected and accounted for. This would allow for a relative positioning not an absolute one – but would allow for comparison and also lower costs.

What is your advice to (aspiring) social entrepreneurs?
Go for it – there are too many challenges to hesitate. The future lies in your hearts and hands. Is it challenging? OF COURSE but the impossible you can do every day; merely miracles take a bit longer.

16.5   Impact Measurement and Management

Impact measurement is an evolving practice and there is no universal standard to follow. However, there is an agreement among important stakeholders such as the European Commission's Expert Group on Social Entrepreneurship (GECES),[21] the G8's Social Impact Investment Taskforce's (now Global Social Impact Investment Steering Group) working group on impact measurement[22]

21 The Expert Group on Social Entrepreneurship (GECES) is a European Commission consultative multi-stakeholder group on social business set up in 2012 and due to exist until 2018. Its Sub-group on Social Impact Measurement had the mission to find an agreement on a European standard in the area of impact measurement.
22 The Global Social Impact Investment Steering Group (GSG) is an independent global steering group catalyzing impact investment and entrepreneurship to benefit people and the planet. The GSG was established in August 2015 as the successor to and incorporating the work of the Social Impact Investment Taskforce established under the UK's presidency

and EVPA for impact measurement, to follow a common process, which we will outline below. Core principles that have come out of these work streams, and which will guide our work on impact measurement going forward, are as follows:

- Impact measurement must be **relevant** to the organization being measured so that it becomes part of their management system and helps them improve their work to **achieve greater impact**.
- Impact measurement also needs to be **proportionate** to the organization at hand, keeping in mind that it is a **means towards an end**, not an end in itself.

These principles have been built according to the main reference in this field, the EVPA *Practical Guide to Measuring and Managing Impact*,[23] given that it has informed the European Standard[24] on impact measurement and the G8 taskforce work. The EVPA Guide adopts a five-step framework as shown in Figure 16.10.

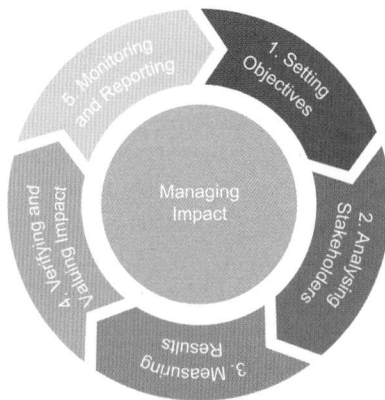

Figure 16.10 The five steps of the social impact measurement process. *Source: Hehenberger* et al. *(2015).*

of the G8. Under the direction of the Social Impact Investment Taskforce, the Impact Measurement Working Group was established in 2014. The Group released the same year: Social Impact Investment Taskforce (2014b).

23 Hehenberger *et al.* (2015).
24 Impact measurement is a key component of the venture philanthropy and social investment model and has been a focal point of EVPA's research and knowledge-building in the past years. EVPA had a leader role in the work of the European Commission's GECES and its Sub-group on Social Impact Measurement. The impact measurement standard is designed to be applicable across Europe – for social enterprises as well as for public and private funders of social enterprise – and is informed by EVPA's Practical Guide; a resource that distils best practice in impact measurement into five easy-to-understand steps to implement impact measurement.

Impact is measured and managed both at the level of the impact investor and at the level of the investee, the social enterprise. The five steps correspond to the sequential order that the impact investor and the social enterprise must follow. This process can be revised at any time by going back through the different steps when new insights and information have been gained during the impact measurement process. It is strongly recommended that both impact investor and social enterprise go through a theoretical simulation of the whole process step-by-step, before they start working on it in practice.

The five steps are as follows and can be developed from both the perspectives of the social entrepreneur and the social investor.

- Setting Objectives: defining the scope of the impact analysis (why and for whom), the level (portfolio of social investments/individual social enterprise) and which is the desired social change to be achieved.
- Analysing Stakeholders: establish an order of priority among the multitude of potential stakeholders to be involved, weighing their contribution to the analysis against the resources available, and including their inputs (if any), activities and potential outputs.
- Measuring Results – Outcome, Impact and Indicators: measuring the output, outcome and impact experienced by the key stakeholders, and pointing out different types of indicators to map the social result of the social enterprise's and social investor's work.
- Verifying and Valuing Impact: verifying that the logical implications are strong enough and that the impact is valued as such also by the key stakeholders – considering quantitative and/or qualitative methods and comparing the results of the work against relevant benchmarks.
- Monitoring and Reporting: collecting data and designing a system to store and manage the data as well as integrating this information into management operations and reporting the data to relevant stakeholders.

The main rationale of impact measurement is to manage and control the process of creating social impact in order to maximize or optimize it relative to the available resources. Once that impact measurement is integrated in the investment management process, managing impact becomes a daily practice. The social expectations related to the investment are compared with the impact measurement's findings, allowing the impact investor to identify what they need to change in their investment management process in order to maximize social impact. The impact measurement process is functional in managing impact with the ultimate objective of funding and building stronger social purpose organizations.

The impact value chain is helpful for distinguishing between inputs, outputs, outcome and impacts as in Figure 16.11.

We have used the definitions shown in Table 16.1 in this chapter.

SPO's Planned Work		SPO's Intended Results		
1. Inputs	2. Activities	3. Outputs	4. Outcomes	5. Impact
Resources (capital, human) invested in the activity	Concrete actions of the social policy organisation	Tangible products from the activity	Changes resulting from the activity	Outcomes adjusted for what would have happened anyway, actions of others and for unintended consequences
€, number of people etc.	Development and implementation of programmes, building new infrastructure etc.	Number of people reached, items sold, etc	Effects on target population e.g. increased access to education	Attribution to changes in outcome. Take account of alternative programmes e.g. open air classes
€50k invested, 5 people working on project	Land bought, school designed and built	New school built with 32 places	Students with increased access to education: 8	Students with access to education not including those with alternatives: 2

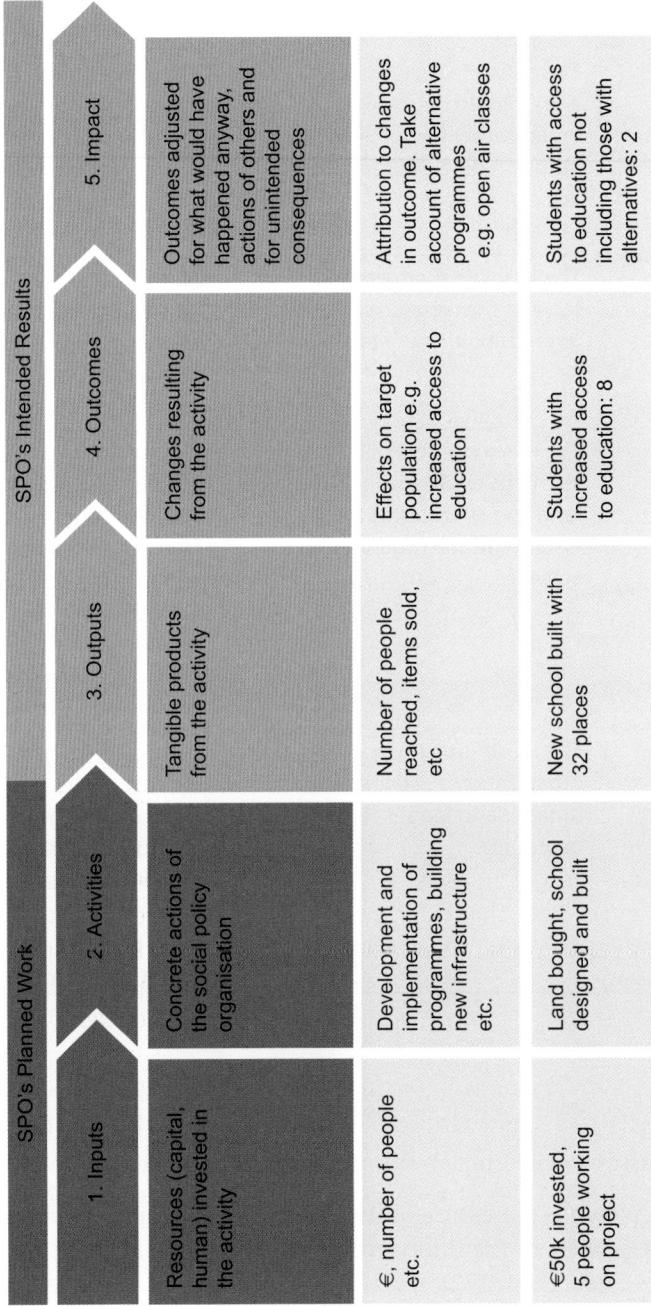

Figure 16.11 The Impact Value Chain.
Source: Boiardi and Hehenberger (2014)

Table 16.1 The Impact Value Chain – Definition of key terms and examples

Inputs:	All resources, whether capital or human, invested in the activities of the organization.	**Example:** The capital and the human resources invested in a social enterprise with innovative solutions to introduce youth in the labour force
Activities:	The concrete actions, tasks and work carried out by the organization to create its outputs and outcomes and achieve its objectives.	The social enterprise finds strategic partners, develops an innovative curriculum based on specialist digital skills, involves and motivates the young unemployed, etc . . .
Outputs:	The tangible products and services that result from the organization's activities.	• Number of persons trained • Number of hours of training provided • Number of persons who have found a job after the training
Outcomes:	The changes, benefits, learnings or other effects (both long and short term) that result from the organization's activities.	• Number of persons who obtained an educational qualification • Number of persons who have a quality job one year after attending the training • Number of persons who declared to feel more confident in their capacities
Social Impact:	The attribution of an organization's activities to broader and longer-term outcomes.	• Positive % contribution to the increase of the fiscal benefits produced by the persons who attended the training • Positive % contribution to the decrease of the youth unemployment rate in a certain geographical area

In order to assess social impact, the outcomes need to be adjusted for:

• *Deadweight*, which is a measure of the number of outcomes that would have happened regardless of the intervention (for example, it will be necessary to calculate the direct contribution made by training to the decrease in the rate of youth unemployment in a certain geographical area given that there was, in the same period, a general trend in the reduction of the number of young unemployed).

- *Attribution*, which is an assessment of the extent to which the action of others have influenced the achievements of the outcomes (for example, other training offered by another organization in the same geographical area and with the same goal).
- *Drop-off*, which accounts for the deterioration of the outcomes over time (for example, in five or ten years how many of those who attended the training on digital skills will still be qualified for a stable job?).
- *Displacement*, which shows the extent to which the original situation was displaced elsewhere or outcomes displaced other potential positive outcomes, the unintended consequences of which could be negative or positive (for example, after training a significant number of young people will find better job opportunities elsewhere, thereby advancing the depopulation trend of the poorest areas).

Impact investors should ensure that the social enterprises in their portfolio do not over claim the social impact produced. To assess impact, it is important to acknowledge and, when possible, to adjust for those factors that contribute to increasing or decreasing the impact of the organization (principle of proportionality). However, arriving at a scientifically accurate impact measure may not be desirable considering the investment required in doing so. Therefore, the above-mentioned principle of proportionality needs to be taken into account. It is better to have a good estimate of impact that is actionable than to get stuck along the way or to collect information that is not used.

We invite readers who are interested in diving deeper into the process to consult the literature referenced and the Appendix to this chapter that contains the synthetic account of the five easy-to-understand steps to implement impact measurement following the EVPA *Practical Guide to Measuring and Managing Impact*.[25]

Managing Impact from the Investor's Perspective

The synthetic review of the five-step impact measurement process outlined in Appendix 5 shows how impact investors can set up a powerful impact measurement system that serves both at the portfolio management and at the social enterprise (the investees) level, and how to constantly revise it in order to maximize its impact on society.

As shown in Figure 16.12, the impact investor uses the impact measurement process as a strategic tool to better manage the impact generated by its

25 Hehenberger *et al.* (2015).

Managing impact in the investment process

Investment strategy	Investment process				
	Deal screening	Due diligence (detailed screening)	Deal structuring	Investment management	Exit
Decide on the overarching social impact objectives of the impact investor– these will guide the investment process.	Assess whether investment opportunity fits with the impact investor's strategy by asking questions detailed in setting objectives.	Dig deeper into questions asked in setting objectives. Perform stakeholder analysis. Verify and value expected results.	Map outputs, outcomes and impacts and decide on key indicators against which progress will be measured. Decide on monitoring and reporting content and frequency and assign responsibilities.	Regularly assess impact results against key indicators. Verify and value reported results at regular intervals. Revise indicators if significant changes are made in the business and impact model.	Perform thorough analysis of impact results against objectives – verifying and valuing reported results.

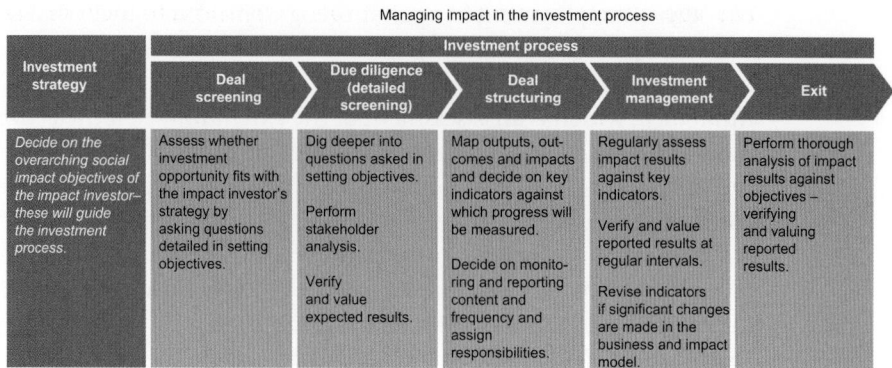

Figure 16.12 Managing impact in the impact investor's investment process. *Source: Hehenberger et al. (2015)*

investments, making the necessary changes whenever the results differs from expectations. The impact measurement process becomes an integral part of the investment process itself – as detailed in the next section of the chapter.

Summary Recommendations for Managing Impact for Social Impact Investors

- An impact investor must formulate its overarching social problem or issue in order to choose investments in social enterprises that can contribute to solving that social issue.
- An impact investor should convince the social enterprise of the value of impact measurement, provide assistance where possible and define with them the responses to the essential questions to help them express their objectives.
- Understanding the current and expected social impact of a social enterprise early in the decision-making process is extremely valuable: it creates a common understanding of the impact of an organization; allows the investor and investee to 'speak the same language'; and facilitates assessment of impact at later stages.
- Alignment of the impact objectives of the different stakeholder involved, such as donors, investors, staff, human resources and social enterprise management, is a priority in order to manage their expectations and coordinate their contributions.
- The definition of portfolio-level indicators may be required to measure how well an impact investor has achieved its objectives as an organization.

- The impact investor should ask the social enterprise to focus on those indicators that are directly related to the social enterprise's theory of change and hence are in line with their operational process. Any additional indicators required for the impact investor to satisfy its impact measurement needs should be collected by the impact investor.
- For an impact investor, it is not enough to just consider the impact achieved by the social enterprise, it is also important to assess the impact of the work of the impact investor on the social enterprise. Impact investors should use independent studies to assess the value they provide to the social enterprise.
- To remove a reliance on 'gut feeling', impact investors should work with the investee to develop an impact monitoring system that can be integrated into the management processes of the organization.

Let's Practise: Case Study

Reach for Change

Reach for Change is a non-profit organization founded in 2010 by the Kinnevik Group to improve the lives of children and young people.[26] Kinnevik Group, an industry-focused investment company with an entrepreneurial spirit, found a way to invest in children and to use the experience and the market knowledge developed by the group to benefit children.

Reach for Change, whose motto is 'innovating a better world for children', finds passionate local entrepreneurs with innovative solutions to pressing issues facing children. The entrepreneurs get support to develop their ideas through an accelerator programme. Those with the highest potential are also invited to join Reach for Change's incubator, where they receive seed funding, networking and advice to transform their ideas into sustainable and impactful organizations improving children's lives. Founded in Sweden, Reach for Change has spread to eighteen countries, supporting hundreds of social entrepreneurs who have, in turn, helped hundreds of thousands of children. Impact management is at the core of the innovative model of Reach for Change.

One of the innovative ideas supported by Reach for Change is *Mattecentrum*, a non-profit organization based in Sweden that offers free of charge maths tutoring to school students both on school premises and online.

The OECD runs a *Programme for International Student Assessment* (PISA), an international study examining 15-year-old students' capabilities in mathematics, natural sciences and reading comprehension. According to

---

26 This practical case was taken from the Reach for Change's Impact Management Experience and Boiardi *et al.* (2016).

the report 'Making Mathematics Accessible to All', based on results from PISA 2012, today more than ever students need to engage with mathematical concepts, think quantitatively and analytically, and communicate using mathematics. One way forward is to ensure that all students spend more 'engaged' time learning core mathematics concepts and solving challenging mathematics tasks. Differences in students' familiarity with mathematical concepts explain a substantial share of performance disparities in PISA between socio-economically advantaged and disadvantaged students. Widening access to mathematics content can raise average levels of achievement and, at the same time, reduce inequalities in education and in society at large.

To tackle the issue of decreasing capabilities in mathematics among Swedish students, Johan Wendt launched *Mattecentrum* in 2008 to promote an equal acquisition of knowledge and to raise awareness and stimulate interest in mathematics. Mattecentrum has since June 2015, when Johan left the organization, been run by secretary general Karolina Lisslö. It is one of the largest free of charge maths tutoring service in Europe, used by more than 350,000 children each month, and involving more than 600 volunteers in Sweden alone. A study performed by the statistics centre Numbers Analytics shows that in schools where students are offered the *Mattecentrum* tutoring services, grades improve by on average 5.4 per cent more than in schools not using the service.

Questions for Discussion

1. Using the information provided about *Mattecentrum*, develop a problem and solution table (Figure 16.13) and an impact value chain (Figure 16.14).

   Make sure that you offer a clear explanation of the logical connections that link activities to the desired outcomes and test the strength of your causal connections by going back from outcomes to activities.

Problem			Solution		
Core problem identified	Root causes of the problem	Consequences of the problem	Your solution	Primary Target group	Other Stakeholders

Figure 16.13 The problem and solution table.

Organization's Planned Work		Organization's Intended Results		
Inputs	Activities	Outputs	Outcomes	Impact
Resources (capital, human, intellectual and social networks) invested in the activity	Concrete actions of the organization	Tangible products from the activity	Changes, benefits, learnings, effects resulting from the activity	Broader social change attributed to an organization's activities

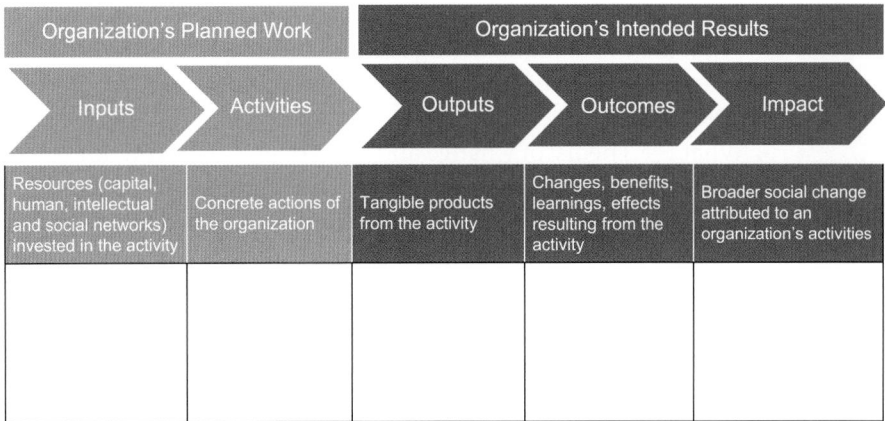

Figure 16.14 Developing an impact value chain.

2. Which problem does *Mattecentrum* want to address?
3. What is the solution offered? Are your connections verifiable?

KEY TAKEAWAYS

- Impact investing (including venture philanthropy) is an investment approach that aims to generate a combination of financial and social returns by providing financial and non-financial support to innovative social enterprises.
- The key components of an impact investing strategy include the social impact it aims to achieve and the financial return expectations. Other considerations flow from these key decisions.
- Impact measurement should be considered a means to an end – a tool that helps both impact investors and their investees achieve greater societal impact. For the social enterprise, this implies including impact as an integral part of its management system. For the impact investor, it means building an impact-centric investment process.
- An impact-centric investment process incorporates a focus on impact from deal screening to exit. The impact investor should manage this process to maximize the achievement of the social and financial return and make the most impactful use of its resources.

END OF CHAPTER QUESTIONS

1. How would you define impact investment?
2. What are the main differences between an impact investor and a venture capital investor?

3. List the key components of the impact investor's strategy.
4. What are the main financing instruments used in the field?
5. Why do you think impact measurement is a required practice in impact investing?
6. What is a Theory of Change and what does it help you do?
7. What is the difference between an output and an outcome?
8. What principles of impact measurement should you take into consideration?
9. Why do you think that many impact investors complain about the lack of high-quality deal flow?
10. What are some important considerations for the due diligence process?
11. What are the key objectives of providing non-financial support to an investee?
12. When is an impact investor ready to exit from an investment?
13. In your opinion, do you think impact investing will become a mainstream strategy in coming years?
14. If so, what are some of the necessary steps in that direction?

FURTHER READING

Clifford, J. (2014). *Proposed Approaches to Social Impact Measurement in European Commission legislation and in Practice Relating to EuSEFs and the EaSI.* European Commission, Directorate-General for Employment & Social Affairs and Inclusion.

Mair, J. and Seelos, C. (2017). *Innovation and Scaling for Impact: How Effective Social Enterprises Do It.* Stanford University Press.

Scarlata, M. and Alemany, L. (2010). Deal structuring in philanthropic venture capital investments: Financing instrument, valuation, and covenants. *Journal of Business Ethics*, 95(2), 121–145.

Vecchi, V., Balbo, L., Brusoni, M. and Caselli, S. (eds.) (2016). *Principles and Practice of Impact Investing: A Catalytic Revolution.* Greenleaf Publishing.

The publications of the EVPA Knowledge Centre: http://evpa.eu.com/knowledge-centre/research-and-tools

REFERENCES

Balbo, L., Boiardi, P., Hehenberger, L., Mortell, D., Oostlander, P. and Vittone, E. (2016). *A Practical Guide to Venture Philanthropy and Social Impact Investment.* The European Venture Philanthropy Association.

Boiardi, P. and Gianoncelli, A. (2016). *The State of Venture Philanthropy and Social Investment (VP/SI) in Europe, The EVPA Survey 2015/2016.* The European Venture Philanthropy Association.

Boiardi, P. and Hehenberger, L. (2014). *A Practical Guide to Planning and Executing an Impactful Exit.* The European Venture Philanthropy Association.

Boiardi, P. and Hehenberger, L. (2015). *A Practical Guide to Adding Value through Non-financial Support.* The European Venture Philanthropy Association.

Boiardi, P., Hehenberger, L. and Gianoncelli A. (2016). *Impact Measurement in Practice: In-depth Case Studies*. The European Venture Philanthropy Association.

Clifford, J., Hehenberger, L., Fletcher, L. and Harling, A. (2015). *Social Impact Measurement in the Framework of a Société d'Impact Sociétal*. BWB Impact.

Hehenberger, L. and Boiardi, P. (2014).*Learning from Failures in Venture Philanthropy and Social Investment*. The European Venture Philanthropy Association.

Hehenberger, L., Boiardi, P. and Gianoncelli, A. (2014). *European Venture Philanthropy and Social Investment 2013/2014 : The EVPA Survey*. The European Venture Philanthropy Association.

Hehenberger, L., Harling, A. and Scholten, P. (2015). *A Practical Guide to Measuring and Managing Impact, 2nd edition*. The European Venture Philanthropy Association.

Kail, A. and Lumley, T. (2012). *Theory of Change: The Beginning of Making a Difference*. New Philanthropy Capital.

Matthews, J., Sternlicht, D., Bouri, A., Mudaliar, A. and Schiff, H. (2015). *Introducing the Impact Investing Benchmark*. Cambridge Associates and Global Impact Investing Network.

Mudaliar, A., Schiff, H. and Bass, R. (2016). *Annual Impact Investor Survey*. GIIN.

Power, G., Wilson, B., Brandenburg, M., Melia-Teevan, K. and Lai, J. (2012). *A Framework for Action: Social Enterprise and Impact Investing*. The Rockefeller Foundation & United Nations Global Compact.

Prahalad, C. K. (2004). *Fortune at the Bottom of the Pyramid*. Wharton School Publishing.

Richter, K. H. (2015). Truth or dare: Transparency by vanguard social investors reveals risks and returns in a maturing market. Retrieved 5 June 2015, from http://karlhrichter.com

Social Impact Investment Taskforce (2014a). *Impact Investment: The Invisible Heart of Markets. Harnessing the Power of Entrepreneurship, Innovation and Capital for Public Good*. Social Impact Investment Taskforce.

Social Impact Investment Taskforce (2014b). *Measuring Impact. Subject Paper of the Impact Measurement Working Group*. Social Impact Investment Taskforce.

Vecchi, V., Balbo, L., Brusoni, M. and Caselli, S. (eds.) (2016). *Principles and Practice of Impact Investing: A Catalytic Revolution*. Greenleaf Publishing.

Whitley, S., Darko, E. and Howells, G. (2013). *Impact Investing and Beyond: Mapping Support to Social Enterprises in Emerging Markets*. Overseas Development Institute.

Let's Practise: Case Study

Oltre Venture

Luciano Balbo is a well-known Italian entrepreneur in the venture capital and private equity business.[27] He has built a successful career after over twenty years spent in the financial markets. He is the founder and chairman of Fondazione Oltre, the first Italian venture philanthropy foundation. Since 2003, Fondazione

---

27 This practical case was inspired by Balbo *et al.* (2016).

Oltre has developed a thorough knowledge of the social sector. In 2006, Luciano Balbo launched the innovative Social Investment Fund – Oltre Venture. The fund (OLTRE I) invests in social enterprises which serve unmet social needs and present credible models of self-sustainability, aiming to realize long-term investments for the benefit of the entire community. Oltre Venture combines strong management and financial skills with a deep knowledge of the social field.

Oltre Venture is one of the first impact investment fund managers in Europe. Since its foundation, it has continuously and proactively supported Italian social enterprises and helped their strategic development.

The first fund, OLTRE I was constituted in 2006, as a *società in accomandita per azioni* – a Limited Liability Limited Partnership – LLLP. OLTRE I focused its investments on companies characterized by highly innovative operating models, economic and financial sustainability and offering high-quality services and/or products at affordable fees. Most of the startups were directly incubated by OLTRE I, supporting entrepreneurs in the design and strategic development of the portfolio companies.

With the experience gathered from the first fund, Luciano Balbo decided to launch Oltre Venture II, which was one of the first funds to have received an investment commitment from the European Investment Fund's Social Impact Accelerator. OLTRE II was authorized by the Bank of Italy on 21 October 2015 and registered as an Italian EuVECA Manager.

Table 16.2 below provides a comparison of the two funds in terms of their main features:

Oltre Venture raised its follow-on fund about eight years after its startup. The fund size has more than doubled, thanks mainly to the commitment of institutional investors and of the EIF. The investor profile has now changed from those initially targeted, who were mainly high-net-worth individuals (HNWI). HNWI and family offices have the advantage of greater flexibility when making investment decisions. But the investment they can commit to is smaller, whilst demanding, at the same time, greater involvement in investment decisions and management. The approach taken by institutional investors is different as they are able to invest larger amounts but require precise procedures to assess and to approve investments, which makes it extremely difficult to close a deal with them.

Oltre Venture II, thanks to its larger size, is able to finance social enterprises at an early stage, when they most need capital to support a step up in capabilities. This contributes to bridging the financing gap between the startup and scaling phase, which affects most social businesses in their development. Oltre Venture I, on the other hand, made small seed-stage investments.

Within the Oltre Venture I portfolio, the three main investments (PerMicro spa, Ivrea24 and Società e Salute Srl) were considered successful ventures, and they became proof of the team's ability to develop and manage new business

Table 16.2 A comparison between Oltre Venture's two funds

Fund name	Vintage year	Timeframe	Investors and Commitment	Legal form	Management Fee	Investment Target
OLTRE Fund I	2006	The fund has a duration of 10 years and an investment period no longer than 4 years.	€8 million raised from 21 investors, mainly from high-net-worth individuals (HNWI) and an important Bank Foundation.	Società in accomandita per azioni (SAPA) (Limited Liability Limited Partnership – LLLP)	Operational expenses covered by the founder	OLTRE I invested in 17 social enterprises belonging to the following sectors, microfinance, temporary social housing, healthcare and job placement. However, their business models were not all fully sustainable and replicable. Three main investments (PerMicro spa, Ivrea24 and Società e Salute Srl) represent 66% of the total portfolio.
OLTRE Fund II	2014	The fund has a duration of 10 years, extendible to 13, and an investment period no longer than 5 years.	Current commitment from private and institutional investors is about €23 million, of which €10 million invested by the	Authorized by Bank of Italy on 21 October 2015 and enrolled at no. 1 of the Register of the Italian EuVECA Managers	3%	OLTRE II investments are mainly directed both to expansion companies with the necessity to grow further and to start-up companies. Only fully sustainable societal impact enterprises are financed. OLTRE II investments will focus on the following sectors. Social sectors: Investments in education, healthcare, social

Table 16.2 (cont.)

Fund name	Vintage year	Timeframe	Investors and Commitment	Legal form	Management Fee	Investment Target
			European Investment Fund. The fundraising will continue until June 2017.			housing, assistance, job placement. Services: Investments in services for individuals, families, elderly and young population. Investments in the most vulnerable areas of the country: Investments in sectors such as agriculture and tourism, as the ultimate aim is to optimize Italy's strengths to promote economic and social development. Any other initiative that might promote social solutions creating a positive impact for the community.

models to attract further investment. In particular, Società e Salute is the fund's star investment, being a financially free-standing investment and a fully replicable business model. In 2009, OLTRE I, as the main shareholder of Società e Salute s.p.a., promoted and founded a network of clinics called Santagostino Medical Centre. These clinics meet a widespread social need offering high-quality medical services at low prices. The centres – nine in Milan and one in Bologna – offer specialist health services in the areas not sufficiently covered by the National Healthcare System (such as Dentistry, Psychotherapy, Speech Therapy) and in areas where standards are low. The centres provide medical care in more than 57 specialties to more than 170,000 patients. The price of an examination is set at €60 and the waiting time is three days. In 2014, the Centro Medico Santagostino attained economic and financial sustainability.

This success story was used as a reference case for the fundraising of Oltre Venture II, where the European Investment Fund (EIF) invested €10 million as anchor investor.

Questions for Discussion

1. *Investor relations:* After the closure of OLTRE I, what would the main elements used to convince an investor to invest in OLTRE II be? What are the risk and opportunities of dealing with the expectations of different kinds of funders, e.g HNWI and institutional investors?
2. What are the risks and opportunities for an impact investor who wishes to directly incubate its own investee startups?
3. Devise a possible scaling strategy for the investment in Società e Salute s.p.a. How can this company achieve greater social impact through its activities?

PART V

HARVESTING AND THE FUTURE OF ENTREPRENEURIAL FINANCE

HARVESTING: THE EXIT

PETER ROOSENBOOM

Rotterdam School of Management, Erasmus University

Investors, such as venture capitalists and business angels, should have the exit and return on their investment in mind from the outset. The main goal of this chapter is to discuss how investors in entrepreneurial firms time the exit of their investments and choose between different exit routes. There are three generic exit routes used by these investors: (1) Initial Public Offerings (IPOs), where some of the shares are sold to the general public and the shares are listed on the stock market, (2) acquisitions (trade sales), where all shares are sold to another company, and (3) buyouts where new investors, employees or management purchase the shares held by current investors.

VIEW FROM THE MEDIA

FINANCIAL TIMES   FT

Delivery Hero shares jump on market debut

Listing is the largest by a European technology business in almost 2 years

JUNE 30, 2017 BY ALIYA RAM

Delivery Hero, the takeaway food app, whet investor appetites in Europe's stirring initial public offering market on Friday, with shares rising 2.9 per cent to €26.25 on the company's debut. The listing is the largest by a European technology business in almost two years and the fourth by a food delivery group since 2014. It follows IPOs by US-based GrubHub, the UK's Just Eat and Takeaway.com, the market leader in Belgium and the Netherlands. Delivery Hero, which is based in Berlin, raised almost €1bn from the offering, which was more than 10 times oversubscribed by investors eager to tap into Europe's lively equity markets. Companies have raised $11bn in the past three months after a slow start to the year, according to data from Dealogic. The company will net €465m from the listing, which it said it would use to pay back loans until it was free of debt and fund expansion. Existing investors such as Berlin-based Rocket Internet, which has faced concerns about losses among its holdings, and hedge fund Luxor Capital welcomed the capital increase. 'My view is that some of the business models in technology are overrated, as though they [have] a monopoly over the internet,' said Alexander Frolov, founder of venture capital firm Target Global, which invested in Delivery Hero in 2013. 'I just think that food delivery, where there are lifetime-long customers, is good.' Lazy diners have driven demand for food delivery apps across the world, which have increasingly sought capital from public markets to fund growth amid growing competition from new entrants such as Amazon and Uber ... On Wednesday Delivery Hero placed almost 19m new shares and 15m existing shares on the Frankfurt Stock Exchange at €25.50 – the top end of its previously projected range. It also sold a further 5m shares held by Rocket Internet, giving it a valuation of €4.39bn. It is still lossmaking, with losses before income taxes of €202m in 2016. Niklas Östberg, co-founder and chief executive, said the company wanted to break even or become profitable from next year. 'We're going to invest and continue to grow and take growth into profitability,' he said. Delivery Hero's float comes amid wider optimism about technology stocks and equities in Europe, where there is a steady pipeline of companies planning to go public ...

www.ft.com/content/c57b3c42-5d68-11e7-9bc8-8055f264aa8b

LEARNING OBJECTIVES

After reading this chapter you will be able to:

- Understand how investors plan their exit strategy.
- Recognize exactly how investors time their exit decisions.
- Appreciate the different choices that investors make between different exit routes.
- Differentiate between the pros and cons of different exit routes.
- Gain an understanding of the going public decision of companies and the IPO process.

Where Are We Going Next?

This chapter will start with a brief overview of the importance of exit markets in Europe and the United States. Next, we will examine how investors time the exit and how they choose between the different exit routes. We will then consider why firms go public and discuss the IPO process. The chapter ends by reviewing the ongoing changes in exit markets in Europe and the United States.

17.1   The Importance of Exit Markets

Venture capitalists and business angels are buy-and-sell investors who look to exit their investments hoping to realize a return. This contrasts with entrepreneurs, who have longer holding horizons and are typically not interested in selling the shares in their company for some time. However, not all investors approach their investments quite so systematically, and many of them are investing under the expectation that, when ready to sell, a buyer for the shares will be found. A lack of preparation at the outset and poor timing can result in poor exit decisions.

There are three generic exit routes used by investors: (1) Initial Public Offerings (IPOs), where some of the shares are sold to the general public and the shares are listed on the stock market, (2) acquisitions (trade sales), where all shares are sold to another company, and (3) buyouts where new investors, employees or management purchase the shares held by current investors. Having well-developed exit markets is of key importance to investors. In this section, we will focus on the exit markets for venture capitalists. Unfortunately reliable statistics for business angels are not available.

Figure 17.1 presents the exit landscape for venture capitalists in the United States during the period between 2007 up to and including 2016. The United States is by far the largest venture capital market in the world and accounts for 60 per cent of the global number of venture capital exits, with an almost 70 per cent share of the worldwide deal volume in exits over this period.[1] Figure 17.1 clearly shows that acquisitions are the most prominent exit route as regards the number of deals and deal volume, followed by IPOs and buyouts. There was a sharp drop in the number and volume of exits in 2008 and 2009 as a result of the global financial crisis. The exit market quickly recovered after that, and in recent years has even exceeded the 2007 levels.

Figure 17.2 shows the exit landscape for European venture capitalists for the years 2007–15. As in the United States, acquisitions comprise the most significant exit route. However, in Europe buy-outs are the second most popular exit route and, in comparison to the United States, there are very few IPOs.[2] Europe also experienced a fall in exit activity in 2008 and 2009, but recovery has been slower than in the United States and is yet to get back to 2007 levels. The European exit market is smaller than that of the United States. This reflects the smaller size of the venture capital industry in Europe. In 2015, 420 exits took place in Europe with a deal volume at cost (i.e. the amount invested) equal to €1.5 billion.[3] This compares to 961 exits in the United States in that year, with a deal volume at exit of $50.4 billion (i.e. using amount paid at exit).[4]

---

1 National Venture Capital Association (2017: 13).

2 Invest Europe (2016)

3 The annual statistics of Invest Europe (formerly the European Venture Capital and Private Equity Association (EVCA)) report 1,109 exits with a deal volume of €2.3 billion for 2015. These numbers include exits via sales of shares in portfolio firms that are already listed, repayment of subordinated loans in silent partnerships (mostly used in Germany), repayment of principal loans, write-offs and divestment via other means. In Figure 17.2 we have ignored these exit routes and only included exits via acquisitions, Initial Public Offering and buyouts (sale to another private equity house, management or financial institution) in order to compare the European exit landscape to that of the United States. At the time of writing, the data on IPO exits for 2016 was not yet available for Europe.

4 The difference in exit volume between Europe and the United States is partly driven by differences in the way the amounts are calculated. Invest Europe calculates this at cost (i.e., it reports on the initial investment) whereas the National Venture Capital Association calculates it at exit prices (i.e. the price that the investment sold for at exit). However, it remains safe to say that the European exit market is smaller than that of the United States.

Panel A: Exit routes in the United States (number of deals)

Panel B: Exit routes in the United States ($ billion)

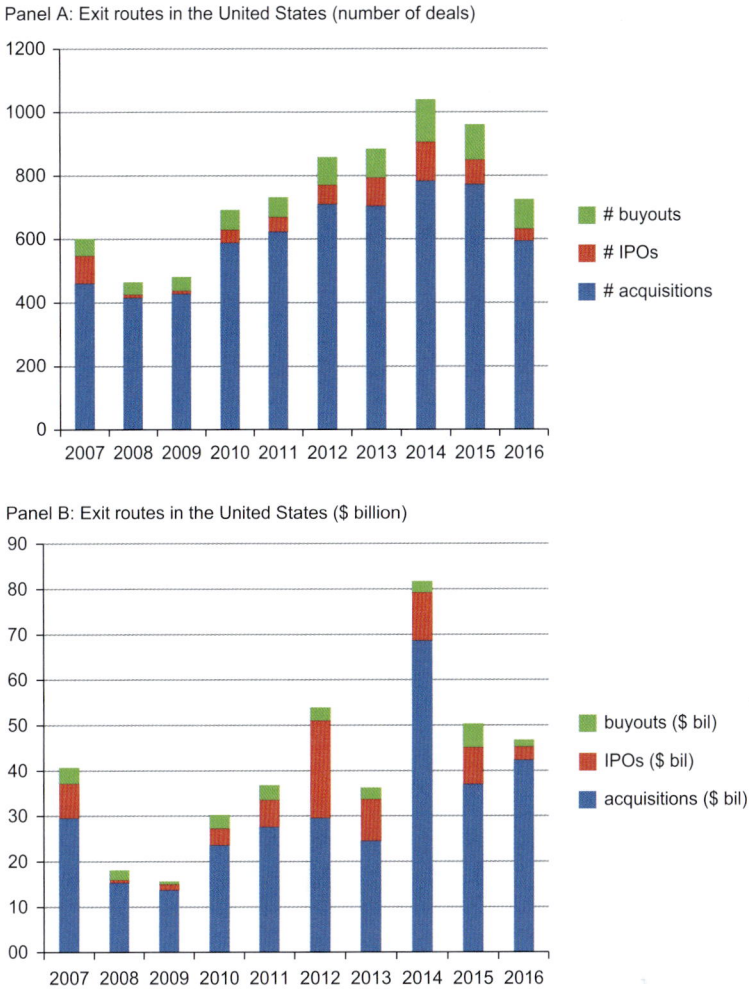

Figure 17.1 Exit routes in the United States.
Panel A: Exit routes in the United States (number of deals).
Panel B: Exit routes in the United States ($ billion).
Source: Based on data from NVCA (2017)

In the rest of this chapter we will consider how investors time their decision to exit and how they choose between the exit routes available to them. In this context, we will discuss the importance of the pre-planning of exits, private contracting, the actions of entrepreneurs and investor backgrounds. We will then continue with a discussion of what is widely viewed as the exit route for the most promising firms in the investor's portfolio (the 'silver bullet'): Initial Public Offerings (IPOs). We will find that not only do IPOs offer a partial exit opportunity to investors but that they are also a momentous occasion for the company. Much of our discussion is based on available academic literature.

Panel A: Exit routes in Europe (number of deals)

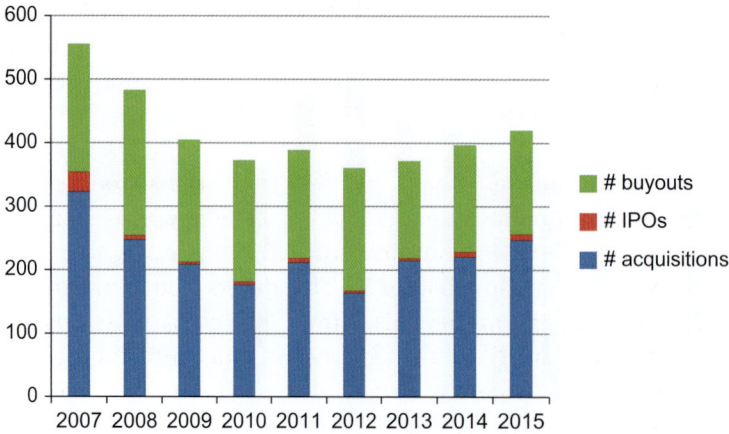

Panel B: Exit routes in Europe (€billion)

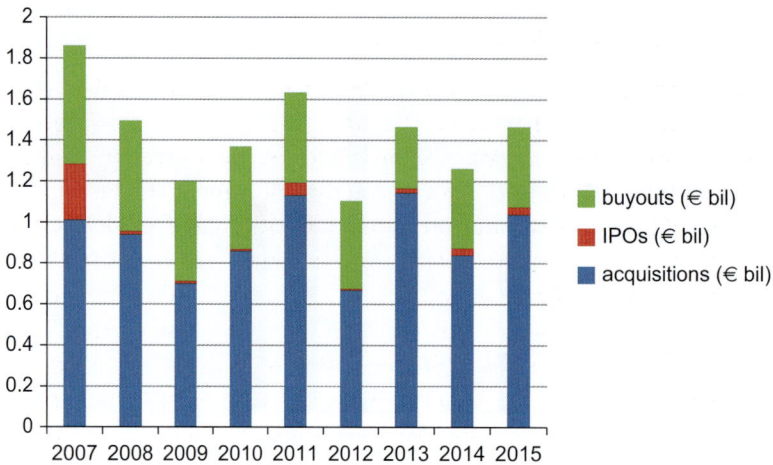

Figure 17.2 Exit routes in Europe.
Panel A: Exit routes in Europe (number of deals).
Panel B: Exit routes in Europe (€ billion).
Source: Based on data from Invest Europe (2016)

This chapter concludes with a discussion of the ongoing changes in exit markets.

17.2   Timing Exits

Investors in entrepreneurial firms are buy-and-sell investors. Having owned their shares for a number of years, they will look to sell them. For example, venture capitalists in the United States hold on to shares in firms for a median of seven years from the first venture capital funding before exiting via an IPO, and a median of four years from the first venture capital funding before exiting via an acquisition.[5] An important decision that investors need to make is at what point to sell the shares in the venture. This decision is complex, and depends on a number of factors, including the success of the venture, the characteristics and actions of the investor, as well as the price that the shares will fetch (market conditions).

Business angels are often seen as less exit-centric than venture capitalists, and tend to make their exit decisions in a less organized way. They can afford to be more patient when exiting their investments because they are investing their own money (as we saw in Chapter 3). This differs from venture capital funds, which are investing the money raised from limited partners (institutional and wealthy private investors) and which pre-plan and contract on exit strategies at the time of investment. Venture capital funds have a limited life-span of typically ten years during which they need to exit their investments to generate a return on investment for their limited partners (see Chapter 4 for more detail).

17.2.1   How Do Deal Characteristics Impact Exit Timing?

Venture capitalists invest in ventures in stages. This implies that, for every investment round, they have the opportunity to decide whether or not to continue to invest in the firm. In other words, every investment round provides them with an exit option. Giot and Schwienbacher (2007) exploit this in their analysis of investment duration using a large sample of 6,000 US venture-backed firms that together had 20,000 investment rounds between 1980 and 2003. They report that later-stage investments, syndicated investments and ventures that have received follow-on investment rounds have faster exits. These ventures tend to be the more successful ones that have achieved (technological) milestones and developed more quickly because of the complementary value-adding services provided by multiple venture capitalists partnering in the syndicate. Moreover, syndicates increase the pool of contacts which helps in the search for a buyer interested in acquiring the venture or certifying the venture's quality at the time of the IPO.

17.2.2   How Do Investor Characteristics and Actions Impact Exit Timing?

The time to exit is also determined by the characteristics and actions of venture investors. In a study that examined the time to exit of European venture capitalists, it was reported that more intense monitoring by the venture capitalist leads to shorter investment durations and therefore faster exits.[6] Venture capitalists with pre-planned exit strategies at the time of investment achieved faster IPO exits in Europe. US venture capitalists that engage in more on-site

---

5 National Venture Capital Association (2017: 30, 31).
6 Félix *et al.* (2014).

monitoring of ventures were able to achieve faster and more successful exits.[7] Young venture capitalists have reputation incentives to rush their portfolio firm into going public to establish a reputation for themselves. This phenomenon has been coined grandstanding.[8]

17.2.3   How Do Market Conditions Impact Exit Timing?

A final and key determinant of exit timing relates to market conditions. Venture capitalists are more likely to exit their investments when general market conditions are good. For example, US venture capitalists take biotechnology firms public when the stock market is peaking and equity valuations are high.[9] Also, improved stock market conditions speed up exit decisions.[10] However, US venture capitalists do not time the market to take advantage of overoptimistic investors. Instead, venture capitalists engage in pseudo market timing: they are more likely to exit their investments at times when overall demand for capital is high, adverse selection costs are low and market conditions are favourable.[11]

17.3   Exit Route Choices

Another important decision involves the selection of the exit route. A number of exit routes exist: (1) Initial Public Offerings (IPOs), (2) acquisitions (also known as trade sales), and (3) selling the shares to management, employees or investors in a buyout transaction. An alternative exit route, should the venture fail, is to write off the investment, but this is a scenario that investors are hoping will not arise. The choice of exit route is closely linked to exit timing, as discussed in the previous section. Sometimes, some exit routes may be more attractive than others because of changing market conditions. For example, during the technology bubble of 1999–2000, venture capitalists were quick to exit their investments via IPOs to take advantage of the high demand for technology stocks that existed at that time.

17.3.1   Characteristics of the Different Exit Routes

Each exit route works differently and has its own pros and cons. There seems to be an exit 'pecking order' among venture capitalists, with preference given to exiting their most profitable investments via IPOs rather than acquisitions or buyouts. The worst investments get written off. Giot and Schwienbacher (2007) confirm that US venture capitalists aim for IPO exits first and select IPO candidates relatively quickly. Business angels, on the other hand, mostly exit via acquisitions and rarely exit via an IPO (see Chapter 3 for more detail).[12]

---

7 Bernstein *et al.* (2016).
8 Gompers (1996).
9 Lerner (1994).
10 Giot and Schwienbacher (2007).
11 Ball and Smith (2011).
12 Mason and Harrison (2002).

Table 17.1 Pros and cons of different exit routes for investors

	Pros	Cons
IPOs	1. Used to exit the best-performing ventures and therefore a profitable exit route 2. Allows (young) venture capitalists to establish reputation via visible exit and to be more successful in raising money from institutional investors for their follow-on venture capital funds ('grandstanding')	1. Only partial exit possible, with remaining shares subject to selling restrictions for some time (lockup period) 2. More public scrutiny and disclosure requirements 3. Transaction costs are relatively high (underwriter fees) 4. Time-consuming to complete 5. Indirect costs (underpricing)
Acquisitions	1. Full exit (all shares can be sold in one transaction) 2. Used to exit a wider range of investments from well-performing ones to distressed ones 3. Lower transaction costs compared to IPOs	1. Potential conflict with entrepreneurs on exit 2. Lower average valuations due to illiquidity discount and wider range of investments that are exited via acquisitions
Buy-outs	1. Partial or full exit possible	2. Exit of last resort: typically if no IPO or acquisition exit was possible at an attractive price

To some extent, this reflects the fact that business angels invest in young, early-stage ventures which are less likely to qualify for IPO exits. We will look at the pros and cons of each exit route in turn, starting with IPO exits. Table 17.1 provides an overview of these pros and cons.

Initial Public Offerings

In the case of an IPO, part of the shares are sold to the general public and the shares are listed on the stock market. To some degree, we can expect angel and venture capital-backed companies to have a stronger chance of going public in comparison with other firms, given that these companies were carefully selected by the investors in the first place and that the investors add value to these companies after investment. Examples of large venture capital-backed IPO exits in Europe include Yandex (Russian search engine Internet firm which went public on NASDAQ in 2011), Zalando (German online retailer which went public on the Frankfurt Stock Exchange in 2014) and Criteo (French online advertising firm which went public on NASDAQ in 2013).

Initial public offerings have the advantage of being a very visible exit. Many young venture capitalists try to establish a reputation for themselves by going public with their ventures in an attempt to attract future flows of capital from institutional investors into their follow-on venture capital funds, a phenomenon called 'grandstanding'.[13] IPOs are also widely viewed as the most profitable exit route. Chaplinsky and Gupta-Mukherjee (2010) constructed the realized exit returns for exited venture capital investments in the United States during 1985–2008 and compared exit returns across different exit routes. They reported that the mean exit return is 99.5 per cent for acquisition exits but 211.7 per cent for IPO exits. While both exit routes produce extreme exit returns (so-called 'strike-outs' and 'home runs'), the IPO (acquisition) exits account for 67 per cent (33 per cent) of the top quartile of returns (home runs) versus 24 per cent (76 per cent) of the bottom quartile of returns (strikeouts). They concluded that IPOs more frequently generate home runs that boost overall fund performance and help to cover the losses on other investments. Achleitner *et al.* (2012) confirm that IPO exits do better than acquisition exits using a North American and European sample of exited investments during 1982–2008. Not much is known about the exit returns for business angels. However, Mason and Harrison (2002) show that in those rare cases where IPO exits by business angels occur they are also within the top-performing investments. In conclusion, it appears that IPOs are used to exit the best-performing ventures. A side benefit for the entrepreneur is that, compared to an acquisition exit, the IPO allows them to stay in control of the company.

There are also disadvantages associated with IPO exits. Initial public offerings only offer a partial exit at the time of the IPO. Investors cannot sell all their shares in the venture at the time of the IPO and are required to hold onto the shares they have not sold in the IPO for some time afterwards because of lock-up agreements. After lock-up expiration, the investors (and the entrepreneurs) are allowed to sell their shares on the open market or in a later acquisition of the firm. The transaction costs associated with IPOs are higher compared to the other exit routes, making it more effective for larger firms. Moreover, IPOs take longer to complete than the other exit routes and need to comply with ongoing disclosure rules. We will return to IPOs in Section 17.4, where we will discuss the pros and cons of IPOs from the company and entrepreneur's perspective and the IPO process in more detail.

VOICE OF THE EXPERT: Javier Perez-Tenessa (Spain)

Co-founder, Honorary Chairman & Former CEO eDreams, Javier worked as a consultant for McKinsey & Company, and later held Senior Manager positions at Netscape Communications, and AOL, where he was responsible for the distribution of Netscape Communicator and the Netcenter portal. Javier has an MS in Aerospace Engineering from the Polytechnic University of Madrid, and an MBA from Stanford

13 Gompers (1996).

University. He has been a Windsurfing Instructor on the Mediterranean Coast and a Tour Guide in the Soviet Union.

What are your thoughts about the IPO process and your advice for entrepreneurs that are looking at the different options to provide liquidity to their investors?

The eDreams IPO was the third time we had generated significant liquidity and returns for our shareholders and the team, having closed two LBOs prior to the IPO. I had also raised public debt twice before for the company, in a process that resembles very much that of an IPO. So in that sense, the IPO was not completely new to me, nor was it going to change my life economically. Completing an IPO was significantly easier than closing any of my prior LBO, Fund Raising or Merger/Acquisition deals. On private deals, there is lots of very difficult due diligence, Q&A sessions, and complex negotiations involving several parties each with different incentives and goals . A CEO in an LBO is a very lonely person. The IPO in comparison is relatively simple. It follows a cookie cutter process, which just needs to be followed, with the same thing being repeated one time after another. Q&A questions are extremely simple in comparison to those with Private Equity or Corporate Buyers. There is also a lot of travelling and lots of glamour involved in the 2–4 week roadshow period, and I think few CEOs will tell you they did not enjoy that. So, when I rang the bell on the floor of the Madrid Stock exchange there was a mixed feeling of accomplishment (after all eDreams was and remains today the only Internet startup in Spain to ever go public on a main exchange) and also of caution on what comes next. Completing an IPO was a personal challenge for me, it was 'the only missing part' on what I considered I had to do in the company, having founded seventeen years prior and taken it to a prominent position worldwide providing solid returns for many. Yet, despite all the advisors in the process (dozens and dozens of bankers, lawyers, consultants), I don't think most teams realize how much being a public company can impact their business. Some of it is positive. Some is also very negative. A public company requires significant risk reviews and some focus is lost on value creation vs. risk reduction. Bureaucracy can creep in, at all levels. "Professional" public company board members and executives can be great, but they can also just be there for the pay, covering their risks, and spending extremely valuable time in Board meetings in meaningless conversations and destroying value. So probably the biggest piece of advice I could give to teams considering and IPO is . . . "Forget the IPO. Think about what it means to be a public company, learn about it from peers, and then decide whether it is worth it".

Acquisitions

Acquisition exits offer the advantage of a full exit for the investors and entrepreneur. They can sell all the shares they own in one go to the acquirer. The acquirer will also have full control of the venture.

However, in most cases acquirers do not come knocking at the door. Investors can guide the entrepreneur and company through the process of finding a buyer. In most cases, the investors will call in the help of business brokers and professional advisors who will put the firm up for sale and use their networks to contact potential buyers. A list of preferred buyers, typically active in the same or related industry as the company that is up for sale, is drawn up and then approached. The purpose is to sell the firm to the highest bidder. A buyer may be interested in the acquisition because it allows them to operate on a larger scale, open up new markets or access new technology, innovations and knowledge. Payment can be made in cash or in shares of the acquiring company. Typically, cash is the preferred means of payment from the perspective of the exiting investor. It may be difficult for the buyer and the exiting investors to agree on a price, in which case the parties agree to a minimum base price and an earnout that pays an additional percentage of the base price to the selling shareholders when certain revenue targets or other milestones are achieved in the period after acquisition. The earnout can be between 10 and 25 per cent of the base price.[14] The parties also need to agree on other terms, such as continued employment of the founders and key employees, how to deal with outstanding employee stock options, non-compete clauses that prevent the founder and key employees from working for competing firms for a certain period of time, specific liabilities and the use of intellectual property.[15]

Having reached agreement on price and terms, the acquirer will instruct their lawyers and accountants to conduct a due diligence investigation of the company. Since the acquirer is incurring costs for due diligence, the parties will typically draw up an exclusivity agreement to prevent the company that is up for sale from negotiating with other potential buyers during this period. It will be impossible for the acquirer to know all there is to know about the company at this stage. For this reason, an escrow account is set up to hold a portion of the price paid to the selling shareholders for a certain period of time, typically one year from the date of the sale, which the acquirer can claim in the event of unexpected claims against the business, such as incomplete litigation and contingent liabilities.[16] Once the period has expired, the remaining monies are returned to the selling shareholders.

As well as having the advantage of a full exit, the transaction costs associated with acquisition exits tend to be lower than for IPO exits. Examples of large venture-backed acquisition exits in Europe include the sale of Supercell, the Finnish developer of the mobile game 'Clash of Clans', bought by Chinese Internet firm Tencent for $8.6 billion in 2016 and the sale of Mojang, the Swedish developer of the game franchise 'Minecraft', to Microsoft for $2.5 billion in 2014.

---

14 McKaskill (2009).
15 McKaskill (2009).
16 McKaskill (2009).

However, there are a number of drawbacks to acquisition exits. First, the entrepreneur loses all control to the acquirer and may have different exit preferences from the investor. This could mean that the entrepreneur is less willing to sell their shares via an acquisition exit. For this reason, investors typically contract on exits with entrepreneurs at the outset. At the time of investment, entrepreneurs may have to agree to grant tag-along or drag-along rights that require them to sell their shares to the acquirer at the same terms as the investors (see Chapter 9 for more detail on term sheets). These exit rights are more commonly used by venture capitalists when they pre-plan an acquisition exit.[17] Angel investors make less use of these contractual exit rights.

The second disadvantage is that the valuations paid on acquisition exits tend to be lower than on IPO exits. For example, Brau *et al.* (2003) report a 22 per cent illiquidity discount on acquisitions when compared to IPOs in the United States. One reason for the lower average for valuations in acquisition exits is that a wider range of ventures qualify for this type of exit. Both well and modestly performing ventures can be exited in this way. Sometimes even distressed firms will undergo acquisition exits. This contrasts with IPO exits, for which only the best-performing ventures qualify. A second reason for the lower prices paid for acquisitions is that the acquirer conducts extensive due diligence beforehand and is more knowledgeable about the venture's industry and technology. This mitigates information asymmetries relating to the venture's value in comparison with IPOs, where investors are less well informed and may periodically overpay for the shares. A third and final reason for the lower average valuation might be that entrepreneurs agree to sell their firm to a larger firm because they realize that their firm may not survive the competition from product market competitors should it stay independent.[18]

Buy-outs

In a buy-out, the investor sells their shares to another investor, the management (the entrepreneur) (see Chapter 13) and/or employees. An example of early-stage investors being bought out by a later-stage investor is BlaBlaCar, the French long-distance ridesharing company. Russian venture capitalist Baring Vostok paid €80 million to buy out some of BlaBlaCar's very early-stage investors in 2016. Buyout exits are more popular among venture capitalists in Europe than in the United States (see Figures 17.1 and 17.2). One advantage of buy-outs is that they allow the investor to exit in part or completely while the entrepreneur retains control. This is different from IPO exits, where the investor can only exit partially (at least initially), and acquisition exits, where the entrepreneur loses control to the acquirer. It is even possible for entrepreneurs or management to increase their control of the firm by buying back shares from the exiting

17 Cumming and Johan (2008).
18 Bayar and Chemmanur (2011).

investor. Should the entrepreneur or management not have enough money of their own, they can team up with an external investor, their employees or raise the money from a bank (personal loan). An added benefit of involving employees in the transaction is that they become part-owners of the firm, incentivizing them to work harder.

It is also possible for the company to buy the shares from the exiting investor. This takes the form of a leveraged recapitalization. The company borrows the money to fund the repurchase of the shares from the exiting investor. It then cancels the repurchased shares. An added benefit of leveraged recapitalization is that the interest paid on the debt is tax-deductible. A disadvantage of leveraged recapitalizations is that it may increase the debt burden on the company to such a degree that it increases the probability of financial distress and limits the flexibility of its operations.

Buyout exits do not offer the most attractive exit route to investors. Typically, the investor will not have been able to find other buyers willing to buy their shares for a good price in the outside market, and has therefore decided to sell to insiders instead. If the investor is able to find external financial buyers (e.g. other business angels or venture capitalists) willing to buy their shares, the buyers may not be willing to pay the same price as that paid by strategic acquirers in acquisition exits. The reason for this is that strategic acquirers can benefit from synergies, thereby increasing their willingness to pay, whereas the financial buyers cannot. Mason and Harrison (2002) provide some evidence of this. They reported on UK business angels selling their shares to other investors in the venture or new third-party investors, particularly in the case of poor or modestly performing investments (the so-called 'living deads').[19] The exit returns for those exits were much lower when compared to acquisition or IPO exits. Achleitner *et al.* (2012), using a sample of exits by North American and European venture capitalists, provided mixed evidence that financial acquirers (i.e. other venture capitalists or financial institutions buying the shares from the exiting investor) generated lower returns when compared to strategic acquirers.

Write-offs

For the sake of completeness, we will also look at write-offs as a potential exit route. Poor and moderately performing investments remain difficult to exit via any of the other routes. Should investors not be able to successfully turn around these ventures, they are written-off as a complete or partial loss of investment. Not surprisingly, write-offs are the exits associated with the poorest investments and biggest losses.[20] In rare cases, a small amount of the investment may be recouped by selling assets. Statistics for European venture capital show that write-offs account for about 20 per cent of the total number of exits during the period from 2007 up to and including 2015.[21] An example

---

19 See Ruhnka (1992).
20 Achleitner *et al.* (2012).
21 Invest Europe (2016).

of a failed startup is Backplane, a social network for celebrities. Founded in 2011, Backplane raised $12 million from Lady Gaga and top venture capitalists such as Sequoia and Google Ventures at around a $40 million valuation. When the cash ran out, venture capitalists were not willing to put more money in. Backplane sold its assets to previous and new investors in 2016 who will try to restart its concept.

17.3.2   Investors and Successful Exits

The choice of exit route is largely driven by the perceived quality of the venture. As we have seen, a pecking order seems to exist: the best portfolio companies exit via IPOs followed by acquisitions, buyouts and, if all fails, via write-offs. However, not all investors are equally good at making successful exit choices. Venture capitalists with better networks are more successful in IPO exits and acquisition exits in the United States.[22] Venture capitalists with more industry specialization[23] and more active involvement[24] make more successful exit decisions in the United States and Europe, respectively. The human capital of venture capital fund management also plays an important role. Dimov and Shepherd (2005) showed that venture capital fund management teams with better general human capital (i.e. education in science and humanities) are more likely to have IPO exits (homeruns), whereas those that have better specific human capital (i.e. MBA, law degree and consulting experience) are less likely to face write-offs (strikeouts). More experienced investors and entrepreneurs are more likely to generate a successful exit both in the United States and in Europe.[25] The fact that there are fewer serial entrepreneurs in Europe explains the lower rate of exit success in Europe compared to that in the United States.

Investors also need to be experienced in handling information problems in exit markets. The greater the degree of information asymmetry between the investor who is selling their shares and the potential buyer of those shares, the higher the likelihood of a partial rather than a full exit. In the case of a partial exit, the exiting investor holds on to some of their shares, which conveys a positive signal to the buyer(s) of those shares. Being able to successfully mitigate information asymmetries and agency costs therefore increases the chances of having a successful exit.[26]

The choice of exit route is also influenced by information. IPO exits are considered to be more suitable for portfolio firms that are easier to value.[27] Acquisition exits might be a better choice for portfolio firms that are subject to higher information asymmetries vis-à-vis public investors.

---

22 Hochberg *et al.* (2007).
23 Gompers *et al.* (2009).
24 Bottazzi *et al.* (2008).
25 Axelson and Martinovic (2015).
26 Cumming and Johan (2008).
27 Bayar and Chemmanur (2011).

In sum, investors who are more experienced and have better skills can add more value to the companies they invest in. As a result, the chances of a successful exit or homerun via IPO exits is increased. Information problems in exit markets influence the choice of exit route and whether or not a full exit can be made.

17.3.3   Combining Different Exit Routes

Until now we have assumed that investors need to opt for one single exit route. However, it is possible to explore two exit routes simultaneously or sequentially in so-called 'dual-track sell-outs', rather than to immediately choose one particular exit route. Brau *et al.* (2010) compare dual-track and single-track sell-outs. They distinguish between private dual-track and public dual-track sell-outs. Private dual-track sell-outs are exits where firms file to go public but are acquired privately before going public. Public dual-track sell-outs are exits where firms go public but are acquired shortly afterwards. Investors can then partially exit via an IPO and fully exit in the subsequent acquisition. IPO exits are, in that case, considered to be delayed acquisition exits. Going public first seems to help to increase the relative bargaining power of firms and thereby to increase the price that acquirers need to pay for the shares compared to the acquisitions of firms that decided to stay private[28] or firms that opted for a single-track sell-out.[29]

Brau *et al.* (2010) note that both types of dual-track sell-out strategies generate higher premiums when compared to single-track sell-outs. However, when compared with single-track sell-outs, private dual-tracks are the most profitable with a 22–26 per cent higher premium versus an 18–21 per cent higher premium earned for public dual-tracks. This shows that investors and entrepreneurs can increase their selling proceeds by following a dual-track exit strategy. Venture capitalists are more likely to follow these profitable dual-track exit strategies.[30]

Let's Practise: Case Study

ACQUISITION OR IPO?

Dual-track sell-outs are becoming more popular. In a dual-track sell-out, two exit routes – typically an IPO and an acquisition – are explored at the same time. Bloomberg reports that 14 out of the 52 US companies (27 per cent) that withdrew their plans for an IPO in 2016 were subsequently sold in the following six months. Of the 14 companies, eight were venture capital or private equity-backed. By comparison, only 11 out of 79 companies (14 per cent) were acquired six months

28 Mantecon and Thistle (2011).
29 Brau *et al.* (2010).
30 Brau *et al.* (2010).

after withdrawing from an IPO in 2015.[31] *Traditionally, dual-track sell-out strategies were more commonly used by private equity investors. However, this exit strategy has gained popularity among venture-backed companies in recent years.*

In Europe, dual-tracks are becoming more common, with companies simultaneously exploring an IPO and an acquisition.[32] *One well-known example of a European company that filed to go public but ended up being acquired is Luxembourg-registered Skype, famous for its voice and video calls over the Internet. The venture capital-backed company did not initially aim for a dual-track process, but once it announced its plans to go public in 2009, it attracted the attention of several potential buyers. Yahoo, Google, Facebook, Verizon, Apple and Microsoft were rumoured to be interested in acquiring the company.*[33] *Skype delayed its IPO plans. Eventually, Microsoft bought Skype in 2011 before it could go public for a price tag of $8.5 billion.*

Questions for Discussion

1. Which companies qualify for dual-track sell-outs?
2. What market conditions might lead companies to opt for dual-track sell-outs?
3. What are the pros and cons of dual-track sell-outs?

17.4   Initial Public Offerings (IPOs) in Detail

In the case of an IPO, a portion of the shares are sold to the general public and these shares are listed on the stock market. This offers a partial exit opportunity for investors. However, going public is also a major milestone in the life of the portfolio firm. In this section, we start by discussing the advantages and disadvantages of an IPO from the perspective of the portfolio firm or entrepreneur. We look in detail at how the IPO process works, and we also explore three anomalies associated with IPOs: in general, IPOs are associated with: (1) high first-day returns (i.e. underpricing), (2) long-term underperformance, and (3) periods of high activity during which many firms go public ('hot issue' markets) followed by periods with less IPO activity ('cold issue' markets). This section concludes by examining the role of venture capitalists and business angels in the context of IPOs.

17.4.1   Pros and Cons of Going Public

Going public is an important decision in the life cycle of a firm. The benefits of being a publicly listed firm include (in no particular order): (1) being able to raise

---

31 See www.bna.com/sale-ipo-companies-n57982082683/
32 See www.ft.com/content/c96004f8-2d25-11e4-911b-00144feabdc0
33 See www.reuters.com/article/us-skype-ipo-idUSTRE6A05N220101101

money in public equity markets, (2) enhancing the reputation of the firm, (3) broadening the ownership base, (4) establishing a market price for your shares, (5) allowing pre-IPO owners to cash out, (6) allowing the firm to pay for future acquisitions using shares as an acquisition currency, and (7) allowing the firm to raise money when other financing sources are depleted or have become too costly. Brau and Fawcett (2006) asked 336 US Chief Financial Officers (CFOs) of companies that have undertaken an IPO, had plans for an IPO but withdrew and firms that remained privately held about their opinion about these benefits. The three benefits perceived to be most important by CFOs are that going public allows firms to use the shares to pay for acquisitions, to establish a market price for the shares and to enhance the firm's reputation. Bancel and Mittoo (2009) surveyed 78 CFOs of European companies that went public. Their results are mostly in line with those of Brau and Fawcett (2006) for the United States. European CFOs, however, responded that the three main benefits of going public are that it allows for enhanced reputation and credibility, financial flexibility and an increase in the shareholder base.

Going public not only brings benefits but is also associated with costs. Going public is expensive. First, there are the direct costs of going public. Going public requires the firm to hire an investment bank that underwrites the IPO. These underwriters typically charge a percentage of the gross proceeds in the IPO. In the United States, the percentage is typically around 7 per cent but lower levels can be found in other countries of the world. There are also the fixed costs of printing the IPO prospectus, legal advice, audit fees, registration fees, etc. that have to be paid when going public. Second, there are the indirect costs of going public. On average, firms that go public sell their shares at an IPO price below the market price on the first day of trading. This positive first-day return is known as 'underpricing'. This creates a cost for the IPO firm: in retrospect, it could have charged a higher price for its shares than it actually did. The firm left money on the table. The level of underpricing averages around 15 per cent historically.

There are also other disadvantages of being a public firm. When a firm goes public it needs to publish an IPO prospectus which includes detailed information about the firm and its performance. Product market competitors of the firm can take advantage of the disclosure of this proprietary information. For example, they can glean new information about the firm's strategy and products. Publicly listed firms also need to comply with disclosure rules after their IPO: they publish (interim) financial statements, issue press releases and hold conference calls with financial analysts. This gives rise to ongoing disclosure costs and a further potential loss of proprietary information to competitors. Another disadvantage of going public is the potential loss of control. As a publicly listed firm, the firm may be targeted in a (hostile) acquisition.

Brau and Fawcett (2006) also asked the CFOs about the disadvantages of going public. The main reasons for not going public are the desire to maintain decision-making control, to avoid ownership dilution, poor market conditions

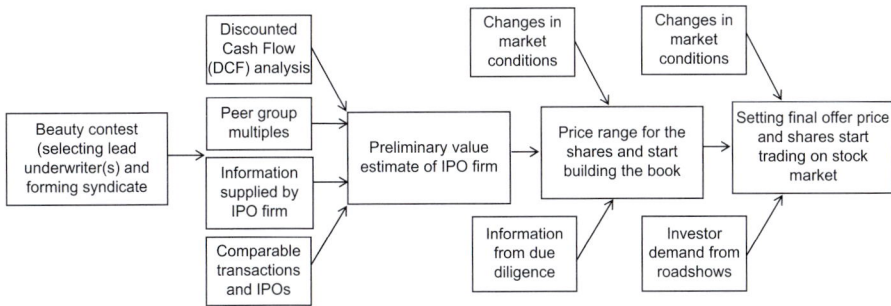

Figure 17.3 The going public process.

and being concerned about disclosing information to competitors. European CFOs indicate that the fees are the major cost of going public.[34]

17.4.2   The Process of Going Public

The process of going public takes about six months from start to finish on average, and is mostly led by the executive directors of the company. Figure 17.3 depicts the IPO process. The process typically starts with a 'beauty contest': the firm approaches several investment banks in order to select one of them to act as the lead underwriter of its IPO. The investment banks pitch their strengths to the firm's management and present their preliminary valuations of the company's shares. Van den Assem *et al*. (2016) show that in the Netherlands on average four to five underwriters participate in this contest. These underwriters typically come up with a preliminary value estimate. There are several considerations to bear in mind when choosing the lead underwriter of the IPO: companies base their choice of lead underwriter on the underwriter's reputation, professionalism, experience, investor client base and whether the firm has an existing business relationship with the underwriter.

The lead underwriter is in charge of forming a group (syndicate) of other investment banks that are going to be marketing the shares in the IPO to retail and institutional investors, distributing the shares between these syndicate members, pricing the shares and, if necessary, stabilizing the stock price in the initial trading period after the IPO. The lead underwriter gets the largest proportion of the fees as compensation for its efforts. The underwriter syndicate purchases the shares from the company at a discount and then sells the shares to retail and institutional investors in the IPO. By doing so, the underwriter syndicate makes a firm commitment to the company that it will buy all the shares offered in the IPO. The discount can be viewed as compensation for bearing the risk that comes with this firm commitment: the underwriter syndicate runs the risk of ending up owning the shares should it fail to resell all the

34 Bancel and Mittoo (2009).

shares to investors. The benefit of the firm commitment for the company is that it is guaranteed to receive the net proceeds of the IPO.

The lead manager then conducts a valuation of the company using Discounted Cash Flow (DCF) analysis, comparable firm values and the valuations of comparable transactions and IPOs. This valuation is based on information supplied by the issuing firm and due diligence by the investment bank. Issuing firms are known to comment on the bank's input parameters or findings, or to bring up specific valuation approaches.[35] Based on this valuation exercise and market conditions, the lead underwriter and issuing firm determine a price range for the shares. For example, Just Eat, the venture capital-backed online takeaway food delivery service founded in Denmark in 2001, was the first ever to join the London Stock Exchange's special 'high-growth' segment with a price range of between 210 pence and 260 pence per share.

After determining the price range, the marketing of the IPO starts in earnest. The lead underwriter and the company's management go on a 'roadshow' to market the shares to large institutional investors. These institutional investors indicate how many shares they would like to buy at what price. This allows the underwriter to build an electronic order book (hence the name 'bookbuilding' is given to this process) of indications of interest from investors and the prices they are willing to pay for the shares. This enables the lead underwriter (also called 'bookrunner') to set a final IPO price based on observed investor demand.[36] The final IPO price is generally set only a few days before the first trading day. The final IPO price does not need to be within the initial price range. Should there be heavy demand for the shares, the final price can be above the upper boundary of the initial price range. In the example of Just Eat, the shares were priced at the top of its price range at 260 pence per share. If there is weak investor demand, the final price can be set below the lower boundary of the initial price range, but it is more likely that the IPO will be withdrawn. In the United States, during the period 1980–2016, the final offer price was set within the initial price range in 51 per cent of cases; in 22 per cent of cases it was set above the upper bound, and in 27 per cent of the cases it was set below the lower bound of the price range.[37] However, in Europe it is very rare for IPOs to be priced outside the initial price range, possibly because European underwriters are less flexible than their US counterparts and think that it scares off investors or, in the case of a price above the upper bound of the range, leads investors to reduce the number of shares they are interested in buying.[38]

---

35 Van den Assem *et al.* (2016).
36 There are also other ways of pricing IPOs. It is possible to price IPOs using auctions (e,g., an auction was used in the Google IPO) or use fixed-price offerings where the price is set by the underwriter and company without first formally collecting indications of interest from investors. However, the book building procedure is by far the most used method to price IPOs worldwide.
37 See the data of Professor Jay Ritter on his website. See https://site.warrington.ufl.edu/ritter/ipo-data/
38 Van den Assem *et al.* (2016).

Most IPOs are oversubscribed multiple times. This means that more shares are demanded by investors than there are for sale. As a result, investors do not get allocated all the shares they asked for. IPOs typically consist of two tranches: an institutional investor tranche and a retail investor tranche. Most of the shares go to institutional investors. Lead underwriters tend to use their discretion by giving more favourable allocations to repeat buyers of IPO shares, investors that have submitted larger bids and investors that have submitted bids via them rather than other members of the underwriter syndicate.[39] After the shares start trading on the stock market, the underwriter syndicate may buy back shares at the IPO price in attempt to stabilize the stock price for weak IPOs that are trading below their IPO price during the first trading month. Pre-IPO owners tend to be subject to lock-up agreements that do not allow them to sell their remaining shareholdings in the firm for a certain number of months and, in the case of some European exchanges, for several years after the IPO. For example, in the Just Eat IPO the company and its selling shareholders were subject to a 180-day lock-up period and director shareholders subject to a lock-up of 360 days following the IPO date, during which they were not allowed to sell shares without the consent of the lead underwriters Goldman Sachs and J.P. Morgan Cazenove.

17.4.3   Three Anomalies Associated with IPOs

There are three anomalies associated with IPOs: IPOs are underpriced, are associated with long-term underperformance and there are 'hot issue' periods when many firms decide to go public. This section discusses each of these three anomalies in turn.

Underpricing

The average first-day return on IPO stocks is positive. This phenomenon is called underpricing: IPO shares are sold at an IPO price which is, on average, 15 per cent below the market price on the first day of trading. This implies that the issuing company leaves money on the table and incurs an indirect cost when deciding to go public. Ex post it could have sold its shares at a higher price. Figure 17.4 shows the average underpricing per year in the United States for the period from 1980 up to and including 2016.[40] It shows that underpricing occurs in every single year but varies over time, ranging from an average of 3.6 per cent in 1984 to an average of 71.1 per cent at the height of the Internet bubble in 1999. From 1980–89, the average underpricing equalled 7.3 per cent, increasing to 14.8 per cent in the period 1990–98, and peaking during the Internet bubble

---

39 Jenkinson and Jones (2003).
40 Professor Jay Ritter offers IPO data on his website. See https://site.warrington.ufl.edu/ritter/ipo-data/

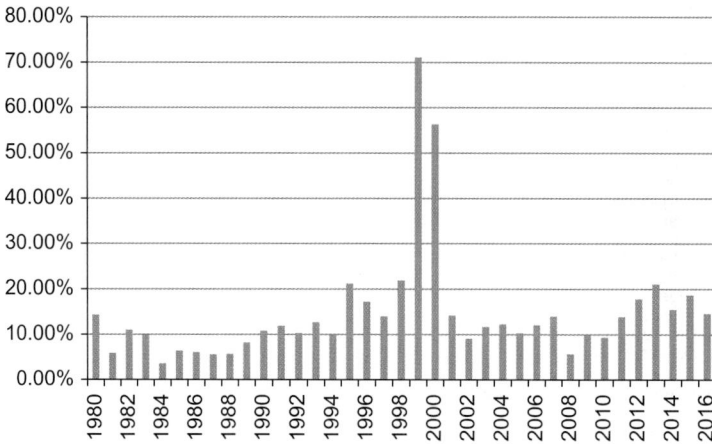

Figure 17.4 Average underpricing per year in the United States, 1980–2016.
Source: Based on data from Professor Jay Ritter available at: https://site.warrington.ufl .edu/ritter/ipo-data/

years of 1999 and 2000 at 64.5 per cent, falling back to 14 per cent in the 2001–16 period. During the entire period of 1980–2016, underpricing averaged 17.9 per cent.

Figure 17.5 shows the average level of underpricing in 51 countries around the world. It shows that underpricing occurs in all countries.

Underpricing is thus a very widespread and persistent phenomenon. What explains the existence of underpricing? Many possible explanations have been proposed. One explanation is that underpricing compensates investors for the risks associated with investing in IPO shares. Uninformed investors, in particular, might be subject to a 'winner's curse'. Let's look at a simple numerical example in which the participation of uninformed investors is required to be able to sell the shares on offer. A company decides to offer 100 shares to the public in its IPO. The value of the shares is either €120 (with 50 per cent probability) or €80 (with 50 per cent probability). There are two types of investors: (1) uninformed investors who apply for 100 shares if the price is fair and zero otherwise, and (2) informed investors who apply for 50 shares if the price for the shares is less than €120 if they know the value of the company to be €120, and zero otherwise. If there is demand from both uninformed and informed investors there will be pro-rata allocation. Should 150 shares be demanded (100 shares from uninformed investors and 50 from informed investors) and only 100 shares be on offer, each investor will receive two-thirds (=100/150) of the shares they asked for. The price for the shares is determined by a fairness condition for uninformed investors (who need to participate in order for the 100 shares on offer to be sold). Uninformed investors do not want to lose money investing in the IPO. If the value of the shares is €120, the informed investors will also apply and the uninformed investors will only receive two-thirds of the shares they demanded.

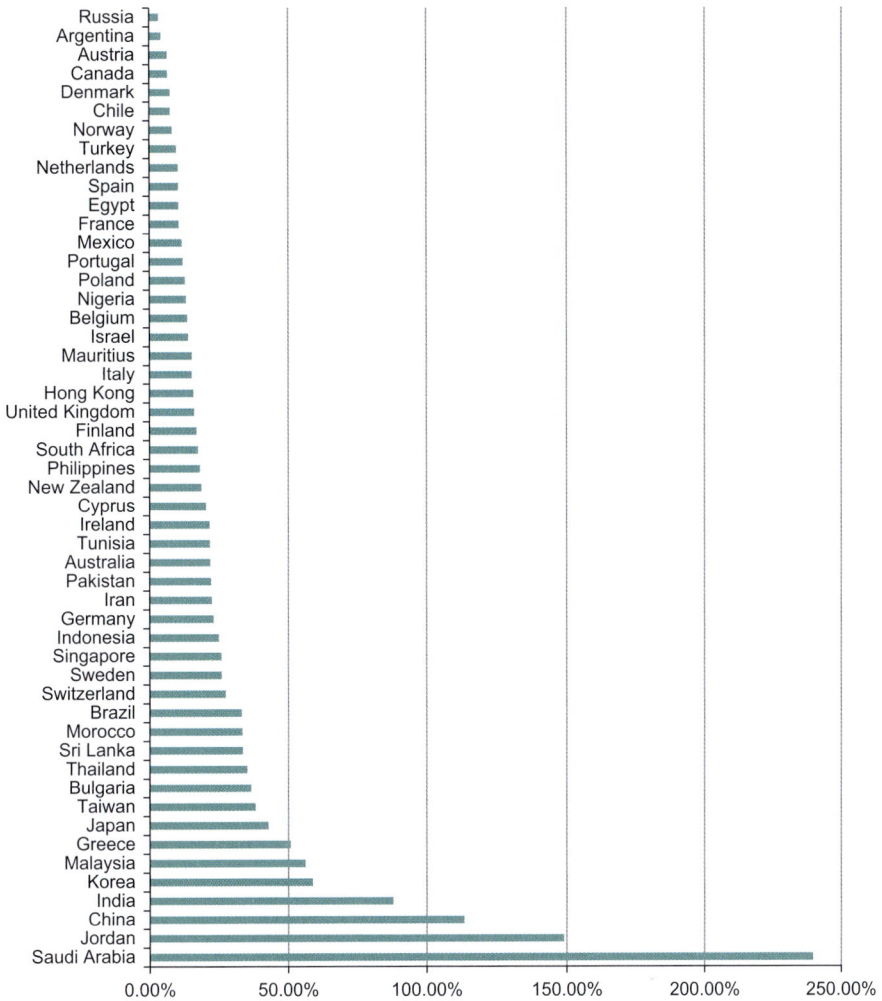

Figure 17.5 Average level of underpricing in 51 countries.
Source: Based on data from Professor Jay Ritter available at: https://site.warrington.ufl
.edu/ritter/ipo-data/

Uninformed investors would then earn $2/3 \times (120{-}P)$ where P denotes the IPO price. If the value of the shares is €80, the informed investors stay out of the market and the uninformed investors get a full allocation and end up buying all 100 shares. In that case, uninformed investors earn $1 \times (80{-}P)$ with P denoting the IPO price. Each of these two scenarios would occur with 50 per cent probability and therefore the expected return for the uninformed investors is denoted as: $0.5 \times 2/3 \times (120{-}P) + 0.5 \times 1 \times (80{-}P)$. In order for uninformed investors to participate in the IPO, this expected return needs to be at least zero. Solving for P shows that the expected return is zero or positive when the IPO price equals at most €96. As a result, the shares need to be underpriced in order to encourage the uninformed investors to participate. They are not sold at the expected value of €100 (=0.5×€80+0.5 ×€120) but at the lower price of €96.

Other explanations suggest that underpricing exists to compensate investors for truthfully revealing their demand for shares in the bookbuilding procedure, or to attract more investors and improve liquidity after the IPO, because it helps to create more news coverage or analyst following for the company and, finally, because the price discount makes it easier for investment banks to sell the IPO shares to investors. Brau and Fawcett (2006) asked CFOs of companies in the United States why they thought underpricing exists. They answered that under-pricing exists to compensate investors for taking the risk of the IPO, to enable the underwriter to curry favour with institutional investors and to ensure a broad ownership base and after-market liquidity. When asked how the level of underpricing might be reduced, the CFOs answered that this could be done by having strong historical earnings, hiring a reputable investment bank to act as the underwriter of the IPO, committing to a longer lock-up period during which the pre-IPO owners are not allowed to sell the shares, or hiring a reputable Big 4 auditor to audit the firm's financial statements.[41]

Long-term Underperformance

In the longer term, IPO stocks suffer from underperformance. Ritter (1991) shows that IPOs in the United States significantly underperform when compared with a set of comparable firms during the three years after going public. A buy and hold strategy of investing in IPO stocks would have left an investor with 83 cents on every dollar invested three years later. The underperformance of IPO stocks has been documented in many other countries since then. For example, underperformance has been found in Australia, Austria, Brazil, Canada, Chile, Finland, Germany, Japan, the Netherlands and the United Kingdom.

There are number of explanations for long-term underperformance. Long-term underperformance can be attributed to overoptimistic investors initially overestimating the probability of 'finding the next Microsoft' and overpaying for the shares at the time of the IPO. Firms take advantage of this window of opportunity and go public at times when investors are overoptimistic. This gets corrected over time. Ritter (1991) indeed finds that companies that go public during such 'hot issue' periods are the ones that perform the worst. Another explanation is that the underperformance can be attributed to the size and book-to-market ratios associated with IPO firms. Brav and Gompers (1997) found that underperformance is not so much an IPO effect: similar sized and book-to-market firms that have not issued equity perform just as poorly. Another explanation for underperformance is that there is a divergence of opinion between investors. Optimistic investors buy shares in the IPO whereas pessimistic investors stay out of the market because of short-selling constraints.

41 Brau and Fawcett (2006).

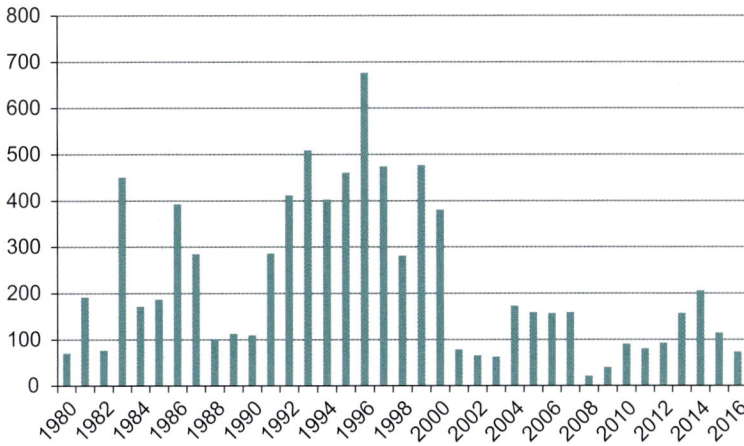

Figure 17.6 Number of IPOs per year in the United States, 1980–2016.
Source: Based on data from Professor Jay Ritter available at: https://site.warrington.ufl.edu/ritter/ipo-data/

It is difficult to sell IPO shares you do not own, or to borrow IPO shares from other investors to sell them with the idea of buying them back later at a lower price. As more information becomes available over time and short-sale constraints become less binding, the divergence of opinion narrows and the stock price starts to decline to more realistic levels. Houge *et al.* (2001) find that proxies for divergence of opinion are associated with poor long-term performance of IPOs. However, Edwards and Weiss-Hanley (2010) show that short selling in IPOs is not as restricted as previously believed.

'Hot Issue' Periods

The number of firms going public fluctuates over time. Figure 17.6 shows the number of firms going public in the United States from 1980 up to and including 2016. The figure shows that the number of IPOs peaked in the period 1996–2000 but has, since then, dropped substantially (also see Section 17.2 on changing exit landscapes). Lowry (2003) tries to understand these fluctuations in the number of IPOs. She develops three hypotheses. First, more firms might go public when general economic conditions improve because they need capital (capital demand hypothesis). Second, adverse selection costs of issuing equity might change over time. Companies might postpone going public at times when information asymmetry problems are severe (information asymmetry hypothesis). Third, firms might go public during periods when overoptimistic investors over value shares (investor sentiment hypothesis). Lowry (2003) finds that more firms go public at times when the aggregate demand for capital is high and investors are eager to buy shares.

17.4.4   The Role of Venture Capitalists in IPOs

The IPO offers venture capitalists and other pre-IPO investors the opportunity to sell part of their shares at the time of the IPO. However, they are only able to sell part of their shares this way. Should they completely cash out, this would send a negative signal to the investors who are considering buying shares in the IPO. It would prompt the question of whether better-informed pre-IPO owners are jumping a sinking ship. Pre-IPO investors, therefore, tend to lock-up their remaining shares and promise not to sell these shares for some time after the IPO. In the United States, the lock-up is typically 180 days (6 months) but in European countries the lock-up period can last for several years. The IPO is therefore a partial exit at best, and existing owners will have to hold onto their shares until the lock-up agreement expires and they are free to sell their shares in the open market. As previously discussed, this is one of the reasons that venture capitalists only exit their most promising ventures via IPOs. They have to continue to hold on to their shares for some time afterwards. Venture capitalists, therefore, have a vested interest in making the IPO a success, and their reputation can help to certify firm quality and lower the indirect cost of underpricing.[42] They can also use their networks to link the company to top underwriters. However, younger venture capitalists, trying to build their reputation through grandstanding, are associated with higher underpricing than established, more reputable venture capitalists.[43] In more recent periods, it has also been shown that venture capital backing and a better reputation are associated with higher not lower levels of underpricing.[44]

The reputation of the venture capitalist is also of significance after the IPO. Krishnan et al. (2011) show that US IPO firms backed by more reputable venture capitalists are associated with better long-run performance. More reputable venture capitalists also continue to be actively involved in the corporate governance of the firm in the post-IPO period. Bessler and Seim (2012) find that venture-backed IPOs in Europe outperform non-venture-backed IPOs. However, when venture capitalists decide to sell after the lock-up has expired, or start distributing the shares they own to their limited partners (who can then decide themselves whether or not to sell the shares), this is typically greeted with a negative stock price response. Also, in the months after the stock distribution to limited partners, stock returns continue to be negative, suggesting that venture capitalists use inside information to time stock distributions.[45] These effects are mitigated when the firm is brought public by a top underwriter or when the venture capitalist has a better reputation.[46]

---

42 Megginson and Weiss (1991).
43 Gompers (1996).
44 Lee and Wahal (2004).
45 Gompers and Lerner (1998).
46 Lin and Smith (1998).

17.5   Recent Developments: Changing Exit Markets

There have been several recent developments that have impacted exit markets (most notably IPO markets) in the United States and Europe. In this section, we will discuss these recent changes.

17.5.1   The Changing Exit Landscape in the United States

The United States remains by far the largest exit market in the world. However, it has lost some ground compared to the early 2000s, since which time countries around the world have improved their entrepreneurial ecosystems and exit markets. Financial globalization, in particular, has helped countries to increase their IPO activity, both in terms of numbers and deal volumes. The United States has not seen the same level of benefit from financial globalization and has lost market share, especially in the market for small firm IPOs.[47] The Jumpstart our Business Act (JOBS) of 2012 has, with some success, tried to turn this trend around in recent years, and the number of IPOs of small firms, in particular, has recovered somewhat.[48] However, US IPO activity remains far below what it was in the 1980s and 1990s, and never fully recovered after the burst of the technology bubble in 2000. During the years 1995–2000, IPOs accounted for more than half of the exits of US venture capitalists, dropping to less than 5 per cent in 2008–9.[49] This may be seen as a cause for concern because, at least traditionally, the IPO market is viewed as a key driver of venture capital investment.[50] Moreover, a well-functioning IPO market allows investors to at least partially exit their investment and use the freed-up money for reinvestment in other venture capital funds and thereby new ventures.

17.5.2   The Changing Exit Landscape in Europe

The decline in small firm IPO activity is not purely a US phenomenon but is also occurring in Europe. Axelson and Martinovic (2015) show that the probability of exit via an IPO has gone down in Europe as well as the US, whereas the

---

47 Doidge *et al.* (2013) show that the drop in US IPO activity is largely caused by the rise of global IPOs in which there is both a domestic and a foreign tranche of shares available (international IPOs) or only a foreign tranche of shares and no domestic tranche of shares (foreign IPOs). They show that the decline in US IPO activity cannot be attributed to a decrease in the economic importance of the United States. Also, more strict disclosure regulations in the United States in the early 2000s (the Fair Disclosure Act of 2000 Sarbanes Oxley (SOX) Act of 2002) cannot explain the drop in small firm IPO activity since it was already abnormally low in the period before these laws came into force.

48 Dambra *et al.* (2015) show that the introduction of the JOBS Act in 2012 increased the number of small firm IPOs in the United States. During the two years after the JOBS Act ending March 2014 IPO volume and the fraction of small firm issuers was at the highest level since 2000 but still far removed from the IPO volume observed in the 1980s and 1990s.

49 Ball and Smith (2011).

50 Black and Gilson (1998).

probability of exit via acquisition has remained stable over time. In Europe, despite the advent of junior stock markets aimed at small firms, small firm IPO activity has been sluggish since the technology bubble burst in 2000. Worsening market conditions, as a result of the financial crisis of 2008 and the Eurozone crisis of 2011, have added to the decline in European IPO activity. Ritter *et al.* (2013) showed that the number of small firm IPOs in Europe has declined over time and that small IPO firms are underperforming, have difficulty in staying profitable and have a higher likelihood of being acquired after going public when compared to large IPO firms in Europe. Many of the junior stock market segments targeted at small and medium-sized firms are struggling or have closed their doors. Only the lightly non-EU regulated Alternative Investment Market (AIM) of the London Stock Exchange is generally considered a success. From its launch in 1995 until April 2017, 3,052 UK companies and 665 international companies listed their shares on AIM, raising more than £42 billion. However, small companies that go public on AIM sell their shares exclusively to institutional investors, and shares in these firms are only thinly traded on the stock market after the IPO. This makes it more similar to a private placement market.[51]

17.5.3   What Explains the Recent Shifts in Exit Landscapes?

There are several explanations for the decline in the number of small firm IPOs. First, several large technology firms, including Google, Facebook and Apple, are acquiring smaller technology firms. As a result, these smaller technology firms no longer go public. They prefer to be bought by larger firms that can help to expedite product launches and realize economies of scope.[52] Business angels prefer acquisition exits for the same reason.[53] Second, firms can raise large amounts of capital privately nowadays in 'private IPOs', sometimes reaching $1 billion or even higher valuations in investment rounds (the so-called 'unicorn' firms). Examples of these privately-held unicorn firms include Uber, Xiaomi, Spotify and Airbnb. These firms can postpone going public for as long as private equity and other institutional investors are willing to continue to finance them privately. Venture capital-backed companies that went public in 2016 had a median time to exit (measured from their initial venture capital funding) of 8.3 years, a 13-year record high.[54] However, sooner or later, investors

---

51 Vismara *et al.* (2012).
52 Gao *et al.* (2013) show that, in contrast to popular belief, the decline in the number of small firm IPOs is difficult to explain by regulatory overreach (e.g. the Sarbanes Oxley (SOX) Act of 2002). Instead, they show that the decline in the number of small firm IPOs results from a structural change where these firms need to become part of larger organizations in order to bring their products to market faster, scale up production and enjoy economies of scope. Also see www.sec.gov/info/smallbus/acsec/hutchinson-goodwin-presentation-acsec -021517.pdf
53 Carpentier and Suret (2015).
54 National Venture Capital Association (2017: 30).

in unicorn firms will also look to exit from their investment. The structural decline in IPO activity in both the United States and Europe reinforces the dominance of acquisitions as an exit route for investors.[55]

KEY TAKEAWAYS

- Investors in entrepreneurial companies are buy-and-sell investors. After having invested in the company for a number of years, they are looking to harvest (or exit) their investment.
- There are three generic exit routes: (1) Initial Public Offerings (IPOs), where part of the shares are sold to the general public and the shares are listed on the stock market, (2) acquisitions (trade sales), where all shares are sold to another company, and (3) buyouts, where new investors, employees or management purchase the shares held by current investors.
- Acquisition exits are the most prominent exit route both in number and volume of exits. The recent decline in the number of firms going public has tilted the exit landscape even further towards acquisitions.
- Timing the exit is complex and depends on the success of the venture and market conditions. Investors that engage in intense monitoring of the companies they invest in or have pre-planned exit strategies tend to achieve faster exits.
- There seems to be an exit pecking order among investors, where they prefer to exit their most profitable investments via IPOs above acquisitions or buyouts. The worst investments get written off.
- Each of the different exit routes has its own pros and cons.
- Information asymmetries in exit markets influence the choice of exit route and determine whether or not a full exit can be made. It is also possible to explore two exit routes simultaneously or sequentially in so-called dual-track sell-outs.
- Initial Public Offerings (IPOs) offer a partial exit opportunity for investors. However, going public is also a major milestone in the life of the portfolio firm. It allows the company access to public capital markets and increases its visibility. However, going public gives rise to direct and indirect IPO costs and ongoing disclosure requirements that comes with being a publicly listed company.

END OF CHAPTER QUESTIONS

1. Since the early 2000s, the number of small companies going public has declined both in the United States and in Europe. What explains this development?
2. What factors influence exit timing decisions?

---

55 Félix *et al.* (2013); Chaplinsky and Gupta-Mukherjee (2013).

3. Initial Public Offerings (IPOs) are often thought of as the 'silver bullet'. Why are the best-performing investments exited via IPOs?
4. Young venture capitalists try to establish their reputation via 'grandstanding'. Explain what the phenomenon of grandstanding entails.
5. Why are some investors better at making exit decisions than others?
6. What are the pros and cons of an IPO versus an acquisition from the perspective of the entrepreneur?
7. What are the advantages of dual-track sell-out strategies?
8. Describe the steps in the going public process.
9. What is underpricing? What are the potential explanations as to why underpricing occurs?
10. Describe how IPOs are a partial exit mechanism for investors. What happens to their remaining shareholdings after the IPO?

FURTHER READING

Axelson, U. and Martinovic, M. (2015). European venture capital: Myths and facts. Working paper, London School of Economics.

Giudici, G. and Roosenboom, P. (eds.) (2004). *The Rise and Fall of Europe's New Stock Markets*. Elsevier.

McKaskill, T. (2009). *Invest to Exit: A Pragmatic Strategy for Angel and Venture Capital Investors*. Breakthrough Publications.

Ritter, J. R. (2003). Differences between European and American IPO markets. *European Financial Management*, 9, 421–434.

REFERENCES

Achleitner, A-K., Braun, R., Lutz, E. and Reiner, U. (2012). Venture capital firm returns from acquisition exits. Working paper, Technische Universität München and Heinrich-Heine Universität Düsseldorf.

Axelson, U. and Martinovic, M. (2015). European venture capital: Myths and facts. Working paper, London School of Economics.

Ball, E. R. and Smith, R. L. (2011). Can VCs time the market? An analysis of exit choice for venture-backed firms. *Review of Financial Studies*, 24, 3105–3138.

Bancel, F. and Mittoo, U. R. (2009). Why do European firms go public? *European Financial Management*, 15, 844–884.

Bayar, O. and Chemmanur, T. J. (2011). IPOs versus acquisitions and the valuation premium puzzle: A theory of exit choice by entrepreneurs and venture capitalists. *Journal of Financial and Quantitative Analysis*, 46, 1755–1793.

Bernstein, S., Giroud, X. and Townsend, R.R. (2016). The impact of venture capital monitoring. *Journal of Finance*, 71, 1591–1622.

Bessler, W. and Seim, M. (2012). The performance of venture-backed IPOs in Europe. *Venture Capital*, 14, 215–239.

Black, B. S. and Gilson, R. J. (1998). Venture capital and the structure of capital markets: Banks versus stock markets. *Journal of Financial Economics*, 47, 243–277.

Bottazzi, L., Da Rin, M. and Hellmann, T. (2008). Who are the active investors? Evidence from venture capital. *Journal of Financial Economics*, 89, 488–512.

Brau, J. C. and Fawcett, S. E. (2006). Initial Public Offerings: An analysis of theory and practice. *Journal of Finance*, 61, 399–436.

Brau, J. C., Francis, B. and Kohers, N. (2003). The choice of IPO versus takeover: Empirical evidence. *Journal of Business*, 76, 583–612.

Brau, J. C., Sutton, N. K. and Hatch, N. W. (2010). Dual-track versus single-track sell-outs: An empirical analysis of competing harvest strategies. *Journal of Business Venturing*, 25, 389–402.

Brav, A. and Gompers, P. A. (1997). Myth or reality? The long-run underperformance of Initial Public Offerings: Evidence from venture and non venture capital-backed companies. *Journal of Finance*, 52, 1791–1821.

Carpentier, C. and Suret, J-M. (2015). Canadian business angel perspectives on exit: A research note. *International Small Business Journal*, 33, 582–593.

Chaplinsky, S. and Gupta-Mukherjee, S. (2010). Exit returns and venture capital investment opportunities. Working paper, University of Virginia and Loyola University Chicago.

Chaplinsky, S. and Gupta-Mukherjee, S. (2013). The decline in venture-backed IPOs: Implications for capital recovery. In M. Levis and S. Vismara (eds.), *Handbook of Research on IPOs* (pp. 35–56). Edward Elgar Publishing.

Cumming, D. J. and Johan, S. A. (2008). Preplanned exit strategies in venture capital. *European Economic Review*, 52, 1209–1241.

Dambra, M., Field, L. C. and Gustafson, M.T. (2015). The JOBS Act and IPO volume: Evidence that disclosure costs affect the IPO decision. *Journal of Financial Economics*, 116, 121–143.

Dimov, D. P. and Shepherd, D. A. (2005). Human capital theory and venture capital firms: Exploring 'home runs' and 'strikeouts'. *Journal of Business Venturing*, 20, 1–21.

Doidge, C., Karolyi, G. A. and Stulz, R. M. (2013). The U.S. left behind? Financial globalization and the rise of IPOs outside the U.S. *Journal of Financial Economics*, 110, 546–573.

Edwards, A. K. and Weiss-Hanley, K. (2010). Short selling in Initial Public Offerings. *Journal of Financial Economics*, 98, 21–39.

Félix, E. G. S., Pires, C. P. and Gulamhussen, M. A. (2013). The determinants of venture capital in Europe: Evidence across countries. *Journal of Financial Services Research*, 44, 259–279.

Félix, E. G. S., Pires, C. P. and Gulamhussen, M. A. (2014). The exit decision in the European venture capital market. *Quantitative Finance*, 14, 1115–1130.

Gao, X., Ritter, J. R. and Zhu, Z. (2013). Where have all the IPOs gone? *Journal of Financial and Quantitative Analysis*, 48, 1663–1692.

Giot, P. and Schwienbacher, A. (2007). IPOs, trade sales and liquidations: Modelling venture capital exits using survival analysis. *Journal of Banking & Finance*, 31, 679–702.

Gompers, P. A. (1996). Grandstanding in the venture capital industry. *Journal of Financial Economics*, 42, 133–156.

Gompers, P. A., Kovner, A. and Lerner, J. (2009). Specialization and success: Evidence from venture capital. *Journal of Economics and Management Strategy*, 18, 817–844.

Gompers, P. A. and Lerner, J. (1998). Venture capital distributions: Short-run and long-run reactions. *Journal of Finance*, 53, 2161–2183.

Hochberg, Y.V., Ljungqvist,A. and Lu, Y. (2007). Whom you know matters: Venture capital networks and investment performance. *Journal of Finance*, 62, 251–301.

Houge, T., Loughran, T., Suchanek, G. and Yan, X. (2001). Divergence of opinion, uncertainty, and the quality of Initial Public Offerings. *Financial Management*, 30, 5–23.

Invest Europe. (2016). *2015 European Private Equity Activity: Statistics on Fundraising, Investments & Divestments*. Invest Europe.

Jenkinson, T. and Jones, H. (2003). Bids and allocations in European IPO bookbuilding. *Journal of Finance*, 59, 2309–2338.

Krishnan, C. N. V., Ivanov, V. I., Masulis, R. W. and Singh, A. K. (2011). Venture capital reputation, post-IPO performance, and corporate governance. *Journal of Financial and Quantitative Analysis*, 46, 1295–1333.

Lee, P. M. and Wahal, S. (2004). Grandstanding, certification, and the underpricing of venture capital backed IPOs. *Journal of Financial Economics*, 73, 375–407.

Lerner, J. (1994). Venture capitalists and the decision to go public. *Journal of Financial Economics*, 35, 293–316.

Lin, T. H. and Smith, R. L. (1998). Insider reputation and selling decisions: The unwinding of venture capital investments during equity IPOs. *Journal of Corporate Finance*, 4, 241–263.

Lowry, M. (2003). Why does IPO volume fluctuate so much? *Journal of Financial Economics*, 67, 3–40.

Mason, C. M. and Harrison, R. T. (2002). Is it worth it? The rates of return from informal venture capital investments. *Journal of Business Venturing*, 17, 211–236.

Mantecon, T. and Thistle, P. D. (2011). The IPO market as a screening device and the going public decision: Evidence from acquisitions of privately and publicly held firms. *Review of Quantitative Finance and Accounting*, 37, 325–361.

McKaskill, T. (2009). *Invest to Exit: A Pragmatic Strategy for Angel and Venture Capital Investors*. Breakthrough Publications.

Megginson, W. L. and Weiss, K. A. (1991). Venture capitalist certification in Initial Public Offerings. *Journal of Finance*, 46, 879–903.

National Venture Capital Association(2017). *NVCA 2017 Yearbook*. National Venture Capital Association.

Ritter, J. R. (1991). The long-run performance of Initial Public Offerings. *Journal of Finance*, 46, 3–27.

Ritter, J. R., Signori, A. and Vismara, S. (2013). Economics of scope and IPO activity in Europe. In M. Levis and S. Vismara (eds.), *Handbook of Research on IPOs* (pp. 11–34). Edward Elgar Publishing.

Ruhnka, J. C. (1992). The 'living dead' phenomenon in venture capital investments. *Journal of Business Venturing*, 7, 137–155.

Van den Assem, M. J., van der Sar, N. L. and Versijp, P. J. P. M. (2016). CEOs and CFOs on IPOs: The process and success of going public. Working paper, VU University Amsterdam, Erasmus University Rotterdam and University of Amsterdam.

Vismara, S., Paleari, S. and Ritter, J. R. (2012). Europe's second markets for small companies. *European Financial Management*, 18, 352–388.

Let's Practise: Case Study

Going IPO Challenges: Candy Crush Saga

On 26 March 2014, King Digital Entertainment went public on the New York Stock Exchange (NYSE). The company was founded in Sweden in 2003 and is the developer of the popular mobile game 'Candy Crush Saga'.

King and early investors, like the private equity firm Apax Partners, intended to sell 22.2 million shares, which would, at the offer price of $22.5, raise just under $500 million and value the company at $7 billion. J.P. Morgan Securities, Credit Suisse Securities and Bank of America Merrill Lynch were acting as the lead book-running managers.

Just hours after pricing, investors lost interest. The stock started trading on the NYSE at $20.5 but then took a dive of almost 16 per cent and closed at a price of $19 on the first day of trading. This turned the IPO of King into a horror story and was one of the worst stock market debuts in 2014.[56] Also, King's competitor, Zynga, maker of the 'Farmville' digital game, saw its shares drop 4 per cent on the same day.

Questions for Discussion

1. What might explain the poor stock market debut of King Digital Entertainment?
2. King Digital Entertainment is an Ireland-registered company founded in Sweden in 2003. Why would a European technology firm opt to go public abroad on the NYSE?
3. King's stock market debut is the exception to the rule. On average, IPOs are underpriced and the market price on the first day of trading is above the offer price. This represents an indirect cost of going public. For example, in the case of Snap Inc., the creator of the popular Snapchat messaging app, its stock market debut in 2017 was a success: the company priced its shares at $17 per share and ended up at $24.48 on the first day of trading (a first-day return of 44 per cent). In retrospect, most companies that go public could therefore have sold their shares in the IPO at a higher price. Why are owners of companies such as Snap Inc. not concerned about leaving so much money on the table?

---

56 See www.cnbc.com/2014/03/26/candy-crush-maker-king-digital-ipo-opens-2050-below-pricing.html

18 THE FUTURE OF ENTREPRENEURIAL FINANCE

LUISA ALEMANY

ESADE Business School

JOB J. ANDREOLI

Nyenrode Business University

This final chapter provides a perspective on recent developments in entrepreneurial finance and how it might evolve in the coming years. The future is, of course, anybody's guess. However, by re-examining the key variables and assessing the impact of their most plausible development, insights can be gained as to the different directions that entrepreneurial finance might take.

The landscape of entrepreneurial finance has changed profoundly in recent years. This change results not only from the decrease in interest rates and the global financial crisis, but seems to be more structural. Since the early 2000s, new sources of funding have arisen, the funding process has changed and the traditional providers of funding have found new players to compete with. However, when we look more closely at these changes, the development of entrepreneurial finance turns out to be shaped to a large extent by a limited number of key drivers, such as technological development and regulatory change. These drivers will keep on shaping society in general and entrepreneurial finance in particular, impacting markets worldwide. It is the push and pull of new avenues that foster entrepreneurial initiatives and their funding.

VIEW FROM THE MEDIA

FINANCIAL TIMES   FT

Cryptocurrency boom upends venture capital

VC investors face a conundrum as money floods into speculative bubble

JANUARY 25, 2018 BY RICHARD WATERS

It is a truism of the venture capital world that even the best ideas can be spoilt with too much money. The extreme discipline needed to build a highly focused team goes out the window, and conflicting incentives creep in when instant riches are on the table.

So what happens when cryptomania invades venture capitalism? New tech projects that would once have struggled to raise a first round of $10m are suddenly awash in a tide of cash. Seven raised $100m or more last year, through what are known as initial coin offerings. The first mega-ICO is now under way in the $1.2bn sought by encrypted messaging app Telegram.

Like the dotcom bubble, most of the money pouring into ICOs will be wasted. But with the possibility that a handful of real businesses will survive to become the next Facebooks and Amazons, it is hard to stand on the sidelines.

This is a boom that should terrify venture capitalists. It has exposed shortcomings in both their funding models and their worldview. They were the ringmasters of the dotcoms: Sequoia and Kleiner Perkins were the only firms to put money into Google – a mere $25m – and rode it all the way to the top. Now, they are jostling for allocations like everyone else.

One sign of this is the revelation that three of Silicon Valley's top venture investors – Sequoia, Benchmark and Kleiner Perkins – are leading the charge into Telegram, with informal commitments of $20m each. Instead of equity, these firms – and other investors – are buying a currency whose value rests entirely on the promise that it will one day support a thriving digital economy inside Telegram.

From the point of view of a venture investor, attuned to backing new technologies, the crypto disruption always looked like a tech story. Blockchain technology offered the chance to build decentralised networks in most areas of the digital economy, circumventing traditional businesses.

The radical potential is still massively underestimated. Banks talk of blockchain technology as something to be tamed and turned into a tool for the back-office, much as the big media companies once saw the internet as merely a useful way to cut their distribution costs.

Ironically, because of the focus on the technology, many of Silicon Valley's top investors missed what has been the bigger short-term disruption: the creation of new money. Bitcoin was always something of a laughing stock in tech circles because of its rudimentary underpinnings: surely it would eventually fall apart, or be overtaken by something designed by serious technologists?

It has not happened that way, at least not yet. But even if bitcoin turns out to have staying power, it does not mean the world needs all (or, indeed, most) of the new cryptocurrencies, each one supporting a different piece of digital activity. Start-ups are not selling coins because they need to, but because it is the easiest way to tap into the flood of institutional money now pouring into crypto.

This has given rise to distortions best seen in the case of Ripple, a six-year old start-up building an interesting piece of technology to grease the wheels of international payments. The technology may or may not find a place in the banking world. A number of institutions have been kicking the tyres, though they have not implemented it yet.

But almost independent of the tech potential, Ripple's currency – called XRP – has taken on a life of its own. Speculators hoping it would become a new international reserve currency bid its value up to more than $100bn (it has since fallen back to about $50bn). No wonder enterprise software companies with staid business models that rely on monthly subscriptions are thinking again, and blockchains in 'verticals' from shipping to manufacturing supply chains are all the rage.

This has created a conundrum for venture investors seeking more than speculative crypto profits from the latest tech innovation. They still need to find – and invest in – real long-term businesses.

The best of these will build communities that unite their developers and wider groups of users in a shared interest. They will have a strong focus on good governance. They will provide real benefits to users and find ways to incentivise mutually reinforcing behaviours that are good for the health of the network, not just the promise of a get-rich-quick scheme.

And, like all valuable new businesses, they will take time to build – not that that will stop the growing speculative crypto bubble.

www.ft.com/content/aa7cd8b4-01ec-11e8-9650-9c0ad2d7c5b5

LEARNING OBJECTIVES

After reading this chapter you will be able to:

- Gain insights into the key drivers of change.
- Appreciate how these drivers have impacted the development of entrepreneurial finance.
- Review the emergence of new forms of financing and learn how providers of funding are changing.
- Understand the position and role of the European Union in these developments.
- Assess how market trends impact the development of the key actors.
- Make your own assessment of the promising future.

Where Are We Going Next?

This chapter looks at the status of the key variables that affect entrepreneurial finance. Predicting the future is far from easy. Even if we combine a description of what we know about entrepreneurial finance with specific perceived paths of development, the future remains an unknown quantity, but it *does* provide us with a point of departure for making more plausible predictions.

This chapter starts by reviewing the key moments in the history of private investments as analysed by the World Economic Forum. This assessment examines the development of private investment from the mid-twentieth century. By assessing these key moments, we can identify three drivers that have affected the development of private financing, namely, regulation, technology and market events. As part of these drivers, we will pay specific attention to the future development of European integration, as the realization thereof can be expected to affect investments and entrepreneurship quite significantly. The final two sections will review the effect of the drivers of change on sources of funding and examine particular trends. We will conclude by reflecting on these perceived changes and raising questions about how the drivers we have identified will continue to shape the future of entrepreneurial finance.

18.1   Key drivers shaping the past

There are several elements that have shaped the past and that will most likely influence the future. Since the mid twentieth century, the development of alternative forms of funding has accelerated. Some key moments in this development are provided by the World Economic Forum, as shown in Figure 18.1. In their broadest definition, alternative investment assets are identified as a non-traditional asset class.[1] However, systematic or scientific documentation of the European alternative finance market is lacking.[2]

As indicated in Figure 18.1, the key drivers of this development are regulatory changes, technological innovation and global market events.[3] These three factors drive the emergence of new capital sources:[4]

- Regulation: where regulation constrains a capital flow for which there is demand, a new source of capital will emerge to fulfil that demand.
- Technology: where technology enables new types of origination, investors will take advantage of those opportunities.
- Markets: changes in demand for capital; where capital destinations develop demand for new forms of funding, investors will innovate to meet it.

All these drivers have an impact, fostering a reaction, creating opportunities or closing doors, bringing new players in or feeding the market dynamics in some other way. The impact will be different for each financial source and application. For example, the enhanced regulatory demands on public companies have increased the number of companies that stay privately funded, thereby creating a higher demand for later-stage funding and the entrance of institutional investors into the area of entrepreneurial finance.[5] Also, the attention of regulators

1 Of which private equity, hedge funds (basically a fancy name for an investment partnership) and venture capital are the most prominent ones, according to World Economic Forum (2016).
2 Wardrop et al. (2015).
3 Footnote 1 in the visual indicates: The firms referenced here are illustrative examples – only space constraints prevent us from mentioning the many other outstanding firms that played important roles throughout the history of alternative investments.
4 Many firms played an important role in the development of alternative finance, the firms referenced here are merely illustrative examples.
5 World Economic Forum (2016).

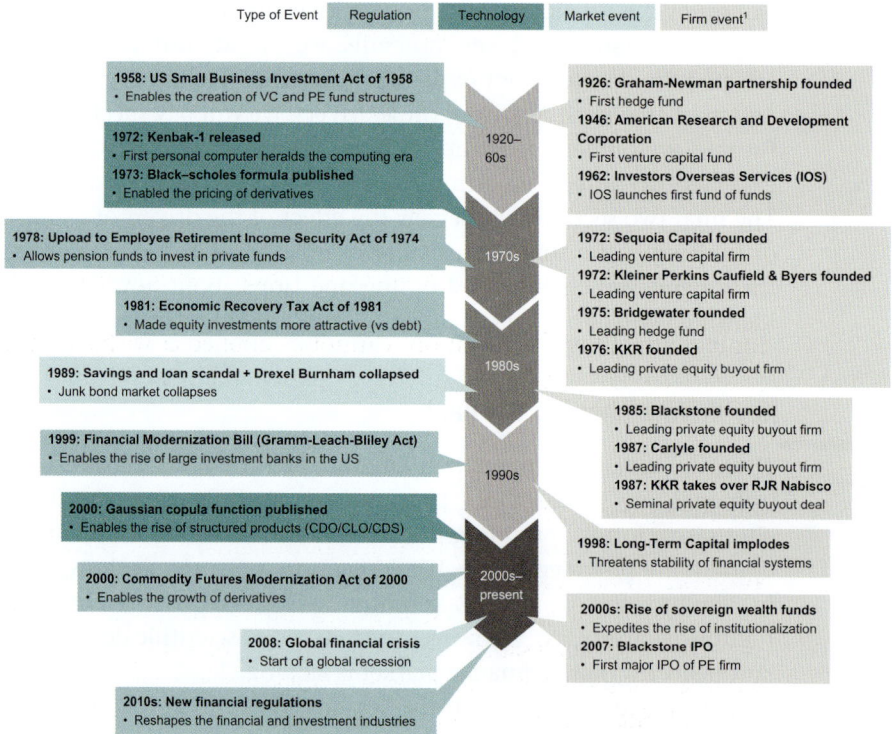

Figure 18.1 Key moments in the history of alternative investments.
Source: World Economic Forum (2016)[6]

has focused on decreasing the risk exposure of banks, creating the emergence of crowdfunding and peer-to-peer (P2P) lending for small businesses that lack the collateral or credit history to meet the requirements to access traditional bank lending.[7]

Changes affecting the European Union also form part of our assessment of the future of entrepreneurial finance (see Figure 18.2), with the extent to which Europe integrates having a potentially significant impact. For example, tariff and non-tariff barriers to trade and financing will arguably have an influence on whether and how ventures are stimulated and funded within the European Union. We will consider this driver in the development of entrepreneurial finance, in parallel with the drivers of regulation.

The key drivers that have shaped the past will arguably have an effect on the future need and ability of ventures to access financing. For a new venture, accessing capital is an essential ingredient of their journey towards growing their markets and consumers and accessing public capital markets. It is a phase in the lifetime of the venture to which the capital asset pricing model (CAPM) or

6 EU IPO Report (2015).
7 OECD (2015).

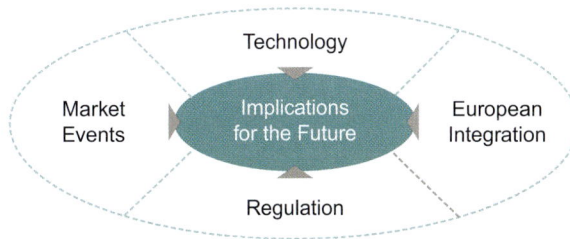

Figure 18.2 Areas likely to affect the future of entrepreneurial finance.

Modigliani Miller's proposition[8] cannot be applied as we haven't come close to perfect markets yet, but we still have financing needs.

18.2 Technology

Following the introduction of the personal computer and the subsequent ongoing improvements in processing power and storage capacity, data became available to analyse markets. Technology made it possible to record, track, move, warehouse and analyse large amounts of data that were previously not available nor analysable. Combining this processing power with insights obtained from academic discoveries enabled investors to more accurately assess and understand investment opportunities.

Technological developments have enabled the origination of new forms of funding, for example, crowdfunding, peer-to-peer lending facilities and mobile payments. Technology often not only enables the transaction itself but also assesses the conditions that justify the transaction (e.g. by carrying out a creditworthiness check). As such, emerging technologies facilitate the gathering, aggregation and analysis of information and also reduce the costs of participating in financial activities.[9]

Technology has proved to play a significant role in transforming finance. It has enabled new forms of funding while, at the same time, disrupting the business models of the traditional financial services industry. Fintech (abbreviation of 'financial technology') refers to all the technology that is used to support financial services. In essence, this has existed for many decades, but recent technological innovation has enabled fintech to do more than merely perform the back-office activities of financial transactions. Over the past decade, fintech innovators have emerged to provide alternative ways of venture funding through:[10]

- Providing highly focused products and services (e.g. UK-based venture Transferwise set up a network of bank accounts, making international payments faster, easier and cheaper).

8 Models used in corporate finance for assessing the expected risk premium. For more information see Principles of Corporate Finance (Brealey et al. 2017).
9 World Economic Forum (2015b).
10 McWaters (2015).

- Automating and commoditizing high-margin processes (e.g. Ginmon, a German initiative that uses 'robo-advisors' to provide wealth management services at a fraction of the cost, as such being able to provide finance to a population that does not meet the wealth management threshold).
- Using data strategically (e.g. UK-based FriendlyScore that assesses the credit-worthiness of individuals based upon their social networking patterns).
- Connecting buyers and sellers through platforms and being capital light (e.g. Lendix, a French marketplace lender that facilitates crowdlending for retail investors and small business owners).
- Leveraging the scale and services of incumbents (e.g. Zervant, a Finnish startup, that provides the SME customers of ING with an online invoicing solution).

A particularly useful lead development is the emergence of blockchain technology, as alluded to in the opening article of this chapter. Blockchain facilitates a globally distributed ledger that can register anything of value.[11] It is the technology that enables transactions to be recorded in an efficient and transparent way while also keeping a permanent record thereof. Communication is fully decentralized, meaning that all databases communicate with one another without having one central database. While users can opt to remain anonymous, each transaction is visible to anyone[12] and remains registered with a time-stamp in all databases. Figure 18.3 depicts the funding process using a blockchain.

Having this blockchain technology available enables parties to transact directly with one another, instead of needing to involve an intermediary (e.g. a bank or rating agencies) to verify their identities, establish trust or perform the necessary activities for completing a transaction (World Economic Forum 2015). Startups can benefit from this technology in a number of ways, all of which relieve them from using the 'man in the middle'. For example, in their quest to raise capital they can bypass valuators, auditors, lawyers and crowdfunding platforms and raise money directly in a peer-to-peer arrangement, using a global distributed share offering.

Blockchain is an example of how technology has enabled new forms of funding. The pace at which technology develops will influence the growth of funding sources and will thereby impact the financing options and funds available to ventures.

18.3   Market Events

The two specific market events mentioned in Figure 18.1 both proved to have been driven by debt market failure. The first occurred in the 1980s, after the junk bond market grew exponentially, at an annual rate of 34 per cent with returns of

---

11 Tapscott and Tapscott (2017).
12 Public or private, dependent upon the blockchain settings.

How a blockchain works

1 A wants to send money to B

2 The transaction is represented online as a 'block'

3 The block is broadcast to every party in the network

4 Those in the network approve the transaction is valid

5 The block then can be added to the chain, which provides an indelible and transparent record of transactions

6 The money moves from A to B

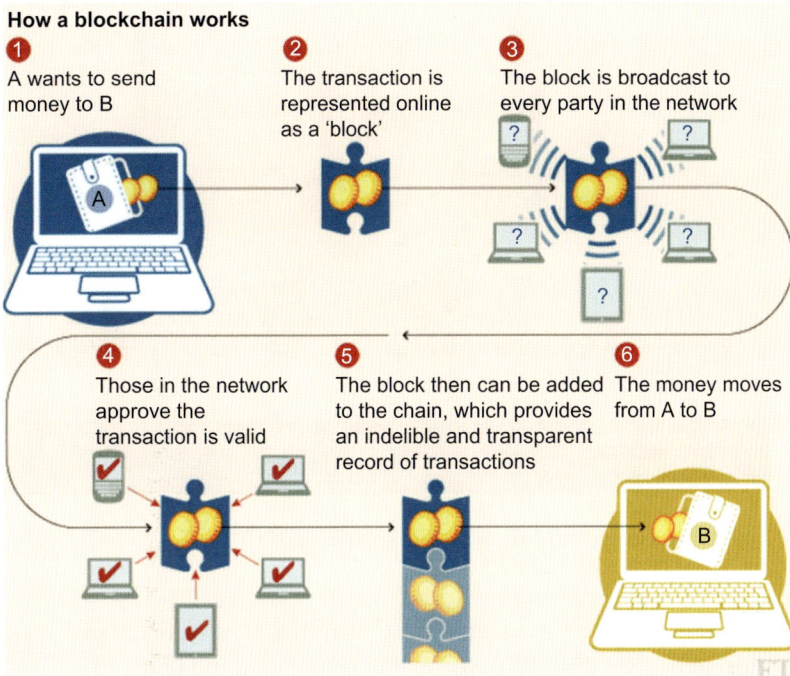

Figure 18.3 How a blockchain works.
Source: Financial Time (2015)[13]

just under 14 per cent. Then, in 1989, a political movement caused the market to temporarily collapse.[14] The second occurrence was the global financial crisis of 2008, which started after the bankruptcy of Lehman Brothers led to a collapse of the real estate market, spreading to the money market, first in the United States and then in Europe and the rest of the world.[15]

Looking at more recent developments, using technology to involve the crowd proved to be of great benefit to new ventures. Crowdfunding is more than just a means of financing ventures as it also allows investors and the public to assess the potential of an initiative. This form of entrepreneurial finance was introduced in the early years of the twenty-first century and gained ground quickly. As well as allowing for more than just funding, crowdfunding also comes in different forms to suit different funding objectives and requirements of the venture. Exact data on the size of the crowdfunding industry remains difficult to obtain, but its growth is exponential (doubling in size every year in Europe). In 2015, crowdfunding reached an estimated volume of $34 billion worldwide,

13 Derived from 'How will blockchain technology transform financial services?' in the *Financial Times*, 3 November 2015.
14 For more information, see 'The Collapse of Drexel Burnham Lambert; Key Events for Drexel Burnham Lambert' (*The New York Times*, 14 February 1990).
15 The Economist (2013).

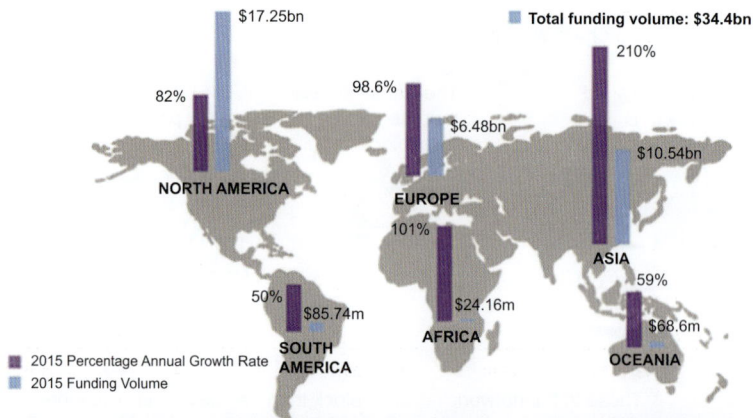

Figure 18.4 Crowdfunding size and growth (2015).[16]
Source: Massolution (2015)

and was expected to overtake VC funding in size in 2016.[17] The size[18] and growth of crowdfunding worldwide is provided in Figure 18.4.

Another key variable pertaining to market events is the recent development in interest rates. Following the financial crisis, the European Central Bank (ECB) decreased the interbank interest rates. For the public this decreases the costs of capital on both equity and debt. At the same time, as we will see in Section 18.4, the Basel Committee for Banking Services increased the amount of capital that financial institutions are required to retain to reduce the risk of an institute failing going forward. Figure 18.5 shows the decline in interest rates since mid 2007. The interest rate decrease was introduced to avert the risk of an economic depression and to counter the risk of deflation.

So while the decreased interest rate made it less expensive to borrow money, the increased capital and liquidity requirements for financial institutions have made it more expensive for them to hold risky assets on their books. This has made it more difficult for SMEs to obtain loans from banks.[19]

18.4   Regulation

Regulation relates to the legal infrastructure that is created and that has a potential impact on new ventures. In general, policymakers have paid more

16 Including P2P/Marketplace Lending as a form of crowdfunding really inflates these statistics, as it consists of 71% of the total, and most companies in the P2P/Marketplace Lending space would not consider themselves to be involved in crowdfunding. Though even without P2P, $10 billion is still an impressive figure (Massolution 2015).
17 Massolution (2015).   18 The realized volume turned out to be €34.44 billion in 2015.
19 World Economic Forum (2015a).

EUROPEAN CENTRAL BANK | BENCHMARK RATE

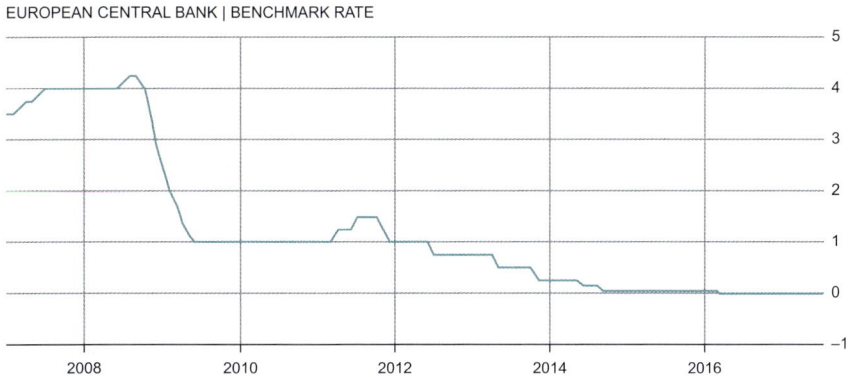

Figure 18.5 Development of European Central Bank interest rate.
Source: Tradingeconomics.com | European Central Bank, (2017)

attention to measures affecting the supply of financing (e.g. tax incentives for investors) than on the demand-side (e.g. coaching of entrepreneurs).[20] The European Commission (EC), however, addresses both, with the aim of decreasing tariff and non-tariff trade barriers in order to grow accessible markets. The effect of this is that ventures are able to promote and sell their offerings beyond national borders to a larger number of customers. On the other hand, decreasing trade barriers also increases competition.[21]

In Europe, 99 per cent of all businesses are SMEs[22] and they are responsible for creating 85 per cent of new jobs and provide two-thirds of total private sector employment. The EC recognizes that SMEs and entrepreneurship are key for ensuring economic growth, innovation, job creation and social integration in the EU.[23]

In view of this contribution, the EC stimulates entrepreneurship, through:

- Creating a business-friendly environment.
- Promoting entrepreneurship.
- Improving access to new markets and internationalization.
- Facilitating access to finance.
- Supporting SME competitiveness and innovation.
- Providing key support networks and information for SMEs.

The EC also recognizes that access to finance is the most pressing issue for many small enterprises. To support growth of SMEs, the EC works on:

- Improving the financing environment.
- Providing information on funding.

20 OECD (2015).   21 Smallbone et al. (2012).
22 Defined by staff headcount < 250 and turnover $\leq €50$ million or balance sheet total $\leq €43$ million (in European recommendation 2003/361).
23 European Commission (https://ec.europa.eu/growth/smes_en).

- Strengthening businesses' rights to prompt payment.
- Accessing finance supported by the EU by means of the single portal on Access to Finance.

Examples of the regulatory impact of the EU on alternative forms of funding are, e.g.:[24]

- The European venture capital funds (EuVECA) regulation.
- The alternative investment fund managers (AIFM) directive.
- The European social entrepreneurship funds (EuSEF) regulation.

The efforts of the EU to harmonize rules and regulations has decreased barriers to trade. However, although the UK is planning to leave the EU and thereby regain sovereignty over its rulemaking, changes in the law are unlikely to sustain their ability to trade freely with the EU.[25]

Another initiative to drive harmonization has been led by the Basel committee. This committee sets standards for the banking sector worldwide. Although the Basel committee does not have the authority to enforce its recommendations in national laws, most EU member countries, and some other countries too, tend to quickly implement the Committee's policies.

The extent to which the European Union develops and operates as a single market, without tariff and non-tariff trade barriers, will have a significant effect on the availability of funding and the ability of ventures to operate cross-border. So far, however, the practices of SME financing sources have not yet proven to be homogeneous across Europe.[26]

18.5 Development of Funding Sources

The consequences of these drivers of change have a comparable outcome: traditional players find themselves flanked by new entrants providing products and services that are either complementary to traditional offerings (such as late-stage venture funding) or in direct competition (such as private debt lending). These outcomes impact key stakeholders in different ways:[27]

- Investors:

  - New players increase competition and drive existing investors to consolidate and differentiate their offering.
  - New types of destinations for capital become available to investors offering different return profiles.

- Society (broader economy and the public): increased funding for entrepreneurs and businesses generally results in more economic activity.

---

24 European Commission (ec.europa.eu/info/business-economy-euro/growth-and-investment/investment-funds_en).
25 Battie (2017).
26 Moritz et al. (2016).
27 World Economic Forum (2016).

As discussed in Part I, new forms of funding have emerged over recent years. The new players are not drivers of change but the consequence of a development in society and the means available. They are attracted to the market as the result of a development, meaning that they can offer a new service or the same service better or cheaper, as result of the drivers identified in Section 18.1.

The emergence of new players and forms of funding provides new opportunities for both investors and entrepreneurs. Along with the already available sources, their form is equity or debt and the investment may be complemented by the active involvement of the investor in the venture. Certainly, the new players have introduced new approaches and business models to funding. While traditionally the focus of investors was purely on obtaining a financial gain, some of these new players aspire to non-financial goals, such as political or social achievements.[28]

How the drivers of change we have identified in this chapter will develop is anybody's guess. The insights we have provided into the existing sources of funding and their potential development does not provide us with conclusive evidence on which to base our predictions about the future. Nonetheless, the data we have gathered does provide some indicators about the future of entrepreneurial finance and thereby allows us to ask better-educated questions.

The following sub-sections will provide an initial assessment of the consequences of the drivers for change on the sources of funding. They also raise questions pertaining to both the development of funding sources and to other aspects of entrepreneurial finance. So, without pretending to offer a complete and comprehensive vision of the future, we provide some pointers as triggers for further discussion.

18.5.1   Incubators, Accelerators and Crowdfunding

Perceived Development

Incubators help aspiring entrepreneurs in the process of developing their proposition and setting up their venture. This form of process support offers the basic facility, simulates peer feedback and provides the opportunity to use its network of former entrepreneurs and corporate partners. Incubators truly nurture the aspirations of their participants and provide a stepping-stone for materializing the venture. The number of incubators has grown as well as their tendency to include traits that are typically associated with accelerators.

Accelerators have proved to be a popular support mechanism for entrepreneurs, allowing them to further develop their ventures and obtain a 'stamp of approval' by associating with an accelerator that has enabled successful ventures in the past. It also has a 'spillover' effect for the community that it is part of. The trend for accelerators is to become increasingly competitive to enter, as can be witnessed by

28 Block *et al.* (2017).

the large number of applicants and the growing scale of their initiatives. Likewise, the number of accelerators has grown strongly, giving rise to the question of whether they will be able to attract the skilled mentors that are so key to their success and who prove their value through the ventures that they support.

Crowdfunding offers a number of different ways in which to gain venture funding, which depend upon the purpose of the crowdfunding campaign, the product of the venture and the goal of the entrepreneur. In this respect, it provides a wide variety of funding possibilities with a relatively low access threshold. The concept of involving a crowd to fund a new venture is gaining interest, not only as form of funding but also for sensing initial market traction. In some cases, follow-on investors will require the setting up of a crowdfunding campaign as a mean of identifying the market interest for a specific offering.

The size and sophistication of companies that use crowdfunding has also increased. The development of equity crowdfunding has also triggered more mature companies to launch crowdfunding campaigns, i.e. companies in the growth stage instead of only the seed stage.[29] This indicates that crowdfunding is more and more considered a viable alternative to other sources of funding. Venture Capital funds and other professional investors are also increasingly investing in crowdfunding campaigns. As regards equity crowdfunding, 14 per cent of startups had this type of institutional involvement in 2016 and this figure is expected to increase.[30] These investors also add value post-funding through their network and expertise. We may increasingly see these equity crowdfunding campaigns led by a professional investor who provides trust to the valuation and who manages the smaller investors.

New crowdfunding funds are emerging, allowing investors to back groups of projects in specific categories instead of focusing on an individual project. Investors partner with a crowdfunding platform to have a seat in the 'first row' on performance indicators, enabling them to select initiatives with potential for further investment.

Questions about the Future

Aspiring entrepreneurs and business partners seem to be increasingly interested in joining incubators. At the same time, the incubators are increasingly adopting some of the traits of accelerators in their quest for venture success, in order to enhance the reputation of the incubator. The question is to what extent incubators will remain a proving ground for aspiring entrepreneurs or whether they will steadily adopt more traits typical of an accelerator.

As interest has grown in participating in accelerators, on the part of both entrepreneurs and corporate partners, the supply of accelerators has grown, inducing the accelerators to specialize in a particular niche. It is uncertain how

29 Based on UK market (Beauhurst 2017).
30 *Financial Times* (16 March 2017).

close the ties between the accelerators and their corporate partners will become, which would have implications for the involvement of the corporate partners in the accelerators' initiatives.

For crowdfunding, the key question is around the development of regulation, within nations and across Europe. Current campaigns have proved to be almost completely confined to national boundaries and the legislation differs from country to country. On a European level, there is no legal framework for crowdfunding.

Crowdfunding is still in its early days. As a result, the track record of equity-based crowdfunding platforms is limited, as an exit typically takes some five years from the launch of the venture. The question for now is whether the ventures that have been funded through equity crowdfunding will deliver on their promise.

18.5.2   Business Angels

Perceived Development

Business angels are private individuals who have largely gained their wealth by being successful entrepreneurs themselves. They are often referred to as 'informals', and finance more ventures than institutional investors with yet smaller amounts. As discussed in Chapter 3, business angels are involved early on in the seed phase of funding and provide so-called 'active money': besides contributing the financial means with which to grow the venture, they are actively involved in supporting the venture through their expert advice and by offering access to their networks.

Analysis of this type of investor reveals that they provide a form of funding that produces less of a scattered effort.[31] It has changed from being a largely invisible activity for entrepreneurs to a system of organized and managed angel groups. The consequence is that these groups have become more professional, sharing their insights and improving their expertise. As a result, they take a more formal approach to valuation and selection. Moreover, as a group, they have a greater investment capacity, enabling them to engage in follow-on investing after the very early stages and to become involved in more and larger deals.

Questions about the Future

Business angels are increasingly organizing themselves – targeting a specific segment, stage or other criterion that they deem of interest – in managed angel groups. Besides decreasing their search costs and allowing them to develop their specific contribution, this increases the funds they have available to support the growth of the ventures that they support. The question is whether the

31 Mason (2017).

benefits of this association will outweigh the possible downside, i.e. whether their size and learning will lead to a 'herd effect' that points to a decreasing diversity in investment approach and a reduction of conventional support for new ventures. Moreover, the introduction of managed angel groups may lead to a greater distance between the investor and the entrepreneur, thereby increasing both the duration of the investment process and the agency costs, giving rise to the question whether the benefits of joining forces outweigh its costs.

Governments recognize the pivotal role that business angels and business angel networks play in growing new ventures. It is, however, unclear how the supporting role of governments, and the European Union in particular, will evolve going forward. How will they, besides tax incentives and co-investment funds, further stimulate the effectiveness of business angels and business angel networks across Europe and create a level playing field?

If the recognition of governments and their support for the grouping of angels is forthcoming, this leads to the question whether business angels will retain their focus on the seed stage or expand it to include more of the growth stage too. If so, they could potentially become competition for VC, which increases the pressure on the added value they need to provide. So, teaming up and professionalizing in the seed stage is already on the cards (European Commission on Business Angels), but will that provide them with an equally compelling proposition to thrive in the growth stage?

18.5.3   Venture Capital, Private Equity and Corporate Venture Capital

Perceived Development

The venture capital and private equity industry in Europe is growing; however, it still lags behind Israel and the United States. As well as being investors, VC and PE funds share many characteristics of the entrepreneurial firms they invest in, as they also need to obtain funding and establish a reputation in the market. In terms of making investments, VC and PE do their best to attract the most successful entrepreneurs to support the funding of ventures.

Overall, Corporate Venture Capital (CVC) investments in Europe made up 6 to 23 per cent of total VC investments in the years 2007 to 2015.[32] The patterns in CVC in Europe are different to those in the United States. While US CVCs tend to get involved in the later stages of venture development, European CVCs investments are more likely to occur in earlier stages due to institutional arrangements.[33]

Venture capital funds tend to compete in increasingly specialized fields, yet on a more global scale. They find themselves in increasing competition with other forms of funding, both in the venture investment and harvesting stages. In the seed stage, new sources of funding, such as incubators, accelerators and

32 EVCA Annual reports, in Block et al. (2017).
33 Colombo and Shafi (2016).

crowdfunding, have emerged and business angel networks have begun to grow their investment size. In the growth and harvesting stages, other funding forms come into play earlier on, such as IPOs, Joint Ventures and Mezzanine Debt. The emergence of new forms of funding, as well as new types of investors, is forcing VC to develop alternative proposals.[34]

Questions about the Future

Europe reveals a growth in VC activity and unicorns. In parallel, the traditionally well-developed VC areas, such as the United States and Israel, show ongoing growth. Given the globalization of VC activity, the question is whether European VC funds will be able to compete adequately with the more established funds abroad.

Equity crowdfunding is rapidly gaining ground. This allows ventures to gather funds without the need to qualify for other forms of early-stage funding or accept the disciplining role of VC funds. While the very early stage of many ventures might not currently be of interest to VCs, the question is whether VCs can match the benefits of crowdsourcing, i.e. sensing the market through building a network and engaging the public. Early research indicates signs of VC and BA adopting crowdfunding.[35]

Competition for VC seems to increasingly come from business angel networks as well. These networks have professionalized and have access to larger amounts of funding. The question is whether VC funds can leverage their capabilities and position themselves to counter the pressure from the extension of other forms of early-stage funding.

In later-stage ventures, VC funds will experience more pressure from PE funds. As the latter leverage their equity investment in LBOs and thereby benefit from the low interest rates, their expected return on capital can be lower as well. Despite having a number of differences, in e.g. funding size and stake in the venture, the question is how VC and PE will divide up the market.

Private equity is particularly challenged by public sentiment in Europe. The question for VC and PE is how the public perception of them will develop over the coming years. In many instances, their involvement is currently perceived as merely benefiting shareholder value, often at the expense of other stakeholders (e.g. employees), while stakeholder value is the prevalent perspective throughout continental Europe. The question is whether the public sentiment can be changed, thereby decreasing the pressure for national protective legislation.

Corporate Venture Capital (CVC) is still quite small-scale in Europe, as opposed to e.g. the United States.[36] From an entrepreneur's perspective, the

34 Lerner (2017).
35 Colombo and Shafi (2017).
36 CVC activity grew on a quarterly basis during 2016. The top-ranking CVC in Europe, Siemens Venture Capital, ranked 16th amongst the most active global CVCs in 2016 (CBInsight 2017).

arguments for searching for a CVC-partner are mixed, including both positive (e.g. extension of network and improved reputation by association) and negative (e.g. decreased agility through lengthier decision-making processes within corporates) aspects. Likewise, from the corporate's perspective, involvement with a startup has positive (e.g. increased feeling for innovations in the market) and negative (e.g. reputation damage should the venture not succeed) aspects. It is unclear whether European corporates will build up their CVC-funds and involve themselves in the venture investment scene while learning from their mainly US counterparts to avoid the typical pitfalls.

18.5.4 Public Sources of Funding

Perceived Development

A combination of the perceived importance of startups for the economy and innovation and the challenges they face in raising funding has lead the European Commission to address this issue in their Horizon 2020-report and COSME projects. Hence, the EC actively supports SMEs and startups in its many programmes by providing grants, loans and guarantees as a limited partner or through their fund of funds.

The EC also supports startups in other ways, e.g. by facilitating networks of entrepreneurs throughout Europe. The EC's involvement mainly centres around three pillars: actions to encourage a bottom-up movement with a strong brand, support activities to strengthen the connectedness and quality of the ecosystem and direct or indirect funding.

For this purpose, the EC dedicated a significant budget to its Horizon 2020 and European Structural and Investment Funds (ESIF). The Horizon 2020 programme has a budget of €80 billion to promote the commercialization, uptake of innovation and support to bring innovation to life. The ESIF dedicates €110 billion to innovation activities, ICT and SME competitiveness.[37]

Questions about the Future

The question of to what extent public sources of funding in Europe can create a level playing field for startups is particularly relevant. This question pertains to both the harmonization of stimulation measures across Europe and the building up of local competencies that will benefit the single market best. So, while having significant budgets to hand, the question is how to avoid spreading European public sources too thinly across the countries and how to stimulate competition in the internal market without hampering early-stage entrepreneurial initiatives.

37 European Commission (ec.europa.eu/growth/industry/innovation/funding_en).

The effectiveness of funding ventures has proven to be higher when public sources of funding are complemented by private funding. The question is to what extent the European Commission will be able to sustain its level of investment while involving private funders in their Fund of Funds. Building an ecosystem in which private forms of funding reinforce one another across Europe is a challenge, for which clarification is needed going forward.

Besides supporting the development of entrepreneurship in the internal market, it is uncertain how the European Commission will facilitate access to finance to provide ventures with access to markets outside the EU.

18.6 Development of Funding and Growing Processes and Harvesting

Besides the changes taking place in funding sources, the drivers of change as mentioned in Section 18.1 will have an impact on the funding and growing processes of ventures, as well as on the alternative routes to entrepreneurship and their harvesting. All these processes have been assessed in Parts II–IV of this book.

As far as funding processes are concerned, the development of blockchain seems to be of particular interest. As this technology enables a shared general ledger, thereby providing a trusted common source, it increases transparency, allows for disintermediation and empowers its users. Because of its newness, the technology still needs to prove itself in the market and governments still need to adopt new legislation to covers its operation. So the question is whether it will actually prove to be able to deliver on its promise and how regulators will deal with it on a cross-national level.

Similarly, blockchain technology will potentially also impact the process of growing a venture. It reduces monitoring and agency costs by increasing transparency and the ability of all stakeholders to continuously monitor the development of the venture, and to keep records of its progress. The technology that facilitates this is the key driver, while regulation is of lesser impact as it largely involves questions of transparency and governance between the parties who are involved. The potential is there; the question is, to what extent the technology will be embraced by the market.

As far as entrepreneurship by acquisition and harvesting are concerned, a crucial variable in Europe will potentially be the public attitude towards maximizing shareholder value and its consequences for the other stakeholders. Furthermore, it is still uncertain whether governments will issue laws that limit the powers of shareholders to the benefit of the other stakeholders. On IPOs, the question remains whether the tightened reporting and disclosure requirements will remain or whether they might even be expanded.

Whilst this book discusses in some detail the development and importance of the various funding sources for growing ventures, there are clearly still many unanswered questions when it comes to 'connecting the dots' going forward.[38] Given the rapid development of entrepreneurial finance over the past decades, and the many variables affecting the availability of and applications for funding sources, we can be certain that the future will prove to be equally as dynamic and exciting!

KEY TAKEAWAYS

- Technology, regulation and market events have impacted the development of entrepreneurial finance in the past and are likely to continue to do so in the future.
- Blockchain offers great potential for significantly transforming transactions by enabling a distributed general ledger that is transparent and registers changes.
- The European Commission is aware of the importance of entrepreneurship and innovation and fosters it through funding and other supporting activities.
- The strengthened capital liquidity requirements for financial institutions make it especially difficult for SMEs to obtain loans from them.
- Developments in the drivers of change have impacted on funding sources, leading to the emergence of new sources and the repositioning of existing sources.
- Regulation and technology (especially blockchain) can be expected to affect the funding and growth processes of ventures.
- Public sentiment regarding the power of the shareholder at the expense of other stakeholders may lead to restraining regulatory pressure.
- The future of entrepreneurial finance proves to be dynamic and promising!

END OF CHAPTER QUESTIONS

1. How do you see the future for entrepreneurial finance?
2. Do any of the drivers of change give rise to new questions about the future?
3. Are there any drivers for change that should be added, or should any of the existing drivers be altered to obtain a better understanding of the development of entrepreneurial finance?
4. What new forms of funding have you encountered or do you expect to develop?
5. What is the role of European integration on entrepreneurship and funding thereof? Can you find evidence to support your view?

38 Reference to a speech made by Steve Jobs (Co-founder of Apple Inc) at the Stanford graduation ceremony in 2011 'You can't connect the dots looking forward; you can only connect them looking backwards. So you have to trust that the dots will somehow connect in your future. You have to trust in something – your gut, destiny, life, karma, whatever. This approach has never let me down, and it has made all the difference in my life.'

6. What role do you foresee for the early sources of funding in relation to the further development of institutional sources?
7. How might public sources of funding deal with their challenge of making it available where it is most effective for entrepreneurship and innovation?
8. How could 'smart contracts' affect the governance of ventures?
9. How do you think that impact investing may benefit from blockchain technology by enabling it to invest where it matters most?
10. How can initial coin offerings (ICOs) help entrepreneurs and investors to harvest?

FURTHER READING

Daniels, C., Herrington, M. and Kew, P. (2016). *Global Entrepreneurship Monitor Special Topics Report 2015–2016 Entrepreneurial Finance*. GEM.

Ferguson, N. (2009). *The Ascent of Money*. Penguin Books.

Kraemer-Eis, H., Lang, F., Torfs, W. and Gvetadze, S. (2016). *European Small Business Finance Outlook June 2016*, EIF Research & Market Analysis working paper 2016/35

Kraemer-Eis, H., Lang, F., Torfs, W. and Gvetadze, S. (2017). *European Small Business Finance Outlook June 2017*, EIF Research & Market Analysis working paper 2017/43

McCulley, P. (2009). *The Shadow Banking System and Hyman Minsky's Economic Journey*. PIMCO.

OECD-publications on *New Approaches to Economic Challenges* (www.oecd.org/naec).

Startup Europe *Partnership monitors* (www.startupeuropepartnership.eu).

World Economic Forum (2015). *Alternative Investments 2020*. WEF.

World Economic Forum (2015). *An Introduction to Alternative Investments*. WEF.

Zhang,B., Wardrop, R., Ziegler, T., Lui, A., Burton, J., James, A. and Garvey,K. (2016). *Sustaining Momentum, the 2nd European Alternative Finance Industry Report*, Cambridge Centre for Alternative Finance.

REFERENCES

Battie, A. (2017). Why the 'Brussels effect' will undermine Brexit regulatory push. *Financial Times*, 12 July.

Beauhurst (2017). *The Deal, Equity Crowdfunding in the UK*. Beauhurst.

Block, J. H., Colombo, M. G., Cumming, D. J. and Vismara, S. (2017). New players in entrepreneurial finance and why they are there. *Small Business Economics*, Doi 10.1007/s11187-016–9826–6.

CBInsight (2017). The 55 most active corporate VC firms globally (www.cbinsights .com/research/corporate-venture-capital-active-2014), 7 March.

Colombo, M. G. and Shafi, K. (2016). Swimming with sharks in Europe, when are they dangerous and what can new ventures do to defend themselves?. *Strategic Management Journal*, 37(1).

Colombo, M. G. and Shafi, K. (2017). When does reward-based crowdfunding help firms obtain external financing. Working paper.

Economist (2013). The origins of the financial crisis (www.economist.com/news/
schoolsbrief/21584534-effects-financial-crisis-are-still-being-felt-five-years-
article) 7 September.

European Commission on Business Angels, (ec.europa.eu/growth/access-to-finance
/funding-policies/business-angels_en).

European Commission on Investment Funds (ec.europa.eu/info/business-economy-
euro/growth-and-investment/investment-funds_en).

European IPO Task Force (2015). *EU IPO Report – Rebuilding IPOs in Europe Creating jobs
and growth in European capital markets*, 23 March.

Lerner, J. (2017). *The Demise of Venture Capital.* Harvard University and Private
Capital Research Institute.

Mason, C. (2017). *The changing nature of angel investing: Some research implications.*
Adam Smith Business School, University of Glasgow.

Massolution (2015). *2015CF Crowdfundig Industry Report*, 31 March.

McWaters, J. (2015). 5 ways technology is transforming finance. World Economic
Forum (www.weforum.org/agenda/2015/06/5-ways-technology-transforming-
finance), 30 June.

Moritz, A., Block,J. H. and A. Heinz, A. (2016). *Financing patterns of European SMEs:
An empirical taxonomy. Venture Capital*, 18(2), 115–148.

OECD (2015). *New Approaches to SME and Entrepreneurship Financing: Braodening the
Range of Instruments*, OECD.

Smallbone,D.,Welter,F. and Xheneti,M. (2012). *Cross-Border Entrepreneurship and
Economic Development in Europe's Border Regions*, Edward Elgar Publishing.

Tapscott,A. and D. Tapscott, D. (2017). How blockchain is changing finance. *Harvard
Business Review*, 1 March.

Wardrop, R., Zhang, B., Rau,R. and Gray, M. (2015). *Moving Mainstream, The European
Alternative Finance Benchmerking Report.* Cambridge Centre for Alternative
Finance.

Williams, A. (2016). Professional investors join the crowdfunding party. *Financial
Times*, 16 March.

World Economic Forum (2015). How will blockchain technology transform financial
services?,3 November.

World Economic Forum (2015a): *Alternative Investments 2020, Regulatory Reform and
Alternative Investments*, WEF.

World Economic Forum (2015b). *The Future of Financial Services*, WEF.

World Economic Forum (2016). *Alternative Investments 2020, The Future of Capital for
Entrepreneurs and SMEs*, WEF.

APPENDIX 1

Examples of Public Support for Entrepreneurship in Europe[*]

Startup Delta

Startup Delta is a not-for-profit public–private partnership created to support, connect and grow the startup community across the Netherlands, together with building connections outside of the country. The partnership was set up in 2014 and was given 18 months to create enough traction to be self-sustainable, which has been achieved.

They are now focused on building even stronger connections globally. One of the key supporters is Neelie Kroes, former EU commissioner for competition and the digital agenda, who became the special envoy for the partnership with the mission of promoting and growing the connections provided to startups in the partnership. This special envoy role has now been handed over to Constantijn van Oranje-Nassau to continue the work.

What Is Different about This Programme?

The partnership has managed to promote the Netherlands internationally as one hub rather than as individual cities. They have also managed to push forward a significant number of regulatory and policy-related actions that needed to be taken to create a more attractive startup environment.

Why Is It Efficient for Entrepreneurs?

The partnership's focus is on building connections and promoting the Netherlands as a whole, rather than simply increasing financing options for startups, as this is seen as the key to scaling up for startups.

Who Have They Helped?

- *Zerocopter.*
- *Takeaway.com.*
- *CryptTalk.*

---

[*] Isidro Laso, Head of Startups and Scaleups Sector (Startup Europe). DG CONNECT. European Commission.

- *App Annie.*
- *Vector Fabrics.*

La French Tech. A Movement Supported by Strong Branding

The French government set up La French Tech in November 2013 in order to develop tech startups in the country and to strengthen its international visibility in terms or startups and innovation in general.

What is Different about This Programme?

La French Tech is not primarily about providing public funds for entrepreneurs. La French Tech belongs to the community, and is a movement supported by strong branding. It also provides a one-stop-shop for all the services offered by France's ministries.

La French Tech has opened several offices around the world with the prime focus on supporting local French startups to grow and scale up. This support may be in the form of coaching, introductions, marketing and sales advice and also raising funding.

Why Is It Efficient for Entrepreneurs?

This support scheme promotes French startups around the world and is opening up new markets for innovative ventures.

Who Have They Helped?

- Deezer.
- Eventbrite.
- Feelunique.
- Lofty City.

Startup Ole

Startup Ole is a two-day international startup and ecosystem builders' event, organized annually in Salamanca, Spain. The format is now been extended to several countries across Europe and Latin America,but the Spanish event is the biggest one compared to the other European and Latin American events. This series of events across different countries and continents will favour the creation of a community across borders.

Startup Ole started as a university students' event for Salamanca University in 2013 and quickly expended to be one of the biggest events in southern Europe. The event now attracts entrepreneurs, investors and ecosystems builders from fifty different countries. It continues to be run by a broad base of volunteers.

What Is Different about This Programme?

Startup Ole is free of charge for startups and investors and is organized as a not-for-profit event by volunteers. Startup Ole is not only an excellent event for facilitating deals between startups and investors, but it also pays special attention to (aspiring) entrepreneurs who are not yet successful. In addition, it also includes a number of activities dedicated to ecosystem builders (accelerators, universities, investors, civil servants) at a European level.

Startup Ole takes place in a very attractive location, Salamanca, which provides an inspirational environment for closing deals between entrepreneurs and investors and for the development of new creative ideas to be launched jointly by ecosystem builders from different places across Europe. More than 700 one-to-one meetings between entrepreneurs and investors took place at the 2017 event using the Startup Ole app. Many more meetings and deals may take place spontaneously, because Salamanca is small enough to become a 'startup city' during the two days of the event which, in turn, ensures high levels of serendipity between the participants at the event.

Startup Ole has been the location of the development of many existing European activities, such as the European Startups Network, Startup Europe Latin America Network, Startup Europe China Network and Accelerators Assembly among others.

Why Is It Effective for (Aspiring) Entrepreneurs?

As part of the event, the volunteers vet those requesting to attend to ensure that the right mix of startups and investors are in attendance. In addition, the volunteers screen the participants in order to suggest face-to-face meetings between certain startups and investors. This proactive approach allows startups to connect with the right investor or ecosystem builder during the two-day event.

High-Tech Grunderfounds (Germany)

High-Tech Grunderfounds is a public–private venture capital investment firm based in Bonn, Germany. The fund provides early-stage seed investment up to market launch. High-Tech Grunderfounds will invest a maximum of €2 million per company and hold this investment for six years with a seven-year disinvestment period. High-Tech Grunderfounds has household names such as the KfW Banking Group, Robert Bosch, Daimier, Deutsche Telekom and RWE Inogy among its investors. The firm currently has over 430 companies in its portfolio with 60 exits already completed.

To be eligible for funding, the company must be classed as a technology-oriented business which is less than a year old and located in Germany. The company must have a promising idea/research that can be converted to a marketable product.

What Is Different about This Programme?

The fund allows very early-stage startups to develop their concept and bring their refined product to market with support and guidance from the fund. The fund stimulates the high-tech startup market and is available to sectors which private funds tend to see as higher risk and require capital investment from the start, such as life science and mechanical engineering.

Why Is It Efficient for Entrepreneurs?

This fund is one of the most active funds in Europe and it allows the public sector to use the private sector's expertise to invest in early-stage startups without taking unnecessary risks. The startups also have an opportunity to access funding in the early stages when funding can be crucial to their survival.

Who Have They Helped?

- *eWings.com.*
- *KonTEM.*
- RAIDBOXES.
- REBELLE.
- Trademob.
- Wunderlist.

APPENDIX 2

Typical Business Angel Term Sheet Clauses[*]

Clause	Sample Detail
Type of security:	Common or Convertible Preferred Stock (Series A)
Dividend:	6% non-cumulative
Conversion:	Preferred shares are convertible at any time to common shares at a conversion ratio of 1:1. Preferred shares are also convertible at an IPO of at least €X million.
Dilution protection:	Weighted average method. This method minimizes the loss of percentage of ownership of a company by an investor due to investments made by other investors in future rounds.
Voting rights:	One vote per share as if the Preferred Stock was converted to Common Stock. A two-thirds vote will be needed to amend the corporate by-laws, issue new stock, incur debt, sell the company or shut down the company.
Redemption:	Stock holder will have the right to force the company to buy back the shares after 6 years.
Registration rights:	If the company completes an IPO, shareholders will be able to register their shares for sale as allowed by law.
Pro rata share offers:	Investor can invest in future rounds of financing in order to retain the same percentage ownership in the company.
Board participation:	Investor will have one seat on the board of directors.
Conditions precedent:	Funding will occur only if due diligence is complete, all legal documents are signed and any special conditions requested by investor are met by the company.
Covenants:	Company management agrees to provide monthly status reports and make financial records available for inspection at any time. Company agrees to abide by all laws and maintain proper insurance.
Expenses:	Company pays for all legal and due diligence expenses regarding this financing round.
Use of proceeds:	Hire CFO and Sales Manager, buy inventory, pay off accounts payable, meet other working capital needs.

[*] Provided by Stefano Caselli.

APPENDIX 3

General Term Sheet

[Company]

Summary of Terms for Sale of Series Seed Ordinary Shares[*]

Company	[*Company*]
Founders	[*Founder 1], [Founder 2], & [Founder 3]*
Investors	[*Lead Investor*] (the '**Lead Investor**') in conjunction with other investors [*Additional Investors*] (the 'Investors') mutually agreeable to the Lead Investor and the Company.
Structure of Financing	The financing will be up to an aggregate of [___] at a fully diluted pre-money valuation of [___], including an unallocated employee share option plan ('**ESOP**') of [ ]%. The Lead Investor will invest up to [___] and would hold no less than [___]% of the Company on a fully diluted basis.
Conditions to Close	(i) completion of confirmatory due diligence and anti-money laundering checks (ii) all employees having entered into service agreements containing IP assignment provisions and (iii) receipt of all necessary consents.
Estimated Closing Date	[*Closing Date*].
Type of Security	Newly issued series seed convertible preferred shares ('**Seed Shares**'), which shall rank senior to all other shares of the Company in all respects [and be provided with the same rights as the next series of preferred stock (with the exception of anti-dilution rights).]
Liquidation Preference	Upon a liquidation, dissolution, winding up, merger, acquisition, sale, exclusive license or other disposal of substantially all of the assets or a majority of the shares of the Company (a '**Change of Control**'), *Option 1*: [the holders of the Seed Shares shall receive the higher of: (a) one times the original purchase price for the Seed Shares; or (b) the amount they

[*] The Seedsummit (www.seedsummit.org) initiative, a community of 30+ institutional and angel investors including founders, was spearheaded by Seedcamp, Europe's Seed fund. Term sheets for many other European countries can also be found on the Seedsummit. The UK Seedsummit documents were drafted by Tina Baker of JagShawBaker.

would receive if all shareholders received their pro rata share of such assets or proceeds.]

Option 2: [(a) the holders of the Seed Shares shall receive one times the original purchase price for the Seed Shares; and (b) all shareholders shall receive their pro rata share of any remaining assets or proceeds.]

[Anti-Dilution Provisions]   [In the event that the Company issues additional securities at a purchase price less than the current Series Seed Preferred conversion price, such conversion price shall be adjusted on a [___] basis.

The following issuances shall not trigger an anti-dilution adjustment: (i) securities issuable upon conversion of any of the Series Seed Preferred, or as a dividend or distribution on the Series Seed Preferred; (ii) securities issued upon the conversion of any debenture, warrant, option, or other convertible security; or (iii) Common Stock issuable upon a stock split, stock dividend, or any subdivision of shares of Common Stock; and (iv) shares of Common Stock (or options to purchase such shares of Common Stock) issued or issuable to employees or directors of, or consultants to, the Company pursuant to any plan approved by the Company's Board of Directors.]

Important Decisions   *Option 1*: [Certain important actions of the Company shall require the consent of the holders of a majority of the Seed Shares (a '**Seed Majority**') or the Seed Director, to include amongst others, actions to: (i) alter the rights, preferences or privileges of the Seed Shares (ii) allot any new shares beyond those anticipated by this investment (iii) create any new class or series of shares having rights, preferences or privileges senior to or on a parity with the Seed Shares (iv) increase the number of shares reserved for issuance to employees and consultants, whether under the ESOP or otherwise (v) redeem or the selling of any shares (vi) pay or declare dividends or distributions to shareholders (vii) change the number of board members (viii) take any action which results in a Change of Control (ix) amend the constitutional documents (x) effect any material change to the nature of the business or the agreed business plan (xi) subscribe or otherwise acquire, or dispose of any shares in the capital of any other company.]

Option 2: [The consent of the holders of a majority of the Seed Shares held by the Investors (an 'Investor Majority' shall be required for the important decisions, substantially in the form listed in Appendix [___]

Conversion

Each holder of Seed Shares shall have the right to convert its shares at any time into ordinary shares of the Company ('**Ordinary Shares**') at an initial conversion rate of 1:1, subject to proportional adjustment for share splits, dividends or recapitalizations [and any anti-dilution adjustments]. The Seed Shares shall automatically convert into Ordinary Shares if (a) a Seed Majority consents to such conversion or (b) upon the closing of a firmly underwritten public offering of shares of the Company.

Pre-emption

All shareholders will have a pro rata right, but not an obligation, based on their ownership of issued capital, to participate in subsequent financings of the Company (subject to customary exceptions). Any shares not subscribed for may be reallocated among the other shareholders. The Investors may assign this right to another member of their fund group.

Right of First Refusal and Co-Sale

The holders of the Seed Shares shall have a pro rata right, but not an obligation, based on their ownership of Seed Shares, to participate on identical terms in transfers of any shares of the Company, and a right of first refusal on such transfers (subject to customary permitted transfers, including transfers by Investors to affiliated funds). Any shares not subscribed for by the holders of Seed Shares would then be offered to the holders of Ordinary Shares.

Drag Along

In the event that a Seed Majority and the holders of a majority of the Ordinary Shares wish to accept an offer to sell all of their shares to a third party, or enter into a Change of Control event of the Company, then subject to the approval of the Board, all other shareholders shall be required to sell their shares or to consent to the transaction on the same terms and conditions, subject to the liquidation preferences of the Seed Shares.

Restrictive Covenants and Founders Undertakings

Each Founder will enter into a non-competition and non-solicitation agreement, and an employment agreement in a form reasonably acceptable to the Investors, and shall agree to devote their entire business time and attention to the Company and to not undertake additional activities without the consent of the Investors. A breach of any of the foregoing restrictive covenants or undertakings by a Founder shall result in immediate dismissal for cause of such Founder.

Founder Shares

Shares held by the Founders will be subject to reverse vesting provisions over three years as follows: [25% to vest one year after Closing and the remaining 75% to vest in equal monthly installments over the next following two years ('the **Vesting Period**').]

During the Vesting Period, any unvested shares shall be automatically converted to deferred shares, provided that if a Founder is a Bad Leaver [all shares held by that Founder shall convert to deferred shares.]

[After the Vesting Period, [a leaving Founder shall offer for sale to the Company (with a secondary purchase option for the holders of Seed Shares) [X %] of shares held (i) at fair market value if not a Bad Leaver, and (ii) at the lower of nominal value or subscription price if a Bad Leaver. The consideration to be received by a leaving Founder on an Exit will be capped at the value of the shares held by such Founder as of the date the Founder leaves.]]

[There shall be acceleration upon double trigger provisions so that if a Founder leaves after a Change of Control, unvested shares may become vested.]

Board of Directors

[The board of directors of the Company (the '**Board**') shall consist of a maximum of three members: the holders of Ordinary Shares may appoint two directors and the holders of Seed Shares may appoint one director.]

The Lead Investor may appoint a non-voting observer to attend meetings of the Board.

Information and Management Rights

The Lead Investor shall receive [weekly/monthly/quarterly] reporting and monthly financial information [and a management rights letter to satisfy its venture capital operating company requirements.]

Documentation and Warranties

Definitive agreements shall be drafted by counsel to the Lead Investor and shall include customary covenants, representations and warranties of the Company (which shall be liable up to a maximum of the investment amount) reflecting the provisions set forth herein and other provisions typical to venture capital transactions. The Founders will also complete a personal questionnaire.

Expenses

Option 1 [The Company shall pay the Lead Investor's fees and expenses in the transaction at Closing, anticipated not to exceed [£XX,000].]

Option 2 [Each party shall pay their own legal and other fees and expenses in the transaction. If the financing does not complete within 60 days or because the Company withdraws from negotiations (except as a result of the Lead Investor making a material change in the terms), the Company shall bear the Lead Investor's legal costs incurred to that date.]

Exclusivity

In consideration of the Lead Investor committing time and expense to put in place this financing, the Company and Founders agree not to discuss, negotiate or accept any proposals regarding the sale or other disposition of debt or equity securities, or a sale of material assets of the Company for 45 days from the date of the Company's signature below.

Confidentiality

The Company and Founders agree to treat this term sheet confidentially and will not distribute or disclose its existence or contents outside the Company without the consent of the Lead Investor, except as required to its shareholders and professional advisors.

Non-binding Effect

This Summary of Terms is not intended to be legally binding, with the exception of this paragraph and the paragraphs entitled Expenses, Exclusivity and Confidentiality, which are binding upon the parties hereto and shall be governed and construed in accordance with the laws of England and Wales.

Acknowledged and agreed:

[Lead Investor]	**[Company Name]**
	[Founder 1]
By:	
Print Name:	By:
Title:	Print Name:
Date:	Title:
	Date:
[Additional Investor]	
	[founder 2]
By:	
Print Name:	By:
Title:	Print Name:
Date:	Date:
	[founder 3]
	By:
	Print Name:
	Date:

Appendix A Capitalization Table

Shareholder	Class of Shares	No. of Shares.	Ownership (%)
[FOUNDER 1]	[Ordinary Shares]	•	•%
[FOUNDER 2]	[Ordinary Shares]	•	•%
[FOUNDER 3]	[Ordinary Shares]	•	•%
Lead Investor	[Ordinary Shares]	•	•%
Additional Investor	[Ordinary Shares]	•	•%
Option Pool	[Ordinary Shares]	•	•%
Total		•	**100%**

APPENDIX 4

Angel Term Sheet

[Company]

Summary of Terms for Sale of Series Seed Ordinary Shares[*]

Company	*[Company]*
Founders	*[Founder 1], [Founder 2],* & *[Founder 3]*
Investors	*[Lead Investor]* (the '**Lead Investor**') in conjunction with other investors (the "Investors") mutually agreeable to the Lead Investor and the Company.
Structure of Financing	The financing will be up to an aggregate of [___] at a fully diluted pre-money valuation of [___], including an unallocated employee share option plan ('**ESOP**') of []%. The Lead Investor will invest up to [___] and would hold no less than [___]% of the Company on a fully diluted basis.
	Note, DELETE on execution version: Each investor is limited to £100,000 in SEIS investment per year. Aggregate SEIS-qualified investment in a company cannot exceed £150,000 in any three-year period. Accordingly, should the aggregate amount of SEIS-seeking investment exceed £150,000, the SEIS-qualified amount for each SEIS investor shall be pro-rated based on his/her investment relative to the round. Two classes of ordinary shares will be issued, one for SEIS investment and the other for non-SEIS investment. For example, if Investor A is investing £50,000 in a £200,000 and all investors seek SEIS, Investor A will receive £37,500 (or 25% of the eligible £150 k) of SEIS shares and the balance, £12,500, in non-SEIS shares. Any division should be included in the term sheet.
Conditions to Close	(i) completion of confirmatory due diligence and anti-money laundering checks (ii) all employees having entered into service agreements containing IP assignment provisions (iii) receipt of all necessary consents

---

[*] The Seedsummit (www.seedsummit.org) initiative, a community of 30+ institutional and angel investors including founders, was spearheaded by Seedcamp, Europe's Seed fund. Term sheets for many other European countries can also be found on the Seedsummit. The UK Seedsummit documents were drafted by Tina Baker of JagShawBaker.

	[and iv) incorporation or re-incorporation in England.]
Estimated Closing Date	[*Closing Date*].
Type of Security	Ordinary Shares [to be issued in two series if EIS qualification is sought].
[EIS]	If requested, the Company will seek to qualify the investment under the Enterprise Investment Scheme.
[Priority Payment on Exit]	[Option 1: If S/EIS **not** enacted or enacted **only for some** of the investors, use for the non-SEIS seeking investors:]

[This provision [will only apply to the Lead Investor] [and] [will not apply to the SEIS Investors].] In the event of a (i) liquidation (ii) sale or (iii) exclusive license or other sale of substantially all of the assets of the Company (an 'Exit'), The [Lead] Investor[s] shall be entitled to receive the higher of:

(i) The financing of €XX,XXX (being the original purchase price paid by the Lead Investor) plus any declared but unpaid dividends; or

(ii) The Lead Investor's pro rata share, based on its ownership of the shares, of such assets or proceeds.

[*If SEIS enacted and SEIS investors excluded from the provision above:* This provision will apply only to the SEIS Investors. In the event of an Exit, the SEIS Investors shall be entitled to receive the investors' pro rata share of assets/proceeds.]

[Option 2: If S/EIS enacted for Lead Investor/all investors, use:]

In the event of an Exit, the Investors shall be entitled to receive the investors' pro rata share of assets/ proceeds.

Important Decisions

[Option 1]

[Certain important actions of the Company shall require the consent of the Lead Investor, to include amongst others, actions to: (i) alter the rights of the Ordinary Shares (ii) allot any new shares beyond those anticipated by this investment (iii) create any new class or series senior to the Ordinary Shares (iv) increase the number of shares reserved for issuance to employees and consultants, whether under the ESOP or otherwise (v) redeem or the selling of any shares (vi) pay or declare dividends or distributions to shareholders (vii) change the number of board members (viii) take any action which results in a Change of

Control (ix) amend the constitutional documents (x) effect any material change to the nature of the business plan (xi) subscribe or otherwise acquire, or dispose of any shares in the capital of any other company.]

[Option 2]

[The consent of the holders of a majority of the Seed Shares held by the Investors (an 'Investor Majority' shall be required for the important decisions, substantially in the form listed in Appendix [___])].

Pre-emption   All shareholders will have a pro rata right, but not an obligation, based on their ownership of issued capital, to participate in subsequent financings of the Company (subject to customary exceptions). Any shares not subscribed for may be reallocated among the other shareholders. The Investors may assign this right to another member of their fund group.

Right of First Refusal and Co-Sale   The Investors shall have a pro rata right, but not an obligation, based on their ownership of Ordinary Shares, to participate on identical terms in transfers of any shares of the Company, and a right of first refusal on such transfers (subject to customary permitted transfers, including transfers by Investors to affiliated funds). Any shares not subscribed for by the Investors would then be offered to the other holders of Ordinary Shares.

[

Drag Along   In the event that the holders of a majority of the Ordinary Shares wish to accept an offer to sell all of their shares to a third party, or enter into a Change of Control event of the Company, then subject to the approval of the Lead Investor and the Board, all other shareholders shall be required to sell their shares or to consent to the transaction on the same terms and conditions, [subject to the liquidation preference of the Lead Investor].

Restrictive Covenants and Founders Undertakings   Each Founder will enter into a non-competition and non-solicitation agreement, and an employment agreement in a form reasonably acceptable to the Investors, and shall agree to devote their entire business time and attention to the Company and to not

	undertake additional activities without the consent of the Investors. A breach of any of the foregoing restrictive covenants or undertakings by a Founder shall result in immediate dismissal for cause of such Founder.
Founder Shares	Shares held by the Founders will be subject to reverse vesting provisions over three years as follows: [25% to vest one year after Closing and the remaining 75% to vest in equal monthly instalments over the next following two years ('the **Vesting Period**').]
	During the Vesting Period, any unvested shares shall be automatically converted to deferred shares, provided that if a Founder is a Bad Leaver [all shares held by that Founder shall convert to deferred shares.]
	[After the Vesting Period, [a leaving Founder shall offer for sale to the Company (with a secondary purchase option for the holders of Seed Shares) [X%] of shares held (i) at fair market value if not a Bad Leaver, and (ii) at the lower of nominal value or subscription price if a Bad Leaver. The consideration to be received by a leaving Founder on an Exit will be capped at the value of the shares held by such Founder as of the date the Founder leaves.]]
	[There shall be acceleration upon double trigger provisions so that if a Founder leaves after a Change of Control, unvested shares may become vested.]
Board of Directors	*Option 1* [The board of directors of the Company (the '**Board**') shall consist of a maximum of three members: the holders of Ordinary Shares other than the Lead Investor may appoint two directors and the Lead Investor may appoint one director.]
	Option 2 [The Lead Investor may appoint a non-voting observer to attend meetings of the Board.]
Information and Management Rights	The Lead Investor shall receive [weekly/monthly/ quarterly] reporting and monthly financial information [and a management rights letter to satisfy its venture capital operating company requirements.]
Documentation and Warranties	Definitive agreements shall be drafted by counsel to the Lead Investor and shall include customary covenants, representations and warranties of the Company (which shall be liable up to a maximum of the investment amount) reflecting the provisions

set forth herein and other provisions typical to venture capital transactions. The Founders will also complete a personal questionnaire.

Expenses

Option 1 [The Company shall pay the Lead Investor's fees and expenses in the transaction at Closing, anticipated not to exceed [£XX,000].]

Option 2 [Each party shall pay their own legal and other fees and expenses in the transaction. If the financing does not complete within 60 days or because the Company withdraws from negotiations (except as a result of the Lead Investor making a material change in the terms), the Company shall bear the Lead Investor's legal costs incurred to that date.]

Exclusivity

In consideration of the Lead Investor committing time and expense to put in place this financing, the Company and Founders agree not to discuss, negotiate or accept any proposals regarding the sale or other disposition of debt or equity securities, or a sale of material assets of the Company for 45 days from the date of the Company's signature below.

Confidentiality

The Company and Founders agree to treat this term sheet confidentially and will not distribute or disclose its existence or contents outside the Company without the consent of the Lead Investor, except as required to its shareholders and professional advisors.

Non-binding Effect

This Summary of Terms is not intended to be legally binding, with the exception of this paragraph and the paragraphs entitled Expenses, Exclusivity and Confidentiality, which are binding upon the parties hereto and shall be governed and construed in accordance with the laws of England and Wales.

Acknowledged and agreed:

[Lead Investor]	[Company Name]
	[Founder 1]
By:	
Print Name:	By:
Title:	Print Name:
Date:	Title:
	Date:
[Additional Investor]	
	[founder 2]
By:	
Print Name:	By:
Title:	Print Name:
Date:	Date:
	[founder 3]
	By:
	Print Name:
	Date:

Appendix A Capitalization Table

Shareholder	Class of Shares	No. of Shares.	Ownership (%)
[FOUNDER 1]	[Ordinary Shares]	•	•%
[FOUNDER 2]	[Ordinary Shares]	•	•%
[FOUNDER 3]	[Ordinary Shares]	•	•%
Lead Investor	[Ordinary Shares]	•	•%
Additional Investor	[Ordinary Shares]	•	•%
Option Pool	[Ordinary Shares]	•	•%
Total		•	**100%**

APPENDIX 5

Measuring and Managing Impact

The five steps to implement impact measurement following the EVPA Practical Guide to Measuring and Managing Impact.[1]

Step 1: Setting Objectives

Step 1 consists of defining the *scope* of the impact measurement process at the impact investor level and at the social enterprise level, and *setting objectives* at both levels. Setting impact objectives goes to the core of the strategy of both the impact investor and the social enterprise. Knowing what impact it wants to achieve is a definitional question, and will be a cornerstone of the investment strategy of an impact investor. Setting objectives is often the most important step of an impact measurement process, as everything else flows from there. Some organizations make the mistake of setting indicators and starting to collect data without knowing exactly what they are trying to achieve. The more clear and specific the objectives, the better the impact measurement can be prepared.

For the impact investor or the social enterprise, objectives should be set at two levels:

(i) Level of the Impact Investor

The *scope* of the impact measurement process depends on the following choices:

- *Motivation for measuring social impact.* An organization can decide to use impact measurement for different purposes, such as strategic reasons, for communication actions, for improving the services provided, etc. These reasons imply different target audiences and outlooks.
- *Resources available* for the impact measurement process. These include the financial, human and technological resources and time.
- *Type of investees* that the impact investor is working with. The maturity, i.e. the stage of development of the social enterprise, will determine the type of information that the social enterprise can provide.
- *Level of rigour of the impact analysis.* This should be aligned with other choices made by the impact investor; the rigour and the methods used will depend, for example, on the scope of the analysis, the quality of the data available, the time and the stakeholders involved. Related to the rigour of the impact

1 Hehenberger et al. (2015).

assessment is the notion of 'impact risk – what is the risk that the impact will not be achieved?

- *Time frame.* The impact measurement can be a provisional analysis to decide whether or not to finance a social enterprise, or an ex-post analysis to assess the outcomes after a programme. The choice of time frame should take into account the estimated length of time required to achieve the most important outcomes.

Impact investors should consider developing their own theory of change as part of their own investment strategy (as outlined in Chapter 16). The investment strategy will determine which social sectors and beneficiary groups will be targeted, hence defining the screening criteria for the investments undertaken.

(ii)   Level of the Social Enterprise

To decide on the objectives at the social enterprise level, it is useful to consider the organization's theory of change. A theory of change shows an organization's path from needs to activities to outcomes to impact.[2] It is a tool that helps describe the change you want to make and the steps involved in making that change happen. The theory of change also depicts the assumptions that lie behind your reasoning and, where possible, these assumptions are backed by evidence. Logic models are grounded in a theory of change and use words and graphics – *the Impact Value Chain* – to describe the sequence of activities thought to drive a desirable change and how these activities are linked to the results the programme is expected to achieve.

These are the main questions that need to be answered by the social enterprise to understand its theory of change:[3]

- What is the *social problem* or issue that the social enterprise is trying to solve? The social enterprise must clarify the nature and extent of the social problem to be tackled, which stakeholders are involved and what is the target audience. For example, offering advanced training in digital skills to unemployed youth in two Spanish regions characterized by a high youth unemployment rate.
- What are the *expected outcomes*? These are represented by what the social enterprise must achieve to be considered successful, e.g. the milestones against which the social enterprise will be measured. For example, the number of individuals who obtained an educational qualification after the training was provided. It is also important to consider the unintended consequences of the social enterprise's activities.
- What are the *key factors in the cause-and-effect relationship*, and the necessary assumptions? Think about and describe how the inputs link to the intervention and then link to the desired outcomes. Briefly describe the basis for the logic model (theory or prior research, or both) along with aspects of the

2 Kail and Lumley (2012).   3 This section is further informed by Clifford et al. (2015).

model, if any, which have been confirmed (or refuted) by previous research. As the intervention is tested by the social enterprise or otherwise, more evidence will be collected to either prove or refute the theory of change, so that the social enterprise may alter its course based on the insights.

- Which *activities* are promoted by the social enterprise to address the social problem? This part includes a detailed description of the activities that the social enterprise will undertake to solve the social problem, to try to effect a change in people's lives. For example, the organization of the partnerships, the developing of innovative training, actions to motivate and involve young people, etc.
- What *resources or inputs* does the social enterprise have and need to undertake its activities, including capital and human resources, time and any other necessary assets? For example, at this stage of the analysis it is advisable to also take into consideration the social investor's contribution to helping the social enterprise with innovative solutions to move youth into the labour force.

Step 2: Analysing Stakeholders

Impact investments generate value for a variety of stakeholders. A stakeholder can be defined as 'Any party effecting and/or affected by the activities of the organization.'

Impact investors should understand and manage:

- The stakeholders' expectations, their contribution to the enterprise and the potential impact the social enterprise projects will have on them.
- The stakeholders' cooperation in the impact measurement process.

The stakeholder analysis applies at both the impact investor and the social enterprise level and it should involve:

- *Identifying stakeholders:* mapping of direct and indirect contributors and beneficiaries, selection of the most relevant stakeholders and a stakeholders' expectations analysis.
- *Engaging stakeholders:* communicating with the relevant stakeholders and verifying whether their expectations have been met. For principles of stakeholder involvement, see Step 4 below.

Step 3: Measuring Results: Outcomes, Impact and Indicators

- At the impact investor and the social enterprise level: the organization should measure its own outputs, outcomes, impact and indicators as per its own objectives (theory of change, etc.); impact measurement at a portfolio level; impact of the social investor's work on the social enterprise.

- At the social enterprise level: the organization should transform its objectives into measurable results via outputs, outcomes, impact and indicators.

The impact measurement process requires the objectives agreed upon in Step 1 to be transformed into measurable results. At both the impact investor and at the social enterprise level, outputs, outcomes, impact and indicators need to be considered.

At the impact investor level, however, it is not sufficient to just refer to the outcome and the impact achieved by the social enterprises in its portfolio but an assessment should be made of the impact of the work of the investor on the investees.

Outputs are the results directly related to the organization's activities and they are generally easier to measure (e.g. hours of training activity, number of participants, etc.)

Outcomes and impact are the positive and negative, expected and unexpected, direct and indirect changes that stakeholders experience and these are generally more difficult to measure.

Indicators are the Key Performance Indicators (KPIs), both qualitative and quantitative, that are used to show progress towards or deviations from outputs or outcomes.

Many established sources list output indicators related to different social sectors and, when possible, the organization should stick to these public databases, such as IRIS, Global Value Exchange and other commonly used repositories of social indicators.

The causal link between output indicators and the achievement of an outcome is sometimes difficult to prove before the enterprise's own evidence has been gathered. If there is acknowledged and independent research attesting that specific outputs do result in specific outcomes, these references can be used to consider the causal link sufficiently strong to sustain the outcome achievement, otherwise the following process to select outcome indicators should be used:

- Define outcomes as change statements, target statements or benchmark statements.
- Select the most relevant, material, useful and feasible outcomes (in achievement not in measurement).
- Select indicators, i.e. identify two or three factors, that provide measurable evidence for a sub-optimal situation.

There are four aspects of a good indicator to keep in mind:

a. Indicators should generally be aligned with the purpose of the organization, although if a potential unintended outcome has been identified, relevant indicators for this outcome may, by definition, not be aligned with the purpose of the organization.
b. Indicators should be 'SMART', i.e. specific, measurable, attainable, realistic and time bound.

c. Indicators should be clearly defined so they can be reliably measured and ideally comparable with those used by others.

d. More than one indicator should be used, with a preference for two or three.

Many interesting methods and approaches are currently under discussion in the field of assessing social impact. However, impact investors and social organizations should be careful to adapt their impact measurement process to their objectives and their financial capacity.

Step 4: Verifying and Valuing Impact

Step 4 helps impact investors verify that there is no over claim on the positive social impact produced, and to what extent the value assessed is correct. In some respects, it can be compared to an audit. The act of verifying and valuing is used to identify the impact with the highest social value, to support the organization in managing impact and focus the resources towards those investees that create the most positive impact on society. This step should occur both at the impact investor overall portfolio level and at the social enterprise level.

At the portfolio impact management level, the social investor needs to verify, with the engagement of the relevant stakeholders including their investees, the effect of the non-financial assistance provided. The impact investors should also constantly verify that the expectations of other stakeholders (donors, investors, staff members) are met so that they can implement the necessary changes to align with those expectations.

At the social enterprise level, it is important to confirm whether the outcomes make sense for the stakeholders involved. It is very important to assess what the direct consequences of the organization's activity are.

There are various methodologies to verify impact. Below we list the more commonly used:

- Desk research is useful for collecting information from acknowledged sources of information (research and knowledge centres, universities, governments) regarding the trends and figures of a given social issue.
- Competitive analysis is a comparative methodology that draws a parallel between the impact results of the social enterprise and other similar organizations in terms of analogous social issues addressed, geographies and populations targeted.
- Interviews or focus groups are useful for creating qualitative benchmarks through addressing neutral questions to a representative sample of the key stakeholders. This format is strongly recommended when the impact investor is assessing the value of non-financial support to the investees. Generally, to give more authenticity to the conversation, it is best to involve a third party facilitator to conduct the interviews or the focus group to ensure that the investees are comfortable providing the most truthful responses.

Finally, a crucial step is understanding whether the outcome was important, i.e. of value, to the stakeholder. Given that space does not allow for the growing number of existing techniques to be listed in this appendix, we have divided the methodologies into two general categories; qualitative and quantitative (monetization):

- Qualitative approaches include storytelling, client satisfaction surveys, participatory impact assessment groups, progress out of poverty index.
- Quantitative techniques for valuing involve converting social value into monetary terms (monetization) using, for example, perceived value/revealed preference and value game or techniques for cost/benefit analysis such as cost-saving methods and quality-adjusted life years calculations.

Although organizations can choose to assess impact using either qualitative or quantitative methods, an impact investor should use both at the portfolio level and should request that each of its investees use a combination of both quantitative and qualitative techniques to assess impact, in a proportion suggested by the rationale for measuring impact in the first place.

Step 5: Monitoring and Reporting

Step 5 consists of monitoring progress against (or deviation from) the objectives defined in Step 1, through the tracking of the concrete indicators set up in Step 3. These results will then have to be reported, i.e. transform the information into formats more fit to be understandable by key stakeholders. Monitoring and reporting are two sides of the same coin: what is monitoring to one stakeholder is reporting to another, e.g. when an impact investor is monitoring the progress of an investee, the social enterprise is reporting relevant data to the social investor. As with the other steps of the Impact Measurement process, impact always has to be assessed at two levels: the impact investor and the social enterprise level.

Monitoring

In order to give substance to the indicators, the organization has to collect data in a systematic way. The impact investor should be collecting and analysing data on:

- Indicators sufficiently specific to measure its progress toward reaching its overarching social objectives.
- Time invested by the impact investor's internal staff and or acquired in the external market to provide non-financial support to its investees.
- The social enterprises that fill the portfolio, according to the objectives and indicators previously defined.

The impact investor will need to verify whether the social enterprise is effectively monitoring its activities and outcomes, e.g. to check whether the selected indicators are appropriate and whether the impact investor is playing a positive and effective role in improving the impact measurement practices of the investee.

If there is any doubt as to whether the impact is happening or not, the impact investor should directly ask the investees and the relevant stakeholders.

At the social enterprise level, the priority is to evaluate the outcomes or the impact that have been achieved as a result of its activities. The social enterprise should also manage impact by using the impact measurement information to decide what actions are needed to increase impact.

Reporting

All the data and information that has been collected and analysed needs to be presented in the most effective way to different audiences. The purpose of reporting and the stakeholder targeted will directly influence the format of the presentation and the content that has to be taken into consideration.

We predict an increased standardization with regard to reporting formats. The current situation is that social enterprises still need to report differently to different funders. Some initiatives (e.g. the German Social Reporting Standard) are trying to overcome this problem, but it is difficult to come up with a unique standard that perfectly adapts to the fragmented nature of the social sector.

Index